About Pearson

Pearson is the world's learning company, with presence across 70 countries worldwide. Our unique insights and world-class expertise comes from a long history of working closely with renowned teachers, authors and thought leaders, as a result of which, we have emerged as the preferred choice for millions of teachers and learners across the world.

We believe learning opens up opportunities, creates fulfilling careers and hence better lives. We hence collaborate with the best of minds to deliver you class-leading products, spread across the Higher Education and K12 spectrum.

Superior learning experience and improved outcomes are at the heart of everything we do. This product is the result of one such effort.

Your feedback plays a critical role in the evolution of our products and you can contact us – reachus@pearson.com. We look forward to it.

Indian Political System

Fourth Edition

Edited by

Mahendra Prasad Singh

Himanshu Roy

Cover Image Courtesy: Photo Division, Ministry of Information & Broadcasting,

Govt. of India, used with permission

Editor—Acquisitions: Kaushal Jajware
Senior Editor—Production: G. Sharmilee

ISBN 978-93-528-6643-4

First Impression, 2018
Current Impression, 2026

Published by Pearson India Education Services Pvt. Ltd, CIN: U72200TN2005PTC057128.

Head Office: 1st Floor, Berger Tower, Plot No. C-001A/2, Sector 16B, Noida - 201 301, Uttar Pradesh, India.

Registered Office: 6th Floor, Tower A, Unit A and B, International Tech Park, CapitaLand Chennai, 200 Feet Radial Road,Zamin Pallavaram, Old Pallavaram Chennai – 600117, Tamil Nadu, India

Website: in.pearson.com; Email: companysecretary.india@pearson.com

Digitally printed in India by Trinity Academy for Corporate Training Ltd, New Delhi in the year of 2026.

Contents

Preface

Himanshu Roy

In the past ten years, since the publication of the third edition of this book, two major changes can be delineated in Indian politics: one, many social laws have been enacted in the legislatures at the Centre and in States under the pressure of democratic upsurge which have democratized liberalism, for example, Employment Guarantee Act, Right to Information Act, Food Security Act, Forest Rights, Civic Rights, Rights for Women, etc., were enacted during Congress regime; and second, at the Centre, and in many States, Bharatiya Janata Party (BJP) has emerged as the dominant party forming the governments, where earlier it was in opposition, which has now led to a shift in the governmentality. The focus now is on new policy formulation, on their effective implementation, on plugging the leakages of resources in development process, on eliminating corruption through transparency, and on actuating efficiency in administration. Moreover, the new governments have involved public in policy formulation, for example, on education, health, governance, environment, and on infrastructure development. The functioning of the administrative agencies are constantly monitored through new technology, review meetings, complaint cells. This has begun to reflect on the results visible in railway, defense, highway projects, in 'Make In India', in 'Start Up India' or in the foreign policy which has been effectively transformed into soliciting global investment in India to make her a manufacturing hub of the world, to generate employment, and skill development for the expanding young population. Furthermore, some of the old policies like Rural Employment Guarantee Act, and Awas Yojna have been rejigged and realigned for better asset creation. The new policies or the realignment of old policies, as indicated above, may speed up creation of rural urban infrastructure, may actuate efficiency and transparency in the functioning of administration or, it may also speed up rural to urban migration and rural-urban stress. Few incremental changes have become visible, such as, disaster management, highway development, etc.

Most importantly, the BJP has co-opted different sections of society in its government, in its party organizations, in its icons, in its programs, and in its ideology. It has become more amorphous and overarching. Its expansion and success has been a reflection of this.

However, the control of governmental power by the BJP at the Centre with Narendra Modi as Prime Minister has unleashed a counter political discourse by his political-ideological opponents. The themes are intolerance, nationalism and socio-economic policies. The reaction is visible in the media, in the parliament, and in many of their micro-macro acts.

This edition, revised and enlarged with two new chapters on health and education policy, will add to the pedagogy on Indian politics.

We thank Kaushal Jajware and Sailza Kumari for their work.

Introduction

Mahendra Prasad Singh

The post-colonial political system in India is founded on two major reconciliations between democracy and capitalism, on the one hand, and parliamentarianism and federalism, on the other. Democracy implies individual rights and liberties, equality, popular sovereignty, and constitutionalism (i.e., rule of law, not only by law, but governments are limited by the constitution). Capitalism is based on property rights and attendant privileges, profit-driven market mechanism, the ideal of economic competition, and the reality of monopolistic and oligopolistic concentration of economic powers. The two are obviously antithetical, yet in the historical trajectory of liberal democracies in the West and in the Third World, democracy and capitalism have coexisted in an indifferent and uneasy coalition. Likewise, parliamentarism and federalism are primarily contradictory. In parliamentary form of government the final chain of command ends up in the Parliament, whereas federalism is premised on division of power between the Parliament and state legislatures and decentralization. Yet Canada, originally and innovatively, in 1867, Australia in 1900, India in 1949, and some other countries like Germany in Europe have tried to combine these two divergent principles and forms of government in their constitutions.

These two aforementioned reconciliations are the products of complexities and diversities of India's composite culture and social structure as also the ideological consensus forged during the nationalist movement and after independence. This ideological consensus attempted to prepare a middle ground between the extremes of capitalism and socialism. The Preamble to the Indian Constitution proclaims a state founded by it to be "a Sovereign, Socialist, Secular, Democratic Republic" and enjoins it "to secure to all its citizens: justice, social, economic, and political; Liberty of thought, expression, belief, faith, and worship; Equality of status and of opportunity, and to promote among them all Fraternity assuring the dignity of the individual and unity and integrity of the Nation". Moreover, Parts III and IV of the Constitution on Fundamental Rights and Directive Principles of State Policy respectively give expression both to the early liberalism centered on bourgeois political rights and later liberalism that opened up to accommodate some economic policy goals aimed at creating a more egalitarian society with at least minimum social securities. The Directives do not really amount to either a full-fledged post-World War II Western welfare state (*e.g.*, Scandinavia, England, Canada, etc.) nor to a Soviet socialist economy. But they certainly give expression to the intention of going beyond classical liberalism *a la* Adam Smith to set up an Indian version of "socialistic pattern" of economic development. The Nehru-Mahalanobis strategy of planned economic development with the state (public sector) seeking to scale the "commanding heights of the economy" became the main ingredients of the new economy. The structure of mixed economy that emerged after Independence allowed both the public sector and the private sector to operate, but the latter came to be increasingly put under a variety of state controls that came to be pejoratively called the "permit-license-quota Raj" by conservatives like C. Rajagopalachari who pleaded for more space and greater freedom for the private sector. The vast agrarian sector, after some land reform measures, remained as a private peasant household production sector. The Indian government under Nehru followed economic policies premised on self-reliance and growth with justice and equity.

With increasing political populism and crisis in the public sector of the economy under the government of Indira Gandhi, Prime Ministers Rajiv Gandhi and P.V. Narasimha Rao, especially the latter, introduced significant measures of economic liberalization, bureaucratic deregulation, public sector disinvestment, and structural readjustment to permit a greater scope for the market, simultaneously opening it up to international competition, investment, and technology. The most comprehensive package of economic liberalization by Indian standards has been brought about by the Rao government and the successive governments have not substantially turned back; if anything, they have gone further in this direction. The Rao government started as a one-party minority government, but subsequently turned into a majority one in the latter half of its mandate. When Rao initiated the major package of economic reforms, his government was in a minority with oppositional majority in the Parliament. So evidently the economic reforms represented a consensus in the party system, at least a dominant consensus with only marginal opposition from the Left and the Right. For the Rao government and the successor coalition governments it was led successively by the Janata Party/Dal, Bharatiya Janata Party (BJP), and Indian National Congress (Indira), BJP under Narendra Modi until 2014 have willy-nilly continued the same economic policies, even though they widely diverged in their socio-cultural policies. Since most of these governments have been coalitional, the economic policies pursued by them have been products of delicate bargaining and balance in steering committees of the coalition cabinets. Even the Hindu Right nationalist BJP, as first majority party to get a single party majority in the Lok Sabha after a gap of 30 years in 2014, has continued the ongoing traditions of federal coalition governments and neoliberal economic reforms. Another notable feature of the economic reforms is that they have come to pass without any formal amendments to the Constitution.

Both capitalism and socialism swear by democracy, each claiming to establish a more genuine democracy. Marxists claim to institute economic democracy in place of empty political democracy of the liberals. They ask what is the use of formal political equality without freedom from hunger and other wants? The liberals retort that men do not live by bread alone! Liberals like John Rawls argue that both liberty and equality are equally important values which cannot be compromised, except that in case of equality a compromise is permissible only in favor of the most disadvantaged sections of the society.

The historical evolution of both liberal democracies and socialist societies shows that the correlation between capitalism and democracy has proved, at least thus far, to be more viable than that between socialism and democracy. However, real democratic possibilities have often been thwarted by both capitalism and socialism in the real world thus far. The experience of socialist countries so far attests that not only democratic freedoms but also economic equality beyond a certain point have in their domains remained a will o' wisp. Capitalist democracies too get very uneasy when the parties of the Left and the Right confront each other with really radical ideological options in a mood to fight it out to the hilt. The Great Economic Depression of the 1930s in the West was the product of the constant fall in the demand in the face of expanding capitalist production due to the repeated failure of a weak working class to win over continuous and significant increase in wages. The period witnessed the collapse of democracy in Germany and Italy and the rise of Nazism and Fascism.

The West emerged from the Great Economic Depression and the Second World War and followed Keynesian economic policies of demand management by expansion of state activities and expenditure, and instituted in the process what came to be known as Welfare State. By the late 1960s the welfare state came to grief due to "stagflation"—galloping inflation outpacing the steady wage expansion of workers and employees and the resultant fall in demand causing recession in the economy. The wars in West Asia and oil-shocks due to heavy increase in the price of the gasoline and petroleum products further intensified the economic crisis.

"Reaganomics" and "Thatcherism" which surfaced in by the 1980s and 1990s spelled the undoing of the welfare state and Keynesianism. The reconciliation of capitalism and democracy in the welfare state proved to be unviable. The restructuring of production globally coupled with the decline of the power of the organized working class to counteract and countervail the power of capital was the result. In most recent elections in the West social democratic parties have registered electoral gains, including power to govern. In India too, the left has declined in parliamentary as well as state assembly elections (notably in West Bengal yielding ground to Trinamool

Congress in 2011 after 34 years of continuous Left Front rule and lost again to it in 2016) in the recent years.

The collapse of communism in 1989 in the Soviet Union and eastern Europe, failure of liberal welfare states and crisis in the social democratic welfare states since the 1970s and 1980s under fiscal overloads and human cupidity by onslaughts of capitalist globalization after the end of the Cold War, have cumulatively tended to produce enormous increase in economic inequalities and disparities among classes and regions *within* as well as *among* nations on an unprecedented scale. Moreover, financial crisis in East Asian miracle capitalist economies in the late 1990s and in metropolitan capitalist centres in North America, European Union, and Japan in 2008-2009 have produced what has belatedly been called the Great Economic Recession.

There is some sign of the economic and political rise of Asia in the post-Cold War world. China, India, and Indonesia have emerged as the fastest growing economies in the world in the 21st century. Despite heavy pressures from Pakistan and China, India in the post-economic liberalization phase has for the first time since the British period and after, scored a rate of annual GDP growth of 5-7 percent. It is spectacular compared to the average growth rate of 1.5 percent in British India and 3.5 per cent in the post-Independence period before the 1990s. The growth rate suffered a setback in 2016-17 due to demonetization of higher value currency and transition to Goods and Services Tax (GDP). But by the year-end of 2017, economic prospects are looking up and would presumably be more robust in the years ahead. What should, however, worry the policy makers is that the high GDP growth is not adequately matched in terms of distributive justice and human development especially measured in terms of education, public health, and poverty. India has been ranked in top 100 among nations in the ease of doing business but also ranks in top 100 in the hunger index.

The world seems to be on the crossroads without any definitive sign whether capitalist globalization resulting in the decline of the nation-state and the triumph of the global market forces will have a field day or neo-Hobbesian political conservatism strengthening the national state protecting its domestic industries which will finally emerge victorious. The democratic dream predicted on participatory democracy and extension of democracy from the political arena to the workplace and family however, has been expanding farther.

The combination of parliamentarianism and federalism in India's parliamentary federal system, has led the politics in India, in the 1980s and 1990s, towards federalizing the predominantly parliamentary regime that had become overly centralized during the long periods of Congress predominance. The 1980s witnessed a phenomenal spurt in the rise of demands for greater state autonomy by parties, movements, and state governments forcing Prime Minister Indira Gandhi to appoint in 1983 the first Commission on Centre-State Relations chaired by Justice R.S. Sarkaria of the Supreme Court and comprising two other commissioners. The Commission submitted its monumental 2-volume report in 1987-88, favoring the strengthening of inter-governmental agencies of consultation and deliberation such as the National (Economic) Development Council, Inter-State Council, Planning Commission, Finance Commission, etc., and constitutionally entrenching those that do not already enjoy such status. It also recommended a fundamental change in the attitude and behavior of federal and state functionaries, especially the Governor, in consonance with the federal value of state autonomy. The BJP-led National Democratic Alliance government appointed the National Commission for Review of the Working of the Constitution (2002) headed by Justice M.N. Venkatachaliah and the Congress-led United Progressive Alliance government appointed the second Commission on Centre-State Relations chaired by Justice M.M. Punchhi (2010) recommended a slew of some of the same federal constitutional reforms as the Sarkaria Commission plus a few additional ones. However, none of these reforms has yet been implemented by the government, including the ones that appointed them.

Nevertheless, the trend of greater federalization of the Indian political system has moved on steadily largely under the impact of party system transformation from one-party dominance to multiparty system with federal coalitional governance since 1989. There has been a reversal of this trend since the 2014 Lok Sabha elections which was spectacularly won by Narendra Modi-led BJP, yet the federal thrust of the system has not been blunted, thanks to the continuing electoral base of some regional parties like All India Anna Dravida Munnetra Kazhagam (AIADMK, belatedly suffering a setback in the demise of its supremo, J. Jayalalitha in December 2016), Biju Janata Dal, and Trinamool Congress, as the oppositional majority in the federal second chamber Rajya Sabha countervailing the governmental majority in the national chamber, Lok Sabha.

Indian federalism is rooted in the country's history and regional diversities. The growing trend of federalization in the past two decades is accounted by at least three factors that have become active in recent times. The first of these is the growing levels of politicization and relative deprivation experienced by the various social groups and regions, especially the peasants and farmers all over the country and some ethnic groups having regional concentration, especially in Assam, Punjab, Jammu and Kashmir. Authoritarian trends in the dominant Congress party and its inability to provide avenues for political mobility to newly politicized groups in some States and also the dissatisfaction of the mass public with it led to the emergence of non-Congress all-India or regional parties, augmenting the trend of federalization.

This leads us to the second factor behind the growing federalization of the Indian polity, namely, the party system's transition from one-party dominance to multi-party system of polarized pluralism and regionalism. This growing diversity in the party system resulted in the multiplicity of parties in control of the two chambers of the Parliament and state legislatures and the various state governments. All these factors and forces together heralded the era of coalition governments at the centre and in some States. However, the growing trend of the absence of intra-party democracy is turning into the Achilles' heel of Indian democracy as it deepens the crisis of democratic and constitutional governance of India and its states.

The judicial behavior is the third factor contributing to the growing trend of federalization. In any federal system the judiciary inevitably emerges as the final adjudicator of jurisdictional conflicts between the federal and State governments. The position of the judiciary is further strengthened if the written federal constitution also contains, as the Indian Constitution does, a written charter of fundamental rights of citizens. Judicial activism over the controversy on the constitutional amendments in India goes back to at least late 1960s (*Golaknath v. State of Punjab*, Supreme Court, 1967) and *Keshavananda Bharati v. State of Kerala*, Supreme Court, 1973). Activism over socio-economic, civic, and environmental issues is a development of the 1980s and 1990s. This has developed in the context of dysfunctionality of the executive and legislative organs of the state. The judicial activism in the federal domain surfaced in the Supreme Court's judgement in *S.R. Bommai v. the Union of India* (1994), in which the Supreme Court for the first time reviewed and declared unconstitutional in some specific instances of the proclamations of President's rule in some states; earlier the Supreme Court had been reticent to look into such cases as "political thickets" within the domain of the Union executive. In the changed ambience, the Patna High Court in 1997, asserted that the courts could even advise the President on whether the constitutional machinery in a state had actually broken down, inviting central intervention. Until now the matter had been under the exclusive purview of the executive (the Governor and the President, in effect the Union Council of Ministers). One may also add that the constitutional offices of the President and Governors are now increasingly becoming more self-conscious about their constitutional responsibilities, especially in the context of "hung" legislatures and coalition or minority governments. A new federal ferment has come to grip the Indian political system.

The process of liberalized capitalism, thus, has resulted into two major transformation; economically, old capitalist production methods and pre-capitalist social formation have been marginalized and market relations have been strengthened and expanded; politically, new party system and federal relations have emerged and social structure has become more democratic. This dynamics of social change and the constant growth of knowledge necessitated a new addition of this book which has been enlarged and revised. Two new chapters have been incorporated and many chapters have been revised.

In the chapters that follow, these general trends in the Indian political system are examined more closely. Part I deals with the historical context and legacies that impinge on the contemporary polity. Beginning with the evolution of the state, the colonial state in India, the section focuses on the role of colonial capitalism that gradually replaced the preceding traditional village-centric economy and decentralized state structure with market economy and modern state having rational-legal bureaucracy and limited representative institutions. The national movement that emerged as a consequence of this rule had different approaches and visions to solve their contemporary problems. It not only freed the country from the colonial yoke but also created the governmental structures for further governance through constitutional mode. The basic principle was liberal-democratic rule premised on capitalist economy under the command of the state, both of which, in essence, were planted by the British.

The governmental structures which Part II deals with are comprised of parliamentary federalism along with the executive and the judiciary. The representative democracy becoming more participatory with the passage of time has not only liberalized the fundamental rights of the citizens but has also brought directive principles concerned with the core issues of development and governance, at par with the fundamental rights in some respects through judicial interpretation and activism. Not only that, it has facilitated the federalization of polity by checking the misuse of powers of the Union executive and has been the motor force of democratization of some of the Constitutional and political bodies in which elements of decay had set in. It also encouraged the legislature to formulate laws that provided impetus to secularization of polity. Simultaneously, it also acted on deterrent against the unaccountable behavior of the political parties and trade unions towards the public in general. Such themes have been discussed independently in Part III with much broader perspectives that also include topics like Panchayati Raj, gender issue, regionalism and electoral process. Basically, all these themes revolve around issues that influence and mobilize considerable number of people or its different segments. Political parties, non-governmental organizations, panchayats, and trade unions play an important role in such mobilization that calls for policy formulation and brings the state face to face with the people.

Part IV deals with such public policies that touches upon the major chunk of population and important areas of society. The discussion brings forth the trends of development in respective fields, points out the flaws in the policies, brings forth the areas of concern and suggests alternative or remedial measures.

Finally, Part V discusses the trends of development in India since Independence and based on it points out its future prospects. The focus is on three aspects: participation of the people in democratization process for determining their own destiny, thrust on global trade and capital flow and global and regional integration of the Indian economy. All the three issues manifest in multifarious ways with no unilinear development.

To sum up, the volume deals with important and topical issues that influence the Indian people and provides a critique and alternative to the public policies and problems of governance.

Contributors

Mahendra Prasad Singh
Professor (Rtd.), of Political Science, University of Delhi.

Himanshu Roy
Associate Professor of Political Science, DDU College, University of Delhi.

S.K. Chaube
Professor (Rtd.), of Political Science, University of Delhi.

Rajesh Kumar Singh
Indian Civil Accounts Service.

K.C. Markandan
Late Professor of Political Science, Guru Nanak Dev University, Amritsar.

Vinod Sethi
Associate Professor (Rtd.), of Political Science, ARSD College, University of Delhi.

Rajvir Sharma
Senior Consultant, Department of Public Administration, IGNOU, New Delhi.

S.N. Mishra
Professor (Rtd.), of Political Science, Indian Institute of Public Administration, New Delhi.

Rajendra Singh
Late Professor of Social Work, University of Delhi.

Sharit Bhowmik
Late Professor, of Sociology, Bombay University.

Bibekbrata Sarkar
Late Professor of Political Science, University of Delhi.

Manju Subhash
Associate Professor (Rtd.), of Political Science, Maitreyi College, University of Delhi.

Subha Pandey
Associate Professor of Political Science, SPM College, University of Delhi.

Kamal A Mitra Chenoy
Professor, Jawaharlal Nehru University, New Delhi.

K.N. Kabra
Professor (Rtd.), of Economics, Indian Institute of Public Administration, New Delhi.

Subir Verma
Professor, FORE School of Management, New Delhi.

Jaytilak Guha Roy
Professor (Rtd.), Indian Institute of Public Administration, New Delhi.

Ashish Kothari
Kalpvriksha, Pune.

Bipan Chandra
Late Professor of History, Jawaharlal Nehru University, New Delhi.

D.L. Sheth
Honorary Senior Fellow, Centre for the Study of Developing Societies, Delhi.

Sunder Raman
Associate Professor (Rtd.), of Political Science, PGDAV College, University of Delhi.

Renu Sethi
Associate Professor (Rtd.), of Political Science, Gargi College, University of Delhi.

Rajni Ranjan Jha
Professor of Political Science, Banaras Hindu University, Varanasi.

Sushma Yadav
Professor of Political Science, Indian Institute of Public Administration, New Delhi.

Pushpa Bali
Associate Professor (Rtd.), of Political Science, Shaheed Bhagat Singh College, University of Delhi.

Satish Kumar Jha
Associate Professor of Political Science, Aryabhatta College, University of Delhi.

Madhu Jha
Assistant Professor of Political Science, L B College, University of Delhi.

Sanju Gupta
Associate Professor of Political Science, JDM, University of Delhi.

Sonali Chitalkar
Assistant Professor of Political Science, Miranda House, University of Delhi.

Indira Chakravarthi
Former Fellow, Nehru Memorial Museum and Library, Teen Murti Bhawan, New Delhi.

Roopinder Oberoi
Assistant Professor of Political Science, K.M. College, University of Delhi.

COLONIAL BACKDROP

1

The Colonial State

Mahendra Prasad Singh

Sketching the historical evolution of the Indian state, particularly the British colonial state, is necessary for an adequate understanding of Indian politics. This task is, however, fraught with methodological problems. This is so on account of the zigsaw puzzle of piecing together the intricate chronological and thematic units in time and place among the diverse state-systems which cover the space. Temporal and theoretical disjunctures often appear impossible to bridge due to the paucity of data and conceptual imprecision. Professional historians may feel inclined to shy away from some of these methodological traps, taking shelter in specialization in the historiography of any specific state of broad periodization of Indian history into ancient, medieval, and modern. But, a political scientist in his long march into history to understand and explain continuity and discontinuities in India's past and present must confront these problems headlong, albeit candidly highlighting the methodological problems in this endeavour. The first part of this paper sketches the evolution of the state in India in terms of the prevailing historiography on the topic. Besides, it seeks to conceptualize and fill in the gaps in the theoretical understanding of the British colonial and post-colonial states in India. The second part presents a critique of the historiography of some states in Indian history. The third part concludes this essay with an outline of the institutional legacies of the states in Indian history of the post-colonial Indian nation-state.

I

We can delineate at least three broad themes of transition having a direct bearing on the evolution of the Indian state. First, there is the transformation of a pre-state social formation based on lineage and tribe in the state. This happened in the Vedic or post-Vedic societies in the North and Sangam period in the South at the dawn of history in these regions. Presumably, a similar transition must have transpired in the pre-Vedic period in the Indus valley and other Harappan and Mohanjodaran sites in the North-West with their centres in Sindh and Punjab, where either a theocratic state or a republican oligarchy is supposed to have existed. While no textual sources are still available for the Indus valley and the Indus script inscribed on archaeological effects remain undeciphered, the tribal and pastoral beginnings are reconstructed from the Sangam literature much in the same way as in the North from Vedic and Buddhist texts. Paradoxically, urban-industrial Indus valley civilization antedates the pastoral beginnings in the Vedic and Sangam periods, the former not very distant in time and place from the Indus valley. It may well be that the Indus culture was the metropolitan centre of the primitive peripheries of the same Indus state to which the pastoral Aryans migrated in hordes from Central Asia. This probably happened at a time when the metropolis were devastated by a natural calamity of great magnitude causing the peripheries to fall into a more primitive existence. Of course, we need historical evidence to corroborate these surmises.

Second, there is the transformation of regional kingdoms into subcontinental states through much of Indian history by a recurrent process of emergence, disintegration, and re-emergence. Beginning with the post-Vedic proto-states (*mahajanapadas*) and their transformation into states in the pre-Mauryan period, among whom Magadha under the rule of the Nandas was the centre of political gravity, the process culminated in the formation of the Maurya state (321-185 BC) in Magadha, the first subcontinental state in Indian history. The *saptang* theory of the state with seven constituent elements—monarch, ministers/bureaucrats, territory/population, fort, treasury, sceptre, and allies—outlined in Kautilya's *Arthashashtra* is commonly regarded as the textual blueprint of this transition. Indologist J.C. Heesterman argues that from the internal evidence of the text itself it appears that there were chinks in bureaucratic procedures, especially in audit and accounts, that betrayed tribal traces making the *mahamatyas* (accountants/auditors) co-sharers in royal powers rather than subordinate to the king. However, what Heesterman makes out to be co-sharing in royal power is easily amenable to an interpretation of autonomy of the officials in a technical field in the first most complex and extensive state in the world until that time. On the decline and disintegration of the Mauryan Empire, smaller kingdoms, and regional states followed that dotted the historical landscapes for a millennium and a half. This period witnessed the phenomenal increase in frequency of the land grants by the state to Brahmans and state officials. This practice resulted in the rise of feudalism. During this period, the important landmarks were the states founded by the Guptas and Harsha (300-700 AD), the Delhi Sultanate (1200-1526 AD), and Vijayanagara (1300-1526 AD). From the third decade of the 16th century to the beginning of the 18th the Mughal state ruled the roost over much of the subcontinent as the most important subcontinental state before the British colonial state that continued until independence in 1947. The Maratha and the Sikh states in the 18th century were the two important states that followed the decline of the imperial Mughals, but they were overtaken by the British colonial state, to which the post-colonial Indian state is the most significant successor.

Third, there is, as already hinted above, the transformation of the 'state'[1] based on British colonial economy and bureaucratic organization into a democratic and sovereign nation-state. This state-system sets off the twin processes of industrialization and democratization that ushered India into the modern world. Western education and capitalist development in the industry were initiated by the British rulers in India that irreversibly undermined the Indian tradition. The British also laid the foundation of the first merit-based bureaucracy in India that replaced the patrimonial bureaucracy of the Mughal and post-Mughal states. All these trends gathered fuller momentum in the post-independence period.

Taking strands from British and Mughal conceptions of monarchical and patrimonial bureaucratic traditions, the British with some modifications erected the viceregal system with first modern structures of bureaucracy and army in India. The British Raj, thus, became the most developed absolutist state claiming to be benevolent in Indian history. Social and cultural historians generally perceive a great deal of continuity between the pre-colonial and colonial periods of Indian history.[2] However, a student of the modern state in India cannot escape discovering a major break in its political-institutional complex with the founding of the British Raj, even though the basically authoritarian viceregal system *prima facie* resembles the ancient and medieval Indian absolute monarchies rooted in the Hindu and Indo-Islamic political ideas. Indeed, by virtue of the British colonial heritage in South Asia, the successor states in the region became heirs to two strands of institutional legacies, those of the viceregal system and the Westminster model of parliamentary government in combination with federalism like Canada and Australia.[3]

During the Raj, however, it was the authoritarian strain of the institutional seed which was more in tune with the traditional state systems of India's past than with the modern British political heritage that flourished. For this reason, it would not be out of place to draw a comparison between the British colonial state in India and the absolutist states of late medieval Europe. Functionally, the colonial state in India was neither comparable to the Bonapartist or Prussian Junker state holding the balance between feudal aristocracy and emergent bourgeoisie[4] nor the Andersonian model of European absolutist state which was essentially a reinforced apparatus of feudal domination of the peasantry.[5] It did not either belong to the category of 'patrimonial authority'[6] or 'patrimonial bureaucratic empire'.[7] It was instead a political instrument of the British imperial or metropolitan capitalist state, and, for this reason, largely undetermined by the mode of production in colonial India. Much like the European absolutist state, the British Raj led to the onset of political and economic forces that produced for the first time in Indian history rational-legal structure of bureaucracy in the Weberian mode. However, due to the crucial factor of colonial intervention in the Indian case the British Raj founded a colonial state dependent on the metropolitan state, but enjoying a large measure of autonomy from the class and ethnic configurations in the colony itself. The colonial state, thus, built up a system of power shaped by a coalition of the dominant classes in the metropolitan state in London supervising over a subordinate coalition of a dominant class—dominant vis-a-vis the colonial class configuration—the adversarial targets of the classes active in the nationalist movement against colonial rule. Thus, whereas the imperial state was functionally and reciprocally conditioned by the full-fledged twin processes of industrialization and democratization, the colonial state in India was ultimately an instrument of the imperial state, but as a state since it was secondarily influenced by the coalition of classes and ethnic groups in the colony. Only with this kind of conceptualization, we can: (1) bring out a sharper focus in the liberal strands in Anglo-American colonialism as distinguished from continental European colonialism; (2) do justice to the incrementally democratic features of constitutional reform in India introduced by the British Parliament pointing towards a parliamentary and federal form of government in the long run; and (3) underline the evolution of consensus during the nationalist movement in favour of the Westminster model and its adoption by Independent India's Constituent Assembly in 1950.

The long-term effect of the British rule both in the Company and the Crown phases was the gradual weakening of the traditional aristocracy (landed classes) and the rise of the middle classes that gradually filled the space vacated by the former. The middle classes 'included university students and teachers, barristers and lawyers, writers and newspaper editors, educated proprietors, and well-to-do traders'. Ironically, it was the princes and *zamindars*, who, after an initial revolt, remained allied with the British Raj, while the middle class (excepting those who joined the bureaucracy) forged an alliance with the Indian industrialists and the peasants against the British.

With the consolidation of the British rule in India, capitalist and pre-capitalist modes of production came to co-exist in a dynamic state of transition to capitalism. This resulted in the gradual destruction of the age-old methods of peasant and craft production under an imperialist regime of capitalism geared to the colonial extraction or revenue and raw materials for metropolitan industrialization and imperial expansion and exploitation of the Indian market for the commodities produced by British industries. Besides, a class of indigenous capitalists within the colony also developed in due course as also a middle class of the new elites educated in colleges and universities established by the British rulers. The industrial working classes also slowly, but steadily emerged in the new industrial towns and cities. Colonial rule, thus, despite its pretentious notions of the 'whiteman's burden' and its extractive and exploitative nature, also generated some unintended consequences, such as the rise of a nationalist movement that weaved a cluster of ethnic groups into a nation for the first time in Indian history, for, though a common cultural consciousness had existed from time immemorial, the nation-state was a modern phenomenon.

Now, moving from the Raj phase of the modern Indian state to its Swaraj phase, we must develop an understanding of the post-colonial Indian state in terms of its continuities and departures from the British Indian colonial state. On attaining political independence in 1947, India turned its back on two aspects of its colonial heritage: (1) the political-institutional legacies of the viceregal model of the bureaucratic state; and (2) the legacies of the political economy of dependency on metropolitan capitalist centres.

The modernizing nationalist elite established the framework of a liberal-democratic state with a parliamentary-federal government, constitutionally guaranteed Fundamental Rights of citizens, and an incipient welfare state promised in the Directive Principles of State Policy. The preamble of the Indian constitution proclaims it a 'sovereign, socialist, secular, democratic republic'. It would be a gross oversimplification to describe this state as an instrument of any dominant class or ethnic group. The Indian state derives its 'autonomy' (in democratic theory) or 'relative autonomy' (in the neo-Marxist theory) from its social/class base from the liberal-democratic constitution under which it has been founded as well as from the fact that, instead of any one class or group ruling over it, only a complex coalition of classes exercise dominance over it. Pranab Bardhan, an economist, argues that in one liberal-Marxist (or neo-Marxist) formulation, a conflict-ridden coalition of three 'dominant proprietary classes'-industrial capitalists, rich farmers, professionals (civil, military, and white-collar)-hold the key to political power in the Indian state. He goes on saying that a wide disparity separates this top two deciles from 'the bottom half of the population living in abject poverty', but the dominant coalition must contend with significant conflicts of interest' within its own ranks which have 'serious repercussions on the fortunes of economic growth, and of the democratic polity'.

To take the tack of the political economy of development, it is a commonplace that colonialism in India created some preconditions for economic and political development, but its primary upshot, beginning with the First World War, was this country's growing multilateral integration with advanced capitalist metropolitan centres of the West on the condition of dependency. On attaining freedom in 1947, the adoption of the Nehru-Mahalanobis strategy of economic development in the Second Five-Year Plan set the basic parameters of planning as rapid industrialization with the accent on a dominant public (state) sector and a self-reliant economy.

These strategies of political-institutional development and economic development together generated a complex dialectics with an immense transformative potential. The principal components of this transformation were: (1) a restructuring of economic dependency on metropolitan capitalism into independent economic development; (2) promoting state capitalist and capitalist developments in the urban sector; (3) transition from semi-feudal agriculture to capitalist farming; and (4) democratization of a largely authoritarian society and polity to begin with, and once this made some headway, federalizing the predominantly parliamentary system established under the 1950 constitution.

Finally, a word about the two major directions of change affecting the Indian state since the 1990s and the unfolding future. Both are related to the somewhat contradictory global trends of economic and political liberalization that gathered momentum in the late 1970s and 1980s. In the Indian context, these developments are manifested on two planes. There is, first the policy of economic liberalization. And, secondly, there are the mounting pressures, for federalizing the predominant parliamentary system to accommodate a greater degree of autonomy for the states in the Indian federal union. Powerful alternative ideologies favouring the market and state governments have come to the fore, though the public sector and the Centre still continue to be powerful yet a series of policy changes have withdrawn, to a significant degree, controls that the state exercised over the private corporate sector and sought to reorient the hitherto inward-looking import-substitution economy by one in which a growing reliance is placed on the private sector, both national and multinational. The new policy thrust has resulted from a constellation of factors in the post-Nehru era, for example, as policy failure on economic front in the public sector bedevilled by huge losses, inefficiency, political populism, and corruption; success of the private sector in industry and agriculture; the emergence of a middle class and a new generation of political elites at the top with favourable orientations towards the Western pattern of capitalist development and consumerism, and so on.

The federalization thrust was earlier broadly confined to the regional elites and the state party systems. The regionalist thrust was buttressed by the rise of 'bullock capitalists' (the term is the Rudolph's, 1987) and the 'Other Backward Classes' (read castes) since the late 1960s. These social and political forces succeeded in pressurizing the then Prime Minister Indira Gandhi to appoint the Sarkaria Commission on Centre-State Relations in 1983, which submitted its monumental two volume report in 1987-88. In the 1989 Lok Sabha elections, the national party system assumed a multi-partisan pattern, breaking out of the mould of a basically predominant party system under the aegis of the Congress party holding the sway most of the time since Independence. The mid-term parliamentary elections in May-June 1991, by and large, maintained the multi-party system of polarized pluralism introduced by the previous Lok Sabha elections in 1989.[8] The federalizing thrust of the new phase of the party system continued unabated through the 1990s and mid-2020s. This makes the search for a new federal consensus an urgent imperative.

II

In this section, we would sketch the historical roots of the post-colonial Indian state. From the beginning, two contradictory as well as complementary patterns of state formation developed simultaneously in Indian history that was continued even by the mighty British colonial state. Centralized bureaucratic administration with direct rule in the territorial core was always complemented by non-bureaucratic modes of incorporation that contended with indirect rule by the central authority in the peripheries. This overarching framework of domination allowed a complex coexistence of the secular and the sacred, the pan-Indian and the region at sovereign cults, like *Dhamma* and *sulh-i-kul* and spiritual cults like *Bhakti* and *Sufi silsilas*, a great tradition in culture and small-group orientations of the village society. Thus, sovereignty in Indian history was ambivalently both crystallized and diffused, centralized and decentralized; it not only allowed appreciable autonomies to groups and regions within the state but also visualized a complex interstate alliance system in the subcontinental interstate configuration in which allies were constituents of the subcontinental super state itself. The network of the federal and state governments established under the 1950 constitution is the first state to rule India directly under a common framework of modern political bureaucratic and economic institutions.

The post-colonial liberal-democratic state in India has sprung from complex historical roots such as these. The immediate inspiration for the democratic, federal and bureaucratic features of the state was, of course, the British rule in India and the British, Canadian, American, Irish, and Australian constitutions. However, the indigenous sociological and ideological influences of the Mughal and Maratha states, the nationalist movement, and the given structures of ethnicity should not be lost sight of. The Mauryan *mahamatta* system and the Mughal *mansabdari* system provide historical antecedents of the British Indian Civil Service and the post-independence all-India services. The ritual sovereignty of the Vijayanagara monarchs, Maratha diarchy between the nominal monarch and the hereditary *Peshwa* (premier) and the *ajnapatra* (ordinance) on the eve of the Maratha conquest in the 18th century, which ordains a 'dualist' authority of 'warriors' and 'ministers' in the administration, may be seen as the indigenous precedent of liberalization of the state structure that may have probably led to the denouement of 'constitutionalism' even without the British and nationalist interventions. The long-span nationalist movement against the colonial rule, that made a moderate appearance in the last quarter of the 19th century and passed through several phases, engendered a pervasive ideological debate and produced a consensus on the constitution and the policy-frame and planning in the new nation. The sprawling caste system and religious and linguistic communities make India a nation of minorities, despite the Hindu majority and the near-majority of Hindi speakers federally. All these legacies and factors together make India an exciting experiment in democracy, economic development, and nation-building.

Notes and References

1. 'Colonial state' is a contradiction in terms-either a country is a colony or a state. However, in view of substantial autonomy of the elaborate apparatus of the British Indian administration 'across the seven seas' form London one is inclined to use the term.
2. AT. Embree (1989, p. 5) for example, observes: "One of the ineluctable facts of Indian history is that fundamental institutions survived, although they underwent great changes, during over 500 years of political domination by Turkic and other Islamic rulers, and during the century and half of British rule in the subcontinent. These changes were sometimes imposed by the rulers, sometimes they were indigenous to India, and it is almost incidental that they took place during a period of foreign rule".
   Dinkar (1962) sees India's composite culture as a synthesis between Aryan, Dravidian. Hindu-Buddhist-Jain,. Hindu-Islamic, and Indo-European cultural streams.
3. Myron Weiner (1989, ch. 3) draws attention to these twin legacies, but calling the second of these a 'British democratic model' glosses over the combination of the parliamentary government with federalism in India as in Canada—1867 and Australia in 1991.
4. Out of the two models of the state—the class dominated and Bonapartist (relatively autonomous from its class-base)—in Marx, the latter is outlined in his 'From the Eighteenth Brumaire of Louis Bonaparte' in Marx, Engels, Lenin (1972, pp. 120–133). See also Tom Bottomore *et al.* (eds.) (1983, p. 53).
5. Perry Anderson (1979, p. 18) interprets the European absolutist state as 'a *redeployed and recharged apparatus of feudal domination*, designed to clamp the peasant masses back into their traditional social position despite and against the gains they had won by the widespread commutation of dues' (emphasis in the original).
6. See Max Weber (1946, p. 298) on the concept of 'Patrimonialism'.
7. On the concept of 'Patrimonial-Bureaucratic Empire' as applied to Mughal state, see Stephen Blake (1979, pp. 77–94).
8. For a discussion of this phase of Indian party system, see M.P. Singh (1992 *a* and *b*) and M.P. Singh and Rekha Saxena (2011)

Bibliography

Altekar, A.S., *State and Government in Ancient India*. Delhi, Motilal Banarsidass, 1958, 3rd ed.; first published 1949.

Anderson, Perry, *Lineage of the Absolutist State*. London and New York, Verso, 1979; first published 1974.

Bagchi, Amiya Kumar, *The Political Economy of Underdevelopment*. Cambridge, Cambridge University Press, 1982.

Bailey, A.M. and J.R. Llobera (eds.), *The Asiatic Mode of Production: Science and Politics*. London; Routledge and Kegan Paul, 1981.

Bardhan, Pranab, *The Political Economy of Development in India*. Delhi: Oxford University Press, 1984.

Basham, A.L., *The Wonder That Was India*. Calcutta: Rupa Paperback, 1981; first published 1954.

Bhattacharya, Sibesh, 'Political Authority and Brahman-Kshatriya Relationship in Early India: An Aspect of Power Elite Configuration'. *Indian Historical Review*, Vol. X, Nos. 1-2 (July 1983-January 1984).

Blake, Stephen, 'The Patrimonial-Bureaucratic Empire of the Mughals'. *Journal of Asian Studies*, Vol. XXXIX (1979).

Bottomore, Tom, *et al.* (eds.). A *Dictionary of Marxist Thought.* Oxford: Blackwell Reference, 1983.

Chandra, Satish, *The 18th Century in India: It's Economy and the Role of the Marathas, the Jats, the Sikhs and the Afghans* (S.G. Deuskar Lectures on Indian History and Culture 1982). Calcutta, CSSS/K.P. Bagchi and Company, 1991.

Chattopadhyaya, Brajadulal, *Making of Medieval India.* Delhi: Oxford University Press, 1994.

Dinkar, Ramdhari Singh, *Sanskriti Ke Char Adhyaya* (Foreword by Jawaharlal Nehru). Patna: Udayachal, 1962, 2nd ed; first published 1956.

Embree, Ainslee T., *Imagining Indian: Essays on Indian History.* Delhi: Oxford University Press, 1989.

Fukazawa, H., 'Maharashtra and the Deccan' in Tapan Raychaudhuri and Irfan Habib *(eds.). The Cambridge Economic History of India.* New Delhi; Orient Longman in association with Cambridge University Press. 1982.

Ghoshal, U.N., *A History of Indian Political Ideas.* Bombay: Oxford University Press. 1959.

Government of India, *Commission on Centre-State Relations, Report,* 2 Vols. Nasik: Government Press, 1987-88.

Habib, lrfan, 'Processes of Accumulation in Pre-Colonial and Colonial India; *Indian Historical Review,* Vol. XI, Nos. 1-2 July 1984 and January 1985.

______, 'Classifying Pre-Colonial'*Journal of Peasant Studies,* Vol. XII, Nos. 2 and 3 July-April 1985.

Heesterman, J.C, *The Inner Conflict of Tradition.* Delhi. Oxford University Press. 1985.

Jalal, Ayesha, *Democracy and Authoritarianism: A Comparative and Historical Perspective.* Cambridge: Cambridge University Press, 1995.

Jayaswal, K.P., *Hindu Polity.* Bangalore: The Bangalore Printing and Publishing Company, 1943; first published 1924.

Jha, Vivekanand, 'Social Stratification in Ancient India'. Presidential Address, Ancient Indian Section. *Indian History Congress,* Calcutta, 28-30 December 1990.

Kautilya, *The Arthashastra* (Edited, Rearranged, Translated and Introduced by L.N. Rangarajan). New Delhi: Penguin Books India (P) Ltd., 1987.

Kosambi, D.D., *An Introduction to the Study of Indian History.* Bombay: Popular Prakashan Private Ltd., 1975, Rev. 2nd ed.; first published 1956.

Kulke, Herman and Dietrnar Rothermund, *A History of India.* Calcutta: Rupa and Co., 1991; first published 1986.

______, (ed.). *The State in India* 100-1700. Delhi: Oxford University Press, 1995.

Kumar, Dharma and Meghnad Desai (eds.), *The Cambridge Economic History of India,* Vol. II, c. 1757-c 1970. New Delhi: Orient Longman in association with Cambridge University Press, 1982.

Marx, Engles and Lenin, *On Historical Materialism.* Moscow: Progress Publishers, 1972.

Misra, B.B., *The Indian Political Parties: An Analysis of Political Behaviour upto* 1947. Delhi: Oxford University Press, 1976.

Moosvi, Shireen, 'The Gross National Product of the Mughal Empire' c. 1600. *Indian Historical Review.*Vol. XIII. Nos. 1-2 July 1986-January 1987).

Mukhia, Harbans, 'Was There Feudalism in Indian History?' *Journal of Peasant Studies,* Vol. XII. Nos. 2 and 3 (1985).

Nettle, J.P., 'The State as a Conceptual Variable', *World Politics,* Vol. XX (July 1968).

Prasad, Beni, *The State in Ancient India,* Allahabad: The Indian Press, 1928.

Raychaudhuri, Tapan and Irfan Habib (eds.), *The Cambridge Economic History of India* Vol. I, c.1200 c.1750. New Delhi: Orient Longman in association with Cambridge University Press, 1982.

Rizvi, S.A.A., *The Wonder That Was India,* Vol. II. Calcutta: Rupa and Co., 1993: first published 1987.

Roy, Kumkum, *The Emergence of Monarchy in North India: Eighth to Fourth Centuries B.C.* Delhi: Oxford University Press, 1994.

Rudolph, Lloyd and Susanne, 'The Regional Kingdom and the Sub-continental Empire in Indian State Formation' in Paul Wallace (ed.), *Region and Nation in India*. New Delhi: Oxford and ISH, 1985.

______, *In Pursuit of Lakshmi: The Political Economy of Indian State*, New Delhi: Orient Longman, 1987.

Sharma, R.S., *Aspects of Political Ideas and Institutions in Ancient India:* Delhi: Motilal Banarsidass, 1991, 3rd ed; first published 1959.

______, *Indian Feudalism;* c. *AD 300-1200*. Delhi: Macmillan of India Ltd., 1980, 2nd ed.; first published 1965.

______, 'How Feudal was Indian Feudalism?' *Journal of Peasant Studies*, Vol. XII, Nos. 2 and (July-April 1985).

______, *Origin of the State in India*. (D.D. Kosambi Memorial Lectures, 1987). Bombay: University of Bombay Publication, 1989.

______, The Segmentary State and the Indian Experience; *The Indian Historical Review*, Vol. XVI, Nos. 1-2 (July 1989-January 1990).

Singh, Mahendra Prasad. 'The Dilemma of the New Indian Party System: To Governor Not to Govern', *Asian Survey*, Vol. XXXII, NO. 4 (April 1992a).

______, 'From Centrist Predominance to Polarized Pluralism: The Post-1989 Party System in India; *Punjab Journal of Politics*, Vol. XVI, Nos. 1-2 (1992b).

Southall, Aiden, 'The Segmentary State in Africa and Asia' *Comparative Studies in Society and History*, Vol. XXX, No. l (January 1988).

Stein, Burton, *Peasant State and Society in Medieval South India*. Delhi: Oxford University Press, 1980.

______, *The New Cambridge History of India: Vijayanagara*. Cambridge University Press in association with Orient Longman, New Delhi.

Streusand, Douglas E., *The Formation of the Mughal Empire*. Delhi: Oxford University Press, 1989.

Thapar, Romila, *A History of India*, Harmondsworth, Middlesex: Penguin Books, 1966.

______, *Asoka and the Decline of the Mauryans*. Delhi: Oxford University Press, 1973, 2nd ed; first published 1963.

______, *From Lineage* to *State: Social Formations in the Mid-First Millennium R.C. in the Ganga Valley*. Bombay: Oxford University Press, 1984.

______, *The Mauryans Revisited* (S.G. Deuskar Lectures on History. 1984). Calcutta: CSSS/ K.P. Bagchi and Company, 1987.

______, *Interpreting Early India*, Delhi: Oxford University Press, 1993.

Veluthat, Kesavan, *The Political Structure of Early Medieval South India*. Hyderabad: Orient Longman, 1993.

Weber, Max, *From Max Weber: Essays in Sociology* (Edited and translated by H.H. Gerth and C. Wright with an Introduction). New York: Oxford University Press, 1946.

Weiner, Myron, *The Indian Paradox: Essays in Indian Politics* (Edited by Asutosh Varshney). New Delhi: Sage Publications, 1989.

Wink, Andre, *Land and Sovereignty in India: Agrarian Society and Politics the Eighteenth Century Maratha Swarajya*. Cambridge University Press in association with Orient Longman, 1986.

2

Colonial Economy

Himanshu Roy

❑ Agriculture

Pre-colonial Backdrop

Agriculture in India has been the bedrock of economy since the Harappan days except in centuries[1] that preceded the post-Vedic society. The unit of agricultural economy since the Magadhan empire, and particularly in the post-Gupta period[2] was the village. A village, away from towns, was considerably autonomous in the sphere of economy and culture. But, it was not a 'republic'. The role of *beparis, mandis, ganjs, haats, melas, etc*., were substantial in linking a village with the market.[3] A village was concerned with the state apparatus, by and large, only at the time of revenue payment. However, it is not to deny the other mundane linkages that existed between a village and the state. The land, by and large, was not the commodity to be purchased and sold. A village had certain customary rights over the village-land which was exercised through *panchayat*. The caste structure was an integral part of this economy which was, by and large, the politico-economic-cultural form of the present day class. Almost every village was horizontally stratified into different castes consisting of certain economically and culturally dominant castes, and certain economically and culturally subjugated castes. It was the economically and culturally dominant castes who used to dominate the village governance through the institution of *panchayat*, and exercised rights on behalf of the entire village. The cultivable land was not communally owned, neither was their agricultural produce. The village was not a commune, neither was the *panchayat*. The *panchayat*, though, on behalf of the entire village community performed numerous kinds of roles, like dispute settlement, development and religious works, maintenance of law and order, etc., and exercised rights over the grazing land, forests, irrigation canals, etc.,[4] but it was never above the caste structure of the village in which dominant castes used to control the affairs. No doubt, the *panchayat* also consisted of individuals of subjugated castes, but it remained an institution of dominance and governance of the dominant castes and, by and large, always played a conformist role. It maintained the property relations of the time existing in the form of horizontal caste structure—*dharma* order—in which the dominant castes enjoyed the customary religious rights, privileges, sanctions, etc., over the land and other forms of property. Though the *panchayat* sometimes went against the interests of the individual peasant families of the dominant castes, the phenomenon of domination-subjugation always continued irrespective of the mergers of tribal aboriginal and foreign invaders into the village society and additions of hundreds of new castes in the system.

The dominant castes could dominate the caste structure and the village governance because the major chunk of the village's cultivable lands were owned by them. The individual peasant families were the customary owners of the land and agricultural tools, like plough, sickle, spade, bullocks, etc. However, the actual ploughing, tilling, sowing, harvesting and thrashing, manuring, etc., were done by the subjugated castes, barring ploughing, did perform other functions of cultivation, but only as their secondary jobs[5]. The agricultural produce that came out of this cultivation was kept partly for revenue payment, partly for *Panchayat*, partly for household consumption and partly for the families of the subjugated castes for their services performed. Though the families of the subjugated castes did possess cultivable land of their own, particularly intermediate castes, like *teli*, barber, potter, iron/gold smiths, etc., enjoyed customary rights over their lands but the amount of their possessions were nominal which did not fetch them substantial grains required by their families in a crop year. Hence, their lands remained their secondary source of earning, the primary source being the grains earned from their *jajmans*. The division of labour in village society was not evident. In some matters, it was overlapping. The peasant families of the dominant castes, for example, performed some subsidiary functions, like cattle grazing, wood collecting, etc. Similarly, the families of the subjugated castes, besides performing the above-said functions including their professional, hereditary functions, like cultivation, making iron tools, ornaments, pottery, shoes, etc., for their *jajmans* also did cultivation for their own families either on their own land or on the land granted to them by their *jajmans* or *maliks* as subsidiary function.

Technologically, agricultural and other kinds of tools required by the villagers had undergone progressive transformation, like three-stage development of water wheels (*rahat*), improved techniques of artificial manuring (mentioned in *Krsi Parasa*), growing number of new crops or the new varieties of old crops, etc., but the pace of development was too slow. The European peasants while struggling against harsh nature developed in leaps and bounds, and possessed more aggressive will, were at constant lookout for better technology, but, the Indian peasantry remained slow, easy-going in technological development[6], which hindered their material prosperity emanating from the technological development. Most villagers had scanty clothes, almost no shoes, lived in mud-thatched houses, ate on leaves or in earthen utensils, cooked in earthen utensils, used straw as mattresses in winter, and so on. The tools used by the peasants, either for cultivation or for handicrafts, saw no improvement for generations. The iron and goldsmiths, for example, kept on using charcoal, instead of coal, in their furnaces. Even their furnaces did not witness change for years. Instead of iron in their crushers, the oilmen used wood to produce mustard oil in the similar way they used to extract sugarcane juice. The cobbler, weaver, potter used same techniques which their forefathers had bequeathed to them. For cultivation, instead of iron, hard wood was used to furrow the fields by poor peasants; wooden buckets and leather bags were used for irrigation, pit wells rather than deep wells were more common in use. It is not that the uses of iron, coal, deep wells, etc., did not exist; rather, their use was spatially widespread across the subcontinent. But their usage in everyday life was lacking. By that time, instead of focusing on technology, people were more dependent on human labour or even on animal power.[7] The gap between the actual cultivation done by a peasant family in a crop year and the total cultivable areas it possessed was far wide which was more due to technological backwardness than anything else. If the total amount of cultivable areas possessed by a peasant family was, say, twenty acres, then the actual cultivation was done only in five-seven acres of land. The technological factors responsible for this gap were also the factors responsible for slow expansion of the cultivable lands in the villages.

Technological development, no doubt, took place in India, but its pace was outmatched by the European society. The political centralization of the European states against the fragmented polity of India compensated the rest of the better things which India had. At this historical backdrop, the British East India Company arrived at the political landscape, defeated its Indian adversaries one by one, expanded its political territory, and finally became the master of the land.

❑ THE TRANSFORMATION

The New Policies

The victory of the East India Company at the battle of Plassey in 1757 led to the formulation of some major new policies for India which saw the beginning of the demise of the traditional village economy and social relations associated to it. The first step in this direction came in the form of New Land Settlement in different stages and in different forms, in different regions. The crux of this policy was the imposition of ever-increasing heavy revenue on the *ryots*, irrespective of failure of crops, and commoditification of land and its produce. The second step was the adoption of policy of Free Trade, the opening up of the Indian market, the vast rural society, to the British industrial goods. The essence of this policy was the elimination of monopoly of trade of the British East India Company restricting it to only administrative roles, and the beginning of the free play of competitive market forces in the Indian society. The third major step was the introduction of Steam Age in India. The essence of this policy was the qualitative transformation of rural society into a classic colony of industrial capitalism of England.[8] The aim was to progressively convert the Indian agriculture into a branch of industry so as to accrue the agricultural produce for the English industrial society. The new policies that took shape in different stages came due to changes in the composition of the British capitalist class which led to changes in their interests in India. The changes were guided by the vilest interests, the consequences of which were the destruction of the traditional economy and social relations, emergence of capitalism in agriculture and the conversion of a section of Indians as the subordinate to the British capital. By 1947, India had sunk deeper into the problems and prospects of capitalism.

Let us now analyze the situation and necessities that led to the formulation of new policies by the East India Company.

In 1757, after the battle of Plassey, the Company, the part of the British mercantile class earned for itself, for the first time, the *zamindari* of the 24 *Parganas* was further extended to the districts of Burdwan, Midnapore, and Chittagong in 1760. By 1765, the entire Bengal, Bihar, and Orissa came under its purview. By 1856, entire India came under unprecedented economic power of the Company. It utilized the opportunity by first imposing an ever increasing heavy revenue on the peasantry and second, by controlling the entire trade and commerce of Eastern India. The excitement of this political and economic power was so intense that the Company had begun to fleece and plunder the Indian traders and peasantry, literally. The phenomenon became so monstrous that even Warren Hastings had to accept this fact. He says, "the government requires so large a proportion of the produce of the country, causes beyond the reach of human control will occasionally operate to render some indulgence in favour of its subjects indispensable, and the formality of agreements will, but ill-justify the vigour of exactions."[9] The rapacious greed of the Company to control the biggest amount of agricultural produce, which was beyond the Company's personnel to collect, in the initial few years of its rule led to two simultaneous phenomena. First, "the lands were ... let out for a year on the best terms procurable. A strict preference was given and every indulgence shown to native inhabitants.... Hereditary *zamindars* were to remain in possession of their *zamindarees* as long this could be done with safety to the revenue."[10] The term of the contract, however, kept changing with minor modifications. Sometimes, it was given to the "highest bidder, whether they were the previous *zamindars* or not."[11] This change in the mode of revenue collection continued in Bengal till 1793 when Permanent Settlement was done by Lord Cornwallis. But, in spite of this settlement, one thing remained unchanged as the highest possible revenue collection by the *zamindars* continued.

The second phenomenon that happened as the result of the first was "the lands … suffered unheard of depopulation by the famine and mortality"[12] which took place within twelve years of Company's rule and even then the collections violently kept up to their former standard had added to the distress of the country and threatened a general decay of the revenue."[13] Though draught, famine, etc., kept on recurring even in the later years of the Raj, the kind of situation Bengal faced in the initial years of the Company rule, that is depopulation of urban centres, fall in agricultural productivity, etc., didn't occur elsewhere with the same ferocity even at the time of transition in Madras and Bombay presidencies, in Sindh, Punjab, etc. In fact, after the New Land Settlement in different parts of India, the urban centres begun to thrive with ever-increasing population, agricultural productivity increased, and trade and commerce picked up with greater intensity.[14] The benefits though went to the British ruling class and his Indian partners, the masses had only the tickle down effect. Nevertheless, the New Land Settlement and later on, the Free Trade and Steam Age turned out to be historically progressive steps.

The New Land Settlement had different forms in different regions. In Bengal, Bihar, sections of North Madras (Northern districts), Orissa, and districts of Varanasi, permanent *zamindari* settlement existed. In parts of Central India and Avadh, temporary *zamindaris* settlement were in vogue. In Bombay, Sindh, Berar, Madras, Assam, etc., constituting 51 per cent of the territory, *Ryotwari* system was applied. In Punjab, parts of Central India, Northwest province, etc., *mahalwari* system existed. These forms of revenue collections were known by the units through which labour produce was sucked out of peasantry. In *mahalwari*, *mahal* was the unit of revenue collection. In *Ryotwari*, it was individual *ryots* who paid the revenue directly to the state. And in *Zamindari*, it were the *zamindars* who collected the revenue from the *ryots* and paid it to the state while keeping a portion for themselves as commission.[15]

For generations, all the three forms had existed in different regions, and in different stages of development in the pre-British India. Now under the British, their nature was transformed and they played a different role.[16] The resettlements of land laid the foundation of capitalism in agriculture and provided an in-built mechanism for the individual mobility to the subjugated castes. The subjugated castes, however, remained by and large subjugated even under the new social milieu. And the dominance of dominant castes continued. Their wealth, power, placement, status, etc., which they had inherited from history helped them in maintaining their position even under the new condition.[17]

The variation in the form of revenue collection that different parts of the country witnessed occurred due to the changing needs of the British. In pre-1973, in Bengal, the revenue collection was auctioned to the highest bidders. This became a practice to collect maximum revenue in the shortest possible time to finance the possible wars that may be waged by the Company in other parts of the country. It was also to ensure "the long-term reproduction of the conditions of appropriation"[18] which had declined in the 1770s and early 1780s. Most of the auction bidders were individuals of dominant castes or members of the Mughal state apparatus who were rich, influential, and powerful. Even after 1793, it was found convenient to continue with the same league of people because being influential, powerful, and rich, they collected and deposited the revenue to the Britishers on time and helped them in maintaining law and order in the society.[19] Their economic and political powers got linked with the British and they developed one state in existence during the British rule as their stake, which once upon a time, was tied up with the existence of the Mughal state. The 1793 settlement, however, proved to be an economic loss to the British, because as per their terms of contract they couldn't enhance the percentage of revenue to be paid to the state. The experience of the pre- and post-1793 periods made the English wiser. They abhorred to repeat the same situation in other parts of the country which came under their rule over the years. To come out of this situation, the best means they planned were to implement *ryotwari, mahalwari,* and the so-called 'permanent settlement' or *zamindari* in which approximately after every 30 years revenue was enhanced. The gap between the Permanent Settlement and other land settlements were more than 15-20 years. The British, in the meantime, had settled down, had no threat to their existence in India, had developed their own state apparatus, and had their fixed source of profit. They were not in a hurry to collect maximum possible revenue in shortest possible time as they did in Bengal. The company, thus, applied the most profitable systems of revenue collection in different circumstances in which it was placed in India from time to time. These systems were neither the figment of its imagination, nor the development of its better understanding of the Indian society.[20] On the contrary; these were the most profitable ventures as these went for in the given circumstances.[21]

While the land settlements were the products of the mercantile needs of the Company, the Free Trade and Steam Age were the products of the needs of the British industrial class who, as the most dominant section of capitalism had arrived on the British political scene in the 1830s. The opening-up of the Indian market in stages, after 1813, and the introduction of steam, after 1853, were the products of the pressure that this class had applied on the Company in India for their interests. The Company had outlived its historic role and was acting as barriers in the path of new class that had emerged in England after the Industrial Revolution. The industrial class, which had two clearly defined roles, no longer requires the commercial monopoly of the Company in India as it was obstructing them in their missions. Ever in search of market, this class found India to be the best dumping ground for their factory-produced products as it was a protected market under the Company. The 1813 and 1833 Acts provided the British industrial class a place for the free play of the market forces. But the inundation that begun after the Acts led to the glut in the market in the absence of the purchasing power of the Indians and finding no other means to come out of this economic rot, they were compelled to create the condition for the growth of purchasing powers of Indians that ultimately led to the beginning of industrial revolution in India.[22] The process began with the introduction of new techniques of cultivation of long-staple cotton yarns and strong silk filatures and got momentum with the introduction of railway and the establishment of textile and jute factories. The British, however, did not let go the benefits of technological development to the Indians without the price. They used these technologies particularly yarn, filature, railway, etc., more for their own benefits than for the Indians. To ward off threat from American textile, they helped in the development of long-staple cotton yarn for their factories in England. Similarly, they used railways for the transportation of military personnel in India, of British factory-produced goods from the port-towns to interior parts, and of agricultural produce and mineral resources from interior parts to port-towns for their shipment to England.

All these policies had wide-ranging impacts on the Indian society. The various inter-dependent and inter-connected forces, these policies unleashed during the course of their existence, led to qualitative transformation of the Indian society that was never witnessed in the past.

The Impact

The three major policies discussed above laid the foundation and expansion of mercantile capitalism in India in almost the first 100 years, and then of industrialist capitalism in the following ninety years. Since the British merchants, and later the industrialists were part of the social forces of Britain of the 18th and 19th centuries, hence it was obvious that their crucial policies were guided by their class interests that finally reduced their affairs to the commoditification of land, to the laws of trade and commerce and to the laws of the capital. Consequently, the first thing they did was to convert land and its produce into objects which began to be purchased and sold. These were given an exchange-value through commercial transactions; the auctioning of revenue to the highest bidders helped in their conversion of bidders into mercantile speculators, hoarders, and usurers which were mostly individuals of dominant castes. This set of people who emerged as class-for-itself in course of time created layers of middle men who were almost the mirror-image of the former albeit on smaller scale.[23] At the bottom of the ladder were the actual cultivators who, in course of time, begun to be converted into bonded labourers, landless peasants, share-croppers, tenant-farmers, agricultural proletariat, etc. Similarly, in the *ryotwari* and *mahalwari* are as the dominant families of the old days emerged as rich peasant proprietors, usurers, hoarders etc., and created almost the replica of social formation that existed in the *zamindari* areas.[24] Majority of the actual cultivators in India, in course of time, begun to lose their property in the battles of competition of wealth and capital that got fillip after the 1830s. The extra-economic concern that had begun before the 1830s compensated the unfinished tasks of uprooting of peasantry through their continued operations. Basically, there was no difference in the objectives of different forms of land settlements while *ryotwari* and *mahalwari* were the caricatures of the French peasant-proprietorship; the *zamindari* was the caricature of English landlordism. In fact, throughout the world, capitalism in agriculture has developed essentially in two forms; one was the French model; and the other was the English model. Both these models were applied in different parts of India. But, being a colony, the models turned out to be caricatures of the originals as the British were interested in their own benefits. Social development was never on the agenda for the British. The development that occurred was the by-product of the policies formulated for the surplus extraction from the Indians.

The land settlements sucked the Indian peasantry to their last grain. For example, in 1764, the revenue collected amounted to ₹8,180,000; in 1771, it went up to ₹23,400,400.[25] But, this was merely the tip of the iceberg, because these were only the officially recorded amounts which were paid to the government. The unofficial amounts extracted by the *zamindars* and the other middlemen were much higher than the official one, and multi-dimensional. The values of the commodities of the *ryots*, for example, collected by the *zamindars*, like milk, oil, curd, earthen utensils, grains, etc., during the family and village festivals were never paid. Similarly, the values of the labour that *ryots* spent on festivities for the *zamindars* were never paid. Above all, the labour spent by the *ryots* on ploughing, irrigating, harvesting, and threshing for *zamindars* were either low-paid or unpaid. The defiant were physically assaulted, including incidents of torching their houses, lifting of cattle, and molestation of women, and so on. The *ryots* having no clearly defined contracts with the landowners, under this system, were subject to all kind of arbitrary extractions. Hastings wrote, "It is the *zamindar's* interest to exact the greatest rent he can from the *ryots*. It is as much against his interests to address the deals by which the *ryots* hold their lands and pay their rents to certain bounds and defences against his own authority."[26] In the *ryotwari* and *mahalwari* areas, "the foundation of such a work was laid by the government itself."[27]As this defined and undefined revenue collection increased in proportion from year to year, so increased the rural indebtedness of the Indian *ryots*. The economic burden, consequently, led to the growth of tension in the peasant families which resulted in the division of landholdings, personal belongings, cattle, agriculture implements, houses, etc. The division of land, however, was the temporary solution from the daily bickerings of the families. In the long run, it didn't benefit the divided peasant families. Due to constant fragmentation of land, generation after generation, landholding per peasant family was considerably declined. As a result, they could not generate sufficient produce to sustain themselves under the laws of commerce and capital. They were compelled to sell or mortgage their lands and other properties to *zamindars, sahukars*, etc., to get some money for family needs. Once the money was borrowed, they were unable to return it and reclaim their lands. Majority of them kept paying the interests which continued for generations. In course of time, the properties of the debtors used to become the properties of the *zamindars, sahukars*, etc. The debtors used to be transformed into bonded labourers, landless peasants, agricultural, industrial proletariat, etc., from which they never redeemed themselves. A survey of the debt data amply demonstrated existence of this phenomenon. For example, in 1911, the Indian debt was ₹300 crore, in 1925, it went up to ₹600 crore, in 1929 it further went up to ₹900 crore, and in 1937, it jumped to 1800 crore.[28] This phenomenon, in fact, under the laws of capitalism operational in agrarian society was bound to occur or else capitalism would have ceased to exist. It created a kind of situation in which either one expanded his properties or gradually lost it. The debt, mortgage, and sale of lands and other properties of one became the wealth and capital for the others. Though, for a brief period, at the time of transition, this phenomenon hampered the growth of agricultural produce to some extent, but it did not continue for long. In course of time, some other persons substituted the former owners and the process of production once again resumed with a new vigour. The fragmentation of lands at one pole and their concentration at other pole continued to recur.

The ascendency of the industrial class on the political landscape of England in the 1830s, however, brought some redeeming features in agriculture in India which begun to be felt since the 1840s. The renovation of old irrigational canals and the construction of new ones, development of river and road communications, construction of barrages to regulate the flow of rivers, scientific development of cotton-seeds, development of agricultural tools, etc., were some of the redeeming features, though these were not short of motivation, "The industrial interests found that their trade declined instead of increasing. For the four years ending with 1846, the imports to India from Great Britain were to an amount of ₹261 million: for the four years ending in 1850, they were only 253 millions ... They found out that the power of purchasing their goods was contracted in India to the lowest possible point ... Then came the short cotton-crop in the United States which caused them a loss of £ 11,000,000 in the 1850s, and they were exasperated at depending on America, instead of deriving a sufficiency of raw-cotton from the East Indies. Besides, they found that in all attempts to apply capital to India they met with impediments and chicanery on the part of Indian authorities ... [Thus] the more the industrial interests became dependent on the Indian market, the more it felt the necessity of creating fresh productive powers in India."[29] Keeping this interest in mind, the British began some limited technological development in India and the benefits of which also trickled down to the *ryots*, though primarily it helped the Indian and British dominant classes. For example, the development of communication increased the intensity of the use of iron in agricultural tools and handicrafts.

Most of the peasant families began to use iron instead of hard wood fitted in the ploughs for furrowing agricultural lands. Similarly, wood or stones used in crusher to produce oil or sugarcane juice was replaced by iron. The wooden buckets and the leather bags used by peasants to draw water from pit-wells or deep-wells for irrigation were replaced by iron buckets. Ropes manufactured out of grass and straw were replaced by jute ropes. Charcoal used by iron and goldsmiths in their blast furnaces was replaced by coal. Woods of *imali, kail,* oak etc., used by potters to bake earthen utensils was replaced by coal. Besides these, the construction of barrages and irrigational canals helped in the conversion of uncultivable and fallow land into cultivable lands and reduced the dependency of peasantry on the unpredictable monsoon. The technological development, thus, helped in enhancing the agricultural productivity and gave boost to commercialization of crops which had already begun due to the demand of revenue in cash.

Apart from these impacts, there were some other consequences of the new policies. There took place a change in the cropping-pattern. Particular areas begun to cultivate specific crops which provided monetary benefits. This was in contrast with the preceding village economy which used to cultivate almost everything required for everyday life. Monetization of crops led to greater circulation of currency. Frequency and volume of transactions of agro-products increased. Money began to play greater role in everyday life. Social relations progressively reduced to cash-nexus. Wage system gradually replaced the old *jajmani* system. Services castes became more professional. Old division of labour gave way to new division. Village life no longer remained attached to typical "combination of hand spinning, hand weaving, and hand-tilling agriculture" as once Marx had remarked. Oilman, cobbler, barber, potter, iron and goldsmiths, etc., no longer remained cultivators but were now regarded as professionals. The traditional disparity between domestic industries and agriculture broke down. The servicing castes could not match the time-saving and cost-effective products of the factories, and thus were doomed irrevocably.

The new class polarization began to substitute the old caste-class polarization. The old dominant-subjugated castes no longer played their respective roles. Though majority of the old dominant castes remained dominant and majority of the subjugated castes remained subjugated, their old defined roles changed. Extra economic coercion was replaced by economic expropriation. Individual's mobility in social hierarchy increased both in volume and frequency. Old concepts of pollution and purity were no longer applicable.[30] Polarization between cultivators and non-cultivators became sharper and irreconcilable with growing number of cultivators getting uprooted from their lands and number of non-cultivators expanding their properties. The situation became such that in 1926, over 10 acres of land in India was into the hands of 24 per cent of the population, while 35 per cent of the population had 1-5 acres of land and 23 per cent of the population had one acre or less of land. Region-wise, Madras had 19 non-working landlords per thousand in 1901. In 1911, it went up to 23 per thousand, and in 1921, it jumped to 49 per thousand. Bengal witnessed an increase of 62 per cent on non-cultivating landlords between 1921-31. On the other extreme, there was a steady increase in the number of agricultural labourers. Madras witnessed an increase of 84 labourers per thousand in 1901-31 period. Bengal had the growth of 50 per cent between 1921-31 period.[31] The above data, however did not reveal the growth of privatization of communal lands of villages appropriated by the dominant class, which increase with the development of productive forces, commercialization of land and its produce, and increasing pressure on land due to population growth.

The changes in the Company and social structure led to the growth of inter-dependence of the villages, from numerous local inter-dependence there emerged a national agriculture tied up with the international economy under the hegemony of the British capital. The social classes that emerged under this hegemony underwent similar transformations. They progressively acquired international character in their world outlook. The inalienated, vegetative, corporate life of the village symbolized by the *panchayat* almost came to an end. The old cultural vibrancy and fatalism that once stalked the countryside were gradually replaced by the Gandhian and Marxian politics. Nationalism and socialism became the keywords of social development.

The British rule in India, as Marx had noted, thus, accomplished a double mission: one destructive, the other regenerating, the annihilation of old Indian society and the transplantation of western patterns in India. Both missions were actuated by the vilest interests. And it must have been sickening to witness the fulfillment of the two missions.[32] But the development of capitalism under colonial system proceeds in this way, as the world history shows, or else it would have ceased to be colonial capitalism for "people who are weak and who are left behind in this march of time invite trouble and ultimately have only themselves to blame."[33]

❑ INDUSTRIES

The Backdrop

Since the Harappan days, the urban industries have been one of the dominant pillars of economy. They played a vital role in the enrichment of material life of Indians and the world community at large, particularly the upper strata of society. In the course of their evolution, they passed through successive phases of ruins and developments, expansions and contracts, qualitative and quantitative technological developments. They had no unilinear continuous growth. The post-Harappan society, for example, till the Buddhist time, had no urban industry. The Mauryan, Gupta, Sultanate, Mughal periods, etc., witnessed the revival and expansion of industrial economy after their interregnums. The industrial economy had relative autonomy from agriculture. The industries were located in the port-towns, in the state and provincial capitals, and in religious centres, particularly after the Gupta period. In the Buddhist and Mauryan periods, however, there was general growth of towns as the monarchical form of state was evolving and the numerous tribal proto-states were being incorporated into monarchical states. The industries were based on commodity production, export-oriented, and catered to the needs of the upper strata of the Indians and foreigners. The craftsmen were either slaves or free professionals working either individually or in *Srenis*. There existed division of works among the slaves working in the *karkhanas*, as it happened during the Sultanate period[34], or among different *Srenis* having expertise into different arts, as it existed in the ancient India[35], or among individuals working within a *Sreni*. A crude kind of wage system was operational. The wages were paid, sometimes every day, sometimes after the completion of work entrusted to a particular *Serni* or to an individual worker. The strength and the size of work place varied depending on the nature of industry and work. Some manufactories consisted of thousands of slaves[36] or free craftsmen, some consisted of twelve, fifteen or twenty workmen. The commodities coming out of the production centres were wide-ranging in nature. Pottery, sword, cotton-cloth, silk and numerous other items comprised the list. Out of this long list of items, textile and pottery were produced and exported even in the Harappan days.[37] In fact, the existence of commodity production industries and trade and commerce presupposes the existence of division of work, specialization and classes which were in vogue in Indian society ever since the Harappan days. The expropriation of surplus produce, from agriculture with ever increasing taxes to maintain ever-increasing luxurious life of the vassals reached its limit as the expansion of new village settlements in hitherto untouched areas stagnated. The stagnation checked the growth of volume of surplus produce. The top-heavy administration, which had grown in the initial years of expansion of agriculture and which sustained itself mainly through agricultural expropriation begun to feel the pinch of the stagnation; and as the stagnation continued, so increased the taxes on the peasantry to maintain their life-styles. While this vicious circle in agriculture continued, the shortage begun to be met by the imposition of heavy taxes on merchants. The merchants, after the initial let out, begun to feel the pinch with ever-increasing demand of wealth by the feudal lords to bridge the deficit of agriculture. The pressure on trade and commerce impacted the industry and the artisans. Thus, begun the economic crisis without any let-up under a dynastic rule. As this crisis deepened, the central authority become weaker in the absence of revenue and military power which were contributed by the feudatories. Simultaneously, the process of carving out independent provinces from the central empire by the powerful feudatories in order to maintain their lifestyle and power begun, thereby, finally leading to the disintegration of the empire. Thus, the crisis emerging from the agriculture and gripping the industry and trade and commerce ruined the

Sultanate and Mughal dynasties as it had ruined the Guptas and post-Gupta dynasties. And by the time the next cycle of revival could bloom fully, the trend had started in Bengal and in other parts of India, there intervened the British East India Company which exploited the political division, captured the political power, and nipped the traditional cycle of economic revival under the traditional dynasties in the bud. Whether the economic revival could have led India to the path of capitalist development, it is difficult to say. But "for most features of economy the meager evidence processed so far suggests continuity rather than sharp change".[38]

The Transformation

The establishment and expansion of the British rule, at first, led to devastation of some of the major industrial centres and unbalanced the relationship between industry and agriculture and trade and commerce in the regions which came under their control. The revival of industry, agriculture, trade and commerce which had begun in the post-Aurangzeb phase at provincial levels, were dislocated. It all began with the extra economic control over production and distribution of goods which was different from the control over the industrial machinery and the production process that happened in England after the industrial revolution. The operational method of the Company has been described vividly by Warren Hastings. He says, "they (the Company and their collectors and chiefs of factories) force advances of money on the weavers, and compel them to give cloths in return at an arbitrary valuation, which is often no more than the cost of the materials, so that the poor weaver only lives by running in debt to his employers and, thus becomes slaves for life."[39] A magnified form of their control could also be observed in the writings of William Bolts which was operational in 1722 in very limited areas and became widespread, engulfing every sector profitable to the Company after 1757. He writes, "A number of these weavers are generally also registered in the books of the Company's *gomastahs*, thus, not permitted to work for any others; being transferred from one to another as so many slaves subject to the tyranny and roguery of every succeeding *gomastah*. The cloth, when made, is collected in a warehouse for the purpose called a *khattah*, where it is kept, marked with the weaver's name till it is convenient for the *gomastah* to hold a *khattah*, as the term is, for assorting and fixing the price of each piece: on which, business is employed an officer called the "company's *Jachendar* or assorter. The roguery practiced in this department is beyond imagination, but all terminates in defrauding the poor weaver, for the prices which the Company's *gomastahs* and in confederacy with them the *Jachendars* fix upon the goods are in all places at least 15 per cent and in some even 40 per cent less than the goods so manufactured would sell for the public bazzar, or market upon a free sale. The weaver, therefore, desirous of obtaining the justifiable price of his labour, frequently attempts to sell his cloth privately to others, particularly to the Dutch and French *gomastabs*, who are always ready to receive it. This occasions the English Company's *gomastabs* to set his peons over the weaver to watch him and not infrequently to cut the piece out of the loom when nearly finished."[40] Since the textile industry of India-cotton cloth, silk, muslin, embroidery, brocades, etc., was world famous, and its products had the maximum demand, therefore, most profitable, hence it was the first target of control. The control over production was further extended to cash crops, such as indigo, spices, jute, tea, coffee, etc.

Actually, the term started with the misuse of *farman* which was issued by the Mughal Emperor in 1717. The *farman* had authorized the Company to trade in Bengal for export and import of goods "without paying taxes and the right to issue passes or *dastakas* for movement of such goods. The Company's servants were also permitted to trade, but were not covered by this *farman*. They were required to pay the same taxes as the Indian merchants."[41] But the Company's servants always misinterpreted this *farman* and indulged in trade and commerce whenever they could manage without paying taxes. They even sold these passes to other merchants which earned them additional revenues. This evasion of tax by the Company's servants was a perpetual source of conflict ever since the *farman* was issued. After 1757, the Company's servants freely engaged themselves in the business and "monopolized the trade to the ruin of the native traders and thousands of weavers.... Warren Hestings said, "The collectors trade with the money they receive in the districts which affects the circulation as commerce of the country."[42] Thus, in the initial thirty years of the Company's rule, it were the Company and its servants who had total monopoly over trade and commerce in Bihar, Bengal, and Orissa. And as the political power of the Company expanded to other parts of the country, their control over trade and commerce as well as over production was extended. But the ferocity of the British rule in Bengal Presidency and the devastation it caused was never witnessed in other provinces. Bengal Presidency faced the severest brunt of their rule because the Company used it as a springboard to catapult over entire India. The revenue collected from Bengal Presidency was used to wage the relentless wars in other parts of the country, for capturing political and economic power. Therefore, the more revenue it could collect, the better it was for the Company as the money provided it more military strength and bargaining power with the native rulers. And it was more or less, with Bengal's revenue that the Company expanded and strengthened its military power, waged war in other parts of India and capturing the country entirely. The more the military wars the Company waged in India and abroad during that period, the more revenue was sucked out. Bengal Presidency being the first area of under the Company's rule, therefore, faced the greatest exploitation and devastation, and was made to bleed white.

The second step of the Himalayan loot of India by the Company came in the form of imposition of heavy taxes "levied on shops, looms, cattle, sundry profession, etc.," besides opium, salt, land, raw cotton, silk, etc.

"Nearly three-fifths of the net revenue are delivered from land", observes Marx, "Out of one-seventh from opium, and upward of one-ninth from salt. These resources, together, yield 85 per cent of the whole receipts". The rest 15 per cent came from all the sundry property and professions levied. The *Motarfa* revenue collected from the Madras Presidency alone yielded £50,000 which was equivalent to the yearly dinners of East India House. The salt revenue collected in 1780-86 yielded £986,450 from which a 'reasonable share' was paid to the Company's servants as emoluments. In fact, one of the motives of the Company to raise the salt tax from 5-50 per cent was to pay higher emoluments to Company's servants to check the malpractices by the servants of the Company by indulging in personal trade for their personal fortune vis-a-vis the Company became a concern for the masters of the Company. "In order to put an end to corruption", Clive, 'the great robber', "proposed that the totally inadequate salaries of the civil servants should be raised and they should be absolutely prohibited from embarking on private trade." As a result, "new regulations were framed for increasing the duties of the Company on salt from 35 per cent to 50 per cent" which was earlier 5 per cent paid by *gentoo* and 2.5 per cent paid by the Muslims at Hooghly on the wholesale price of salt transported into the interior parts of the country. This taxation monopoly of the Company over salt trade and payment of 'reasonable share' as emolument from the net profit from salt to Company's servants continued till 1857 and further, in different forms. The Earl of Albermarle gives a vivid description of the corruption that was practiced in salt trade in those days in the following words: "A great proportion of the salt for inland consumption throughout the country is purchased from the Company by large wholesale merchants at less than four rupees per *maund;* these mix a fixed proportion of sand, chiefly got a few miles to the south-west of Dacca, and send the mixture to a second, or counting the government as the first, to a third monopolists at about ₹5 or 6. This dealer adds more earth or ashes, and thus passing through more hands, from the big towns to villages the price is still raised to ₹8-10 and the proportion of adulteration from 25-40 per cent... The Indian masses, thus, paid not only the higher amount for salt to the merchants' coffer, but also ate sand, ash, etc., more than salt and paid dearly to the merchants' coffer in terms of health which the Company brought along with its rule."

The third step of the Company in this direction came in the form of seizure of wealth of native rulers, merchants, and bankers. The local rulers, whether in the countryside or in the towns, were directly/indirectly forced to part with heavy amount to the Company's masters and servants, officially and privately, in the form of precious commodities, like stones and metals as well as landed property of importance. And it is a well-known fact that the Nawabs of Bengal including Mir Jafar and Mir Qasim paid lakhs of rupees to the Company and its officials. Beside this, the investment of Indian merchants and bankers, in the industries and trade and commerce, were also seized. Their movable/immovable property, whichever they could lay their hands on were confiscated. Even the property of the craftsmen, guild masters, textile-workers were seized, and were returned only after payment of bribe in the form of money, gold, silver or precious gem stones. The services performed by the barbers, cobblers, washermen, servants or the craftsmen, privately or officially for the Company's personnel were either low paid or never paid. The defiant were brutally thrashed in public as well as in private, jailed, dragged in streets behind the horse-drawn carriages or their hands chopped off. The ferocity of their rule was so intense that within twenty years of their existence as paramount power in Bengal Presidency the manufacturers, *ryats*, bankers, merchants, and other common people bled to white and threatened to cause the decline of the Company's ever-increasing amount of revenue collection, services performed, and the rapacious greed of the Company and its personnel. As a result of this, the Company was forced to mend certain ongoing state of affairs. The first step was to abolish numerous petty costume *chawkies*, through which the Company and its personnel were collecting heavy revenue from Indian merchants, officially and privately, and which was hampering the net profit of the Company's masters as a lot of amount was being pocketed away be the Company's servants. This withdrawal of custom *chawkies* provided some limited opportunities of trade to the Indian merchants. The second step was to stop the seizure of private property of the craftsmen and weavers, in general, in order to maintain production level of textiles, silk, muslin, pottery, embroidery, brocades, etc. Since these products had high demand and value in the world-market, hence to maintain the Company's economic fortune, it was necessary on their part to check the decline of the produce on the condition that a fixed amount was to be paid to the Company, or like throwing open the trade to the natives for a fixed period who had advanced money to the salt-farmers for its distribution to the labourers on the condition that a fixed amount of salt, at a fixed price, was to be delivered to the Company. Certain other reforms, such as fixing the prices of the articles and making it public, fixing the duties to be paid to the Company by the native merchants, or providing security to the commodities of the native merchants to reach the destinations unmolested, etc., were implemented. Thus, these highly-motivated reforms though provided some limited opportunities to the Indians to amass some lost wealth to a limited extent were intend to revive the dying trade and industries to keep the Company's revenue flowing which was vital for them, for their political and economic existence in India. It was also because "the British, by then, were in a secure position, over-shadowing all the others as the largest single buyer and for some varieties of superior cloth virtually the only buyer. Extra-market means and restraint on producers were no longer strictly necessary to ensure a monopsonistic structure.[43]

The consequences of the rule, till the mid-19th century, were profound and multi-dimensional. Rather than constructive, it was mainly destructive. The constructive aspect, as it begun after 1785-86, was limited to few technological developments in sectors, like the cotton-industry (baling presses), silk-industry (filature machine), mint (steam-machine), watch-repairing, shipping (steam-engine and intensive and extensive use of iron), etc., integrating the Indian market through higher volume of trade and commerce, growth of urban centres, and so on.[44] Though these introductions of new technologies were highly motivated for cost-effectiveness, time-saving, better competitive product, etc., nevertheless these laid the material condition for the future development of modern industrial economy in India after the 1850s. The technological changes after 1785-86 didn't replace the old organization of labour by the modern wage-labour system. The monopoly of the Company, dominated by merchants rather than by industrialists, in trade and commerce in India and its forcible rule over the Indians has hampered the industrialization in the other sectors of industries which didn't serve the immediate interests of the Company and, in which it did not feel threatened by other European competitors were the main factors in checking the growth of the modern wage system. The workers in these industries, as in others, though timely paid, were not free to choose their masters. They were forced to the subsistence level wages in contrast to freedom to choose their masters who employed them at higher wages in the earlier days. The company systematically eliminated/subjugated the Indian merchants/bankers. By extra economic coercion, it eliminated the traditional craftsmen, textile workers, and other traditional workforce. The forced labour, reduced wages, increased price of resources required by the workforce, for manufacturing cotton, etc., introduction of limited technology, increased prices of grain (rice), imposition of taxes, like *motarfa* on loan, etc., forced the traditional workers to abandon their profession and seek asylum in villages, which consequently, led to the depopulation of towns, like Murshidabad, Dhaka, Patna, Lucknow, Tanjore, etc., in the first three decades of the Company's rule. This time, the economic factors become more effective than the extra-economic ones, and more rapid changes took place than occurred after the beginning of the free-trade and the steam age. Marx in his observation in 1853, noted, "It was the British intruder, who broke up the Indian loom and destroyed the spinning wheel. England began with driving out the Indian cottons from the European market; it then introduced twill fabric into Hindustan and in the end inundated the very mother country of cotton with cottons. From 1818-36, the export of twill fabric from Great Britain to India rose in the proportion of 1 to 5,200. In 1824, the export of British muslins to India hardly amounted to 1,000,000 yards, while in 1857 it surpassed 64,000,000 yards. But, at the same time, the population of Dhaka decreased from 150,000 inhabitants to 20,000. This decline of the Indian towns celebrated for their fabrics was by no means the worst consequence. British steam and science uprooted over the whole surface of Hindustan, the union between agriculture and manufacturing industry."[45] In fact, right from 1757, prior to the decline of high-value export goods and other items, the process of de-industrialization had begun. Though there was massive growth of Calcutta, Madras, and Bombay, as these towns were the seats of commerce and administration, as well as some new administrative centres, including Chapra, Munger, etc., the overall trend was declining at least during the first three decades of the Company's rule.

The elimination/subjugation of the Indian merchants/bankers from trade and commerce gave a fatal blow to the wealth of the country. Renowned Indian bankers, like Monahar Das, Dwarka Das, Bolaki Das, Fateh Chand, Jagat Seth, and others, who used to operate business from Delhi to Dhaka through *hundi* system, and chain of *kothi* established in all major towns, were gradually eliminated from the commercial and banking activities. The seizure of their property and snapping of their link with the industrial workforce led to the flight of urban workforce as the advance payment made to the working people for purchasing the raw materials required for manufacturing goods, stopped. This had provided security to the artisans in the form of existence of permanent customer (the bankers/merchants who had advanced the loan), the security vis-à-vis the fluctuating market (the amount of money advanced totaling to the price of goods in the market), and the security at the time of family's financial crisis when they could approach the bankers/merchants for monetary help. Once this system was snapped and was replaced by coercion and forceful appropriation of their labour, the working class began to desert their profession and the place of their livelihood. Though the third grade Indian moneylenders and merchants, who used to operate as retailers, continued to operate in the subjugated condition in the *quasbas* and *ganjs* but they were not in decisive position to arrest the general trend of decline.

The elimination of political rulers of India further hampered its industries particularly the industries related to luxury goods and war utilities. The production of war materials and luxury goods, such as swords, helmets, body armours, gold and silver embroidery, high-value metal pottery, etc., were hampered as the class of traditional consumers of these commodities were in flux. The ongoing political disturbances in India creating insecurity to the caravans carrying the goods further aggravated the problem. The return of the titular kings and Nawabs after the 1850s and the creation of new *zamindars* didn't help much in bringing old glory to these industries. At least, the glory never returned. The new political class didn't enjoy the same power and privilege, in the absence of traditional political system that the old feudatories had. As a result of this vital difference between the pre- and post-1757 political rulers, even these branches of industries were affected, adding further number of unemployed Indians to the total population of the country.

Thus, the beginning of the British rule was the beginning of the destruction of the traditional industries and its support base, namely, merchants/bankers and feudatories at one pole, working people at the other pole, and towns in general. It was the beginning of the Himalayan loot of the Indians and the pauperization of its people without any sign of substantial technological innovations and new industrial products till the 1840s. The available data clearly show this. "Between 1772/93-1796/97 and 1818/19-1823/24 … While spinners' wages in Malda and eight other residences remained stagnant at ₹2.5 per month, the average price of raw cotton went up from. ₹12.8 to ₹16.5 per month and that of rice from ₹0.62 to ₹1.02 per *maund*. The weavers were getting from the English East India Company prices which were from 6 per cent to 83 per cent less than what private traders were offering. In 1974, weavers were incurring a loss of about 10 per cent to 30 per cent because of the difference between the Company's purchase price and raw material and labour input costs. The Company used its dominant position to fix the terms of exchange, pushing down the share of wages towards the subsistence level."[46] This state of affair was not limited to Bengal only, neither was it limited to only one segment of the workforce (the weavers), but it was spread to the entire British India and the industrial workforce. The wealth 'sucked out of the workforce and the natural resources of India were shipped to England, enriching the coffers of the masters of the Company and the political rulers of that country'. The trade and commerce linking every town, *Quasba, ganj* and *haat* with metropolis, like Calcutta, Bombay, and Madras was the medium. The military force was the midwife that helped trade and commerce to come into existence. The imports of different goods in Calcutta and the share of different provinces by sending these goods to Calcutta between 1812/13-1835/36 can be seen in Tables 1 and 2.[47]

The tables show: (1) an overall growing integration of national market, linking Calcutta with different towns of India; and (2) the nature of imports. Between 1812-36, there had been an overall growth in the value and per centage of trade. From ₹27.9 million, 83 per cent of the trade, it went up to ₹55.3 million, that is, 92 per cent of the trade. The import of commodities, including indigo, opium, raw cotton, raw silk, textile, sugar, and saltpetre were meant for either industries in England or for sale in the highly profitable European market. The benefit of this kind of trade was obviously, going into the pocket of the British ruling class either in India or in England. And the brunt was being borne by the working populace of Bengal Presidency, in the initial years, and later on by the working population of other parts of the country.

The shameless plunder of India facilitated the growth of Industrial Revolution in England which could have been delayed in the absence of wealth required for the research. The emergence of the Company as the paramount power in India in 1757 and the beginning of Industrial Revolution in 1760 was not merely a coincidence or chance. The Industrial Revolution which gave birth to the industrial capitalist however, killed the very Company and the merchant class which had helped in giving birth to it.

The Company's India loot activities, nevertheless, helped the economic integration of the country. The linkage of the metropolis with the provincial

TABLE 1 Imports into Calcutta from the interior of the Presidency (Percentage of total trade by value)

	Value (million ₹)	Indigo	Raw Silk	Raw Cotton	Sugar	Saltpetre	Bilalr	Opium	Banaras	Cotton	Textiles	Silk	% of total trade
1812-13	27.9	26	9	4	3	*	—	—	—	—	41	—	83
1813-14	25.6	29	7	14	4	1	—	—	—	—	28	—	83
1814-15	32.0	32	11	11	5	1	—	—	—	—	28	—	88
1815-16	39.5	39	7	11	4	1	—	—	—	—	38	—	90
1816-17	48.8	18	3	15	7	3	—	—	—	—	38	—	90
1817-18	na	13	8	*	9	*	—	—	—	—	43	—	89
1818-19	39.7	17	4	18	12	2	—	—	—	—	49	—	79
1819-20	53.2	20	15	8	9	5	—	1	—	24	—	3	85
1820-21	46.1	17	16	10	8	5	—	2	—	21	—	4	83
1821-22	50.4	18	17	9	7	4	—	1	—	21	—	6	83
1822-23	47.7	24	16	6	7	3	—	1	—	22	—	6	85
1823-24	40.5	20	17	5	6	6	—	2	—	21	—	6	8.
1824-25	54.2	20	15	8	7	3	—	17	—	11	—	5	86
1825-26	58.0	27	15	5	4	3	—	19	—	13	—	5	91
1826-27	51.4	16	16	12	7	5	12	—	4	12	—	6	90
1827-28	54.0	28	14	7	4	2	15	—	5	8	—	5	88
1828-29	53.3	18	19	7	8	3	15	—	5	7	—	4	86
1829-30	51.9	26	15	7	8	3	15	—	6	4	—	4	88
1830-31	52.3	25	16	6	5	4	17	—	7	4	—	6	9
1831-32	47.8	25	13	5	4	5	17	—	8	4	—	8	89
1832-33	49.9	27	12	6	3	5	18	—	7	4	—	7	89
1833-34	48.5	20	14	6	5	6	17	—	8	3	—	10	89
1834-35	50.2	22	11	8	6	4	18	—	9	3	—	7	88
1835-36	55.3	18	7	22	3	3	23	—	12	1	—	1	92

Sources: Computed by Marcia Frost, Department of Economic History, University of Pennsylvania from *Report of the internal and External Commerce of Bengal,* 1812.13 through 1835-36, India Office Records, P/174/24-47.
na: data missing; *: Less than 1%.

TABLE 2 North India's share of the internal trade of the Bengal Presidency (based on customs collections)

	Bengal presidency (million of ₹)	Major Stations' share of upper provinces customs										5 Delhi stations	8 provinces stations	Value of upper provinces trade (million ₹)
		%upper provinces	Kanpur	Faru-khabad	Allahabad	Bareilly	Agra	Mirzapur	Meerut	Banaras	Ghazipur			
1815-16	69.4	49	14	8	10	7	27	9	9	7	7	—	—	19.4
1816-17	7.7	47	12	8	11	6	31	8	12	7	9	—	—	22.9
1817-18	8.2	43	12	9	11	7	33	8	11	6	8	—	—	a
1818-19	8.1	41	8	6	7	7	36	8	14	6	6			16.3
1819-20	a	—	—	—	—	—	—	—	—	—	—	a —	—	—
1820-21	7.6	47	13	5	7	4	36	8	14	5	6	—	—	21.7
1821-22	7.9	44	11	6	6	5	38	10	10	6	7	—	—	22.2
1823-24	6.4	47	10	6	6	6	41	10	9	5	7	—	—	19.0
1824-25	6.6	44	7	6	6	6	41	11	8	6	8	—	—	23.8
1825-26	6.1	46	10	6	6	8	39	11	6	5	7	—	—	26.7
1826-27	5.7	49	8	5	7	5	41	14	6	6	8	—	—	26.7
1827-28	6.2	49	7	4	5	5	47	10	8	6	6	—	—	26.5
1828-29	6.2	49	8	5	5	6	47	10	6	6	6	18	—	26.1
1829-31	7.1	49	7	3	13	4	32	6	5	4	4	20	—	30.9
1831-32	6.5	61	6	2	14	3	28	6	7	4	4	16	9	29.2
1832-33	7.1	68	5	2	16	4	27	6	6	4	4	16	8	33.9
1833-34	6.0	62	6	3	14	4	25	7	6	5	5	13	10	30.1

Source: Computed by Marcia Frost, Department of Economic History, University of Pennsylvania from *Report of the Internal and External Commerce of Bengal,* 1812-13 through 1833-34, India Office Records, P/174/24-47.
a: data missing.

towns and villages for procurement of agricultural and industrial commodities facilitated by the development of steam-powered tug boats, flotilla, etc., which revolutionised river communications, created an integrated national economy based on the inter-dependence and inter-connectedness of the different scattered and autonomous production centres. And further linked the national economy, as a subjugated partner, to the English-European capitalist economy.

Thus, the period 1757-1857 saw momentous changes brought about by the numerous policies of the British, including *dadni* system (upto 1770s), contract system or *khatbandi* regulation (1770s to 1780s), the direct agency system (1793-1814), limited Free Trade (1814-34), and Free Trade (1834 onwards). It was momentous because it witnessed the beginning of systematic and cruelest destruction of the Indian political ruling class, merchants and bankers, industrial workforce, and industries and towns through the above-mentioned policies adopted from time to time. It was a degrading period, because it witnessed the transformation of a land from an independent, sovereign, chiefly exporting country to a subjugated country chiefly exporting commodities satisfying British interest, and then, to an importing country inundated with English twists and cotton stuffs'. It was the period which laid the foundation of converting India into a classic colony.

But, in spite of these transformations, there was no fundamental change in the organization of labour, neither was there any mass qualitative technological change in the production of commodities, except in the selected few areas discussed here. The "production and trade occurred within organizational forms and patterns which predate 1757 ... Nor is there much evidence of dramatic technological change in either crafts or agriculture."[48] The Company threatened by the decline of revenue after the initial years of brutal rule tried to revive to a limited extent the old system of advance payment to the salt farmers and others through Indian merchants on given terms. But, overall, its rule remained mainly destructive, the formation of integrated national market and its linkage as subordinate partner to the international capitalist economy notwithstanding. The constructive aspect of the British rule could take place in substantial form only after the second half of the 19th century.

The growth of the modern, large-scale industry in India was the product of the necessity of the British industrial capitalist class. The inundation of the Indian society with English twists and cotton stuffs that had started since 1813 (the year of limited Free Trade) and it gathered momentum after 1834 (the year of Free Trade Act) that sunk down the exchange rate of rupees, reduced the power of consumption of the Indian masses and contracted the market of British goods could not have continued for long unless the ruling class of Britain would have revived the power of consumption of the Indian population which could become possible by establishing large-scale industries and providing jobs to millions of jobless workers. The requirement of the industrial resources (mineral resources, raw cotton, jute, silk, etc.) for churning out finish goods further created the necessity for the development of better transportation facilities which could rapidly carry the resources from village, town, and mines to ports for shipment to England. Thus, the dependency of the British ruling class on the Indian market and raw resources forced it to lay the foundation of modern large-scale industries and transport system. While the first problem (shrinkage of market share) was the creation of the Company's rule, the latter (the raw sources) was the requirement of the class that had come up as a result of general movement of society towards industrialization since the time of Industrial Revolution.

The result of these two necessities led to the establishment of jute and cotton mills and development of iron and coal mines between 1850-55 along with the introduction of railway in 1853. In 1879, there were 56 cotton mills in India. The number of jute mills, mainly owned by the European, rose to 20 in 1882. In 1880, 56 coal mines were operating the country. The number of cotton mills increased to 144 during 1894-95. In the same year, the number of jute mills rose to 29 and that of coal mines to 123 in the same year. In 1913-14, the number of cotton mills rose to 264 and that of jute mills to 64. Between 1890 and 1914, new industries, like petroleum, manganese, mica, and saltpetre, came into existence. Some rice and timber mills were also started. In addition, "engineering and railway workshops, iron and brass foundries, also grew rapidly."[49] The growth of railway like that of jute, textile, coal mine, etc., was faster than the other sundry industries, like paper, matches, or the heavy industry. From the first line built between Bombay to Thane in 1853 to the last built in 1846-47 during the British Raj, the density of rail lines grew to 159 per 10,000 sq km and all but few districts in remote regions were served by railway. Already at the beginning of First World War, India had the third largest railway network in the world. Similarly, by that period it had the largest jute manufacturing industry and the fourth largest textile industries. Between 1914-18 and 1939-45, due to the World Wars, there was comparatively faster growth of profit in the industries than in the preceding years of the wars. The value of exports of manufactured jute, for example, was £18,849 in 1913-1914 which rose to £35,101 in 1918-19. The port and cement registered production of 84,000 tons, about half the quantity imported in 1914. Similarly, the expansion of production capacities of old industries, creation of new and different kind of industries, like paper, sugarcane, matches, iron and steel, chemical, etc., and the growth in numbers of established industries, like jute, cotton were considerable. And not only that, "during the inter-war period, Indian manufacturing output grew at a rate well above the world average being exceeded during the whole period by only four of the 28 countries. India's manufacturing output grew at rate well above the world average being exceeded during the whole period by only that of the UK, the US and Germany."[50] However, in spite of these now rapid, now low growth of industries in India at the time of independence remained largely non-industrial and one of the poorest countries of the world. Industrialization could not engulf the entire sectors of economy nor its total effect was cumulative; rather the rate of industrialization was much slower than the rate of 'dis-industrialization' in the sense that employment generated by the modern industries fell far short of ruin it did to the traditional industries employing millions. The factor mainly responsible for this kind of growth was the class interest of the British. Some other minor factors, like lack of technical education in India, unsuitability of British imported machines to Indian environment, etc., also hampered proper growth.

Since the development of industries in India was the product of necessities of the British ruling class, therefore, the expansion of the industries was largely guided by these necessities. And throughout the British rule, we find that only those industries could develop, and with the desired intensity, which were desired by the British, barring the years of the world wars in which they were forced to concede the development of some new industries due to the military engagement of England, disturbances of sea routes and conversion of India into the military theatre of England in the east of Suez. As a result of this need, there grew mainly railway, cotton, jute, and coal industries which served their interests. There was a virtual absence of heavy and chemical industries, manufacturing machine tools, sulphuric acid, fertiliser, railway engines, ships, aeroplanes, automobiles, petroleum products, etc., which were against their interests. The existence of great demand of textile in the world market providing heavy profits to the British, and the labour-intensive nature of these industries providing jobs to millions, which was necessary for reviving the purchasing power of the Indians in order to sell the British manufactured goods, were the main responsible factors for the establishment of cotton and jute industries. Its establishment and growth were further facilitated by abundant coal-iron reserves in India, which were extracted from the pits at a very cheap price due to the supply of cheap labour-power, and constant supply of cheap raw cotton and jute. The low wages and the abundance of low-priced raw resources put the cost of manufactured goods very favourably vis-a-vis the Europeans and Americans. The demand of the Indian goods, therefore, was very high. Since India was a colony, hence the profit was being accrued by the British. Contrary to this, the setting up of heavy and chemical industries were either discouraged or not initiated due to economic fear. The low wages and cheap resources could have put the Indian heavy/chemical industries in a far better position than the British and could have paved the way for all-round development which could have been detrimental to the interest of the British.

The methods that were employed to check the growth of the industries were mainly financial and control over management, imposition or removal of tariffs on goods imported into and exported from India, and deliberate check on the spread of technical knowledge in general. While the latter policy adopted by the British, hampered the growth of scientific-technological knowledge, research work, etc., required for manning the industries, the former two policies checked the expansion of production capacities, creation of economic/industrial infrastructure, and other such facilities required for the economic development of masses. Since capital is required for the establishment and growth of industries in capitalist society, therefore, the absence of capital meant absence of industries. The British ruling class did this successfully through various budgetary expenditure, tariff boards and management control. The expenditure on education was lowest, the duty imposed on the Indian goods in England undesired by the ruling class was heavy and that of desired goods was lowest. The goods coming into India was either not taxed or lowly taxed. The role of the banks in giving loans to the Indians' controlled industries was dismal, while the loans asked by the British was easily given, that too on soft interest. On the other hand, if loans were given to Indians they had very high rate of interest. The pressure of the Indian political masses put upon the British in this regard didn't affect the overall scenario much. It simply restrained the British, to some extent, in closing their economic tentacles over the Indian industrialists. Except for few modifications here and there, like increase and decrease of tariff, extension and withdrawal of subsidies, expansion and withdrawal of control of British capital and personnel from management, etc., which were being done from time to time after observing the overall political and economic situation in India, England, and the world, there was no fundamental, qualitative change in the state of affair.

The impact of industrialization on the Indian society was multi-dimensional, the most important being the creation of three different urban social classes, namely, the industrial proletariat, bourgeoisie, and petty-bourgeoisie. Among the three the proletariat was numerically the most superior, followed by the petty-bourgeoisie and bourgeoisie. The interest of the proletariat and the Indian capitalists were antithetical, while the former was for abolition of capital and all modern property relations, stood for higher wages, better working and living condition, social security, etc. The latter stood for having more share in the total surplus value appropriated by the British and were anti-change vis-a-vis proletariat. The middle class vacillated between the two and lived in two minds. The one minor section aligned itself with the proletariat, the other major section joined the Indian capitalists. Nevertheless, all the three classes viewed the existing colonial rule as the principal political contradiction and fought jointly and separately against the British regime. The economic contradictions between the proletariat and the Indian capitalists were shelved temporarily, at least it was not brought to the fore.

The proletariat that grew out of the womb of old society mostly comprising the traditional weavers, craftsmen, and poor backward sections of the society swelled in numbers as the years rolled by. From the modest beginning of few hundred in the 1850s, working in jute and textile mills of Bombay and Calcutta it swelled to 951,000 in 1914 working in 2,681 registered companies and again to 17,000,000 in 1940 working in 9,000 factories of different nature. Tables 3 to 5[51] show the evolution of jute and textile industries in India from 1854-1914. It can be noted that technology used, like looms and spindles provided opportunities to the traditional weave and spinners.

Compared to the total Indian population, this number was a mere fraction of the populace. But in terms of militancy and consistency it outmarked every other class. Its condition of working was horrible and was not different from the condition of the working class in England, as noted by Engels in 1840s. The wages were meager, to the lowest subsistence level. And in the absence of trade unions it practically could not register any substantial growth till 1918 unlike the Charterists of England of 1830-40s. Though right from 1870 onwards, workingmen's club and associations begun to grow, and the journals espousing their cause begun to publish, but nothing concrete emerged either in terms of economics or politics. They continued to live in hovels, the children, males, females, all crouching together in small shanty rooms without any proper ventilation, lavatory, water, etc. Their diet consisted of *sattu*, rice, *litti*, salt, chilli, etc. They were forced to work for 18-20 hours a day in smoked, dirty factories, suffered from diseases, like

TABLE 3 Number of mills, looms and employment in Indian jute industry 1854-55 to 1913-14

Year	No. of mills	No. of looms	Aveage daily employment	Average no. of looms per mill	Averge employment per mill
1854-55	1	N.A.	N.A.	N.A.	N.A.
1868-69	5	950	N.A.	190	N.A.
1883-84	23	6,132	47,863	266.6	2,081.0
1893-94	28	9,580	69,179	342.1	2,470.7
1903-04	38	18,400	123,869	484.2	3,259.7
1913-14	64	36,050	216,288	563.3	3,379.5

TABLE 4 Growth of the cotton mill industry in India (1875-76 to 1913-14)

Year	No. of mills	No. of spindles (thousands)	No. of looms (thousands)	Average daily employment (thousands)
1875-76	47	1,100	9.1	N.A.
1883-84	79	2,002	16.3	60
1893-94	142	3,650	31.1	130
1903-04	191	5,118	45.3	185
1913-14	271	6,779	104.2	260

Source: In Table 3, data before 1883-84 from D.R. Wallace, *The Romance of Jute "A Short History of the Calcutta Jute Industry,* 1855-1927 *and edn,* 1928). *Data for* 1883-84 *and after, from Moral and Material Progress and Condition of India.*

Data on the Cotton textile industry given in Table IV come from the annual reports of the Bombay Millowners Association.

TABLE 5 Regional distribution of cotton mill capacity in India 1875-76 to 1913-14 (per cent)

	Mills			Spindles		
	Bombay city	Elsewhere in Bombay Presidency	Elsewhere in India	Bombay city	Elsewhere in Bombay Presidenc	Elsewhere in India
1875-76	61.7	21.3	17.01	74.3	13.4	12.4
1883-84	54.4	21.5	24.1	67.5	13.6	18.8
1893-94	48.6	21.1	30.3	55.5	14.7	29.8
1903-04	41.4	28.3	30.4	49.5	20.1	30.3
1913-14	31.4	36.2	32.5	44.4	25.8	29.9
	Looms			*Employment*		
1875-76	87.9	6.6	5.5	—	—	
1883-84	73.6	14.1	12.3	60.0	15.0	25.0
1893-94	58.8	19.3	21.9	54.6	14.6	30.8
1903-04	53.2	22.3	24.5	48.6	20.5	30.8
1913-14	46.8	332.2	20.98	42.3	26.2	31.5

Source: *Annual Report,* Bombay Millowner Association.

tuberculosis, skin disease, etc., lean and thin, rag-tagged, but most humane this class of humanity suffered from all kinds of destitution. Cultural and caste differences, continued linkage of workers with the villages and land (at least in the first generation) checked their strength of collective bargaining which perpetuated their poverty. Illiteracy and lack of the critical comprehension of the functioning of the capitalist system checked them from political participation almost till the end of 19th century. It was only after the First World War that they could form powerful trade unions at national level and participated in the freedom struggle. Their leadership was, by and large, dominated by the middle class. From among the workers who could rise to the position were sucked into the ethos and methods of struggle of the middle class. Thus, the working class, in spite of vast numerical superiority, consistency, and militancy could not pose a powerful alternative, independent of bourgeoisie and petty-bourgeoisie as the Paris communards had done. On the contrary, instead of taking their movement, at their own strength, to the logical conclusion they remained (at least the majority) mere supporters of different political parties. Since their support was vital to pressurize the government for conceding concessions, hence every political party vied with each other for enlisting their support. The working class, politically speaking, could not form a "class for itself". They remained spellbound by the *vibhutis* (political leaders of different political parties). The era of *Lokaavtar* remained a distant dream.

The bourgeoisie, in contrast to the numerical strength of the workers, consisted of a fraction of the population, was most organized and a class that was conscious of its interests. Their umbilical cord was tied up with the British and European capitalism right from the 1850s, and they operated as their junior partners at system-level. The history of their subordination, in fact, started from 1757, when, after the systematic elimination of independent, powerful Indian merchants, the petty-Indian merchants, the retail suppliers of commodities in *ganj, quasba*, and *baat* began to play second fiddle to the British canoe for their economic survival. This economic tendency continued even after they began to convert their wealth in establishing modern industries, and gradually becoming part of the modern industrial capitalist process. Their politics emanating from their economic status, was the politics of compromise and gaining concessions. Since the economic interest of the British and the Indian capitalists was fundamentally the same, formation of capital, therefore, the use of political movements was limited to pressurize the British to concede some economic benefits rather than to go for revolutionary reconstruction which they could have done like the American Revolution of 1776, but which they didn't do due to the fear of the working class or state repression. They maintained a distance from political struggle to save themselves from the probable colonial state reprisal. The history of 1757 and 1857 worked very deeply in their minds.

It is well known that the Indian capitalists not only compromised with the British, but also with the nawabs, *zamindars*, and kings. The latter (a number of them) had converted themselves into merchants and industrialists; the former required them as supplier of finance (share holdings), raw resources for the industries, and seller of finished commodities in the villages. Thus, the common economic interest and a common ideology of wealth between the two branches of top capitalist strata (industry and agriculture) hampered the socio-economic transformation in the agricultural sector as well. The Indian capitalists never intended a radical rural-urban social transformation and, like the German bourgeoisie of 1848, they betrayed the working class and peasant movements that had built up over the years. They were the reflection of the social status quo. Their struggle against the British was the struggle of a bigger share in surplus value which the transfer of political power in 1947 gave them. It meant for them the removal of all colonial economic restraints, like tariff, loan, aid, management control, etc., which had hampered their economic maneuverability and checked them in expanding their capital. The fight of the Indian capitalists was the fight for removal of these economic restraints. It was never intended to share the benefits of technological development with the working class. The workers working in the factories of the Indian capitalists were never paid higher wages than the workers in the factories controlled by the British. The working and living condition remained the same. In fact, the workers of jute and cotton mills which were generally controlled by the Indians were the worst sufferers both in terms of wages and physical existence. Not only this, the Indian capitalists vehemently opposed the factory legislations in the ground that it will harm the Indian capitalists, that is, it is intended to give leverage to the British capitalists. The workers' strike in the factories of the Indian capitalists was as recurrent as in that of the British. The Indian capitalists, in fact, with less paid-up capital than the British were the biggest exploiters. The economic necessity of rapid capital formation was the reason behind this severest exploitation which could be done only by pushing the wages to the lowest subsistence level and increasing the working hours, the phenomenon that was prevalent in the initial years of capitalism. The hike in wages in the initial few years after the First World War was the result of trade boom, growing organized pressure of the workers and the technological improvement. The strike of the workers could have led to huge losses during a period when there was a general trade boom. In order to get benefit out of this opportunity, it was felt senseless by the capitalists to face organized workers almost everyday. The massive capital formation during the war years, the technological improvement and the reduced intervention of the state due to war constraints in the management leading to productivity further removed the hitch in the wage hike. Consequently, "wages in industrial centres rose steadily until 1921. In Bengal jute mills, by 1920, wages rose by 50 per cent over the 1914 wage level, and in Bombay, for the first time, a wage rise of 10 per cent in 1919 followed by quick rise till 1921 when there was nearly 130 per cent increase over the 1914 level."[52] But, in spite of this progress, the workers were still being dragged "through blood and dirt, through misery and degradation."

The late historical arrival of Indian bourgeoisie, that too under the colonial system, put them under so many constraints. Unlike the European-American counterparts, they could never enjoy the freedom of free trade and limited state. The colonial state always discriminated between the Indian and British capitalists. While the British enjoyed all the support and benefit for their expansion of the empire from this state and financial institutions, the Indian capitalists always suffered at the hands of the monstrous, monolithic structure. However, among themselves, the Indian capitalists enjoyed a brief era of free competition in the sense that they competed against each other freely, without any monopolistics domination. The monopoly among the Indian capitalists was yet to emerge. And, it could emerge only after the First World War. From the 1850s to the 1920s, for almost seventy years, the Indian capitalists thus enjoyed among themselves a phase of non-monopolistic competition, an era of free competition. The huge profit made during the First World War and in subsequent years altered the form of capitalism. From free competition stage it passed to monopolistic stage. The profit made during these years (for example, the rates of net profit to paid-up capital of the jute mills of Calcutta was given as 58 per cent in 1915; 75 per cent in 1916; 49 per cent in 1917, and 73 per cent in the first half of 1918)[53] out of free competition was channelized and invested in different branches of industries by few capitalists who succeeded in eliminating others in the race of capital, which, later on, gave them leverage in management. The growth of financial institutions, like banks after 1920s and their growing roles in the industrial development provided further impetus to their tightening control over different branches of industries. The financial oligarchy that grew after the 1930s finally sealed the fate of free competition. Thus, "a dozen individuals" writes Asok Mehta about those days of Bombay, "by their control over banks, insurance companies, and investment trust, occupy commanding position in the industrial life of Bombay. Sir Purshottam Das Thakur Das and his cousin Sir Chunilal Mehta, between them, hold directorships in every trust and in well-nigh every important concern in Bombay. They have facilitated or frustrated as it suited them many an amalgamation and absorption. Prem Chand Brothers, Jeejeebhoy Brothers, Cowasji Jehangir, in their ways exert similar influence, thanks to their financial power."[54] Similarly, Tatas controlled numerous cotton mills and power and electric companies besides controlling one iron and steel works and airway company. The British already had their own trusts and cartels. Another feature of capitalism that was growing at this period was the growing volume of import of capital in India from England which had gradually replaced the other import items like cotton goods as primary importable commodity. Now, it was capital which was the primary import item. In 1933, as per the estimate of British Associated Chambers of Commerce, £1,000 million was invested in India. The role of finance capital within India and the import of capital from England further intensified the loot of India. The more capital was invested; the severe was the intensity of exploitation. As a result, the loot of India in the last 20 years of British Raj was manifold more than the loots put together in the preceding 50 years, like the loots that had begun after the 1850s was many times more and higher in intensity than the loot that begun after 1757. The different successive stages and forms of capitalism within the colonial system, thus, brought greater misery and degradation to Indians which finally culminated in the most inhuman Bengal famine of 1940s. But parallel to this, capital kept on expanding. The petty traders, through accumulated wealth of trade and commerce of the pre-1850s channelized their wealth in the modern industries of the post-1850s period, became petty industrialists. From petty industrialists they became monopolistic, financial oligarchies. Thus, the force that was let loose in the post-1757 period saw its maturity by the 1930s. The Indian capitalists, like an island, had arrived on the scene with the essential requisites of developed capitalism in the sea of famine struck humanity.

The third class, the modern, urban middle class was the first to arrive in urban India. While the proletariat and the bourgeoisie arrived after the 1850s, the middle class arrived in the 1820s itself after the 1813 Act when the British took conscious decision to spend money in education as a policy to produce brown skins who can handle the expanding administrative and trading functions of the Company and can act as interlocutors between the British and Indians. Even prior to 1813, the Company's personnel in order to understand Muslim and Hindu laws of the land which were necessitated in order to do business had opened two educational institutions, one at Calcutta and another at Varanasi. But they were mere peanuts. However, the process that begun after 1813, became intensified after the 1820s creating a vast strength of multi-layered middle class in India, which in course of its rule first helped the social reforms movement and then pioneered the political agitation for *swaraj*. The social reforms which broke the backbone of the evils of Indian society preceded by the economic necessities of trade and livelihood, encouraged the traditional Indians to join new educational institutions. The help of liberal philanthropists silently supported by the business community in order to expand consumers of the British commodities gave further push to this process. The beginning of industrialization acted as another milestone in spreading education. The new method of production and distribution required updated knowledge, both technical and theoretical, which forced the British to set up universities in industrial centres. The establishment of nationalist schools and colleges in the first decade of 20th century and later provided another boost to education. Thus, the economy followed by education steeped into liberal humanism and rationalism created a class that was urbane, suave, articulate, and yet volatile. It helped the demise of the Raj that had created it.

The educated unemployed that were created out of Macualay's policy over the years gradually became restless. Even those in administration were discontented with the discriminatory treatment meted out to them. The power of comprehending the functioning of the system that they developed after learning the English alphabet put them at forefront of agitation. The economic discontentment clubbed with the power of knowledge and their own frustration with the colonial system provide the fertile ground for the nationalist mass movement that begun to rock the system from the first decade of the 20th century. Their existence in every town, in every nook and corner of the country, organizing and teaching the workers, peasants and their own inactive class brethren gave power to the movement. However, as a class they resembled the characters portrayed in Harishankar Parsai's story, *Ek Madhyam Vargiya Kutta*. They barked at the sign of approaching danger that emanates in the capitalist and colonial society. The prospect of unemployment, the alienation and the guilt-consciousness of non-contribution to the society all created fear in them. But, at the same time, the fear of losing property, job or the fear of state-repression, harassment of family members, etc., restricted them from active participation. Majority sympathized with the cause of workers and peasants or the cause of freedom yet majority never participated actively for the cause. Since they belonged to the propertied groups, like rich gentry, traders, peasants, salaried professional, hence the fear of present and future haunted them strongly. Even those who didn't belong to the propertied group, but had some property in the past looked at the past instead of looking at the present and future. The ideology, like that of Hindi maxim 'my grandfather had eaten *ghee*, smell my palm' operated very strongly.

The political parties and associations that sprang up were virtually controlled by the middle class, particularly the top layer, as it were they who had helped in creating these organizations. They enjoyed decisive, crucial, decision-making powers, had indirect/direct linkage (barring the Communist Party) with the magnates of the industries, land, and trade. The policies that were formulated and adopted particularly by the Congress and Muslim League helped the development of capitalism rather than the cause of workers, as Bhagat Singh had rightly pointed out. The brief rule of the Congress and Muslim League in 1937 and the transfer of power ten years later proved him right. Thus, from social reforms movement of the 1820s to the transfer of political power in 1947, the middle class remained at the centre-stage of leadership. From motivating the British rulers to abolish *sati* to forcing them to transfer political power through workers' and peasants' mobilization, the middle class helped building a society in which certain liberal political rights became the creed of future governance.

To conclude, the impact of the British rule on Indian industries was multi-faceted. It travelled through mercantile capitalism to industrial capitalism, and from free competitive capitalism to monopoly capitalism. In course of its journey, the different stages of growth had different kind and intensity of impact on the Indian socioeconomic structure. In the first stage that lasted up to 1853, the Company operated by and large, within the traditional parameters of production, and organization of labour system. The second stage marked the beginning of industrial revolution in India, the growth of free competitive capitalism, and its replacement by monopoly capitalism in the 1920s. The social classes that grew as a result of this economy, passed through numerous stages of development reflecting more or less the changing features of capitalism. While the Charter Act of 1813 and 1834 saw the growth of educated, urban middle class, and the beginning of social reform movement, the 1850s saw the growth of industrial bourgeoisie and the proletariat. The decade 1920 and after began to witness the growth of real workers' and peasants' movements in India. In between the 1850s and the 1920s, there were important sporadic revolts of peasants in various pockets of India which had considerable impact on the psyche of the masses as well as on administration, but it fizzled out in a year or two unlike the movements that began from the beginning of the 20th century. While the focus of the social reform movement was the elimination of caste and sex-based exploitation that had gripped the upper castes of the Indian society in course of history, the focus of the political movements, beginning from the first decade of the 20th century, was the elimination of the British rule. In between these, two social and political contradictions, there was another important contradiction that haunted the Indian masses since the beginning of 1757. The struggle between the peasant and *neo-zamindars* in agricultural sector and between the proletariat and bourgeoisie in the industrial centres, the continued now open, now subtle struggle, were equally important contradictions which were glossed over due to the existence the of British Raj. The development of mechanized transportation, hotels, and *dhabas* which facilitated the weakening of caste and cultural differences gave national character to the localized peasants' and workers' movements by linking them with common organizations. The common national education and the capitalist economy had already prepared the ground.

The British rule, as Marx had observed, with all its ulterior motives, thus, laid the promise for the material and moral emancipation of the Indians and put them into the comity of civilized humanity. As an unconscious tool of history, as a chaser of commodities and market, it battered all the Chinese Walls of local seclusion, self-sufficiency, caste, sex and cultural differences of the Indian society, and gave her a cosmopolitan character of production, distribution, and consumption.

Notes and References

1. For Pastoral Economy of the Vedic Society, See Romila Thapar, *From Lineage to State*, Delhi, 1990, pp. 24–27.
2. See D.D. Kosambi, *An Introduction to the Study of Indian History*. Bombay, 1956, pp. 222, 281.
3. For the Role of Market Forces in Rural India, See Sanjay Subrahmanyam (ed.), *Merchants, Markets and the State in Early Modern India*. Delhi, 1990, Chaps. VII, VIII.
4. For the *Role* of Village Panchayat, See John Mathai, *Village Government in British India*, 1915, p. 19: Burton, Stein (ed.). *Essays on South India*. New Delhi, 1976, pp. 69–70.
5. For the Upper Castes' Role in Agricultural Production, See Dharma Kumar (ed.). *The Cambridge Economic History of India, 1757-1970*, Vol. II, Delhi 1982, p. 10; Burten Stein (ed.). *The Making of Agrarian Policy in British India: 1770-1900*. Delhi, 1992, p. 40.
6. See Dharma Kumar (ed.), *op. cit.*, p. 16.
7. *Ibid.*, p. 1933.
8. See Bipan Chandra, *et. al., Freedom Struggle*, Delhi, 1992, p. 7.
9. Warren Hastings, *Historical Documents of British India*, Vol. I. Delhi, 1985, p. 160.
10. *Ibid.*, p. 150.
11. *Ibid.*, p. 15.
12. *Ibid.*, p. 12.
13. *Ibid.*
14. See Dharma Kumar (ed.), *op. cit.*, Chap. III.
15. B.H. Baden-Powell, *Administration of Land Revenue and Tenure in British India*, New Delhi, 1978, Chap. 8.
16. R.P. Dutt. *India Today*. Bombay, 1947, Chap. 8, Satish Chandra, *Medieval India: Society, the Jagirdari Crisis and the Village*, Madras, 1982, p. 105.
17. Burten Stein, No. 5, pp. 9–10.
18. *Ibid.*, p. 120.
19. *Ibid.*, pp. 38–39.
20. There is no denying of the roles played by Thomas Munro and the Utilitarian Ideology but even these two factors, in course of time, turned into profitable ventures.
21. Dharma Kumar (ed.), *op. cit.*, p. 41; Burten Stein (ed.), *op. cit.*, pp. 68–78.
22. K. Marx and F. Engels, *On Colonialism*, Moscow, 1978, p. 52.
23. Burton Stein, No. 5, p. 42.
24. *Ibid.*, p. 49.
25. Bipan Chandra, *Modern India*, New Delhi, 1986, p. 185.
26. Warren Hastings, *op. cit.*, pp. 144–145.

27. *Ibid.*
28. Quoted in A.R. Desai, *Social Background of Indian Nationalism*, Bombay, 1981, p. 60.
29. K. Marx and F. Engels, *op. cit.*, pp. 52–53.
30. See M.N. Srinivas, *Social Change in Modern India*, Delhi, 1977, pp. 22–28.
31. Quoted in A.R. Desai, *op. cit.*, p. 54.
32. K. Marx and F. Engels, *op. cit.*, pp. 52–53.
33. Jawaharlal Nehru, *The Discovery of India*, Delhi, 1986, p. 306.
34. See D.D. Kosambi, *op. cit.*, p. 34.
35. See Jawaharial Nehru, *op. cit.*, p. 113.
36. See D.D. Kosambi, *op. cit.*
37. *Ibid.*, p. 56.
38. Dharma Kumar (ed.)., *op. cit.*, Vol. II. Delhi, 1982, p. 9.
39. Warren Hastings, *op. cit.*, Vol. I. Delhi, 1985, p. 18.
40. William Bilts, quoted in Warren Hastings, *op. cit.*, p. 18.
41. Bipan Chandra, *Modern India*, Delhi, 1986.
42. Warren Hastings, *op. cit.*, p. 18.
43. S. Bhattacharya in Dharma Kumar (ed.), *op. cit.*, p. 288.
44. See *Ibid.*, pp. 242–375.
45. K. Marx and F. Engels, *op. cit.*, pp. 38–39.
46. Quoted in Dharma Kumar (ed.), *op. cit.*, pp. 288–289.
47. Quoted in Tom G. Kessinger, *"North India"*, in Dharma Kumar (ed.), pp. 253–255.
48. Tom G. Kessinger, in Dharma Kumar (ed.), *ibid.*, p. 267.
49. Quoted in A.R. Desai, *Social Background of Indian Nationalism*, Bombay, 1981, pp. 104–105.
50. Morris D. Morris in Dharma Kumar (ed.), *op. cit.*, p. 609.
51. Quoted in Morris D. Morris, *"The Growth of Large-Scale Industry to* 1947" in Dharma Kumar (ed.), *Ibid.*, pp. 569–576.
52. D.R. Gadgil, quoted in B.B. Sarkar, *Nationalism and Marxism in India*, Delhi, 1990, p. 5.
53. Qutoted in B.B. Sarkar, *Ibid.*, p. 4.
54. Asoka Mehta, quoted in A.R. Desai, *op. cit.*, p. 114.

STRUCTURE

3

Constituent Assembly and Its Vision of the Future

S.K. Chaube

The purpose of this chapter is to examine the basic concepts of the Indian constitution in their historical perspective. No other method has been found as suitable for the purpose as the study of the Indian Constituent Assembly, the mother of the Indian constitution.

The task is admittedly difficult. It involves a study of the constitutional progress as well as the political struggle of India leading to the establishment of the Constituent Assembly and also its problems. The mind and working of the Assembly will be better understood in this setting than through any mechanical analysis. The developments in the Indian politics, even during the prolonged working of the Constituent Assembly, form a part of this setting no less vital than the collective political and socio-economic background of the members of the Constituent Assembly. It is also to be remembered that the collection of a vast store of data from the constitutions of other countries formed the comparative background of the Indian constitution.

Until the beginning of the Second World War, British schemes for constitutional reform in India were confined to the grant of responsible government within the British Empire and under British supervision. And the major obstacle to the grant of responsible government was considered to be the so-called 'Indian problem', by which the British constitutionalists referred to the organic heterogeneity of the Indian community and the reluctance of the princes to sacrifice their rights and status. The core of the Indian problem was, however, unmistakably considered to be the Hindu-Muslim communal rivalry reflected in the Congress-League differences on the political future of India. As Reginald Coupland wrote, "of cardinal importance" was not the division between British and Indian India, but the conflict between the Congress and the Muslim League, "more strictly, the Hindu-Muslim schism which that conflict reflects."[1]

In his "restatement" on India, Coupland, however, admitted[2] that the British "had deliberately widened" the Hindu-Muslim schism. Positive encouragement to separation in the constitutional set-up indeed started with the Morley-Minto Reforms (1909) which granted separate electorates to the Indian people with the first installment of responsible government. The Montagu-Chelmsford Report considered the system as repugnant to democracy but, in view of "the promises given and renewed by secretaries of state and viceroys"[3] recommended its retention and even extension. The Government of India Act, 1919, gave separate electorates to Muslims, Sikhs, Indian Christians, Anglo-Indians, and Europeans. Among the Hindus, the non-Brahmins of Madras and Marhattas in Bombay had reservation of seats in their respective provincial legislatures. A provision was made for nomination of depressed-class Hindus to ensure them adequate representation.

The Simon Commission (1928) recommended the continuation of separate electorates for Muslims, Sikhs, Anglo-Indians, and Europeans. Reservation of seats was recommended for the depressed classes and Indian Christians (the latter had so long enjoyed separate electorate). So was recommended the abolition of the reservation for the non-Brahmins of Madras though reservation for Marhattas was allowed to stay. The Commission commented that the separate representation of the communities and special interests was "the most noticeable feature of the Indian electoral system."[4] The Government of India Act, 1935, extended the franchise to cover about 15 per cent of the population, but retained and further extended the system of separate electorates to a total of 18 categories.

The Cabinet Mission Plan

The Coupland Plan which came after the failure of Cripps Mission directly influenced the Cabinet Mission, which came to India in March 1946 and took no time to realize that the whole constitutional problem of India boiled down to the communal question. The Cabinet Mission held a conference at Simla to bring about an understanding between the Congress and the Muslim League. Since the effort failed, the Cabinet Mission "decided that immediate arrangements should be made whereby Indians may decide the future constitution of India."[5]

The Cabinet Mission proposed a representation of 292 from British India exclusive of the three chief commissioners' provinces and British Baluchistan (whose total representation would be four). It rejected the expedient of universal adult suffrage as it would lead to a "wholly unacceptable delay in the formation of the new constitution" and had the constituent assembly elected by the provincial legislative assemblies which themselves had been elected under the Government of Indian Act 1935, according to which not more than 15 per cent of Indians had the right to vote.

So far as the electoral provisions were concerned the constituent assembly was, therefore, made of men who represented the relatively propertied section of Indians. The political developments in India, however, had led to an overwhelming victory of the Congress in most of the provincial legislatures in elections that took place in early 1946 and its consequent prodominance in the constituent assembly.

Following was the relative position of parties among the British Indian representatives to the Constituent Assembly, when it first met.[6]

Out of 296 members from British India 75 were Leaguers (all Muslim), there being five non-League Muslims. In section A, Rafi Ahmed Kidwai won a Muslim seat from UP with a Congress ticket. The other Congress Muslim (in a general seat) in section A was Asaf Ali, the member from Delhi. In section B, out of 23 Muslims three were non-Leaguers, two with Congress tickets (from NWFP—Abul Kalam Azad and Abdul Ghaffar Khan) and one Unionist (from Punjab). In section C, 35 Muslim members were Leaguers, one from Krishak Proja Party (A.K. Fazlul Huq, whose difference with the League was difficult to trace). Fifteen members were women, of whom three were Muslim, all Leaguers. The age of the members ranged between 25-75.

The Congress position was sound in section A with 164 seats out of a total of 190 while Muslim League had 19 seats. In section B, the League captured 19 seats, whereas 10 seats went to Congress, three each to Panthik Akali and the Unionist Party (Punjab). In section C, the League and Krishak Proja Party own 36 seats, though Assam returned a Congress majority (7:3). The Independents ranked seventh in section A and first in section B. In section C, one seat went to the Communist Party and one to the Scheduled Castes Federation.

The most significant point about the status of the constituent assembly is that it was convened not by any national provisional government, but by the British government who regarded it merely as a conference of the delegates of the major political parties in this country. This was exactly what Reginald Coupland had suggested a few years earlier, though recommending a smaller size. The restrictions were imposed on the constitution-making body obviously on the assumption that, unless guided by the British, the Indian communities would fail to arrive at any agreed formula regarding the constitution. The limitations on the powers of the constituent assembly to change the composition and procedure of work and even given its own interpretation to the clauses of the Cabinet Mission's statement could be disregarded only when complete communal harmony was reached. Until then any attempt of the parties to modify any of the provisions of the Cabinet Mission Plan was destined to be unsuccessful as the British parliament still retained the right to veto over the transfer of power. The procedure of constitution-making in India was, thus, intended to be similar to that in Canada and Australia, where notwithstanding the people's approval of the constitutions, their legal authority was sanctioned by the British parliament. The transfer of power was conditional upon the acceptability of the constitution to the League as well as the British government.

Scope of the Interim Government

"While the constitution-making proceeds", declared the Cabinet Mission, "the administration of India has to be carried on. We attach the greatest importance, therefore, to the setting up at once of an interim government having the support of the major political parties."[7]

The scope of the interim government was only fit to carry on the administration of British India until such time as a new constitution can be brought into being.[8] At the Simla conference between Cabinet Mission and the Indian leaders (5-12 May 1946), negotiations for replacing the Viceroy's Executive Council by an Interim ministry of fourteen members (six Congress nominees including a scheduled caste Hindu member, five League nominees, and three representative members of other communities to be nominated by the Viceroy) were held. The talks failed. The Congress insisted on its right to nominate two nationalist Muslims from its own quota which Jinnah rejected.

The viceroy renewed his efforts to form an interim government on 22nd July 1946, granting the Congress freedom to nominate six members (including a scheduled caste Hindu). The Muslim League would nominate its five members. Three other members (a Parsi, a Sikh, and an Anglo-Indian) would be nominated by the Viceroy. Distribution of portfolios would be decided after the parties agree to join. The viceroy was sure that such a government would enjoy the status of a dominion government with least interference by the British government.

Jinnah rejected even this offer as it was not based on Congress-League parity and as he apprehended that the Congress would not follow the "convention" of respecting minority interests in a cabinet under its dominance. On 8-10 August 1946, the Congress Working Committee accepted the offer of the interim government and evasively repeated their acceptance of the Cabinet Mission plan "in its entirety."[9] The Viceroy immediately requested the Congress President Jawaharlal Nehru to form the interim government. Nehru sought the cooperation of Jinnah who objected to the status of the interim government.

Amidst this situation, the personnel of the interim government were announced on 24th August. Most of the members were Congressites, three members belonged to the Sikh, the Indian Christian, and the Parsi communities. Of the Congress members, one was a scheduled caste Hindu, three were Nationalist Muslims. Two seats remained vacant. A communique said that the Viceroy's Executive Council had resigned. It also stated that five seats would be allotted to the Muslim League whenever it agreed to join the government.[10]

On the same day, Viceroy Wavell, in a radio broadcast, desired that the work of the constituent assembly should begin as early as possible. On 20th November, a government press note said that it had been finally decided that the preliminary meeting of the constituent assembly would be held at

New Delhi on 9th December. On the same day, invitation was sent to all members of the constituent assembly to attend its session. Jinnah declined the invitation.

The Constituent Assembly Meets

On 9th December 1946, the Constituent Assembly met in the constitution Hall, New Delhi, at 11 o'clock in the morning. According to the program set by the Congress Experts Committee, J.B. Kripalani, Congress President, proposed the name of Sachchidananda Sinha, the senior-most member of the Constituent Assembly, for the temporary chairmanship of the Assembly. The chairman took his seat with perfect dignity and immediately started the business. He read three congratulatory messages from aborad, gave his ruling on an election dispute concerning the member from Baluchistan and nominated Frank Anthony as his deputy. B.N. Rau read out Sinha's address. A total of 207 members presented their credentials on the same day.

On the next day, a resolution was moved by Jawaharlal Nehru, and seconded by Govind Ballabh Pant, proposing the provisional adoption of Central Legislative 'Assembly rules and standing orders' until permanent rules were framed. It was passed after some discussion. So was passed another resolution confirming the existing organization of the Constituent Assembly office pending final decision of the Assembly.

The Constituent Assembly declared its firm and solemn resolve to proclaim India as an independent sovereign republic and draw up for her future governance a constitution for a union of the territories of British India, the Indian states, and such other parts of India as were outside British India and the states as well as such other territories as were willing to be constituted into the independent sovereign India. Therein the said territories, whether with their existing boundaries or with such others as might be determined by the Constituent Assembly and, thereafter, according to the law of the constitution, would possess and retain the status of autonomous units together with residuary powers.

The sovereignty of the constitution would be derived from the people who secure justice, equality, and freedom. "Adequate safeguards shall be provided for minorities, backward and tribal areas, and depressed and other backward classes." The constitution would maintain the integrity of the territory of the republic and its sovereign rights or land, sea and air according to justice and the law of civilized nations.[11]

The next meeting of the Constituent Assembly was scheduled on 20th January, 1947.

When the second session of the Assembly started, the debate on the Objectives Resolution continued. Jayakar said that as the Muslim League had not so far shown any intention of joining the Constituent Assembly, it was of no use further holding up the Objectives Resolution. Nehru wound up the debate on 22nd January. He regretted the delay, but considered it justified, "because we have always balanced two factors. One, is the urgent necessity of reaching our goal, and the other, that we should reach it in proper time and with as great unanimity as possible." However, "there has been waiting enough". The Objectives Resolution was carried unanimously.[12]

The second session also disposed of some routine work, like setting up of the Steering Committee, Advisory Committee on Minorities, Tribal Areas and Fundamental Rights, Business Committee, and Union Powers Committee, electing Harendra Kumar Mukherjee as the Vice-President and passing the budget of the Assembly.

Partition

The final refusal of the League to join the Constituent Assembly created a critical situation. On 20th February, Prime Minister Attlee, made a vital statement in the Parliament. He regretted that there were still differences among the Indian parties which were preventing the Constituent Assembly from functioning as a fully representative body, though the British government desired to hand over their responsibility to authorities established by a constitution approved by all parties in India in accordance with the Cabinet Mission's plan. "The present state of uncertainty is fraught with danger and cannot be indefinitely prolonged. His Majesty's government wish to make it clear that it is their definite intention to take the necessary steps to effect the transference of power to responsible Indian hands by a date not later than June 1948." But, if it should appear that such a constitution would not have been worked out by a fully representative assembly before that time, the British government would have to consider, "to whom the power of the Central government in British India should be handed over, on the due date, whether as a whole to some form of Central government for British India", or in such other way as may seem most reasonable and in the best interests of the Indian people[13].

Although the final transfer of authority might not take place until June 1948, preparatory measures must be taken in hand in advance. As the first of such measures, Attlee announced the termination of the war-time appointment of Wavell and the appointment of Mountbatten who will be entrusted with the task of transferring to Indian hands responsibility for the Government of India.

Mountbatten was only too eager to arrive at a prompt solution of the "Indian problem", "within six weeks of his arrival and after constant and ceaseless effort, Lord Mountbatten had produced a plan which marked the first stage towards the transfer of power."[14]

After detailed and complete consultation with the Indian political leaders, on 3rd June 1947,[15] Mountbatten declared that British government was formulating the new plan, though it had no intention of attempting to frame any ultimate constitution for India which was "a matter for the Indians themselves". The plan did not preclude "negotiations between communities for a United India". Yet, "any constitution made by this (Constituent) Assembly cannot apply to those parts of the country which are unwilling to accept it." Partition was, therefore, inevitable by implication, though negotiations for a united India was not ruled out.

In order to ascertain the wishes of the people of Bengal and the Punjab, the plan provided that the representatives of the Muslim-majority districts and the representatives of the other districts to the provincial legislative assemblies would sit separately to decide whether the provinces would be partitioned. If even one part of a particular provincial legislature decided in favour of partition, the province would be partitioned. If both parts agreed to remain united, they would decide to which constituent assembly they would belong. The legislative assemblies of Sindh and British Baluchistan would also, at special meetings, decide which constituent assembly they would join. The British government considered the position of NWFP as "exceptional". "Two of the three representatives of this province are already participating in the existing Constituent Assembly. But, it is clear, in view of its geographical situation and other considerations that if the whole or any part of the Punjab decides not to join the existing Constituent Assembly, it will be necessary to give the North-West Frontier Province an opportunity to reconsider its position." So, there would be a referendum in that province.

In the predominantly non-Muslim province of Assam, the Sylhet district had a majority of Muslims. In case of a decision for partition of Bengal, Sylhet would get a referendum to choose whether it would or would not join the Muslim part of Bengal. If Sylhet, along with the contiguous Muslim majority areas of adjoining districts were to join "Eastern Bengal", the rest of Assam would continue in the Constituent Assembly.

Consequent upon the possible partition, the number of representatives to which each area would be entitled was as follows:

Province	General	Muslim	Sikh	Total
Sylhet district	1	2	a	3
West Bengal	15	4	a	19
East Bengal	12	29	a	41
West Punjab	3	12	2	17
East Punjab	6	4	2	12

Following the mandates given to them, the representatives of the various areas would either join the existing Constituent Assembly or form a new constituent assembly. British policy in respect of the Indian states remained as under the Cabinet Mission's plan. It was proposed to introduce legislation shortly to implement the transfer of power on the basis of dominion status, the dominion(s) having the right to opt out of the Commonwealth.

The most important change introduced on the 3rd June plan in the working of the Constituent Assembly was the abolition of the communal veto. So far as the communal question was concerned, the Constituent

Assembly of India could work independently. The Constituent Assembly was, thus, promoted to the status of a really free body, though its authority would still apply to the states only to the extent of their negotiated acceptance of it. Transfer of power remained subject to an agreement between the British government and the successor authority or authorities on matters arising out of the transfer of power.

Acceptance of the 3rd June declaration involved the partition of the country, consequent upon the splitting up of the Constituent Assembly into two parts. Sindh, Baluchistan, and after referendum on 20th July 1947 which was boycotted by the Khudai Khidmatgar Party, the North-West Frontier Province went wholly to Pakistan. The Punjab, Bengal, and Assam (after a referendum in Sylhet on 14th July 1947) were divided. This brought down (East) Punjab's representation to the Indian Constituent Assembly to 6 general, 4 Muslim, and 2 Sikh and (West) Bengal's representation to 15 general and 4 Muslim. On 22nd July 1947, by a government press note, the Governor General fixed the representation of Assam minus Sylhet (a part of which remained with Assam) at 6 general and 2 Muslim.

New elections took place in West Bengal, East Punjab and Assam. All general seats in West Bengal and Assam went to the Congress and some sitting members were dropped. The only communist member, Somnath Lahiri, lost his seat. B.R. Ambedkar returned from Bombay, with a Congress ticket in the vacancy caused by the resignation of Jayakar. All Muslim seats of Bengal went to the League. In East Punjab, all general seats and one Sikh seat went to the Congress. The other Sikh seat went to the Akali Party. The four Muslim seats went to the League. In the new house, the total strength of British Indian representatives came down to 229.

Transfer of Power

The Indian Independence Bill was introduced in the British Parliament on 4th July 1947 in order to create two "independent dominions", making a technical departure from the Statute of Westminster, which had merely provision for dominions. The Act defined the Indian Constituent Assembly as the Constituent Assembly, "the first sitting whereof was held on 9th December 1946", modified by the exclusion of the members representing the territories due to be included in Pakistan.

Section 6, sub-section 1 of the Act provided that, "The legislature of each of the new dominions shall have full power to make laws for that dominion, including laws having extra territorial operation." This would necessarily imply that no law and no provision of any law made by the legislature of either of the new dominions would be void or inoperative on the ground of its repugnance to the law of England, or to the provisions of any Act of the British Parliament, including the Indian Independence Act itself, or to any order, rule or regulation made under any such act. The powers of the dominion legislatures would include the "power to repeal or amend any such act, order, rule or regulation insofar as it is part of the law of the dominion" (Section 6, Sub-section 2).

Sub-section 3 of Section 6 gave unlimited power of assent to the Governor-General "in His Majesty's name to any law of the legislature of that dominion." Disallowance by His Majesty or reservation for His Majesty's signification of a law would no longer apply in case of the two dominions. It was in this respect that the Indian Independence Act was a definite improvement on the Statute of Westminster. No law of the British Parliament and no order-in-council passed after 15th August 1947 would be automatically operative in the dominions (Sub-sections 4 and 5).

This unlimited legislative competence of the Assembly would cover constitutional legislations for the dominions (Section 8, Sub-section 1). Sub-section 2 of Section 8 provided that "except insofar as other provision was made by or in accordance with a constituent law", enacted by the Constituent Assembly of the dominion, each of the new dominions and all provinces and other parts thereof shall be governed as nearly as may be in accordance with the Government of India Act, 1935. The provisions of the 1935 Act, and the orders-in-Council, rules and other instruments made thereunder would, so far as applicable, and subject to any express provisions of the Indian Independence Act and with such omissions, additions, adaptations, and modifications as might be specified in orders of the Governor-General, have effect accordingly. This meant that, so long as Constituent Assembly did not interfere, the Governor-General-in-Council was competent to make alterations, adaptations, modifications, etc., of the Government of India Act, 1935, in order to run the administration.

According to provision (1) of the Section, these powers of the Governor-General would in no way imply the control of Parliament over the dominion legislatures. Provision (2) removed the power of Governor-General and governors to act in individual discretion. Also, provision (3) laid down that "the powers of the federal legislature or Indian legislature under that Act (i.e., Government of India Act, 1935), as in force in relation to each dominion, shall in the first instance be exercisable by the Constituent Assembly of the dominion in addition to the powers exercisable by that Assembly under Sub-section 1 of this section." The ordinary legislative authority of the dominion was, thus, also vested in the Constituent Assembly. On the whole, the total legislative functions and authorities of the successor government were vested in the Constituent Assembly.

In order to make the transfer of power "smooth" and utilize Mountbatten's services in the transition period, the Congress leadership proposed that Mountbatten would continue as the Governor-General of India for some time. They authorized the President to chalk out the programme for the Independence Day celebration. On 14th August, at 11 pm the Constituent Assembly met and decided upon the formalities of the transfer of power. As the clock struck twelve, the President and members stood up and took the pledge of service to India and its people. Then the President proposed "that it should be intimated to the Viceroy that:

1. The Constituent Assembly has assumed power for the governance of India, and
2. The Constituent Assembly of India has endorsed the recommendation that Lord Mountbatten be the Governor-General of India from 15th August 1947, and that this message be conveyed to Lord Mountbatten by the President and Pandit Nehru.[16]

On 15th August 1947, Mountbatten addressed the Constituent Assembly, after reading out a historic royal message of greetings to the Constituent Assembly of India.

On 20th August 1947, the President appointed a committee to consider the Indian Independence Act, the adaptations of the Government of India Act, 1935, the rules and standing orders of the Legislative Assembly, the rules and standing orders in force in the Constituent Assembly, etc., and report on the procedural matters."[17]

In view of the report, the House passed a resolution moved by K.M. Munshi to the effect that the Assembly's functions would be:

1. To continue and complete the work of constitution-making which commenced from 9th December 1946, and
2. To function as the dominion legislature until a legislature under the new constitution came into existence.

These changes were brought into effect by the Governor-General through the India Provisional constitution (Second Amendment) Order, passed on 6th October 1947.

Foundations of the Constitution

The last and the most important act of the drama was played on 26th January 1950, when the Governor-General gave the following proclamation in the Durbal Hall of the Government House at 10.30 am.

> "Whereas the people of India, having solemnly resolved to constitute India into a sovereign democratic republic, adopted, enacted and gave to themselves on the twenty-sixth day of November 1949, in their Constituent Assembly, the constitution of India;
>
> "And whereas it has been declared by the said constitution that India, that is Bharat, shall be a union of states comprising within the union the territories which were hitherto the governors' provinces, the Indian states and the chief commissioners' provinces;
>
> "And whereas the, twenty-sixth day of January 1950 has been fixed for the commencement of the said constitution;

> "Now, therefore it is hereby proclaimed that on and from this, the twenty-sixth day of January 1950, India, that is Bharat shall be a sovereign democratic republic, and the union and its component units, the states, shall exercise all powers and functions of government and administration in accordance with the provisions of the said constitution."[18]

The Constituent Assembly was partly elected by the popularly-elected provincial legislatures and partly filled by representatives of the states, about one-half of whom were the rulers' nominees and the rest elected through a greatly restricted franchise. Everywhere popular franchise was limited by property qualifications.

In India, a strong political factor had emerged by the time the Constituent Assembly was convened. That was the party system. It is in, and through the political parties that the socio-economic forces in India had crystallized. A proper characterisation of the Indian Constituent Assembly, therefore, can be made not by any mechanical inquiry of the individual property background of the members, but by an objective study the concerted growth of social, economic, and political forces in this country.

The most fundamental of them were: (1) a parliamentary government, (2) a politically centralized but culturally diversified federal state, and (3) a dynamic social order, whose connotation varied from man to man.

The most outstanding influence that is perceptible is that of the Government of India Act, 1935, with its 321 articles and 10 schedules.

Yet, at least in some respects, the new Indian constitution was going to be different from the Act of 1935. For instance, the Act of 1935 did not contain any bill of rights, whereas the Cabinet Mission scheme itself provided for one. The protection of minority and tribal interests, a cornerstone of the Cabinet Mission scheme, had been left, by the 1935 Act, under the special responsibilities of the Governor-General and the governors. India having decided to adopt a republican government, there was need to make new arrangements for such thing as well as to redefine the position of the chief executives at the Centre and the units along with their discretionary powers. There was also the Congress commitment to linguistic reorganization of provinces.

A major issue before the fathers of the Indian constitution was the establishment of social justice between the various religious and social groups to which the Indian leaders had already been committed. The most complicated situation existed within the Hindu religious institutions, the solution of which had long been overdue. Social problems within the Muslim community were also grave, but due to several political reasons the fathers of the Indian constitution could not attack them with the vigour with which they did the Hindu social problems. In fact, the issue of minority rights, quite paradoxically, stood between the government and social reforms of the minority communities.

But the greatest problem before the Constituent Assembly in the post-partition era was economic in nature. An industrial revolution had already set in, producing a consequential class contradiction. Largely fed by the financial assistance of the propertied classes, the Congress had to meet the demands of private property, paying at the same time equal attention to the amelioration of the condition of the poor workers and peasants, which in this underdeveloped economy had already become unbearable.

Now, let us examine the political thinking in India around 1947 that witnessed the making of the Indian constitution.

At the end of the Second World War, Indian industry was far more organized than at any time before. Consequently, tremendous pressure was being exerted by it, on the government, for moulding the national economic policy in its interests. The biggest and most controversial issues, on which private Indian business felt it necessary to speak out and assert the right to property, were economic control and nationalization. The attitudes of Indian businessmen to these questions, however, were sometimes contradictory.

Indian businessmen, for instance, were well-aware that the system of controls that had been introduced during the war could not be done away with; on the other hand, it could be utilized to serve the purpose of a newly-emerging economic order that was state-capitalism.

On the assumption, therefore, that the future economy of our country would be largely state-directed it endorsed "progressive strengthening of the present system of controls, in scope and character, so that not only may it strengthen the smooth transition to peace economy, but may also become the instrument of long-term economic planning in our country."[19]

But the real controversy on Indian planning had started with the publication of what is commonly known as the Bombay Plan, a product of the deliberations of a group of big industrialists led by G.D. Birla, which rejected the "Soviet-type socialism". The Bombay Plan was in essence a capitalist plan with the state control unavoidable in the middle of the 20th century.

The Economic Programme Committee of the National Planning Committee struck a compromise between state socialism and private enterprise. It promised equal opportunities to all classes of people and special opportunities for the backward. Private enterprise was not to be abolished, but at the same time basic industries were to be expanded under public sector. While land would be exploited on the basis of cooperative farming, *zamindari* was to be abolished. Small-scale industries would be promoted through cooperatives, especially in the rural areas. It was on the basis of these recommendations that the Industrial Policy Resolution of 1948 was drafted.

Integration of Indian States

Participation of a handful of princely states in the proceedings of the Constituent Assembly, however, did not imply their merger with the Indian union or their obligation to accept the Indian constitution. On the basis of the Cabinet Mission's plan a state department was set up with V.P. Menon as its secretary on 5th July 1947. Patel, the presiding minister of the department, assured the princes in his inaugural speech, that "we are no enemies of the princely order."[20] On 25th July, Mountbatten, in an address to the Chamber of Princes, endorsed Patel's appeal for accession.

Long and arduous negotiations between the state department and the states followed. These negotiations certainly involved a tremendous pressure tactics in order to counteract the fissiparous tendencies of several princely states. Two major points that emerged out of such negotiations were the signature of three categories of instruments of accession (covering defence, external affairs, and communication) and a Standstill Agreement with each state (which would make possible the continuation of all treaties and obligations between the crown and the states).

The transfer of power on 15th August 1947 made the princes realize their position, 547 states had joined the Indian union, though a number of them were yet unrepresented in the Assembly. Hyderabad, Junagarh, and Kashmir were still outside the orbit.

After 15th August, a new process of integration was initiated by the state ministry with the object of democratizing the governments of the states and linking them up with the Indian administration either by merger with neighboring provinces or by "unionisation" in groups. A few states were brought under the administration of chief commissioners. Most of the princes, on pain of popular revolts and even, in some cases, of "communist menace," readily handed over power.

The fascinating story of the integration of the Indian states is beyond the scope of this work. It would be sufficient to state here that this integration was almost wholly attained outside the Assembly through negotiations with the rulers of the states and their official representatives. The Constituent Assembly indeed provided a forum for such negotiations; technically, however, all agreements were based on the consent of the Government of India on the one hand and the rulers on the other.

On 26th November 1949, Patel announced in the Constituent Assembly that all the states and unions of states had accepted that constitution of India. The President of the Assembly, on the same day, duly took note of the fact that "the constitution as it stands practically makes no difference so far as the administration and distribution of powers among the various organs of the state are concerned between what were the provinces and what the Indian states were before. They are now more or less on the same footing and as time passes whatever little distinction still exists is bound to disappear."[21]

Fundamental Rights

Religious rights became a central point of minority rights. On 26th March 1947, the sub-committee on fundamental rights adopted a modified version of Munshi's draft article on the freedom of conscience and the right to freely profess and practise religion. Such rights would not include economic, financial, and political activities associated with the religious activities. The sub-committee adopted Ayyar's clause about communities being free to set up their religious institutions. The two women members, Amrit Kaur and Hansa Mehta were, however, opposed to this form of religious right which would block the long-needed reforms of the practices, like *devdasi* and child-marriage. The objections led to the removal of the right to "practise" religion.[22]

The house readily accepted Munshi's amendment that notwithstanding the religious freedom, the state would be able to legislate for the purpose of "throwing open Hindu religious institutions of a public character to any class or section of Hindus", as well as for social welfare or reforms.

The question of religious instructions in educational institutions underwent several drafting operations. Adopting B.N. Rau's draft the Advisory Committee recommended that religious instruction would not be compulsory in "any school maintained or receiving aid out of public funds" (Clause 16).

The recommendation was broken into three parts in the Draft constitution: (1) No religious instruction would be given by the state in the educational institutions "wholly maintained out of state funds", (2) religious instructions was made optional in an institution receiving aid from or recognized by the state, and (3) a community or denomination could yet give such instruction "outside the working hours".

The Fundamental Rights Sub-committee also accepted the proposal of Rau to incorporate the right of religious denominations to manage their affairs, and to own, acquire, and dispose of property, in the teeth of opposition of Masani and Shah.[23] Munshi's proposal for freedom from taxation for religious purpose was also accepted. On 7th December 1948, however, the rights of denominations were subjected to "public order, morality or health."[24]

In line with Ambedkar's suggestion, the Fundamental Rights Sub-committee on 26th March 1947 proposed that the state would not recognize any religion as state religion.

The problem of minorities had several and confusing dimensions. Because of the long Gandhian commitment of the Congress members, there was a general eagerness for constitutionalizing prohibition.

The framing of a set of fundamental rights was implied in the Objectives Resolution that had been adopted by the Assembly as well as the Cabinet Mission's scheme. Moreover, most of the members were determined to have "uniform fundamental rights" providing at the same time safeguards for minorities and backward classes and areas.

Clause 2 of the sub-committee's report said that the existing laws and ordinances inconsistent with the given fundamental rights would be abrogated to the extent of such inconsistency. The state would also not pass in future any law prejudicial to the fundamental rights. Clause 22 elaborated the constitutional remedies to be secured from the courts. The Supreme

Court was given the power to enforce such rights. Such power included the power to issue directions in the nature of the writs of *habeas corpus, mandamus*, prohibition, *quo warranto*, and *certiorari tiorari*. The right to secure remedies would not be suspended unless "when, in the case of rebellion or invasion or other grave emergency, the public safety may require it". The union legislature by law could restrict these rights in the case of the armed personnel. Broadly, the committee classified the justifiable right under seven heads: (1) citizenship, (2) equality (including abolition of untouchability), (3) freedom (including the right to life), (4) religion, (5) culture and education, (6) miscellaneous (including the right to property), and (7) constitutional remedies.

Every person born in the union or naturalized according to its laws would be a citizen of India. Irrespective of race, religion, caste or sex, citizens would have equality vis-a-vis the state and access to places of public importance, though separate provision might be made for women and children. There would be equality of opportunity in public services. Untouchability was to be abolished and heritable titles would not be conferred by the state. Subject to public order and morality, or in case of grave emergency, the restrictions imposed in the interest of the security of the country, freedom of speech and expression, peaceful assembly, associations or unions, movements and residence was to be granted. No person was to be deprived of his life or liberty without due process of law, in the eye of which all citizens were equal. Subject to regulation by the law of the union, trade, commerce, and inter-dependence among the citizens or units would be free, though units could impose reasonable restrictions in public interest. Trafficking of human beings, forced labour, and employment of children below the age of 14 in factories, mines, and other hazardous works were to stop. Full religious freedom as well as the rights to maintain their own religious institutions was granted to all communities, subject to public order, morality or health, and other constitutional restrictions, *e.g.*, against conversion through coercion or undue influence. Cultural and educational rights of all communities were duly granted. Among miscellaneous rights, right to property was not to be taken away except by law, for public purposes and against payment of compensation.

In the Fundamental Rights Sub-committee in spite of Rajagopalachari's contention that the provision of universal adult franchise in the fundamental rights part would amount to an encroachment on the constitutional structure of the country, which was being thrashed out by other committees, the principle was "unanimously" accepted. Elections were to be universal, free, and controlled by an independent commission. The Minority Rights Sub-committee in April 1947 endorsed them.

The Advisory Committee recommended to the Assembly the grant of voting right to all citizens at the age of 21, the conduct of voting by secret ballot and the superintendence and control of elections to be left under an election commission.

On 16th June 1949, the Constituent Assembly adopted the principle of universal adult franchise in the form of an amendment (Article 289B). By an earlier amendment (Article 289A) voting right was granted irrespective of religion, race, caste, sex or any of them.[25]

The machinery of elections was evolved in an interesting way. It was the Minority Rights Sub-committee which had insisted upon a neutral and autonomous election commission to conduct free elections. The Advisory Committee endorsed the formula and the Draft constitution of February 1948 provided, in Article 289, for a union election commission, whose personnel would be appointed by the President, and an election commission, for each state, whose personnel would be appointed by the governor, to superintend, control, and direct the elections. But on 15th June 1949, Ambedkar moved an amendment in the Assembly envisaging "a radical change in the proposed system". The new plan was to have an integrated election commission, with members appointed by the President and wanted, in the language of Ambedkar, "centralize the election machinery in the hands of single commission to be assisted by regional commissioners, not working under the provincial government", but under the central government. The change was found necessary "because today we find that in some of the provinces of India, the population is a mixture".

Directive Principles

After the Fundamental Rights Sub-committee completed its discussions and formulations, Rau drafted its report to the Advisory Committee. At the very beginning of the meeting of the Advisory Committee an interesting confrontation took place between Munshi and Rau. By a stroke of drafting ingenuity, Rau had provided in the introductory clause in the chapter on the rights, that any existing or future law inconsistent with the rights guaranteed "in this constitution" would be invalid. Munshi pointed out the difference between the rights in "this part" as originally decided by the Fundamental Rights Sub-committee and rights in "this constitution" as drafted by Rau. Obviously, Rau's draft was an attempt to provide judicial guarantee to the rights guaranteed in the other parts as well. The Advisory Committee made no mistake about it and changed Rau's version.[26]

The effect of the amendment proposal was that no law made by the state in discharge of its duty under the principles of social policy would be invalid on ground of its inconsistency with the justifiable rights. This proposal also was not accepted by the Drafting Committee.

The most important point about the directive principles of social policy is that, they had never been discussed in the Constituent Assembly before the Draft constitution was presented. If their origins are to be found in the rather academic benevolence of B.N. Rau, their adoption "may be considered as a golden compromise between the desire of Congress to achieve a social revolution" and the pressure of the vested interests.

Assessment

Granville Austin finds in the fundamental rights and directive principles "the core of the commitment to social revolution" of the India.[27] It is difficult to accept the view without reservations.

The concepts of equality and freedom are indeed revolutionary and have great social content. But, it is doubtful whether the fundamental rights in the Indian constitution proceeded much further than that. Secularism has long been accepted to be a condition of political stability, and India certainly can claim a great credit on account of this achievement. So is property, a symbol of a stable polity. But these are concepts which Europe achieved by 1848, one hundred years earlier than the making of the Indian constitution. The social revolution in 1948 should evidently have a different content from the social revolution in 1848.

The abolition of untouchability was common in the Munshi and Ambedkar drafts. Presumably, on Ambedkar's insistence, restriction of caste, etc., on the use of wells and places of public use was removed. But, when Munshi moved that "No impediments to marriages between citizens shall be based merely upon differences of religion", the resolution was defeated 5-4. Ambedkar's resolution to remove difference between "legitimate" and "illegitimate" children was defeated 6-3.

Munshi's "rights of workers" was shifted into social policy. K.T. Shah wanted the right to employment. It was not granted.

The main outlook of the constitution, therefore, is political in spite of the directive principles. Two other major features of the fundamental rights under the constitution are:

1. At least some of the basic rights of the constitution are closely linked with the state and government structures of the country. Citizenship is indeed closely linked with the state and government of a country. But the fact that the right to franchise found no place in part III of the constitution, freedom of trade, practically became a constitutional instrument of integrating the Indian polity and the right to property had to be safeguarded by the requirement of the President's approval to every state legislation encroaching upon property, which are distinct pointers to the trend of a modern state towards centralism. The incorporation of a uniform set of fundamental rights into the Indian constitution itself is a part of this process.

   The deliberate rejection of "due process of law" in favour of "the procedure established by law" speaks eloquently about the constituent assembly's intention not to make the judiciary a super-legislature. Yet in India, as in the USA, the judiciary has not only assumed the power of judicial review, but also challenged Parliaments' power to amend the fundamental rights. The power was asserted first in the case of *Golaknath vs. the State of Punjab*, and was taken a step further in the case of *Keshavananda Bharati vs. the State of Kerala*.

2. If the fundamental rights in the Indian constitution contributed to the development of a massive political superstructure in India, its place in determining the intra-governmental power-relation is no less significant. The most elaborately written constitution as it is, the Indian constitution allots rather than limits space for the functioning of the judiciary as guardian of the constitution. Parliament ultimately is the master of the rights, which was never intended to be unalterable.

Structure of Federal and State Government

The compulsion of what had always been regarded as the core of the Indian problem being absent, a trend towards centralization became irresistible. Yet the new Indian situation did not at all rule out the necessity of a federation. The composite character of the Indian social organization was too real to be ignored. Besides, the provincial aspirations aroused by the previous reforms were heading towards their logical culmination. A federal structure of state with considerable autonomy for the provinces and regions was, therefore, a historical imperative though the union was certainly going to be much stronger than what had been anticipated by the Cabinet Mission.

The two most important committees responsible for the formulation of the state structure of India were the Union Constitution Committee and the Union Powers Committee. Both were chained by Nehru and overlappingly manned by most of the stalwarts. Three days after Mountbatten's declaration on 6th June 1947, the Union Constitution Committee decided that: (1) the constitution would be federal with a strong centre, (2) there would be three exhaustive lists of powers, the residuary powers lying with the Union in the pattern of the 1935 Act, (3) the states would be on par with the provinces in respect of the federal legislative list, subject to the consideration of any special matter which might be raised when the lists would be fully prepared, and (4) the executive authority of the federation would be coextensive with the legislative authority.[28]

According to the Union Constitution Committee, the federal government was to consist of (1) a President elected by the members of both the houses of the federal legislature through proportional representation by means of single transferable vote, (2) the two houses of parliament, and (iii) a federal judicature. There would be a vice-President to act for President in contingencies. There would be a council of ministers appointed by the President, who would follow the cabinet principles. There was no mention of ministerial responsibility to the legislature. The tenure of the office of the president was six years. The upper house of the Central Legislature was based on federal principles, mainly, though not more than ten of its members would be nominated by the president in consultation with the universities and scientific bodies. Other members would be elected by legislatures of units. Out of the total strength of this house (Council of States) one-third would retire every two years, making it a permanent body. Its total strength would not be more than half of the strength of the lower house (House of the People) elected through universal adult franchise.

Direct election of the president, it was thought, "would not be desirable, first because we want to emphasize the ministerial character of the government, that power really resided in the ministry and in the legislature and not in the president as such. At the same time we did not want to make the president just a mere figurehead, like the pre-Fifth Republican French president. We did not give him any real power, but we have made his position one of great authority and dignity."[29] Second, election of the President by the whole people would mean a big waste. So the committee suggested the indirect election of the President. The President, however, would be elected not only by the members of the union legislature, but also by the members of the provincial legislative assemblies. This system was not evolved solely out of any regard for the federal principle, but also because the President's election by only the central legislature was considered to be on a too narrow basis.

The Draft constitution published in February 1948 provided, in the centre, for a council of ministers to aid and advise the President, though the conformity of the President with their advice remained outside the jurisdiction of a court's enquiry. Ministers were to hold office during the pleasure of the President (Article 62/2) and were to be entirely responsible to the House of the People (Article 62/3). There was no reference to any discretion of the President.

The Drafting Committee in October 1948 decided that as it was well-established convention in a parliamentary government that the ministers would be in office so long as they had the support of the legislature, the above proposal was unnecessary.

Presenting the Draft constitution in the Assembly, Ambedkar clearly said that, What the Draft constitution proposes is a parliamentary system.

In this constitution, there is placed at the head of the Indian union a functionary who is called the President of the union. The title of the functionary reminds one of the President of the United States. But beyond identity of names there is nothing in common between the form of government prevalent in America and the form of government proposed under the Draft constitution.[30]

"Under the parliamentary system of government, there are only two prerogatives which the king or the head of the state may exercise. One is the appointment of the Prime Minister and the other is dissolution of parliament. With regard to the Prime Minister, it is not possible to avoid vesting the discretion in the President. The only other way by which we could provide for the appointment of the Prime Minister without vesting the authority of discretion in the President is to require that it is the house which shall in the first instance choose its leader, and then, on the choice being made by a motion or a resolution, the President should proceed to appoint the Prime Minister. "If the president made a wrong choice, the legislature could express no confidence." With regard to the dissolution of the houses, Ambedkar said, "there again there is no definite opinion so far as the British constitutional lawyers are concerned."

Ambedkar concluded, "I think these are purely prerogatives and they do not come within the administration of the country."[31]

The Union Constitution Committee in early July 1947, at first, decided to have 25 members of the Council of States from functional constituencies, or panels and other members elected by lower chambers of provincial legislatures on the basis of the strength of population of provinces (one representative for one million, up to five millions, above which one representative for every two millions, subject to a maximum of 25 representatives).

The final shape of the Council of States emerged out of an amendment moved by Ambedkar, on 3rd January 1949, in the Assembly. The wide range of nomination constituencies was reduced to men of "letters, arts, science, and social service," the number of nominated members being reduced from 15 to 12.[32]

Only one of the replies from the Provincial Constitution Committee members (Katju) had required a second chamber for a unit legislature. Rau's draft of the provincial constitution left the scope for bicameral legislatures in some provinces, if the members of the Constituent Assembly from the province so chose. When the Provincial Constitution Committee met, some provinces were found to be demanding two chambers. The committee finally decided to have, normally, one chamber, and two chambers in exceptional cases. The question of the need for a second chamber was referred to a subcommittee (Kher, Sitaramayya, Subbarayon and Katju) which recommended that the strength of the second chamber should not exceed 25 per cent of the strength of the first chamber. Representation to the provincial second chamber was to be, on the Irish model, functional, up to a half, the other half being filled up by election from the lower chamber of the provincial legislature and nomination by governors.[33]

The Draft constitution provided for election of one-half of the total strength of the upper house of a state from five panels of candidates from universities, literature, arts, science, various professions, and social service. A special representation of trade, commerce, industry, women, and labour was abolished from both the union and state second chambers.

The whole episode gives an estimate of the indecisiveness which the Constituent Assembly suffered from over the question of the second chambers. India inherited the second chamber from the British days. With the introduction of the federal idea into Indian politics, a second chamber had been taken for granted at the central level. Yet, explaining the purpose of the second chambers in the union legislature, N.C. Ayyangar could only say that, "The most that we expect the second chamber to do is perhaps to hold dignified debates on important issues and to delay legislation which might be the outcome of passions of the inoment."[34] But never was the justification of a second chamber in a unit sufficiently established. Ultimately, the decision was left to the provincial representatives of the assembly to be taken separately.

The joint meeting of the union and provincial constitution committees recommended on 10th June 1947 that high court judges should be appointed by the President of the union in consultation with the Chief Justice of India, the provincial governors and the provincial chief justices. To appoint the chief justice of a province, the President was to consult the chief justice of India, the provincial governor, and other judges of the Supreme Court and the high courts as he deemed necessary. The Provincial constitution Committee accepted the suggestion.

The Ad-hoc Committee on the Supreme Court, appointed by this committee, whose report was appended to the report of the latter, recommended that, "A Supreme Court with jurisdiction to decide the constitutional validity of acts and laws was a necessary implication of any federal scheme. This jurisdiction might not, however, belong exclusively to the Supreme Court". Other courts might enquire into the validity of acts and laws as well.[35]

The Union Constitution Committee accepted the recommendations of the Ad-hoc Committee on Supreme Court that the Supreme Court would have: (1) exclusive jurisdiction over centre-unit and inter-unit disputes, (2) ultimate jurisdiction on matters arising out of the union government's treaties with foreign states, (3) concurrent jurisdiction with high courts on disputes relating to fundamental rights, (4) appellate jurisdiction similar to that of the Privy Council, and (5) advisory jurisdiction. However, the Ad-hoc Committee's recommedation about a panel of advisers for recommending the appointment of the Supreme Court judges was turned down. The president was given the full authority to appoint the judges in consultation with the chief justice and other judges, as necessary. The joint meeting of the union and provincial constitution committees on 10th June 1947 decided that the judges of high courts would be appointed by the president in consultation with the Supreme Court judges. The fourth session of the Assembly passed the reports. But, on Ayyar's resolution, the high courts were given the powers to issue writs on cases involving fundamental rights and of superintendence and control of the lower courts.[36] The controversy over the writ-issuing powers was, thus, finally solved. With a view to adding to the dignity of the highest courts, another amendment of Ayyar made the Supreme Court judges liable to removal on the address to the President of India by the two houses of the parliament.[37]

The Draft constitution of February 1948, for the first time, upheld that the central judiciary would not be separate from the state judiciaries. In the list of union powers it put the "Supreme Court of India" instead of the "federal judiciary."[38] Following the Ad-hoc Committee's recommendations the Supreme Court was given original, appellate, and advisory jurisdictions.

Considering the intensity of the "Indian problem" which was very close to explosiveness one is bound to appreciate the strong and centralized state-structure that the Constituent Assembly of India evolved into. In several ways the governmental machinery itself helped this centralization. So did some of the special features of the Indian government.

A significant special feature is the "discretion" of the governor. The concept of discretionary power of the governor underwent several changes. In B.B. Rau's model Provincial constitution the governor was expected to be working, generally, following the adive of the ministers, except on a few occasions, *e.g.* the choice of the ministers, protection of minorities and maintenance of law and order. If in any case, the ministerial advice was disregarded by the governor, the ministers might resign, and the governor was advised even to dissolve the legislature and call for another election. The "discretionary" power would "in such cases have at least the effect of bringing the issue before the electorate."[39]

According to clause 9 of the Provincial constitution Committee's report, the governor would act in his discretion in the following matters:

1. The prevention of any grave menace to the peace and integrity of the province or any part thereof,
2. The summoning and dissolving of the provincial legislature,
3. The superintendence, direction, and control of elections,
4. The appointment of the chairman and the members of the Provincial Public Service Commission and of the Provincial Auditor General.

The Special Committee, with Jawaharlal Nehru as the chairman, which recommended the appointment of a governor[40] rather than election on 11th April 1948, opined that "all references to the exercise of functions by the governor in his discretion should be omitted from the Draft constitution."

While the Drafting Committee dropped the "discretion" of the governor in the appointment of minister, the governor's "pleasure" to determine their tenure was retained. The Drafting Committee held that such "pleasure" was limited in scope by the confidence of the legislature. The other fields of the governor's discretion were retained.[41]

The house discussed President's power of suspension of the constitutional remedies for the violation of rights (part III) on 4th August 1949. Kamath and Kunzru moved for restriction of the scope of this suspension to a few articles relating to freedom. On Ambedkar's request, the article was held over[42] and placed on the day on which an amendment to Article 277 (requiring the president to lay before parliament every proclamation of emergency as soon as possible) was passed. The modified draft article restricted the scope of suspension to only those rights which might be mentioned in the proclamation (an amendment very close to Kamath's) and required the suspension order to be placed in parliament as soon as possible. The suspension might also be operative "in the whole of the territory or a part of it."[43]

The last stroke of emergency on the states' autonomy came in the revised and renumbered Draft constitution that was placed in the House in November 1949. A new Article (No. 365) declared that non-compliance of a state government with the directions of the centre would be considered a "failure" of the state, following which by implication, president would have the power to declare "constitutional breakdown".

Conclusion

In India, the Cabinet Mission plan, first, set up the Constituent Assembly; the 3rd June 1947 statement of Mountbatten then split it and the Indian Independence Act finally gave it not only the status of a sovereign constituent assembly, but also the power to control a provisional government. The Constituent Assembly, in its final form was, therefore, very much different from the constituent assembly that had been anticipated by the Cabinet Mission.

Born with a peculiar stigma, it was confronted not only with the task of drafting a constitution for India, but also with the odd job of making the most important political decision for the country, namely, the state's structure. No other constituent body in the world has had to make such an important decision in as much as each of them merely recorded the achievements of the revolution through which the major political decisions has already been reached.

Partition of the country gave the Assembly a sense of direction which its earlier sessions lacked. If the partition was the result of circumstances that developed outside the Constituent Assembly of India, the other major decisions were also taken according to the several political notions that had taken shape in the course of the national movement, particularly, on the platform of the Indian National Congress which commanded an overwhelming majority in the Constituent Assembly. Those notions, in 1947-49, crystallized in a strong federation and a parliamentary government. It was left to the changing political situation in the country to determine how "strong" the centre of this federation would be. The rather long duration of the Constituent Assembly was contributory to the emergence of this strongly unified political organism. Beginning with the hazy idea of a loosely federated India, the members of the Constituent Assembly moved a long way to reach a tangible unity effectively mitigating all local aspirations.

It was imperative of the social forces of the time that India would emerge into a strong and organized political entity. Ambedkar effectively stressed this social imperative when, during the presentation of the Draft to the Constituent Assembly, he severely criticised the orthodox demand for a village-centric policy, "I am glad that the Draft constitution has discarded the village and adopted the individual as its unit."[44]

That the application of the principle of parliamentary government was somewhat crippled at the unit level, was due to the "strong centre" growing stronger. But, when it was a question of the nature of the union government, the decision of the leadership was firmly for a parliamentary type. The state-level governmental set-up was the result of a compromise between centralism and parliamentary government. On the details, however, the leadership had no clear picture, except the somewhat bitter memory of the provincial administrations in the short period before the Second World War. The formulation of the details was initially left to one of the ablest Indian bureaucrats, B.N. Rau, whose acquaintance with the Indian constitutional developments was more through the Reforms Office than through the judiciary.

The original drafts of the union and provincial constitutions formulated by Rau were almost wholly based on the models of the Government of India Act, 1935, and the dominion constitutions. Some of their basic assumptions, therefore, inevitably clashed with the republican and anti-executive notions of the Congress leaders. The result was the intervention of the lawyers, like Ayyar and Ayyangar in the question of the union constitution and a somewhat unsatisfactory compromise on the question of the provincial constitution. On the question of minority representation to the legislature and the executive the Swiss constitutional precedent was, for a while considered. But, as the minority problem took a new turn, the scheme was dropped.

Besides the minority question, the states formed almost the only element of the "Indian problem." Here, the Constituent Assembly had a very little part to play. It only registered whatever the states/ministry worked out in its "negotiation" with the rulers.

The "limited" and "political" achievement of the Constituent Assembly in India consisted installing the disintegrationist forces of India which flowed during the latter part of British rule and encouraged by the fact of partition. It consolidated the unity of India including the native states. It put an end to the cancerous problem of minorities. In short, it cut the Gordian knot of the classical "Indian problem", though the merit of the surgery appears to be dubious. In any case, the present political map of India was drawn in the Constituent Assembly and a parliamentary-federal democracy was set up to preside over it.

This was bound to be so. Right from the beginning the makers of the constitution had no illusion about their aim. On several occasions they made it clear in the Assembly that the constitution was going to be nothing more than a political document.

Truly, the work of the Constituent Assembly was the reflection of the political developments that took place on the national political arena. Yet, the national revolution of India was not complete in the period of work of the Assembly. As a result, the Constituent Assembly was found to be doing a balancing act between the claims of stability and adaptability. Placed between its own commitment to widespread socio-economic reforms, repeatedly though rather vaguely promised, and the pressure of the propertied class, it upheld the claims of property and at the same time confirmed its promises for socio-economic reforms through the directive principles and left the door open for land reforms in certain states where the programme had already been initiated.

A number of important developments took place during the rather prolonged functioning of the Constituent Assembly and were reflected in the constitution.

A very important feature of the constitution was the transitional character of several provisions, among which those relating to the units of the federation are most remarkable. The parliament got absolute power to change the territorial boundaries of states. The integration of princely states was not obviously complete. The problem of linguistic reorganization of states was unsolved.

The social forces of the time permitted exactly this much and no more. The stable and independent political order that was most urgently needed for the full flowering of Indian economic prosperity was ensured by the two epoch-making incidents of transfer of power and framing of the constitution. Right to property was ensured to the extent that a welfare state could afford to ensure.

If the constitution has great omissions, the mistakes of the commission are not quite insignificant. Complaints of complicating details in the constitution have been raised very often and by many, including Jennings. In the constitutional document several provisions are overlapping; some may even be considered superfluous.[45] Understandably, the radicals of the country, specially the socialists, demanded the constitution to be amendable by an ordinary legislative procedure.

The claim is valid as far as it goes. For, every Constituent Assembly has a mind which can be understood in the light of the concrete political and socio-economic forces of the time and place. The limitations of these forces, therefore, are bound to be attached to the constitution it produces, and to be exposed gradually with the passage of time.

Notes and References

1. R. Coupland, *The constitutional Problem in India*, Part III, London, OUP, p. 16.
2. R. Coupland, *India-A Restatement*, London, OUP, 1945, p. 69.
3. *Report on Indian constitutional Reforms*, p. 150.
4. *Report of the Indian Statutory Commission*, Vol. I, Government of Great Britain, 1923, p. 200.
5. *Cabinet Mission's Statement*, 16 May 1946, para 3.
6. Figures based on *IAR*, 1946, Vol. II, and the *Hindusthan Yearbook*, Calcutta, 1947.
7. *Cabinet Mission's Statement, op. cit.*, para 23.
8. *Ibid.*, para 3.
9. *AIR*, 1946, Vol. II, p. 105.
10. *The Statesman*, 25th August 1946.
11. *CAD*, 10th December 1946, Vol. I, p. 57.
    Undoubtedly, the Objectives Resolution was a confederal document of the democratic aspirations of a newly-freed people and the departing British imperial rules. Yet it was basically a political document and had no economic outlook.
12. *CAD*, Vol. II, p. 305.
13. *AIR*, 1947, Vol. I, pp. 142–143.
14. V.P. Menon, *The Transfer of Power*, Calcutta, Orient Longman, 1957, pp. 353–357.
15. *AIR*, 1947, Vol. I, pp. 143–146.

16. *CAD*, Vol. V, p. 10.
17. *Ibid.*, pp. 29, 57.
18. *The Gazette of India Extraordinary*, 26th January 1950.
19. *The Eastern Economist*, New Delhi, 14th January 1944.
20. *The Stateman*, Calcutta, 6th July 1947.
21. *CAD*, Vol. XI, pp. 987–988.
22. The proceedings of the subcommittees are found in B. Shiva Rao's, *The Framing of India's constitution, Select Dowments*, Vol. II, IIPA, 1966 pp. 122 and 165. Powerful support were also accorded to Kaur and Mehta by A.K. Ayyar.
23. *Ibid.*, p. 123.
24. *CAD*, Vol. VII, p. 859.
25. *Ibid.*, Vol. IX, pp. 931–932.
26. B. Shivarao, *op. cit.*, pp. 215–216.
27. G. Austin, *The Indian constitution*, London, OUP, 1966, p. 50.
28. *Union constitution Committee's File.*
29. *CAD*, Vol. IV, p. 734.
30. *Ibid.*, Vol. V, p. 32.
31. *Ibid.*, Vol. VII, pp. 1158–1159.
32. *Ibid.*, p. 1202.
33. *Provincial constitution Committee File.*
34. *CAD*, Vol. IV, p. 927.
35. *Report of the Ad-hoc Committee on the Supreme Court.*
36. *CAD*, Vol. IV, p. 889.
37. *Ibid.*, p. 895.
38. *Draft constitution of India*, p. 192n.
39. B.N. Rau, *India's constitution in the Making*, Calcutta, Orient Longman, p. 170.
40. B. Shivarao, *op. cit.*, Vol. IV, p. 411.
41. *Ibid.*, pp. 67 and 81.
42. *CAD*, Vol. IX, p. 186.
43. *Ibid.*, Vol. X, p. 523.
44. *CAD*, Vol. VII, p. 39.
45. Sen, a leftist academician thought that the Indian constitution was "a copy-book text borrowed indiscriminately from alien sources" (vide *his Paradox of Freedom*, Calcutta, Vidyalaya Library, 1958, p. 8).

4 Constitutional Amendment and Socio-Political Implications

Sunder Raman

❑ Introduction

A Constitution is a system of fundamental laws or principles for the governance of a nation. It differs from a statute in that a statute must provide, at least to a certain degree, the details of the subject it treats, whereas a constitution usually states the general principles and framework of the law and government.[1] Permanence and generality are the main characteristics of most of the constitutions in the world. As a rule, a constitution does not deal in detail, but enunciates the general principles and directions, for the framers of a constitution cannot anticipate conditions which may subsequently arise in the progress of a nation or establish all laws which may be necessary from time to time to do justice to the changing conditions of a community. It is not practicable for a written constitution to specify, in detail, all its objects and purposes or the means by which they are to be carried into effect; nor is such an exercise considered necessary or desirable. On the other hand, it is considered unwise to provide immutable rules for future exigencies which are at best dimly perceived and which can be best dealt with by the legislature keeping in view the unfolding circumstances. Besides, a modern democratic constitution not only establishes the basis of the governmental system, but also serves as an effective means of public welfare, and this warrants its adaptability more than anything else.

The idea of a rigid constitution is logically untenable; for human societies grow and develop with the passage of time and, unless a provision is made for such constitutional readjustments as the internal development of society requires, they must stagnate and retrogress. Moreover, a constitution that does not provide for a formal method of amendment, leaves room for unconstitutional and violent changes. C.J. Friedrich rightly observes that "a well-drawn constitution will provide for its own amendment in such a way as to forestall, as far as is humanly possible, revolutionary upheavals."[2]

In view of the need for changes in the constitution of India, the framers of the constitution did not opt for a very rigid procedure for amendment as is usually the case with federal constitutions, and preferred a "facile procedure." However, they did not make the procedure so easy that it made the constitution unstable. They tried to strike a balance between constitutional stability and change. Unlike many written constitutions which have only one procedure for affecting "any change of any kind in any part of the constitution," the constitution of India provides for a variety of procedures to amend it, a feature which has been commended by KC Wheare, for the reason that uniformity in the amending process imposes "quite unnecessary restrictions on the amendment of parts of a constitution."[3]

Procedure of Amendment

The founding fathers of our constitution intended our Parliament, elected on the basis of universal adult suffrage, to be powerful enough to make quick changes in the constitution when needed for social and economic transformation. Therefore, they made several provisions of the constitution amendable by a simple majority of Parliament. Part XX of our constitution consisting only of Article 368 which deals with the power of Parliament to amend the constitution and procedure therefore. It reads as under:

> *368. Power of Parliament to amend the constitution and procedure therefore ...*
>
> (1) *Notwithstanding anything in the constitution, Parliament may in exercise of its constituent power amend by way of addition, variation or repeal any provision of this constitution in accordance with the procedure laid down in this article.*
>
> (2) *An amendment of this constitution may be initiated only by the introduction of a Bill for the purpose in either House of Parliament, and when the bill is passed in each House by a majority of the total membership of that House, and by a majority of not less than two-thirds of the members of that House present and voting, it shall be presented to the President who shall give his assent to the Bill and thereupon the constitution shall stand amended in accordance with the terms of the Bill.*
>
> Provided that if such amendment seeks to make any change in:
>
> (a) *Article* 54, *Article* 55, *Article* 73, *Article* 162, *Article* 241, *or*
>
> (b) *Chapter IV of Part V, Chapter V of Part VI, or Chapter I of Part XI, or*

(c) *Any of the Lists in the Seventh Schedule, or*
(d) *The representation of States in Parliament, or*
(e) *The provision of this article, the amendment shall also require to be ratified by the Legislatures of not less than one half of the States by resolutions to that effect passed by those Legislatures before the Bill making provision for such amendment is presented to the President for assent.*

(3) *Nothing in Article* 13 *shall apply to any amendment under this article.*

(4) No *amendment of this constitution (including the provisions of Part III) made or purporting to have been made under this article (whether before or after the commencement of Section* 55 *of the constitution (Forty-second Amendment Act, 1976) shall be called in question in any court on any ground.*

(5) *For the removal of doubts, it is hereby declared that there shall be no limitation whatever on the constituent power of Parliament to amend by way of addition, variation or repeal the provisions of this constitution under this article.*[4]

In the given text, the amplified marginal heading to the article, clauses 1 and 3 and amendment in clause 2 indicated by italics, were inserted by the 24th Amendment Act, 1971/and clauses 4 and 5, by the 42nd Amendment Act, 1976.[5]

The constitution provides for three categories of amendments. The first category includes those amendments which can be affected by Parliament by a simple majority which is required for passing any ordinary law. The amendments contemplated in Articles 4, 169, para 7(2) of Schedule V and para 21(2) of Schedule VI fall within this category and are specifically excluded from the purview of Article 368 which is the specific provision in the constitution dealing with the powers and procedure to amend the constitution. Those amendments which can be affected by Parliament by a prescribed 'special majority' constitute the second category. And the third category consists of those amendments which require, in addition to such "special majority", ratification by at least one-half of the States legislatures.

Amendment by a Simple Majority

The following constitutional provisions can be amended by a simple majority at the instance of the Union government:

1. Admission of a new state under Article 2, along with the consequential amendments in Schedule I (which defines the territory of a State) and Schedule IV (which deals with the allocations of seats to a State in the Rajya Sabha);
2. Provisions relating to the citizenship of India; Article 11;

3. Provisions relating to the exercise of executive power by a State or its Officers in respect of a matter over which Parliament has power to make laws: Article 73(2);
4. Provisions relating to the salaries and allowances of ministers: Article 75(6) and the consequential amendments to Schedule II;
5. Provisions to the salaries and allowances of the Speaker and the Deputy Speaker of the House of the People, and the Chairman and the Deputy Chairman of the Council of States: Article 97 and consequential amendments to Schedule II;
6. Provisions relating to salaries and allowances of the Members of Parliament Article 106;
7. Provisions relating to the number of judges in the Supreme Court; Article 124(1);
8. Provisions relating to the privileges, allowances and rights of judges of the Supreme Court; Article 125(2);
9. Provisions relating to appeals to the Supreme Court: Article 133(3);
10. Provisions relating to review of the judgements of the Supreme Court; Article 137;
11. Provisions relating to the salaries and allowances of the Comptroller and the Auditor-General: Article 148(3), and the consequential amendments to Schedule II;
12. Provisions relating to the composition of the Legislative Councils: Article 172(2);
13. Provisions relating to the salaries and allowances of the judges of the High Court: Article 22(2) and the consequential changes in Schedule II;
14. Provisions relating to English language; Article 343(3);
15. Provisions relating to the language to be used in the Supreme Court and the High Courts: Article 348(1);
16. Provisions relating to the creation of Legislature and Council of Ministers for a Union Territory: Article 239 A;
17. Provisions relating to the administration and control of the Scheduled Areas and Scheduled Tribes: Para 7 of Schedule V; and
18. Provisions relating to the administration and control of Tribal Areas: Para 21 of Schedule VI.

In addition to Parliament's power to amend the constitution in the aforesaid areas, the State Legislative Assemblies also have the power to amend Article 164(5) which relates to the salaries and allowances of ministers in the States.

Strictly constitutionally speaking, the amendments in the aforesaid areas cannot be called constitutional amendments, because, for these amendments, the procedure laid down in Article 368 (which specially deals with amendments of the constitution) is not required to be followed. However, it is averred here that these are amendments to the constitution inasmuch as the constitution stands amended, albeit by simple majority.

Amendments at the Instance of the State Governments

The amendments at the instance of the state governments fall under two categories: (1) some of the provisions of the constitution can be amended at the instance of a State, and (2) some can be amended in consultation with the states. The provisions relating to the Upper House in a state fall under the first category. Whether a State will create or abolish an Upper House, entirely depends on the will of the state. When, under Article 169, a state assembly passes a resolution by a majority of not less than two-thirds of its members present and voting for having or abolishing its Upper House, the Parliament may pass a law in this behalf by a simple majority. Once such a law is passed, the constitution stands amended.

The provisions relating to the formation of a state and alteration of the boundaries or name of a state fall under the second category. Under Articles 3 and 4, Parliament has the power to form new states and alter the boundaries and names of the existing states. It can also make consequential changes in Schedules I and IV. Parliament can do so by passing a law by a simple majority. But, no such Bill can be introduced in Parliament except on the recommendation of the President. When such a law is going to affect the area, boundary or name of a state, the bill has to be referred to the legislature of the affected state for its views thereon within such period as may be specified in the reference (this period may be extended by the President). Once such a law is passed, the constitution stands amended accordingly.

Amendment by Two-thirds Majority and with the Concurrence of Half of the States

The following constitutional provisions can be amended by a two-third majority and with the concurrence of half of the states:

1. Mode and manner of the election of the President of India: Articles 54 and 55;
2. Extent of the executive power of the Union: Article 73;
3. Extent of the executive power of the States: Article 162;
4. Constitution of a High Court for a Union Territory: Article 241;
5. Provisions relating to the Union judiciary: Chapter IV of Part V of the constitution: Articles 124-127;
6. Provisions relating to the High Courts: Chapter V of Part VI of the constitution: Articles 214-231;
7. Provisions relating to the distribution of legislative powers between the Union and the States: Chapter I of Part XI of the constitution of India: Articles 245-255;
8. Provisions relating to the three lists: Schedule VII;

9. Provisions relating to the representation of states in Parliament: Article 80 and Schedule IV; and
10. Provision relating to the amendment of the constitution: Article 368. For the amendment of the aforesaid provisions of the constitution, the procedure laid down in Article 368 has to be followed.[6]

The provisions other than those which have been discussed under the previous two heads can be amended by a special majority vote in Parliament, i.e., by a majority of the total memberships of each House of Parliament and by a majority of not less than two-thirds of the members of each House present and voting. For the amendment of these provisions, no ratification by the States is required.[7]

Assent of the President

In each of the aforesaid cases, an amendment of the constitution can be initiated only by an introduction of a Bill in either House of Parliament, and in each case, the assent of the President of India is obligatory. Without the assent of the President the constitution cannot be amended.[8]

Constitutional Amendments Assailed and the Shifting Judicial Stance

The first attack on Parliament's power to amend the constitution came in *Slzankari Prasad*[9] case, soon after the constitution was promulgated. In this case, the First Amendment Act was erroneously assailed on the ground that it infringed upon the right to property, a Fundamental Right (then), and attracted the prohibition of Article 13(2) of the constitution. In fact, the first constitutional amendment which caused curtailment of Fundamental Rights was enacted by the Provisional Parliament, the same body as the Constituent Assembly (which continued to function as Parliament till the new Parliament was elected after the first general elections in 1952). The amendment was, therefore, for act of the same persons who had made our constitution. On 5th October 1951, the Supreme Court unanimously declared the impugned Act valid on the ground that the power in exercise of which the Amendment Act had been passed, was a constituent power and the validity of the exercise of that power was not within the reach of judicial process. Again, when the Seventeenth Amendment was challenged in the *Sajjan Singh*[10] case, the Supreme Court examined *inter alia* the scope and reach of the amending power and arrived at the conclusion that the Court's earlier decision in the *Shankari Prasad* was correct.

The Supreme Court, however, in 1967, usurped the power of judicial review of constitutional amendments by the narrowest margin when it declared in the *Golaknath*[11] case that the Fundamental Rights could not be abridged or taken away even through the process of constitutional amendment. Notwithstanding, earlier decisions of the Court, the majority led by

Chief Justice K. Subba Rao and Hidayatullah Justice in this case misconstrued Articles 368 and 13(2) and came to the conclusion that Article 368 was controlled by Article 13(2).

The government passed the 24th Amendment[12] to supersede the *Golaknath* decision. The Amendment provided that the power of Parliament to amend the constitution was to be found in Article 368; the amending power was a constituent power; Parliament could amend any part of the constitution, including Part III; it was obligatory for the President to give assent to a bill amending the constitution; and the provisions of Article 13 would not be applicable to any amendment of the constitution. The 24th Amendment tried to bury the *Golaknath* decision completely. One wishes that *Golaknath* had passed off as a solitary bad event in our constitutional history, but that was not to be, *Golaknath* turned out to be the beginning of the intra-governmental discord over the amending power.

In 1972, the Supreme Court was called upon to consider the validity of the 24th, 25th, and 29th Amendments in the famous *Kesavananda Bharati*[13]case. The *Golaknath* decision was also reconsidered. *Kesavananda* provided yet another opportunity to the Supreme Court to rule upon the limits of the amending power. In this case, the *Golaklnath* decision was over-ruled to the extent that the Court conceded wider amending powers to Parliament and lifted the embargo of Article 13 placed by the earlier Bench in the *Golaknath* case. But the Court interpreted the 24th Amendment and, consequently, Article 368 in its own way. It upheld the validity of 'the 24th Amendment Act, but at the same time declared that on the basis of certain implied limitations, the amending power could not damage or destroy the basic features of the constitution. The decision opened a Pandora's box and created uncertainty, as it did not specify the basic features of the constitution. In fact, the Court widened the basis of *Golaknath's* limitation and, thereby, the scope of judicial review.[14] Instead of resolving the controversy raised by the *Golaknath* case, the Supreme Court through *Kesavananda* redefined the argument advanced in the earlier case.[15] It prevented the Fundamental Right plus much more from being damaged or destroyed by constitutional amendment.

In 1975-76, during the period of internal emergency, the government enacted the 39th Amendment Act which *inter alia* inserted Article 329(a) to validate the election of the Prime Minister and to wipe off appeals and cross-appeals in the election dispute that were lying before the Supreme Court of India. The validity of the 39th Amendment was assailed on the ground that it had violated the basic structure limitation laid down in the *Kesavananda Bharati* case. The 39th Amendment was impeachable on moral and political grounds, but it could not have constituted the basis for judicial invalidation. However, the Court held that since the Amendment had not made any change in Article 368, the 24th Amendment which laid the law in respect to the amending power could be applied only as it was interpreted by the majority of judges in *Kesavananda*. In sum, the *Kesavananda* judgement was considered as binding on the Supreme Court, and the *Election* case[16] was decided accordingly. The counsel for the government was left with a limited scope for arguing in favour of the 39th Amendment, and his argument rested on the slippery ground that the impugned parts of the 39th Amendment did not damage or destroy the basic structure of the constitution. Consequently, the impugned parts of the 39th Amendment were struck down on the basis of basic structural limitations, although there was no unanimity on the basis features that had been violated by the amendment and each judge chose his own path to invalidate the amendment.

The decision in the *Election* case provided a new dimension to the theory of basic structure limitation. It declared that the amending power was subject to the theory of separation of power; that the amending power could not become a judicial power; and that there was a difference between the constituent power and the amending power.[17]

Just as the 24th Amendment was enacted to supersede the *Golaknath* decision, the Parliament added clauses (4) and (5) to Article 368 through Section 55 of the 42nd Amendment to nullify the effect of the *Kesavanada* decision. According to the two clauses, no court could question any amendment of the constitution on any ground and there were to be no limitations on the constituent power of Parliament to amend the constitution. The 42nd Amendment Act was a firm communication to the Supreme Court to the effect that the Parliament had an absolute power to amend the constitution. Section 4 of the 42nd Amendment Act amended Article 32(c) to give preponderance to all the Directive Principles of State Policy over the Fundamental Rights laid down under Article 14, 19, and 31 and the government also demonstrated that it needed an unfettered amending power to bring about revolutionary socioeconomic changes in society[18]. Subsequently, when the Amendment was substantially repealed by the Janata Dal government, the above-mentioned Sections 4 and 55 of the Amendment Act remained unaltered, because the Congress with a majority in the Rajya Sabha refused to give its approval to the proposed changes in respect to these two sections.

It was hoped that the 42nd Amendment would take care of the basic features theory and bring an end to the conflict between the government and the judiciary over the amending power. But that did not happen. Sections 4 and 55, *inter alia*, came for judicial review in the *Minerva Mills*[19] case and the Supreme Court affirmed the theory of basic structure and revived the *Kesavananda* judgement. After the 24th Amendment, the *Golaknath*-decision had stood over-ruled, and after the 42nd Amendment the *Kesavananda* decision should have ceased to exist. But the apex court through *Minerva Mills* case elbowed Section 55 out and brought back *Kesavananda*.

Further, the Supreme Court in *P. Sambamurthy v. State of Andhra Pradesh* invalidated Clause 5 along with its provision of Article 371-0 which had been introduced in the constitution by the 32nd Amendment Act, 1973; the provision, the Clause 5 had empowered the State Government of Andhra Pradesh to modify or even nullify an award given against it by the Administrative Tribunal constituted under Clause 3 of the same Article. The five-member bench headed by Chief Justice Bhagwati declared the impugned part as shocking and subversive of the principles of justice; the Court held that it was violative of the basic structure doctrine and therefore, was unconstitutional. Thus, the Supreme Court knocked down yet another constitutional amendment, an amendment that had existed for twelve long years.

The above discussions clearly show that there has been a steady usurption expansion of judicial review power since the *Golaknath* case. The Supreme Court through *Kesavananda*, and subsequent cases seems to have firmly established its power of invalidating constitutional amendments. However, it must be acknowledged that the Supreme Court has not interfered in many cases on the basis of "basic structure" doctrine; in particular, it has allowed the socio-economic changes to take place through the constitutional amendments.

Constitutional Amendment and Social Change

Various constitutional amendments have been enacted to bring about important socio-economic changes. In fact, the government had to take the help of Article 368 to implement agrarian reforms, soon after the launching of our constitution. From the very beginning, many social legislation and executive actions were held invalid by the Court. Consequently, the constitution had to be amended to overcome the difficulties created by these judicial decisions. Every amendment has been brought about with some specific purpose. The amendments which aimed at ushering in an new egalitarian social order are the First, Fourth, Seventeenth, Twenty-fourth, Twenty-fifth, Twenty-sixth, Twenty-ninth, Thirty-ninth, Fortieth, Forty-second, Forty-fourth, Forty-seventh, Forty-ninth, Fifty-first, Sixty-fifth, and Seventy-third to Seventy-eighth.

The first major challenge to the constitution came when the Supreme Court held the abolition of *Zamindaris* as void in *Kamenshwar Singh vs. State of Bihar*[20], *Ramesh Thaper vs. State of Madras*[21]and *Motilal vs. State of U.P.*[22] The Court invalidated the Bihar Land Reforms Act, 1950, on the ground that it discriminated between the rich and poor in determining the compensation for acquired property. The Court held that the compensation provided in the Act was unjust/inequitable and in some cases illusory. The government was committed to protect such legislation and, therefore, came forward with the First Amendment[23], the main object of which was to secure fully the constitutional validity of *Zamindari* and *Jagirdari* laws in general, and of certain specific State Acts, in particular. For this purpose, the amendment added Articles 31-A and 31-B. The famous IX Schedule also came into being to preclude the judicial review of the Acts in the Schedule.

Like the First Amendment, the Fourth Amendment[24] also intended to bring the constitutional provisions in line with the new social order.

The difficulties arose once again because decisions of the Supreme Court in cases, like *State of West Bengal vs. Bela Banerjee*[25], *Owarkudas Shriniwas vs. Sholapur Spinning Co. Ltd.*[26] and *State of West Bengal vs. Subodh Gopal.*[27] The Court had given a very wide meaning to clauses (i) and (ii) of Article 31 regarding the limitation against compulsory acquisition of property. State's power needed re-definition in this context, so as to distinguish it from cases in which the operation of regulatory or prohibitory laws of the state resulted in deprivation of property. Further, the judicial decisions interpreting the Fundamental Rights had raised serious difficulties in the implementation of social welfare programme such as fixing the limit on agricultural holdings, conferment of rights on tenants, proper planning of urban and rural areas, clearance of slums, etc. The state also required power to take over commercial or industrial undertaking or other property in the public interest. Furthermore, the government wanted certain Acts to be protected and, therefore, wanted to include them in the IX Schedule.

The Fourth Amendment nullified the decision in the *Bela Banerjee* case. It declared that the adequacy of compensation for acquiring private property could not be justiciable.

The amendment also clarified the right of Parliament or state legislature to make laws introducing State monopoly in any trade or commerce. The government was committed to see that the right to property did not come in the way of social revolution. The first and the fourth amendments were in pursuit of this object. When Kerala Agrarian Relations Act, 1961, the Madras Land Reforms Act, 1961 (fixation of ceiling on land), the Rajasthan Tenancy Act, 1955, and the Maharashtra Agricultural Land Act, 1961 (ceiling and holding), were struck down by the judiciary, the need for yet another constitutional amendments was thus felt. The definition to term 'Estate', in Article 31-A, was found lacking. According to the Supreme Court, it did not include lands held under *ryotwari* settlement and also other lands which figure in land reforms enactments. The situation became rather complicated as the term 'Estate' had come to be defined differently in different states. The Seventeenth Amendment Act[28] was passed to get over all these difficulties. The amendment defined 'Estate' widely by substituting old sub-clause (1) of clause (2) of Article 31(A) with a new clause and added 44 statutes relating to land reform in the Schedule. The Supreme Court though struck down the various legislative enactments it upheld the power of Parliament to amend the fundamental rights in *Shankari Prasad vs. Union of India* in 1965.[29]

An unfortunate situation arose in 1967 when the Supreme Court in the *Golaknath* case[30] revised its earlier stand and declared that the fundamental rights could not be impaired or taken away even through the process of amendment. This was an erroneous decision, to say the least. It created a political impasse, and Indira Gandhi who had just established herself in the internecine struggle ordered the mid-term poll. The election was fought to seek popular sanction from the electorate on the issue of parliamentary competence to amend the constitution, to implement the various socio-economic programmes. Indira Gandhi secured more than two-third majority and that enabled her government to pass the Twenty-fourth, the Twenty-fifth, the Twenty-sixth and the Twenty-ninth Amendments.

The Twenty-fourth Amendment was passed to nullify the effect of the *Golaknath* case, and to assert Parliament's right to amend the fundamental rights. The amendment made it abundantly clear that the Parliament had the power to amend any part of the constitution, including the fundamental right. The Supreme Court in the *Bank Nationalization*[31] case held that the properties taken over by the state like banks and other industrial units should be paid compensation according to the market-value. The government had not proposed to pay the fourteen nationalized banks the compensation according to the market value and, therefore, the Supreme Court invalidated the nationalization. To surmount the difficulties created by the decision, the Twenty-fifth Amendment was passed in 1971. The amendment substituted the word 'compensation' by the word 'amount' and forbade the courts to go into the question of quantum of compensation. The Twenty-fifth Amendment also authorized the government to make laws to give effect to the Directive Principles specified in clauses (2) and (3) of Article 39. They were not to be declared void on the ground that they took away any of the fundamental rights guaranteed by Articles 14, 19, and 31. Thus, Article 31(c) sought to subordinate the fundamental rights to prevent concentration of wealth and to have economic programmes that could subserve the common good.

Indira Gandhi was committed to abolish Privy Purses of the erstwhile rulers. She described the Privy Purses as "anachronism" and got the princes derecognized and abolished their special privileges and privy purses through Presidential order. This Presidential order was challenged in the Supreme Court and the Court gave its ruling against it. The Twenty-sixth Amendment was subsequently enacted in December 1971, to nullify the court decision and to abolish the privy purses and special privileges of the princes. The amendment was justified by the Prime Minister and the Law Minister on the ground that it was necessary to transform the economic and social structure of the Indian society.

The Twenty-ninth and Thirty-fourth Amendments also belong to this category of amendments (made for socio-economic change). The Twenty-ninth Amendment included Kerala Land Reforms Act, 1969 and 1971, in the Ninth Schedule of the constitution which empowered the state government to take over the land in excess of the ceiling without paying compensation at the market value and the Thirty-fourth Amendment (1974) provided constitutional protection to all the 17 land reforms Acts passed by different states.[32]

Another important constitutional development took place when the Twenty-fourth, Twenty-fifth, and Twenty-ninth Amendments were challenged in the Supreme Court in the *Kesavananda Bharati* case. The Supreme Court though reversed its earlier decision in the *Golaknath* case and upheld Parliament's right to amend the constitution including the fundamental rights, it held that the basic structure or framework of the constitution could not be amended. The Court, thus, put fetters on Parliament's power to amend the constitution. (The Supreme Court has reaffirmed its faith in the doctrine of basic structure in the subsequent cases.)

Again, with a view to giving effect to progressive measures the government enacted Section 5 of the 39th Amendment Act (1975) and the 40th Amendment Act (1976). Both the Amendments added 38 and 64 new entries in the Ninth Schedule respectively. Besides the Acts relating to land reforms, the aforesaid section of the 39th Amendment *inter alia* inserted the Industries (development and regulation) Act, 1951, the Mines and Minerals (regulation and development) Act, 1957, the Monopolies and Restrictive Trade Practices Act, 1969, the Maintenance of Internal Security Act, 1971, the Cocking Coal Mines (nationalisation) Act, 1972, the General Insurance (nationalisation) Act, 1972, the Sick Textile Undertakings (taking over of management) Act, 1972, the Coal Mines (taking over management) Act, 1973, and the Foreign Exchange Regulation Act, 1973 in the Ninth Schedule to pre-empt litigation. Similarly, the 40th Amendment *inter alia* gave protection to certain Central laws such as the Smugglers and Foreign Exchange Manipulators (forfeiture of property) Act, 1976, the Urban Land (ceiling and regulation) Act, 1976, the Essential Commodities Act, 1955, and certain provisions of the Motor Vehicles Act, 1939, by placing them in the Ninth Schedule. When the progressive legislations conceived in the interest of the public are allowed to be challenged in the court of law, the very purpose of enacting those stands are defeated.

The much discredited Forty-second Amendment was brought about with a view to revising the constitution. The comprehensive amendment did not leave any important area untouched. It *inter alia* sought to reassert once and for all the supremacy of Parliament and its plenary powers to amend any provision of the constitution; incorporated in the preamble the words 'Socialist' and 'Secular'; prescribed fundamental duties for the citizens and established primacy of the Directive Principles over certain fundamental rights.

The Forty-fourth Amendment omitted the right to property from the list of fundamental rights to enable the Parliament to go ahead with socio-economic measures unimpeded. On the suggestion of the state governments of Assam, Bihar, Haryana, Tamil Nadu, Uttar Pradesh, West Bengal, and the Administration of the Union Territory of Goa, Daman, and Diu to include some of their Acts relating to land reforms in the Ninth Schedule. The Forty-seventh Amendment Act, 1984, inserted as many as fourteen entries in the Schedule.

A couple of amendments have been made to help the development of tribal areas and representation of tribal people in the legislatures. The Forty-ninth Amendment provides constitutional sanctity to the autonomous

District Council in the State of Tripura, meant to ensure rapid development of tribal areas and self-governance by the tribes. The Fifty-first Amendment changed Article 330 to provide for reservation of seats in the Lok Sabha for Scheduled Tribes in Meghalaya, Nagaland, Arunachal Pradesh, and Mizoram, and Article 332 to provide for similar reservation in the Legislative Assemblies of Nagaland and Meghalaya.

The Sixty-fifth Amendment has brought in a qualitative and comprehensive change in Article 338 of the constitution. It provides for a high level five-member National Commission for Scheduled Castes and Scheduled Tribes to investigate and monitor all matters relating to the safeguards provided for the scheduled castes and scheduled tribes under the constitution and law. It has also been vested with the power to recommend suitable measures for the protection, welfare and socio-economic development of the scheduled castes and scheduled tribes.

The Sixty-sixth Amendment added a further group of land reform enactments passed by the State legislatures of Andhra Pradesh, Bihar, Gujarat, Himachal Pradesh, Karnataka, Kerala, Madhya Pradesh, Maharashtra, Orissa, Rajasthan, Tamil Nadu, Uttar Pradesh, West Bengal, and Union Territory of Pondicherry to the IXth Schedule of the constitution, so that they could remain outside the purview of judicial review.

Moving on to the landmark Seventy-third Amendment of the constitution, it may be mentioned that the successive governments have been making efforts to revitalise the Panchayati Raj institutions in India. In 1989, Rajiv Gandhi's government introduced the 64th constitution Amendment Bill in Parliament and, likewise, in September 1990, the V.P. Singh government introduced the 74th constitution Amendment Bill, but these efforts did not fructify because to the dissolution of the Lok Sabha. It was only during P.V. Narasimha Rao's tenure as Prime Minister, the government succeeded in passing the 73rd constitutional Amendment. This historic amendment provides for an elaborate system of establishing panchayats as units of self-government; it has added Articles 243-A to 243-0 and a fresh Schedule XI enumerating the powers and functions of Panchayati Raj institutions. The constitutional amendment *inter-alia* provides for a three-tier model of Panchayati Raj and reservation of seats for scheduled castes, scheduled tribes, and women in the panchayats. It also provides for constituting a Finance Commission, for each state, to look after the financial position of the Panchayati Raj institutions.

Again, the 74th Amendment is an important one. It deals with the establishment of municipalities as a part of the constitution. The amendment details the powers, duration, election, finance, and other related matters of different types of municipalities. It has added the Twelfth Schedule to the constitution, wherein 18 subjects are mentioned for the municipalities to handle.

The Seventy-sixth Amendment has been enacted to raise the reservation quota of government jobs and seats for admission in educational institutions in favour of socially and educationally backward classes to 69 per cent in Tamil Nadu. Further, the Amendment Act has been included in the IXth Schedule to save it from judicial scrutiny. This has been done at the behest of Tamil Nadu government. All the political parties in Tamil Nadu without exception put pressure on the Union government for its enactment; no political party wanted to miss an opportunity to have political mileage. However, this Act was assailed on the basis of *Indra Sawhney v. Union of India* before the apex Court.

The Seventy-seventh Amendment has added a new sub-section 4(a) to Article 16 of the constitution to enable the state to make any provision for reservation in matters of promotion in government jobs in favour of scheduled castes and scheduled tribes, if it is of the opinion that they are inadequately represented in services under the state.

The Seventy-eighth Amendment has been made to insert land reforms Act once again of various States in the IXth Schedule to give them constitutional protection from judicial invalidation. The Amendment adds 27 land reform acts bringing the total entries to 284 in the IXth Schedule.

And, finally, the Eighty-first constitution Amendment Bill, popularly called 'Women's Reservation Bill', has been drafted in consonance with the commitment made by practically all the political parties in their election manifesto favouring 1/3rd reservation of seats for women in the Lok Sabha and the State assemblies. It also forms part of the Common Minimum Program of the government. It is averred that one-third reservation is essential to empower women and strengthen the Indian democracy. In fact, more than one million women have already begun their political careers at the Panchayati Raj level, and when the women's reservation Bill is passed by Parliament, it will further help the cause of women's participation in the decision-making bodies.

The above discussion clearly reveals the objects and purposes of enacting various constitutional amendments. Judicial invalidation of good number of socio-economic legislative measures resulted in the enactments of aforementioned constitutional amendments. However, the enactment of such large constitutional amendments in the past decades cannot be justified. Undoubtedly, while some of the amendments were a natural product of evolution of the new political system, there were others which sub-served only the political power. By way of illustration, it may be mentioned that the purpose of rushing through 38th constitutional Amendment was only to prevent inquiry into the constitutionality of the proclamation of internal Emergency on 26th June 1975, and the following 39th Amendment was masterminded to oust the jurisdiction of courts retrospectively any petition challenging the Prime Minister's election. The much discredited 42nd Amendment was brought about to institutionalize Emergency; it whittled down fundamental rights and made serious inroads into our democratic polity. Many have also questioned the wisdom of enacting anti-defection law and blatantly discriminatory 59th Amendment. There are also amendments which have not only enlarged the size of Schedule IX, but have also changed its content. There is, in fact, something called "politics of IXth Schedule".

Summation

To sum up, it can be said that the founding fathers of our constitution were keen to bring about socio-economic revolution in free India through constitutional means and for that, they deliberately provided for a flexible procedure. However, they did not make the procedure so easy that it made the constitution unstable.

Part XX of our constitution containing Article 368 deals with the power to amend the constitution and the procedure therefor. The multiple mechanism provided, therein, has its own advantages. The original Article 368 and the subsequent modifications to it through 24th and 42nd constitutional Amendments leave no scope whatever for any kind of limitation on the amending power.

However, the Supreme Court decided to put limitations on the amending power while handing down its decision in the *Golaknath* case in 1967, and in 1973, it introduced the 'basic structure' limitation through *Kesavananda*. The subsequent decisions of the apex Court only reaffirm and reiterate the *Kesavananda* judgement.

The successive governments have passed constitutional amendments to bring about important socio-economic and political changes, on the other, certain amendments smack of only politics and politicking. Also, it has been noticed that on many occasions, when national interest demanded, the ruling party received wholehearted support from the opposition for the passage of constitutional amendments.

In fact, there are two views about amending the Indian constitution. One, the constitution has failed to deliver, and it needs to be changed lock, stock, and barrel; and two, the constitution has served us well by and large, and the successive governments have been able to bring about significant changes through the available mechanism under the constitution. Hence, the present arrangement is satisfactory. The second view is supported here, as the constitution alone cannot bring in qualitative changes either in the society or in the functioning of the government. Even the best of constitutions may not be of help so long our society is afflicated with illiteracy, poverty, corruption and lawlessness, and we the people remain 'soft'. This sentiment has been succinctly expressed by Sabyasachi Mukherji, a former Chief Justice of India in the following words: "The root cause of India's failure in many fields is not in the structure of the constitution, but because we have not imbibed the requisite culture of living by constitutional morality, respecting law and order and the principle of accountability."

He further added, "The constitution was intended to bring about substantial changes in Indian society. In 1947, we achieved the goal of national independence, but the parallel goal of social, cultural, and economic revolution is still in the process."

NOTES AND REFERENCES

1. See 11 American Jurisprudence, pp. 602–603.
2. Carl J. Friedrich, *constitutional Government and Democracy* (Calcutta, 1966), p. 430.
3. K.C. Wheare, *Modern constitutions* (London, 1951), p. 143.
4. Text, *constitution of India* (New Delhi, 1977), p. 160, Clauses (4) and (5) in Article 368 were included vide Section 55 of the constitution (Forty-second Amendment) Act, 1976. However, the two clauses have been struck down by the Supreme Court of India in the *Minerva Mills* Case (1980).
5. See the constitution (Twenty-fourth Amendment) Act, 1971 and the constitution (Forty-second Amendment) Act, 1976.
6. The elaborated explanation of Article 368(2) has been taken from Dewan, Abrogation of forty-Second Amendment, New Delhi, 1978, pp. 6–7.
7. See Article 368 of the *constitution of India* (text).
8. The constitution (Twenty-fourth Amendment) Act, 1971 amended Article 368 to make the assent of the President obligatory. In fact, the assent could have been done away with.
9. *AIR*, 1951, SC, p. 458.
10. *AIR*, 1965, SC, p. 845.
11. *AIR*, 1967, SC, p. 1643.
12. Constitution (Twenty-fourth Amendment) Act, 1971.
13. *AIR*, 1973, SC, p. 1461.
14. See the impact of *Kesavananda* decision (*AIR*, 1973, SC, p. 1461).
15. See *Kesavananda*.
16. *AIR*, 1975, SC, p. 2299.
17. See *Election* case (*AIR*, 1975, SC, p. 2299).
18. See constitution (Forty-second Amendment) Act, 1976.
19. *AIR*, 1980, SC, p. 1789.
20. *AIR*, 1951, SC, p. 392.
21. *AIR*, 1950, SC, p. 124.
22. *AIR*, 1950, SC, p. 257.
23. The constitution (First Amendment) Act, 1951.
24. The constitution (Fourth Amendment) Act, 1955.
25. *AIR*, 1954, SC, p. 110.
26. *AIR*, 1954, SC, p. 119.
27. *AIR*, 1951, SC, p. 92.
28. The constitution (Seventeenth Amendment) Act, 1964.
29. *AIR*, 1951, SC, p. 458.
30. *AIR*, 1967, SC, p. 1643.
31. KC. *Cooper vs. Union of India*. *AIR*, 1970, SC, p. 564.
32. The constitution (Thirty-fourth Amendment) Act, 1974.

5

The Nature of the State

Rajesh K. Singh

The centrality of the state in today's life cannot be over-emphasized. From birth to death an individual lives under the constant shadow of its imposing and overwhelming structure. The omnipotent character of the state has been beautifully summarized by Ralph Miliband in the opening lines of one of his celebrated books:

> 'More than ever before men now live in the shadow of the state. What they want to achieve, individually or in groups, now mainly depends on the state's sanction and support... It is for the state's attention, or for its control, that men compete; and it is against the state that beat the waves of social conflict. It is to an ever greater degree the state which men encounter as they confront other men. This is why, as social beings, they are also political beings, whether they know it or not. It is possible not to be interested in what the state does; but it is not possible to be unaffected by it.'[1]

Needless to say that from time immemorial, such an important structure of our society has drawn the attention of a whole lot of thinkers. Traditionally systematic and rigorous study of the state belonged to political philosophy. More recently, it has been taken up as a subject by social sciences. The philosophers of the Renaissance and Enlightenment, as well as Hegel, shaped the thinking of the state, before social scientists took up the subject in the nineteenth century, particularly the political economists and German historical sociologists, whose great figures were Marx, Weber, and Otto Hintze.

But, unfortunately, this intellectual tradition did not continue for long, and until the Second World War the study of the state was totally done from legal and constitutional approaches. An empirical study of the state was not positively considered because the concept was said to be too broad.

In Western Europe and the United States, the concept of state fell into disuse of academic circles in the twentieth century, especially during the behavioural revolution. Thus, in this context, it is correct to say that the state is now being slowly rediscovered by political and sociological theorists, or to put it in Theda Skocpol's terminology, the debate is on "Bringing the State Back In."[2]

Theda Skocpol believes that the state as an area of study has suddenly become quite important since the last decade. The omnipresent nature of the state has become one of the unavoidable facts of today's life, not only for the industrialized countries (both capitalist and socialist), but also for the developing ones. "For most (if not all) of the Third World countries, state building is the *sine qua non* for independence and development."[3]

The post-colonial states have been studied and analyzed both within the liberal and the Marxist paradigms. In this context interpretations have ranged from the liberal to the neo-liberal, on the one hand, and from the Marxist, to the neo-Marxist, on the other. In this essay, we would be discussing both the liberal and the Marxist viewpoints on the Indian state.

❑ Liberal Interpretation of the Indian State

Surveying the literature on the post-colonial state in India one encounters a sort of loss of surveyability due to the divergence of ideological proclivities and conceptual frameworks underlying the major academic works on the topic. These diverse perspectives have ranged from the liberal and neo-liberal to the Marxist and neo-Marxist. First, we propose to survey major theories and paradigms of the state within the liberal and neo-liberal traditions of research.

The first thing noticeable in the early liberal discourse on Indian politics is the virtual conceptual absence of the category of "state". The preferred category was the "government". This may perhaps reflect the political scientific traditions in Anglo-American countries that essentially on the study of government in contrast to the continental European traditions in law and political science that have always preferred the term "state" to the government. But, since the late 1970s, there has been a conceptual shift in the Anglo-American political science to the state. This shift is also reflected in the more recent works emanating from the liberal perspective on the Indian state. A close, look at the state and its internal structural dynamics is noticed for the first time in the libral discourse of Indian politics in the works of Rajni Kothari,[4] Lloyd, and Susanne Rudolph,[5] and M.P. Singh.[6] A precursor was the work of Norman D. Palmer.[7] An early study of the secular nature of the Indian state was carried out by Donald Eugene Smith.[8]

State and Society

Reminiscent of, though not replicative of, the state-civil society dichotomy in Hegel and Marx, the state-society relations in the context of the study of the Indian state have been highlighted in some more recent works of Atul Kohli and Francine Frankel. In a sense, this perspective is a "primitive" point of theoretical departure to analyze significant dimensions of Indian politics by juxtaposing the twin amorphous concepts of the *State* and *Society* and patterns of interaction between the two.

Kohli's main problem is to comprehend and explain the paradox of the growth of centralization and powerlessness at the centre. This problem is sought to be X-rayed both at the district and the state levels. The crux of the problem is identified as the following: "Political turmoil not only threatens the prospect for establishing legitimate and coherent authority, but also undermines the government's ability to facilitate socio-economic development."[9]

Kohli defines the crisis of governability in the Indian context with reference to the following dimensions: "(1) the absence of enduring coalitions, (2) policy ineffectiveness, and (3) an incapacity to accommodate political conflict without violence".[10] Kohli goes on saying, "A government whose power rests on fluctuating coalitions and whose leaders repeatedly fail to fulfil their stated goals and to control politically directed violence will be deemed to be a government with low capacity to govern".[11] His findings underline the growing disjuncture between centralization and development in the post-Nehru era. Centralization may temporarily aggrandize the personal powers of leaders but it seriously erodes the legitimacy of the state and its developmental power.[12]

A major weakness of Kohli's study is that even though it probes into the crucial factor of the role of political parties and their declining standards of performance and institutionalization in explaining the crisis of governability, he almost completely blacks out a focussed treatment of governmental organs, like the legislature, the executive, and judiciary. This omission appears strange in a book that purports to study the crisis of governability!

A more sophisticated theoretical framework for analyzing state-society relationship is offered by Francine R. Frankel in the introductory and concluding essays in Francine R. Frankel and M.S.A. Rao (eds.), *Dominance and State Power in Modern India: Decline of a Social Order.*[13] Both the editors as well as authors have been more successful in analyzing the contemporary dialectics between the state and social structures than their historical dynamics and evolution that often appear to be elliptical and vulnerable to abstracted empiricism.

This theoretical approach sets up a dichotomy between the state and the civil society, but does not take this separation to a complete logical dissention that may become too unrealistic and reified. Instead, the two categories are kept sufficiently porous for osmotic interpretation. Domination is neither exclusively associated with the state nor is social domination solely regarded as traditional and state domination solely modern. It is a very promising and empirically more valid theoretical approach to analyze state-society relations.

State and Party System

In liberal theory and ideology, political party is the most vital link between the civil society and the state. This is in contrast to the Marxist ideology and theory in which the party is absolutely appropriated by the state apparatus: indeed it subjugates both the state and the civil society, jettisoning the autonomy of both. In the early, post-independence liberal political science literature on Indian politics, studies of parties and party systems were conducted in relation to society and government. One does not really find any self-conscious attempt to theorize the party/party system variable within the framework of any theory of the state. Works of W.H. Morris-Jones[14] and early writings of Rajni Kothar[15] illustrate this point. In Kothari's classic *Politics in India*[16] there is hardly any discussion of the Indian state as such, except for a passing but precocious comment:

> To no small degree, the state has become the arbiter of society. This is not to deny the autonomy of social and economic factors in the development process; indeed, it seems likely that with increasing diversification of centres of power, this autonomy will increase.[17]

A similar tendency is evident in Morris-Jones' writings. Even though he made such seminal remarks as "The character of the political system of any modern state is substantially dictated by the manner in which political forces are organized in a party system,"[18] he did not ever seek to theorize about the Indian state, except for studying such vital institutions of the state as the Parliament and the party system. Rajni Kothari, in his later writings, concerned himself with condensed analytical focus on the Indian state. But, this happened in a period when the theoretical ideologue of the "Congress system" had become disillusioned with the Indian model of development, mainly during the ascendancy of the Indira Gandhi government and, subsequently, the Emergency regime which she imposed. Reflecting on this period in particular, Kothari[19] found fault with the distortions in the Indian model of democratic nation-building in which "horizontal aggregation" at the top came to be juxtaposed by "a deliberate strategy of vertical *disaggregation*. Politicization and challenges from the bottom met with a response from the top that was essentially premised on the politics of populism from the top."[20] A crisis of institutions and a crisis of values together produced the proclivity for personalized power on the part of those in government and for the cult of "oppositionalism" or "the tendency of the opposition to subordinate other goals to the simple aim of displacing those who happen to be in power."[21]

Some more contemporary studies of some formal and informal institutions of the state and government continue to lament the phenomenon of "deinstitutionalization", but they are not as pessimistic as Kothari's conclusions (the Rudolphs[22], Myron Weiner[23], James Manor[24] and M.P. Singh[25]).

State, Economy and Society

Perhaps the most comprehensive and internally differentiated theoretical framework for analyzing Indian politics in which the state, in relation to the economy and society, receives a fuller treatment has been put forward by the Rudolphs in their more recent work *In Pursuit of Lakshmi: The Political Economy of the Indian State.*[26] In this theoretical perspective, the Indian state is depicted as embedded in group and class pluralism and its expanding role in the mixed economy is attributed to the historical legacies of the strong sub-continental state traditions of Mughal and British India as also to the strategy of economic development devised by the post-colonial modernizing elites. But, as the state was expanding in the economy, the society was undergoing a parallel process of the gathering momentum of politicization and the emergence of the typically Indian phenomenon of "demand groups" and organized interests also typical of Western liberal democracies.

As all this was happening, the political institutions were themselves declining in their efficacy: the Congress party, the parliament, the judiciary, the federal structures, and so on. All these developments had serious consequences for the autonomy of the state. In the Indian context they identify two major sources of threat to the autonomy of the state, namely, from the social forces, and from the state elites themselves which they call the phenomenon of "state for itself'.[27] In their estimation, the Indian state has oscillated between autonomous and constrained patterns. To quote the Rudolphs:

> 'Over the four decades since independence, state capacity and autonomy declined. The decline encompassed both authoritarian and democratic regimes. The long-run deterioration in state capacity and autonomy was associated with the deinstitutionalization of both political parties and state institutions.'[28]

The Rudolphs conclude this study with the following perceptive, but contingent observation:

> Like Hindu conceptions of the divine, the state in India is polymorphous, a creature of manifold forms and orientations. One is the third actor (between the capitalist and working classes) whose scale and power contribute to the marginality of class politics. Another is a liberal or citizens' state, a juridical body whose legislative reach is limited by a written constitution, judicial review, and fundamental rights. Still another is a capitalist state that guards the boundaries of the mixed economy by protecting the rights and promoting the interests of property in agriculture, commerce, and industry. Finally, a socialist state is concerned to use public power to eradicate poverty and privilege and tame private power. Which combination prevails in a particular historical setting is a matter of inquiry.[29]

❑ The Marxist View of the Indian State

The uniqueness of the Marxian analysis of the state lies in the fact that it is not only a political, but also a social analysis. The Marxian theory views the state not as a result of some abstract idea of political will or sovereignty, but as an embodiment of the social dynamics resulting from either the constant change or relative stability of a mode or modes of production and the consequent class configuration.

Although the idea of a relatively autonomous state as such was present in Marx's own writing, he "himself did not attempt to set out a comprehensive and systematic theory."[30] He has given, what can be said, at best an outline of a theory of state which contained both the "instrumentalist" as well as the "structuralist" arguments.

The instrumentalist argument of Marx was readily endorsed by the orthodox Marxists who believed that "the executive of the modern state is, but a committee for managing the common affairs of the whole bourgeoisie". Regarding this, Miliband opines that "this is a more complex statement than appears at the first sight, but it is a summary and lends itself to over-simplification. However, it does represent the core position of Marxism on the subject of the state."[31] But, there is a strong evidence to show that after the disappointments of the revolutions of 1848, Marx himself increasingly abandoned this view. In the *Eighteenth Brumaire* Marx put forward a more complex theory which tells that the bourgeoisie on its own keeps itself away from power because they are shrewd enough to perceive that in this way their interests may be better served. "This is the origin of the neo-Marxist idea of the state being 'relatively autonomous' of the dominant economic class even though it acts on behalf of the latter and safeguards its interests."[32]

The Miliband[33]-Poulantzas[34] debate, which is also known as the 'instrumentalist' *vs.* 'structuralist' debate, revolved around the concept of the 'relative autonomy' of the state and not only created the ground work for the neo-Maxist school, but also made rich contributions towards its literature. Over the years, the thinkers of this school widened their scope to take up the case of the developing societies which were earlier denied their legitimate place. To use Poulantzas' terminology, the "specificity of political" in these developing societies has forced these neo-Marxist thinkers to see the whole reality in a new light. "Marxism primarily fashioned in and for a *burgeoisl* capitalist context has, to say the least, to be adapted to the very different circumstances subsumed under the notion of underdevelopment."[35]

All these factors have forced some neo-Marxists in the recent years to study these developing societies in their own right and improvise the theory applied to advanced capitalist states to suit an entirely different environment. Thinkers, like Hamza Alavi, Anupam Sen, and Pranab Bardhan, all neo-Marxists, have done the same and quite efficiently so. In the coming pages, while analyzing the Indian state, we would be discussing them is some detail. But first, we will start with the classical orthodox Marxist interpretation.

The viewpoints of this interpretation would conceptualize of a ruling-class coalition and see the state as an instrument in the hands of that coalition. With different interpretations the members of the coalition as well as its leader would vary, but the framework would remain the same. The Communist Party of India (CPI), for instance, characterized the Indian state as a national bourgeoisie state. The class of nationalist bourgeoisie does not include the monopolists who tend to compromise with feudalism and imperialism. The CPI ideologues believe that due to their participation in the anti-imperialist struggle, certain sections of the bourgeoisie have become progressive in their outlook. It is because of this class that the Indian state has been able to take up progressive steps. The CPI believes that the Indian state can take up any anti-monopolistic measures, provided that it has a political will to do so.[36]

The Communist Party of India (Marxist) views the Indian state as "an organ of the rule of the bourgeoisie and landlords led by the big bourgeoisie who are increasingly collaborating with foreign finance capital in pursuit of the capitalist path of development."[37] Similarly, with a slight variation, the Communist Party of India (Marxist-Leninist) views the Indian state as a semi-colonial and semi-feudal state. The CPI (ML) theoreticians observe' that "the characteristic features of new government in the name of independent India was a continuity of the old regime, of the social and economic order, the same administrative machinery of imperialism, the same bureaucracy, and the police."[38] Hence, they conclude that the reforms brought by the subsequent governments "have not changed the foundations of the Indian society in general and the ruling classes in particular. There is no change in their foundations of power."[39] They view that the comprador bourgeoisie has mortgaged India into the hands of the foreign capitalists.

Other Marxist theoreticians, like A.R. Desai, Moin Shakir, and Ajit Roy also formulated, though in a more sophisticated way, similar instrumentalist view regarding the state. A.R. Desai, for example, seeks to demonstrate that despite contrary appearances, the state in India is a capitalist state. Similarly, Ajit Roy observes the Indian state as essentially the organ of the dictatorship of the Indian monopoly bourgeoisie and the rural bourgeoisie.[40] The neo-Marxists, on the contrast provide us with an interpretation which shrugs off the instrumentalist orthodoxy and throws a refreshing light on the concerned subject.

Thanks to a belated discovery of Gramsci, there is a greater willingness now to recognize the "relative autonomy" of the Indian state. Ironically enough the recognition carne at a time when the state was rapidly losing its autonomous character. Nevertheless, the autonomous character of the state remains an important quality of the post-colonial Indian state. The aforesaid recognition came with its accessory which is a realization that there are multiple ways to build capitalism, including the passive revolution.

Hamza Alavi was one of the first neo-Marxists to argue that a post-colonial state, like India has a relative autonomy vis-a-vis the civil society.

The predominance of dependency theory of the late 1960's was epitomized in Hamza Alavi's work on the "overdeveloped" post-colonial state. He gave an important insight into the analysis of the state in the post-colonial societies. He gives proper emphasis on the historical specificity of post-colonial societies, "a specificity which arises from structural changes brought about by the colonial experience and alignment of classes and by the superstructures of political and administrative institutions which were established in that context and secondly from radical realignments of class forces which have been brought about in the post-colonial situation."[41]

To take up the first point, Alavi observes that the post-colonial state dispenses with the mediation of politics because the state is overdeveloped. It denotes a superstructure which is capable of dominating all the indigenous social classes. According to Alavi, the colonial state:

> ... had to create a state apparatus through which it can exercise domination over all the indigenous social classes in the colony. It might be said that the superstructure in the colony is, therefore, over-developed in relation to the structure in the colony, for its basis lies in the metropolitan structure itself from which it is later separated at the time of independence.[42]

The state which is inherited by the post-colonial society, consequently remains so powerful that Alavi wonders that "the excessive enlargement of powers of control and regulation that the state acquires extends far beyond the logic of what is necessary in the interests of the orderly functioning of the peripheral capitalist economies over which the state presides, and specific needs of each of the dominant classes."[43]

Apart from the colonial legacy, the structure of the society obviously helps the state to maintain its autonomy. The peculiar class structure within the peripheral capitalist system seems to provide the answer. "In peripheral capitalist societies, we are presented with a pattern of class formation and class alignment that is different both from that of the advanced capitalist countries and that of Lenin's picture of non-colonized Russia awaiting in bourgeois revolution."[44] Alavi finds a plurality of "fundamental classes" in peripheral capitalist societies and observes that none of them can be designated unambiguously, as the "ruling class". Thus, there is no single class potent enough to dominate over the affairs of the state.

Hamza Alavi comes as the forerunner among the neo-Marxist thinkers who have specifically theorized about the peripheral capitalist societies of the Indian subcontinent. Although his main concerns are Pakistan and Bangladesh, he has several important things to say about India. The common past of all these countries begets them several qualities which run across the present political boundaries. While certain formulations of Alavi, like when he talks about a military-bureaucratic ruling class alliance, are appropriate for Pakistan and Bangladesh only and cannot be applied to India with ease, his other formulations can be generalized. His thesis focuses on mainly two factors: (1) the overdeveloped state apparatus; and (2) the relatively weak societal forces, which gives rise to the relative autonomy of state in these societies has been widely accepted as a reality by the other neo-Marxists.

Bardhan follows the footprints, but showing an alert mind goes beyond Alavi in the sense that he discovers that not only the colonial-state, but even the pre-colonial state was overdeveloped in India. To quote Bardhan:

> Some Marxist scholars have traced the extraordinary powers of control and regulation vested in the state to the colonial administration ruling an alien land. But *this overdeveloped state actually goes back* to *pre-colonial days and was certainly evident during the peak of the Mughal rule* in *India.*[45]

The centrality of the state is an established fact for Bardhan too. He thinks that the state in the developing society is even more important than they are in the west.

> In the countries of delayed industrialization, the state has usually played a more active role, as the history of south, central and eastern parts of Europe, as contrasted with the western, clearly shows.[46]

At the time of independence, Bardhan opines, the Indian state acted "neither at the behest of nor on behalf of the proprietary classes."[47] But, over the years, the autonomy of the state has declined owing to various constraints and "as a consequence, today the autonomy of the Indian state is reflected more often in its regulatory than developmental role."[48]

Anupam Sen comes next in the line. His work deals more specifically with the nature of the state and the social formation in India.[49] Through a historical study, he has tried to argue that it is "because of the nature of the evolution of its social formation", that the Indian state has been able to play an independent role vis-a-vis the civil society. The post-colonial state in India is still autonomous because of the multiplicity of modes of production. The Indian society is at the same time partly feudal, partly capitalist, and partly Asiatic. This puts obstacles in the way of any class emerging as the dominant class. This ensures the state's autonomy. The multiplicity of "fundamental classes" in these societies is present in Anupam Sen as well as in all other neo-Marxists working on India. The most controversial point in Sen's work is that it still finds the 'Asiatic Mode of Production' (AMP) valid in India. The insufficiency of the AMP as a tool for analyzing the Asiatic societies has long been recognized and today no serious Marxist scholars apply it to study these societies. However, Sen has retained it and quite explicitly so.

Achin Vanaik, accepting almost all the formulations of his fellow neo-Marxists, goes a step further when he analyzes the relationship between the Indian state vis-a-vis foreign capital and declares that the Indian state is autonomous not only internally (vis-a-vis the civil society), but externally (vis-a-vis the foreign capital) also. He has firm belief in the indigenous economic infrastructure which sustains the pressures from abroad. So much so that he thinks that even the ongoing economic liberalization is not going to alter the situation as "it is from a relatively stronger position than in the past and in a careful and cautions manner" that the Indian economy is approaching it. However, this is a field in which, there is a need for a considerable amount of study. At present, the Indian economy is in a flux and nothing definite can be predicted about it.

Although Vanaik does not include the Indian middle classes in this ruling class alliance, he recognizes the pivotal role they play in the Indian politics and economy, and rightly so. He observes:

> There is not enough recognition of the fact that this demographic uniqueness has played a significant role in enabling the Indian economy to pursue an internally oriented path of growth with considerable insulation from the world economy, thus reinforcing the state's autonomy.[50]

From the foregoing analysis, we see that it is the neo-Marxists who have the most profound grasp of the nature of the state in India and its autonomous character, quite interestingly, the liberals who seem to be most persuasive and logical in their argument, are, precisely speaking, not the liberals in its classical sense, but actually the neo-liberals, a school which finds itself in close vicinity of the neo-Marxists.

Today, we encounter a situation where the liberals seem to be more radical and the Marxists more liberal—the former represented by the neo-liberals, like Rudolphs, and the latter by neo-Marxists, like Alavi, Bardhan, and Anupam Sen. A sort of convergence of perspectives is taking place.[51] While the liberals are increasingly using the vocabulary of the neo-Marxists, the latter are gradually recognizing the "specificity of political" (*a la* Paulantzas). Both the views today give the state the position which it deserves. The Rudolphs, for example, recognized the utmost centrality of the state in India when they talked about the phenomenon of "state for itself". They observe that between the capital and the labour, the state in India has emerged as the "third actor". The "state for itself", on various occasions, jealously guards its own interests to the detriment of the other two actors. The Rudolphs also recognize that the autonomy of the Indian State has declined over the decades since the independence. But the reasons, for them, are quite different from the ones provided by the neo-Marxists.

For the Rudolphs, it is mainly because of the "deinstitutionalization of both political parties and state institutions"[52] that the autonomy of the Indian state has declined. The neo-Marxists bring in a much more sophisticated approach to define the autonomy and its decline. The rich tradition of the Marxist theorizations about the state comes very handy here.

The neo-Marxists reviewed here have shed the deterministic fallacy of the orthodox Marxists who are prone to *reducing* the state to the class, but they are yet a long way from recognizing the areas of choice, of indeterminacy, and of unintended consequences in much of social, economic, and political relationships. They also fall prey to a tendency of using the conceptual blinders of class such that they fail to come to terms with the complexity of the Indian social formation. For example, they tend to take a rather dismissive view of caste, ethnicity, religion, etc., as well as the forces of nationalism in India and the contemporary world.

But, it would be unjust to say that the neo-Marxists are just following a trodden path. No, they are not. They have opened the windows and doors of the fortress created by the orthodox Marxists and have let in fresh air and light. As shown in the introduction of this chapter, they have tried to adapt themselves to the new situations which they confront in the peripheral capitalist societies like India. At least they are trying, and in the right direction.

The state in India still retains its autonomous character, though it has much less than the amount of autonomy that it had inherited from the colonial state. Over the decades, constraints have increased but the state still manages to have a relatively autonomous arena of operation. As one observer concludes: "In post-colonial societies, the hegemonic position by a single dominant social class has not yet been achieved due to their transitional nature and this hegemonic position must be created for capitalism to grow on native soil."[53]

Ever since the independence, capitalism has been growing gradually in India with the state as the biggest capitalist around. The scenario has changed drastically now. The economic liberalization has created the conditions for a rapid growth of capitalism in India. Whether or not a single class emerges in the process to dominate the state apparatus is open for debate. But there are factors which would still impede the process. To name a few, these are divisive forces of ethnicity, language, religion, caste, region, urban-rural divide, etc. In India, these factors show amazing resilience and longevity. And even if, in a long drawn process, a dominant class emerges, as the neo-Marxist debate has shown, it is in the interest of the dominant class coalition itself that the state retains its autonomy.

Notes and References

1. Ralph Miliband, *The State in the Capitalist Society.* London: Quarlet Books, 1973, p. 31.
2. Theda Skocpol, "Bringing the State Back in: "Strategies of Analysis in Current Research". Peter Evans, *et. al.*(eds). *Bringing the State Back in*, Cambridge University Press, 1985.
3. Kola Olugbade, 'State in the Third World', Foreign Affairs Reports, Vol. XXXII, Nos. 7-8, July-Aug 1998,p.46
4. Rajni Kothari, "The Crisis of the Moderate State and the Decline of Democracy", Peter Lyon & James Manor, (Eds.) *Transfer and Transformation: Political Institutions in the New Commonwealth.* Leicester University Press, 1983.

5. Lloyd Rudolph and Susanne Rudolph, *In Pursuit of Lakshmi: The Political Economy of the Indian State,* New Delhi: Orient Longman, 1987, Ch. 3.
6. Mahendra Prasad Singh, "The Crisis of the Indian State: From Quiet Developmentalism to Noisy Democracy", *Asian Survey,* Vol. XXX, No. 8, August, 1990.
7. Norman D. Palmer. *The Indian Political System,* Boston: Houghton Mifflin Company, 1961.
8. Donald Eugene Smith, *India as a Secular State;* Princeton University Press, 1966.
9. Atul Kohli, *Democracy and Discontent: India's Growing Crisis of Governability.* Cambridge University Press. 1991, p. 304.
10. *Ibid.,* p. 23.
11. *Ibid.*
12. *Ibid.,* pp. 397–398.
13. Francine Frankel and M.S.A. Rao, (Eds). *Dominance and State Power in Modern India: Decline of a Social Order.* 2 Vols. Delhi: Oxford University Press, 1989 and 1990.
14. W.H. Morris-Jones, *The Government and Politics of India.* New Delhi: Universal Book Stall, 1989: and *his Politics Mainly Indian.* New Delhi, Orient Longman. 1978. First Published in 1964 by Hutchinson University Library.
15. Rajni Kothari. "The Congress System in India", *Asian Survey,* Vol. IV, No. 21, December 1964; His *Politics in India.* Boston: Little, Brown & Company, 1970; and his "Congress System Revisited: A Decennial Review", *Asian Survey,* Vol. XIV, No. 12, December, 1974.
16. Kothari, *Politics in India,* No. 15.
17. *Ibid.*
18. Morris-Jones, *Politics Mainly Indian,* No. 14.
19. Kothari, No. 15, pp. 38–39.
20. *Ibid.,* p. 40.
21. *Ibid.,* p. 42.
22. Rudolphs, No. 5.
23. Myron Weiner, *The Indian Paradox: Essays in Indian Politics* (Ed.) by Ashutosh Varshney. New Delhi, Sage, 1989.
24. James Manor, "Parties and the Party System", Atul Kohli. *India's Democracy: An Analysis of State Society Relations.* New Delhi, Orient Longman, 1991. First published by Princeton University Press in 1988.
25. M.P. Singh, No. 06; and his "the Dilemma of the New Indian Party System: To Govern or not to Govern?" *Asian Survey,* Vol. XXXII, No. 4, April 1992.
26. Rudolphs. No. 5.
27. *Ibid.,* pp. 62–63.
28. *Ibid.,* p. 224.
29. *Ibid.,* pp. 400–401.
30. Henri Lefebvre, *The Sociology of Marx,* Translated from the French by Nobert Guterman. London, Allan Lanes Penguin Press, 1963, p. 123.
31. Ralph Miliband, "The State', in Tom Bottomore (Ed.) *Dictionary of Marxist Thought* (Blackwell Reference, 1983), p. 464.
32. Pranab Bardhan, *The Political Economy of Development in India,* New York, Basil Blackwell, 1984, p. 33.
33. Ralph Miliband, *The State in Capitalist Society.* London: Weidenfeld & Nicolson, 1969. Cf. His "The Capitalist State-Reply to Nicos Pulantzas", R. Blackburn (Ed). *Ideology in Social Science,* London, Fontana, 1972, and *Marxism and Politics.* Oxford: Oxford University Press. 1977.
34. Nicos Poulantzas, *Political Power and Social Classes,* London: New Left Book, 1973, pp. 331–340.
35. Ralph Miliband, *Marxism and Politics.* Oxford: Oxford University Press, 1977, p. 29.

36. Mohit Sen, "Indian Monopoly-Necessity and Possibility of Elimination", *Monopolies and Public Policy,* Delhi: People's Publishing House, 1972, p.57.
37. Quoted in *SUCI-CPM* Polemic. Calcutta, Gandabi, 1984, p. 71.
38. T. Nagi Reddi, *India Mortgaged,* Anantpur, 1978, p. 10.
39. *Ibid.,* p. XXII.
40. Yogendra Yadav, "Theories of the Indian State", *Seminar,* No. 367, March 1990, p. 18.
41. Hamza Alavi, "The State in Post-Colonial Societies", Kathleen Gough and H.P. Sharma. (Eds). *Imperiatlism and Revolution in South Asia,* New York, Monthly Review Press. 1973, p. 147.
42. *Ibid.,* p. 147.
43. Hamza Alavi, "Character of State in Pakistan". V.D. Chopra (Ed). *Studies in Indo-Pak Relations,* New Delhi, Patriot Publishers, 1984, p. 43.
44. Hamza Alavi, "State and Class", Hamza Alavi and T. Shanin (Eds). *Introduction to the Sociology of Developing Societies,* London, Macmillan, 1982, p. 297.
45. P. Bardhan, No. 32, p. 37.
46. *Ibid.*
47. *Ibid.*
48. *Ibid.*
49. Anupam Sen, *The State, Industrialization and Class Formations in India: A Neo-Marxist Perspective in Colonialism, Underdevelopment and Development,* London, Routledge & Kegan Paul, 1982.
50. Achin Vanaik, *The Painful Transition: Bourgeois Democracy in India,* London,Verso, 1990.
51. See Nicos Poulantzas. "Towards a Democratic Socialism", David Held, *et al.* (Eds). *States and Societies,* UK, Basil Blackwell, 1983.
52. Lloyd Rudolph and Susanne Rudolph, No. 5, p. 224.
53. Srikant Dutt, *Viewpoints on the Third World,* Delhi, Allied Publishers, 1988, p. 10.

6

Fundamental Rights and Directive Principles of State Policy

K.C. Markandan

The Fundamental Rights and Directive Principles had their roots deep in the struggle for independence. And they were included in the constitution in the hope and expectation that one day the tree of true liberty would bloom in India. The Rights and Principles, thus, connect India's future, present and past, adding greatly to the significance of their inclusion in the constitution, and giving strength to the pursuit of the social revolution in India.

In the Directive Principles, however, one finds an even clearer statement of the social revolution. They aim at making the Indian masses free in the positive sense, free from the passivity engendered by centuries of coercion by society and by nature, free from the object, physical conditions that have prevented them from fulfilling their best selves.[1] To do this, the State is to apply the precepts, contained in the Directive Principles when making laws. These principles are not justiciable, a court cannot enforce them, but they are to be, nevertheless, 'fundamental in the governance of the country'.[2] The essence of the Directive Principles lies in Article 38, which echoing the Preamble, reads:

> The State shall strive to promote the welfare of the people by securing and protecting as effectively as it may a social order in which justice, social, economic, and political, shall inform all the institutions of a national life.

Although the Fundamental Rights and Directive Principles appear in the constitution as distinct entities, it was the Assembly that separated them; the leaders of the independence movement had drawn no distinction between the positive and negative obligations of the State. Assuming that the constitutional conflict between the Fundamental Rights and Directive Principles of State Policy is real, one way to resolve it would be to study the background in which these rights and principles were incorporated in the original constitution with the actual intention of founding fathers in regard to them. Instead of doing that, the judiciary starting with the decision in the *Golak Nath* case (1967) (which put the power to amend the Fundamental Rights beyond Parliament's purview) chose to interpret the constitution according to their varying lights and in the process destroyed its intrinsic harmony. The executive and the legislature have, on their part, disfigured the document through a series of amendments calculated not so much to resolve the apparent conflict between the constitutional provisions, as to assert their own supremacy over the judicial arm of the government. The constitution has become a plaything in the hands of its own creatures, namely, the organs, institutions and functionaries provided by it.

The main question today is, how the constitution can be saved from further misinterpretation and mutilation. In fact, had the constitution been correctly understood, both in letter and spirit, no conflict would have arisen. The constitution is a sterling document drawn up after mature consideration by some of the best minds of the time. Some critics have called it a bagful of borrowings, a jumble of contradictions. But if they are borrowings, they have not been taken mechanically. In fact, the two most remarkable features about the content and style of the constitution are the precision in the choice of works and the avoidance of any redundancy.

It is less than charitable to assume that the founding fathers lacked the sense to realize that situations would arise when the Fundamental Rights and the Directive Principle's might conflict. Article 31 includes the fundamental right to property enforceable in a court of law, while Article 39, clauses (b) and (c), provide for acquisition of property for the purpose of equitable distribution, but makes it non-enforceable in law. If this be a contradiction, a further question that arises is whether the judiciary, entrusted with enforcing Article 31 should prevent the executive and the legislature from performing their constitutional function under Article 39 (b)[3] and (c)[4] even when that function conflicts with Article 31. It was never the intention of the framers that what might appear in the context of today as an inevitable conflict to become a conflict at all. Their intention when they framed what appears to be "conflicting provisions" was that the judiciary would normally enforce the fundamental right to property under Article 31, but when the State chose to acquire property for purposes of equitable distribution under Article 39(b), the judiciary would, by a process of harmonious interpretation, allow the State to discharge its constitutional function, instead of asserting its own right to enforce the Fundamental Rights. In other words, the principle adopted was that the extent of the enforceability of Article 31 would depend on State action under Article 39(b) and (e). In fact, it was even thought of at one stage of the Constituent Assembly deliberations that an explicit provision should be made in the constitution that in the case of conflict between the Fundamental Rights and Directive Principles, the latter should prevail.[5] But then this proposal was given up as unnecessary and redundant on the ground that the various organs of the government, created under the constitution, would be responsible enough to work in a complementary manner performing their prescribed functions without coming in conflict. Only, what was considered as redundant at that time has now come to be proved for in the constitution, although in a different manner and with a limited objective, in the shape of the new Article 31(c). This article enjoins that State action under Article 39(b) and (c) shall override the Fundamental Rights, more particularly the right to property under Article 31. To the extent state legislatures too are expected to follow the Directive Principles, the new Article 31(c) empowers these legislatures as well to make laws in pursuance of the Directive Principles, which would have an overriding effect on the fundamental right to property. In fact, it would be legitimate to extend the ambit of the legislative power under Article 39(b) and (c) even to municipal authorities because they are also instruments for implementing the Directive Principles.

The artificial nature of the present day conflict between the Fundamental Rights and the Directive Principles would be clear if one looks into the historical circumstances in which they came to be incorporated in the constitution. The Fundamental Rights Sub-committee was entrusted with the task of framing the Fundamental Rights as well as the Directive Principles. It would be worthwhile to recall in this respect that both part III and IV were originally designated and drafted as Fundamental Rights. The Committee had a long list of rights including political, social, economic, and so on. A scrutiny of this list reflects that the rights fell into two categories: (1) those that could be assured to the citizens without any serious difficulty, and, hence enforceable in a court of law, and (2) those that were for some reason or other, difficult to be ensured and, therefore, impracticable to be legally enforced. It was clear that a special effort would have to be made by the government to secure the second type of rights for the citizens; as such, till these were capable of realization, there was no point in making them enforceable in a court of law. So, it was obvious that as and when the State was in a position to ensure to the citizens these rights (which were termed as the Directive Principles of State Policy) and laws were enacted for this purpose, they should become rights in the same manner as the Fundamental Rights. In other words, when the Directive Principles become realisable, they should also become enforceable. Thus, the intention clearly was to enlarge the chapter on Fundamental Rights by a progressive transfer to it from that part of the constitution dealing with the Directive Principles.

Strictly speaking, there is no conflict between the Directive Principles of State Policy as non-enforceable rights and Fundamental Rights as enforceable ones. The Fundamental Rights cannot be whittled down, but at the same time the purpose cannot be achieved by treating the Directive Principles as things of no consequence at all. It is here that courts on the one hand and the executive and the legislature on the other should endeavour to harmonize the Directive Principles with the Fundamental Rights. Positively also the Directive Principles enjoys a judicial status because of the nature of the principles contained in it. They being 'fundamental in the governance of the country', it devolves on the judiciary to see to their fulfilment. Also, as it is the duty of the State to apply these principles in making laws, it is incumbent upon the judiciary not only to interpret the laws made thereunder but also to see to their faithful compliance.

Right from the time the constitution came into force, the State has been directing its policy towards the fulfillment of all the objectives contained in the Directive Principles of the State Policy with a varying degree of success. Generally speaking, there has been considerable amount of difficulty in securing the social ideals for more than one reason. For instance, some states are reluctant to introduce prohibition[6] for if they did so, it would suffer a serious loss in revenue which it could not otherwise offset. In the case of securing for the citizens a uniform civil code,[7] there is the difficulty of reconciling the vast number of varying practices. Adequate protection to Scheduled Castes and Scheduled Tribes from social injustice and exploitation is difficult in view of the existing prejudices against them. Article 45 of the constitution envisages the provision of free and compulsory education for children up to the age of 14 years, within a period of 10 years from the commencement of the constitution. This object has not met with success, not so much because of slackness on the part of the central as well as the state governments, or non-availability of funds, but because of the following three factors beyond the control of the aggregate state:

1. Difficulties of bringing sufficient numbers of girls to school.
2. Extreme backwardness of certain areas and certain sections of the population in matters of education.
3. Wastage due to parents discontinuing their children from attending school immediately after they are able to earn for the family. For this reason, more than one-half of the children never reach class IV, and hence fail to gain permanent literacy.

The framers of the constitution were clear that though the Fundamental Rights could not be abridged or taken away by a law made by the State, they could be by an *amendment* of the constitution. Accordingly, the term "law" in Article 13(2) was not to take in, in its inclusive definition, an amendment to the constitution. The doubt over this kicked up in *Golak Nath's* case was not all that new. It needs to be recalled that to clarify this position, the Constituent Assembly unanimously decided on an amendment on 29th April 1947, to the effect that although the Fundamental Rights could not be abridged or taken away by law, they could nevertheless be curtailed by an amendment of the constitution.[8] It might then be asked why the constitution, as finally adopted, did not make this provision explicitly. The answer lies in the fact that the Drafting Committee which examined this matter found that such a provision was unnecessary in as much as no Article or part of the constitution was exempted from the purview of the amending clause of the constitution.[9] While the Fundamental Rights as incorporated in the constitution were not to be abridged or taken away, they were to be subject to the constitutional law. That was the reason why the term "law" was defined in Article 13, clause 3(a), rather elaborately. If this basic scheme of the constitution had been appreciated by the judiciary, they would not have gone the way they did in the *Golak Nath* case, nor would it have been necessary for the Parliament to bring forth a series of amendments to the constitution.

Directive Principles and Fundamental Rights—Written Words and the Spirit of the Constitution

From the foregoing pages, it is reasonable to come to the conclusion that there cannot be a conflict between the Directive Principles of State Policy and the Fundamental Rights in the Indian constitution. The framers of the constitution had intended to provide these two chapters so that they may supplement and complement each other. This is evident not only from the records of the Constituent Assembly, but also from the written words and phraseology of the constitution. As already pointed out, the framers of the constitution had a long list of rights from which they have picked up some to be put in the chapter on Fundamental Rights and some others to be put in the chapter on Directive Principles of the State Policy. Since some of the rights could be ensured to the citizens without much difficulty to the individuals they have put them as Fundamental Rights and made them enforceable by the courts of law. As for the other set of rights, since they anticipated difficulty in ensuring them for the people of India straightway, the difficulties, such as finance, difficulties consequent on social customs and traditions, the founding fathers had thought of putting them in another chapter. Because of these difficulties, they further thought that it may be prudent to make them non-enforceable in the courts of law. Lest they should be looked upon by the judiciary as less important than Fundamental Rights, the framers of the constitution took a realistic view and made to Directive Principles non-enforceable in the courts of law. If the Fundamental Rights are important because they are so entailed, the Directive Principles are equally important because the framers have said that the Directive Principles are "fundamental in the governance of the country" and "it shall be the duty of the State to apply these principles in making laws."[10] As a matter of fact, one could think of the Directive Principles as more important than Fundamental Rights, because the former are concerned with conferring certain rights for the society as a whole as against the latter which are concerned with the conferment of the rights for the individuals. Certainly society is more important than the individual. As the arguments presented above state, that truly speaking, the Directive Principles are more fundamental than Fundamental Rights from the point of view of the constitution since the ideas enshrined in it, 'Justice, Social, Economic, and Political', are loftier in conception and seek to secure to the individual tangible benefit of great significance than Fundamental Rights.[11] It was suggested by B.N. Rau that in case of conflict between Fundamental Rights and the Directive Principles the former should be made subservient to the latter, otherwise the framers of the constitution might be accused "of sucking the Bill of rights".[12] Evidence to this effect which was the intention of the founding fathers is also available from the Constituent Assembly records. Sir B.N. Rau, to recall, suggested through an amendment, the incorporation of an Article as a preface to the chapter on Fundamental Rights and the Directive Principles of State Policy to the effect that as and when the two parts appear to come in conflict the Directive Principles would prevail.[13] This preface was not provided for in the constitution explicitly because it was felt by the founding fathers that it would be redundant. It was also felt that it would be quite obvious that the rights of the individual would certainly be less important than the rights of society and that in case of conflict, the individual rights should be subordinated to the social rights. Read in this context, it was certainly the intention of the framers of the constitution that the individuals had Fundamental Rights, but as and when the government of the day passed a legislation in order to confer a social right in pursuance of the Directive Principles of State Policy, the Fundamental Rights of the individual would cease to be operative. This was how the framers of the constitution wished the judiciary to view the Fundamental Rights and the Directive Principles of State Policy. Unfortunately, however, as the judiciary could not appreciate this position and constantly took the view that the Fundamental Rights were more important than Directive Principles of States Policy, a conflict arose. To the judiciary the Directive Principles had not much of relevance viewed in relationship with the Fundamental Rights. This position, therefore, necessitated the constitution Twenty-fourth and Twenty-fifth amendments.

The above-mentioned amendments are in reality redundant and unnecessary, because what has been sought to be achieved by these amendments is already implicit. In fact, these amendments have been necessitated due to the interpretation of the judiciary contrary to the intention of the founding fathers. If these two amendments, although pointed out as redundant, had not been effected, there would have been a never-ending conflict between the judiciary on the one hand, and the executive and legislature on the other. The judiciary would always give primacy to Fundamental Rights and set aside relegating to the background Laws made by the executive and the legislature in pursuance of a Directive Principles of State Policy. The government, on the other hand, by amending the constitution would try to clarify the position.

The position of the Fundamental Rights *vis-à-vis* the Directive Principles of State Policy, therefore, appear to be that the Fundamental Rights should be enforced by the judiciary so long as they do not conflict with the Directive Principles of State Policy. But, once such a conflict arises, the judiciary ought to withdraw to allow the Directive Principles to prevail. Secondly, the Fundamental Rights should be enlarged by translating the Directive Principles into laws. Also, The Fundamental Rights could be whittled down or even totally effaced by an amendment of the constitution. It follows that the Fundamental Rights were not meant to be sacrosanct or transcendental. These were incorporated in the constitution of free India to signify, first, the emancipation of the country from the British rule and, secondly, the right of the minority communities to be protected against any possible tyranny of majority rule. Those who framed the constitution did not intend to pit these rights against the Directive Principles of State Policy. Rather, they expected that the organs of government would interpret and use these rights in a manner that would help implement the Directive Principles. The framers of the constitutions saw no incongruity, nor any possibility of a conflict, between Parts III and IV of the constitution. The Fundamental Rights embodied in Part III are intended to secure the main objectives of the constitution enumerated in its Preamble, that is, "social, economic, and political justice". These very words occur in Article 38 which is the main plank of Part IV thereby implying that there is no conflict between Parts III and IV.

Directive Principles of State Policy: Nature and Significance

A novel feature of our polity is the inclusion of a chapter on Directive Principles of State or Social Policy as an integral part of the constitution. They are deliberately included by the framers of the constitution to bring about, primarily, a desired socio-economic pattern of society into existence.

❑ Origins

In the nineteenth and twentieth centuries the recognition of the Fundamental Rights of man, in the constitutions of states, became a general principle of constitutional law of the civilized states. The constitution of Egypt of 19th April and of Abyssinia of 6th July 1931 contained declarations of rights of individuals. The declaration of Fundamental Rights was also found in the Latin American constitutions. The enunciation of social and economic policies became a regular feature in the constitutions framed in the post-war years recognizing thereby that justice was to be secured not only in the political field for the individuals alone, but also in the social and economic spheres, for the society as a whole. The state was, therefore, called upon to play a more positive role to achieve the common good without sacrificing the good of the individual. The practice with regard to the enumeration of social and economic policies within the framework of the constitution has not been uniform. It has varied from country to country depending upon its social and economic progress.

Constitutional Precedents

The constitution of the Principality of Liechtenstein[14] of 5th October 1921, and the constitution of the Spanish Republic of 9th December 1931, both professing the Roman Catholic religion are out of those constitutions which had provided for social and economic matters, and require special mention. In the constitution of Liechtenstein, the chapter commencing with the 'Directive' provides that the supreme duty of the State was to advance the public welfare, goes on to include in its fourteen articles, matters relating to education, public health, industrial and agricultural labour, public utilities, natural resources, currency, credit and taxation, poor relief, social insurance, and reform of the legal system. The Spanish 'directives' was an improvement on the Liechtenstein 'directives' in the sense that it broadened the 'directives' by including in matters relating to the family and culture apart from social and economic matters. The enunciation of social and economic policies, however, found a distinctive place in the constitution of Ireland which came into force on 29th December 1937.[15] A distinction was made in it between 'Fundamental Rights' relating to personal rights and other rights relating to the family, education, private property and religion and Directive Principles of Social Policy which contains social and economic matters. The Irish constitutional provisions relating to social and economic matters, thus, made a significant advancement[16] in this regard in comparison to other constitutions of the world. It made a distinction between justiciable and non-justiciable rights and found a place in the constitutional documents for non-justiciable rights which was till then unknown. The title given to the provisions of this chapter as "Directive Principle of Social Policy" and their being non-justiciable in character not only enlarged the scope of the 'Directives', but also it applicability.

Case for its Provision

It is worthy to note here as to what principles should be kept in view while laying down the 'Directives' in the constitutional framework; what should be the basic contents; and in what manner should they be stated. First and foremost consideration is to avoid any sort of partisan zeal. Secondly, that 'Directives' should appeal to popular imagination. Thirdly, the 'Directives' should not occasion violent and lasting controversy. The function of the provision contained in the 'Directives' is to give a particularly solemn sanction and status to principles which are regarded of great importance. In regard to the content, it should be said that no model 'Directives' could be set for adoption by all countries. The most that could be done is to lay down certain generally acceptable objectives. Writing about Indian 'Directives' Where says:

> "Difficult to justify to the practical minded British observer, perhaps, is the large section embodying the 'Directive Principles of State Policy'. As these principles cannot be enforced in any court, they amount to a little more than a manifesto of aims and aspirations. In this matter of declarations of rights and of Directives of State Policy, the Indian Constituent Assembly has followed the Irish constitution and European practice rather than the less colourful and more legalistic documents which serve as constitution for other members of the Commonwealth.
>
> One thing is certain. If these declarations of liberal principles, strange as they may seem in a legal document to British eyes, help the Indian constitution on its way and assist its people in working their government, they are more than justified. This is the biggest liberal experiment in the government of men by themselves that has ever been tried."[17]

Apart from the Irish constitution wherein the distinction between rights justiciable and non-justiciable were made, Sir. B.N. Rau also found a similar distinction recognized by Dr. Lauterpacht in his 'International Bill of the Rights of Man'. The substantial provisions of the Bill were in two parts; Part I dealt with rights meant to be enforced by the ordinary courts, and Part II dealt with rights incapable of or unsuitable for such enforcement. Impressed with that distinction in Fundamental Rights as justiciable and non-justiciable in the Irish constitution and reinforced by Dr. Lauterpacht's recognition of the same, Sir B.N. Rau suggested for adopting in the Indian constitution the Irish plan[18] and separating the two classes of rights: Part A dealing with Fundamental Principles of State Policy, and Part B with Fundamental Rights. The suggestion of Sir B.N. Rau could not find any acceptance for even if a list of rights could be prepared for inclusion in the Indian constitution to further divide them in to justiciable and non-justiciable rights was indeed a difficult task. The difficulty in dividing rights into justiciable and non-justiciable was also pointed out by the Sapru Committee.[19] Sir Alladi Krishnaswami Ayyar also stressed the need for making a distinction between rights which were justiciable and rights which were merely intended as 'a guide and directive objective to State Policy'. On the other hand, K.M. Munshi was not very particular in making any distinction between justiciable and non-justiciable rights and including the latter in the constitution. Ultimately, the Fundamental Rights Sub-committee resolved that a distinction should be made in the list of Fundamental Rights as justiciable and non-justiciable. The Sub-committee examined the Directive Principles of Social Policy on 30th March 1947. According to the first set of 'Directive Principles of Social Policy as framed on 30th March 1947 by the Sub-committee was: "The principle of Social Policy set forth, in this part, are intended for the general guidance of the appropriate legislatures and governments in India (hereinafter collectively called as the State). The application of these principles, in legislation and administration, shall be the care of the State and shall not be cognizable by any court.[20] On the next day, 31st March 1947, the Sub-committee decided to insert the following Preamble to the Directive Principles of Social Policy:

> "The principles of social policy set forth in this part are intended for the general guidance of the State. The application of these principles in legislation and administration shall be the care of the State and shall not be cognizable by any court".[21]

The members went on to adopt the provisions based on Rau's draft of the effect that the State should raise the level of nutrition and the living standard of the people, and promote international peace and justice dealings between nations.[22] Certain changes and counter-changes were made during the next several weeks, but in general, the first stage of drafting the Directive Principles was over. The Minorities Sub-committee suggested two changes in the clause relating to non-justiciable rights as framed by the Fundamental Rights Sub-committee. Two other changes effected by the Advisory Committee in the list of non-justiciable rights recommended by the Fundamental Rights Sub-committee were (1) Clause 33[23] was given the sub-title 'Preamble' and the rest a subtitle 'Principles', and (2) the substitution of the world 'are not' for the words 'shall not be' in the second sentence of Clause 33.[24]

The second stage in the framing of the principles took place on the Assembly floor in November and December 1948, during the debate on the Draft constitution. An earlier debate-held in August 1947, on the occasion of Sardar Patel's presentation of the Advisory Committee's Supplementary Report, was of little consequence.

The assembly's attitude towards the draft revealed two major reactions: one that the Directives did not go far enough towards establishing a socialist state and the other that they should have placed greater emphasis on certain institutions. By November 1948, there were scores of amendments to the Principles as a consequence to these two major reactions. Some Assembly members sought to make the promotion of cottage industry a government responsibility and make it a duty of the State to prevent the slaughter of cattle and to improve animal husbandry and agriculture. In the Assembly, Dr. Ambedkar admitted, 'a considerable amount of feeling'[25] in favour of government encouragement for cottage industries, and this forced him to accept an amendment placing the promotion of cottage industries, and this forced him to accept an amendment placing 'the promotion of cottage industries' in the Directive Principles.[26] The provision pertaining to the improvement of agricultural and animal husbandry techniques and the prohibition of cow slaughter was also added. The prohibition of liquor and harmful drugs (*e.g.*, opium) also became a fundamental principle of governance.

The second major reaction to the draft principles was that they did not go far enough in encouraging a socialist society. In this respect, most of the amendments were voted down in the Assembly and in the Congress party meetings were withdrawn by the initiators. Those substantive amendments reaching the Assembly floor were not adopted because the majority of the members held with the 'oligarchy' that the Principles should be kept general, leaving enough room for the people of different ways of thinking to reach the goal of economic democracy.[27]

Nature of the Directives

Chapter IV of the Indian constitution relating to the Directive Principles of State Policy was the subject of animated discussion in the Constituent Assembly. On the one hand, one member preferred to label it as "pious expressions" and "pious superfluities", another member characterized it as 'vague' and 'adrift'. A third linked it to 'a cheque on a bank payable when able' because of its non-justiciable and non-binding character, a fourth took it to be analogous to an 'election manifesto' and as such there was no place for it in the constitution, and a fifth member called its inclusion in the constitution as 'undemocratic' and 'opposed to parliamentary democracy' and went to the extent of suggesting its deletion from the constitution. On the other hand, Professor Shibban Lal Saksena[28] considered it to be 'an important chapter laying down the principles which would govern the policy of the State;' Pandit Thakur Das Bhargava[29] regarded it to be the 'essence of the constitution and justified the way the Directives were worded, and S.V. Krishnamurthy Rao[30] deemed it as containing 'the germs of a socialist government' and he said that the part relating to the Directives in the constitution should come in immediately after the Preamble.

One member went to the extent of pointing out that the chapter on Directives was "one of the most cardinal, important, and creative chapters of the constitution." Pandit Hirday Nath Kunzru[31] did not attach any 'value' to any of the Principles included in the Chapter on Directive Principles, and T.T. Krishnanamachari, a member of the drafting committee, preferred to label it as 'a veritable dustbin of sentiment.' V.S. Sarwate (United States of Gwalior-Indore-Malva-Madhya Bharat) was, however, inclined to believe that 'all the principles given in this chapter are of such a nature that they are fundamental, that they are basic, and that efforts to implement them to the fullest extent would have to the taken as long as society goes on.[32] Members also criticized the distinction made between justiciable and non-justiciable rights. For instance, Somnath Lahiri (Bengal, General) observed:[33]

> "It is rather difficult to make a distinction between what are justiciable rights and what are not. For instance, when we make a provision that people should have the right to work, that is, unemployment should not be allowed to exist on our country, it would be social rights. If you make it an inalienable provision of our Fundamental Rights, naturally it will have to be justiciable. Similarly, take the question of nationalization of land. If one wants to say that the land belongs to the people and to nobody else, that would be a social and fundamental right no doubt...it will also be a

justiciable right. Therefore, it is rather arbitrary to make any distinction between what are justiciable and what are social and economic rights".

Promath Ranjan Thakur (Bengal, General) said:

"I do not know why economic Fundamental Rights should not be included in these justiciable rights., Economic rights are essential while framing a country's constitution and they must also be made justiciable".[34]

Renuka Ray (West Bengal, General) said:

The provision that no person shall be deprived of his property save by authority of law with the details about compensation when property was taken by the State for public purpose in accordance with law, should be put under directives and not under rights which are justiciable and enforceable in courts of law.[35]

Vishwambhar Dayal Tripathi also thought:

"There is no ground for thinking that the Directive Principles of State Policy as embodied in the Draft constitution would at all affect the future structure of society in India.'[36]

Members also expressed the view that in the absence of provisions in this chapter making it obligatory, it was quite possible that none of these provisions might ever be realized in their life time.[37] To overcome this difficulty, Krishna Chandra Sharma (U.P., General) suggested the addition of a provision to the Directives to the effect that any law made in contravention of these Principles shall to the extent be void'.[38] He added that it would give jurisdiction to a court of law, though only a negative right to the people, to move a court that a law which went against the interests of the people should be declared void. On 4th November 1948, Dr. Ambedkar merely stated what the Directives were like and justified their inclusion in the constitution.

From the discussion in the Constituent Assembly, the following points emerge in respect of the Directive Principles of State Policy:

1. That the Directives are like Instruments of Instructions to the legislature and the executive and as such could be justified for inclusion in the constitution;
2. That the Directives cannot or will not be ignored by any responsible government or any legislature elected on the basis of universal suffrage for the sanction behind them is not the courts but the electorate;
3. That the Directives lay down the ideal of economic democracy.

Article 37 brings forth a three-fold characteristic of the Directives, namely;

a. That the Directives shall not be enforceable by any court;
b. That the Directives are fundamental in the governance of the country despite the fact that the judiciary cannot see to their effective compliance;

c. That it shall be the duty of the State to apply these principles in making laws.

As regards to the language used, it shows the binding nature of the duties of obligations of the State towards the constitution. Excepting for the language used in four Articles (Articles 43, 44, 45 and 51) the latter Part of Article 47 and the first part of Article 48, wherein the word 'endeavour' is used, it seems to be in the nature of Commands—institutional orders to the State asking it to perform certain specific functions, that is, social, economic, cultural, etc. The term, 'primary duties' indicates that the directives are a sort of duty is used in Article 47. The word 'strive', used in Article 38, was interpreted by Dr. Ambedkar to mean that it had binding character.[39] Judged in the context, therefore, the word 'endeavour' used in Articles 43, 44, 45, 51, and parts of Articles 47 and 48 would also mean that the State has got to put its best efforts in order to achieve the objectives mentioned therein.

It is important to take into consideration, how and for what purpose, the Directives came to be incorporated into the constitution, for assessing the nature and significance of the Directives.[40] It has already been noted that the Directives came to be incorporated in constitutions to ensure social and economic democracy in addition to political democracy. Directives partake the nature of the rights, but are different from the rights contained in the chapter on Fundamental Rights. Part IV confers on the people Positive Rights while Part III grants to the people Negative Rights, rights not to be harmed and it is easier for the law to prevent the infliction of harm than to enforce positive benefits. It is because of practical difficulty of enforcement of positive rights that Article 37 states that these rights 'shall not be enforceable by the courts'. It is undesirable for the court to order the state to do any particular work and the exchequer may not have enough money to implement them or pay damages for failure to do so. It is for this reason that Part IV has not set, save in one instance, namely, Article 45, a time limit for their fulfillment.

It is also worthy to recall that Part III and Part IV were originally designated as Fundamental Rights. The Fundamental Rights Sub-committee recommended 'the list of Fundamental Rights should be prepared in two parts, the first part consisting of Directive Principles of Social Policy.'[41] Sardar Vallabhbhai Patel also came to the conclusion that Fundamental Rights should be divided into two parts, the first part justiciable and the other non-justiciable.

To know the real nature and significance of these rights, all the above considerations have to be borne in mind. It is incorrect to consider them wholly as rights, duties, and obligations or even as principles though they partake the nature of each one of them. They are rights which the individual enjoys in his collective capacity by virtue of being a member of the Welfare State. Similarly, they are duties of the State to establish social order in which social, economic, and political justice would prevail. They are duties in the moral sense and the constitution enjoins that the State shall perform these duties in the absence of legal enforcement. Directives are not obligations merely though they partake its nature. It is not even mere principles as the heading shows, but unlike the principles, Directives are binding in character. Directives are in the nature of duties, which the constitution calls upon the State to perform to achieve a Welfare State. Directives aim at achieving social and economic democracy. They are directives from the constitution to the State, asking it to perform certain duties fundamental in character with the assurance that in the performance of these duties there shall be no compulsion by individuals acting through the judiciary.

Further, it could be said that some critics have given exaggerated importance to the statement that 'the principles enunciated in this part are not enforceable by a court of law' restricts the real nature and significance of the Directives in the Indian constitution. But, they seem to forget that there are such things like conventions in the constitutional matters and the same are not enforceable through courts and they are often of equal value and effect with legally enforceable principles. Today the generally accepted view is that a rule is a legal rule not because it is recognized by the courts of law, but because it prescribes a norm of conduct.

The significant expression contained in Article 38 "Justice, social, economic, and political" gives the proper key to the understanding of the nature and significance, on the base of which the entire structure of the Directives has been built. The Directives in the Indian constitution lend flexibility to the written constitution, by enabling it to adjust according to the circumstances. It was for this reason that the Prime Minister characterized the Directives as representing something "dynamic" as against Fundamental Rights which he said represented something "static". Directive Principles are the deliberate formulation of national policy. They were not formulated by any particular political party or any particular organ of the government, but by the representatives of a nation who assembled to lay down the constitution for the government of the country. They indicate to the people of the country as to what the State might do for them and what it seeks to achieve. Directive Principles also constitute a pledge by the framers of the constitution to the people of India and failure would bring not only breach of faith, but would also render a vital part of the constitution a dead letter. Truly speaking, the Directive Principles are more fundamental than Fundamental Rights from the point of view of the constitution since it contained the ideals, 'Justice, social, economic, and political'. It is for this reason that both in the Objectives Resolutions and in the Preamble to the constitution the ideal of "Justice, social, economic, and political" is mentioned prior to the securing of guarantees under Fundamental Rights.

Another important thing to be noted is with regard to the nature of Directives and that is their enunciation in a general and non-detailed way, unlike the other constitutions in which provisions of economic and social matters are laid in a detailed manner. It also lends flexibility to the constitution and enables different governments to achieve the ideas contained in the constitution with varying methods of approach without resorting to alterations and amendments in the constitution.

Analysis of the Articles

There were initially sixteen Articles of the constitution, from 36-51 that dealt with the Directive Principles. The 42nd Amendment added three more articles, namely, 39A, 43A, and 48A; modified clause (f) to Article 39; and a small usual change in Article 49. These cover a wide range of state activity embracing economic, social, legal, educational, administration, cultural, and international issues.

Article 37 confers non-enforceable rights on any person and imposes non-enforceable obligation on the State. The principal object in enacting the Directive Principle appears to have been to set standards of achievements before the legislature and the executive, the local and other authorities, by which their success or failure could be judged. The key to the Directive Principles is found in Article 37 which states, "The provisions contained in this part shall not be enforceable by any court, but the principles therein laid down are nevertheless fundamental in the governance of the country and it shall be the duty of the State to apply these principles in making laws".

Article 38 provides that the State shall endeavour to promote the welfare of the people by effectively securing and protecting a social order in which social, economic, and political justice shall inform all the institutions of national life. Article 39 particularises certain objectives, it provides that the State should direct its policy towards securing the right of the citizens, men and women, to an adequate means of livelihood, that the ownership and control of the material resources of the community be so distributed as best to subserve the common good, that the economic system should not result in the concentration of wealth and the means of production to the common detriment, that there should be equal pay for equal work for both men and women; that the State should endeavour to secure the health and strength of workers, men and women, and to ensure that the tender age of children is not abused and that citizens are not forced by economic necessity to enter avocations unsuited to their age and strength, and that childhood and youth are protected from exploitation and from moral and material abandonment. Through the 42nd Amendment made in 1976, free legal aid was provided to those denied by reason of economic or other disabilities. These and other directions are designed in Part IV to bring about a Welfare State.

Article 40 directs that the "State shall take steps to organize village *panchayats* and endow them with such powers and authority as may be necessary to enable them to function as units of self-government".

Article 41 directs the State within the limits of its economic capacity and development to make effective provision for securing the right to work, to education, and to public assistance in case of unemployment, old age, sickness, and disablement and in other cases of undeserved want. Article 42 directs the State to make provisions for just and humane condition of work and maternity relief. Article 43 provides that the State should endeavour to secure to all workers, by legislation, economic organization, or in any other way, a living, wage, conditions of work ensuring a decent standard of life, and the full enjoyment of leisure, and social and cultural opportunities. A new Article 43A, was inserted through 42nd Amendment to ensure through legislation .the participation of workers in management. Article 44 provided that the State should endeavour to secure a Uniform Civil Code for the citizens.

The Directive Principles lay considerable emphasis on education. Article 45 directs the State to make effective provisions for securing the rights to education. It directs that the State shall endeavour to provide within a period of ten years from the commencement of the constitution, free and compulsory education for all children less than fourteen years of age. The directive contained in Article 45 has not been fulfilled, though primary education has been made increasingly free and compulsory. Article 46 directs the State to promote special care, the educational interests of the weaker sections of the population, and in particular the Scheduled Castes and Scheduled Tribes, and shall protect them from social injustice and all forms of exploitation. According to Article 46, the State was at liberty to do anything to achieve that object so long as no other provision of the constitution was contravened; but Article 46 could not override Articles 15(1) and 29(2), nor could an exception be read into those Articles in favour of the backward classes. It has been held that Article 46 did not permit the State to discriminate in favour of Harijans so as to contravene the Fundamental Rights guaranteed by Article 15(1).

Article 47 directs the State to regard the raising of the level of nutrition and the standard of living of its people as among its primary duties. It deals not only with raising the standard of living of the people, but also directs that the improvement of public health should be a primary duty of the State and in particular, "the State shall endeavour to bring about prohibition of the consumption except for medical purposes, of intoxicating drinks and of drugs which are injurious to health."

Article 48 directs the State for the organization of agriculture and animal husbandry. According to Article 49 it should be the obligation of the State to protect every monument, place and objects of national importance.

A new Article, 49A, was inserted during the 42nd Amendment. Under this Article, the State would endeavour to protect and improve the environment and safeguard the forests and wildlife of the country.

According to Article 50, the State shall take steps to separate the judiciary from the executive. Many of the States have implemented this directive either wholly or in part. Article 51 directs that the State shall endeavour to promote international peace and security, maintain just and respectful relations between nations, foster respects of International law and treaty obligations, in the dealings of organized peoples with one another, and encourage the settlement of international disputes through arbitration.

Attitude of Executive, Legislature and Judiciary towards Fundamental Rights and the Directive Principles of State Policy

It emerges from the foregoing discussion that the Fundamental Rights are in the nature of general duties which the State is obliged to perform for the benefit of the individual and that the Directive Principles of State Policy are in the nature of specific duties which the State undertakes to do for the good of the society as a whole. A conflict between the two sets of rights, either directly or indirectly, seems to be apparent. A conflict, even if it arises, becomes magnified indeed with the constitution of an independent judiciary charged with the function of safeguarding the Fundamental Rights of the Individual as against the duty of the legislative and executive organs of the government of looking after the welfare of the society as a whole. The judiciary might try to avoid a conflict by refusing to take cognizance of the Directives on the ground that they are non-enforceable in character but it would be drawn into it, for the simple reason that the Directives form a part of the constitution. A situation may arise when the State in due discharge of its duty, under the Directive Principles, may make law prejudicial to Fundamental Rights, or an aggrieved individual in support of his rights cites the Directive Principles. In either case, there is room for conflict between the Fundamental Rights and Directive Principles of State Policy or, in other words, between the executive and legislature on the one hand and the judiciary on the other. If such a situation arises that court is bound to give preference to the former for they are enforceable in character. The State, on the other hand, bound by its 'duty' would give preference to the Directives.

It should be pointed out that there is no inherent conflict between the rights contained in Parts II and IV and the attitude of the courts towards the directives would not have been so hostile if the real meaning of the words 'shall not be enforceable' used in Article 37 had been comprehended. When Sir B.N. Rau suggested the inclusion of these directives, he did not anticipate any conflict between the provisions of the two chapters, but with the elevation of the status of the 'directives' as 'fundamental in the governance of the country' and the substitution of the word 'duty' for the word 'care' left the possibility of a conflict between Fundamental Rights and Directive Principles. He, therefore, suggested that in case of conflict the 'directives' should prevail. The words 'shall not be enforceable' used in the chapter on Directives were not really meant to offend the judiciary or to restrict its ambit as the guarantor of the Fundamental Rights of the individuals. It is not correct to say that the judiciary being charged with the function of safeguarding the rights of individual would be oblivious to the rights of the society as a whole.

The occasion for a conflict between the 'Directive Principles' and the 'Fundamental Rights' however came before the judiciary for the first time in the case, *State of Madras vs. Champakam Dorairajan* in 1951.[42] The petitioner, a Brahmin lady, contended that the Madras Communal Government Order violated her Fundamental Rights under Article 15(1) which prohibits discrimination on grounds only of religion, race, caste, sex, and place of birth and Article 29(2) which protects the citizens from denial of admission into any educational institution. As against this, the State of Madras contended that such a discriminatory treatment was justified under Article 46 of Part IV which imposes a duty on the State to promote the educational and economic interests of the weaker sections of the population, and in particular, of the Scheduled Castes and Scheduled Tribes. In this regard, Chief Justice Rajamannar gave his view and Justice Viswanath Sastri supported his views by saying that Article 37 expressly states that the provision of Part IV shall not be enforceable by any court. The rights conferred by Articles 15(1) and 29(2) are made justiciable by Articles 32 and 226 of the constitution.

Justice Somasundaram, however, dissented from the other two judges and drew the attention of the latter part of Article 37 which emphasized the 'fundamental character' of the 'Directives'. He observed:[43]

> "Article 46 of the constitution is a very relevant and important Article to be considered in this connection. This is placed in the chapter relating to Directive Principles of State Policy. Article 37 states that though the provisions in that part are not enforceable in court, nevertheless the principles therein are fundamental in the governance of the country. Article 46 may not override Articles 15(1) and 29(2) in Part III. Articles 15(1) and 29(2) must be read with Article 46 of the constitution. In distributing the seats, State can take into account the fundamental principles embodied in the Article which it cannot ignore."

The Supreme Court rejected the above contention and held:[44]

> "The chapter of Fundamental Rights is sacrosanct and not liable to be abridged by any legislative or executive Act or order, except to the extent provided in the appropriate Article in Part III. The Directive Principles of State Policy have to conform to and run subsidiary to the chapter of Fundamental Rights".

In *Om Parkash vs. State of Punjab*[45], 1961, the Punjab High Court rejected the contention that the provision of Part IV could not be enforced by any court, Article 46 could not override Article 29(2); and the High Court of Bombay in *Jagwnat Kaur vs. State of Bombay*,[46] 1952, following the Supreme Court's decision in the Champakam Dorairjan's case, 1951, subordinated the Directives to Fundamental Rights. The following points, therefore, emerge from the above decision:

1. The Directive Principles of State Policy cannot override the provisions in Part III as the latter are made enforceable by appropriate writs or orders or directions under Article 32, whereas the former are expressly made unenforceable by any court.
2. The chapter on Fundamental Rights is sacrosanct and not liable to be abridged by any legislature or executive Act or order, except to the extent provided in the appropriate Articles in Part III.
3. The Directive Principles of State Policy have to conform to and run subsidiary to the chapter on Fundamental Rights.
4. The State action under Directive Principles is subject to the legislative and executive powers.
5. The State action under Directive Principles is also subject to the limitations conferred on the State under different provisions of the constitution, an inference of which there is no basis.

In other words, the attitude of the judiciary towards the Directives was not only to make it subordinate, but also not to give effect to it if it came in conflict for the mere reason that the Directives are 'not enforceable' in a court of law. Thus, the Full Bench of the Bombay High Court in *Fram Nusserwanji Balsara vs. State of Bombay 1950*,[47] wherein the legislative competence of the Bombay Legislature to enact the Bombay Prohibition Act in view of Article 47 was questioned held that Article 47 could not confer legislative competence where it was otherwise lacking. In *Ajaib Singh vs. State of Punjab*,[48] 1952, when Article 51 was cited in support of the petitioner's contention, Justice Bhandari of the Punjab High Court held that "Article 51 cannot empower the Parliament to make a law which can deprive a citizen of India of the Fundamental Rights conferred upon him".

In *Biswambhar vs. State of Orissa*,[49] 1953, when Article 51 of Directives was cited, Narasimhan, CJ., observed that Article 51 being in the chapter dealing with Directive Principles is not enforceable in this court in view of the express bar of Article 37."

The verdict of the Supreme Court in the *Champakam Dorairjan's* case resulted in the amendments of Article 15 of the constitution. Thus, although the Supreme Court had given its verdict, subordinating the Directive Principles to Fundamental Rights on the interpretation of the clause 'not enforceable in the courts of law' Parliament by amending the constitutional provision relating to Fundamental Rights impressed upon the judiciary that in the view of the State the Principles enunciated in Part IV, were more sacrosanct than the rights contained in Part III and in case of conflict between the two Parts, the latter has to yield to the former. After the amendment, however, the Courts could not reconcile with the discrimination in educational matters under Article 46. Article 31 was thrice amended (First, Fourth, and Seventeenth, to give effect to agrarian and economic reforms envisaged under the Directives in Article 39, and more especially in 39A).

It is worthy to note, however, that after the first and fourth amendment there was increasing recognition of the fact that although the Directives were non-justiciable in character, the courts were to recognize their importance for the reason that the Directives formed a vital part of the constitutional document. The Directives were no longer to be set aside or ignored when it came into conflict with Fundamental Rights. In *M.H. Quareshi vs. State of Bihar,*[50] 1958, the Supreme Court maintained that although the Directives should conform to and run subsidiary to the chapter on Fundamental Rights, it would not reject the Directive Principles, but would give it a harmonious interpretation provided that the Executive and the Legislature do not take away or abridge the Fundamental Rights while implementing the Directive Principles.

While in the cases discussed in the preceding paragraphs, the outlook of the judiciary in regard to Fundamental Rights vis a-vis the Directives came up in the first instance before the High Court, the Supreme Court was directly confronted with the question four times till this day. For the first time, the question came up on the case *Shankri Prasad vs. Union of India and the State of Bihar 1951.*[51] In this case, the validity of the constitution (First Amendment) Act, 1951, which inserted, *inter alia,* Articles 31A and B in the constitution came to be questioned. This amendment was made under Article 368 of the constitution by the Provisional Parliament. The Supreme Court held in that case (Patanjali Sastri, J., speaking for himself and Hiralal, C.J., Mukerjee, Das, and Chandrasekhra Ayyar, J.J.) that Parliament had power to amend Part III of the constitution. The Court came to that conclusion on two grounds, namely: (1) the word 'law' in Article 13(2) was one made in exercise of legislative power; and (2) there were two Articles, i.e., 13(2) and 368, each of which was widely phrased, and, therefore, harmonious construction required that one should be so read as to be controlled and qualified by the other, and having regard to the circumstances mentioned in the judgment. Article 13 must be read, subject to Article 368.

The question came up for the second time in *Sajjan Singh vs. State of Rajashtan,*[52] 1964 in the context of the validity of the constitution (Seventeenth Amendment) Act. The Supreme Court by a majority of 3:2 (Gajendragadkar, CJ., Wanchoo, and Raghubar Dayal, J.J.) for the majority and Hidayatullah and Mudholkar, J.J. for the minority upheld:

1. The correctness of the decision on Sankari Parsad's case although the correctness of the decision in that case was not questioned;
2. That the Seventeenth Amendment did not require ratification under the provision to Article 368 because of its indirect effect upon Article 226, etc.; and
3. That the power conferred by Article 368 included the power to take away Fundamental Rights guaranteed under Part Ill; that the power to amend was very wide and could not be controlled by the literal dictionary meaning of the word 'amend' and the word 'law' in Article 13(2) did not include amendment of the constitution made in pursuance of Article 368. Therefore, they doubted the competence of Parliament to make any amendment to Part III of the constitution.

The question came up for the third time in the case of *Golak Nath and others vs. the State of Punjab*[53] in connection again with the constitutional validity of the constitution's Seventeenth Amendment. Opportunity, therefore, was availed of to constitute a Special Bench of eleven judges of the Supreme Court to consider the correctness of the decision of the Supreme Court in the Sankari Parsad's case, which was accepted as correct by the majority in Sajjan Singh's case.

The Supreme Court, in its judgement in the Golak Nath's case, delivered on 27th February 1968, by a majority of 6:5 held *inter alia*: (1) that Parliament has no power to amend any of the provisions of Part III of the constitution so as to take away or abridge the Fundamental Rights enshrined; (2) that amendment is 'law' within the meaning of Article 13(2). Actually, there were two judgements on behalf of the majority and three on behalf of the minority. Subba Rao, C.J. on behalf of himself, Shah, Sikri, Shelat, and Vidialingam, J.J. held:(1) that the power of the Parliament to amend the constitution is derived from Articles 245, 246, and 248 of the constitution and not from Article 368 thereof which only deals with procedure. Amendment is a legislative procedure; (2) that amendment is law within the meaning of Article 13 of the constitution and therefore, it is void; and (3) that the parliament will have no power from the date of their decision to amend any of the provisions of Part III of the constitution as to take away or abridge the Fundamental Rights enshrined therein.

The judgement in the *Golak Nath's* case resulted in a serious situation, apart from the fact that the interpretation of the Supreme Court was erroneous. To get over this difficulty and to show what exactly the spirit of the constitution was, the Twenty-fourth and Twenty-fifth amendments to the constitution were affected. The Twenty-fourth amendment to the constitution is the result of the Supreme Court's judgement in *Golak Nath's* case. In it, the Supreme Court reversed its previous judgement by a narrow majority, its own earlier decisions upholding the power of Parliament to amend all parts of constitution including Part III relating to Fundamental Rights. The constitution's Twenty-fourth Amendment[54] had made five changes in the basic document:

1. A new clause is added to Article 13 to the effect that Article 13 would not be a bar to amendment of Part III of the constitution under Article 368.
2. A new clause is added to Article 368 emphasizing the fact that Article 13 would not debar the amendment of the constitution, including Part III, sought to be made under Article 368.
3. An alteration in the marginal heading to Article 368 provides not only the procedure for amendment of the constitution, but also empowers Parliament to amend the constitution.
4. A clause is added to Article 368 specifying clearly, that under the constitution, Parliament could, in the exercise of its constituent power amend by way of addition, variation or repeal any provision of the constitution in accordance with the procedure laid down under Article 368.

5. A clarificatory provision is made in the existing provision to Article 368 to the effect that it would be obligatory on the part of the President to give assent to a constitution Amendment Bill when it is presented to him after it had been passed by the two Houses of Parliament and in cases where ratification by the requisite number of State Legislatures is required, after that had been obtained.

The Twenty-fifth amendment in effect wrote into the constitution that in case of conflict between the Fundamental Rights and Directive Principles of State Policy, the latter shall prevail. The Twenty-fifth amendment shut out the jurisdiction of the court by holding that once a legislation was declared to be in pursuance of the implementation of the Directive Principles of State Policy even if it conflicted with any Article relating to Fundamental Rights, the courts could not entertain the case. Under the Twenty-fifth amendment, it was possible even for the State Legislature to override Fundamental Rights if it sought to implement the Directive Principles of State Policy. However, a distinction was made between the power vested on the Parliament and the power vested on the State Legislatures in the matters of giving primacy to Directive Principles of State Policy. Whereas, in the case of Parliament a mere declaration by it that a contemplated legislation was for the purpose of implementing Directive Principles of State Policy was sufficient to shut out the court's jurisdiction, in the case of the State Legislatures, it was necessary of the State Legislatures that a declaration so made shall be approved and assented to by the President of India.[55]

The *Golak Nath* judgement and the 24th and 25th constitution Bills which sought to nullify its effect came up before the Supreme Court's scrutiny in the *Kesavananda Bharati's* case is 1973. The Special Bench held by a majority of 7 : 6 on 24th April 1973, that the constitution empowered Parliament the right to alter, abridge or abrogate the Fundamental Rights guaranteed by the constitution. The Court held that the part of the constitution (Twenty-fifth) Amendment Act, 1971, establishing the primacy of the Directive Principles of State Policy of the Fundamental Rights in respect of certain articles was valid although the second part of the Act which said that 'now law containing a declaration that it is for giving effect to such policy shall be called in question in any court on the ground that it does not give effect to such policy' was held to be unconstitutional and void. In other words, 'the Supreme Court for the first time accepted the primacy of the Directive Principles over Fundamental Rights', rejecting, however, the denial of the Court's jurisdiction to pronounce its verdict on the validity of law passed in pursuance of the Directive Principles of State Policy.

While partial primacy of Directive Principles over Fundamental Rights came about as a result of the Fundamental Rights cases, its total primacy came about in an entirely different manner and under altogether different circumstances. It was made a part of a package of comprehensive constitutional changes brought about through the constitution (42nd) Amendment and during the period of emergency. The clamour for constitutional changes came in the wake of Allahabad High Court's judgement, setting aside the election of Prime Minister Indira Gandhi to the Lok Sabha in 1971, and, consequently, Parliament enacting the constitution (Thirty-ninth) amendment empowering it to set up a new forum for resolving disputes relating to the election of the President, Vice-President, the Prime Minister, and the Speaker. During the consideration of the Thirty-ninth Amendment Bill, the Law Minister Gokhale observed that the time had come to have a fresh look at the whole fundamental structure of the constitution so that it could be altered to meet the changed circumstances. A constitution Bench of the Supreme Court, however, unanimously upheld on 7th November 1975, the election of Indira Gandhi to the Lok Sabha, setting aside the High Court judgment of 12th June.

Meanwhile, in a submission made by the Central Government that the 1973 judgement of the Supreme Court in the *Kesavananda Bharati's* case, holding that the basic structure of the constitution could not be altered or reviewed, a full Bench of the Supreme Court was convened on 10th November 1975. The plea taken for the review was to decide a large number of cases involving nationalization of coal mines, textile units, and sugar factories as well as court jurisdiction in disputes involving administrative personnel. On 12th November, however, Chief Justice A.N. Ray announced that the review bench had been dissolved.

Three new Directives were added to the existing Directive Principles through the constitution (42nd) Amendment. Those were:

1. *Article 39A—Equal Justice and Free Legal Aid:* The State shall secure that the operation of the legal system promotes justice, on the basis of equal opportunity, and shall, in particular, provide free legal aid, by suitable legislation or schemes or in any other way to ensure that opportunities for securing justice are not denied to any citizen by reason of economic or other disabilities.
2. *Article 43A—Participation of Workers in Management to Industries:* The State shall take steps, by suitable legislation or in any other way, to secure the participation of workers in the management of undertakings, establishments or other organizations engaged in any industry.
3. *Article 49A—Protection and Improvement of Environment and Safeguarding of Forests and Wildlife:* The State shall endeavour to protect and to improve the environment and safeguard the forests and wildlife in the country.

Article 39A reflects the increasing recognition of the fact that legal aid is now regarded as an essential part of the administration of justice. In England, the first Legal Aid Act was passed on 30th July 1949.

Article 48A reflects an increasing awareness of people all over the world of the need to preserve the environment from pollution, especially in the urban areas. Smoke, industrial waste, deleterious exhaust fumes from motor cars, and other combustion engines are injurious to the health and well-being of the people and foul atmosphere. The preservation of forests and their renewal by afforestation has long been recognized in India as of great importance both with reference to rainfall and to prevent erosion of the soil by depriving it of forests which protect it. The preservation of wild-life is looked upon as necessary for the 'preservation of ecological balance.'

The Janata Party which came to power in 1977 sought to confine, through Clause 8 of the constitution (44th) Amendment Bill, 1978, the protection afforded to Article 31 C only to laws giving effect to the policy of States towards securing the Directive Principles specified in Clauses (b) and (c) of Article 39. This would have had the effect of restoring that Article to the form to which it stood before the amendment made to the Article by the 42nd Amendment Act. But, this part of the Bill which was adopted by the Lok Sabha on 23rd August 1978, was rejected by the Rajya Sabha. So much so that in the 44th Amendment Act as finally adopted by the Parliament on 7th December 1978, this provision remained unaffected.

The judiciary still clings to the basic feature argument and despite the 42nd amendment, has held in Minerva Mills and Vaman Rao's cases that the primacy of Directive Principles over Fundamental Rights in its entirety cannot be sustained.

The government's attitude was also the verdict of the Supreme Court in Minerva Mills and Vaman Rao's cases in the matter of primacy of the Directive Principles over Fundamental Rights needs a comment. A careful reading of the statement of objects and reasons of the 44th Amendment Bill would reveal that their difficulty in accepting the primacy of the Directive Principles over Fundamental Rights was that it was affected through an amendment during "emergency" and not during the normal circumstances. The revival of basic structures are meant on the part of the judiciary in the aforesaid cases was for the same reason. The taste of the emergency, it should be remembered, was too bitter to be forgotten for both the judiciary and the government. In short, their non-acceptance of the primacy of Directive Principles is due to political reasons rather than to legal and constitutional.

Notes and References

1. This is one aspect of 'positive' freedom as described by 1. Berlin, *Two Concepts of Liberty*, Oxford: Claredon Press, 1958, p. 16, when he writes, "The positive" sense of the word "Liberty" derives from the wish on the part of the individual to be his own master. I wish life and decisions to depend on myself not on external forces of whatever kind".
2. Article 37, *constitution of India*.
3. Article 39, Clause (b) provides that state shall in particular, direct its policies towards securing that "the ownership and control of the material resource of the community are so distributed as best to subserve the common good."

4. Article 39, Clause (c) provides "that the operation of economic system does not result in the concentration of wealth and means of production to the common detriment".
5. K.C. Markandan, *Directive Principles in Indian constitution,* Allied Publishers, Bombay, 1966, p. 148.
6. Article 47, *Constitution of India*
7. Article 44, *Constitution of India*
8. *Constituent Assembly Debates,* Vol. III, Annexure to the Appendix of the Discussions, dated the 29th April 1947, p. 440.
9. "Does Article 13 debar amendment of the constitution, Part III?" K.C. Markandan, *Journal of constitutional and Parliamentary Studies,* October 1970.
10. Article 38, *constitution of India.*
11. K.C. Markandan, *op. cit.*, p. 148.
12. B.N. Rau, *India's constitution in the Making,* p. 333.
13. Sir B.N. Rau's remarks on Part III of the Draft of 7th October 1947, and the proposed amendments in "A Letter to the President of the Constituent Assembly," dated 11th November 1947, see Appendix III also.
14. The constitution of the Principality of Liechtenstein, which was passed by the Diet of the Principality on 24th August 1921, approved by the reigning Prince, Johann II. On 2th October 1921, and finally signed on behalf of the Prince on 5th October 1921.
15. Declaration embodying a programme of social, economic or cultural reform also found a place in the constitution of the Irish Free State (Saorstát Éireann) Act of 1922. Articles 10 and 11 related to free elementary education and the nationalisation of the natural resources of the country.
16. Writing about the declaration of Fundamental Rights and incorporation of Directive Principles of Social Policy in the Irish constitution, Donald O'Sullivan observed: "Large sections of the new constitution consist of declarations of homiletic character concerning personal rights, and the family, education, private property, religion, directive principles of social policy. Many of these are so vague that they could not possibly be impleaded in the courts and it is difficult to see what purpose they serve in such a document."
17. K.C. Wheare, "India's New constitution Analyzed," *Allahabad Law Journal,* 21, 1950.
18. B.N. Rau, *India's constitution in the Making,* Edited by B. Shiva Rao, pp. 248–250.
19. constitutional Proposals of the Sapru Committee, p. 257.
20. Minutes of the Fundamental Rights Sub-committee meeting of 30th March 1947, *President's Collection.*
21. Minutes of the Fundamental Rights Sub-committee meeting of 31st March 1947, *President's Collection.*
22. Clauses 9, 10 and 12 of the Supplementary Report.
23. Clause 33: The Principles of policy set forth in this part are intended for the guidance of the state. While these principles shall not be cognizable by any court. They are nevertheless fundamental in the governance of the country and their application in the making of laws shall be the duty of the State.
24. *Constituent Assembly Debates,* Vol. V, pp. 406–407.
25. *Constituent Assembly Debates,* Vol. VII, p. 535.
26. Article 43 of the constitution. The amendment that Dr. Ambedkar accepted was moved by I.A.R. Chettiyar, *Constituent Assembly Debates,* Vol. VII, p. 532.
27. *Constituent Assembly Debates,* Vol. VII, No. 9, pp. 494–495.
28. U.P., General.
29. Punjab, General.
30. Mysore, General.
31. U.P., General.
32. *CAD,* Vol. VII, No. 13, dated 25th November, 1948, p. 596.

33. *CAD*, Vol. III, No. 2, dated the 20th April, 1947, p. 384.
34. *CAD*, Vol. III, No. 2, dated the 29th April, 1947, p. 383.
35. *CAD*, Vol. VII, No. 5, dated the 9th November, 1948, p. 357.
36. *CAD*, Vol. VII, No. 5, dated the 9th November 1948, p. 370.
37. Professor K.T. Shah expressed this view, *CAD*, Vol. VII. No. 9, 19th November, 1948, p. 479.
38. *CAD*, Vol. III, No. 2, dated 5th November, 1948, p. 230
39. *CAD*, Vol. VII, No. 9, dated November 1948, p. 495.
40. *Parliamentary Debates* (Lok Sabha) Part II, 18th May 1951, Cols, 9013–9014.
41. Letter from Sardar Patel to the President of the Constituent Assembly, dated 23rd April 1947 (*CAD*, Vol. III, No. 2 Appendix, p. 422).
42. *AIR*, 1951: Madras, 120; and *AIR*, 1951: S.C. 226.
43. *AIR*, 1952: Bombay, 461.
44. *AIR*, 1951: S.C. 226.
45. *AIR*, 1951: Punjab, 93.
46. *AIR*, 1952: Bombay, 461.
47. *AIR*, 1951: Bombay, 210–217.
48. *AIR*, 1952: Punjab, 309.
49. *AIR*, 1957: Orissa, 247.
50. *AIR*, 1958: S.C. 731.
51. The case came up on 5th October 1951, 1952 S.CR. 89.
52. 1965 *I.C.S.R. 933.*
53. (1967) 2 S.C.J., 486.
54. See Appendix (i) in K.C. Markandan, *Aspects of Indian Polity,* Vol. II Jalandhar: ABS Publications, 1990).
55. Article 31C as amended by the 25th constitution Amendment Act. See Appendix in K.C. Markandan, *Ibid.*

7

The Parliament

Mahendra Prasad Singh and Roopinder Oberoi

❑ Introduction

Looking back to the historical roots of Indian Parliament, we do not find feudal antecedents like the Lords and Commons in the United Kingdom and the Estates in France. Ancient *Sabhas, Samitis,* and *Vidhatas* in the North and the self-governing local institutions in South India in the pre-modern times may be regarded as hoary antecedents, but they were presumably instruments of direct democracy rather than those of representative democracy.[1] Moreover, *Panchayats* is also supposed to have existed in the past before their statutory revival after independence in rural communities, but they are essentially instruments of local self-government.[2] In addition, the Sultans of Delhi were supposed to be elected by the Turkish and Afghan nobles, and liberal and orthodox factions in the Mughal court in alliance with the monarch influenced the state policy as well as successions.[3] But they lacked the crystallization and institutionalization of medieval European political institutions.

Hence, the historical antecedents of the Parliament must be found in the Government of India Acts of 1909 and 1935, and their feebler predecessors in the post-1857/58 period during the British Raj.[4] But, these British Indian experiments suffered from two basic limitations. First, these bodies were elected (earlier mostly nominated) on an extremely limited franchise based on property and education. Second, they lacked legislative autonomy from the executive power of the Governor-General and Governors. The Nehru Report (1928) and Sapru Report (1945) produced by leaders of the nationalist movement abortively advocated parliamentary federalism with certain degree of proportional representation. The Constituent Assembly retained this basic framework sans proportional representation in the 1950 constitution. The historical importance of the first Parliament elected in 1952 is that its popular chamber, the Lok Sabha, was the first legislative body in India elected on universal adult franchise and endowed with complete legislative autonomy unencumbered by any undue executive prerogatives to interfere with the legislative process; second, the Parliament is the first full-fledged national institution representing the free will of the entire Indian nation historically bedeviled by a recurrent pattern of political divisiveness and fragmentation. Third, it is the first institutional mechanism created as a built-in device for political and socio-economic change in a country whose only experience of change was through rebellion, wars, and dynastic revolutions. The principle of government based on popular and parliamentary sovereignty purports to provide an instrument of change through electoral and institutional politics among groups and classes. In the contexts of articulation of political demands for new bases of legitimacy, participation, integration, and distribution during the nationalist movement and the post-independence period the Parliament has become the formal focal point of allegiance and resolution of conflicts in the political system.

For reasons of their different patterns of institutional evolution and constitutional system, Britain and the United States feature the contrasting constitutional doctrines of parliamentary supremacy and judicial supremacy, respectively. The American constitutional doctrine of separation of powers among three more or less coequal organs of government—executive, legislature, and judiciary—does not create a supreme legislature; it circumscribes the powers of the legislature through a system of checks and balances among the three governmental organs. The principle of parliamentary supremacy as it has evolved in Britain has at least the following four corollaries: There is no legislative authority higher than the Parliament, there is no limitation on the scope of the legislative competence, no Parliament can bind its successor, and no court can declare enactments of Parliament invalid.[5]

Parliamentary sovereignty in India is modified by a number of circumstances and factors specific to India. First, the combination of a parliamentary system with a federal system in the Indian constitution entails the resultant division of powers between the Union Parliament and state legislatures. The simplistic legal view of the constitution earlier tended to argue that state legislatures are basically non-sovereign, but the more comprehensive constitutional and behavioural view holds that, except during periods of constitutional emergencies, state legislatures' competence is protected by a written constitution interpreted by an independent judiciary. Besides, the balance of political forces in the political system also puts practical constraints on the purely legal view of the constitution and opens up the possibility of new constitutional conventions. Second, the constitution incorporates the guarantees of Fundamental Rights of citizens and Directive Principles of State Policy that amount to constitutional limitations on the powers of the Parliament. Although the Directives, unlike the Fundamental Rights, are not legally enforceable by courts in the normal way, the courts have indeed invoked them in interpreting the constitution, and thus clothed the Directives with selective legal sanction in an indirect way.

Third, as a corollary of the first and the second points, the principle of judicial review of the acts of the Parliament/State Legislatures and Executive(s) is an integral part of the Indian constitutional system. It is this perspective that explains not only the great concern with the independence of the judiciary in the constitution, but also the expanding scope of judicial review in the recent decades. Fourth, there are some temporary and special constitutional provisions (*e.g.*, Articles 370-6, 371-A-l and G relating to the states of Jammu and Kashmir, Nagaland, and Mizoram) arising out of peculiar problems of regional autonomy and national integration. They are limitations on unilateral powers of the Parliament.

From the foregoing it is evident that the Indian constitutional system is a mixed one: while the parliamentary part of the government directs attention to the supremacy of the Parliament in the system, the federal part, coupled with constitutionally entrenched Fundamental Rights and Directive Principles of State Policy and traditions of regionalism in the country, compromise parliamentary supremacy by complementing it with constitutional supremacy featuring judicial review.

❑ LEGISLATIVE-EXECUTIVE RELATIONSHIP

Consistent with the principle of parliamentary government, the Indian Parliament, like its British counterpart, presents the picture of fusion rather than separation of legislative and executive powers. The President being, by and large, the figurehead and the Parliament normally being under the thumb of the majority party led by the Prime Minister, the principle of parliamentary sovereignty has really come to mean the executive or cabinet domination of the Parliament. The growth of disciplined party system in parliamentary systems may be regarded as a functional response to the structural necessity of maintaining a stable parliamentary government. For a parliamentary government, unlike a presidential executive of the American type, springs from the Parliament itself, instead of being elected directly by the people and is perpetually dependent on the confidence of the parliamentary majority.

In addition, the Parliament has also yielded ground to the executive in the field of law-making. Most bills are drafted by civil servants and piloted in the Parliament by ministers. Private members' bills form a negligible proportion of legislation.[6] Besides, the government often presents legislative *fait accompli* to the Parliament in the form of presidential ordinances, although one must hasten to add that these are constitutionally expected to be used sparingly and only in pressing circumstances. The constitution also expects them to be replaced by legislation at the earliest convenience.[7]

The committee system in parliamentary system is, generally, less vigorous than in presidential systems. For parliamentary committees are overshadowed by the cabinet, which, in a sense, is itself the most important committee of the Parliament. *In contrary,* presidential systems feature a stronger committee system as the presidential cabinet is external to the legislature. The committee system in the Indian Parliament is no exception to this rule. Moreover, it has introduced a new committee system in the early 1990s designed to enhance the quantum and quality of committee work in the legislative process and parliamentary scrutiny and control of the executive. (This new committee system is discussed in a subsequent section of this chapter).

Besides these developments, practical difficulties and executive greed tend to shorten the duration of parliamentary sessions[8] to say nothing of parliamentary procedures that put limit on the length of parliamentary debates.[9] These trends in India (and elsewhere) have given rise to the thesis of the decline of the Parliament as a sovereign decision-making body.[10] However, this decline of the Parliament's law-making function does not signal the utter irrelevance and impending atrophy of the legislative branch of the government. Parliament still performs the important function of representing the mass public in the governmental process and of legitimising the formation, maintenance, and actions of government. Moreover, in the event of the party system failing to throw up a majority party government, the powers of the Parliament (and the President) may come into a less constrained play, as happened with the minority governments of Indira Gandhi (1966-71), Chaudhary Charan Singh (1979-80), and those in the aftermath of the 1989 parliamentary elections. During these minority/coalition governments, the powers of the Parliament have tended to increase.

Parliament and Judiciary

The fusion of legislative and executive powers typical of the parliamentary systems does not extend to the judiciary. For the concern with judicial independence is as old as the conflict between the absolute monarchy in Britain and the Parliament in the 17th century. However, it would be wrong to say for this reason that the parliamentary system is based on a limited principle of separation of powers between the Parliament and the cabinet, on the one hand, and the judiciary, on the other. Indeed, in their original intent, both the parliamentary and presidential systems seem to be more concerned with the idea of designing a judiciary which is sufficiently independent of the legislative and executive branches of the government (even though the judges are actually appointed by the executive) than with creating a judiciary with full-scale and overriding powers of judicial review, which is actually a feature of the federal system, whether in combination with presidential or parliamentary system. This is evident from the fact that even in the American presidential-federal system the Supreme Court did not actually derive the power of judicial review from an express provision of the constitution. It invented this power subsequently and circumstantially from a written constitution and the federal context that made it an umpire for purposes of interpreting an evenly matched written constitution. Article 13 of the Indian constitution expressly provides for judicial review inasmuch as it declares all extant and future laws inconsistent with or in derogation of the Fundamental Rights in Part III of the constitution null and void.[11] Moreover, the court naturally becomes the arbitrator in cases of dispute between the federal and state governments over their respective legislative competence and over the residuary powers which, under the constitution, belong to the union Parliament (Part XI of the constitution and the 7th Schedule).

However, the power of judicial review in India is *prima facie* somewhat limited than in the United States. For under the 'due process' clause of the American constitution (5th and 14th amendments) the court has assumed enormous power of judicial review of any law depriving a person of his liberty save by the due process of law determinable by the court itself. In contrast, the Indian constitution has opted for the 'procedure established by law' in place of the due process of law: 'No person shall be deprived of his life or personal liberty, except according to procedure established by law' (Article 21). The Indian Supreme Court earlier held the view that left the matter entirely in the hand of the legislature so far as the establishment of the legal procedure was concerned (*Gopalan Vs. State of Madras*, 1950). The current view of the court is, however, different. Since the *Maneka Gandhi Vs. Union of India* case (1978), the court has come to hold the view that almost verges on due process inasmuch as it expects that fundamental freedoms under Article 19 and life and personal liberty under Article 21 must not be subjected to a legal restriction and a procedure that is arbitrary, unfair or unreasonable.

The Indian political system has witnessed phases of headlong collisions between the executive swearing by the principle of parliamentary sovereignty and the judiciary seeking to assert its independence and power of judicial review. Lloyd I. Rudolph and Susanne H. Rudolph (1987, ch. 3) metaphorically term it "The Struggle over Stateness; Judicial Review versus Parliamentary Sovereignty." Under Nehru and early years of Indira Gandhi, the conflict centred on a government seeking to promote land reforms, to bring about abolition of Privy Purses of former princely rulers, nationalization of banks, etc., and a Supreme Court purporting to protect Fundamental Rights. There followed an extremely suspenseful drama of a series of parliamentary legislations, adverse judicial reviews, and constitutional amendments by the Parliament to get around the judicial reviews putting limitations on the power of the Parliament. In constitutional terms, the conflict shaped up as one between the executive pleading for the primacy of the welfare goals of Directive Principles of State Policy and the Supreme Court clinging to the jurisprudence of the original intentions of the founding fathers of the republic and express provisions of the constitution in relation to the Rights and the Directives. The judges argued, among other things, that all parts of the constitution were designed in perfect harmony with the chapter on Fundamental Rights, and that all legislations and constitutional amendments contravening them must be constitutionally invalid. In the 1970s (pre-Janata phase) during the hegemonic premiership of Indira Gandhi the confrontation between the executive and the judiciary took the unsavoury form of a self-serving Prime Minister hell bent on perpetuating herself in power by virtually dismantling the framework of the liberal-democratic state through constitutional amendments and repressive administrative measures. Under extreme pressure, the Supreme Court conceded to the executive on some points, but it did continue to somehow hedge in its power of judicial review.

The major landmarks in this story of confrontation are the *Golaknath* case (1967), the 24th constitutional amendment (1971), the *Keshavananda Bharati* case (1973), the 42nd constitutional amendment (1976) during the Emergency, the *Maneka Gandhi* case (1978), and the *Minerva Mills* case (1980).[12] During the period of Nehruvian consensus (1952-64), which was structurally buttressed by the predominance of an internally democratic and pluralist Congress party at national as well as state levels, the Supreme Court had pursued 'harmonious construction' of the constitution's Directive Principles (Part IV) and Fundamental Rights (Part III). Hence, confrontation between the Parliament and the judiciary was avoided. From 1967-77, a series of changes in the political system brought about recurrent conflicts between the two. The wave of political turmoil witnessed during this decade included the first major breach in Congress predominance at state level and reduced majority at the national level in 1967, the split in the Congress party in 1969, the restorat ion of Congress predominance under Indira Gandhi within a highly centralized and internally undemocratic party organization in 1971-72 onwards, the anti-corruption movements in Gujarat, Bihar, and subsequently almost whole of North India in the first half of the 1970s, and the internal Emergency (1975-77). It was in this political backdrop of growing authoritarianism on the part of the executive that the Supreme Court asserted in *Golak nath* that the Parliament's amending power under Article 368 did not extend to the chapter on Fundamental Rights, which was amendable only by a new Constituent Assembly. The Parliament overrode the *Golak Nath* case through 24th amendment by making Fundamental Rights amendable by it. The Supreme Court upheld the 24th amendment, conceding that even the Fundamental Rights were amendable by the Parliament, but then added a caveat that the power to amend does not extend to destroying the 'basic structure' or 'essential features' of the constitution developed in 1950. The Emergency regime of Indira Gandhi mounted the most serious assault on constitutional government through the 42nd amendment. It aimed, among other things, at undoing *Keshavananda* by barring the Supreme Court from reviewing constitutional amendments: 'there shall be no limitation whatever on the constituent power of Parliament to amend' the constitution. The *Minerva Mills* restored *Keshavananda* by striking down two clauses of the 42nd amendment on the ground that it sought to destroy the basic structure of the constitution by: (1) prohibiting judicial review of a legislation contravening Fundamental Rights on the specious ground that such a legislation was to give effect to the Directive Principles;

and (2) proscribing judicial review of constitutional amendments. The court declared judicial review, among other features, as part of the basic structure of the constitution and, hence, indestructible.

Bicameralism

In a parliamentary system, the collective responsibility of the council of ministers to the popularly elected chamber gives it a special status vis-a-vis the second chamber. But the second chamber is still valued as a forum for deliberation and debate and amendatory restraints on the popular passions of the first chamber. In addition, with the growing volume of legislation in a modern state, the second chamber may also be used as the chamber for the initiation of legislation to lessen the burden of the first chamber, so that by the time a bill reaches the first chamber, the major initial and time-taking scrutiny would have already been done. In a parliamentary-federal system, the second chamber acquires an added relevance as the house giving representation to be units of the federation.

The Rajya Sabha seems to be originally designed by the makers of the constitution with a certain measure of ambivalence with regard to the two axial principles of government: (1) parliamentarism, and (2) federalism. At first glance, it appears that the Rajya Sabha is typically a parliamentary second chamber: (1) It gives representation to the states on the same principle of the proportion of population as in the Lok Sabha rather than equal representation as federal units irrespective of their size; (2) It is legally subordinate to the Lok Sabha so far as collective responsibility of the council of ministers to the Parliament and money bills are concerned; (3) Even though it has been given equal powers with the Lok Sabha in legislation and constitutional amendment, the provision for a joint session of the two chambers, in cases of conflict, would mean that the Lok Sabha with its larger membership would usually win, barring one-party majority or multi-party coalitional majority cutting across the two houses. Most commentators seem to have taken this line of interpretation, one even going to the extent of arguing that instead of being cast as a defender of state rights, the Rajya Sabha instead can only take away the rights of the states by resolving through a 2/3rd majority that: (1) the Union Parliament legislate in national interest on a subject enumerated in the State List, and (2) the Central government create a newall-India service.[13] Even W.H. Morris-Jones (1957) in his classic study of the Indian Parliament fails to find any appreciable federal relevance for the Rajya Sabha:

> "The Upper House is a Council of States of the Union and its members are elected by the State Assemblies. This, however, does not seem to have made the floor of the Council a battle-ground between Centre and States; a defence of 'states-rights', an expression of regional demands, is just as likely to be heard in the other house' (p. 256)."

K.V. Rao (1961), too, takes a critical view of the utility and relevance of the Rajya Sabha. Even as a parliamentary second chamber, Morris-Jones (1957) did not find the Rajya Sabha greatly relevant or useful: similar in members' socio-economic and political career backgrounds as well as in rules of procedure, the Rajya Sabha 'provided neither for technical revision nor for a wider and more leisurely debate'. The only saving grace for the Rajya Sabha as a second chamber that Morris-Jones found were two: (1) The government that had started using it as the site for first initiation of bills in conjunction with the Lok Sabha to lessen the burden of the primary initiation in the Lok Sabha; and (2) the Rajya Sabha was 'beginning to try its wings as a forum for grand and soaring debate'. (Though the two houses have similar procedure, the debate in the Rajya Sabha is less restrictive time-wise on account of its smaller size.)

The Rajya Sabha today does not function in a way radically different from what Morris-Jones portrayed in the 1950s. However, the federalization of the party system in the 1980s at the state level since 1989 at the national level has invested the Rajya Sabha with greater potentiality as a federal second chamber. Indeed, we are inclined to argue that even the modest designed Rajya Sabha in the constitution can have a greater federal relevance that the commentators have generally attributed to it. This is for the following reasons. First, it has equal powers with the Lok Sabha in the federally important matter of constitutional amendments. Second, the joint sitting of the two houses, instead of always dividing on the house-basis, may shape up in a more complex way in terms of coalitions among parties and groups in the Parliament as a whole. This may bring victory to the point of view championed by the Rajya Sabha. Third, the Rajya Sabha can block the intentions of a federal government to legislate in a certain contingency on a State List subject and to create a new all-India service. So, it would appear that the essential parliamentary interpretation of the powers of the Rajya Sabha was a by-product of the one-party dominant system in the early decades of the Indian republic. The federal relevance of the Rajya Sabha is likely to increasingly become more salient with the growing regionalization and federalization of the political system.

An amendment in law, in the early 2000s, abolished the residence or domiciliary requirement for Rajya Sabha members in relation to the State of the Union they were elected from in view of the fact that they were often elected on false certificates in this regard. A case, arguing that this will destroy the credential of the Rajya Sabha as the federal second chamber, was rejected by the Supreme Court. By the same amendment voting in Rajya Sabha elections has ceased to be by secret ballot on the consideration that open voting by MLAs in these biannual elections will discourage/stampout cross party voting in violation of party discipline. Strange logic, to say the least as it may only increase the price of the vote of an MLA in the Rajya Sabha elections.

The Speaker

The Rajya Sabha is better served by a politically more neutral presiding officer (the Vice-President of India) than the Lok Sabha. The Deputy Chairman of the Rajya Sabha and the Speaker and Deputy Speaker of the Lok Sabha are neither required to disaffiliate themselves from the parties on whose ticket they are elected nor is the Speaker allowed an uncontested return to the house in re-election. The Speaker of the British House of Commons snaps party tie on being elected to the office and extends the courtesy of an uncontested return to the house. We would do well to develop these salutary conventions to make the presiding officers more effective instruments of impartial and orderly conduct of business in the house. This will reduce the frequent recourse to judicial review of Speaker's decisions in disputes under the Anti-Defection Law (1985). Such cases have been multiplying recently.

Parliamentary Privileges

Parliamentary privileges of the members have been another controversial problem often leading to litigation. After guaranteeing freedom of speech in Parliament (subject only to the constitution and procedure of Parliament) and immunity from any legal procedure for speech and vote in Parliament or any committee thereof, the constitution proclaims:

> "In other respects, the powers, privileges, and immunities of each House of Parliament, and of the members and the committees of each House, shall be such as may from time to time be defined by Parliament by law, and until so defined, shall be those of that House and its members and committees immediately before coming into force of Section 15 of the constitution (Forty-fourth Amendment Act, 1978" (Article 105-3).

Until 1978, these privileges and immunities were declared by the same Article to be 'those of the House of Commons of the Parliament of the United Kingdom'.

Chetakar Jha makes a strong plea, citing the opinion of the Press Commission, for definition and codification of parliamentary privileges in a law. He also cited the case of *M.S.M. Sharma Vs. S.K. Sinha,* arising out of the Bihar legislature, in which the Supreme Court concurred with the Bihar Legislative Assembly that publication by the press of an expunged portion of the proceedings of the Assembly constituted the breach of privilege of the House. He considers it 'disturbing' as it not only smacks of intolerance, but also suggests that the right to freedom of speech and expression is subordinate to the parliamentary privileges. He also considers it repugnant to open government. The case for the codification of parliamentary privileges has over the years become, if anything, more pressing.

The uncodified nature of parliamentary/legislative privileges has continued to cause problems over the years. It led to a confrontation between the U.P. Assembly and the Allahabad High Court (*Keshav Singh v. Speaker of U.P. Assembly, 1965*) and between the *Tamil Nadu Assembly* and the editor and his colleagues of *the Hindu* newspaper early in the 21st century. The question of parliamentary privileges also came ahead in the JMM bribery case in the Supreme Court in connection with a confidence vote against the Congress government headed by P.V. Narasimha Rao in the late 1990s. The problems are somehow provisionally settled by the Supreme Court, but codification would make the situation less problematic and more settled.

Parliamentary Committees

Historically, the parliamentary Committee system in India may be traced back to the Montagu-Chelmsford reforms that led to the Government of India Act, 1919. The Indian Legislative Rules made under sub-section 67(1) in the section 129A of the Act and the standing orders of the legislative assembly made by the Governor-in-Council under sub-section 67(6) of the same Act, provided for the appointment of several committees. The standing orders provided for the committees, namely, the committee on petitions relating to bills, select committee on Amendments of standing orders, and select committee on bills. There was also a provision for Public Accounts Committee and a joint committee on bills. These committees also served as standing advisory committees attached to various departments of the Government of India. Purely advisory in nature, the committees were neither free from government interference nor were they endowed with privileges.

After the adoption of the constitution (1950), the committee system was significantly restructured in numbers and powers and privileges.

Committees are a microcosm of the reflecting the political complexion. They were small and compact groups of 20-30 member interacting regularly over an issue to hammer out a consensus or 'nearconsensus' in otherwise highly polarized positions in the House (for changes see the section below). They are a device to streamline the function of the legislation. In a relatively relaxed atmosphere away from the cameras, details are laid bare which provides acceptability and finesse to the also serve as an alibi for inaction and postponement of controversial bills, and often times; it is a springboard for a prelude to purposeful legislative action.

A good deal of parliamentary business is transacted in the Committees as the timely disposal of the Houses is savant and insufficient to make a through and detailed examination of the varied and voluminous legislative proposal. The magnitude, complexity and multifarious nature of work done by the parliament can be assessed by the fact that India's first 13 parliaments passed more than 3,200 bills. However, due to coalition governments, there has been a relative fall in the number of legislative and consequent reliance on ordinance which it can be considered as a travesty of democracy.

The New Committee System

Ministry-based specialized standing committees for detailed scrutiny of expenditure, administration, and policy by Parliament is probably the most important reform in parliamentary government in the last quarter of the 20th century. In 1979, the Birtish House of Commons moved in this direction by formally establishing fourteen departmentally related select committees, to which a fifteenth, Liaison Committee, consisting of chairmen of department-based and other select committees, was added in 1980. The committees were empowered to send for persons and governmental records, enlist services of specialists, and appoint sub-committees, in respect of three departments (home affairs, treasury, and foreign affairs). The developments have been viewed positively by the participants as well as by the Procedure Committee's formal inquiry ten years after the establishment of departmental select committees. The reform has also been welcomed by the media and the pressure groups. The journalists are much better informed about the parliamentary process than they were before these reforms. The pressure groups, generally, see themselves 'as forming a triangle of influence, the other two corners of which are occupied by departmentally-related Select Committees and the media'.[14]

Following the recommendations of the Royal Commission on Financial Management and Accountability chaired by Allen Lambert, the Canadian Parliament also streamlined its Committee system in 1989. The reformed departmentally-related standing committees then introduced are empowered to review and report on statute laws, programs and policy objectives and their implementation, expenditure plans and their implementation, and performance of the departments falling within the purview of the parliamentary committees.[15]

The Indian Parliament made a beginning with three select subject committees one each on agriculture, science and technology, and environment and forests in 1989,[16] Encouraged by the experiment, the Rules Committee in its Third Report of the Lok Sabha in March 1993 recommended the establishment of 17 standing select committees of Parliament for the various ministries and departments. The committees were formally inaugurated on 31st March 1993.[17] Established under Rule 331C the members of the committees are nominated by the Rajya Sabha Chairman and Lok Sabha Speaker and their chairman are appointed by the Speaker. The Committee membership is for a year.[18] While this allows for a larger number of MPs to gain experience of committee work, the turnover is too quick to allow deeper interest and specialization. It may not be a bad idea to make the membership of committees co-terminus with the term of a Lok Sabha.

Each of these committees consists of 45 members (30 from Lok Sabha and 15 from Rajya Sabha). Party representation in committees broadly reflects their parliamentary strength. The expectation of the Rules Committee is that consensus culture would prevail in the committees, but in case a member wants, 'he can be allowed to give a dissenting note or minutes of dissent'.[19]

The experience so far confirms this norm. As Subhash Kashyap, presumably on the working of the three pioneering select committees, observes:

> "There does develop in these committees a distinct committee approach to looking at problems of administration. This approach can be easily distinguished from the approach on the floor of the house. In short, though the strength of the political parties in the house may be the basis for nomination to the committees, it does not affect the functioning of the committees in any way impairing its impartial and non-partisan approach".

The chairmanship of some of the committees is allocated to the Rajya Sabha as also to opposition parties. In addition to the usual stuff of committee concern, both the Speaker and Rajya Sabha chairman may refer any 'other matters of the concerned ministeries' to them. In deference to the government's view, policy matters are not supposed to be discussed by the committees 'for the present'. Also, 'ministers would not be called before the committees'. Besides, 'while the committees could discuss matters of basic and important policies referred to them, they would, however, not discuss minor details, like appointments, transfers, day-to-day administration, etc'.[20]

The committees are instruments of Parliament, not of government. Their role is advisory; obviously they are not meant to dislodge the cabinet, only to improve their performance by scrutiny and control. The formulation of policies is the province of government which it does with Parliament's government which it does with Parliament's approval. The committees are meant 'to examine and oversee the implementation of policies by the administration'. To conclude with Kashyap:

> 'Without weakening the parliamentary system, the concept of departmentally related standing select committees provide to parliament sharper and more effective surveillance tools, restore the balance between parliament's legislative and deliberative functions and its role as a representational body, and above all, save valuable parliamentary time to the mutual advantage of both parliament and government'.

Notes and References

1. For these Vedic political institutions which gradually lost their popular character and tended to become aristocratic before suffering a decline, see R.S. Sharma (1991) and Romila Thapar (1984). On self governing local institutions of *Brahumadeyam* villages *(sabhas)* and *nagarams* of traders and local institutions of peasant villages *(urs)*, See Burton Stein (1980), and Kesavan Veluthat (1993).
2. The tradition of *panchayats* goes back at least to the *Mahabharata*. See the 'Sabha Parva', V. 81.
3. See I.H. Qureshi (1971 & n.d.) and Satish Chandra (1979).

4. For a historical sketch of constitutional reforms in India in the British period, see MV Pylee (1984) and Subhash C. Kashyap (1992), ch. 1.
5. The classic formulation of the British constitutional doctrine of parliamentary sovereignty was made by A.V. Dicey (1885). For a classic statement of the American constitutional principle of judicial supremacy, see Charles A. Beard (1912).
6. Private members' bills are not only rarely introduced but are also unlikely to be enacted.
7. See Pushpa Bali (1989).
8. Parliamentary sessions are usually three in a year and they generally tend to get shorter *over* time.
9. Limits of time on parliamentary debates may be prescribed by the Speaker 'after taking the sense of the House'. Parliament (India) (1989), p. 10. Such limitations are regular and frequent.
10. The decline of Parliament' thesis was originally formulated by Lord Bryce in 1921 in his classic *Modem Democracies* (relevant chapter excerpted in Philip Norton, ed., 1990, ch. 3). The phenomenon is mainly attributed to stricter parliamentary party discipline, rise of the Press and extra-parliamentary class and group organizations, complexity of policy issues and legislations in the Parliament, loss of 'class' and calibre in the bulk or parliamentarians etc. Part of the decline in his estimation is also psychological, stemming from exaggerated hopes 'entertained of the services they [legislatures] were to render' (p. 53). And, partly the decline was a function of the passing out of historical moments of insurgent idealism in new societies transplanting parliamentary institutions: 'The next generation did not in days of peace rise to the standard set in the days of conflict' (p. 53). Yet Bryce's conclusion is not entirety pessimistic. The utility which Mill and Bagehot saw in them remains, if perhaps reduced' (p. 56). This residual utility of the Parliament is seen by Bryce in its representative role and 'the watchful supervision needed to ensure honest and efficient administration' (p. 56). To a modern reader even these claims may appear a bit exaggerated though not entirely hollow.
11. To quote Lal Narain Sinha (1993, pp. 134–135); "Previous laws were continued by Article 372, but by the very term of this article, these laws continued only on the extent that they were consistent with the present constitution. Limitations were imposed directly by numerous Articles of the constitution and also by valid enacted laws. Whenever limitations were to be imposed, the extent of the limitation, thus abridging the right and the nature and the contents of such right, were indicated so as to make the provisions of the constitution dealing with the freedom of trade, commerce, and intercourse within the territory of India. Likewise. Part III deals with certain aspects of freedoms, the rights and liberties of the individual. The plenary powers of legislature are granted by detailed provisions of Part XI dealing with the legislative relations between the Union and the States beginning with Article 245. This clearly corroborates the oft-stated cliche that the Indian constitution is a 'lawyers' paradise".
12. For more details, see the relevant constitutional amendment Acts and the relevant volumes of *All India Reporter* for the Supreme Court judgments.
13. If my memory serves, this argument was made by Professor Chetakar Jha in his lectures on Indian politics in Patna College which I attended as an undergraduate student in the early 1960s.
14. British House of Commons (1990, 2 Vols.). The quote is from Vol. 1, Clause 219. Available with Parliament Library, New Delhi.
15. Information obtained through the courtesy of the Shastri Indo-Canadian Institute's Library in New Delhi.
16. Subhash C. Kashyap (1990, p. 2275).

17. *The Journal of Parliamentary Information,* Vol. XXXIX, No. 1 (March 1993), Editorial.
18. Parliament (India) (1992 and 1993).
19. *Ibid.*
20. *Ibid.*, The quotes are from, p. 5.

Bibliography

Austin, Granville, *The Indian constitution: Cornerstone of a Nation*. Bombay: Oxford University Press, 1966. Bali, Pushpa, *A Case Study of the Major Presidential Ordinances in India,* Ph.D. dissertation, University of Delhi, 1989.

Beard, Charles A., *The Supreme Court and the constitution* (With an Introduction and Bibliographies by Alan F. Westin). Engelwood Cliffs, N.J.; Prentice-Hall, Inc., 1962. First published in 1912 by Macmillan.

Bryce, Lord, The Decline of Legislatures' excerpted from his *Modern Democracies,* II, pp. 367–377 (1921) in Philip Norton (ed.), *Legislatures.* Oxford; Oxford University Press, 1990.

Dicey, A.V., *An Introduction to the Study of the Law of the constitution* (With Introduction by E.Ç.S. Wade). Delhi; Universal Book Traders, 1994, Indian Reprint of 10th ed. by Macmillan 1959. First published 1885.

Government of India, *The constitution of India,* New Delhi, Ministry of Law and Justice, Preface, date 15th August 1989.

House of Commons (U.K.), *Second Report from the Select Committee on Procedure, Session 1989-90. The Working of the Select Committee System together with Proceedings of the Committee Relating to the Report, Minutes of Evidence and Appendices,* London: HMSO, 23rd October 1990, 2 Vols.

Jha, Chetakar, *Indian Government and Politics: A Political Commentary,* Patna, Novelty & Company, Preface date 26th January 1960.

Kashyap, Subhash C., *Our Parliament: An Introduction to the Parliament of India,* New Delhi, National Book Trust, India, 1992, 2nd ed.; First published 1989.

———, 'A New Parliamentary Initiative: Subject-Based Standing Committees of Parliament', *Economic & Political Weekly,* Bombay, 6th October 1990.

Morris-Jones, W.H., *Parliament in India,* London: Longmans Green, 1957.

Norton, Philip (ed.), *Legislatures.* Oxford Readings in Politics and Government Series, General Editors: Vernon Bogdanor and Geoffrey Marshall. Oxford University Press, 1990.

Parliament (India), *Rules of Procedure & Conduct of Business in Lok Sabha,* New Delhi, Lok Sabha Secretariat, 1989, 7th ed.

———, *Rules Committee (Tenth Lok Sabha), First Report,* New Delhi, Lok Sabha Secretariat, August 1992.

———, *Rules Committee (Tenth Lok Sabha), Minutes Relating to the Second Report of the Rules Committee,* New Delhi, Lok Sabha Secretariat, March 1993.

Pylee, M.Y., *constitutional History of Indian 1600-1950,* New Delhi, S. Chand & Company Ltd., 1984 rev. 3rd ed. First published 1967.

Qureshi, I.H., *The Administration of the Sultanate of Delhi,* New Delhi, Oriental Books Reprint Corporation, 1971, 5th rev. ed. First Preface date 1942.

———, *The Administration of the Mughal Empire,* New Delhi, Janaki Prakashan, New Delhi.

Rao, K.Y., *Parliamentary Democracy of India: A Critical Commentary* (Foreword by K.M. Munshi). Calcutta, The World Press Private Ltd., 1961.

Sharma, R.S., *Aspects of Political Ideas and Institutions in Ancient India,* Delhi, Motilal Banarsidass Publishers Pvt. Ltd., 1991, 3rd ed., First published 1959.

Sinha, Lal Narain, *Indian constitution: A Fresh Look, An Analysis of Some Salient Aspects*, Patna, Malhotra Bros., 1993.

Stein, Burton, *Peasant State and Society in Medieval South India*, Delhi, Oxford University Press, 1980.

Thapar, Romila, *From Lineage to State: Social Formations in the Mid-First Millennium H.C. in the Ganga Valley*. Bombay, Oxford University Press, 1984.

The Journal of Parliamentary Information, Vol. XXXIX, No. 1, March 1993, Special Number 89th Inter Parliamentary Conference, New Delhi, April 1993.

Veluthat, Kesavan, *The Political Structure of Early Medieval South India*, Hyderabad, Orient Longman, 1993.

Federalism: Constitution and Dynamics

Mahendra Prasad Singh

❑ Parliamentary Federalism

Even if this argument is accepted that the parliamentary-federal system established under the 1950 Indian constitution is in many ways not only a unique federal union in contemporary comparative politics, but also the one uniquely suited to the Indian conditions,[1] we cannot wish away the fact that India in the 1980s and 1990s has been faced with an overwhelming challenge of federalizing its predominantly parliamentary system. Working a pure parliamentary system (e.g., United Kingdom) is difficult enough. But the problems are compounded manifold when the system combines the parliamentary principle of government with the federal one, and seeks to transplant it in a post-colonial nation. Even though, neither the ideas of federalism and republicanism[2] nor those of nominal monarchy and effective premiership[3] are alien to Indian history, India owes substantially to the modern West for its contemporary experiments with parliamentary federalism. For reasons not far to seek, both the British colonial rulers and the emergent nationalist elites who inherited power from them contrived constitutions that created a system of parliamentary paramountcy with a limited federal component. The British, due to the compulsions of colonial administrative centralization, and the nationalists, on account of the fissiparous tendencies prevalent through the Indian history and due to the trauma of religious communal frenzy and the partition of the country did it. Sure enough, in the last days of their rule, the British offered a scheme of loose confederation in the Cabinet Mission Plan as a sequel to the Simon Commission Report. But it fell on the hard rock of intransigence between the Indian National Congress and the Muslim League. And earlier, the federal components of the Government of India Act, 1935, had remained a dead letter for the refusal of the princely rulers of the native Indian States to join hands with the nationalists in working the new constitution. The Congress itself turned back to the promise of a loose federal union in its 1946 election manifesto. It outlined the objective of centralized federal union in the Constituent Assembly when it became evident that partition was inevitable.[4]

Thus, despite its great cultural and regional diversities and historical patterns of disunity, indeed, in a very real sense, because of it, in 1950 India adopted a heavily centralized system of parliamentary federalism under the dual impacts of the British colonial and nationalist interventions.

The constitution established an "amicable union" combining parliamentary federal features. In many ways, it is a unique federal constitution in comparative federalism. It ensures Union's legislative supremacy not on the Union List, but also on the Concurrent List and residuary legislative jurisdiction; even on the State List the Union Parliament can legislate in specified and exceptional circumstances. The Union executive power overrides State executive power outside the area of exclusive legislative jurisdiction of the States. The constitution ensures Union Parliament's supremacy and initiative in taxation, in constitutionally anticipated emergencies, in all-India civil and police services (which are recruited and trained by the Union government, and then allocated to the State governments), in judicial administration, and in constitutional amendments. Even the very existence of a State is contingent on the will of the Parliament which enjoys overriding powers with regard to redrawing the map of India and reorganization of State boundaries. However, it is evident from the reorganization of States over the years that the formal parliamentary power, in this regard, had been subject to the powerful mass movements for the creation of unilingual States much against the will of the Central government. Moreover, since the constitution went into effect, there has been a further expansion of the powers and functions of the Central government. For example, the Industries (Development and Regulation) Act (1951) expanded the power of the Central government under Entry 52 of the Union List to a number of industries (included in Schedule I) limiting or overlapping the power of State governments over industries under Entry 24 of the State List. Entries to Schedule I are indeed further extendable by Union executive order.[5] However, barring constitutional emergencies, the Union and State governments in their respective jurisdictions coordinate, which is what federalism essentially means. And, with the growing diversification and regionalization of the party system, Centre's interventions in State governments is becoming less viable and more restrained. Moreover, of late, especially since 1989, State governors are beginning to show some signs of independence as "federal" rather than just being Centre's agent.[7]

The Dynamics of Causation

This paper analyses the impact on India's parliamentary-federal system of the following seven factors in the past 42 years of its working: (1) styles of

Prime Ministerial leadership, (2) judicial and moral authority and structures, (3) party system, (4) regional disparities, (5) ethnic identities, (6) class formation in the emerging structures of the mixed capitalist and State capitalist economy, and (7) economic planning and centrally sponsored schemes of development. Needless to say, like all variables in social sciences, the foregoing, too, are partly overlapping and enmeshed, but their independent casual effects are analytically amenable to delineation.

Among the constitutional-political and public-policy variables, the Prime Ministerial leadership style has been a factor of greater salience in India than in some other political systems that combined the parliamentary and federal systems (e.g., Canada in 1867 and Australia in 1901). Even similar party systems, in terms of the structure of electoral competition, have produced a different political dynamics under varying premiership styles. For example, the party systems under Jawaharlal Nehru and Indira Gandhi were structurally both one-party dominant systems. However, the former was more pluralistically structured while the latter was heavily personalized and centralized. Of the socio-economic factors, especially regional disparities and ethnic and class identities, these had been less salient than the political variables to begin with, but they have been becoming factors to gathering momentum over the years. Combined with regionalism, ethnic and class factors mounted a great deal of institutional and mass pressures in favour of further federalization with an increased degree of State autonomy in the 1980s. States' autonomy demands and movements multiplied. While most of the earlier mass movements related to the Sates in the 1950s and 1960s were for linguistic reorganization of State boundaries, movements over the 1970s and 1980s veered around the issues of constitutional restructuring to provide greater powers and revenue resources for the States. By the late 1980s, some of these movements took a turn for religious fundamentalism and secessionism. The Sikh fundamentalists in Punjab, Muslim fundamentalists in Jammu & Kashmir, and linguistic ethnics in Assam came to rule the roost in these States, virtually paralyzing the democratic process. Forces of secessionism were neither new in Punjab and Jammu & Kashmir nor were they absent in some other States (e.g., Madras/Tamil Nadu, some Northeastern states) earlier. However, over the 1960s and 1970s, the dominant regional parties in these States had turned their back on secessionism and joined the national mainstream. The 1980s witnessed, two parallel developments, both mounting tremendous pressures towards federalization. With the number of non-Congress state governments increasing over the decade, chief ministers of these States held conclaves in Vijayawada, Bangalore, Calcutta, and Srinagar, demonstrating an impressive orchestration not only of the all-India parties, like Communist Party of India (Marxist) and Janata Party, but also of regional parties, like Telugu Desam, National Conference, and Akali Dal. (Such a conclave of Bharatiya Janata Party CMs also took place in the early 1990s.) Besides, regional mass movements in states, like Punjab, Kashmir, and Assam in the late 1980s came to be captured by fundamentalists and secessionists to the discomfiture and ambivalence of the dominant regional parties in these States, i.e., Akali Dal, National Conference, and Assam Gana Parishad.

Premiership Styles

The evolution of premiership styles has yielded at least three major models: (1) Parliamentary, (2) Patrimonial, and (3) Federal. Nehru, Lal Bahadur Shastri, and Indira Gandhi (until the 1969 Congress split) displayed a premiership style that may be termed Parliamentary. The parameters of this political framework were defined by a more or less collective leadership among the stalwarts in the cabinet even though the Prime Minister clearly towered over them, autonomous set of Chief Ministers, especially in the rimland states, and a clientelist pattern of voting behaviour under the tutelage of dominant caste and community leaders. However, the Congress party ruled at the Centre as well as in overwhelmingly large number of states. And the Prime Ministers were widely popular leaders having participated in the national liberation movement or being members of the Nehru dynasty or closely associated with it. The dominant Congress party, with its inheritance of the mass nationalist movements against the British Raj, was itself the New Raj, but it held regular organizational elections at various levels and annual All India Congress Committee conferences. So, even though the federal tensions were often exacerbated, the system of one-party dominance worked essentially within the parliamentary framework.

With Indira Gandhi's rise to undisputed leadership in the Congress party and the country after the 1969 Congress split with her right-wing senior colleagues and the 1971 Lok Sabha and 1972 State Assembly elections, a new premiership style came into being, even though the structure of competition among parties formally continued to be a one-party dominant one. A series of changes followed. The area of collective cabinet leadership tended to narrow and eventually zeroed in on the Prime Minister. The patron-client network of voting behaviour at the level tended to erode under the twin pressures of competition among political elites and social mobilization and politicization at the mass level. Challenged by the Syndicate faction within her party, Indira Gandhi bypassed the intermediary structures of power within the party and State governments and made a direct personalized mass appeal to the electorate through the government-controlled electronic mass media, bureaucratic apparatus, and a handpicked pack of party bodies that passed as party organizations. Central interventions in State governments under Article 356 of the constitution providing for "President's rule" and legislations through presidential ordinances multiplied manifold (Table 1). The executive backed by a docile parliamentary majority and with some regional and Communist parties' support, sought to ride rough shod over the judiciary. A powerful mass movement led by the non-Congress and non-Communist opposition parties gathered momentum. The intelligentsia

TABLE 1 President's Rule in States and Presidential Ordinances (1950-91)*

	PRs		POs	
Year	*Cases*	*Average per Year*	*Cases*	*Average per Year*
1950-65	9	9/15 = 0.6	110	110/15 = 7.3
1966-76	32	32/11 = 3.0	146	146/11 = 23.3
1977-79	16	16/3 = 5.0	34**	
1980-84	16	16/3 = 5.0		
1985-89	6	6/5 = 1.2		
1990-91***	8	8/2 = 4.0		

Notes: President's rule was promulgated in Jammu and Kashmir in 1986 following the expiry of six months of Governor's rule under Section 92 of the constitution of Jammu and Kashmir. Similarly, in 1990, again in the same State President's rule followed the expiry of six months of Governor's rule. President's rule in Punjab declared in May 1987 was extended several times almost for four years necessitating a constitutional amendment for this purpose. It was finally revoked after the controversial Assembly elections in the State in February 1992.

Sources: Adapted from Government of India, *President's Rule in the States and Union Territories* (New Delhi:

Lok Sabha Secretariat, 1991), Appendix IV; supplemented by *Asian Recorder*, Vols. XXXVI (1990) and XXVII (1991). Pushpa Bali, *Case Study of the Major Presidential Ordinances in India 1950-1980* (Ph.D. thesis, Department of Political Science, University of Delhi, 1989), pp. 418–449. For detailed studies of President's rule, *see* B.D. Dua, *Presidential Rule in India, 1950-1974: A Study in Cris Politics* (New Delhi: S. Chand & Co., 1979), and Davinder Kaur *A Political Study of President's Rule in the Indian States*, 1966-1984 (Ph.D. thesis, Department of Political Science, University of Delhi, 1989).

* I have so constructed the categories as to correspond, as far as possible, to the Prime Ministerial terms of Nehru—Shastri, Indira Gandhi, Morarji Desai, Indira Gandhi's second coming, Rajiv Gandhi, and post-1989 Prime Ministers.

** Until 10th November 1980 only.

*** There has been a marked decline in the incidence of Presidents rule since the 1990s. *See* M.P. Singh, "Towards a More Federalized Parliamentary System in India: Explaining Functional Change", *Pacific Affairs*, Vol. 74, No. 4, Winter 2001-02: 553-568.

in the press and the universities also grew critical. Faced with these pressures mounted by the federal and judicial organs of the State, the press, and the extra-parliamentary mass movements, the executive reacted by authoritarian constitutional amendments concentrating power into the office of the PM, proclamation of a national emergency under Article 352 of the constitution, and large-scale arrests of the opposition leaders. With all these developments, the federal features of the political system, limited even at the best of times, came to be seriously whittled down. Indeed, even the Parliamentary features were seriously eroded by an excessively centralizing drive on the part of the Prime Minister. It is for these reasons that this phase of Indira Gandhi's premiership is best described as patrimonial one.'[8]

After her defeat in the 1977 Lok Sabha elections and her electoral restoration in the 1980 mid-term polls, Indira Gandhi was a bit chastened. But her imperious style, reinforced by her augmented international prestige, continued by and large. Rajiv Gandhi, who succeeded her after her brutal assassination in October 1984 and won by an electoral landslide the same year, was a breeze of fresh air. He was less inclined to topple non-Congress State governments. He also showed a greater respect for the judiciary and the press. He entered into a series of formal and informal accords with dominant regional parties in Punjab, Assam, Mizoram, Tripura, and Jammu and Kashmir and continued his mother's informal understanding with the All-India Anna Dravida Munnetra Kazhagam (AIADMK) in Tamil Nadu.

However, before he could seriously execute his promised reforms in the Congress party aimed at weeding out the corrupt "middlemen" and holding organizational elections, he was himself caught up halfway through his mandate in the alleged kickbacks in the defence purchase deals with the Swedish firm Bofors (his personal involvement remains as yet unestablished in the inconclusive probes). Moreover, Punjab Accord remained unimplemented due to political and judicial intractability. Besides, Punjab, Kashmir, and Assam were overtaken by the spreading dragnet of terrorism and secessionism. And, finally, Rajiv Gandhi lost in the 1989 Lok Sabha elections and, after a brief but impressive spell as the leader of the opposition in the Parliament, was brutally assassinated in a terrorist bomb blast by suspected Sri Lankan Tamil terrorists in Sriperambudur in Tamil Nadu in the run-up to the midterm polls in May 1991.

The federal Prime Ministerial style of leadership was presaged by the Janata phase (1977-79) and carne into a fuller play after the 1989 Lok Sabha elections and the elections in 1991, 1996, 1998, 1999, 2004, and 2009. The Prime Minister's now have to contend with not only a multi-party system at the Centre, but also with some powerful regional and all-India parties, other than the one in power at the Centre, ruling the roost in some States.

Judicial and Moral Authority Structures

Federal systems are especially hungry for judicial and moral interventions in the political process to rescue them from the mire of illegitimacy and excessive partisan conflicts and coercion. The judiciary and the Presidency are the two obvious candidates for such a role in the Indian political system: one, the repository of condensed judicial authority, the other, endowed with a great moral authority in the federal domain by virtue of his federal electoral college and the expectations of the framers of the constitution about his non-partisan role in a strictly Parliamentary (i.e., nominally constitutional) framework. Despite Presidents Rajendra Prasad's and Zail Singh' pleas or threats to the contrary,[9] all the incumbents so far have stayed put in the parameters of a constitutional Presidency. Indeed, the Parliamentary system normally precludes an activist or interventionist conception of the Presidency beyond the pale of moral persuasion and sagely advice. In India's institutional parameters of a parliamentary-federal system, the ultimate moral and judicial sanction rests with the Supreme Court, which under Article 131 of the constitution enjoys exclusive original *legal* jurisdiction in all federal and inter-state disputes, and under Article 143 an *advisory* jurisdiction on any "question of law or fact" of "public importance" referred to it by the President.[10]

Federal nature of the Indian constitution is a major source, among others, of the judicial review not only of laws but also of constitutional amendments enacted by the Parliament and State legislatures. Judicial review, in turn, has also significantly impacted the dynamics of the Indian federal system. Neither the constitution nor the conflicts between the Parliament and judiciary for supremacy have established in India a system which is identical with the system of parliamentary sovereignty (any other source of law and constitution is subordinate) as in Great Britain or with the system of judicial supremacy ("the constitution is what the judges say it is") in the United States. One may perhaps venture to say that India has established a system of constitutional supremacy. For within the constitutional text itself, there are express limitations placed on the power of the Parliament and that of judicial review.[11] The parliament and the Supreme Court 'each enjoy considerable, say, on where the constitution really stands and what it actually means.' The Supreme Court first sought to extend its power of judicial review of legislations under Article 13 to constitutional amendments in Part III of the constitution on Fundamental Rights by declaring them unamendable (*Golak Nath vs. State of Punjab,* 1967). The Parliament reacted by inserting an additional clause into Article 13 by the constitution (24th Amendment) Act, 1971, Section 2: "Nothing in this article shall apply to any amendment of this constitution made under Article 368". The judiciary in its judgement in *Keshavanada Bharti vs. State of Kerala* (1973) conceded that the Parliament can amend any part of the constitution, but it bounced back to entrench the constitution by qualifying that in doing so the Parliament cannot alter its "basic structure" or "essential features". Its power of judicial review was reiterated by the Supreme Court in the *Minerva Mills vs. Union of India* (1980).[12] This is inevitable in a written constitution with federal division of powers, Fundamental Rights, and federally shared amending process.

It is interesting to observe that the ebb and flow of parliamentary and judicial power have varied with the changing nature of the party system. Periods of one-party dominance have seen the judiciary, generally, acquiesce in and accommodate the socio-economic reforms and constitutional amendments enacted by the Parliament (e.g., the Nehru era). Or else, such periods of one-party dominance under a more populist and centralizing Prime Minister have seen the Parliament seeking to clip the wings of the judiciary, with the latter retreating from its contention that Part III of the constitution on Fundamental Rights is beyond the pale of the amending power of the Parliament, yet holding tenaciously to the doctrine of the unamendability of the "basic structure" or "essential features" of the constitution. The *Golak Nath* judgement came in the year of the Fourth General Elections which witnessed the first major breach in the system of one-party dominance. The inherent unity in diversity of the Indian society, the current multi-party system of polarized pluralism, and the tremendous pressures for federalizing the predominantly parliamentary system are likely to enhance the federal relevance of the judicial organ of the state. But excessive reliance on the judiciary for settlement of *political* disputes and its consequential politicization would reduce its judicial relevance and efficacy.

Party Systems

There is also a significant factor in the nature of the party system, which has been in transition. One such transition was from the one-party dominant system to the two-party system in 1977, when only two parties, Janata and Congress, accounted for above 80 per cent of both votes and seats. For a brief period in the wake of the 1969 Congress split, the minority Congress government of Indira Gandhi had survived with the support of CPI and some regional parties, but the hangover of the Congress predominance was too recent and breach in it too short to give rise to a federal premiership style. During the Janata Dal phase, even though this party came to power simultaneously in New Delhi and some major and smaller North Indian States, factionalism among the five constituent parties that had merged to form it had an added federal dimension to it, as the two major constituents, the Bharatiya Lok Dal and Bharatiya Jana Sangh, divided among themselves the States ruled by the Janata Party. Besides, the Congress continued to control Andhra Pradesh and Karnataka in the South, and so did the AIADMK in Tamil Nadu, and the Left Front to West Bengal.

The post-1989 party system became a multi-party system; in Giovanni Sartori's terms, a system of "polarized pluralism".[13] Two governments followed in quick succession in the Ninth Lok Sabha. The National Front government was a minority coalition government of the Janata Dal, Congress (Socialist), Telugu Desam, Dravida Munnetra Kazhagam (DMK), and Asom Gana Parishad and supported, without joining government, by the Communist Parties and the Bharatiya Janata Party (BJP). Its successor Janata Dal (Socialist) minority government was supported from outside the government by the Congress party. Following the mid-term polls in 1991, the Congress formed a minority government led by the veteran P.V. Narasimha Rao that somehow completed its mandate of five years. The Prime Minister had to contend not only with an issue-based support from the BJP and National Front-Left parties alliance, but also had to make a tight-rope-walk in the context of the most diverse set of State governments formed by Congress and non-Congress parties since Independence. All these developments obviously put a high premium on a federal style Prime Ministerial leadership. In subsequent elections in 1996, 1998, 1999 and 2004 coalition/minority government led by Janata Dal, BJP or Congress were formed continuing to demand federal premiership style of leadership.

To sum up, the trajectory of party system evolution has passed through at least six stages: (1) Predominant Party System-I (1952-69); (2) Multi-party System-I (1969-71); (3) Predominant Party System-II (1971-77); (4) Two-Party

System (1977-84); (5) (a stillborn) Predominant Party System-III (1984-1989); and (6) Multi-party System-II (1989-todate).[14] The transition from one–party dominance to a more competitive, pluralist party system has been a factor contributing to the greater federalization of India's predominantly parliamentary system.

Regional Disparities

In addition to being a political arrangement for democratic governance of societies marked by unity in diversities, federalism is also an economic mechanism for reduction of regional disparities by federal financial transfer and reallocation of resources. Indian States are divisible into six major categories of economic development measured by per capita income, with Punjab at the top (₹1586) and Bihar at the bottom (₹645). The national average happens to be ₹874, and the averages for Groups A, B, C, D, E and F States stand at ₹1445, ₹1071, ₹939, ₹812, ₹712, and ₹262, respectively, as per the *Report of the Finance Commission, 1978.*[15] Such sharp regional disparities have led the States not only to take divergent positions on the criteria for federal fiscal transfers but also more lately for a new constitutional reallocation of powers and revenue resources between the Centre and the States. For example, the criteria for the distribution of income tax between the two levels of government and among the States have been highly contentious. More industrialized States, like Maharashtra and West Bengal have advocated for a greater weightage for the criterion of the place of collection of the tax, while poorer and more populous states have emphasized population as the major criteria. Neither is foolproof. In case of a large business enterprise, income earned in a number of States is usually declared in the metropolitan city where its head office is located. On the other hand, population may not always be a valid indicator of the financial needs of a State. A less populous State, like vast but arid Rajasthan may, at times, require larger revenue for development than a more populous one.[16] Moreover, some states endowed with rich mineral resources, but, otherwise, poor have been agitated over lower royalties for their minerals and inadequate share in the industrial exploitation of their resources (e.g., Assam and Bihar). Similarly, agriculturally rich States have been uptight about Food Zones restricting movement of grain across the nation freely and the pricing mechanism for the agricultural sector.

By and large, there have been three channels for federal financial transfers to States: (1) assured fiscal devolution from the divisible pool of taxes and duties on recommendations of the Finance Commission under Article 275 of the constitution; (2) discretionary plan assistance (loans and grants) from the Centre to the States recommended by the Finance Commission (under Article 282) and by the Planning Commission; and (3) discretionary grants to the States for Centrally-sponsored projects of development and administration under the Planning Commission dispensation. There has been a growing trend over the years for a larger proportion of federal transfers to be made through the Finance Commission than through the

Planning Commission. For example, where 24.4 per cent of resources in the Third–Five Year Plan were transferred through the Finance Commission, 48.9 per cent through the Planning Commission, and 22.7 per cent through other means; the respective figures in the Sixth Plan period stood at 61.1 per cent, 38.9 per cent, and 14.6 per cent. The pattern of change is consistent across the various plans.[17]

Finance Commissions have evolved approaches, with some variations, for devolution of taxes divisible between the Centre and States and grants-in-aid by the former to the latter in which the population of States loomed large among the criteria for tax revenue devolution (80 per cent for income tax in the Fifth Finance Commission Report) and revenue-expenditure gap and special problems of the States for grants-in-aid. The Ninth Finance Commission, in its first Report for 1989-90, recommended a modified Gadgil formula, whereby income tax and union excise duties may be distributed among States in accordance with this ratio: (1) 20 per cent on the basis of population; (2) 50 per cent on the basis of distance of the per capita income of a State from the highest per capita income State multiplied by its population; (3) 12.5 per cent on the basis of a State's per capita income multiplied by its population; and (4) 12.5 per cent on the proportion of poor people in the State to the total poor population nationally.[18]

However, in the formula for Central assistance to the States recommended by the Planning Commission and approved by the National Development Council in December 1991, population continues to be given more weightage, alongside, of course, some other criteria: population (60 per cent), per capita income (25 per cent), and performance (7.5 per cent). Moreover, of the 25 per cent weightage given to per capita income was made to conform to the "deviation method" such that higher the allocation of Central assistance, lower the per capita income of a State than the national average.[19]

Ethnic Identities and Class Formation

To take the tack of ethnic identities and class formation, it is only natural that modern class formation in a country of India's size and diversity is marked by sharp regional variations and pre-capitalist residues. The classes of capitalists, middle class professionals, and industrial workers have been more prone to form national federations than the farmers, peasants, and agricultural workers. But, all these class organizations have been marked by factionalism along regional and party lines. Trade unions have been especially susceptible to "colonization" by political parties and inter-union rivalries. In the short run, primordial or ethnic identities bedevil class interests and organizations. Moreover, there have been dominant regional parties thriving on linguistic and religious identities in some States, besides some national or all-India parties predominantly based on religious and caste identities.

Three recent developments are particularly noticeable in this context. One refers to the rise by the mid-1960s of a prosperous peasantry, predominantly comprising the "Other Backward Castes" (GBCs so-called to distinguish them from the Scheduled Castes/Tribes). Economically, they happen to be the major beneficiaries of the post-Independence land reforms and the green revolution. Socially and educationally, they have made some advance, but their representation in government employment, universities, and the press is still disproportionate to their size. This gave rise to the controversies and agitations around the New Reservation Policies of the National Front and the Narasimha Rao Congress government. Politically, they emerged as a dominant group in the Janata Party/Janata Dal, especially its Bharatiya Lok Dal/Dalit Mazdoor Kisan Party/Lok Dal constituents and splinters. The taste of political power in periods of Janata ascendancy only whetted their political appetite, but Janata Dal has become splintered into Samajvadi Party (U.P.), Rashtriya Janata Dal (Bihar), Biju Janata Dal (Orissa), Janata Dal (Secular) (Karnataka), and Janata Dal (United) with Samata Party elements in Bihar as the nucleus.

The second development, in this connection, is the rise of the regional bourgeoisie and professional middle classes. These classes, often in collaboration with the peasants and farmers brought about by the late 1970s and early 1980s far-reaching electoral realignments in some States displacing the Indian National Congress by some regional parties, otherwise, not very different from the Congress sociologically and ideologically, except for OBC and regional biases, e.g., Telugu Desam in Andhra Pradesh, Asom Gana Parishad in Assam, Janata Party/Dal in Bihar, U.P., Haryana, Karnataka, etc.

The third development is the emergence of Hindu revivalism in the late 1980s under the aegis of Vishwa Hindu Parishad, Rashtriya Swayamsevak Sangh, and Bharatiya Janata Party in several States, especially in the Hindi belt. Riding on this revivalist wave, the BJP came to power, off and on, in Madhya Pradesh, Rajasthan, Himachal Pradesh, and Uttar Pradesh, Maharashtra (in coalition with Shiv Sena), and Gujarat. Initially, a party of urban Hindu refugees from Pakistan and traditional middle class urban Hindus, the BJP in recent years has extended its support-base to rural areas as well.

All these features and factors have significantly affected the patterns of federal politics. For one thing, the gradual growth of separate class and ethnic political mobilization put the multi-class, multi-ethnic, catch-all strategy of political mobilization under severe strain. The decline of one-party dominant system allowed a freer play to the federal forces of the polity. For another thing, it was not only the parliamentary party system that was increasingly federalized, but also the States component of the party system came to be diversified with a large assortment of non-Congress parties forming governments in a sizeable number of States. The electoral support of these non-Congress regional and all-India parties is strongly associated with: (1) areas of agrarian and industrial modernization, and (2) communal and caste mobilization by these parties. Though the Congress still remains the largest and most widely spread national party, seeking to simultaneously appeal through its policies to the bourgeoisie, the middle classes, the workers, and the poor in urban and rural areas. It also seeks to address to all regions of the country across the board. In the long-run and in the final crunch, it may settle down to be a party of the bourgeoisie and the middle classes and still manage to garner a sizeable measure of electoral support if and when the hold of communal, caste, and regional parties on the middle classes and the regional bourgeoisie declines. The other two enduring party formations may be a party of peasant proprietors and of the communists supported by industrial and agricultural workers.

Strategy of Economic Development

The relationship between the strategy of economic development adopted in India and federalism is, generally, not yet fully appreciated. But, it is plausible to argue that the structure of mixed economy (consisting of a dominant Public/State sector and a Private sector) and a state-led strategy of industrialization have had a centralizing impact on the federal system during the Nehru and Indira Gandhi premierships up at least until the mid-1970s. Due to political and economic pressures, both the Nehruvian model of economic development and the gloss of political centralization put on it by Indira Gandhi was challenged during the Janata phase (1977-79). The return of Indira Gandhi in 1980 and the succession of Rajiv Gandhi in 1984 did not mean a return to pre-1977 conditions. Both initiated policies of liberalizing the heavily regulated economic regimes of the Nehru and the first Indira Gandhi eras. And, after the uncertainties of two minority governments between the 1989 Lok Sabha elections and the 1991 mid-term polls, the Narasimha Rao government greatly accelerated the pace of economic liberalization. Reorientation in economic policies was not without its impact on federal dynamics in the 1980s, even though the ushering in of a multi-party system in 1989 has initially been a factor of greater moment. However, the contradiction between a centralized federal polity and the new economic reforms has been perceptively brought out by Amal Ray:

> "If the objective of the new reforms is to enhance competitiveness of the Indian economy and so its efficiency, then this precludes the concentration of governmental power at one level or private power in a few monopoly houses. The ethos of competition has to be enforced through economic as well as political behaviour. And competition would require the maintenance of certain protected powers for the respective partners and, therefore, a certain dualism in the federal system."[20]

Economic Planning and Centrally-sponsored Development Schemes

In classical federal thought and institutional design and practice, planning was either unanticipated or considered antithetical to federalism. In modern Indian political thought and policy formulation, however, planning was considered as essential strategy for national economic growth and industrialization under the aegis of the independent Indian nation-state. Early on after independence, a Planning Commission was set up by a decision of the Central government, a practice that came to be emulated by the State governments that followed suit by establishing similar commissions or boards that came to work in tandem. Similarly, a non-statutory body developed in the National Development Council to facilitate final political consultations between the Union government and State Chief Ministers on the plan document. This exercise in "economic federalism" in itself may not have led to excessive centralization. But financial superiority of the Centre, coupled with the State governments' reluctance to tax the farm sector for obvious political reasons, led to the unfolding of Centrally-sponsored schemes of economic development jointly administered by the Central and State governments. Central financing and guidelines for and monitoring of these schemes, implemented mainly through State governments, have resulted in an enormous increase in the activities, powers, and influence of the Central government not only in areas of concurrent, but also exclusively State subjects. This is not only unique to India; this trend of "cooperative federalism" has been observed in other federal systems as well. In the USA, in the 1980s the "New Federalism" of President Ronald Reagan initiated the process of reversing this trend by transferring responsibilities and funds to the State governments.

In more recent years, the Centre has been transferring the Centrally-sponsored schemes to the States on the plea of lack of funds. But it has to initially continue to finance them because the States say they do not have funds either. Thus, at the 43rd meeting of the National Development Council in December 1991, it was decided that 113 such schemes, as recommended by the Narasimha Rao Committee, would be transferred to the States with the existing mode of their financing.[21] The future of such schemes would appear to be bleak because of current financial crunch and the new, more conservative economic policies stepped up since 1991 by Prime Minister P.V. Narasimha Rao and Finance Minister Manmohan Singh and more or less continued by successive governments of India, at varying faces without change of direction.

Territorial Convolution

An interesting dimension of federalization in India concerns territorial and cultural matrices of India's sub-continental polity: Indian history is replete with a constant interplay between the imperial and regional centres of power. During the British Raj, the colonial State first consolidated a centralized Viceregal system incorporating the British Indian provinces under its direct rule and the princely/native Indian States under their paramountcy. It subsequently started the processes of devolution of power: and federalization in stages. So, when the 1950 constitution established a centralized federal Union, it was not an instance of independent States federating, but one of the virtually unitary State decentralizing itself. The "territorial federalism" in India does not only have the pressure of size to federalize (as in Australia), but also the additional components of language, religion, and tribe. The linguistic basis for the organization of the Indian National Congress in disregard of the then existing multilingual State boundaries was accepted by its leadership as early as the beginning of the Gandhian era in the 1920s. Besides, regional movements in the Bengal Presidency led to the carving out of the provinces of Bihar (Hindi-speaking) and Orissa (Oriya-speaking in 1912 and the bifurcation of the latter in 1936. With the lapse of paramountcy of the British Crown over the native Indian States in 1947, the Government of India combined diplomacy and "police action" to effectuate the integration of these States with the newly created Indian Union. The constitution of India first created several categories of States to take into account the variety and complexity of units, thus, amalgamate (but subsequently reduced them into "States" (28) and "Union Territories." (7). Shortly after Independence in 1947, movements for linguistic reorganization of States appeared in several States. The National Congress leadership as well as the States Reorganization Commission Report (1956) preferred the maintenance of multi-lingual; States for cultural homogenization. However, under the pressure and persistence of linguistic, religious, and tribal movements the Central government yielded, creating the States of Andhra Pradesh (Telugu-speaking), Tamil Nadu (Tamil-speaking Karnataka (Kannada-speaking), Gujarat (Gujarati-speaking), Maharashtra (Marathi-speaking), Punjab (Punjabi-speaking with a Sikh-majority), Haryana (Hindi-speaking), Himachal Pradesh (Hindi-speaking), all in the 1950s and 1960s. This process of territorial reorganization extended to the North-East in the 1970s, culminating the emergence of the so-called "seven sisters" States and Union Territories in the North-East. In the 1980s, sub-regional movements based tribal or ethnic identities, acquired salience in several states. Such movements includes Gorkha National Liberation Front in the Darjeeling hill district of West Bengal, Bodoland agitation in Assam, Jharkhand Mukti Morcha in the Chhotanagpur region in South Bihar, and some other tribal areas in the adjoining states including West Bengal, Orissa, and Madhya Pradesh.To meet these sub-regional demands, a new federal innovation of an autonomous Regional Development Council has been made in Darjeeling and Bodoland. Earlier, when the Telangana sub-regional agitation in Andhra Pradesh was at its peak in the 1970s, this device was first introduced there with good results. Since then, the idea also gained ground in Vidrabha and Ladakh regions in Maharashtra and Jammu and Kashmir. In addition, a new experiment in federal convolution has been made in the North-East, where several States until recently had a common Governor and there still is an inter-state development council, named, North-Eastern Council (NEC).

Moreover, inter-state disputes have been flaring up around almost all rivers that flow through more than one State. Such disputes over Satluj and

Cauvery rivers have recently soured relations between Punjab and Haryana, Tamil Nadu and Karnataka, and involved multiple mechanisms of conflict resolution including the executive heads of governments at the two levels, special tribunals, and eventually the Supreme Court. In the early years of the republic, political devices for disputes settlement were more frequent and effective. Recourse to political methods were facilitated by the prevalence of Congress dominance in New Delhi as well as in most of the States. Political reconciliation was also facilitated by the existence of towering leaders of the anti-colonial nationalist movement or new charismatic leaders. The Congress party under Nehru had nurtured a breed of reconciliatory leadership well-versed in democratic resolution of disputes. Such an approach was also encouraged by Article 262 of the constitution, which provides for parliamentary enactment "for the adjudication of any dispute or complaint with respect to the use, distribution or control of the waters of, or in, any inter-State river or river valley". Subsequently, the Parliament enacted the Rivers Board Act and the Inter-State Water Disputes Act for this purpose. In recent years, however, there is a growing trend towards a cleavage between the party in power in New Delhi and other parties in power in some States (e.g., the conclaves of the non-Congress Chief Ministers in the first half of the 1980s). This trend explains why the earlier experiment of inter-State consultations in the four Zonal Councils consisting of all States in one region during the Congress predominance has fallen into disuse. One notices at present a growing reliance on judicial resolution of inter-state disputes.

Proposals for Structural Reforms

In the deliberations on the plethora of demands of constitutional restructuring by various political parties and State governments, a number of proposals for greater federalization of India's predominantly parliamentary system have emerged. These proposals are mainly related to the office of the Governor, the second chamber of the Parliament, autonomous federal instrumentalities mediating between the Central and State governments, decentralization of the planning process, and the local political systems in rural and urban areas below the State level with a view to strengthening them as a third effective tier added on to the two-tier federal structure. Rasheeduddin Khan pleads for "a comprehensive review and necessary recasting alterations, modifications and changes of the constitutional provisions, and the functioning aspect of the Centre-State relations, by a National Assembly, especially constituted for this purpose, representing a cross-section of public opinion, drawn from different political parties, public organizations, and expert groups."[22] This chapter is premised on the assumption that amendments to the 1950 constitution and a chastened sense of national purpose on the part of the political elites would be an adequate response to the growing crisis of governability.

Executive Federalism

The office of the Governor has perhaps been the most contentious one in the Centre-State confrontations over the misuse of "President's rule" in States. Some parties and States governments have indeed gone to the extent of demanding its outright abolition. The Sarkaria Commission Report (1987-88) was seized with the problem of gubernatorial reforms, but was beset with the dilemma of ensuring States' autonomy, on the one hand, and maintaining the existing links between the two levels of government. It could not come up with a satisfactory way of combining the contradictory principles of a strong parliamentary Centre and strong State governments, a theme rhetorically emphasized by all Indian leaders, including Indira Gandhi. The Commission's resolution of this dilemma did not go beyond exhorting the establishment of sound federal conventions and normative patterns of behaviour on the part of the Governor and the Union Horne Ministry and the Cabinet respecting State autonomy.[23] A Canadian political scientist, Douglas V. Verney, has made a proposal that offers a way out of this dilemma of wedding a responsible parliamentary government with a "responsible" federalism. Verney seeks to slightly modify the existing Inter-State Council such that the President replaces the Prime Minister as the Chairman of the general body of the Council, while the Prime Minister continues to chair its standing committee. "The full President in-Council could then act as a federal buffer between the Union cabinet and the Governors. President's rule could initially be via the President-in-Council and not the Home Minister."[24] This could remove the sting of illegitimacy now surrounding a Central intervention in a State as the Inter-State Council is representative of both sets of governments. But, this device of responsible federalism is limited to "executive federalism" in the sense that the Inter-State Council brings together only the heads of the executive, whether of the Government of India or of the States. And this only gives a constitutional recognition and a constitutional structure, although this in itself may be a qualitative quantum jump to such informal devices as the Chief Ministers', Governors', Ministers', Secretaries', Speakers' conferences that have become a regular practice, though they work by consensus rather than voting.

Legislative Federalism

A proposal for an effective exercise in "legislative federalism" has been made by the leading Indian political scientist Rajni Kothari. That the Rajya Sabha is a weak second chamber, federal in composition and name but largely "unfederal" in potentiality, is an old story. To make it a truly federal chamber, Kothari proposes that it may continue to be indirectly elected by State legislatures as now, but its electoral college may be expanded to include the district councils. Renamed as Pradesh Sabha (which, in fact, literally means the same as Rajya Sabha), the federal second chamber "should speak for the lower levels."[25] This proposal would, of course, go a long way in federalizing the Parliament. However, it is notable that an almost total irrelevance of the Rajya Sabha observed by W.H. Morris-Jones in his classic study on the Indian Parliament[26] in the early years of the Republic, has been changing in later years. The principal factor of change has been the differentiation in the parliamentary party system as well as the overall transformation of the party system. The Congress dominance of early decades in both chambers subsequently gave way to different parties holding sway in them, e.g., when the Congress lost in 1977 to the Janata Party, it still continued to enjoy a majority in the Rajya Sabha and effectively blocked some constitutional amendments sponsored by the Janata government. Moreover, with the Party system becoming one of a multi-partisan polarized pluralism since 1989, parliamentary power not only in the Rajya Sabha, but also in the Lok Sabha has become more manoeuvrable to the federal forces in the polity. Regional and nominally national parties have been playing decisive balancing role in federal coalition governments since 1989.

Autonomous Federal Instrumentalities

Another package of constitutional reforms came in 1987-88 from the Commission on Centre-State Relations (chaired by Justice R.S. Sarkaria). Instead of dividing parliamentary powers on a more effective federal pattern between Lok Sabha and Rajya Sabha, the Sarkaria Commission proposes the constitutional entrenchment and/or strengthening of a series of points of autonomy in the federal government. These federal instrumentalities are the Inter-Governmental Council, National Economic Development Council, Finance Commission, and Planning Commission, all proposed to be invested with constitutional status, permanent existence, and regular secretariats.[27] Of these four bodies, the first two are political and economic in scope representing the executive branches of the two levels of the government, with the Prime Minister chairing. The latter two bodies consist of experts nominated by the Union Executive. So far, only the recommendations relating to the IGC has been implemented in 1990 under Article 263 of the constitution that had thus far remained unused. A National Development Council exists, but it does not have a constitutional status. The Planning Commission continues to be a creature of the Union Executive without a constitutional entrenchment. The Finance Commission does enjoy a constitutional status, but it is presently appointed by the President only in every five years to recommend on the patterns of sharing finances between the Central and State governments.

Democratic Decentralization

"Democratic decentralization" in India has come to mean two things: (1) strengthening of local political systems as contrasted with the national and state political systems; and (2) decentralized planning involving local participation. A huge corpus of political and administrative thought has accumulated in India since independence on these two inter-related dimensions. But most of it still remains ideological and rhetorical with scanty implementation.

Local Political Systems

The important landmarks in the evolution of local politics in the post-Independence period are the Community Development projects initiated with much fanfare in 1952, the Balwantrai Mehta Committee Report on Democratic Decentralization (1957), the Panchayati Raj Acts in the late 1950s and 1960s in various states mostly modelled on the Balwantrai Mehta Committee Report on Panchayati Raj (1957)[28], and the Panchayati Raj and Nagarpalika constitutional Amendment Bills (1989) proposed by the Rajiv Gandhi government towards the end of its mandate, but defeated by the opposition majority in the Rajya Sabha. The idea was put into the constitution by the Congress minority government headed by P.V. Narasimha Rao in the form of the 73rd and 74th Amendments (1992-93). These amendments are models, like the Directive Principles which become binding on States only when the State Legislatures enact them into State laws. All States have revamped their Panchayati Raj institutions by now.

The Balwantrai Mehta Committee Report recommended a three-tier structure of Panchayati Raj. The Asok Mehta Committee Report expressed preference for a two-tier structure.[29] Most existing Panchayati Raj Acts enacted by various state legislatures still follow the three-tier structure of rural local self-governing bodies below the state level. Typically, there are councils at district, block, and village-cluster levels, known by various nomenclatures and semantically close to, say, Zila Parishad, Panchayat Samiti, and Gram Panchayat. The most frequently lamented malaise of Panchayati Raj are: (1) their non-functioning character; (2) conflict between the elected heads of the councils and the civil officials; and (3) domination of Panchayati Raj Acts bodies by the dominant castes and classes in collusion with the officials such that the development funds are siphoned off, resulting in infrastructural developments only on paper and depriving the depressed demographic targets of development. To an extent, these three charges are contradictory. If PR bodies are non-functioning, there would be little bone of contention between the officials and representatives. And, if they are in collusion with each other, there cannot be much conflict among them. The basic problem is that PR bodies are still waiting for a firm institutional functioning. Their inadequate performance is at least partly due to the failure on the part of state governments to devolve more powers and revenues to them. Besides, the voluntaristic vitality of the Indian rural society is presently at a low ebb.

However, there has recently been enthusiastic discussion of a more successful attempt at reviving the Panchayat Raj in at least three states: West Bengal, Karnataka, and Andhra Pradesh. Moreover, the lot of these bodies appears to be relatively better also in Gujarat and Maharashtra than in many other states. West Bengal's Left Front government showed, even without structural reforms, a state government willing to hold regular elections and involve panchayats in development work and land reforms can make a qualitative improvement in the situation. The Janata government in Karnataka and the Telugu Desam government in Andhra Pradesh brought about new Panchayat Raj legislations in the 1980s. The Karnataka Zila Parishad and Mandai Panchayat Act (1985) established a three-tier structure with a Zila Parishad, Taluk Panchayat Samiti, and Mandal Panchayat. The Zila Parishad is the key-body in the structure and is partly elected and partly nominated. Its *Adhyaksha* (Chairman) is elected from amongst its members for a term of five years and receives the salary of a Minister of State. From the official side, the Chief Secretary of the Zila Parishad is a bureaucrat of the rank of a Deputy Commissioner. The new PR Act (1986) in Andhra Pradesh also established a three-tier structure with a Zila Praia Parishad, a Mandai Praja Parishad, and a Gram Panchayat. Alongside the Zila Praja Parishads at the district level, there are Pranalika Abhivrudhi Mandals (District Planning and Development Councils), since then replaced by Abhivrudhi Sameekasha (Review) Mandals (1987) in response to the criticism that in its earlier form it overshadowed and weakened the Zila Praja Parishads and, thus, went against the spirit of democratic decentralization. The Zila Praja Parishad consists of a Chairman (directly elected), Presidents of MandaI Praja Parishads of the district, and Members of the Parliament and Members of the Legislative Assemblies from the district without voting right. In addition to local taxes and grants from government and non-governmental agencies, the main source of fund for Zila Parishads is a certain per capita grant from state governments in both Karnataka and Andhra Pradesh. The Karnataka Act provides for the appointment of a Finance Commission by the state government to recommend on the financing of PR bodies.[30] The post-73rd Amendment (1993) conforming laws largely maintain these features.

The Asok Mehta Committee Report is emphatic on the district as the key-unit in PR and local level planning, and directs elections to these bodies, and adequate transfer of funds to them. To deliberate on the recommendations of this Committee, a Chief Ministers' conference was called in Delhi in August 1979. As a sequel to this, the Centre prepared a model PR Acts, but most States are yet to bring about a properly modelled enactment.[31]

Municipal governments in India are also, by and large, in a state of decay. Outside the metropolitan cities, corporations, and municipalities are mostly superseded and corrupted to the core. Administratively, they are not entirely non-functioning, though they operate at subsistence level outside the VIP areas. Their representative character is in double jeopardy because of frequent superseding and overly delayed elections.[32] However, two aspects of city government and politics in India point to a newly emerging scenario and deserves close observation.

First, the metropolitan cities in India are emerging as an important element in the federal dynamics. They often directly enter into negotiations with the federal government not always intermediated by the State government. Secondly, they are acquiring demographic profile and cultural orientation that are often at variance with those of the States in which they are located. Though this often leads to tensions and conflicts between the ethnics dominant in the State and the migrants from other cultural regions or States to the city (e.g., the Maharashtrian Shiv Sena in Bombay and their anti-South and anti-North Indian stance and activities), yet it also reflects the emerging cosmopolitan culture in the metros. They may, in due course, become the nuclei of a new identity and orientation common all over the nation cutting across linguistic, religious, and tribal identities. But the progress in this direction is slowed by the tendency of ethnic migrants to the city to settle in ghettos of ethnically grouped new colonies, maintenance of strong social and economic bonds with the folks back home, and nativistic political movements by the locals, that is, Shiv Sena in Bombay. It may appear too far-fetched to visualize a territorial reorganization of India dispensing with the present state boundaries in favour of metropolitan zones cutting across ethnic and cultural boundaries.

Decentralized Planning

Decentralized planning has been a creed of planning thought in this country almost since the beginning of the planning process.[33] There is, however, very little practice of it below the state level yet. Lack of will at the state level, lack of initiative and skills at the grassroots level despite growing levels of education and politicization are the main hurdles to decentralized planning. There are conflicting views on the proper area-unit for decentralized planning in more or less appropriate units by various protagonist. But, a wider consensus seems to be developing in favour of the district as a planning unit. Commenting on the practice in various states, a former member of the national Planning Commission observed:

> "Whatever decentralized planning that is practised at the distinct level, is done essentially by the bureaucracy by putting together the various schemes undertaken by the different departments within the parameters set at the state level. In quite a few cases, this can even be descended as district planning done at the state level. Even planning at a regional level such as for hill areas in Uttar Pradesh is reduced essentially to the putting together of schemes undertaken by various departments at the state level and at best monitoring of the flow of resources into the region on account of such schemes."[34]

Nonetheless, the need for decentralized planning for a more appropriate use and distribution of resources with local/grassroots participation can hardly be gained.

Concluding Observations

To conclude, we examined India's political dynamics through the conceptual prisms of a combination of parliamentary and federal institutional imperatives. What has emerged from our analysis is that, though the 1950 constitution continues to be a predominantly parliamentary one with subsidiary federal features, the political system in its actual working has been becoming more federal than a mere reading of the constitutional text may imply. There is also a growing pressure for a greater federalization of the system by constitutional amendments. In this concluding section, we intend to argue that we may indeed go further and see the ongoing political ferment in terms of the conceptual polarities of majoritarianism versus consensus models of democratic politics.[35] The consensus model seeks to break the majoritarian ethos of parliamentary democracy by a multiplicity of mechanisms for generating consensus by fabricating pluralities or concurrent "majorities". Federalism itself is only one of such devices. Other emerging features of this consensus model may be noted in passing: recourse to coalition and/or minority governments, judicial activism, and the growing reliance of the system on the judiciary for settling not only inter-state and federal disputes, but also those arising in ethnic diversities and class and regional disparities of the society. Prime Minister P.V. Narasimha Rao's preference for the flexibility of consultations on some issues in the National Integration Council and all-party meetings over exclusively formal bodies, like the Inter-Government Council, reliance on technocrats over politicians for policy-making in the areas of finance, agricultural pricing, and so on. David Taylor sees in Hindu political revivalism and resurgence of Bharatiya Janata Party (BJP) in the late 1980s and early 1990s, a trend towards "social majoritarianism."[36] This is indeed a reaction against the consensus model gradually evolving since Independence. The Congress predommance in the Nehru and pre-1977 Indira Gandhi eras was indeed built on a voting bloc of minorities: Muslims, Sikhs, Harijans, and tribals. The Hindu communal leaders tended to decry it as "minorityism".

The present political ferment and the gathering conflicts may also be seen as the building up of a tension between the representative and participatory strains of the Indian political system. What makes the situation particularly difficult is that the system is facing overwhelming participatory pressures at the same time as it is still struggling to establish its representative character. Representative institutions established under the constitution are facing a trial due to the vitiation of the electoral process by money and muscle-power, criminalization of politics, pervasive political corruption, bossism in political parties, religious fundamentalism, separatism and terrorism, and persisting social and regional disparities. Participatory demands have been mounting enormous pressures in the form of social and political movements of all kinds: agrarian class radicalism of Communist Party of India (Marxist-Leninist) or the so-called "Naxalites", communal revivalist and secessionist militant organizations in Jammu and Kashmir and Assam, "demand groups"[37] of peasants and industrial workers, environmentalists and grassroots mobilization groups. The party system and institutions of representative democracy are yet to come to terms with these participatory pressures in a coherent and institutionalized pattern. Only a concerted strategy of institutional reforms with an accent on federalization and electoral and party reforms alongside a sustained economic development would enable the system to tide over the persisting political and economic crises.

Notes and References

1. K.R. Bombwall, *The Foundations of Indian Federalism* (Bombay: Asia Publishing House, 1967), ch. 1, surveys a wide range of interpretations of the Indian federal Union and makes the above point. Granville Austin. *The Indian constitution: Cornerstone of a Nation* (Bombay: Oxford University Press, 1966) calls Indian federalism "the amicable union"; it goes on to argue: "The (Constituent) Assembly, in fact, produced a new kind of federalism to meet India's peculiar needs" (p. 186).
2. Romila Thapar, *From Lineage to State: Social Formation in the First Millennium B.C. in the Ganga Valley* (Bombay: Oxford University Press, 1984) mentions Kuru-Pancala, Licchavis, and Vrjjis as *ganasanghas* (approximately, republican-federations) rather than full-fledged monarchies (p. 69).
3. The post-Shivaji Maratha state in the 18th century showed tendency towards the evolution of a new type of state in medieval India in which the Maratha ruler with his capital at Satara was reduced to being a nominal monarchy, while the hereditary prime minister, the Peshwa, "established his own government at Poona, which was *de jure* subordinate to, but *de-facto* dominant of Satara; hence a diarchy at the Central government". See H. Fukazawa, "Maharashtra and the Deccan: A Note", in Tapan Raychaudhuri and Irfan Habib (eds.). *The Cambridge Economic History of India, Vol. I,* c. *1200-c. 1750* (New Delhi: Orient Longman in association with Cambridge University Press, 1982), pp. 198–99.
4. Chetakar Jha, *Indian Government and Politics: A Political Commentary* (Patna: Novelty & Co., 1960), ch. l. For the text of the manifesto, see A.M. Zaidi (ed.), *Promises to Keep: Election Manifestos of Indian National Congress,* 1937-1985 (New Delhi: Indian Institute of Applied Research, 1986), pp. 24–32.
5. Harish K. Puri, "Centre-State Relations in India: A review of Sarkaria Commission Report". *Punjab Journal of Politics,* Vol. XIII, Nos. 1-2 (1989), p. 34.
6. The "purest" case, unconfounded by other factors, illustrating this point is the Left Front governments in West Bengal ruling since 1977 undisturbed by the Presidential Damocles' sword. Tamil Nadu's All India Anna DMK CMs M.G. Ramacharndran and Jayalalitha enjoyed a similar peace, but that was more because of their alliance with the Congress party ruling at the Centre.
7. The recent roles of Governors S.S. Barnala in Tamil Nadu and M.M. Thomas in Nagaland are cases in point. Both showed some independence from the Centre. This raised furors in the Parliament and the Press, indicting their conducts as violative of the spirit of the constitution. Both had to go. Barnala resigned while Thomas was removed.
8. This Weberian term was earlier used in the context of Indian federalism in the Indira Gandhi era by Bhagwan D. Dua, "Federalism or Patrimonialism: The Making and Unmaking of Chief Ministers in India". *Asian Survey,* Vol. XXV, No. 8 (August 1985).

For an authoritative exposition of "patrimonialism", see Reinhard Bendix, *Max Weber. An Intellectual Portrait* (Berkeley: University of California Press, 1977), p. 345.

9. On Rajendra Prasad, see Granville Austin, *The Indian constitution: Cornerstone of a Nation, op. cit.*, pp. 139–143. On the Zail Singh episode, see *India Today*, Vol. XIII. No. 7 (15th April 1988), pp. 72–8o; and *Link*, Vol. 29, No. 40 (10 May 19B7), pp. 6–8.
10. Examples of Presidential references to the Supreme Court for its advisory opinion are: (1) Delhi Laws Act, 1912; Ajmer Merwara Extension of Laws Act, 1947; Part C States Laws Act, 1950; (2) Kerala Education Bill, 1957; (3) the transfer of the Berubari Union to Pakistan and Cooch Behar enclaves to India by an Indo-Pakistan Prime Ministers' agreement in 1960; (4) the Union Bill to amend the Sea Customs Act, 1878, and the Central Excise Act, 1944, in 1963, (5) Parliamentary/legislative privileges or the Keshav Singh case in 1964; (6) abolition of privy purses or *Madhav Rao Scindia v. Union of India* Case, 1970; (7) Presidential election, 1974, (8) Special Courts for Emergency Excesses bill, 1978; (9) Jammu and Kashmir Settlement Bill, 1982; (10) Cauvery Water dispute, 1990s. The reference up to 1978 are discussed in Pushpa Bali. *The Advisory Jurisdiction of the Supreme Court of India* (M. Phil, dissertation in Political Science, University of Delhi, 1980). The latest case in the Satluj-Jamuna link canal dispute between Punjab, Haryana, and Rajasthan in 2004.
11. See for example, Article 13, 370, 371A, 371G, Seventh Schedule, List II, State List; Ninth Schedule, substitution of the American constitutional doctrine of "due process of law" by that of "procedure established by law" in Article 21; Article 13(4), Article 31A., etc.
12. For a more detailed and authentic version of these judgements, see the volumes of the All India Reporter for respective years. For the most well-rounded view of the Supreme Court's exposition of the limitations on Parliament's amending power in some essential features of the "basic structure" of the constitution, see *Minerva Mills Ltd. v. Union of India in AIR, (1980)*, Supreme Court Section. Vol. 67 especially, pp. 1795–1811.
13. Giovanni Sartori, *Parties and Party Systems:* A *Framework for Analysis*, Vol. I, Cambridge: Cambridge University Press, 1976, ch. 6.
14. Not all these phases of party system evolution are adequately conceptualized and analysed. The better studied phases are Nos. (1), (2), (3), (4), and (6). See Rajni Kothari, *Politics in India* (New Delhi): Orient Longman, 1970), ch. 5: W.H. Morris-Jones, *Politics Mainly Indian* (New Delhi: Orient Longman, 1978 for No. 1. See M.P. Singh, *Split in a Predominant Party: The Indian National Congress in* 1969 (New Delhi: Abhinav, 1981), ch. 4, for No. 2; the Rudolphs, *In Pursuit of Lakshmi; The Political Economy of the Indian State* (New Delhi: Orient Longman, 1987), chs. 4 & 5 for Nos. 3 & 4 and M.P. Singh, "To Govern or Not to Govern? The Dilemma of the New Indian Party System", *Asian Survey*, Vol. XXXII. No. 4 (April 1992) for the early years of Nos. 6.
15. *Report of the Finance Commission*, 1978, p. 146, an abstracted Table reproduced in Prabodh Kumar Jha, *Federal Finance in Developing India*, Delhi: Capital, 1983, p. 281.
16. Hemlata Rao, *Centre-State Financial Relations: Criteria of Federal Fiscal Transfers and Their Application in India* (New Delhi: Allied, 1981), ch. 2.
17. Prabodh Kumar Jha, *op. cit.*, p. 137.
18. Hemlata Rao, *op. cit.*, ch. 2.
19. Government of India, *First Report of the Ninth Finance Commission* (For 1989-90) (New Delhi: Ministry of Finance Press, July 1988), p. 29. See also Hemlata Rao, "Financial Relations", *Seminar*, No. 357 (May 1989), a special symposium issue on Indian federalism.
20. Amal Ray, "New Economic Policy and Indian Federalism", *Working Paper-II*, Bangalore, Indian Institute of Management, no date, pp. 6–7. The passage by Ray

is from John Kincaid, "From Cooperative to Coercive Federalism", *The Annals of the American Academy*, May 1990.

21. *Asian Recorder*, Vol. XXXVIII, No. 4, 22-28, January, 1992, pp. 22113–4.
22. Rasheeduddin Khan, *Federal India: A Design for Change,* New Delhi, Vikas Publishing House, 1992, p. 57.
23. Government of India, Commission on Centre-State Relations (Chairman Justice R.S. Sarkaria), *Report, Part I,* Nasik: Government of India Press, 1988, ch. 5.
    For an evaluation of the recommendations of the Sarkaria Commission Report, see M.P. Singh, "Whither Indian Federalism? The Sarkaria Commission Report and Beyond". *Punjab Journal of Politics,* Vol. XIII, Nos. 1-2, 1989, pp. 17–31.
24. Douglas V. Verney, "Responsible Government and Responsible Federalism: Parliamentary Government in Plural Societies", *Typescript,* Department of Political Science, York University, Toronto, 1990, p. 14.
25. Rajni Kothari, *Democratic Policy and Social Change in India: Crisis and Opportunities,* Bombay, Allied Publishers, 1976, p. 106.
26. W.R. Morris-Jones, *Parliament in India* (London: Longmans, Green, 1957), did not find much relevance for the Rajya Sabha as a *federal* second chamber on account of its weak power and its representation to the states proportional to population rather than on the basis of equality as federating States irrespective of their size, even though it is indirectly elected by state assemblies. Even as a *Parliament's* second chamber. Morris-Jones did not find the Rajya Sabha much relevant or useful. For similar to the Lok Sabha in members' socia-economic and political career backgrounds and the Houses' rules of procedure the Rajya Sabha "provides neither for technical revision nor for a wider and more leisurely debate", p. 257.
27. Sarkaria Commission Report, *op. cit.*, ref. 24. Each of the 21 chapters are surned up as major recommendations at the end.
28. See G. Rama Reddy, *Patterns of Panchayati Raj in India,* Delhi, Macmillan, 1977; and R.B. Jain (ed.), *Panchanyati Raj,* New Delhi, Indian Institute of Public Administration, 1981.
29. Government of India, *Report of the Committee on Panchayati Raj Institutions* (New Delhi Ministry of Agriculture and Irrigation, Department of Rural Development, 1978, (Chairman Asoka Mehta), pp. 4–6.
30. S.N. Mishra, "New Thrust in Democratic Decentralization" *Typescript,* New Delhi, Indian Institute of Public Administration, 1987.
31. *Ibid.*
32. Study of city politics in India is yet to become a mainstream concern in Indian political analysis, at any rate to the same extent as the study of rural politics. For some good early case studies, see Ali Ashraf, *The City Government of Calcutta: A Study of Inertia,* Bombay, Asia Publishing House, 1966 published for Institute of Public Administration, New York); Donald B. Rosenthal (ed.). *The City in Indian Politics,* Faridabad: Thompson Press (India) Limited, 1976, etc.
33. As in the area of Panchayati Raj, there exists a great deal of administrative thought and enthusiasm among Indian administrators and academics about decentralized planning. See among others, M. Vivekananda, *Planning Unit Areas for Integrated Rural Development* (New Delhi: Ashish Publishing House, 1980); Shreekant Sambrani and K.R. Pichholia, *Area Planning: Precepts and Practices* Ahmedabad: Centre for Management of Agriculture, Indian Institute of Management, 1983; and Kamta Prasad, *Planning at the Grass-Roots,* New Delhi: Sterling Publishers, 1988.
34. C.R. Hanumantha Rao, "Decentralized Planning: An overview of Experience and Prospects in India" *Typescript* of a paper presented at the National Seminar on Nation-Building, Development Process and Communication: In Search of India's Renaissance, New Delhi, 3-7 December, 1988, p. 11.

35. For conceptual theoretical elaboration of the "majoritarian" and "consensus" models of democracy, see Arend Lijphart, *Democracies: Patterns of Majoritarian and Concensus Government in Twenty-One Countries,* New Haven: Yale University Press, 1984.
36. David Taylor made this point in a talk on Democracy in South Asia in the Department of Political Science, University of Delhi, in March 1992.
37. Lloyd and Susanne Rudolph, In *Pursuit of Lakshmi: The Political Economy of the Indian State, op. cit.*, ref. 14, have formulated the concept of "demand groups" to emphasize the differece between the pressure group politics in India, where such groups often tend to take recourse to direct action or politics of the street in pursuit of their demands, and such politics in the U.S. based on lobbying through institutional channels.

9

Federalism: Elite and Nationalities

Himanshu Roy

This chapter discusses Indian federalism, primarily, in terms of movements launched by people in the pre-and post-independence India under the banners of different political organizations or independent of them against the 'democratic centralism' of the ruling class, and for the decentralization of power-economic and political, not in the narrow sense of the words, Centre and provinces, Union territories and autonomous councils which are merely the forms of the essence. But in a broad sense, this means that the right of the people to decide their own destiny. The chapter analyses the roles of different classes and their interests both in pre-and post-independence period. The chapter, however, presents only the broad contours of class relations between the various sections of bourgeoisie, on the one hand, and between the bourgeoisie and the masses, on the other, that are cloaked under federalism since 1935, when for the first time, it was partly actuated as a political programme. The paper does not belittle the traditional approach of looking at federalism from constitutional paradigm which has its own value.

To begin with, federalism, as we understand it today, came into existence after the emergence of capitalism as a dominant mode of production. Its formation in a given society was the result of various factors which need elucidation. But the most important out of it is the importance of market under capitalism. The treatment of society as market and individual as consumer are the requirements of capitalism for the sale of commodities. This compels the owners of commodities to be ever in search of new markets; but simultaneously, they equally require control over their old markets for the same reason as noted above. These twin necessities bring the competing bourgeoisie (unequal/equal) within a nation or of different states to a market sharing arrangement. As a result, they enter into a written contract among themselves and set up an entire paraphernalia of state woven around it with certain powers to intervene in case of dispute. The taxes, area of market, etc., to be shared among different sections of the bourgeoisie, however, themselves depend upon their respective strengths and bargaining power. The more powerful a section, the greater the share it enjoys over the market area, taxes, etc., and the vice-versa. Here, a rider may be added while discussing the roles of various sections of bourgeoisie within a nation. In societies such as India, where capitalism arrived late on the historical scene due to many, complex, interwoven factors, there emerged two sections in the Indian bourgeoisie—oligopoly and regional. It was their economic and political strengths in the given circumstances that ultimately decided the nature of their sharing arrangement of market, taxes, etc.[1] In the American case, which is considered as classical, the situation was somewhat different. Beginning their history with capitalism, that too as one of the precursors and without facing the nightmare of past generations, the emergence of bourgeoisie as a class for itself was early in history. At the time of their constitution in 1787, they were untouched with the phenomenon of oligopoly versus regional. On the contrary, it were the equal, competing bourgeoisie of different sovereign states that came together to create a central executive committee with only those powers that were required to protect the collective interests of all regions, while keeping the powers of their regional committees intact, except, for those which were transferred to the centre. Therefore, even after decades of capitalist development that subsumed many powers of the region there are still substantial powers left with the regional committees. But, despite the differences between the two societies, India and the USA, the twin necessities of the bourgeoisie as enumerated earlier remain common. Coming back to the basic, the contract entered into among the bourgeoisie is, by and large, irrevocable until and unless the secessionist bourgeoisie emerge powerful enough to break away from the main body either through bullet or ballot.[2] In political terms, this contract for them is called 'federalism'. It is defined as a polity where power between centre and provinces are divided through written constitution. In federalism, constitution is supreme, and where there exists an independent judiciary bestowed with the powers, granted by the constitution, to dispense justice in case of dispute either between provinces or between provinces or centre. The history, however, does not terminate here; rather it begins in the sense that the great mass of society begin to play assertive role in the body politics. Here, it will be appropriate to add that in the formation of federal polity, apart from the roles of dominant classes which are decisive, there are also other factors, such as pursuit of political power either by individuals or political parties that come into the play.

The bourgeoisie, the most enlightened class of the society, and revolutionary in character in the given period of history, helped in training the great mass of society against economic and social oppressions in their fight against feudalism and colonial capitalism. This training further sharpened by the new social milieu unleashed by capitalism, either through revolutionary technological development, socialisation of productive forces, new work culture or modern education, has now turned out to be a political Frankenstein for the bourgeoisie. The Lockean concept of democracy was compelled to shed its form under the constant onslaught of this trained mass. From 'democratic centralism' of the Lockean variety the polity turned towards democratic decentralism of the Ruosseausque variety, not wholly but considerably. The ideology of Utilitarianism and Positive Liberalism helped in 'liberalising democracy and democratising liberalism' to use Macphersonian metaphor in the early phase of mass struggle. Later on, Marxism as an ideology and praxis fixed the death knell on the Lockean form of democracy in different stages, in different societies. The bourgeoisie, however, are not a bunch of fools who granted politically decentralized polity to the masses on a platter. In fact, there have been long, arduous battles between the economic and brute coercive force of the bourgeoisie, on the one hand, and the numerical strength of the masses, on the other, for the empowerment of people. Ultimately, it was the strength of the masses that tilted the power equations in their favour, in stages, after many defeats. The bourgeoisie in the changed social milieu thought better to throw some political crumbs in order to keep their property relations intact which is primary to them. It was also designed to localise the issue rather than let it become social. Federalism, thus, an integral part and one of the forms of political democracy formed in particular circumstances become a mass reality.

In India, in its political form, it began with the Lucknow Conference of the Congress in 1916 where federalism was accepted, for the first time, as the future polity of India and was incorporated in the political and constitutional programmes. In 1920, the Congress accepted the principle of linguistic provinces[3] under the pressure of the nationalities, which was an indirect recognition to the nationality question that was asserting for the formation of linguistic provinces. In 1927, the Government of India and India Office were flooded with memoranda for recognition of nationalities (Oriya, Kannada, Andhara, Tamil, Bengali and Jharkhand) and formation of linguistic provinces.[4] They were requested to forward these memoranda to the Simon Commission which was set up to suggest the future shape of the Indian polity. Earlier, in 1921, the Madras, Bihar, and Orissa Legislative Councils had accepted, in principle, the formation of linguistic provinces.[5] In 1942, in the Quit Indian resolution, the Congress promised, "the largest measure of autonomy for the federating units"[6]. The crux came in 1946 when the Dravid Kazagham submitted a memorandum to the Cabinet Mission asking for sovereign, independent Dravidstan[7] and the Communist Party of India (CPI) proposed for "17 sovereign National Constituent Assemblies based on the national homelands of various Indian peoples"[8] and stood for "a voluntary union of national states". The Congress, too, promised for a federation based on the "willing union of its various parts", the parts themselves being constituted on the necessary homogeneity of language and culture.[9] After the partition and transfer of power, the Congress, however, turned renegade. It abhorred the very principle of 'willing union', 'willing partners' and linguistic provinces that it had promised in its election manifesto of 1946. Though the concept of 'willing union' was not to be decided by the plebiscitary politics at the grassroots by the Constituent Assembly dominated by the Congress which, in turn, was controlled by the High Command yet the quantum of autonomy envisaged in the manifesto was substantial. The Congress in post-partition phase opposed the concept of linguistic provinces and all that on the ground that they will fan up sub-national consciousness, the existing administrative setup is a good instrument for country's unity which has taken root like a living vital organisms and has served the useful purpose of bringing people together. It viewed the demand of linguistic provinces as separatist and disruptive tendency to be rigorously discouraged.[10] The States Reorganisation Commission appointed in 1953 almost reiterated the same reasons.[11] The mass pressure, however, compelled the government to recognize the provinces on the linguistic principle first, in 1956 and subsequently, in 1971 and in 1987.[12] Not only that the government was on further compelled to create different categories of Councils within the existing provinces under the series of Accords it signed with the leaders of the movements that took place from time to time in different pockets of the country the last three being the Leh, Jharkhand and Bodoland Councils.

Administratively, the process of democratic decentralization in India began from the 1892 Act when the country was a British colony. The subsequent Acts of 1909,1919 and 1935 provided further impetus to the process. The enactment of these Acts were the product of sustained mass pressure that grew under the leadership of the Congress demanding, first, political reforms, and then, *Swarajya*, and, finally, *Purna Swarajya*. Under these Acts, there was ever-increasing participation of the people in the election process as the restrictions on participation were gradually eased up under the subsequent Acts. The formation of a limited federal polity under the 1935 Act that was implemented only in the British provinces (and not at the Centre and in the princely states) was the culmination of the decentralization process in colonial India. Under this Act elections were conducted for the formation of the elected provincial government in which the Congress participated under its declared strategy of 'pressure-compromise-pressure' or 'struggle-truce-struggle'. The Act laid the essence of the federalized polity for independent India that was created between 1946-49. After 1947, except for some cosmetic changes, the substance of the 1935 Act remained the same. The most perceptible change was the right granted to all people transcending property and educational qualifications to elect representatives for governance under the Indian constitution in 1950. But in practice, even this right became a caricature as the role of muscle and money-power increased in the after-independence years. It is a well-known fact that the poor strata of rural India particularly, considerable sections of Scheduled Castes and

OBCs were denied participation in electoral process. And as the standard of politics itself degenerated to the level of 'animal politics', there was nothing constitutional to safeguard even this right, except for the Moral code of Conduct of the Election Commission which, till few years ago, was a whimper. The judiciary, the branch of the executive committee has, by and large, remained only a moot spectator. Actually, the centre is so power-packed that right from altering the boundaries of the provinces to dismissing the provincial governments, and from appointing the governors, to distributing the taxes to the states it can do anything except for dissolving the masses. This situation compels the students of Indian federalism studying it from traditional approach to call it 'quasi-federalism'. Few, however, have dared to call it 'cooperative federalism'. The explanation of this dichotomy lies in understanding the social forces that shaped the constitution.

In the decades after the 1820s, the modern pan-Indian elites began to emerge on the politico-economic firmament of the country along with the elites of different nationalities in different geographical parts of the country. The Free Trade era and later on, the Industrial Age broke down the secluded village life of the pre-capitalist society and helped in the development of two simultaneous trends, pan-Indianness and nationality formation, reinforcing each other on the same plane. The formation of the nationalities in the earlier stages of the capitalist development was concentrated mainly in the coastal regions and in some other pockets of the country and from among these nationalities emerged: the members of the pan-Indian elite, but mostly dominated by Gujrati, Marwari and Parsi traders and industrialists. While "the national movement was built up by harnessing the forces of regionalism",[13] as the States Reorganization Commission of 1953-55 was later on to observe in its report, the nationalities pressurized the pan-Indian elites to agree to their demands and then, together they fought the British for their joint interests. The separation of Bihar and Orissa from Bengal and, later on, of Orissa from Bihar, agreement over the formation of linguistic provinces and distribution of power between centre and provinces as envisaged in the Cabinet Mission Plan were integral part of this phenomenon. Nationality formation in India, contrary to the general understanding, did not precede the pan-Indian formation. In fact, as stated here, both kinds of formations emerged simultaneously. What actually happened as a result of the uneven capitalist development was the formation of some nationalities earlier, while the others were yet to emerge which could materialize only after the post-independence era and when capitalism expanded in other backward regions. The regional, historical identities of language, culture, phyche, etc., began to coalesce under the new productive powers, economy and administrative set-up that led to the formation of nationalities. But, simultaneously under the same condition, they also began to transcend their nationality barriers. It was only then that the Congress could come into existence in 1885 which was like a United Front in which different nationalities along with the pan-Indian elites came together to fight the principal contradiction, the British, while being equally protective about their own interests. And over the years it developed into a well-knit pressure-compromise-pressure arrangement based on 'mutual convenience', as Aladi Aruna, the spokesman and the then Law Minister in the DMK government was later on to say on the autonomy of nationalities and India's unity.[14] Not only that the two determinants grew in strength and balanced each other till partition and transfer of power disrupted the evolving structure and helped in establishing the absolute hegemony of the pan-Indian bourgeoisie. The legacy of development till 1946, however, could not be obliterated. Pressure of nationalities, once again, started building up for concessions first, in the form of constituting linguistic provinces and various categories of Councils and second, in the demand of financial and administrative autonomy. But the most important legacy was that there was no emergence of one or a group of nationalities dominating over the rest; neither was there any constitutional administrative, political or economic discrimination against anyone based on the nationality. Even the imposition of Hindi as the official language of the country had, for all practical purposes, no impact.

All these political struggles among the two sections of the bourgeois or among the bourgeoisie of different nationalities were essentially the reflections of their economic contradictions hidden beneath the labyrinth of autonomy/secession versus centralism/unity, linguistic province vs. existing provinces, etc. In fact, politics for them was merely an instrument to be used to deliver the economic goods which were best reflected in their business associations and chambers of commerce fighting each other for the supremacy over market, trade and commerce industries, and revenue. For an instance, the Federation of Indian Chambers of Commerce and Industry (FICCI) dominated by the pan-Indian bourgeoisie, in a communication to the Department of Planning and Development, Government of India, "opposed the principle of regionalization of industries"[15] and urged that the "private enterprises should be given the full freedom and facilities to establish industries in places most suitable for such development".[16] The Southern India Chamber of Commerce (SICCI) dominated by the Chettiars, on the other hand, "contended that economic planning should have not an all India, but a provincial basis."[17] It urged the Madras government, on the eve of the budget session in 1946, to "do everything possible to improve the trade and industries and help to retain as big a slice of them as possible for the benefit of the sons of the soil."[18] Similarly, the bourgeoisie of the Andhra nationality represented by the Andhra Chamber of Commerce resented "the indifference shown towards Andhra Commercial, industrial and banking interests by the Southern Indian Chamber of Commerce,"[19] represented by the Tamil bourgeoisie. The transfer of power in 1947, finally, established the supremacy of the pan-Indian bourgeoisie by providing them exclusive control over "banking, insurance, stock exchanges, petroleum, mining and airways, most initiative in industry and finace."[20] They, nevertheless, coopted the bourgeoisie of different nationalities, in phases, as per their strength.

The formation of nationalities and the pan-Indian community at the level of labouring masses- the hoipolloi- too began, like the bourgeoisie, simultaneously under the new productive forces, economy and administrative set up. At the one hand, the destruction of their cottage industries and uprootment from soil, their migration to towns and conversion into, mostly, wage-earners were compelling them to coalesce under the historical identities, at least, in the initial years of their new vocation, in order to fight for their livelihood against the oppressors, principally, the British; on the other-hand, their fight against the British or even against the Indian bourgeoisie was bringing them closer to other nationalities which was further accentuated by the modern transportation and the living conditions of the cities. Those who were still in the villages, too, did not remain unaffected. The gradual expansion of market economy and its impacts were constantly felt by them. Coupled with these factors, the role of the media, modern education, and the alienating role of the administration hastened the process. Consequently, from the first decade of the 20th century the pan-Indian feelings made their presence felt which were ultimately visible in the success of the political movements which, in turn, were possible only when people transcended their barriers of nationalities. But, equally important is the point that this pan-Indian feeling were still nascent and restricted to a narrow percentage of population in relation to the total strength of the country. Women in villages, tribals, outcastes, and vast sections of peasantry were still out of its fold. They were more rooted in their history, culture, language and local needs. Even the first generation wage-earners, industrial and non-industrial, had deep roots in their castes and nationalities; and it were these factors that kept on pressing the British and pan-Indian bourgeoisie not only for linguistic provinces and their autonomy/secession, but also lead to quarrels among the nationalities such, for example, as between Bengalis and Biharis in the first decade of the 20th century. Mishra and Pandey have provided a fine analysis in their book[21] of the various factors that led to the movement in Bihar for its separation from Bengal. One of the factors was the decline of agriculture as a source of livelihood and absence of private enterprises which could have substituted the agriculture as a source of livelihood. So the only course left for the Biharis, particularly the educated ones was to join the government service which was dominated by the Bengalis. And unless Bihar becomes a separate province they could not hope to find jobs. This was resented by Bengalis as they perceived that separation of Bihar will hamper their job prospects. Consequently, they opposed the separation of Bihar from Bengal. This led to acrimony and bitterness between the two nationalities. The second factor was the identity crisis of the Biharis who had no separate recognition independent of Bengalis. Sachidanand Sinha, one of the prominent leaders of Bihar, has given a vivid account of the humiliation he faced in England.[22] Bengalis too looked upon Biharis with contempt which created serious resentment among them. All these factors ultimately led to the movement for creation of a separate province of Bihar.

In the last decade of the 20th century, though the situation was vastly different from that of colonial India, but still we find a replica of the past occurring in the pockets of India which are relatively backward as they witnessed the arrival of capitalism at a later stage. It is true that under the rule of the Indian bourgeoisie, in an unequal collaboration with the Transnational Corporations, the society has made vast strides in productive forces, economy and administrative set up yet due to the uneven sectarian growth there are numerous pockets of India which are still lagging far behind either in infrastructural facilities, job opportunities or in administrative efficiency. There is no doubt that today's peasantry, wage-earners, women, tribals, dalits, etc., are no longer the same as they used to be in the 1920's or in the 1940's having undergone substantial transformation in the mobility, economic condition and consciousness, yet their condition in the tribal and hilly areas are not at par with the rest of India. They are still rooted in their historical identities. The pan-Indian feeling, which today exist in greater percentage of population and in greater geographical parts, do not sway them much. Neither the formation of the linguistic provinces, which lessened the contradictions of the older nationalities, have solved their problems. They are yet to finalize their relationships with the Indian bourgeoisie as majority of the older nationalities did. Though after the formation of the different categories of councils with different quantum of power bestowed to them, some of them have settled down with their new administrative and economic arrangements, like Gorkhas in Gorkhland, Laddakhis in Leh, etc., yet there are many who are agitating for separate provinces or seeking secession, such as United Liberation Front of Assam (ULFA) in Assam, or National Socialist Council of Nagaland (NSCN) for greater Nagaland, etc. They are the new nationalities that grew in the womb of older linguistic provinces, mostly concentrated into the tribal and hilly regions of the country, towards whom we now turn our discussion to.

The development of capitalism in dimension and intensity in post-colonial India has tended to form new nationalities in the tribal and hilly areas. Earlier, these were less intensely penetrated due to the uneven economic development. These new/evolving nationalities are witnessing the same transformative processes which the older nationalities had undergone in the past as the transformative process includes the process of stratification of peasantry, their gradual uprootment from soil and conversion into wage-earners, migration to towns, etc., formation of bourgeoisie, coalescing of historical identities, changing consciousness and mobility, etc. In short, the formation of nationalities and new classes within them having varying needs are being replicated. Though at crossroads, they may not fit into the conventional Stalinist definition of nationality, but they possess the social and secular heritage of identity that binds them together, at least, during the agitation. Apart from that, there exists commonalities of economic and political interests irrespective of the varying class interests, including decentralization of power, availability of infrastructural facilities, etc., that make them stand on one platform against the hegemonic bourgeoisie. The elite among them, the medium/small scale industrialists and the various categories of business lobbies-traders, shopkeepers, transporters, etc., like their brethren's in 1946, as quoted earlier, desire "everything possible to improve the trade and industries to retain as big a slice of them as possible for the benefit of the sons of the soil". Their economic compulsion in the capitalist society compels them to seek control over market, share in surplus value, access to revenue, opportunities for capital investment and a sympathetic government of their own to attend to their grievances. Lack of such opportunities and benefits bring them into confrontation with the hegemonic bourgeoisie of different layers. Since they are economically/politically weak vis-a-vis the dominant bourgeoisie and numerically a peanut vis-a-vis peasantry and wage-earners the local bourgeoisie are unable to do anything at their own. Consequently, they turn to other strata of society for support and, in turn, include some of the demands of the masses. Not only that they prop up the historical roots to cement the cultural-identity to bind and to generate the feelings of oneness between the bourgeoisie and the masses to stand as one united body against the administration. Even crocodile tears are shed by the elite in case of causalities during the agitation. Strikes, street marches, blockades and organized violence are used to bring the hegemonic bourgeoisie to a negotiated settlement; and once they arrive at a satisfactory settlement the movement is called off. In case the settlement is not arrived at the movement lingers on interruptedly.

On the other hand, the hegemonic bourgeoisie, first, attempt to ignore or downplay the movement. But, if it gathers momentum and becomes persistent, they attempt to isolate/deflect/frustrate it by using the bogey of foreign hands or use the state power as shock absorber. Only when all these methods fail to deter the agitators they come at the negotiating table. Formation of linguistic provinces in the past, and various types of councils at present are the results of such mass pressure.

The other two important determinants in such movements are the wage-earners, particularly the non-industrial urban wage-earners, and peasantry who constitute the bulk of a nationality and on whose participation or lack of it depends on the success or failure of the movements. Basically, the economic interests of wage-earners and peasantry are antagonistic to each other as they represent two different historical eras.[23] While the wage-earners are the emerging social force, peasantry are its decaying constituents. It's only after negating the peasantry that wage-earners come into being with capitalism playing the role of the midwife. The development of capitalism, the negation of peasantry and the emergence of wage-earners are parts of the same social matrix. The essential demands of the peasantry are land to the tillers, easy credit, and accessibility to market, higher support prices for their commodities, subsidized electricity, irrigational facilities, fertilizers, seeds and all that which facilitates their working on the land. In short, they stand for land and capital to maximize their gains in order to survive in the competitive milieu, or else they would be doomed irrevocably. The wage-earners, on the other hand, seek job opportunities, better wages, less hours of work, better health and living condition, participation in management, post-retirement benefits and all that which are linked with human life. Their working condition set in the social environment of assembly line production vis-a-vis the individualistic nature of work of peasantry attached with their pieces of land makes them class-for-itself. These economic needs, nature of working conditions and world-outlooks led Marx to call peasantry a 'sack of potatoes' and wage-earners, a class that has to conquer the world. Though he was aware about the peasants' revolutionary role in history, but he equally believed that they facilitate the development of capitalism by creating the material condition for the production of wage labour; and that their existence' wrecks the proletarian revolution.

But both these constituents mediated by political organizations fight the bourgeoisie, local and hegemonic, for their varied as well as common interests, the common interests being the development of infrastructural facilities, decentralisation of power, etc. Since the local bourgeoisie themselves fight the hegemonic bourgeoisie for their class as well as common interests of the society, hence the contradictions between the local bourgeoisie and the masses get subdued for the time being and the fight between the hegemonic bourgeoisie and the entire nationality becomes the principal contradiction. The movement that ensues acquires different forms of struggle and the settlement that follows depend upon its strength. If there occurs a negotiated settlement on the demands of the nationality to the satisfaction of broad strata of society the movement is called off, or it fades out in course of time and the society relapses into its old contradictions of masses vs. local/hegemonic bourgeoisie. If the settlement does not work out to the satisfaction of the broader strata/sections of society or in absence of such settlement the movement may acquire the form of 'terrorism', as it is known in the official parlance. It may also develop into 'anti-foreigners', 'anti-outsiders' movements. Bihar in the first decade of the 20th century,[24] Bodoland,[25] Arunachal Pradesh,[26] Assam, etc., in recent months/years are some of the illustrative cases. In Bihar, the contradictions between different classes reflected in the form of caste struggles got subdued once the movement began for the formation of separate province. They all united, temporarily, against the British, pan-Indian bourgeoisie and Bengalis to demand a separate state of Bihar. But, once the demand materialised, their subdued contradictions came to fore as usual. In Bodoland and Assam, the movement not only became 'terroristic' but also adopted anti-Santhals and anti-Bangladeshis postures. In Arunachal Pradesh, the anti-Chakma, anti-Hazong issues have provided issues to the agitations which may acquire various proportion in the coming days.

On the constitutional side, the "prefectural federalism" that was granted by the 1935 Act and taken over by the Constituent Assembly after July 1947 with certain modifications has been described as "quasi", "cooperative-federalism", etc. To some extent, these descriptions may be true keeping in mind the practical application of development programme's, maintenance of law and order, etc., which are mainly done by the provinces. Nehru, the liberal democrat who had attended the Lucknow Conference of 1916, where for the first time federalism as a constitutional and political framework for the country was agreed upon, sparingly used Article 356, now the much abused one. All together he used this Article seven times since 1950. The rise of anti-Congress forces in subsequent years, however, not only witnessed the misuse of Article 356, but also numerous other Articles of the constitution as a tool in the hands of centre to crush the federal aspirations of the people. The 'quasi' and 'cooperative' aspects of Indian federalism as described by the constitutional experts are essentially based on the division of powers between the centre and provinces and on their smooth functioning, which normally happens when the same party is in power at both the levels. The different parties' rule at provinces and centre makes the constitutional aspect of federalism, by and large, useless, at least, in practice, particularly when provinces begin demanding greater autonomy in their functioning. The centre resorts to Articles, like 275, 282, 256, 257, 355, 288, 254 (2), etc., apart from Art 356. Even institutions, like Finance Commission, Planning Commission, etc., are used in pursuit of absolute power by the centre. In a nutshell, the unitary aspect is so pervading that constitutionally the centre can do anything with the provinces except for dissolving the people. But the fear of revolt of the people is the only restraining factor that checks the centre from moving towards absolute power. There has been no democratisation of constitution as far as the functioning of the federal aspect is concerned either in abrogation of the pernicious articles or in their lesser usages. The only change has been the addition of new amendments for the creation of new provinces out of old ones, and the abolition of categories (A, B and C) among the provinces that existed in the original constitution.

The American concept of 'indestructible union' has been the ideal of the Indian big bourgeoisie right from the pre-independence days. But the pressure of the nationalities that grew over the years demanding reorganization of provinces, autonomy or even secession compelled the big bourgeoisie to adopt, at least, the verbiage of "willing union" of "willing partners" to which they never reconciled to in practice. A weak centre with strong provinces having the right to self-determination as envisaged in the Cabinet Mission Plan were anachronism to them as this democratic structure of polity restricted their control over market, access to revenue, opportunities for capital investment and over administration to attend to their grievances. The deeds of the Muslim League on the eve of the transfer of power were a god-sent opportunity for the big bourgeoisie to strike back at the local bourgeoisie of different nationalities with the bogey of 'civil war' and loss of property. They preferred to do away with a 'moth-eaten' and 'truncated market' of Pakistan rather than to live with a weak centre and restricted market. Subsequently, the Cabinet Mission Plan was torpedoed, formation of Pakistan was agreed upon and a strong centre with overriding powers was created with no right of self-determination to nationalities. The transfer of power provided them uncontrolled leverage over the state machinery which they lacked earlier, and which was used whenever their interests were threatened. The question of compromise on secession, therefore, never entered their vocabulary.

Neither has secession been on the agenda of the masses. Had it gripped the masses and become the material force, the right to secession would have been either incorporated into the constitution or the bourgeois machinery would have been ripped apart. Since it has remained intact and the right to secession does not exist in the constitution it can safely be concluded that only a fringe population is affected by the idea of secession that are either co-opted or crushed by the bourgeoisie. However, if the right to secession is not on the agenda of the masses it does not mean that this right is not to be incorporated into the constitution. But, in the contemporary power structure, if this right is to be incorporated with a corresponding mechanism of referendum and is to be made applicable in practice, as it happened in Quebec in Canada, the nationalities with widest active participation of the masses have to jointly fight for it. The bourgeois society wouldn't hand it over to them on the platter.

Notes and References

1. For details, see Central, State and Concurrent Lists of the Indian constitution.
2. The Quebec in Canada almost seceded from the Canadian federalism but for the last minute rejection by the voters.
3. See Suniti Kumar Ghosh, *India's Nationality Problem and Ruling Classes,* Calcutta, 1996, p. 22.
4. *Ibid.*, pp. 16–17.
5. *Ibid.*, p. 17.
6. *Ibid.*, p. 23.
7. *Ibid.*, p. 17.
8. Quoted in *Ibid.*, p. 18.
9. *Ibid.*, pp. 14, 16.
10. *Ibid.*, pp. 13–14.
11. *Ibid.*, p. 14.
12. *The constitution of India,* Government of India, Ministry of Law, Justice and Company Affairs, Official Language Section, New Delhi, 1991, p. 63;
13. Quoted in Suniti Kumar Ghosh, *op. cit.*, p. 23.
14. *The Hindustan Times,* New Delhi, 9th June, 1996, p. 5.
15. Quoted in Suniti Kumar Ghosh, *op. cit.*, p. 21.
16. Quoted in *Ibid.*
17. *Ibid.*, p. 20.
18. Quoted in *Ibid.*
19. Quoted in *Ibid.*
20. *Ibid.*, p. 15.

21. Girish Mishra and Braj Kumar Pandey, *Sociology And Economics of Casteism in India,* Pragati Publications, New Delhi, 1996, pp. 22–38.
22. *Ibid.*, pp. 30–31.
23. For a detailed analysis of workers' and peasants' role in history, their demands and impacts, etc, see Himanshu Roy, "Peasantry Against Socialism: A Theoretical Perspective", *Science and People,* No: 3, No. 2, March 1992, pp. 57–71.
24. Girish Mishra and Braj Kumar Pandey, *op. cit.*
25. *India Today,* 15th June 1996; Sanjay Hazarika, "Land Question Behind Bodo-Santhal, Conflict", *The Times of India,* New Delhi, 3rd July 1996.
26. *Revolutionary Democracy, op. cit.*, pp. 67–70.

10

The Judiciary: Supreme Court

Vinod Sethi

Justice is the basic human law for any civilized society to ideally function. Upholding the law is, in fact, the first essential, the first guidepost. Neither a nation nor a state can survive unless it provides an efficient justice delivery system capable of alleviating the concerns of the people within reasonable time frame.[1]

The judiciary has assumed only such roles as would enable it to fulfill the ideals of the constitution. The role of Courts is not just to interpret laws, but to safeguard the rights that legitimately belong to the people. It must be independent, efficient and active if democracy has to have a meaning for the people of India.[2]

In a modern nation state, judiciary plays an important role of interpreting and applying the law. In a country with a written constitution, the judiciary upholds the supremacy of constitutional provisions. In India, within the framework of supremacy of the constitution, parliamentary democracy and a quasi-federal set-up, the judicial system is unitary in nature with the highest court being the Supreme Court of India.

From the very beginning of national movement, in the late 19th century, there was a demand for independent Supreme Court with considerable jurisdiction, which was to be an important ingredient of the machinery of state of independent India. This demand continued with Hari Singh Gaur's attempt to establish a Supreme Court in Governor's Councils in the 1920s. This demand found its expression in the Nehru Report of 1928, which proposed important additions to the existing judicial system.

The White Paper of 1933 proposed a Supreme Court parallel to that of the Federal Court which was to hear appeals from provincial courts, provided that appeal did not lie in the Federal Court. This proposal was rejected by the Joint Committee and subsequently abandoned by the colonial rulers.

Under the Act of 1935, an All India Court, named, the Federal Court was set up. It consisted of one chief justice and a number of other judges as Her Majesty's government deem necessary. From 1937-50, constitutional questions were dealt with by the Federal Court while ordinary civil and criminal appeals went to the Privy Council.

When the question of Supreme Court came to be discussed in the Constituent Assembly, it was clear that the powers of both Federal Court and Privy Council were to be vested in one court. After independence, the new constitution substituted the Federal Court by Supreme Court. The framers of the Indian constitution wanted judiciary to correspond with the broad political philosophy of the country. They were mindful of the implications of a written constitution and conceived of judicial independence within the parameters of such a constitution.[3]

The framing of draft provision establishing the Supreme Court was done by an *ad hoc* committee of five members including B.N. Rau, K.M. Munshi, M.L. Mitter, Varadacharian and Alladi Krishnaswamy Ayyar. This report was later submitted to the Union constitution Committee.[4] It was accepted by the Constituent Assembly with an exception of the rule applicable for choosing the judges of the Court.

The Supreme Court was idealized by the Constituent Assembly because the Court was seen as an extension of the rights; it was to be an arm of the social revolution; and as the guardian of the constitution, it would be the expression of the new law created by Indians for Indians.[5] In other words, the Supreme Court is envisaged with widespread functions as an apex court in judicial hierarchy and at the same time interprets the constitution. It is a guardian of Fundamental Rights (Article 32), adjudicates upon the controversies between the states and centre-state(s) (Article 131) and is the ultimate court of appeal having constitutional (Article 132), civil (Article 133), and criminal jurisdiction (Article 134). It has the power to supervise the working of the entire judicial system and maintains uniformity of law ensuring high standards set by the framers of the constitution.

"The Supreme Court", wrote Bryce saying of the U.S. constitution, 'it the living voice of the constitution, that is the will of the people expressed in the fundamental law they have enacted. It is, therefore, the conscience of the people, who have resolved to restrain themselves for hasty and unjust actions by placing their representatives under the restriction of a permanent law. It is the guarantee of minority who when threatened by the impatient vehemence of a majority, can appeal to this permanent law, finding the interpreter and enforcer thereof in the court set high above the assaults of factions'.[6] This view was endorsed by many leaders of the Constituent Assembly.

Organization of the Court

The members of the Constituent Assembly wanted to keep the judicial system strong and independent. Austin has rightly observed, "The subject that loomed largest in the minds of Assembly members when framing the judicial provisions, was the independence of the court and two closely related issues, the powers of the Supreme Court and judicial review. The Assembly went to great lengths to ensure that the courts would be independent, devoting more hours to debate to this subject then to almost any other aspect of provision. If the beacon of the judiciary was to remain bright, the courts must be above reproach, free from coercion and from political influence".[7]

Further, many judges have observed that independence of judiciary is a necessary element for efficient functioning of the judiciary. Justice Khanna went on to say, 'since persons who are to decide disputes should not susceptible to pressures of the citizens and of the state, independence of the judges has come to be accepted as an essential trait of the democratic society."[8]

The constitution has made due provisions for ensuring independent judiciary by providing security of tenure and fixed remuneration. At the same time, the Parliament has been given the power to make laws regulating the constitution, organization, jurisdiction, and powers of the Supreme Court.[9] The original constitution provided for seven judges besides the chief justice but, with progress of time, due to increase of workload, he made the Parliament to amend the constitution Article 124(1). The Parliamentary Acts have been raising over the years, and in terms of the Supreme Court (number of Judges) Amendments Act, 2008, it now stands at 30.

To ensure fair appointment of the judges, the constitution in Article 124(2) provided for the judges to be appointed by the President in consultation with such judges of the Supreme Court and High Court as he may deem necessary. Further, consultation with the chief justice of India by the President has been made obligatory.[10] While appointing judges, emphasis has been made on experienced judges.[11] The 80th Law Commission Report recognized the influence of politics in Supreme Court, and it stated, 'any revelation of any tendency or inclination to hobnob with ministers and political personages should not be considered for the post of a Supreme Court judge.'[12]

The constitution has not provided for any procedure for the appointment of Chief Justice of India. An unbroken convention of appointing the seniormost judge of the Supreme Court as Chief Justice of India was followed till the 1970s. The Law Commission criticized this procedure for appointment. It later set down some criterion for the appointment of Chief Justice. It stated, 'For the performance of the duties of Chief Justice of India, there is needed not only a judge of ability and experience, but also a competent administrator capable of handling complex matters that may arise from time to time, a shrewd judge of men and personalities above all, a person of sturdy independence, and towering personality who would on the occasion arising, be a watchdog of the independence of judiciary. It is well accepted that the qualification needed for a successful Chief Justice are very different from the qualifications which go to make an erudite and able judge. The considerations which must, therefore, prevail in making the selection to this office must be basically different from those that would govern the appointment of other judges of the Supreme Court.'[13]

The government acted on the recommendations of the 14th Law Commission Report only in 1973, and for the first time the appointment of chief justice entered into controversy. Justice A.N. Ray was appointed as the chief justice of India superseding three senior judges of the court, Justices J.M. Shelat, K.S. Hedge, and A.N. Grover, all of whom resigned. This sparked off controversy in the political circles, Bar Associations, and some ex-judges. The then Union Law Minister Mohan Kumaramangalam, who was responsible for this appointment, later wrote in utmost candour: 'It is entirely within the discretion of government of the day to appoint a person considered in its eyes as most suitable to occupy the highest judicial office in the country and to take into consideration his philosophy, his outlook in life.'[14]

H.M. Seervai, an eminent constitutional export remarked that, our judiciary was, and was intended to be, a non-political judiciary on the English model and the American view of judges for their known political views was foreign to the judicial traditions which we have inherited.'[15]

The act of supersession of judges was repeated by the government in January 1977. Justice Khanna was denied the right to become the Chief Justice of India stating that his tenure would be short-lived as he would retire soon. To many, his suppression was due to his opinion in *habeas corpus* case (1976). Justice H.M. Beg was appointed the Chief Justice of India. This controversy surfaced during the Emergency period, and it died down because of the announcement of general election and resignation of Justice Khanna.

Once again in 1978, eminent lawyers from the Bombay Bar Association stood up against the appointment of Justice Y.Y. Chandrachud as the Chief Justice of India. This eroded the principle of seniormost judge becoming the Chief justice of India. The Janata Dal government defended its action and took the view that violation of the principle of seniority in the appointment of Chief Justice would be undermining the independence of judiciary. This controversy led the jurists to look into this problem more seriously.

Justice Bhagwati, in the historic judge's case remarked, 'Appointment of judges is a serious process where judicial expertise, legal learning, life experience, and high integrity are components. If the appointment of Judges is made with these considerations weighing predominantly with the appointing authority, then we have a truly independent judiciary committed only to the constitution and to the people of India.'[16]

It is believed that the Chief Justice should be appointed through a due process where sitting judges form a committee to recommend the name of the Chief Justice to the executive authority which can end political interference. Upendra Baxi has suggested a collegium consisting of the Chief Justice and eminent jurists who should recommend the name of the successor.

In response to the long-standing demand for a National Judicial Commission, the Union Cabinet in 2003 decided to set up a National Judicial

Commission for the appointment of judges of the Supreme Court and High Courts. The Commission will be chaired by the Chief Justice of India and would comprise of two senior-most judges of the Supreme Court, the Union Law Minister and eminent citizens.[17]

Article 124(3) deals with the constitutional provision for qualification of appointment of judges. No person shall be qualified for appointment as a judge of the supreme court unless he is a citizen of India, and: (1) has been for at least five years a judge of High Court or two or more such courts in succession; or (2) has been for at least ten years as an advocate of a High Court or of two or more such courts in succession; or (3) in the opinion of the President, a distinguished jurist. It is, thus, possible to appoint an eminent non-practising academic lawyer as a judge in the Supreme Court. This provision has been inspired by the American example, where distinguished law teachers have often been appointed to the Supreme Court and they have proved to be successful judges.[18] Till date, nobody has been appointed as per clause (c), though, for appointment, it has given wider choice to the President.

POST SCRIPT

The process of appointment of Supreme Court and High Court Judges as provided for in Articles 124 and 217 of the constitution has undergone some changes under the case law yielded by the Supreme Court judgment in the Supreme Court Advocates on Record, for the Union of India (1993) and its advisory opinion in re-Presidential Reference (1999. According to these rulings, the advice of the collegiums of judges chained by the Chief Justice of India (CJI) has become binding on the President of India for appointment of judges of the Supreme Court and High Courts. The Union Executive has expressed the intention of bringing about some changes in this procedure to give the executive representations in the process of deciding who are to be appointed. A National Judicial Commission with consisting of the CJI as the chain and two senior must judges of the Supreme Court, the Union Minister of Law and Justice and one eminent person nominated by the President of India after consulting the CJI has been proposed by the Nation; Commission to Review the Working of the constitution on in its Report (2002). But, so far it has not been implemented.

The framers of the Indian constitution attached much significance to the provisions relating to the tenure of the judges for protection of the independence of judiciary. Article 124(2) states that the judges of the Supreme Court hold office until they attain the age of 65 years. There were proposals during Chief Justice P.N. Bhagwati's and Chief Justice Ranganath Misra's term that retirement age should be increased to 70 years. This ensures bringing new talent from time to time, and to act according to contemporary socio-economic needs.

A Supreme Court judge can resign from office by writing to the President. He can be removed from the office by a procedure provided in clauses 4 and 5. Article 124(4) provides for the President to remove a judge by way of an address to the effect, being proved for misbehavour and incapacity. The order must be supported by a majority of the total membership of both the Houses and by a majority of not less than two-thirds of the members present and voting. The address should be presented to the Parliament only after the alleged charges of misbehaviour and incapacity has been investigated by an impartial tribunal.

In 1993, a case against Supreme Court Justice Ramaswamy was investigated for financial regulations during his tenure as the Chief Justice of Punjab and Haryana High Court. Though the investigation[19] *proved to a very large extent, his impeachment failed to get through in the Parliament. This had also instigated a spate of litigations against the Government of India.*[20] *Till date, no other Supreme Court judge had to go through such indictment.*

There have been incidences of protest against appointment of Chief Justices. Questions raised in some quarters when Justice M.N. Punchi, one of the senior most judges, was to become the Chief Justice of India.It was said that he had sought favour from Haryana Chief Minister in a land allotment case for his family.

Justice A.S. Anand, the Chief Justice of India, was accused of misrepresenting his age and was asked to step down, failing which a case under sections 420, 406 and 471 of IPC would be filed, along with a writ of quo warranto directing him to deposit ₹3 crore for usurping the office of the Chief Justice even after attaining the age of superannuation.[21]

He was also accused of using his position to get a favourable order from a subordinate judge, for his wife and mother-in-law in a suit that had been barred by limitation. Justice J.S. Verma was also in a controversy, as a newspaper alleged that some money was paid to his daughter in England by a Hawala accused. However, all such reports were dismissed as scandalous.

The complete independence of the judiciary is possible when their remuneration is guaranteed by the constitution. Article 125 and five second schedules deal with remuneration of the judges including their allowances and privileges. In addition to residential accommodation, the judges draw a salary of ₹30,000 p.m., and the chief justice draws ₹33,000 p.m.[22] *None of these can be varied to his disadvantage after his appointment to the Court. These matters are now regulated by the Supreme Court Judges (Condition of Service) Act 1958. But, these allowances and salaries of the judges can be reduced in times of grave financial emergency.*

As a matter of fact, the exchequer is burdened with substantial expenditure on each judge. The privileges of the judges include a free furnished residential accommodation in VIP areas with round the clock security. They are also provided with free medical and library allowances and an air-conditioned car. Their personal staff includes a personal assistant, stenographer, and attendants. Their other privileges include an office at their residence with a free telephone. These privileges are provided to protect the independence of judiciary.

To maintain the dignity of the apex court and to secure its independence, the judges have been disqualified from action or pleading in any court within the territory of India (Article 124, clause 7) after retirement. But the retired judges have been appointed as chairmen of different commissions, which the government constitutes from time to time. Though the Law Commission has criticized such appointments, the members and chairman of the Law Commission itself are appointed from among the retired judges. However, many judges have roaring practice of arbitrators, and their earnings surpass even some of the leading members of the Bar.

Article 126 provides for acting Chief Justice. Article 127 talks for appointment of ad hoc judges in the Supreme Court with the prior consent of the President. While attending the Supreme Court, the ad hoc enjoys the power and privileges equal to a Supreme Court judge. Till date, no such appointments have been made. Article 128 provides that an ex-judge can be appointed as the judge of the Supreme Court by the Chief Justice with prior consent of the President.

Though the framers of the constitution made all possible efforts to ensure an independent and strong judiciary, it could not escaped controversy. The controversies regarding appointments, court's power to veto legislative and executive acts, and judicial activism have shown signs of stress and strain. However, it has still maintained its independent nature.

The Supreme Court is a court of record under Article 129. The court of record is one where the judicial proceedings are kept for further testimony, having evidentiary value. They are not to be questioned when produced before any court. The court has the power to punish those who are guilty of contempt of court.[23] *A legitimate criticism of the judiciary or the judge in his capacity as a judge is permissible. Contempt of court is, when there is undue interference in the proceedings or administration of the court. The court can punish the contempt by fine or imprisonment.*[24]

In Arundhati Roy's case[25] *the court felt that judiciary is under constant threat and is being undermined from within and without. It observed that the confidence of citizens should not be undermined. The criticism that undermines the court unfairly could not go unpunished under clock of freedom of speech.*

Article 130 of the constitution allows the Supreme Court to have its seat in Delhi.

It also allows the Chief Justice to seek permission from the President to change its seat to some other place.

Jurisdiction of the Court

The Supreme Court of India enjoys a commendable position with its wide jurisdiction and powers which no apex court of any other country enjoys.

Sir Alladi Krishnaswami Ayyar remarked in the Constituent Assembly: "The Supreme Court of India under the constitution has wide powers, more than the highest court, in any other federation. The criticism, if at all, can only be that the powers of the Supreme Court are not wide enough, but that they are too wide."[26] The decisions of this court are binding on all the courts within the territory of India as stated in Article 141. The Supreme Court is assigned with original, appellate, and advisory jurisdiction by the constitution.

Original Jurisdiction

This refers to the cases that directly originate in the Supreme Court. The court, in its original jurisdiction, is not entitled to entertain any suit where both the parties are not units of the federation. If any suit is brought either against the state or the Government of India by a citizen, that will not lie within the original jurisdiction of the Supreme Court, but will be brought in the ordinary courts under the ordinary law.

Article 131 of the constitution explains the original jurisdiction of the Supreme Court. The courts has the power to decide on dispute arising between: (1) the Government of India and one or more states on the other hand; (2) the Government of India and one or more states on the one hand; and (3) between two or more states *inter se,* insofar as the dispute involves any question (whether of law or fact) on which the existence or extent of a legal right depends.

This jurisdiction does not extend to treaties signed before the commencement of the constitution, and its scope does not extend to: (1) complaints as to interference with inter-state water supplies referred to statutory tribunal mentioned in Article 262 with Inter-state Water Disputes Act, 1956, S. 11 (XXXXIII); (2) matters referred to the Finance Commission (Article 280); (3) adjustment of finances between the union and states (Article 290); and (4) a reference to the Supreme Court under Article 131 read with Article 363(1).

The first suit brought before the Supreme Court was between *West Bengal vs. Union of India* (1963)[27] to declare the unconstitutionality of the Coal Bearing Areas Act 1957. It was dismissed by the Court. In *State of Bihar vs. the Union of India,*[28] in 1970 the court held that dispute must arise in the context of constitutional and legal right and not of political character. This was further upheld by Justice Y.Y. Chandrachud, saying, 'It is competent for the state governments to bring suits of the present nature under Article 131 and by this, state governments are raising a legal and not political issue.'[29] In the *State of Karnataka vs.* the *Union of India,*[30] Karnataka challenged the Union Government's power of appointing inquiry commission where the Court considered the scope of Article 131 and interpreted the article magnanimously.[31]

In *State of Karnataka vs. State of Andhara Pradesh,*[32] the Supreme Court was asked to adjudicate the issue of raising the height of Amatti dam to 512 m. The Court examined the provisions of Inter-state Water Dispute

Act, 1956, to determine whether the issue would fall under Article 131 or is barred by Article 262. Dispute between riparian states located in inter-state river basin relating to no implementation of the binding award of the Water Dispute Tribunal has nothing to do with rising of fresh water dispute. This is a question of execution and implementation of already adjudicated dispute.

In *State of Haryana vs. State of Punjab and Others*[33] the issue was not of inter-state water dispute, but of claim of Haryana that the State of Punjab should construct the Sutlez Yamuna Link Canal. It is not a water dispute, hence not barred by Article 262.

As per Article 71(1) of the constitution the Supreme Court exercises original jurisdiction on matters relating to election of President and Vice-President where its decision is final.[34] The election of V.V. Giri as President and G.S. Pathak as Vice-President of India, in 1969, was challenged in the Supreme Court. Justice S.M. Sikri upheld the election of V.V. Giri and G.S. Pathak.

Appellate Jurisdiction

As a court of appeal, the Supreme Court is a final appellate tribunal of the land. The power of reviewing and revising the orders of lower courts and tribunals by the Supreme Court is called as the appellate jurisdiction.

Article 132 provides that all appeals from High Court will lie with the Supreme Court. Also, it involves a substantial question of law as to the interpretation of the constitution, and also, if the Court certifies that substantial question of law is involved. The procedure for grant of certificate is laid down in Article 134(A) which has been inserted by the 44th Amendment Act of 1978. Further, in *Election Commission vs. Venkata Rao,*[35] the Court held that even if a single Judge delivers a judgement, on the issue of a certificate, an *appeal* can *lie* in the Supreme Court.

Article 133 provides for civil appeals in the Supreme Court if it involves substantial question of law or in the opinion of High Court the subject matter involved in the dispute was valued to ₹20,000 or more, the matter can be entertained by the Court. This was deplored by the 44th Law Commission Report[36] which stated 'the article should be amended with the object to remove discrimination based merely on value of the property and equal chance be given to both rich and poor litigant to appeal in the Supreme Court'. Accordingly, this article was amended in 1973,[37] by the Thirtieth Amendment Act.

Article 134 provides for an appeal to the Supreme Court from the decision of High Court if the High Court: (1) has on appeal reversed the order of acquittal of an accused person and sentenced him to death; or (2) has withdrawn for trial before itself any case from any court subordinate to its authority and has in such trial convicted the accused person and sentenced him to death; and (3) certifies that the case is fit for an appeal to Supreme Court. Once again it was maintained that certificate should be granted only in exceptional cases.[38]

Besides the jurisdiction as noted above, the constitution provides for appeal by special leave under Article 136. This appeal is entertained by the court only when special circumstances are shown to exist. In *Dhakeshwari Cotton Mills Case*[39] principles were laid down for granting appeal by special leave. The then Chief Justice Mahajan observed: 'It being an exceptional and overriding power naturally it has to be exercised sparingly and with caution and only in special and extraordinary situations. The constitution having trusted the wisdom and good sense of the judges is itself a sufficient safeguard and guarantee that the power will only be used to advance the cause of all justice. When the court reaches the conclusion that a person has been dealt with arbitrarily and has not been given a fair deal to a litigant, then no technical hurdles of any kind like the finality of finding of facts or otherwise can stand in the way of exercise of this power because the whole intent and purpose of this article is that it is the duty of this court to see that injustice is not perpetuated or perpetrated by decisions of courts and tribunals because certain laws have made the decisions of these courts and tribunals final and conclusive.'[40]

However, in matters related to criminal appeal unless special circumstances are shown to exist or when substantial and grave injustice has been done, leave to appeal is not granted.[41] The jurisdiction extends to all judgements from any court of tribunal as and when it feels the interference of the court is necessary.

Seven judge bench in *Konkan Railway Corporation Ltd. vs.* Ms *Rani Construction Private Limited*[42] discussed the scope of SLP. Justice S.P. Barucha held that for an order properly to be a subject matter of Special Leave to Appeal under Article 136 must be an adjudicatory order, an order that adjudicates upon rival contentions of parties, and it must be passed by an authority constituted by the State by law for the purpose in discharge of state's obligation to secure justice to its people.

If SLP is summarily dismissed such dismissal does not bar other parties from filing special leave petition against the judgement.[43]

The Supreme Court under Article 137 has the power to review any judgements pronounced by the court. It can be done on the ground that there is error or the court's attention has not been drawn as a particular statutory provision. The normal principle that judgements pronounced are binding unless substantial and compelling character make it necessary to review and revise its decisions. The court can also override its decisions for compelling reasons as fresh horizons[44] may reveal as a result of new ideas and developments. The court, while reviewing its decisions, should uphold the changing ideas of the society.

Advisory Jurisdiction

The power of consulting the Supreme Court by the President, on a matter affecting the nation is termed as advisory jurisdiction.

Article 143 of the constitution explains that the advisory jurisdiction and states: If the President at any time feels that a question of law or fact of public importance has arisen such that it is expedient to obtain the opinion of the Supreme Court. H.M. Seervai has said 'although the advisory opinion given by the Supreme Court has high persuasive authority, it is not law declared by it within the meaning of Article 141.'[45] The Supreme Court in *U.P. Legislative Assembly vs. State High Court* expressed its view that advisory opinions are not binding on the President or the courts. But eminent jurists including Justice Y.R. Krishna Iyer and Lawyer Soli Sorabjee hold the view that advisory opinion is binding on the President.[46] Till date, nine cases have been sent by the President for advisory opinion.[47]

Major constitutional crisis was witnessed when the Election Commission was attacked for it decision not to conduct elections in Gujarat. The Gujarat Assembly, which was constituted in March 1998, was to end by February 2003. On 19th July 2002, the Chief Minister recommended the Governor to dissolve the Assembly. The Election Commission started the election process, but due to unrest in the State it felt that conducting the elections was not possible before 3rd October 2002. The Presidential reference was made as the last session of the Assembly took place on 3rd April 2002, and Article 174 provides that six months should not elapse between the two sessions. Hence, mandatory provisions of the constitution were not followed by the Election Commission. The Supreme Court held that Article 174 does not apply where the house is dissolved under Article 356.[48]

The Supreme Court is the guardian of Fundamental Rights under Article 32.

Article 139 provides that Parliament by law can confer on the Supreme Court powers to issue directions, orders, or writs including the writs mentioned in Article 32(2), for any purpose other than Fundamental Rights.

The power of issuing constitutional writs is regarded as original jurisdiction of the Supreme Court as petition can be directly filed in the apex court.[49] Moreover, under Article 32, the Court confines itself to the question of infringement of Fundamental Rights, and once it is established, the court is duty-bound to give him relief.[50]

The Supreme Court has also been assigned some extra-judicial functions. In the absence of the President and the Vice-President of India, the Chief Justice and in his absence the seniormost judge acts as the President. In 1968, Justice M. Hidyatullah was the acting President of India when V.V. Giri and Chief Justice Subba Rao contested the presidential election.

Judicial review is the power of judiciary to review any act or orders of the Legislative and Executive wings and to pronounce upon the constitutional validity when challenged by the affected person. This power is based upon a simple rationale that the constitution is the supreme law of land and any authority, if it ventures to go beyond the limitation laid down by the constitution, it will be curbed.

The doctrine of judicial review is a contribution of American constitutional system. This was acquired by the American Supreme Court in *Marbury vs. Madison* case of 1803 when Chief Justice Marshall announcing the verdict remarked that any law violating the constitutional provision is null and void. Since then it got strongly embedded in the constitution, and judicial supremacy got established.

In India, the Government of India Act, 1935, gave the power of judicial review to the Federal Court, but its scope was limited to the extent that it could review only the provisions of the act which provided for distribution of powers between the Union and Provinces. The constitution provides for distribution of power among states and the centre, separation of power among the governmental organs, and Fundamental Rights, which has widened the scope of judicial review.

The constitution does not refer to the concept of judicial review because the framers realized that there were inherent drawbacks of this doctrine. In the first place, it may set at naught the will of the people expressed through the Parliament. Secondly, judicial review inevitably opens the floodgates of litigation involving huge expenditure and loss of time and consequent delay in the implementation of government programmes, and, thirdly, the judiciary is responsible to none and is not answerable for consequences of its decisions.[51]

Justice Patanjali Shastri states, 'Our constitution contains express provision for judicial review of legislation as to its conformity with the constitution, unlike in America, where the Supreme Court has assumed extensive powers of reviewing legislative acts under 'due process' clause in the Fifth and Fourteenth Amendments.'[51] This is, especially true as regards the Fundamental Rights as to which this court has been assigned the role of sentinel; while the out naturally attaches great weight to the legislative judgement, it cannot desert its own duty to determine finally the constitutionality of an impugned statute.[52]

There are specific provisions in the constitution which provide for judicial review, though the Supreme Court has enumerated certain rules for applying this doctrine. According to H.M. Seervai:[53]

1. There is a presumption is favour of constitutionality. A law will not be declared unconstitutional unless the case is free from all doubts and onus to prove that it is unconstitutional lies with the petitioner who has challenged it.
2. When the validity of law is questioned, it should be upheld to protect parliamentary sovereignty.
3. The Court will not raise constitutional questions if a case is capable of being decided on other grounds.
4. The Court will not decide a larger constitutional question when is required by the case before it.
5. The Court will not hear an objection as to the constitutionality of a law by a person whose rights are not affected by it.

6. A statute cannot be declared unconstitutional merely because it is not consistent with the spirit of the constitution.
7. In assessing the constitutionality of a statute, the court is not concerned with the motives-*bonafides* or of the legislature, but the law must be upheld whatever a court may think of it.
8. Courts should not pronounce on the validity of an Act or part of an Act which has not been brought into force, because till then the question of validity would be merely academic.

The independent India had to go through many controversies leading to institutional rivalry between the legislature and judiciary. Though the power of judicial review had its limitations, it was viewed as a challenge to the supremacy of legislature leading to many constitutional amendments. Dr. Ambedkar had earlier remarked, 'The Constituent Assembly in making the constitution has no partisan motive. Beyond securing a good and workable constitution, it has no axe to grind. In considering the articles of the constitution, it has an eye on getting through a particular measure. The future Parliament, if it met as a Constituent Assembly, its members will be acting as partisans seeking to carry amendments to the constitution to facilitate the passing of party measures which they have failed to get through in the Parliament by reason of some article of the constitution which has acted as an obstacle in their way. The Parliament will have an axe to grind while the Constituent Assembly has none.'[54]

But Pandit Nehru, a staunch supporter of Parliamentary sovereignty, has remarked with a different tone,'No Supreme Court and no judiciary can stand in judgement over the sovereign will of Parliament, representing the will of the entire community. Ultimately, the whole constitution is a creation of the Parliament.'[55]

By interpretation and amendment, the constitution underwent many vital changes. The process began with the First Amendment Act, 1951,[56] which abolished the *zamindari* system. This act was challenged in the *Shankari Prasad* case[57] on the ground that this has infringed Fundamental Rights. The Court rejected the petition and stated that the Parliament is authorized to amend any part of the constitution including the chapter on Fundamental Rights. This was upheld by a majority judgement in the *Sajjan Singh* case[58] where the 17th Amendment Act 1964 was challenged on the ground that it violated Fundamental Right under Article 31A. The landmark judgement professing judicial activism came in 1967, when the 1st, 4th and, amendments were challenged in the *Golak Nath* case.[59] The court by majority of 6-5 held that the Parliament does not possess the authority to amend the chapter on Fundamental Rights with respect to Article 13(2) embedding the doctrine of judicial review and giving way to due process of law.

In fear of non-implementation of its social legislations, the Parliament through an ordinance in 1969 nationalized 14 banks under Banking Companies (Acquisition and Transfer of Undertakings) Ordinance. This Act was challenged by R.C. Cooper[60] on the ground that it violated Articles 14 and 3i(2).

Once again in 1970, the President by an executive order abolished the institution of ruler's privy purses. This was challenged by Madhav Rao Scindia.[61] Both these ordinances were declared unconstitutional by the court.

In response to these setbacks, the Parliament framed the constitution (24th) Amendment Act, 1971, and due amendments were made in Articles 13 and 368 to provide the authority to the Parliament to amend any part of the constitution. By the (25th) Amendment Act, 1971, Article 31 was amended to remove obstacles laid down by the court in the Bank Nationalization case. Further, the 26th Amendment Act, 1971, was made to abolish the institution of rulers' privy purses. The government defended its action by stating that these were necessary amendments which would transform socio-economic structures of the society.

In the *Keshvanand Bharati* case,[62] the constitutional validity of the twenty-fourth, twenty-fifth, and twenty-ninth amendments came up for judicial review. The court, by limiting the power of amendment, held that the Parliament does not possess the authority to amend the basic structure of the constitution though the concept of basic structure was not explained. The Supreme Court was moved to review its decision, but the bench was abruptly dissolved by the chief justice. In 1975, the 39th Amendment Act, relating to electoral matter, was challenged in the historic election case.[63] The Court dismissed the petition, and it was held that they had adhered to the theory of basic structure.

The 42nd amendment of the constitution placed limitations upon the exercise of the power of judicial review. They were:

1. The power of the centre was increased by transferring certain provisions from the State List to the Concurrent List.
2. The power of the Supreme Court and High Courts were curtailed. With respect to Articles 14, 19, and 31, Parliament can make any law to implement Directive Principles of State policy.
3. The powers of the Supreme Court was further curtailed by stating that 'no amendment of this constitution made or purporting to have been made under this article shall be called in question in any court on any ground.'
4. The validity of central law was to be decided by the Supreme Court (Article 141A) and not by High Courts (Article 228A) and subsequently the validity of the state law could be decided only by High Courts.
5. The power of issuing writs for implementation of Fundamental Rights were curtailed to the effect that these writs will not be issued unless substantial injury has taken place and also if alternative remedy is provided under any law.
6. Minimum seven judges of the Supreme Court should sit for the purposes of determining constitutional validity of central law. It cannot be declared unconstitutional unless two-thirds majority of judges decide and for the High Court there had to be five judges to determine the constitutional validity of a law.

7. Further, the appointment procedure of High Court was dealt extensively.
8. It was also stated that the decisions of any administrative tribunals can be questioned or challenged only in the Supreme Court under Article 323B.

The subsequent amendments, the 43rd and 44th amendments, did restore the lost glory of judiciary and the threat of judicial supremacy was reduced, the judiciary was forced to look into the democratic values of the constitution and interpret them more generously. The 44th amendment:

1. Deleted Right to Property from the chapter as Fundamental Rights and placed it under Article 300A.
2. Fundamental Rights were to be duly protected.
3. The powers of judiciary were partially restored by repealing Articles 131A and 226A. The power of judicial review to the courts was restored.

In the *Minerva Mills* case,[64] the Court struck a balance between Fundamental Rights and Directive Principles of State Policy by placing Article 39B and C above the chapter on Fundamental Rights. It was further held by Justice Bhagwati, 'It is for the judiciary to uphold the constitutional values and to enforce constitutional limitations.'

The Court has also been called upon to exercise its power of judicial review in cases relating to Presidential rejection of clemency for death sentence.[65] The Court has upheld the decisions of the President.

Justice Krishna Iyer, spoke of judicial review in the following words: "No power in the republic is irresponsible or irresponsive, the people in the last resort being the repositories and beneficiaries of public power. But two constitutional limitations exist in our constitutional system. The court cannot intervene everywhere as an omniscient, omnipotent or omnipresent being. And when the constitution has empowered the nation's executive, excluding by implication judicial review it is presumptuous this court to be a super power unlimited. The second limitation conditions all public power, whether a court oversees it or not. That trust consists in the plurality of public authorities. All power, howsoever majestic and dignified wielding it, shall be exercised in good faith with intelligent and informed care and honestly for public well being.[66] Further he held that "the magnificent concept of judicial review is at its best when kept within the framework of broad principles of public policy and tested by the intentionality of the statute."[67]

The working of the Supreme Court during the first three decades can be described as an arena of struggle between the legislature and the judiciary in relation to Fundamental Rights[68] and power of amendment. *The Maneka Gandhi* case[69] gave new impetus to the concept of liberty. During this period, the Court adopted a strategy of coordination enhancing the glory of the institution and practised self-restraint. Many political observers and jurists have held that judiciary will always avoid a confrontation between popular sovereignty and independent judiciary.[70]

The institutional rivalry dominated the Indian political process and judiciary till the 1980s. The advocates of parliamentary sovereignty blamed the judiciary for non-implementation of their programmes aimed at the weaker sections, i.e., the poor and distressed people, of the society. This led to the outflow of new ideas and dimensions in the minds of the socially progressive judges, like Justice Krishna Iyer[71] and Justice P.N. Bhagwati.[72] They led the movement to protect the socially oppressed classes with programmes, like legal aid, as provided in Article 39A of the constitution inserted by the 42nd amendment and institutions including Lok Adalat and public interest litigation. This added a new dimension in thealready existing jurisdiction and power of the judiciary.

The role of the Supreme Court in enforcement of fundamental rights is internationally recognized. In the first constitutional case before the Supreme Court, *A.K. Gopalan vs. State of Madras,*[73] Mr. Justice Fazal Ali and Justice Mukherjee, while interpreting Article 21 of the constitution in their dissenting opinion, felt that natural justice is a part of the procedure established by law. In *Maneka Gandhi vs. Union of India,*[74] Gopalan was reversed. It was held that procedure under Article 21 must be reasonable and fair. In *Madhav Hoskot vs. State of Mahrashtra,*[75] the Court said, "free legal aid service to the poor was an essential element of any just and fair procedure".

In *Hussainara Khatoon vs. Home Secretary State of Bihar,*[76] the Court held that a procedure that kept under trails in custody for long periods of time was not warranted by Article 21. In *State of Maharashtra vs. Ravikant Patil,*[77] the Court liberally interpreting Article 21, held that handcuffing and parading an undertrail was prohibited. Justice Sujatha Manohar felt, 'Although torture is not expressly countermanded by the constitution, Article 21 clearly provide protection against it'.[78] In *Bandhua Mukti Morcha vs. Union of India,*[79] the Supreme Court directed the union government to release the bonded labourers giving a wide meaning to right to life and personal liberty under Article 21. In *Unni Krishnan vs. State of Andhra Pradesh,*[80] the Court held that right to life and liberty included right to receive free education up to the age of 14 years. In *Ranganath Mishra vs. Union of India*[81], the Court treated a letter written by the former Chief Justice as a writ petition directing the State to educate its citizens as a matter of fundamental duties so that a right balance may emerge between rights and duties. In *State of Gujarat vs. Pravin Manghabhai,*[82] the Court directed the State to make proper security arrangements in courts and for judicial officers.

The Supreme Court, while interpreting Article 21, has held that it does not merely include traditional procedural due process, but would also include whole gamut of economic rights such as food, housing, health and education.[83] In *State of Bihar vs. L.K. Advani,*[84] the Court held that reputation of an individual is a part of one's life. A good reputation is an element of personal security, and is protected by the constitution equally with the right to enjoyment of life and liberty.

In *S.K. Mastana Bee vs. Supreme Courts G.M. South Central Rail,*[85] the Supreme Court went to the extent of saying that denial of pension to a helpless, poor and illiterate widow of petty employee was violation of Article 21 when she did not know about the family pension.

Justice R.C. Lahoti in *Javed vs. State of Haryana,*[86] said, "it is well established that right to life and personal liberty includes right to enjoy all materialistic pleasures and procreate as many children as one pleases." But Fundamental Rights are not to be read in isolation. They have to be read with the Directive Principles in Part IV and Article 51A where in it is a duty to keep population within reasonable bonds.

Protecting the right to healthcare under Article 21, the Supreme Court took *suo motu* notice of gruesome tragedy in which 25 mentally challenged patients were chained and housed in an Asylum House at Eravidi in Ramanathapuram district of Tamil Nadu.[87]

There have been several cases where the Supreme Court has upheld the right to clean environment as an integral part of right to life and personal liberty.[88]

Whether the evidence collected by video conferencing is within the ambit of procedure established by law. This was the subject matter of a debate in *State of Maharashtra vs. Dr. Praful B.Desai.*[89] Let's take more recent examples of SMS/MMS through mobile phones. Do they violate right to privacy? Or, are they admissible as evidence (e.g., the DPS MMS case, and the case of Anara Gupta, which was raked by media of obscene CD of beauty pageant Miss Jammu). Article 21 includes right to livelihood and to live with human dignity. Livelihood means, which are not illegal, immoral or opposed to public policy, are protected by Article 21.[90]

In *PUCL vs. Union of India,*[91] the Court held that 'Fundamental Rights are dynamic concepts and have no fixed contents. Most of them are empty vessels into which each generation must pour its content in the light of its experience. The constitution is required to be kept young, energetic and alive. Accordingly, the attempt of the Court should be to expand the reach and ambit of fundamental rights rather than accentuate their meaning and content by the process of judicial construction. Interpreting Article 19(1)(a), the Court said, "right to information is an integral part of freedom of speech and expression. This includes voter's right to know the antecedents/assets of the candidates contesting elections of Parliament and Legislative Assemblies".

In *T.R. Rangarajan vs. Government of Tamil Nadu,*[92] the Court held that right to strike is not a fundamental right or a statutory right. Similar opinion was expressed by the Delhi High Court in *Delhi Public School vs. DPS Karamchari Union*[93] that employees have no right to protest within the school premises and if they wish to protest, they should do outside the school. The Supreme Court upheld the principle of gender justice in *Vijay Lakshmi vs. Punjab University* (2003) 8 *SCC* 440),[93] Punjab University rules which provided for reservation for appointment of women candidates in a women college, a woman superintendent of a women's hostel and a woman doctor for a women's college, were challenged as violative of Articles 14 and 16 of the constitution. The Court held that the classification was reasonable, and it has a nexus with the object sought to be achieved which is precautionary, preventive and protective measure based on public morals and particularly in view of the young girl students to be taught. The Court set aside the majority, judgement of the Punjab and Haryana High Court which had struck down the rule as violative of Article 14 in *M.C. Sharma vs. Punjab University*.[95]

In different cases the Supreme Court has held that the classification is reasonable if it is found on an intelligible differentia which distinguishes or things that are grouped together from others left out in the group; and secondly, such differentia has a rational relation with the object sought to be achieved.[96]

The Supreme Court in *Onkar Lal Bajaj vs. Union of India*[97] held that enmass cancellation of allotment of retail outlets, dealership, distributorships of petroleum products on the basis of newspaper reports that the allotments were on the basis of political affiliations was not correct. The Court said that such decisions must stand test of judiciousness and impartiality and must avoid arbitrariness and capriciousness. Enmass cancellation without application of mind was arbitrary and, hence, violative of Article 14.

In *TMA Pai vs.State of Karnataka*,[98] it was held that the Fundamental Right of a citizen to establish an educational institution and in particular a professional institution is not absolute. They are subject to regulations and reasonable restrictions. The right to establish is guaranteed, but not right to get recognition and affiliation. In *Government of Maharashtra vs. Deokar's Distillary*,[99] the Court held that citizens have no fundamental right to caryon trade and business in liquor.

The role of judiciary to merely interpret and declare the law was the concept of a bygone age. It is no more open to debate as it is fairly settled that the Courts can so mould and lay down law formulating principles and guidelines; as to adopt and adjust to the changing conditions of society with the ultimate objective being to dispense justice.[100]

Lok Adalat

Lok Adalat is a voluntary agency. It settles disputes between the parties outside the courts with the help of public-spirited lawyers and like-minded citizens. It was established by Legal Services and Authorities Act, 1987. It has been given the widest possible jurisdiction, and it can take up any matter, pending in any court including the apex court. The Lok Adalat is guided by legal principles including principles of justice, equality, and fairplay. The judicial officers of the area and other such members possessing such qualifications conduct the affairs of Lok Adalat. It is being urged by many that Lok Adalat has therapeutic role to fulfill in aid of justice. So, the legal system must encourage the government and voluntary agencies should reach out to aid them, and the parties must trust them so that it can share the burden of accumulated litigation of the courts.

Seeing the popularity of the 10k *adalats* the Government introduced the Legal Services Authorities (Amendment) Act 2002[101] which provided for setting up of permanent Lok Adalats with pecuniary jurisdiction upto ₹10 lakhs as a part of compulsory pre litigative mechanism for conciliation and settlement of cases relating to public utility services.

Rules were framed under Legal Services Authorities Act, 1987 which deal with the remuneration and mattes regarding fee and other allowances to be paid to the Chairman and other staff members of the permanent 10k Adalat, terms and conditions of their service, resignation and removal and procedure to be followed in case of their removal from office.[102]

Public Interest Litigation

Public Interest Litigation (PIL), or Social Action Litigation (SIL) as termed by Upendra Baxi, is an offshoot of liberalized rule of *locus standi*. The traditional rule of *locus standi* was based on the fact that judicial remedy can be sought only by those who have suffered an injury on account of violation of a legal right by some public authority. The PIL chose to liberalize this rule by making it clear that any person who suffers an injury, but is unable to reach the court is helped by public-minded citizens to reach the court to seek justice.

The institution of PIL originated in the U.S. in mid-1960s. Legal aid to these litigations were provided by private foundations. The PIL cases centred around issues relating to civil rights, liberties, and problems of the distressed. This provided representation to those previously unrepresented groups.

The PIL is considered to be an offshoot of social forces where freedom suffered in the cruel hands and public participation was required to check the system. It was an opportunity for like-minded citizens to participate and reaffirm their faith in the legal process. The petition can be filed by any voluntary agency or a member of the public. However, the court must satisfy itself while accepting the petition and see that the person is acting *bona fide* and not for personal gain or profit.

The PIL involves issues connected with environmental protection, and a set of evolved fundamental rights including right to free legal aid, right against torture, right to humane treatment in prison, etc., reflecting the human dimension of the PIL. Further, it extended its domain in a delicate task of mediating between social actualities and social change. Issues, like degraded bonded labour, humiliated inmates of protective homes, women prisoners, custodial violence, and other victimized groups are attracting remedial attention of the courts. For this, Article 32 emerged as a forum of PIL in the recent years, and it has become a byword for judicial involvement in social, political, and economic affairs of the society.

The movement of liberalization of *locus standi* started with the *Bar Council of Maharashtra vs. M.V. Dabholkar*,[103] where the Bar Council was stated to be an aggrieved party. Further, the judiciary directed to government agencies to be responsive to public grievances. In the *Fertilizer Corporation*

Case,[104] it was held that in a society where freedom suffers from atrophy activism is essential for participative public justice. Some risks have to be taken and more opportunities opened for the public-minded citizen to rely on the legal process and not be repelled from it by narrow pedantry now surrounding *locaus standi*.

As litigations became very expensive, the affected persons joined together to fight for a common cause. Justice Krishna Iyer has observed in the *Akhil Bhartiya Shoshit Karmachari Sangh* (*Railway*)[105] case, 'Our current procedural jurisprudence is not of individualistic Anglo-Indian mould. It is people-oriented and envisions access to justice through class actions, PIL, and representative proceedings. Indeed, little Indians, in large numbers, seeking remedies in courts through collective proceedings instead of being driven to an expensive plurality of litigations is an affirmation of participative justice in our democracy. We have no hesitation in holding that the narrow concept of cause of action and person aggrieved and individual litigation is becoming obsolescent in some jurisdiction.'

The PIL received the required recognition in the *S.P. Gupta*[106] case who was not an aggrieved person. The court observed that the basis of judicial redressal was personal injury caused by an act or omission of the state or a public authority which is contrary to the constitution or the law, any member of the public acting *bona fide* and having sufficient interest can maintain an action for redressal of such public wrong or public injury.

The *Asiad workers*[107] case further strengthened the rule of *locus standi* in the PIL.

The PUDR was an organization for the protection of human rights which sought to enforce labour laws for the unorganized construction workers of projects concerning the Asian Games. Justice Bhagwati held that strategy has to be evolved for relaxing the traditional rule of *locus standi* so that justice becomes easily available to the lowly and the lost. Judicial activism has become the root of PIL and this was reflected in various other cases.

PIL has limitless field. Every PIL case is not propelled by any urge for vindication of the rights of the disadvantaged, exploited or victimised groups. It is intruding into areas previously immune from judicial intervention. In its early career, PIL was used as a struggle against domination and abuse of power for vindicating human rights of the deprived and the depressed sections of community. Today, PIL is considered as a legal action initiated in a court of law, for empowerment of public interest or general interest. In a PIL, public or a class of the community has pecuniary interest or some interest by which their legal rights are affected.[108]

The PIL is no more limited to enforcement of human rights of the oppressed or victimised groups who cannot on their own move the court for redressal of their grievances. One can file a PIL for better conditions of work for subordinate judiciary,[109] enforcing a ban on smoking at public places,[110] controlling noise pollution during festivals,[111] checking ragging in universities,[112] electoral reforms,[113] suggesting irregular allotment of petrol pumps etc.[114] Lawyers have challenged commercial transactions of public sector institution,[115] judicial review of appointments of government counsels,[116] challenging bail to certain persons,[117] or to misuse of public property.

Justice B.N. Kripal in *BALCO Employees Union vs. Union of India*[119] said, "There is in recent years, a feeling which is not without foundation that PIL is now tending to become 'publicity interest litigation' and has tendency to become counter-productive". He also said, "PIL is not a panacea for all wrongs".

In a recent case, the Supreme Court said with anguish that the PIL was being misused by a lawyer in Maharashtra to blackmail someone. This has been a sad reflection on members of the legal profession and is almost the black spot on the noble profession.[120] There have been instances of publicity interest litigations or private interest litigations all pushed by vested interests for their own motives.

PIL has done enormous good. In addition, the benefits of the system are also worthy of consideration. Access locus is highly liberalized, in fact almost eliminated; cost is minimal to the point of being zero; speed is much faster than any other normal litigation; procedural thicket is avoided altogether; disposal is more mass as opposed to individual and lateral; and awareness is greater because of a multiplier effect.[121]

The Supreme Court with its wide jurisdiction and powers reflects the concern with providing social equality and rule of law. In India, the apex court has acted judiciously in changing socio-economic structure and the progress of a nation has depended on its decisions. The existence of this court gives a feeling of security among the citizens. It acts as an independent authority which puts check on extreme actions and upholds the constitutional values. It has adhered to values enshrined in the minds of the framers of the constitution.

Unfortunately, the apex court has not escaped controversy because of various reasons. Lately, the contempt of court cases have shown the sensitivity or the high handedness of the judges. The court has at last woken up to the repeated charges of human rights violations by law-enforcing agencies. Further, loads of cases and delays in judgement have reflected the loopholes of the judicial system.[122]

As a democratic institution, the judiciary is answerable to the people. As Justice Krishna Iyer observed,[123] "all public power is people's trust and so even judicial power has a fiduciary component. Executive power is accountable to the Parliament and the Parliament to the people, judicial power is neither accountable to the executive nor to the Parliament in any direct sense. The judiciary by deriving its power from the constitution, its accountability to people cannot be negated. Unfortunately, these ethnics have not been adhered to by judiciary and, therefore, whenever natural calamities struck the different parts of the nation, it remained a spectator and could not reach the people at the grassroots level, be it the Bhopal tragedy or the Narmada *Andolan*."

Many areas of the court need to be reformed, like the code of conduct of judges, transfer of judges, and rigidity of the system to ensure and preserve its position as the guardian of the constitution and the protector of the basic rights of the individual and society at large.

There is a great need to revamp the judicial system so that people can get access to justice and speedy justice. The experiment of Lok Adalat has met only with a limited success. Most cases referred to Lok Adalat are those where the state has to pay and it agrees to pay for an early settlement.

The Supreme Court of India should inspire alternate dispute settlement machinery, where public can redress its grievances and not burden it with special leave petitions. The judges should write brief judgements and give early decisions. In a few cases, judgements are pronounced only when a judge is to retire; otherwise, they remain reserved for unlimited period. Quality of judges and ability to handle cases with speed and honesty should be the criterion in selection. Unfortunately, politics has entered even in appointments. One finds that judges, like ministers, also come from different High Courts representing different castes, class, or religious backgrounds. It would be worthwhile to restrict the time for arguments. It need not be stressed that a lot of time is wasted by a few senior lawyers who keep arguing for days and many other cases suffer.

There is a need to reform even the legal profession, which has made access to Supreme Court virtually impossible for millions in this country. Long and tardy procedure with further uncertainty, whether the matter would be taken up or not on a particular day, keeps the poor away from approaching the Supreme Court. Time has come when either we reduce the cases that can come up before the Supreme Court or have its benches in different regions. The sitting judges should not be appointed for commissions of inquiry.

There has been a feeling in a section of legal luminaries that judiciary is interfering in things which are actually in the domain of executive or the legislature. On the other hand, Dr. Sri Ram Khanna points out 'when people stand helpless and watch their elected representatives bargain their interests for personal gains, they have no option but to look at the judiciary to step in those matters that concern the public as a whole. At this stage, they will go to anyone who listens to them and that is the environment in which PIL system actually started'.[124] (*Judicial Governance and PIL supra notes 121*). According to Chief Justice Lahoti, one of the main reasons why the hopes of the common man has high vis-a-vis the Indian Judiciary, is because the judiciary is perhaps the only remaining wing of governance that still continues to perform its functions with integrity without fumbling. "When other pillars of the building crumble the remaining pillar has to bear the additional burden and must be willing and alert enough to shoulder this responsibility efficiently."[125]

The large number of cases in courts and large number of cases being filed everyday are suggestive of the people's confidence in the judiciary.

They have the faith that the justice will be done. Unlike other institutions of governance, judiciary stands apart because of certain unique features. First, it is also accessible; it is receptive and responsive to the seekers of justice. Second it listens to everyone. The Courts do not take a decision until both sides of a case have been heard. Third, each decision taken by the judge is accompanied by reasons, which in itself provides for a very high level of accountability. These reasons are guarantees against the possible whims of arbitrariness of judges.[126]

Why judiciary has not been able to live up to people's expectation is on account of doubts about the capability of the judiciary. These doubts are because of delays in deciding cases, and also because of instances of corruption that have started occurring in judiciary (though they are rare). Finally, accusations have been made about the credibility of the courts. Justice Lahoti feels that any system of justice, to be effective, needs to have a proper procedure to follow and the reasonableness of the procedure take its toll in terms of time. According to the 120th Report of the Law Commission, we need 10 times the existing strength of judges to clear the backlog in the Supreme Court, High Courts, and subordinate court the sanctioned strength judges is 26, 704 and 13, 204, respectively. In contrast, the actual numbers are 22, 496 and 11, 103 in that order. The gap is glaring. As far as pending cases are concerned, there are 26,750 in the Supreme Court 31,88,000 in High Courts and 2.28 crore in subordinate courts. The system begs for alteratives, innovation and severe analysis and reform.

At the end, the fact remains that for the success of Indian democracy people still have their faith and hope in an independent judiciary and our Supreme Court has not entirely disappointed them.

Notes and References

1. Chief Justice R.C. Lahoti 'Can the Judiciary Meet the Expectations of the People' Dr Kailash Nath Kunjru Memorial Lecture, *India Habitat Centre Newsletter*, August 2004, p. 9.
2. *Ibid.*
3. D.S. Claire, 'Judiciary: An Estimate', in Sunder Raman (ed.), *Indian Government and Politics*, Delhi, Allied Publishers, p. 151.
4. Report of the *ad hoc* Committee of the Supreme Court, dated 21st March 1947, was attached to as an appendix to the Union constitution Committee.
5. Granville Austin, *The Indian constitution: Cornerstone of a Nation*, Bombay, Oxford University Press, 1972, p. 164.
6. Quoted in M. Imam, *The Indian Supreme Court and the constitution*, Delhi, Eastern Book Company, 1968, p. 16.
7. Austin, *op. cit.*, p. 164.
8. H.R. Khanna, *Judiciary in India and Judicial Functions* (Calcutta: Ajoy Law House, 1985), p. 16.
9. D.O. Basu, *Introduction to the constitution of India* (Delhi: Prentice-Hall of India: 1992, 14 ed.), p. 267.

10. *S.P. Gupta vs. Union of India*. 1982 SCC, 149; *All India Judges Association vs. Union of India. AIR*, 1993, SCC, 2493. Incidentally while appointing Justice Ramaswamy to the Supreme Court, the President ignored the Chief Justice of India. Except Ms Fatima Bibi, Ms Sujatha Manohar, Ms Ruma Pal no other woman has become a judge of the Supreme Court.
11. In September 1977, Justice D.A. Desai of Gujarat High Court was appointed as Judge of Supreme Court, and with his appointment three senior judged of Gujarat High Court were superseded.
12. Law Commission, *Method of Appointement of Judges: The 80th Report*, 1979, p. 29. Justice Y.R. Krishna Iyer was a Home Minister in the First Communist Government of Kerala, though, he himself was an independent candidate.
13. Law Commission, *Reform of Judicial Administration: the 14th Report*, Vol. 1, 1956, p. 39.
14. M. Kumaramangalam. *Judicial Appointments*, Delhi, Oxford and IBH Publishing Co. 1973, p. 83.
15. H.M. Seervai, *constitutional Law of India*, Vol. II, Bombay, N.M. Tripathi Pvt. Ltd., 1976, pp. 1418–19.
16. *S.P. Gupta vs. Union of India*, 1982, SCC, 149.
17. *Times of India*, 7th May 2003.
18. *Consituent Assembly Debates*, Vol. VIII, p. 254; *Law Commission Report*, p. 36.
19. A three-member committee was constituted by the parliament. The members were Justice P.B. Sawant, sitting Judge of Supreme Court: Justice P.O. Desai, Chief Justice of the Gujarat High Court; Justice O. Chinappa Reddy, Retd. Judge of the Supreme Court.
20. *Sub-committee on Judicial Accountability vs. Union of India*, 1991, SCC, 699; *Krishna Swami vs. Union of India*, 1992, (2) Scale 311; *Sarojini Ramaswamy vs. Union of India*, 1992 (2), Scale 257.
21. In reference S.K. Sundram, *AIR*, 2001, S.C., 2374. Supreme Court had *suo moto* issued a contempt notice of the advocate.
22. The salaries of the judges of both Supreme Court and High Courts have been enhanced by the constitution Act of 1986 (54th Amendment).
23. The procedure is subject to the provisions of the Contempt of Courts Act, 1971.
24. On 23rd January 1994, the Supreme Court sentenced three UP policemen for three months simple imprisonment for beating and kicking an undertrial in the Supreme Court premises. The judges said, 'The sanctity of the highest court of the land has been reduced to that of a torture chamber. This is the culmination of a police culture and is a symbolic attack against the rule of law.' *Sunday*, 20-26, February, 1994, New Delhi, pp. 10–12.
25. Arundhati Roy,(2002) 3 SCC 343.
26. *Constituent Assembly Debates*, Vol. XI, pp. 836–837.
27. *State of West Bengal vs. Union of India*, *AIR*, 1963, SC Section, p. 1241.
28. *State of Bihar vs. Union of India*, *AIR*, 1970, SC Section, p. 1446.
29. *State of Rajasthan vs. Union of India*, *AIR*, 1978, SC Section, p. 68.
30. *State of Kamataka vs. Union of India*, *AIR*, 1978, SC Section, p. 68.
31. A.R. Antulay v. R.S. Nayak. *AIR*, 1988, SC Section, p. 1531.
32. *AIR*, 2001, SC, p. 1560. See also, *State of Rajasthan vs. Union of India*, *AIR*, 1977, SC, p. 1361.
33. State of Haryana v. State of Punjab, *AIR*, 2002, SC, p. 685.
34. *Dr. N.B. Khare vs. Election Commission of India*, 1958 SCR, p. 648; *Baburao Patel and Others vs. Dr. Zakir Hussain and Others*, 1968; 2SCR, p. 133; *Shiv Kirpal Sigh vs. Y.Y. Giri, 1971, 2 SCR, p. 197; Charan Lal Sahu vs. Fakhruddin Ali Ahmed and Others*, *AIR*, 1975, SC Section, p. 1288; *Charan Lal Sahu vs. Neelam Sanjiva Reddy*, 1978,3, SCR, p. 1; *H.Y. Kamath vs. G.S. Pathak*, 1970, 3, SCR, p. 334.
35. *Election Commission vs. Venkata Rao*, *AIR*, 1953, SC Section, p. 210.

36. Law Commission, *The Appellate jurisdiction of the Supreme Court in Civil Matters:* The 44th Report, 1971, p. 6.
37. *Damodar Valley Corporation vs. Damodar Valley Corporation Displaced Employees' Union*, *AIR*, 1993, SC Section, p. 2478.
38. *Rajan Sinha vs. State of Bihar*, *AIR*, 1991 SC Section, p. 1377.
39. *Dhakeshwari Cotton Mills Ltd. vs. Commissioner of Income Tax*, 1955, 1, SCR, p. 941.
40. *Union Carbide India Ltd. vs. Union of India*. *AIR*, 1984, SC, p. 101: *M.P Singh vs. Union of India*, *AIR*, 1990, SC, p. 1098; *Sampat Singh vs. State of Haryana*, 1993 1, SC, p. 561; *Sterling Computers vs. M and N publications Ltd*., 1993, 1, sec, p. 445; *Damodar Valley Corporation vs. DVC Displaced Employees' Union*, *AIR*, 1993, SC, p. 2478.
41. *Jugal Kishore Prabhatilal Sharma vs. Vijendra Prabhatilal Sharma*, 1993, 1, SCC, p. 114.
42. Konkan Railway Corporation v. Rani Construction, *AIR*, 2002, SC, p. 778.
43. *Delhi Administration vs. Madan Lal Nangia*, *AIR*, 2003, SC, 4672.
44. *A.R. Antulay vs. R.S. Nayak*, *AIR*, 1988, SC, p. 1531; *All India Judges Association vs. Union of India*, *AIR*, 1993, SC, p. 2493; *Savita Kumar vs. Union of India*, 1993, 2, SCC, p. 357.
45. H.M. Seervai, *op. cit*., p. 1515.
46. Justice V.R. Krishna Iyer, *Current Pathological Problems of India*, Delhi, Capital Foundation Society, 1993, p. 42.
47. Delhi Laws Act of 1912 and 1951, SCC, p. 747; Kerala Education Bill 1958, SCC, p. 956; Indo-Pak Agreement relating to Berubari Union; 1960, SCC, p. 845; Sea customs Act. 1963, SCC, p. 1960: UP Legislative Assembly v. State High Court 1965, SCC, p. 745; Presidential Election, 1974, SCC, p. 1682; Special Courts Act, 1978, SCC, p. 478; Special Deference No.1, referred as Ram Janambhoomi Babri Masjid matter; 1993, SCC, p. 642; Cauvery Water Disputes Tribunal, 1993, Supp., 1 SCC, p. 96.
48. Gujarat Assembly Election Matter, *AIR*, 2003, SC, p. 87.
49. *Romesh Thapar vs. State of Madras*, *AIR*, 1950 SC, Section, p. 1241.
50. *Kharak Singh vs. States of Uttar Pradesh*. *AIR*, 1963, SC, p. 1295; *Nilabati Behra vs. State of Orissa*, 1993 2, SCC, p. 746.
51. R.E.S. Sarkar, 'Judicial Review', in M.M. Shakhdher (ed.). *Framework of Indian Politics*, Delhi, Gitanjali Publications, 1983, p. 101.
52. *State of Madras vs. V. G. Row*, 1952, SCR, p. 605.
53. H.M. Seervai, *constitutional Law of Indian*, Bombay, N.M. Tripathi, 1975, pp. 54–57.
54. *CAD*, Vol. VII, pp. 43–44.
55. *CAD*, Vol. IX, p. 1495.
56. As a result of judgements declared in *Romesh Thapar vs. State of Madras*, 1950, SCR, p. 1957; *Brij Bhushan vs. Delhi*, 1950, SCR, p. 605; *Chmpakam Dorairajan vs. State of Madras*, 1951, SCR, p. 525.
57. *Shankari Prasad vs. Union of India*, *AIR*, 1951, SC, p. 458.
58. *Sajjan Singh vs. State of Rajasthan*, *AIR*, 1965, SC, p. 845.
59. *Golak Nath vs. State of Punjab*, *AIR*, 1967, SC, p. 1643.
60. *R.C. Cooper vs. Union of India*, *AIR*, 1970, SC, p. 564.
61. *Madhav Rao Scindia vs. Union of India*, *AIR*, 1971, SC, p. 530.
62. *Keshavanand Bharati vs. State of Kerala*, *AIR*, 1973, SC, p. 1461.
63. *Indira Gandhi vs. Raj Narain*, *AIR*, 1975, SC, p. 2299.
64. *Minerva Mills Ltd. vs. Union of India*, 1980, 1, SCR, p. 287.
65. *Kehar Singh vs. Union of India*, 1989, 1 SCC, p. 204. *Jumman Khan vs. State of U.P.*, 1991, 1 SCC, p. 752.
66. *Krishna Gauda vs. State of A.P.*, 1976, 2, SCR, p. 1776.
67. Madhukar vs. J.C. Rajani, 3, SCR, p. 837.
68. *Rudal Sah vs. State of Bihar*, *AIR*, 1983, SC, p. 186; *Sebestian M. Hargry vs. Union of India*, *AIR*, 1984, SC, p. 1026; *Bhim Singh vs. State of J&K*, *AIR*, 1986, SC, p. 494;

A.S. Mittal vs. State of U.P., AIR, 1989, SC, p. 1570; *Sabeli, a Women's Resources Centre vs. Commissioner of Police*, Delhi, *AIR*, 1990, SC, p. 513.

69. *Maneka Gandhi vs. Union of India, AIR*, 1978, SC, p. 579.
70. *Tamil Nadu N.V.V.N.U.P. Sangam vs. Union of India, AIR*, 1990, SC, p. 1316; *DTC vs. DTC Mazdoor Congress, AIR*, 1991, SC, p. 101; *Sterling Computers Ltd. vs. M&N Publications Ltd.*, 1993, 1 SCC, p. 445; *Indian Airlines Corporation vs. Capt. K.C. Shukla and Others*, 1993, 1. SCC, p. 17; S.C. upholding the dismissal of BJP governments by presidential Ordinance on 11th March 1994.
71. *Processual justice to the People; Report of the Expert Committee as Legal Aid* (Ministry of Law, Justice and Company Affairs, Govt. of India, New Delhi, 1973).
72. *Report on judicature: Equal justice-Social justice* (Ministry of Law, Justice and Company Affairs, Govt. of India. New Delhi,1978).
73. *AIR*, 1950, SC, p. 27.
74. *AIR*, 1978, SC, p. 597.
75. *AIR*, 1978, SC, p. 1548.
76. *AIR*, 1979, SC, p. 1360.
77. (1991) 2 SCC 373.
78. Sujatha Y. Manohar: Judiciary and Human Rights, *AIR*, 1996, SC, p. 1295.
79. *AIR*, 1984, SC, p. 802.
80. 1993 SCC 645.
81. (2003) 7 SCC 133.
82. (2003) 9 SCC 268.
83. *C.E.S.C Ltd. Vs. Subhash Chanda Bose, AIR*, 1992, SC, p. 573.
84. (2003) 8 SCC 361.
85. (2003) 1 SCC 184.
86. (2003) 8 SCC 369.
87. *Annual Survey of Indian Law*, 2003 Indian Law Institute.
88. *M.C. Mehta vs. Union of India* (2003) 10 SCC 719 where in notice of non-compliance of its orders by the Agra Municipality on removal of solid wastes were issued.
89. (2003) 4 SCC 601.
90. *Times of India, 12-1-2005.*
91. (2003) 4 SCC 399.
92. (2003) 6 SCC 581.
93. *AIR*, 2002, Delhi 36.
94. (2003) 8 SCC 440.
95. *AIR*, 1997 P H 87.
96. *John Vallamattom vs. Unin of India* (2003) 6SCC 611; State of M.P. vs. Gopal D. Tirhani (2003) 7 SCC 83; *Javed vs. State of Haryana* (2003) 8 SCC 369; *Welfare Association vs. Ranjit P.G. Gohil* (2003) 9 SCC 358; *State of Haryana vs. Jai Singh* (2003) 9 SCC 114.
97. (2003) 2 SCC 673.
98. (2002) 8 SCC 481.
99. (2003) 5 SCC 669.
100. *Rupa Ashok Hurra vs. Ashok Hurra* (2002) 4 SCC 388 at 413.
101. Act 37 of 2002 Gazette of India 12-06-02 Part II SI (Extra) SI 40.
102. Permanent Lok Adalat (Other Terms and Conditions of Appointment of Chairman and Other Persons) Rules 2003, GSR 3 (E) 2-1-2003 3(1) Extra SI 3. See Annual Survey of Indian Law 2003, Indian Law Institute p. 755.
103. *Bar Council of Maharashtra vs. M.Y. Dabholkar*, 1975, 2, SCC, p. 702.
104. Fertilizer Corporation Kamgar Union and others vs. Union of India. *AIR*, 1981, SC, p. 344.
105. *Akhil Bhartiya Soshit Karamchari Sangh, vs. Union of India, AIR*, 1981, SC, p. 298.
106. *S.P. Gupta vs. Union of India, AIR*, 1982, SC, p. 1473.

107. *P.U.D.R. vs. Union on India, Ibid., AIR*, 1982, SC, p. 1473.
108. *Justice S.R. Pandian in Janata Dal vs. H.S. Chaudhary, AIR*, 1993, SC, 892.
109. *All India Judges Association vs. Union of India, AIR*, 1992, SC, p. 165.
110. In reference of Noise Pollution (2001), SCALE, 481.
111. *Vishwa Jagriti Mission vs. Central Government* (2001), 3, SCALE, 503.
112. *Union of India vs. Association of Democratic Reforms,* 2001, 3, SCALE, 503.
113. *Common Cause vs. Union of India* (1996), 6, SCC, 530.
114. *N. Parthasarthi vs. Controller of Capital AIR*, 1991, SC, p. 1420.
115. *Harpal Singh vs. State of U.P.* (1993), 4, JT SC, 1.
116. *R. Rathman vs. State Distt. Crime Branch, AIR*, 2000, SC, p. 1851.
117. *Jayalalitha vs. Government of Tamil Nadu, AIR*, 1999, SC, p. 2330.
118. *Guruvayur Devsom Managing Committee vs. C.K. Rajan* (2003), 6, SCALE, 401.
119. *AIR*, 2002, SC, p. 350; See also *Chairman & MD BPCL vs. S.P. Guruja, AIR*, 2003, SC, p. 4536.
120. Justice Arijit Pasayat and Justice S.H. Kapadia of the Supreme Court fined ₹25,000 as fine on the litigant. 'Bitter PIL: Is it for Private Good or Public Welfare?' *Times of India,* 10th January 2005.
121. Dr. Abhishekh Manu Singhavi 'Judicial Governance and Public Interest Litigation' Rajiv Gandhi Foundation, Habitat Focus, *Newsletter* of India Habitat Centre, September 2004, pp. 5–6.
122. *Sunday,* 20-26 February 1994, p. 10.
123. Justice Y.R. Krishna Iyer, *Jusitce at Crossroads*, Delhi, Deep and Deep Publications, 1992, p. 266.
124. Judicial Governance and P.I.L. See *supra note* 121.
125. See *supra note* 1.
126. *Ibid.*

11

The Union Executive

Mahendra Prasad Singh

❑ The Background

Historically, one can delineate at least two divergent lines associated with the evolution of the executive system in India: (1) the monarchical, and (2) federal-republican. The federal republican *gana-sanghas* appeared in the ancient India, but were soon supplanted by monarchies. Republican parliamentary-federal executive finally came to be established only in independent India under the constitution framed in 1950. The main institutional strand in the Indian history has been monarchical and viceregal executive continuing from the ancient through the medieval to the British period. There were at least six variants of this monarchical executive system: (1) monarchical executive within the framework of centralized bureaucratic state during the Mauryan period; (2) decentralized feudal monarchies in the post-Mauryan period; (3) decentralized segmentary state monarchy in the early medieval South India; (4) a diarchical feudal post-Shivaji Maratha state in the 18th century in which the Maratha ruler with his capital at Satara was reduced to being a nominal monarchy, while the hereditary prime minister, the *Peshwa,* with his *gaddi* at Pune, became the dominant power; (5) the Mughal monarchy within the framework of feudal patrimonial bureaucracy; and (6) the viceregal executive within the framework of centralized bureaucratic state in colonial India. The viceregal system of executive subsequently came to be supplemented by rudimentary parliamentary and cabinet systems based on limited franchise and legislative responsibility introduced by the British.

The Union Executive

Independent India adopted a modified version of the Westminster model of government. The most fundamental modification was, of course, the combination of the parliamentary system with federalism and Fundamental

Rights of the citizens and Directive Principles of State Policy. This created the federal imperative that the Westminster model does not know. Another equally important departure is the replacement of monarchy by a republican presidency, although the two are functionally comparable in their limited and strictly nominal role for all practical purposes and their pomp and pageantry. This feature is best described by Walter Bagehot by his celebrated distinction between the 'dignified' and 'efficient' parts of the executive played by the monarch and the Prime Minister and his cabinet. This is similar though not identical with the roles of the President and the Prime Minister/Cabinet in the Indian system. A second feature of the Westminster model adopted in the Indian constitution and convention without any modification is the fusion of powers between the executive and the Parliament which technically means the President-in-Parliament, and the Prime Minister and his council of ministers spring from the Parliament itself. The Prime Minister is the fulcrum of the cabinet, which is collectively and individually responsible to the Parliament, specifically to the Lok Sabha. This feature of the cabinet system is buttressed by the party system. The party or coalition of parties enjoying majority in the Lok Sabha forms the government. This lends ideological and programmatic homogeneity to the cabinet. This is further reinforced by Prime Ministerial and Presidential prerogatives with regard to the formation of the government, dismissal of ministers, and the dissolution the Lok Sabha. A third feature of this model is the independence of the judiciary from legislative and executive control. Even though the judges are appointed by the executive and are impeachable by the Parliament, the constitution takes great pains to ensure that they function without fear or favour. Parliament's power of impeachment of the President and judges and President's powers of pardon and reprieve in criminal cases are essentially, or at least partly, judicial functions. But the judicial power is mainly the preserve of the judicial organ of the state, which forms a unified hierarchy of federal, state, and local courts of India. A fourth feature of the Union executive in India is that the ultimate responsibility of the cabinet goes beyond the Parliament to the electorate at large. Over and above, the presidential prerogative tempered by parliamentary majority, the final recourse in the last analysis is the will of the people expressed in electoral mandate and public opinion. The President is elected by an Electoral College consisting of the elected members of both the houses of Parliament and elected members of the Legislative Assemblies of the states. He has, thus, a federal constituency that transcends the Parliament. The Prime Minister basically springs from a parliamentary base, but given the nature of electoral politics and the party system, it is evident that more often than not that in case of a particular party coming to power who will form the government. This is also often true of coalitions or fronts of parties. Thus, even though a prospective Prime Minister may be seeking election from a narrow parliamentary constituency, he campaigns as a national leader in the entire country. It is by virtue of this plebiscitary feature of elections that the Prime Minister comes under the real focus of power in the parliamentary as well as federal spheres of the government. With the growing fragmentation and regionalization of the party system, the nature of elections may change such that it may become increasingly obscure as to who may be campaigning as prospective Prime Ministers. To that extent, this situation may demand an institutional substitute for the parliamentary-federal salience of the Prime Minister's role, *e.g.*, election of the party leaders at a national convention of parties as in Canada. Or else, designation of the leaders of the fronts of parties prior to the national electoral campaign. These reforms will find a federally aggregative effect to the electoral campaign.

President and Prime Minister

It is clear from the foregoing discussion that the Indian constitution establishes an executive at the federal level that comprises a constitutional or nominal Presidency with an effective Prime Minister and his cabinet. Article 53 proclaims that 'the executive power of the Union, shall be vested in the President', and Article 74(1) provides that 'there shall be a Council of Ministers with the Prime Minister at the head to aid and advise the President who shall, in the exercise of his functions, act in accordance with such advice'. The President thus, cannot ever rule the country unaided by council of ministers. According to Article 75(1), 'the Prime Minister shall be appointed by the President. The other Ministers shall be appointed by the President on the advice of the Prime Minister'. Although the constitution does not mention political parties here, according to the established conventions of the British, Canadian, Australian, New Zealand, and (now since independence) the Indian political systems, it is evident that the President's choice of a Prime Minister is normally limited to the leader of the party with a majority in the Lok Sabha, or to that of the largest single party or coalition of parties therein. Thus, only when the party system fails to throw up an obvious choice in the leader of the majority party (as, for example, after the fall of the Janata Party government in 1979, and in government formations since the loss of Congress predominance in 1989) can the President have some active role and discretion in this matter. Article 75, (2) and (3) makes the seemingly contradictory provisions that the ministers shall hold office during the pleasure of the President' (2) and 'The Council of Ministers shall be collectively responsible to the House of the People' (3). This seeming contradiction, plus the absence of the mention of the Prime Minister in the above clauses, dissolves in view of the convention of the constitution in parliamentary systems the world over that the head of the state is bound by the structure of the majority on the floor of the popularly elected house of the Parliament. The same holds true of the lower chamber. It is shared by the President and the Prime Minister, with the view of the Prime Minister holding majority in the Lok Sabha prevailing. The President can have discretionary power in the matter only when a Prime Minister has evidently lost majority in the house. Now, with the 42nd and 44th constitutional amendments, in fact, the foregoing convention in India has become part of the written constitution in as much as Article 74(1) expressly requires the President to act in accordance with the advice of the Council of Ministers; at most the President may require the Council of Ministers to reconsider such advice once more 'either generally or otherwise' and after such a reconsideration he is constitutionally bound by the advice. This is true of Emergency provisions in the constitution as well as of constitutional amendment Acts. In contrast to Governors (Article 163, Section 1), the constitution does not expressly give any discretionary powers to the President.

The foregoing construction of the powers of the President and the Prime Minister/cabinet is consistent with the expectations of the Constituent Assembly and the major thrust of academic commentaries as well as the behaviour of the incumbents of both the highest offices of the land (*e.g.*, Chetaker Jha, 1960; K.V. Rao, 1961; and Granville Austin, 1966). This does not mean, however, that this interpretation has gone entirely unchallenged either by commentators or by some incumbents of the Presidency. Alan Gledhill, for example, presents an alarmist view of the President's power to assume dictatorial control of the government. Granville Austin paraphrases Gledhill's apprehensions of the murky prospects thus, only to subsequently dismiss it:

> 'A President who has been aggrandizing his powers learns that Parliament intends to impeach him. During the stipulated lapse of two weeks between the notice of, and the movement of, the impeachment motion, the President dissolves Parliament. If a new Parliament is elected, writes Professor Gledhill, the President need not to summon it for six months. In the meantime, the President may dismiss his ministers and appoint others of this choice, himself governing the country by Ordinance during this period. This situation could easily justify a proclamation of emergency, and in this manner the President could step by step take over control of the nation'.

He rejects this argument out of hand, and persuasively so:

> 'The President could not dissolve Parliament without the advice of his Prime Minister, in the first place. Nor could his other hypothetical actions be described as constitutional. That a President or a Prime Minister, perhaps with the backing of the armed forces, could assume power in India is possible, but that would be revolution. And, as Sir Ivor Jennings has written, constitutions do not contemplate revolutions. If the Federal Executive in India becomes autocratic it will be because Parliament and body politic

have defaulted in their responsibility and have acquiesced in their own downfall, because the intent of the constitution has been 'constitutionally' circumvented'.

At least two past Presidents have also questioned the strictly nominal interpretation of the President's role under the constitution. Dr. Rajendra Prasad, the first President, in a note to the first Prime Minister, Jawaharlal Nehru, on 18th September 1951, conveyed his desire to exercise his own discretion in assenting to Bills, sending messages to Parliament, and returning Bills for Parliament's reconsideration. This view of President's power was firmly opposed by Nehru, Attorney General M.C. Setalvad, and A.K. Ayyar, a member of the Constituent Assembly.[1] Prasad never acted upon his intention, but raised the issue again in the context of non-comparability of President's power to that of the British Crown, arguing that in Britain the monarch can do no wrong (as he/she acts always on the advice of ministers), whereas the President is both elective and impeachable. Besides, he pleaded that 'our conditions and problems are not on a par with the British'. President Prasad went on amplifying:

> 'The British constitution is a unitary constitution in which the Parliament is supreme, having no other authority sharing its power of legislation except such as may be delegated. Our constitution is a federal constitution in which the powers and functions of the Union Parliament and the State Legislatures are clearly defined and the one has no power or right to encroach upon the rights and powers reserved to the other'.

In view of all this, he wished it to be investigated as a matter of academic debate 'the extent to which and the matters in respect of which, if any, the powers and functions of the President differ from those of the sovereign of Great Britain'.

The Zail Singh-Rajiv Gandhi open confrontation over President's powers occurred during the last months of Singh's presidency (summer and monsoon of 1987). The controversy had been brewing for a long time. It centered initially around the violation of Article 78 of the constitution which provides:

> 'It shall be the duty of the Prime Minister: (1) to communicate to the President all decisions of the Council of Ministers relating to the administration of the affairs of the Union and proposals for legislation; (2) to furnish such information relating to the administration of the affairs of the Union and proposals for legislation as the President may call for; and (3) if the President so desires, to submit for the consideration of the Council of Ministers any matter on which a decision has been taken by a minister but which has not been considered by the council'.

In the midst of media reports and speculation that the Prime Minister was neither calling on the President nor did the Home Ministry oblige him by supplying a copy of the Thakkar Commission Report on Indira Gandhi's assassination despite repeated requests. Rajiv Gandhi claimed in the Parliament that he was regularly meeting the President and briefing him on all important affairs of the state. A letter purportedly written by the President contradicting it leaked out to the press. It raised a furore in the Rajya Sabha, but the Vice President R. Venkataraman, acting as the Chairman of the upper chamber, 'ruled out any discussion on the subject, upholding the principle of confidentiality of communication between the President and the Prime Minister'. The problem subsequently became more complicated with the revelations of alleged payment of kickbacks to 'Indian contacts' by the German firm HDW in the supply of SSK submarines and to the Indian ministers and bureaucrats in the supply of Howitzer guns by the Swedish firm Bofors to the Indian army. The opposition mounted a public outcry against the Prime Minister, seeking his resignation. The opposition parties, Congress dissidents, and some prominent luminaries of the legal and journalistic professions began lobbying the President to either dismiss the Prime Minister or to give permission to prosecute him for the alleged involvement of his government in corruption and moral turpitude. They found that Zail Singh not only a President willing to listen and seeking legal advice in and outside the government (mostly outside), but also keen to negotiate politically an alternate Prime Minister to replace Rajiv Gandhi and his own candidature for a second term as President with the support of the opposition and Congress dissidents. Only two days before handing over the presidency to the President-elect R. Venkataraman, Zail Singh finally replied to a letter by journalist Rajinder Puri expressing his inability to grant permission for Rajiv Gandhi's prosecution.[2]

A federal dimension to the mode of indirect election of the President (*e.g.*, association in the process of the elected members of state legislatures) plus frequent appeals to the President for intervention in matters affecting the state governments may convey the impression that he may have some discretionary federal role independent of his nominal parliamentary role as the head of the federal state. But, in a parliamentary-federal state any such independent federal role can be exercised only by the judiciary without jeopardizing the parliamentary component of the government at the Centre.

Two years after the Zail Singh episode, his successor, R. Venkataraman, was also called upon to decide on a similar petition by Shanti Bhushan, a Supreme Court advocate, for Rajiv Gandhi's prosecution on the same charges. In consultation with the Attorney General, the President dismissed the petition, as the charges were based on newspaper reports and surmises, which had been held by Bombay High Court earlier as hearsay rather than evidence. The Attorney General veered to the position that the Supreme Court's ruling in Karunanidhi's case would suggest that the Chief

Minister (and, therefore, the Prime Minister) might be deemed to be a public servant under the anti-corruption Act, 1986, and the Governor (and, therefore, the President) could remove a Chief Minister (and, therefore, a Prime Minister) for proven charges of corruption. Besides, he also argued that in terms of the R.S. Naik case, the President or the Governor should decide independently of the Council of Ministers in sanctioning such prosecution. However, both these positions could be assailed in appropriate proceedings'. The President has wondered aloud what an incumbent without legal training would do in such cases:

> 'If the President had to decide such issues in his sole discretion, he could hardly distinguish between evidence and hearsay, nor could he judge whether the ingredients of an offence had been made out by the applicant. If he relied on his secretary who often times was an administrative officer and not one trained in law, his advice could not be of much value. If the President consulted the law officers of the Government, he could not be sure if the advice was not partisan. Nor could he consult judges since they had to decide the case later if sanction was issued. Consultations with non-official lawyers would hardly be proper since it involved sensitive charges against the head of the administration. I hope the Supreme Court will some day ponder over all these matters'.

A few months later, C. Subramaniam wrote to the President drawing his attention to the Comptroller and Auditor General's observations in his report on the Bofors gun deal and urged him to examine the matter, as the Supreme Commander of the Armed Forces, outside the purview of Article 74(1) of the constitution and act on his 'own independent conclusions'. President Venkataramen found nothing in the constitution which gave validity to the suggestion. He said:

> 'It is well known that the President is only a titular head of the Armed Forces and cannot issue any direction to the Forces except through the Ministry of Defence. In my view, the constitution of India did not envisage the President as an appellate authority over the government, but only as a symbol of State with defined powers'.

Despite a federal electoral college for election of the President, the construction of Presidential power in Indian constitutional law and practice has developed within the framework of parliamentary principle of government. In fact, this is in conformity with the functional requirement of unity and cohesion of the Union executive in the parliamentary mode with subsidiary federal roles. The advent of a multiparty system and federal coalition governments have, however, significantly changed this scenario typical of one party dominance or even single-party majority governments in New Delhi. The new development has increased the moral maneuverability of the President and Governors. The coalition partners and supporters in the Parliament and state legislatures/governments have also seriously constrained the authority and power of the Prime Minister. This has also diluted the collective responsibility of the Union Cabinet to the Parliament and added a more effective federal dimension to the whole framework of government of India than ever before.

The Prime Minister and the Cabinet

An important thing about the cabinet system in India is that, except for the procedure of its formation, almost everything else about it has been left to conventions. This is essentially in conformity with the Westminster model of cabinet government. This constitutional vacuum in India, as in Britain, has been left to be plugged by the party system. There has, of course, grown an intricate web of conventional and legal administative procedures and organizations centering around the cabinet (*e.g.*, cabinet committees, Prime Minister's Office, cabinet secretariat, etc.) within the government itself. However, the role of the Prime Minister and the way Council of Ministers works are basically determined by the balance of forces in the ruling party, or parties in case of a coalition government, and in the party system at large. Besides the factional balance of forces in the party and configuration of parties in the system, a Prime Minister is also constrained in government formation to take into account, at least to an extent, ethnic and regional factors. But, these considerations are always mediated by political factors. If the Prime Minister happens to be in a commanding position in the party, there are few fetters on his powers of appointing and dismissing ministers and conducting the working of the Council of Ministers. This was, by and large, true of Nehru after Patel's death in December 1950 and prior to the Chinese aggression in October 1962. The PMs usually enjoy the leeway in bypassing the Council of Ministers/Cabinets as whole bodies, or even the cabinet committees, and get away with deciding informally in consultation with a few senior colleagues, who may constitute a sort of 'inner cabinet' or 'kitchen cabinet'. The foregoing was also characteristic of Indira Gandhi after her massive mandates in the 1971 mid-term elections and 1972 State Assembly elections.

One can, indeed, delineate at least three models of Prime Ministerial leadership in India. The first, typical of the Nehru era, may be called for want of a better term, 'pluralist parliamentary premiership. It coincided with the single-party dominant 'phase under the aegis of the Congress both at the federal and state levels. For this reason, the Prime Minister of India operated within a political framework that, despite the federal division of powers, almost resembled the parliamentary system. The second model of Prime Ministerial power may be called 'neo-patrimonial parliamentary premiership'. This was exemplified by Indira Gandhi at the height of her power, mainly 1971 to the end of internal Emergency in 1977. The Congress party enjoyed predominance during this phase in New Delhi and also in most of the states, but with a difference.

Unlike the pluralist power structure and internal democracy in the party in the Nehru era, Indira Gandhi's Congress dispensed with organizational elections following the great split of 1969; state Chief Ministers and *Pradesh* party presidents came to be nominated by the Prime Minister herself. With this centralization of power in the Prime Minister's hands, she also gave the call for 'committed' bureaucracy and judiciary. The Prime Minister's Secretariat (later renamed by Morarji Desai as PMO) was greatly expanded to buttress her enormous powers. The third model of Prime Ministerial style may be designated as the 'federal' parliamentary one. It was presaged by the Janata government (1977-79) and the Rajiv Gandhi government (1984-89), which, despite the persistence of oligarchical tendencies in the two respective parties, were more amenable to federal pressures than any other preceding governments. The four (later five) major parties that merged to form the Janata Party—Bharatiya Jana Sangh, BharatiyaLok Dal, Congress (Organization), Socialist Congress for Democracy-functioned as four oligarchical factions at the Centre, but state-level groups had better chances of being heard and considered in New Delhi than, say, in the highly-centralized and oligarchic power structure of the Congress Party led by Indira Gandhi. The Congress (Indira) under Rajiv Gandhi continued to be oligarchical and undemocratic, but his relations with non-Hindi state units of the party and non-Congress state governments were generally more informed by the federal principle than those with Congress units and governments in the Hindi-speaking regions. The federal premiership style came to have a fuller denouement in the post-1989 period.

With the range of variation sketched above, the Prime Minister must act as to use a cliché, the keystone of the cabinet arch. Observers, who have worked in the Prime Minister's, Secretariat, tell us that his role as the executive head of the government mainly clusters around initiation, coordination, and monitoring of policies. An effective Prime Minister is the one who keeps himself as free and available as possible for consultation and policy initiation and coordination. In Chetakar Jha's opinion, 'a Prime Minister without any specific portfolio is more desirable than the present practice. The British Prime Minister does not hold any'. L.N. Sharma, too, regards coordination as his 'most important responsibility'. This is particularly true of governments and countries with greater departmental autonomy, such as Britain and the older Commonwealth than India, especially under powerful Prime Ministers, like Jawaharlal Nehru and Indira Gandhi, who like the grand Mughals tried to implement almost everything important by themselves. With what we have called 'federal' Prime Ministers above, coordination and arbitration between and within ministries, and between the Centre and the States, assumes greater importance, without, however, relegating their role in major policy initiatives to the background. With the growing complexity of the government, policies in increasingly larger number of areas are now formalized in national policy statements and approved by the Parliament for longer term implementation by ministries. Ministers, especially in finance and technological areas, now seem to enjoy a quantum of autonomy which was previously unknown.

Parliament, Party, and Mass Public

Beyond the Presidency and the cabinet, Prime Minister's role may well be conceptualized as a series of concentric circles of power and influence spanning the parliament and the civil society. The classical role of the Parliament in the convention mode as the independent maker and unmaker of the constitution and government and the seat of legislative initiative has been arrogated by the party whip and the government and the administration. The Indian Parliament is no exception to this universal trend of the decline of Parliament. Even the committee system in a parliamentary system cannot compete with the committee system in the American Congress. For the separation of the U.S. President and his cabinet from the Congress allows vigorous committee work in the legislative process. On the contrary, committees in a parliamentary system are overshadowed by the cabinet, which is, in fact, the most important committee of the house, so to say. The Indian Parliament has introduced a new full-fledged system of departmentally-related standing committees since the spring of 1993. It will strengthen the committee system, but hardly reverse the role of the Parliament beyond being: (1) the instrument of legitimization of the government shaped by political processes and forces, and (2) the forum for focusing on important public issues and mitigation of public grievances.

The institutional imperatives of India's parliamentary-federal system significantly determine the Prime Minister's relations and role in the party and the mass public. In the periods of transition from the anti-colonial nationalist movement to national governance (1947-50), from the 'Nehru-Patel duumvirate',[3] to the former's supremacy in the dominant Congress party (1950-52), and from one durable premiership to another (1964-1970, when Shastri and Indira Gandhi in quick succession, succeeded Nehru), the organizational wing of the Congress tended to acquire some salience and even tried to assert its supremacy vis-a-vis the parliamentary wing. However, forcing the issue into direct confrontations, both Nehru and Indira Gandhi in their respective periods of ascendancy were soon successful in establishing the supremacy of the parliamentary wing over the organizational wing and of the Prime Minister over the party as a whole. The organizational wing again displayed a flurry of sponsored activity under the benevolent authoritarian shadow of Prime Minister, Indira Gandhi, to facilitate the political induction of her sons, Sanjay's and, after his death, Rajiv's, in the first half of the 1980s. After Rajiv's tragic assassination in 1991, when the veteran P.V. Narasimha Rao was called upon to abandon his plans of political retirement and head the party, he departed from the practice of *ad hoc* nomination of organizational units under Indira and Rajiv Gandhi and held organizational elections in the party in 1992 after a lapse of twenty years. However, he implemented the principle of 'one man one post' only in the state units of the party, and continued to hold the office of the national Congress President. Moreover, organizational elections were again postponed in subsequent years. The organizational wing did not, therefore, emerge as a locus of any autonomous power. Feeble challenges to Rao's position and policies, if at all, surfaced either from a few of his own cabinet colleagues (*i.e.,* Arjun Singh, Sharad Pawar, and R. Kumaramangalam) or from some state Congress presidents (*i.e.*, Narain Datt Tewary in U.P. and Vazhapadi Ramamurthy in Tamil Nadu). All had to go. These challenges to the Prime Minister's position in the party and the government are attributable to the federal tensions.[4] They coincide with the transition from single-party dominant system to multi-party system of polarized pluralism since the 1989 Lok Sabha elections, since the early-1980s in the states component of the party system.

The federal tensions found fuller expressions in the Janata Party government (1977-79) and National Front government led by Janata Dal (1989-90). Prime Ministers Moraji Desai and V.P. Singh were forced to contend with extra-parliamentary party leaders and powerful cabinet colleagues on much more liberal terms than any previous Congress Prime Minister. However, when it came to the crunch, both Desai and Singh, despite the fact that they represented smaller factions in their parties than some of their cabinet colleagues, were able to easily dismiss and dispense with Charan Singh and Devi Lal, respectively, in swift actions. These more powerful cabinet colleagues in the party had to cool their heels out in the cold when they crossed swords with the Prime Ministers, inherently more powerful in the government. The Prime Ministers, had, however, to eventually pay a heavy price. The Desai government fell victim to factional feuds. While the Singh government survived the factional conflict, it fell shortly thereafter due to other reasons (*i.e.,* withdrawal of support by BJP, which had been supporting it from the parliamentary floor without joining it). Janata Party President Chandra Shekhar and National Front chairman N.T. Rama Rao played only a second fiddle to Prime Ministers, Desai and V.P. Singh (the latter himself was the convener of the National Front).

As effective head of the government, the Prime Minister, especially in an one-party government easily dominates the electoral process and the party's political process. Elections are virtually plebiscites between prospective premiers. In the period intervening between elections Prime Ministers and his rivals in the ruling and opposition parties often organize mass rallies to demonstrate their strength in intra-party bargains and competitive inter-party mass mobilizations with an eye on the coming elections. Left parties and BJP often demonstrate their hold over trade unions and trading centres and white-collar employees, respectively, by calling for *bandhs* in a particular state or the nation at large. Mass movements occasionally spread out like Prairie fires spilling out the confines of the party and electoral processes, leading to major shifts in the political realignment of the mass electorate and changes in the party system (*e.g.*, around the 1967 general elections in the major North Indian states and Tamil Nadu; in 1977 when Congress lost power to Janata Party in New Delhi and major states in North India; in 1989 and 1991 when Congress predominance suffered another major breach at the national-level to National Front, with BJP and Janata Dal emerging as two other major parties alongside Congress, opening up a wide space for coalitional politics and minority governments between these three 'pivot' parties and leftist and regional parties). By 1998-99 these three pivot parties were reduced to two Indian National Congress and Bharatiya [Janata Party on account fragmentation of Janata Dal into several regional splinters in Bihar, Orissa, U.P., and Karnataka, and its decimation in Gujarat. As a result, the national party system configuration has tended to become dualistic-BJP-led National Democratic Alliance (NDA) and Congress-led United Progressive Alliance (UPA). The two fronts have been led by Atal Bihari Vajpayee and Sonia Gandhi respectively. The two UPA governments were headed by Prime Minister Dr. Manmohan Singh, Sonia Gandhi's nominee by virtue of her positions as the Congress party president and the UPA convener. The Prime Ministers are always the major protagonists in these confrontations in party politics and mass movements. The role of the mass media and the use of professional advertising agencies in electoral campaigns and mass mobilizations have also becoming increasingly important since the 1970s. These trends have specially intensified since the 1980s.[5]

In sum, the Indian federal executive has functioned predominantly in the Prime Ministerial mode so far, with the parliamentary component of the government providing the major active component than the federal one. But, with the growing regionalization of the party system, especially since 1989, the Prime Ministers have been required to operate within a political framework with increasingly active federal component. Besides, over the years, the salience of the politics of mass rallies, and occasionally of mass movements, has become more evident in the party system and lent a plebiscitary favour to the electoral politics. This strand of mass politics is more typical of the unorganized sectors of the economy and polity according to Lloyd and Susanne Rudolph, and is marked by what they call 'demand groups', distinct from pressure groups inasmuch as the former are more likely to use anomic and non-institutional channels. The test of statesmanship lies in institutionalizing the party system and restoring the efficacy and esteem of the organs of the government within a more federalized parliamentary system. With much greater salience of regional parties in the 2014 general elections, the statesmanship of the Indian political leadership would be much in demand in the times ahead.

Notes and References

1. See also Reba Som (1994) for a more recent discussion of the episode with some additional documentation.
2. See Prabhu Chawla (1988).
3. The term 'Nehru-Patel duumvirate' is Michael Brecher's (1966).
4. Sharad Pawar was shifted from the Union Defence Ministry to the Chief Ministership of Maharashtra. Tewary and Ramamurthy were highly critical of the soft stance of Prime Minister Narasimha Rao towards Mulayam Singh Yadav government in U.P., and the Jayalalitha government in Tamil Nadu, and the alleged neglect of Congress party's interest in the two states. Kumramangalam was dismissed for open criticism of Prime Minister's policies. The Prime Minister was constantly needled by Arjun Singh on the Babri Masjid demolition and on the violation of 'one man one post' principle by Narasimha Rao himself by combining Prime Minister's office with party presidentship. Following Congress debacle in Andhra Pradesh and Karnataka in Assembly elections in 1994. Arjun Singh resigned from the cabinet presenting a litany of his oft-repeated charges against the top party leadership. On crossing this *Lakshmanrekha* (Rao's favourite metaphor in the context of party discipline), Rao suspended Singh from primary membership of the party. Expressions of support for Singh mainly came from Ramamurthy, Tewary, Digvijay Singh (Madhya Pradesh CM), A.K. Anthony (Kerala), and Kalpnath Rai (Eastern U.P). Singh has since rejoined Congress and was the HRD Minister in the Manmohan Singh government.
5. On the post-1989 party system, see M.P. Singh (1992a and b).

Bibliography

Austin, Granville, *The Indian constitution: Cornerstone of a Nation,* Bombay, Oxford University Press, 1966.

Brecher, Michael, *Nehru's Mantle: The Politics of Succession in India,* New York, Praeger, 1966.

Chawla, Prabhu, 'The Conspiracy that shook Rajiv Gandhi', *India Today* (New Delhi), 15th April 1988.

Gledhill, Alan, *The Republic of India,* London, Stevens and Sons, 1951.

Jha, Chetakar, *Indian Government and Politics: A Political Commentary,* Patna, Novelty & Co, 1960.

Prasad, Rajendra, *President's Speech While Laying the Foundation Stone of the Building of the Indian Law Institute.* New Delhi, 28th November 1960. Indian Law Institute, typescript.

Rudolph, Lloyd & Susanne H., *In Pursuit of Lakshmi: The Political Economy of the Indian State,* New Delhi: Orient Longman, 1987.

Rao, K.V., *Parliamentary Democracy of India: A Critical Commentary,* Calcutta, The World Press, 1961.

Singh, Mahendra Prasad (ed.), *Lok Sabha Elections* 1989: *Indian Politics in 1990s,* Delhi, Kalinga Publications, 1992a. 'From Centrist Predominance to Polarized Pluralism: The Post-1989 Party System in India'. *Punjab Journal of Politics,* Vol. XVI., Vos. 1-2 (1992b).

Singh, M.P. and Rekha Saxena, *India at the Polls: Parliamentary Elections in the Federal Phase,* New Delhi, Orient Longman, 2003.

Sharma, L.N., *The Indian Prime Minister*, Delhi, Macmillan Company of India Ltd., 1976.

Som, Reba, 'Jawaharlal Nehru and the Hindu Code: 'A Victory of Symbol Over Substance?' in J.S. Grewal and Hugh Johnston (eds.), *The India-Canada Relationship: Exploring the Political, Economic and Cultural Dimensions*, New Delhi, Sage Publications, 1994.

Venkataraman, R., *My Presidential Years*. New Delhi, Indus, An imprint of Harper Collins Publishers India, 1994.

12

Governor: Powers and Position

Renu Sethi

The Governor plays the key role as a constitutional head of the state and a custodian of the constitution. This chapter examines the important constitutional provisions relating to the powers and functions of the Governor; how these powers have been exercised since the commencement of the constitution; how to safeguard and ensure the smooth working of parliamentary democracy in states even in the most difficult situations.

Each state in India has a Governor in whom, as per Article 154 of the constitution, all the executive powers of the state are vested. This power is to be exercised by him in the same fashion as the President in case of the executive powers of the Union "either directly or through the officers subordinate to him in accordance with this constitution." The pattern of governments in the states in the Indian Union is of the parliamentary type. The executive head designated as the Governor is a constitutional ruler and acts on the advice of the ministers who are responsible to the lower house of the state legislature. M.V. Pylee observes, "As in the union, the government in the states is also organized on the Parliamentary model. The head of the states is called the Governor; the head of the state government is called the Chief Minister who is counterpart in the State, of the Prime Minister of India." His office is not subordinate or subservient to the government of India, nor is he accountable to them for the manner in which he carries out his functions and duties. He holds an independent constitutional office which is not subject to the control of the government of India.

❑ Appointment of Governor

Article 155 provides the "Governor of a state shall be appointed by the President by warrant under his hand and seal." He is removable by the same authority. But, in actual practice, he is appointed by the Central government, which means by the party in power at the Centre [Prime Minister]. But two conventions have generally come to govern his nomination." One, the Central government ordinarily consults the state concerned before announcing the appointment so that he is acceptable to the concerned state ministry. It is a sound practice though it has been flouted on several occasions. For instance, the appointment of the West Bengal Governor Dharamvir against the wishes of the then chief minister. In Bihar, the controversy arose when M.P. Sinha, the then chief Minister, protested against the appointment of Nityanand Kanungo as the Governor. In the appointment of Sri Prakasa in Madras, and Kumaraswami Raja in Orissa, the respective Chief Ministers were not consulted. The Chief Ministers of Tripura and Uttar Pradesh protested when Romesh Bhandari was appointed Governor in those states. Jayalalitha strongly opposed the appointment of M. Chenna Reddy and S.S. Barnala as Governor of Tamil Nadu.

Before the fourth general elections of 1967, no importance was given to this convention, because in the Centre and in almost all the states, Congress was the ruling party. It assumed vital importance after 1967 when coalition governments came into being in different states. There arose a controversy between the Congress government at the Centre and the non-Congress governments in various states over the meaning of consultation. If it is consultation and not the consent of the Chief Minister or the state cabinet, there is no logic in it. Thus, in actual practice, Article 156 meant that the Governor was appointed by the Prime Minister in consultation with the Home minister.

Another convention is that the incumbent of this office comes from outside the concerned state. This, again is a wholesome arrangement, because such an incumbent does not have his local political roots and affliations and would, thus, be free from state level party politics. But this convention has also been violated in some cases. For instance, Ujjal Singh, Punjab (1966), Karan Singh, Kashmir (1965), J.E. Wodeyar Bahadur, Mysore (1956), H.E. Mukherjee, West Bengal, and Vasantdada Patil in Maharashtra were appointed Governors.

National Commission to Review the working of the Indian constitution under the Chairmanship of Justice N.M. Venkatachalaiha recommended, a committee consisting of the Prime Minister, Home Minister, Speaker of the Lok Sabha and the Chief Minister of the concerned State should select the Governor. Instead of confidential and informal consultation, it is better that the process of selection is transparent and unambiguous.

The executive powers of the state are vested in the Governor and all executive actions of the state have to be taken in the name of the Governor. Though the Governor holds office during the pleasure of the President [Art. 156], the period is limited to a term of five years. However, the person can be reappointed as the Governor of the same state or of some other state. His term can also come to an end by resignation or dismissal by the President.

By the Seventh constitutional Amendment, 1956, it has been provided that the same person can be appointed Governor for more than one State.

Qualifications: Any citizen of India, who is 35 years of age or above, is eligible for the office of the Governor [Art. 157]. He is debarred from holding any other office of profit or being a Member of the Parliament or any State legislature [Art. 158].

The Governor is paid a monthly salary of ₹35,000 and is provided a rent-free official residence, Raj Nivas. He is entitled to all allowances and privileges as were enjoyed by the Provincial Governor at the commencement of the constitution. Parliament has the right to make laws relating the emoluments, allowances, and privileges of the Governor. However, the emoluments and privileges cannot be diminished during the term of office [Art. 158(3)], except during financial emergency under Article 360.

❑ Constituent Assembly Debates

When the Constituent Assembly discussed the question of the head of the State four alternative methods of selecting the Governor were suggested before the final decision was taken:

1. Election by adult suffrage.
2. Election by the members of the Legislative Assembly either by proportional representation, or otherwise.
3. Selection by the President out of a panel prepared by the Legislative Assembly.
4. Appointment by the President.

General discussion in the Constituent Assembly revealed that the election of the Governor on the basis of universal adult suffrage was incompatible with the parliamentary form of government as was adopted for states where head of the state has to be only a constitutional head. Several members of the Constituent Assembly criticized the direct election as inappropriate, an anomaly and absurd. B.R. Ambedker, on behalf of the Drafting Committee, made the position clear and stated, "We feel that the powers of the Governor were so limited, so nominal, his position so ornamental that probably very few would come forward for elections." Direct election of the Governor would have created constitutional crisis as it would have clashed with the directly elected Chief Minister. His election would also create problem of leadership at the time of general election. Apart from a possibility of clash between the Governor and the Council of Ministers, the direct election of the Governor creates serious problem of leadership at the time of a general election. During election, a political party will have to rally round a leader. Who will be the leader, a candidate for the Governor or for the office of the Chief Minister? Discussions on the floor of the Assembly revealed that the co-existence of a directly-elected Governor and directly-elected Chief Minister might lead to friction. Election by the Legislative Assembly would make the Governor a nominee of the ruling party, and he would always be trying to appease the Assembly, for his own election. Therefore, this was also not acceptable to many. H.V. Kamath opposed the panel system on the ground that if the President somehow did not choose the very first nominee and chose the third or fourth, the legislature of the state would certainly have grouse against the man chosen by the President, because he had been chosen in preference to the first man. After having discussed all the proposals, framers accepted Brajeshwar Prasad's amendment for the appointment of the Governor by the President "by warrant under his hand and seal," thinking it to be the "lesser most evil", an instrument of maintaining "common links" between the Centre and the states and a cogent factor establishing "harmony, good working, and balanced relations between the provincial cabinet and the Governor."

Experience of administration from 1947-49 had convinced the framers of the fact that the disintegrating forces were quite strong in India, preservation of country's unity, security, and solidarity was vital, therefore, the Governor should act as constitutional nexus between the Union and the states. It was Nehru's dream that only eminent, non-partisan, and non-political men could be selected for the dignified post the Governor. However, it has seldom come into operation. The Administrative Reforms Commission had recommended that a person, who can be trusted to rise above party prejudices and predilections should be considered for the post. But Governors have been unashamedly appointed in total disregard of these norms. Most of the appointees have been active politicians whose loyalty to their party often reflected in their actions and conduct. In some cases, the defeated candidates of the Congress party had been appointed governors. N. V. Gadgil, H. V. Pataskar, V. V. Giri, M. M. Jacob, the Governor of Meghalaya, Krishan Kant, Governor of Andhra Pradesh, K.V. Raghunatha Reddy, the Governor of West Bengal, Motilal Vora, Sudhakar Nayak, Shiv Shankar, Bali Ram Bhagat, Krishna Pal Singh, Sheila Kaul, and others, were in this category. Thus, one finds that those who were rejected by the electorate were rewarded with the Governorship as a consolation prize. Kailashpati Mishra, S.S. Bhandari, Kaidarnath Sahani, K.R. Malkani were rewarded by the NDA government. In the year 2004, R.L. Bhatia in Kerala, Buta Singh in Bihar, Naval Kishore Sharma in Gujarat, Balram Jhakar in Rajasthan and S.C. Jamir in Goa were appointed by the United Progressive Alliance led by Manmohan Singh. There are instances where Chief Minister of certain states were appointed Governors to make room for their successors. Arjun Singh, Moti Lal Vora, Chenna Reddy, Surjit Singh Barnala, S.M. Krishna, Sushil Kumar Shinde, Madanlal Khurana, S.C. Jamir fall in this category. It is often alleged that such Governors misuse their powers and act as tools in the hands of the Central government and destabilize the state governments of opposition parties. Accusations by the former Uttar Pradesh Chief Minister Mayawati against the Governor Romesh Bhandari on the law and order situation in the state are not totally baseless. Besides these, another category of governors is of retired civil servants who are considered "favourite boys" of the Central government, *e.g.,* Dharmvir, B.N. Chakravarty, Raghukul Tilak, Jagmohan, Vishnu Sahai, L.P. Singh, Govind Narayan, Romesh Bhandari, General K.V. Krishna Rao, Naresh Chandra, P.C Alexander, T.N. Chaturvedi, Rama Devi, Ved Marwaha, V.C. Pande, A. R. Kidwai, and other. In brief, we can say that mostly Governorship is reserved for the party men. Nath Pai rightly maintained that the office of the Governors was degraded by the Centre by making it a patronage and largesse. The fact that the standard of appointment of Governors is deteriorating day after day has forced persons, like E.M.S. Namboodiripad, Bhupesh Gupta, and C. Annadurai to ask for its abolition. Namboodiripad said that it had become a fifth wheel.'

Speaking in the Constituent Assembly on the choice of the Governor, Nehru observed: "I think it would be infinitely better if the Governor was not so intimately connected with the local politics of the province; and would it not be better to have a more detached figure, obviously—a figure that must be acceptable to the government of the province and yet he must not be a part of the party machine of that province. But, on the whole, it probably would be desirable to have people from outside, eminent people, sometimes people who have not taken too great a part in politics." Three decades later Sarkaria Commission on the Centre-State relations recommended the following: (1) It is desirable that a politician from the ruling party at the Union is not appointed as Governor of a State which is being run by some other party or a combination of other parties, (2) In order to ensure effective consultation with the State Chief Minister in the selection of a person to be appointed as Governor, the procedure of consultation should be prescribed in the constitution itself by suitably amending Article 155.

To sum up, we can safely say that to ensure efficient and impartial discharge of the limited discretionary powers by the Governor, it is a must that fair-minded men of high calibre and integrity are appointed.

Powers and Functions of the Governor

Executive Powers: Under Article 154 of the Indian constitution, the executive powers of the state are vested in the Governor and shall be exercised by him either directly, or through officers subordinate to him. The Governor appoints the Chief Minister of the state and other ministers are appointed by the Governor on the advice of the Chief Minister. Ministers hold office during the pleasure of the Governor [Article 164]. The constitution provides that it is the duty of the Chief Minister to communicate to the Governor all decisions of the Council of Ministers relating to the administration of the affairs of the state and proposals for legislation [Article 167]. The Governor can ask the Chief Minister to submit for the consideration of the Council of Ministers, any matter on which decision has been taken by a minister, but which has not been considered by the Council. Article 165 empowers the

Governor to appoint Advocate General of the state. He also appoints the members of the State Public Service Commission [Article 316].

As far as the states of Bihar, Madhya Pradesh, and Orissa are concerned the constitution confers special responsibility on the Governor to see that a minister is placed in charge of tribal welfare [Article 371]. In Assam, also he enjoys certain special powers with respect to the administration of tribal areas [Sixth Schedule]. All executive actions of the government of the state shall be expressed to be taken in the name of the Governor [Article 166].

Legislative Powers: Governor enjoys extensive legislative powers in the state. Article 168 makes the Governor a part of the state legislature. Governor may summon, address, prorogue, and dissolve the Legislative Assembly [Article 174]. The Governor can address and send messages either to the house or houses of the state legislature [Article 175]. Under Article 176, the Governor, at the commencement of the first session after each year, addresses the Legislative Assembly or in case of a state having a legislative Council, both houses assembled together, and inform the legislature of the causes of its summons.

President Shankar Dayal Sharma, inaugurating the Conference of Governors in June 1997, said: "In the ordinary course, an address under this [Article 176] represents the policies and programmes proposed to be implemented by the Council of Ministers and invites the attention and consideration of the legislature in this respect". However, it is argued that the circumstances are materially different when a government is asked first to seek a vote of confidence. In such a situation, the question arises whether the address under the above Article should not focus exclusively on the true cause of the summoning to the legislature, *i.e.*, to enable the Assembly to determine whether it has the confidence in the Council of Ministers. If the Council of Ministers succeeds in securing a vote of confidence, it remains open to them to advise the Governor to make an address under Article 175(1) of the constitution, whereby the policies and programmes of the Council of Ministers could be indicated. Alternatively, if the Council of Ministers fails to secure a vote of confidence and if another Council of Ministers is installed in its place, the successor Council of Ministers retains the option of advising the Governor to address the legislature under Article 175(1) of the constitution. All considered, would the foregoing approach not be desirable?

When a Bill has been passed by the state legislature, it has to be presented to the Governor. He shall declare either that he assents to the Bill or that he withholds his assent therefrom or that he reserves the Bill for the consideration of the President [Article 200]. The Governor may return a non-money Bill with a message for reconsideration of the whole Bill or parts of it. He may suggest amendments. The legislature must consider his suggestions without delay. If the Bill is again passed by the legislature or without amendment and presented to the Governor for assent, the Governor shall not have the power to withhold assent any more. In other words, he shall be bound to give his assent. The Governor, under Article 213, can promulgate ordinance during the recess of the legislature if he is satisfied that there exist circumstances which make it necessary for him to take immediate action. Such an ordinance has the same force and effect as an Act of the state legislature. The ordinance ceases to operate at the expiry of six weeks from the reassembly of the legislature unless a resolution approving it is passed by the legislature.

The Governor can nominate a member of the Anglo-Indian community if they are not adequately represented in the legislative assembly [Article 333]. He can also nominate persons to the Legislative Council who have special knowledge or practical experience in the fields of literature, science, art, cooperative movement and social service [Article 171(5)].

Judicial Powers

Article 161 says that the Governor of a state shall have the power to grant pardons, reprieves, respites or remissions of punishment or to suspend or remit or commute the sentence of any person convicted of any offence against any law relating to a matter to which the executive power of the state extends. In case of A.M. Nanawati, the Governor of Maharashtra granted remission and ordered his release, four years after he was awarded life imprisonment. This order was issued by the Governor in consultation with the Chief Minister because of exceptionally good conduct of Nanawati in jail and a distinguished record of service in the Indian Navy.

The Governor is entitled to be consulted by the President of India in matters related to appointment of the judges of the State High Court [Article 217].

The Governor has the power to sanction prosecution of a minister or an MLA under the Prevention of Corruption Act. There has been considerable debate whether this power is to be exercised by the Governor on the advice of the Council of Ministers or in his discretion. After A.R. Antulay's case where Governor P.C. Alexander had accorded his permission to prosecute the former, a new controversy surfaced in the Fodder Scam case involving Bihar's former Chief Minister Laloo Prasad Yadav. The then Bihar Governor A.R. Kidwai had accorded sanction to the CBI to prosecute the Chief Minister. In Tamil Nadu, Jayalalitha had challenged in the Supreme Court of India the power of the Governor M. Chenna Reddy to sanction her prosecution.

The apex court said, "If the Governor cannot act in his own discretion, there would be a complete breakdown of the rule of law as much as it would be open for governments to refuse sanction in spite of overwhelming material showing that *prima facie* a case was made out."

Emergency Powers

Article 356 empowers the Governor to send a report to the President that the constitutional machinery in a state has broken down or that the state cannot function in accordance with the provisions of the constitution. On receipt of the report, President may assume to himself all or any of the functions of the government of the state [President's rule]. Article 356 has been used more than hundred times to impose President's rule in different states.

Discretionary Powers

To understand the discretionary powers of the Governor, let us once again read Article 163 of the constitution, which states: '(1) There shall be a Council of Ministers with the Chief Minister at the head to aid and advise the Governor in the exercise of his functions, except insofar as he is by or under this constitution required to exercise his functions or any of them in his discretion. (2) If any question arises whether any matter is or is not a matter as respects which the Governor is by or under this constitution required to act in his discretion, the decision of the Governor in his discretion shall be final, and the validity of anything done by the Governor shall not be called in question on the ground that he ought or ought not to have acted in his discretion'. Article 163[2] confers on the Governor blanket discretion to decide, when they are required to act in discretion. There is no such mention of discretion in case of the President. The Governor can act in his discretion: while the President is bound by the advice of the Union Council of Ministers. The 42nd constitutional Amendment Act, 1976, makes it further clear that the president has no discretion under Article 74.

The survey of state politics reveals that the governors have exercised their discretion under certain circumstances on following matters:

Appointment of the Chief Minister;
Dismissal of the Chief Minister and the Council of Ministers;
Suspension of the Legislative Assembly;
Dissolution of the Legislative Assembly;
Recommending to the President to issue a proclamation of emergency;
Seeking information from the Chief Minister relating to legislative and administrative matters;
Directing the Chief Ministers to submit for the consideration of the Council of Ministers any matter on which a decision has been taken by any individual minister;
Returning a Bill passed by the state Legislature for reconsideration;
Reserving a Bill passed by the state legislature for the assent of the President;
Seeking instructions from the President before promulgating an ordinance on certain matters;
Sanctioning the prosecution of the Chief Minister or other ministers under the Prevention of Corruption Act;

Recently the Supreme Court of India in a land mark judgement held that the Governor is not a mere titular head, he can accord sanction for the prosecution of a minister for an offence even after the council of ministers had refused such permission. A five-member bench of the constitution consisting of Justice Santosh Hegde, Justice S. N. Variava, Justice B. P. Singh, Justice H. K. Sema and Justice S. B. Sinha, said, "Democracy itself will be at stake if the government refuses to accord sanction for prosecution against ministers in matters where *prima facie* a clear case for prosecution was made out. It would then lead to a situation where people in power may break law with impunity safe in knowledge that they will not be prosecuted as requisite sanction will not be granted."

While exercising judicial powers, the Governor can act independently.

Special powers of Governor of Assam in matters relating to tribal areas are also discretionary.

Governors of Nagaland, Sikkim, Arunachal Pradesh, Mizoram, Meghalaya, and Tripura have also been given special powers where they can act in discretion.

How this discretion has been exercised by different Governors would also reveal what role they have played in state politics. Have they merely acted as the constitutional heads or as the agents of the Central government?

In matters relating to the appointment of Chief Minister the Governor has no discretion where the Chief Minister enjoys the absolute majority in the Legislative Assembly. Further, in cases, where the person is the leader of a coalition or united front formed before the election, the Governor has no choice but to invite that person to form the government. The question of discretion arises where no party gets absolute majority in the Legislative Assembly elections. In such situations, who should be invited to form the government?

After the 1952 elections in Madras, no party secured absolute majority in the Legislative Assembly. T. Prakasam formed the United Democratic Front and staked the claim before the Governor, Sri Prakasa, to form the government. But the Governor invited C. Rajagopalachari, leader of the single largest party, namely, the Congress, to form the government. In Rajasthan, after the 1967 elections, Congress could win only 89 seats in the Assembly of 184. Opposition parties forged a united front against the Congress and claimed the support of 92 MLAs under the leadership of Maharawal Luxman Singh. Two days later, the Governor Sampurnanand announced that he had decided to invite Mohan Lal Sukhadia, leader of the Congress Party, to form the government. This led to mass protests and the leader of the opposition paraded 93 members of the State Legislative Assembly before the President of India at the Rashtrapati Bhawan. In Haryana, after the 1982 elections, the Congress could muster the support of 42 MLAs in the House of 90. Devi Lal, leader of the combined opposition, with the strength of 45 MLAs staked his claim to form the government. Haryana Governor, G. D., Tapase invited him to the Raj Bhawan to prove his claim in two days, by 24th May 1982. Bhajan Lal, leader of Congress Party, claimed that he should be given the first chance to prove his majority as the Congress was the single largest party in the house. Surprisingly, Governor Tapase administered the oath of office to Bhajan Lal as the Chief Minister without even waiting for Devi Lal. The Governor also allowed one month time to Bhajan Lal to prove his majority.

Priority of single largest party over post-election alliance is a clear convention supported by the Sarkaria Commission and President R. Venkataraman, but it has often been disregarded. Most recently, Governor Krishna Pal Singh of Gujarat, who ignored Suresh Mehta's demonstration of his majority, dismissed the government and paved the way for Shanker Singh Vaghela. Likewise, after the 1996 elections, in Uttar Pradesh, no political party could secure clear majority in the 425 member assembly. BJP emerged as the single largest party with 176 seats. Romesh Bhandari, the Governor of *Uttar Pradesh,* refused to invite Kalyan Singh, the leader of the BJP, to form the government. The Governor wanted full satisfaction to the effect that a stable government could be formed in the State. It was only in March 1997, that Bhandari invited Mayawati, leader of the Bahujan Samaj Party and the BJP combine, to form the government. Discretion relating to the appointment of the Chief Minister is also exercised when there are defections from one party to the other.

The Sarkaria Commission has recommended that in states, where there is no clear majority with any single party, the Governor should invite leader of the alliance of parties that was formed before the elections. Thereafter, chance should be given to the single largest party staking claim to form the government with the support of other parties and independents. Next in order should be the leader of the post-election alliance of parties claiming support of other parties joining the government and some supporting it from outside without joining the government should be given the chance.

Another area, where governors exercise discretionary power is in dismissing a ministry. Where Governor is satisfied that the ministry has lost the confidence of the legislature, he may dismiss the government. This may be due to the split in the ruling party or on account of defections or withdrawal of any constituent party from the alliance/united front. Since it is the duty of the Governor to see that the government of the state is carried on in accordance with the provisions of the constitution, he is duty bound under his oath to exercise discretion. There are instances where ministries enjoyed the support of majority in the Legislative Assembly yet the governors felt that they should not continue in office.

In 1957, E.M.S. Namboodiripad was sworn in as the first Communist Chief Minister by Governor B. Ramkrishna Rao in the state of Kerala. The government decided to eliminate corruption, introduce land reforms, and make vital changes in the administration of the state by associating large number of people and the party workers. V.R. Krishna Iyer, who later became a judge of the Supreme Court of India, was the law minister in the Namboodiripad government. He streamlined the working of courts and withdrew frivolous cases against workers and introduced radical reforms in various departments. The opposition parties, namely, the Congress, P.S.P., and Muslim League, called for civil disobedience movement in June 1959, to bring down the first communist ministry. Roman Catholic Church and the Nair community which opposed the educational reforms of the communist government in the Kerala Education Act also engineered an agitation against the communists. The Governor of Kerala sent a report to the President stating that the law and order situation in the state was deteriorating and there was insecurity for the people, therefore, it was difficult to carry on the administration of the state in accordance with the provisions of the constitution. The Central government dismissed the Kerala government though it enjoyed the support of majority in the State Legislative Assembly. In 1976, Tamil Nadu Governor, K.K. Shah, recommended the dismissal of DMK government under Chief Minister M. Karunanidhi on the ground that the government had indulged in serious acts of maladministration, corruption, and misuse of power for partisan ends. It had failed, he alleged, to follow the instructions of the Central government in relation to the emergency. Karunanidhi's government had comfortable majority in the legislative assembly, but it was dismissed. In 1993, four state governments ruled by the Bharatiya Janata Party were dismissed after the demolition of the Babri Masjid on 6th December 1992.

At the 1995 Governors' conference, the President constituted a committee of governors on minorities under the chairmanship of Khurshid Alam Khan, Governor of Karnataka. Terms of reference for the committee included: to record such observations and reflections as might be of use to the Central and state governments in better securing the well being of minorities towards fulfilling the ideal enshrined in the preamble of the constitution. Other members of the committee were Mohammed Qureshi, Governor of Madhya Pradesh, Romesh Bhandari, Governor of Uttar Pradesh, M.M. Jacob, Governor of Meghalaya, Krishna Pal Singh, Governor of Gujarat, Justice (Rtd.) Fatima Beevi, Governor of Tamil Nadu, and Justice (Retd.) S.S. Kang, Governor of Kerala.

In 1997, a serious controversy arose relating to the law and order situation in the state of Uttar Pradesh. The Union Home Minister Indrajit Gupta said in a statement that there was state of anarchy in the state and law and order situation was going from bad to worse. Romesh Bhandari, the Governor of the state, denied the charge and gave facts and figures to show that the situation in Uttar Pradesh under the President's rule was better compared to earlier times and other States. BJP gave a notice of motion for Governor's recall in Lok Sabha, while Romesh Bhandari and Indrajit Gupta brought disrepute to their respective offices by publicly confronting each other on the law and order situation in Uttar Pradesh. Speaker P.A. Sangma, set a healthy precedent for parliamentary democracy in admitting the BJP's motion for debate. On the same issue, another controversy arose between the Uttar Pradesh Chief Minister, Mayawati, and the Union Defence Minister Mulayam Singh Yadav.

In West Bengal, after the 1967 elections, Left Wing parties won 151 seats in 280 member Legislative Assembly. Governor Dharmvir invited Ajoy Mukherjee, leader of the Front, to form the government. But, soon

P.C. Ghosh, Food Minister in Ajoy Mukherjee's government withdrew support from the ministry and formed an independent Progressive Democratic Front. Ghosh met Governor Dharmvir and staked his claim to form the government with the support of the Congress Party. On 6th November 1967, the Governor asked the Chief Minister to convene the Legislative Assembly to prove his majority on the floor of the house before 23rd November 1967. Mukherjee's ministry rejected the date and suggested 18th December 1967, as the earliest convenient date for Assembly session. The Chief Minister said that since the legislators were involved in the paddy procurement drive of the government, it would be inconvenient to call them. Ajoy Mukherjee's government requested the President to seek advice of the Supreme Court on the discretionary powers of the Governor on the following issues:

1. Whether the Governor has authority to dismiss the Council of Ministers without taking the verdict of the legislature?
2. Can the Governor, on the basis of information available to him that the Council of Ministers does not enjoy the confidence of the legislature, in his individual discretion dismiss the ministry?
3. Is the Governor bound to act on the advice of the Council of Ministers in matters of summoning of legislature or can be disregard the advice of the Chief Minister on the date of summoning the Assembly and insist on a particular date?
4. If the Chief Minister fails to comply with the advice of the Governor, can the Governor dismiss the Chief Minister on the ground of non-compliance of the advice tantamount to violation of them constitution?

Governor Dharma Vira under his discretionary powers dismissed the Left Front government on 21st November 1967, and on the same day invited P.C. Ghosh to form the government. Interestingly, there have been many cases where Governors in different states did not even give three days time to the Chief Ministers to prove their majority on the floor of the house. On 2nd July 1984, when 12 legislators of the ruling National Conference in Jammu and Kashmir Assembly decided to withdraw their support to Farooq Abdullah ministry, Governor Jagmohan dismissed the ministry the same evening. Governor did not allow Abdullah even a single day to prove his majority on the floor of the house. Not only this, he also invited G.M. Shah to be the new Chief Minister of J&K. Similarly, in Andhra Pradesh, when N. Bhaskar Rao, Finance Minister in the N.T. Rama Rao's Telugu Desam ministry defected with some MLAs and resigned from the ministry on 12th August 1984, the Governor Ram Lal dismissed the N.T. Rama Rao ministry on 14th August 1984, and also appointed N. Bhaskar Rao as the Chief Minister of Andhra Pradesh. N.T. Rama Rao advised the Governor to summon the Assembly on 18th August, but the governor did not oblige. On the other hand, he allowed one month's time to N. Bhaskar Rao to prove his majority. Again in 1995, when Telugu Desam leader and Andhra Chief Minister N.T. Rama Rao was in hospital, his son-in-law Chandrababu Naidu arranged a coup and split the party.

Governor Krishna Kant secured Rama Rao's resignation from the hospital bed. Krishna Pal Singh, Governor of Gujarat, did not give any time to Chief Minister Suresh Mehta and invited Shanker Singh Vaghela, in October 1996, to form the government. Illustrations of such nature are available in almost all states where governors have exercised discretion in dismissing the Chief Ministers. Recently Prakash Singh Badal, Chief Minister of Punjab, accused the Centre for dismissing all Akali governments before their full term.

The Supreme Court, in the Assembly dissolution case, felt that the majority of the Chief Minister should, generally, be tested on the floor of the house. Floor test was reasonable to avoid unnecessary political controversies about the misuse of power. The Sarkaria Commission has suggested that the Governor cannot dismiss the ministry so long it enjoys the majority in the Legislative Assembly. He must not allow them to remain in power if they lose the majority in the Assembly. But, if the Assembly is not in session or is prorogued he should advise the Chief Minister to summon the Assembly as early as possible, say between 30-60 days depending upon the circumstances and the exigencies.

The power to dissolve Legislative Assembly is vested with the Governor. Normally, the Assembly should not be dissolved before the period of five years, but the growing political instability due to defections or fast realignments in political groups makes it necessary to seek fresh mandate from the public. Interestingly, in Kerala after 1965 Assembly election no political party or group was in a position to form the government. Hence, the Governor had no choice, but to dissolve the house without even the first session. Similar situation had arisen in Uttar Pradesh after the 1996 elections. Governor Romesh Bhandari refused to call any party to form the government. The Assembly remained suspended till the BSP and BJP decided to form an alliance and form the government. It is interesting to note that BJP had opposed the BSP-Congress combine in the Uttar Pradesh Assembly elections. In March 1997, Atal Bihari Vajpayee said in Lucknow, "The BJP has decided to close the BSP chapter. The BSP should have allied with us in Punjab if it wanted our cooperation in Uttar Pradesh."

Punjab Chief Minister Gurnam Singh resigned in November 1967, and recommended to the Governor that Assembly may be dissolved. But the Governor did not accept the advice and installed another ministry. Similarly, in 1971, Hitendra Desai, Chief Minister of Gujarat, when he lost the majority recommended to the Governor to dissolve the Assembly. The Governor did not accept his advice; whereas in 1971, the Punjab Governor D.C. Pavate dissolved the Punjab Assembly on the advice of Chief Minister Prakash Singh Badal and in West Bengal the Governor dissolved the Assembly on the advice of Ajoy Mukherjee.

In a parliamentary model, the head of the state should accept the advice of the Chief Minister and order fresh elections. At the time of annual conference of Governors on 20th November 1970, President V.V. Giri had set up a committee of five governors under the chairmanship of Kashmir

Governor Bhagwan Sahay to study the constitutional powers of the governors relating to the appointment of Council of Ministers, summoning and dissolving of Legislative Assemblies and failure of constitutional machinery in the state and to suggest guidelines for Governors to meet such problems other members of the committee were the Uttar Pradesh Governor B. Gopala Reddy, the Kerala Governor M.V. Vishwanathan, the Maharashtra Governor Ali Yavar Jung, and the former West Bengal Governor S.S. Dhawan. In October 1971, the committee submitted a 73 page report and disapproved the idea of laying down rigid guidelines for state governors, as doing so was considered unconstitutional, because under the constitution no authority was vested with the power to issue any directions to the Governor or lay down any rules for his guidance. The committee expressed the feeling that greater degree of political discipline on the part of legislators and parties, rather than strict observance of a set of rules by governors, would prevent erosion of democracy and ensure stability of administration. The committee suggested that in order to assist the governors in evolving healthy conventions with respect to all these issues a special wing in President's secretariat must be set up to collate and make available authentic information regarding political and constitutional developments in all states from time to time.

There has been some criticism of the power of Governor to reserve a Bill passed by the state legislature for President's assent under Articles 200 and 201. A study made by the Indian Law Institute reveals that in almost all cases the Governor reserved the State Bill for President's assent on the advice of the State cabinet. On the contrary, D.C. Gupta feels that Council of Ministers will not advise the Governor to reserve any Bill for the President's assent as the same is passed by the state legislature with its concurrence. If any Bill is so reserved, the decision is taken by the Governor in his discretion. Vinod Sethi still goes a step further when he says, "It is quite likely that Governor may reserve a particular Bill in his discretion contrary to the advice of State cabinet."

P.V. Rajamannar, Chairman of the Inquiry Committee on Union-State Relations, has severely criticized the manner in which the Governors have exercised their powers. Chapter VIII of the Report, from pages 119-31, provides a well documented case that the Governor, keeping in traditions with the British parliamentary system, should be bound by the advice of the council of ministers. In 1977, West Bengal government had also submitted a memorandum to the Prime Minister underlying *inter alia* the misuse of powers by the state governors. West Bengal government had witnessed a controversy even on omitting certain paragraphs from the Governor's address to the Assembly.

Role of Governor

The role of Governor has become one of the main issues in the Centre-State relations. While the office of the Governor remained free from public controversy during 1950-67, it became highly controversial after the fourth general elections of 1967 which ushered in an era of coalition politics. The thinking that the Governor was a mere constitutional figure had proved true and served the country well during 1950-67. This was mainly due to three reasons. First, after the promulgation of the new constitution when governments were formed in the states in the wake of first general election the top Congress leaders of the states took over as Chief Ministers and only second rank leaders were appointed as governors. For instance, G.B. Pant took over as the Chief Minister of Uttar Pradesh, B.C. Roy of West Bengal, and Srikrishna Sinha of Bihar. Governors appointed in these States though illustrious persons, were not of comparable eminence. Second, the Indian political scene was dominated by a single party, namely, the Congress for a long period, 1950-56. During this period, the Congress party held sway at the Centre and in most of the states, and if and when there was a constitutional crisis in any state, which was resolved in the intra-party forum according to the directions of the Congress high command, and the Governor, had very little chance of using his discretionary powers. The office of the Governor remained non-controversial. In cases where one ministry went out of power the installation of another did not prove tumultuous. Except in states, like Kerala where President's rule was introduced thrice, i.e., 1957, 1959, and 1964; it was promulgated once in each of the following: Punjab in 1951, PEPSU in 1953, Andhra Pradesh in 1954, Travancore-Cochin in 1956, and Orissa in 1961. The third reason, why the Governor acted as figure head was that they took their cue from the President who acts according to the aid and advice of the Prime Minister and his cabinet. The governors were so powerless during this period that some of them lamented over their fate and wondered whether the office they held was of any consequence or significance at all. In his article, titled *The Governors at Work,* K.V. Rao has quoted Sarojini Naidu, one time Governor of UP, as "bird in a golden cage". Sarojini Naidu became the Governor of Uttar Pradesh immediately after independence. Patabhi Sitarammaya observed that he had no public function to perform except "making fortnightly reports to the President".

A major change occurred after the fourth general elections of 1967. The political situation changed when Congress party lost the majority support in some states and opposition parties, in some cases, as many as 12-13, formed united fronts to take control of the government machinery. The only uniting factors amongst these parties was opposition to the Congress and a desire to wrest power. All united fronts were a marriage of convenience and were the products of naked struggle for power and offices; and the moment hope of gaining something in the government was lost, the support to the government by some of the constituent units of the united front was withdrawn; the united front was wrecked and the ministry went out of office. From March 1967 to March 1972 governments in different states fell from power more than two dozen times, President's rule was introduced about fifteen times. On the eve of the fifth general election of the State Assemblies, seven states were under Central rule. Those states are, Bihar, Gujarat, Punjab, Mysore, Manipur, West Bengal, and Tripura. During that period, emergence of new regional parties and political defections were the order of the day, and MLAs changed their loyalties as often and as freely as a man would change dress in a day. These developments gave rise to chronic instability in several states; there could be no such thing as the "collective responsibility" of the Council of Ministers to the Legislative Assembly. As a consequence, the Governors were called upon to exercise their discretionary powers more frequently. Provisions of Article 163 [l], that the Governor would discharge his functions with the "aid and advice" of a Council of Ministers, became inoperative. A party or parties which benefited from the Governors' conduct in a particular situation appreciated his decision and the others which lost in the game of power-politics became his bitter critics, irrespective of the impartiality of his decision. Under such situation, it was difficult for the Governors to act impartially because the office they held has of a political nature. On certain occasions, they took different decisions in identical constitutional situations and this naturally led to the conclusion that they were acting under Central pressure to promote or protect the political interest of the ruling party, namely, the Congress. The period was popularly known as 'Aaya Ram, Gaya Ram' period, the term which gained currency in Haryana due to frequent defections. As a result, the governors were called upon to exercise their discretionary power more frequently. In other words, they acted as agents of the Centre. The manner in which they exercised those powers has had direct impact on Union-State relations. After 1967, controversies regarding the role of Governor became alarming. In the states of Rajasthan, West Bengal, Punjab, M.P., Haryana, Uttar Pradesh and Kerala role of governors in appointing chief ministers or suggesting for imposition of President's Rule or dissolution of Assemblies raised several questions about their position, partisan attitude, and constitutional status. Another interesting development regarding the role of Governor which deserves a mention is the manner in which Charan Singh, Union Home Minister in the Janata Party government in 1977, dismissed nine state governments ruled by the Congress party after the defeat of Congress party in the Lok Sabha elections. Three years later, on the same logic, Indira Gandhi dismissed nine state governments on the ground that the Janata Party had lost mandate to rule in the states due to defeat in the Lok Sabha elections.

Role of Governor as Chancellor had also attracted public debate in some states. In December 1995, Shankar Dayal Sharma, President of India, had constituted a committee under the chairmanship of P.C. Alexander, the Governor of Maharashtra and Goa, to examine the role of the Governor as Chancellor, keeping in view the experience obtained in various states, and record such observations and reflections as might make for more efficacious discharge of the functions of the Chancellor with a view to improving the standard of higher education in tune with the priorities and resources of state government; and to prepare a report for being placed before the President. Other members of the committee were Krishna Kant, Governor of Andhra Pradesh, K.V. Raghunatha Reddy, Governor of West Bengal, B.R. Bhagat, Governor of Rajasthan, and Mahabir Prasad, Governor of Haryana. The report of the committee was circulated in the 1997 governors' conference.

These developments were really unfortunate and eroded the credibility of our federal structure. It destroyed the very basis of two sets of government at the Centre and in the states. There is a need to develop our institutions so that the federal structure can be strengthened. There is a noticeable trend in favour of regional parties and coalition groups. If the Centre would misuse its power to dismiss democratically elected governments for partisan ends, the whole democratic fabric would be destroyed or would be in jeopardy.

At a National Debate on the Term of Governor, Justice Kuldip Singh, former Judge of the Supreme Court and the Chairman of Delimitation Commission of India, felt that in cases where the Central Government wants to remove the governors, natural justice demands that they should be told the grounds for their removal. Senior Advocate and Member of Parliament R.K. Anand speaking at the national debate said that RSS governors misused their office and brought shame to the high office. He said despite several *strictures* by the Supreme Court against Gujarat Government the Governor continued to shield the Chief Minister for political reasons. Senior Advocate and former President of the Supreme Court Bar Association K.K. Venugopal felt that the convention should be developed that the governors should tender their resignations whenever there is change of the Central Government as it is done by the Attorney General, Solicitor General, etc. They are men of integrity and independence. P.H. Parekh, President of the Supreme Court Bar association, questioned the utility of the Office of the Governor when politicians are appointed and they misuse their office. In fact, they serve no useful purpose and become a burden on the tax payers. Dr. Vinod Sethi felt that only men of integrity, independence and high qualifications should be appointed as governors.

National Commission to Review the working of the constitution under the Chairmanship of Chief Justice M. N. Venkatachaliah observed that a fixed tenure of five years should be introduced coupled with a provision for impeachment by the State Legislature as it is in case of the President. He stressed the suggestions were aimed at investing the office of the Governor with the requisite dignity and integrity and making the Governor an independent and fair arbiter of a dispute. The Panel felt that it was essential to retrieve and restore the glory and dignity of the office.

❑ Conclusion

The era of coalition politics in states expanded the scope of discretionary powers of the governors with regard to several matters. In June 1997, the focus of the Conference of governors and political leaders convened by the President was mainly on the theme: "The role of constitutional head when, following an election, no party or combination of parties appears to have secured a majority." The issue has relevance both at the Centre and in the States in the present era of coalition governments.

The President of India while inaugurating the governors' conference said that the outcome of the elections of the eleventh Lok Sabha and the Uttar Pradesh State Assembly in 1996 have led to conjectures that hung Assemblies and even Lok Sabha could be a recurrent feature in India's political life. This has a bearing on the image of our country. We have to bestir ourselves to prove that there are institutions and systems which can efficiently and confidently deal with the phenomenon of hung legislatures. This conference should signify the capability and determination of higher leadership to effectively manage any problem, however, intractable it may seem. This will be in keeping with our country's prestige as an advanced parliamentary democracy.

President Shankar Dayal Sharma said, "In my view it is of utmost importance that in the given situation the constitutional head functions with due impartiality, independence, constitutional propriety, transparency, and upholds national interest as paramount." Underlying the agenda of the Conference, he listed some questions that deserve answers. These are as follows:

1. Ought the leader of the government that has failed to secure a majority in general election be obliged to tender his resignation and that of the members of his Council of Ministers, and if so, when: (1) immediately on the outcome of the election being apparent, or (2) on the new house being notified as constituted, or (3) only on an indication from the constitutional head?
2. On the composition of the new house being clear, *i.e.,* the party position being known, should the constitutional head wait for some party or combination of parties to approach him with a claim to form a government. If so, for how long should he wait for such an initiative? In the interim period, *i.e.,* until the decision of formation of the new government is taken, should any restriction or restraint be observed by the caretaker government? If so, what should be the restrictions or restraints to be observed by the care-taker government?
3. Should the constitutional head himself take the initiative towards consulting political parties on their being in a position to form the government? If so, what may be the criteria on which the constitutional head should satisfy himself that the leader of any particular party or combination of parties qualifies for an invitations to form a government.
4. Should a leader so invited to form the government be asked to seek a vote of confidence in the relevant house? If so, should a period be stipulated for doing so, and, if so, what would be a reasonable period for this purpose?

5. In the period up to motion of confidence being voted either way, for or against, should the government be obliged to observe any restrictions or restraints, and, if so, what should these restrictions or restraints be.
6. When a government is formed on the basis of support from more than one party, and the support to the government is indicated to have been withdrawn by one or more of the parties, it being evident that viability of the government may have been materially impaired. Should the constitutional head: (1) take no immediate cognizance of the withdrawal of support, leaving it for concerned party to move a motion of confidence in due course, or (2) ask the Council of Ministers to seek a vote of confidence from the relevant house? If so, what would be the reasonable period to be stipulated for the purpose, or whether any restrictions or restraints would be advisable to be observed by the government for the interim period?
7. If a particular configuration of political parties forms a government, and, then, following the withdrawal of support by one or more of its supporting parties, that government suffers a defeat in the relevant house, but the same configuration of political parties re-forms and there is no alternative government possible, and it being evident that the reformed configuration enjoys a majority, what are the factors that need to be kept in mind for an appropriate decision in the matter?
8. What steps should be taken to safeguard and ensure that the institution of the constitutional head is enabled to function as an impartial and independent constitutional authority?

In the year 2004, some interesting developments took place in respect of the role of Governor. The UPA government of Dr. Manmohan Singh dismissed the four state governors for their RSS links, namely, Kedarnath Sahani [Goa]; Vishnukant Shastri [Uttar Pradesh]; BabuParmanand [Haryana] and Kailashpati Mishra [Cujarat]. The Centre has said before the SC that the President has unfettered powers to order the removal of governors and it cannot be questioned in any court.

NOTES AND REFERENCES

M.V. *Pylee, constitutional Government in India,* 1960, p. 457.
Hargobind Pant vs. Raghukul Tilak, AIR, 1979, SC, p. 1109.
S.R. Maheshwari, *State Governments in India*,1979, p.35.
M.V. Pylee, *op. cit.*, p. 459.
H.V. Kamath and K.Y. Munshi, *Constituent Assembly Debates (CAD)*, Vol. 1. p. 462.
CAD, Vol. III, p. 468.
M.V. Pylee, *op. cit.*, pp. 459–460.
CAD, Vol. III, p. 429
H.V. Kamath, *Ibid.*, p. 430.
Jawaharlal Nehru, *Ibid.*, p. 455.

The Hinsustan Times, June 15, 1997.

Lok Sabha Debates, Vol. 6, 1967, col 2793.

D.C Gupta, *Indian Government and Politics,* 1983, p. 381.

CAD, Revised edition, Vol. III, pp. 445–446.

A.R. Antulay. State of Maharashtra, 1984, 2 SCC 183; After the Governor's sanction the Chief Minister was charge sheeted and arrested by the CBI in July 1997.

Times of India, 6th November 2004, p. 8.

Chief Ministers of Delhi,Haryana,mahrashtra and Rajasthan who met at the Jaipur criticized the use of Article 356 for narrow political ends. *The Times of India,* June 26, 1997.

Times of India, 6th November 2004, p. 8. Madhya Pradesh Governor Bhai Mahavir granted sanction to prosecute two former Ministers in Digvijay Singh's cabinet Bishnu Ram Yadav and Rajinder Kumar Singh who had allegedly allowed the release of 7.5 acres of land illegally to the earlier owners even though the area had been acquired by the Indore Development Authority, under Section 197 of the Criminal Procedure Code even after the Council of Ministers had decided not to accord sanction for their prosecution.

In July 2004,Governor V.C. Pande of Arunachal Pradesh dissolved the Legislative Assembly and recommended the imposition of President's Rule in the State as several members from ruling party has crossed over to the Opposition. Next day he again wrote to the President withdrawing his recommendation for imposition of the President Rule in the State as his earlier was under duress and undue pressure. Thereafter three contradictory reports were sent to the President.

India Today, June 16, 1997, p. 4.

Commission on Centre-State Relations (Chairman, Justice R.S. Sarkaria), 1987, ch. 1. pp. 135–137.

The Times of India, June 14, 1997.

S.R. Bommai and others. *The Union of India and Others,* 1994, 3 SCC1.

India Today, 15th March 1997, pp. 26–27. In their desperation to get rid of President's rule, and to have a share in power the B.J.P. with 176 legislators as against 69 of the B.S.P. accepted Mayawati's terms for the formation of a coalition government on a rotational basis. A novel formula was evolved to break the political impasse. The B.S.P. was to rule up to 21st September 1997, and, thereafter, the B.J.P. was to lead the coalition, see *The Hindustan Times, Sunday Magazine,* 7th September 1997.

S. N. Jain and Alice Jacob, "Presidential Assent to State Bill: A Case Study", *Journal of Indian Law Institute,* January-March 1970, p. 151.

D.C. Gupta, *op. cit.*, p. 374.

Vinod Sethi, "Centre-State Relations: Presidential Veto Over State Legislation", *Indian Political Science Review,* Vol. XII, No. 2, July 1978, p. 242.

Sarojini Naidu, *Selected Letters,* 1890-1940,edited by V. Pranjape, 1997, p. 80.

Report of the Capital Foundation Society National Debate 12th July, 2004 published in *Pioneer, Hindu* and some other newspapers on 13th July 2004.

Shivraj patil replying to a short duration discussion in Lok Sabha on removal of governors denied that the government's action were politically motivated and that it had not consulted the State government while appointing new governors.

In *B.P. Singh vs Union of India* in which removal of four governors by the Presidential order of 2nd July 2004 was questioned in the the Supreme Court of India. See Times of India on 1st October 2005 and 26th January 2005.

13

Bureaucracy and Development

Rajvir Sharma

Bureaucracy occupies a central place in the context of development process of a country like India. However, its role has been visualized and analyzed in different ways by different people. But mostly, the opinion is that the bureaucracy plays a leading role in the formulation and administration of development plans, policies, programmes and projects. At the same time, it is pointed out that bureaucracy is also responsible for the slow progress of social and economic change. Many dysfunctional attributes of bureaucracy are brought to our notice. Nonetheless, it cannot be denied that bureaucracy has a lot of influence and even control over the policies of the state. It is in this context that the role of bureaucracy in the socio-economic change can be traced in independent India.

At the time of independence, India faced a large number of issues, *viz.*, poverty, hunger, squalor, illiteracy and ignorance, unemployment, ill-health, inequalities of income, regional imbalances, etc. These problems required immediate attention to be solved. Moreover, the problem of scarcity of resources was also acute. Neither had we adequate financial and physical resources, nor was there an adequately trained manpower. In such a situation, the need for optimum utilization of existing resources was imperative. Furthermore, the human and capital-resources were to be augmented. In this context, the policy-makers decided to opt for planning as a strategy of development. The problem before India was not merely of economic developments that refer to increasing production of goods and services or growth. We were to ensure a mechanism of distributive justice encompassing all elements of social justice with special emphasis on alleviation of poverty, equality of opportunity, provision of mass employment, health and education, etc. In other words, the leaders and the administration were to contend with satisfying basic needs of the masses in general and the underprivileged in particular. Development, thus, was to be seen in a comprehensive perspective which impinges upon social, economic, political, and cultural aspects. It was realized that this gigantic task could not be completed without: (1) the direct and leading intervention of the state in the social and economic affairs; and (2) the development of adequate and appropriate administrative structures and behaviours. Both of these considerations required formulation and implementation of development plans, policies, programmes, and projects together with the creation of a responsive, result and achievement-oriented administration. In other words, the dreams of the poor could be shaped in to reality through the mechanism of bureaucracy insulated from colonial attitudes and behaviour or imbued with democratic, empathetic and goal-oriented attitudes, skills and habits. This could not be done without making conscious efforts for administrative development and development of administration. Let us see now as to how India has proceeded on the path of development administration in terms of capabilities and capacities. The statement subsumes the achievements and failures of bureaucracy also.

Approaches and Strategies of Rural Development

It is evident from what has been mentioned above that development for us was to be a multifaceted exercise-building-up large public sector to play a role of 'commanding heights' in industrial, agricultural, scientific and technological progress, and laying special emphasis on redistribution of national income and wealth in order to realize constitutional goals of equity, justice, and freedom. Priority was naturally given to poverty-alleviation, concentration of wealth into the fewer hands, and employment generation. The focus on rural development, hence, was the consequence. Let us now examine, first, the response to the problems of rural development in light of the following legislative policy and strategic initiatives:

1. Land-reforms: legislation and implementation.
2. Community development programme.
3. Democratic decentralization.
4. Approaches to rural poverty-alleviation and employment creation.
5. Decentralized planning.
6. The shift in the approach in 1990s.

❑ Land Reforms: Legislation and Implementation

At the time of independence, transforming the political economy of rural India was one of the most important jobs of public administration.

The land, the sole important source of income for the rural population, was owned by a handful of *zamindars* and or *jagirdars*, and rest of the rural people worked as either tenants or landless labourers inclusive of bonded labourers. This was the deprived or underprivileged sections of the Indian rural society that constituted the majority. This perpetuated the exploitative relations between the privileged few and underprivileged majority. In order to put an end to all this, minimization of levels of inequality between social classes became a prerequisite. It required priority development of backward and deprived social strata and abolition of mass-poverty. The importance of land reforms in this context need not be over-emphasized. While these reforms aim at augmenting agricultural output leading to rapid economic growth, more employment generation and distributive justice also intended to eliminate discriminative and exploitative social and economic structure. The major elements of land-reforms policy in India are: (1) abolition of intermediaries; (2) tenancy reforms; (3) land ceiling and distribution of surplus land; and (4) consolidation of land holdings. The most revolutionary step in the direction of terminating intermediary tenures was the abolition of the *zamindari* system as a result of which an estimated 20 million farmers were brought into direct relationship with the state and were conferred ownership-rights. The tenancy reforms followed the policy of land to the tiller, security of tenure and regulation of rent. The First Five-Year Plan document suggested the following steps in this context:

1. Fixing the rent at 20-25 per cent of the gross produce.
2. Termination of tenancy by mutual consent only.
3. The land surrendered by the tenant voluntarily should be deemed to be surrender in favour of the state which can distribute that land to the landless people. However, these recommendations did not find favour with the state governments. They sought to provide security of tenure through regulating laws. However, even these laws, for most part, in most states remain unimplemented for political, social, and administrative reasons. Though leasing of land is permitted only in case of widows, minors, unmarried women, physically and mentally challenged, and members of the armed forces, yet the system of absentee landlordism is not completely out of use even in other cases. Thanks to the connivance between the revenue staff and the land owners at the grassroots level.

Another measure was aimed at restricting the size of landholdings through legislation. The first phase covering the period of 1960-72 witnessed many states passing the ceiling laws. However, there was no uniformity in these laws in terms of unit of application and acreage fixed. The implementation of these laws brought to the surface many weaknesses and deficiencies. Hence, the Central Land Reforms Committee was set up to review the agrarian question in 1972 pursuant to whose recommendations a Chief Ministers' conference in the same year prepared national guidelines which included: (1) low ceilings for a family of five members depending upon irrigation and cropping pattern of land; (2) limited exemption from the preview of the ceiling fixed; and (3) implementation of these laws from retrospective effect. The surplus land was to be assigned preferably to landless agricultural workers belonging to the members of Scheduled Castes/Scheduled Tribes, particularly. In order to enable these allottees to do profitable cultivation, the Government of India also initiated a scheme of financial assistance or subsidy to a maximum of ₹8000 per allottee including the assistance from IRDP, NREP, RLEGP, etc. The productivity of land and income of the people were also sought to be improved through consolidation of landholdings. It may be pointed out here that there has been an 'implementation lag' for various formal structural and informal relational factors. The land-reforms legislation, thus, achieved its objects partially.

❑ COMMUNITY DEVELOPMENT PROGRAMME (CDP)

Another major programme with a view to changing the socio-economic conditions of the village community as one unit was launched in India in 1952. The Community Development Programme (CDP) was initiated to achieve the following aims and objectives:

1. To develop local leadership and self-governing institutions.
2. To develop, in total, the human and capital-resources of rural areas.
3. To increase agricultural production in order to raise the living standards of the rural people.
4. To ensure a change in the rural mindset, creating in them an ambition for higher standards. The programme was administered at all levels, i.e., national, state, district, block, and the village. The main unit of development was the block. Without going into the details of the programme, we may try to see the impact on poverty-removal. Several scholars, like S.C. Dube, Oscar Lewis, Wilson, and others, and vaious institutions, like the UNESCO, U.N. Evaluation Mission, Programme Evaluation Organization of the Planning Commission and Balwantrai Mehta Committee have gone into the question of achievement and failures of the CDP. In the opinion of the U.N. Mission, the CDP was "one of the major experiments of the 20th century, the results of which is of world-wide interest and represents an effort of an unprecedented magnitude to establish a progressive system of agriculture in a land of impoverishment and hierarchical (caste) society". Toynbee described it as "one of the most beneficent revolutions in the peasantry's life that have been known so far to history". Indeed, it was the first comprehensive programme for socio-economic change with machinery different from the revenue administration set-up. It underlined that: (1) development has to be people-centred based on comprehensive planning and, sustained and long- term investments form the government; and (2) the need for technical and technological inputs, besides the trained personnel for the development of rural areas. Resultant to the CDP was the setting up of credit-societies, primary schools, hospitals and dispensaries, maternity and child-welfare centres, etc. However, the CDP could not achieve the

objective of socio-economic reconstruction of rural India because: (1) it benefited the rich farmers more than the poor; (2) bureaucratic red tape, lack of coordination and inter-departmental rivalries became part of the administrative performance; and (3) the objective of self-reliance and people's participation could not be obtained.

❑ DEMOCRATIC DECENTRALIZATION

Democratic decentralization was the consequence of the recognition of the aforesaid weaknesses of the CDP by the planners and the administrators. The Planning Commission, in the Second Five-Year Plan, proposed the need for creating a well-organized democratic set-up or administration at the district level in which village *panchayats* were to be organically linked with popular organizations at the higher levels. Subsequently, the Balwantrai Mehta Committee recommended a three-tier *Panchayati Raj* structure with adequate resources, authority, autonomy, and executive machinery. Norman D. Palmer, A.H. Hanson, Janet Douglas, and Henry Maddie described it as not only an innovation, but also a revolution.[1] It was interpreted as the most exciting experiment in democratic decentralization in any developing country and India's distinctive contribution to the theory and practice of local government. The *Panchayati Raj* institutions were entrusted with three major functions, namely, administrative, political, and developmental. However, the initial enthusiasm towards these institutions began to decline on account of bureaucratic hostility and political apathy, along with non-devolution of sources of revenue, etc. It was a 'God that failed' by the 1970s. Nevertheless, it galvanized the average citizen in the rural areas and succeeded in devising a development strategy for the people. People's participation in development programmes, though it remained a distant dream, continued as a foundation for future development thought and strategy. It is evident from the constitution of the Asoka Mehta Committee in 1977 to review the working of the *Panchayati Raj* system in all its aspects. It renewed interest not only in the decentralization of political power, but also in the people-centered approach towards development to unlock the process of change and growth. This committee opined that the formulation of structural functions and the utilization of financial, administrative, and human resource in PRIs should be determined in the emerging functional necessity of management of rural development. The "new approach" focussed on the functional necessity of administrative decentralization. The committee suggested a two-tier structure: (1) the *Zila Parishad* should serve as the first point of decentralization and the unit of planning, and (2) the *Mandal Panchayat* below the district as the implementing agency. In its view, the PRIs should be the instruments of people's empowerment and their voice. To serve this purpose, the vulnerable sections of rural society were to be given more representation, and all development functions in a district which are now being performed by the state government should be assigned to the *Zila Parishad* which should be provided, among other things, with a professionally-trained team for the preparation of district plans. The committee also suggested that all the staff with decentralized functions should be under the supervision of the *Zila Parishad*. In fact, the committee visualized a separate development administration having decentralized functions along with a composite *Zila Parishad* Secretariat. Another major recommendation among the 132 recommendations it made was the automatic transfer of funds to *Zila Parishad* to implement all transferred development functions. Thereafter, the Committee on Administrative Arrangements for Rural Development set up by the Planning Commission on 31st March 1985, studied the role of *Panchayati Raj* Institutions and their relationship with the proposed administrative set-up and pointed out the need for entrusting them with planning, plan-implementation, and monitoring of rural development programmes. The plan at the district level, in its view, should be prepared by the district planning board and the *Zila Parishad* should review and authenticate it. The thrust of both the Ashoka Mehta Committee and the CAARD was on priority to rural development, eradication of poverty and all-round improvement in the rural economy through people's empowerment and their participation. The L.M. Singhvi Committee (1988), Sarkaria Commission (1987-88), Thungon Committee (1988), further reiterated the arguments for strengthening the *Panchayati Raj* bodies. Consequently, the 64th and 74th constitution Amendment Bills were introduced in 1989 and 1990, but could not be adopted by the Parliament[2]. Finally, the Central government was able to receive Parliament's approval to the 73rd constitution Amendment Act in December 1992. The 73rd constitution Amendment Act provides for addition of Article 243A and of Part IX, besides the addition of the Eleventh Schedule which incorporates a list of 29 powers and functions of the PRIs. The other central features of this Act are: (1) uniform three-tier structure with regular elections to the PR bodies; (2) provision for a state finance commission; (3) scope for assigning the task of formulation and implementation of plans for development and social justice to the PRIs; and (4) making the PRIs a truly representative body of the people in general, and the vulnerable sections in particular. However, after the close scrutiny of the Bill, one cannot help conclude that the success of the PR system is still left to the discretion of the state governments. Besides, it does not define the relationship between the PRIs and local-level bureaucracy. "Due to the lack of defined roles for the two", opines M. Wadhwani, both used to move in different directions due to the lack of proper coordination. Unfortunately, the present amendment to the constitution has also left this problem untouched and authorized the state legislatures, as in many other areas, to make suitable provisions. While concluding, we may mention that for the success of the PRIs, we would need the strong political will of the state government and also to change the assumption that the problems of socio-economic development of the people can be resolved through the machinery of the state government. This statement can be further examined in the light of the approaches adopted for rural development and removal of pervasive poverty followed in India so far. The question is whether to prepare a structure for participation in making the decisions and implementation, thereof, or to use the traditional bureaucratic machinery for this task and continue with the strategy of conceiving and administering development programmes from above. In pursuing the rural development policy, these and many other approaches have been adopted from time to time. Mainly, these can be analyzed in terms of the policy objectives and programmes. For convenience, they are being put in Chart 13.1.

In all, more than 20 development programmes for rural areas were launched with a number of administrative agencies to implement them. However, the programmes have not been able to make much impact on the social and economic life of the underprivileged population in the countryside because of centralization of development initiative, lack of resources with the states and lethargic attitude of the states to implement them, lack of coordination at the Central, state, and district levels, *ad hocism* in the formulation and implementation of programmes, indifference of beneficiary groups at the grassroot levels, lack of credibility competence and commitment on the part of bureaucracy, lack of sound management information system, etc.[3] The development experience of the last four decades also convinced that centralized planning and action has largely failed to yield the desired result and create an intended impact on the eradication of poverty. Hence, the focus changed in the 1970's and 1980's to decentralized planning. The Planning Commission consistently underlined the need for the same along with the recommendation of various other commissions, committees and the working groups, namely, the ARC, Sarkaria Commission, Dantwala Committee, Dr. C.H. Hanumantha Rao working group, etc. How far we have moved in this direction needs to be analyzed in the some detail. The need, rationale, machinery and progress are some of the issues which require our attention.

❑ Decentralized Planning

The rationale of decentralized planning lies in: (1) failure of centralized planning, (2) diversities, details and information costs, (3) socio-political aims, like people's participation, and (4) coordinated departmental efforts. The desirability of district planning arises from the need for optimization of results from the same plan outlays by integrating the efforts of numerous departments and agencies. The system would produce better coordination and consistency. It would usher in an era of participative development ensuring effective strategy of collective development articulation in collective interest. Ultimately, it might mature into collective self-empowerment. The decentralized planning was taken as an instrument, over a period of time, for changing the rural power structure and social consciousness. Here the assumption is, it would lead to better monitoring and evaluation of programmes and projects. Moreover, planning shall be in tune with the felt needs of the people. S.N. Mishra points out, "decentralization can lead to

CHART 13.1 Policy Objectives and Programs

Sl. No.	Approach	Programme	Objectives
1.	Community Approach	(A) Community Development Programme (2nd October 1952) (B) National Extension Service (2nd October 1953)	The programme was broad-based and aimed at initiation of the process of socio-economic formation of the villages.
2.	People's Participation	Democratic Decentralization (1959)	Promoting self-reliance among the people by enabling them to achieve intensive and continuous development in the interest of the entire population. The CDP was sought, thus, to be made a people's programme with government's participation.
3.	Area Development approach	(A) Intensive Agricultural Development Programme (1961). (B) Intensive Agriculture Area Programme (1964). (C) Drought-prone Area Programme (1972) (D) Command Area Development (1974).	Initiating steps to: (1) Increase agricultural production; (2) assuring reasonably high prices for agricultural produce; and (3) use of improved and modem technology. Intensive agricultural development of the area as a whole. Integrated area development programme in agriculture through soil and moisture conservation, irrigation and aforestation. Making scientific, efficient and economic use of irrigation potential and construction of roads.
4.	Target Group Approach	(1) Small Farmers' Development Agency (1971) and Marginal Farmers' and Agricultural Labourers' Development Agency (1972). (2) Integrated Tribal Development Project (1972)	Growth with social justice.
5.	Employment generation	(a) Crash Scheme for Rural employment (1971) (b) Food for Work Programme (1977) (c) National Rural Employment Programme (1980) (d) Rural Landless Employment Guarantee Programme (1983) (e) Training of Rural Youth for Self-employment (1979) (f) Development of Women and Children in Rural Areas (1982)	Creation of employment opportunities for the rural unemployed and under- employed.
6.	Minimum Needs Approach	Minimum Needs Programme (1973)	Social development and social infrastructure with emphasis on elementary education, health, nutrition, water supply, housing, roads, etc.
7.	Integrated Rural Development Approach	Integrated Development Programme (1978) inclusive of all ongoing rural development programmes	To serve as a major instrument for poverty alleviation.

greater social justice. It is visualized that such control over determination of priorities and use of resources exercised by the people would mean greater social justice as a much greater number of people would be involved in the decision-making process."[4] Echoing the same sentiments, Paulo Freire avers by saying, "the basic elementary criterion is whether or not the society is a being for itself. If it is not, the other criteria indicate modernization rather than development."[5] In the words of Dr. C.H. Hanumantha Rao, "Decentralization of planning and decision-making has become urgent with the changes in the orientation and structure of development planning over the last two decades as would be evident from the large number of beneficiary-oriented schemes and area-development schemes."[6] As for objectives of local level planning, the working group on district planning mentioned three, *viz.*, "increasing production, reducing unemployment and alleviation of poverty."[7] In recognition of this context and framework, many states established district level planning machinery, mainly of the following types.[8]

1. District Planning Boards/Committee/Council;
2. District Development Board/Committee/Council;
3. District Planning and Development Council; and
4. District Planning and Monitoring Committee.

These bodies are concerned with the following functions:

1. Determining the major objectives of the district plan;
2. Formulation of major strategy and thrust of district plan;
3. Compilation of data-demographic, agro-climatic, socio-economic, and infra structural, etc.;
4. Modification of the ongoing programmes and projects;
5. Proposals for removal of inter-block disparities;
6. Assessment of unemployment/underemployment and proposals for manpower planning and budgeting;
7. Proposal for interlink ages between various projects and programmes;
8. Proposals for organization and management to ensure that no implementation gap exists;
9. Assessment of resources available from the state, center, local bodies, financial institutions, voluntary organizations & NGOs;
10. Analysis and proposals regarding relationships and links between the district plan and regional and state development plans.

With some variations, the planning bodies in various states prepare annual, five–years, and perspective *plans alongside* the *functions of coordination, monitoring* review, evaluation, implementation, etc. It may, however, be mentioned that district planning has proved to be relatively a failure because the administration has not made any serious efforts to deal with the problems related to district planning, though many commissions and committees have focused on them from time to time. Some of the obstacles may again be reiterated. First, there is a gap between responsibility and authority, insofar as the district-level government has no autonomy to take decisions on plans, projects or programmes. Secondly, there is inadequacy of financial powers at the district level. Thirdly, the PRIs have been rendered redundant and irrelevant to articulation of peoples' needs giving precedence to bureaucracy in the formulation, and implementation of departmental schemes. Besides, adequately trained and competent planning personnel are also not there. This was clearly brought out by the Dantwala Committee when it observed, "in majority of states, no attempt seems to have been made to improve personnel resources at this level. Even in the case of states, which have set up something like district planning machinery, the composition of staff reflects that there has been no serious attempt to induct technical skills in planning. The staffs who have been appointed in these units perform only routine secretarial functions, assisting the District Development Council under the collector, but do not provide much technical support in the tasks of plan-formulation, monitoring, review, and evaluation. Thus, in many states, the district planning cell consists of district planning officer assisted by statistical and research assistants and clinical staff mainly look after the implementation of the district plan in a routine manner."[9]

Other questions gaining attention are: What after varying experiments with socio-economic development approaches and methodologies appear to be mostly inadequate to remove poverty and unemployment? And, what is the future role of the planning and administration, especially in the context of ongoing economic reforms in India? It is proposed to examine these issues in the light of changes of paradigms of development initiated by the government in the 1990s.

❑ Shift in Development Strategies Since the 1990s

The experience of the past four decades of socio-economic development suggests two things. One, that India was able to achieve the targets of economic and technological development to a large extent, but it failed to make progress on social justice and development. Two, India faced severe balance of payments (BoP) constraints in the late 1970s, and 1980s. This proved that state and its machinery, which expanded phenomenally on account of command economy or semi-command economy established through centralized planning and leading deterministic role on the part of the state, is not an appropriate answer to the solution of the problems of the poor. In other words, it is being increasingly recognized that the days of 'big government' are over and that the state should play the role of a facilitator of development rather than playing that of an interventionist one. It should keep itself away, as far as possible, from being a producer or provider of goods and services, since the job of the state is to govern, and not to do business. However, it is not only a part statement of the truth as total acceptance of this view would be tantamount to abdicating social responsibility on the part of the state. It would mean that the ideas of equity, social justice, and social welfare would recede to oblivion. It cannot be an acceptable proposition. While the open economy approach could be inescapable in the face of the public sector remaining an enclave and in perpetual state of infancy leading to inefficient and ineffective performance, it would be anybody's guess that the poor shall be left to fend for themselves. The dysfunctional characteristics of the structure and behaviour of bureaucracy, *viz.*, inefficiency, non-competitiveness, lack of creativity and imagination, ineffectiveness, lack of trust in the capabilities and capacities of the masses, status and authority-orientation, corruption, unresponsiveness and lack of professional ethics and professionalism, etc., are enough reasons to make the development concept free from the bureaucratic chains and promote peoples' initiative including the enhanced role to private industry and business. The idea behind the privatization of economic development is the re-emergence of the validity of Keynsian economics and trickle-down theory. It is being assumed that the problems of poverty and unemployment would be addressed by the expanding industry, trade and business. The process would involve opening up of Indian economy and abolition of the system of licence, permit and quota raj. The new role of the state, as envisaged in the economic reforms, would have to concentrate on removing hurdles from the way of the investors and regulating the new development process to protect the interests of the deprived and the exploited. This is being conceived through the initiation of economic reforms since 1991 and adjusting policies to the new demands of marketization. The social developmental role of the state is also being reminded simultaneously. The economic reforms under the new paradigms consist of two parts:[10] (1) Short-term stabilization policies for correcting imbalances in the balance of payments through devaluation, improving macro-economic balances through curtailment of government expenditure, monetary liquidity, and market-liberalization (eliminating subsidies/price-controls); and (2) Long-term economic reforms, *e.g.*, deregulation of industry, liberalization of trade, elimination of protective tariff-barriers, privatization of financial institutions and public enterprises, streamlining of state sector, privatization of social programmes, and rationalizing the tax system.

The question is how far we have responded to these economic reforms. It can be mentioned in this context that a number of reforms have been undertaken, some of which can be mentioned as follows:[11]

1. Downward adjustment of value of rupee;
2. Liberalization of foreign trade regime;
3. Cutting down tariffs;
4. Liberalization of policies in respect of trans-border capital-flows;
5. Abolition of industrial licensing in a large number of cases;
6. Opening-up of the earlier forbidden areas to private enterprises;
7. Multiple steps towards financial sector and fiscal reforms.

Imperatives for Planning and Bureaucracy

This process of liberalization and privatization has to be simultaneously supported by reallocating roles to planning and administration. The process of dismantling of controls, regulations and administered prices, and adoption of EXIM, and EXIT policies notwithstanding, planning shall play a crucial role in redefining the role of the state. This is evident from the stipulations of the Eight Five-Year Plan when it says, "in view of the need to build massive infrastructure, existence of significant number of poor and underprivileged, existence of severe imbalances in the course of development, government will have to play a role and that role will have to be planned out. The government will have to step in for creation of supply of essential inputs, like power and creation of infrastructure where private initiative is not adequate. It will have to continue to run programmes for the poor and the weaker sections. Programmes for social welfare, population-control, environment protection, health, and education, at least at the primary level, will continue to be the responsibility of the government for quite some time."[12] Further, the role of planning will subsume the following functions:

1. Reorienting governance for speedy service delivery;
2. Controlling and regulating the monopoly tendencies;
3. Suggesting interventions for expanding the market and making it work more freely, competitively and with accessibility to big and small;
4. Efficient redeployment of resources released from disinvestments in public enterprises;
5. Planning for protection of consumer interests, removal of hurdles in free movement of goods, supportive legal framework, etc.;
6. Social investment and organizing the poor for self-development with assistance of the government and the voluntary and non-governmental organizations;
7. Search for ways and means of making the least, but the most effective interventions for the poverty-alleviation and social justice;
8. Preparing a perspective plan to formulate views on a longer period of development;
9. Review and evaluation of technological development and its impact on the unemployment;
10. Reorientation of development policies programmes and projects to inculcate developmental-orientation, rather than dependency-orientation, among the people by creating peoples' institutions with peoples' empowerment.

With changing role of planning and decline in "big government", bureaucracy cannot remain unaffected. Some of the implications can be visualized as follows;

1. Decline in the size, authority, power and status of bureaucracy which may result in inbuilt opposition of bureaucracy, albeit in a concealed manner, to the success of the new economic policy;

2. Emphasis on administrative reforms;
3. Creation of responsive, empathetic, competitive bureaucratic mechanisms.

In sum, it can be mentioned that the first four decades of independence and development till 1990 assigned a central role to bureaucracy in development and nation-building, but the 1990s are visualizing a supportive rather than directional and commanding role to public administration. It is also true that Indian development process has been rich in the intent and content, but poor in performance.

NOTES AND REFERENCES

1. For details, see Henry Maddie, *Panchayati Raj: A Study of Rural Local Government in India,* Longman. 1970; Norman D. Palmer. *The Indian Political System,* Hougton Mifflin; Hanson and Janet Douglas, *India's Democracy,* Delhi, Vikas, 1972.
2. For details, see *CAARD Report,* Department of Rural Development, Ministry of Agriculture, Government of India, December 1985; *L.M. Singhvi Committee Report on Panchayati Raj and District Planning,* Ministry of Personnel, Public Grievances and Pensions, Government of India, July, 1988; *Sarkaria Commission Report on Centre-State Relations,* Government of India, Vol. II, July 1988; *Thungon Comunitte Report,* Gol, 1988.
3. See Kamal Nayan Kabra, "Leadership and Development: Some Reflections in the Indian Context," *Indian Journal of Public Administration,* Vol. XL, No. 3, July-Sept., 1994, pp. 279–86.
4. S. N. Mishra, *Participative Management and Rural Development,* Mittal Publications, 1992.
5. Paulo Freire, *Pedagogy of the Oppressed,* Seabury Press, New York, p. 161.
6. See the Foreword written by C.H. Hanumantha Rao to the *Report of the Working Group 011 District Planning,* Vol. I, May 1984.
7. *Ibid.,* p. 25.
8. *Ibid.,* pp. 52–53.
9. See *Dantwala Committee* (Committee on Block-level Planning) Report, Planning Division, 1978.
10. Perspective Planning Division, "The Indian Planning Process and an Agenda for its Reorientation", Occasional papers, 1994, p. 11.
11. See *Ibid.,* p. 12.
12. See *Ibid.,* pp. 12–13.

14

Ombudsman in India

Rajni Ranjan Jha

The institution of Ombudsman has become a standard part of the democratic system in many developed countries of the world. It is a mechanism of grievance redressal available to the people against the functioning/actions of those in the government service. Geofrey Sawer has tried to trace the origin of this institution to the offices of Censor and Tribune of the ancient Roman Republic, but for all practical purposes the roots of Ombudsman office in modern times may be traced to the 1809 constitution of Sweden. Etymologically, the Swedish word 'Ombud' refers to a person who acts as a spokesman or representative of another person. In Swedish public law, however, Ombudsman means an appointee of the Parliament of Sweden for the supervision of the administration.'[1] After the idea became popular in Sweden and other Scandinavian countries, any complaint handling mechanism in some countries began to be given the name of Ombudsman.[2] As a result, the committee of the International Bar Association formulated a standard definition of the term Ombudsman in 1974 which says:

> 'An office provided for by the constitution or by action of the legislature or parliament and headed by an independent, high level public official who is responsible to the legislature or parliament, who receives, complaints from aggrieved persons against government agencies, officials, and employees or who acts on his own motion, and who has the power to investigate, recommend corrective actions, and issue reports.'[3]

❑ Mechanisms of Grievance Redressal

Ombudsman is viewed as an improvement upon the existing system of grievance-redressal. Traditionally, the grievance-redressal is available to an individual in various forms, such as: departmental self-control, administrative tribunals, legislative remedy provided through the members of the House by asking questions on the floor of the House, for example the adjournment motion, the system of ministerial accountability, etc. For one reason or the other, these methods proved inadequate to meet the requirements of individual complainants. Though the traditional function of legislature since long has been the redressal of grievances, as a body, it is not suitable for paying due attention to innumerable number of small grievances of people.[4]

The Ombudsman is also preferred to the judicial remedy, because court procedure is usually taxing, time-consuming, expensive, tension-creating, protracted and slow-moving. One of the important features of the judicial procedure is that the initiative must come from one of the concerned. The court until PIL, since the early-1980s, had no *suo motu* jurisdiction to initiate investigation into any matter on its own. For a vast majority of people, especially in a third world country, like India, seeking remedy through courts is a choice of despair.

Further, the judicial methods have not been modelled in such a manner that these can effectively tackle the grievances of the people arising as a result of day-to-day contact with government machinery. Besides, in some cases, people have a grievance which cannot be redressed through the proper application of law only. The complainant may be actually interested only in the proper accommodation of his interest and not in getting a remedy in strictly legal terms. In fact, he seeks a mediator who can negotiate and settle a satisfactory remedy for him.'

Owing to the above deficiencies of the traditional system of grievance-redressal, the Ombudsman has emerged as an alternative institution. It answers the main problem before the modern administrative system, that is, how to provide the citizens with an alternative institution within the democratic framework which enjoys their confidence and to which he can have easy access for the redressal of his grievances. It is also equally important to ensure that the review of administrative action by the said institution is cheap, quick, thorough, and impartial.[5]

Salient Features of Ombudsman

Ever since its emergence in Sweden, the office of the Ombudsman has been so closely associated with the parliament that it has been regarded as an extended "arm of legislature, though an appointee of parliament, the Ombudsman enjoys independence from the legislature itself."[6] In some countries, like Britain and some provinces of Canada, there are designated committees of the House to coordinate and assist in the functioning of the Ombudsman. The Ombudsman is not only independent of the legislature, but of the executive wing of the government as well. Independence and autonomy in functioning is the most striking element of the system. The apt remark of Bernard Frank that the Ombudsman must be free from any control by any officer and, if he is subject to supervision, then whatever he may be, he is not an Ombudsman very well assesses the significance of independence guaranteed to this institution.[7]

Objectivity

Apart from independence, objectivity is another hallmark of the Ombudsman system. The institution is primarily based on the principle of impartial investigation by an authority entirely independent of the administration. To be successful, therefore, an Ombudsman must continue to operate independently and with objectivity, competence, efficiency, and fairness.

The Ombudsman has the authority to criticize and expose all agencies, officials, and public employees. Normally, he is not empowered to criticize courts and their personnel, legislative bodies and their personnel and the chief executive and his personal staff.[8] At the same time, he has the freedom of investigating complaints relating to governmental action or inaction.

Suo motu Power

A very important and unique element of the Ombudsman system is the *suo motu* power enjoyed by most Ombudsmen in various countries of the world. Under this, the Ombudsman has the authority to act on his own initiative, reopen and undecided case and pursue it to the end. He may start investigation on the basis of reports gathered through various communication agencies, like newspapers, radio, television, etc. For initiating investigation the Ombudsman does not need to be approached by the concerned parties. However, this important power is not available to the Ombudsman in Britain and France.

Informal Procedure

The procedure of investigation conducted by an Ombudsman is quite informal in nature. It is expeditious and inexpensive as well. Generally, he is empowered to call for information from any quarters and has the authority to inspect almost all government documents and files.[9] Thus, Ombudsman ensures that all the necessary facts have been placed before it in connection with a case under investigation.

Ombudsman and Courts

The difference between the Ombudsman, on the one hand, and the courts and administrative tribunals, on the other, needs to be understood and highlighted. Apart from *suo motu* power of the Ombudsman, no counsels for presenting the point of view of a complainant are required in the Ombudsman institution. Nothing of the sort of court-like trial takes place in the office of Ombudsman. Many matters of maladministration, such as receiving no reply to an application, leisureliness in replying to mail, tardiness or bias in making a decision, not giving sufficient information on a decision, etc., are such matters that are generally not subject to review by courts or are not serious enough to warrant the high cost of the court review are usually dealt with by the Ombudsman.[10]

Poor Man's Tribune

The investigation by Ombudsman is not only informal, but also inexpensive. The procedure of complaints, at least in a majority of places where the office functions, involves no cost to the complainant.[11] The complaints of the aggrieved persons is accepted through a letter or a toll-free telephone call in some countries.[12] Once a complaint is filed, the Ombudsman's machinery starts functioning in a free and quick manner. Another quality of the institution is that the Ombudsman is easily accessible. Under the Ombudsman system, justice is provided to the ordinary people virtually at no or relatively low cost. Thus, even those people who cannot afford to approach a court of law because of lack of means can think of getting their grievances redressed through the office of the Ombudsman. No wonder that the Ombudsman has sometimes been hailed as a "poor man's tribune." Justice through Ombudsman is, thus, cheap, quick, and virtually free of botheration and risk.

Power to Recommend

Except for Sweden and Finland, the Ombudsman in most of the other countries has only power to recommend, report, and suggest.[13] He has no power to enforce his decisions. His function is essentially to persuade and not to command. He tries to seek solution of a problem through a process of investigation and conciliation. His authority and influence come from the fact that he is appointed by, and has the authority to report to one of the main organs of the state, usually the Parliament or to the President.[14] After making the report to the concerned authority, he makes his report public.[15] Someone has rightly pointed out that persuasion and publicity are the chief weapons through which the Ombudsman works. Commenting upon the question of providing enforcement power to the Ombudsman, Guy Powles, the former Chief Ombudsman of New Zealand, once remarked, "To give him such (enforcement power) would be to depart from the peculiar and valuable characteristics of the institution."[16]

Confidentiality

Maintaining confidentiality is one of the most important aspects in the entire functioning of the Ombudsman. The name of neither the complainant nor the official complained against is disclosed either during or after investigation. It creates confidence among both the parties concerned and helps, in many cases, in arriving at a negotiated settlement. Confidentiality also rules out the possibility of repraisal, which, in very many cases, prevents people from approaching such institutions for grievance-redressal.

In any discussion on Ombudsman, a fact worth taking note of is that he deals with only minor administrative matters and not with questions concerning policy decisions which fall within the exclusive jurisdiction of the legislature and executive in state.[17] The Ombudsman not only functions as a watch-dog of the people's interest and well-being, but his very presence goes to augment the official functioning; it injects a double dose of care and vigilance into the public dealing of administration. It, thus, has "tonic effect" on the administration.

The Ombudsman has been created to observe, to investigate, to criticize the functioning of the government and, if need be, to negotiate a solution for the aggrieved complainant. It has been observed that his attitude is sympathetic towards persons perplexed by life and victimized by officialdom. Walter Gellhorn rightly maintains that the "Ombudsman is, as it were, lithe Auditor-General of human relations accounts."[18] He is citizen's defender. Others regard his role as that of an "administrative doctor,"[19] who treats complaints arising from the omissions and commissions of the excessive bureaucracy in the public sector.

Ombudsman in India

The idea of Ombudsman attracted the attention of political leaders, administrators, social scientists, journalists, and jurists in India in a serious manner in the early-sixties of this century, more precisely, after the publication on the report of "justice," the British section of the International Commission of Jurists in England. This report was known as Wyatt report. The institution of Ombudsman in India recommended, in 1962, by the Committee on Ombudsman of the third All India Law Conference, New Delhi, was discussed at the third All India Law Ministers' Conference, and, also at Madras Bar Association, Madras, in October 1963. Making a convocation address at the Indian Institute of Public Administration, in New Delhi, on 15th July, 1963, the then Chief Justice of India, Justice P.B. Gajendragadkar, lent his powerful support to the cause of an Ombudsman for India on the ground that the confidence of the public is the main asset to a public administration and that the establishment of such an institution would create a sense of confidence in the people that their grievances would be looked into.[20]

The question of having an Ombudsman for India was for the first time raised in the parliament on 3rd April 1963 by L.M. Singhvi, and an eminent jurist and later India's High Commissioner in the U.K., while participating in a debate in the Lok Sabha on the demands for the grants of the Ministry of Law. In the meantime, the Government of Rajasthan appointed an eight-member committee under the chairmanship of H.C. Mathur to suggest administrative reforms. In its reports submitted to the government, sometime in September 1963, the Committee recommended the appointment of an Ombudsman, or a Commissioner to enquire into complaints against high officials, including Ministers of State.[21] Sometime later, while addressing the All India Congress Committee at Jaipur on 3rd November 1963, Prime Minister Jawaharlal Nehru stated that he was seized seriously of the problem of combating corruption in administration. Further, he said that "the office fascinated him since the office had the overall authority to deal with charges even against the Prime Minister and commanded everybody's respect and confidence. Nevertheless, he felt that in a big country, like India, the system might not provide the right solution."[22]

Meanwhile, a parliamentary committee on the Prevention of Corruption headed by K. Santhanam was constituted in 1962 "to review the problem of corruption and make suggestions." On the recommendation of this committee, the Government of India established the office of the vigilance commissioner at the Central level to deal expeditiously with cases of corruption in the Central and All India Services. But the Vigilance Commission was deficient on two counts. First, the cases of corruption concerning public men but debarred from its jurisdiction. Secondly, it was constituted to look into alleged cases of corruption only. Thus, the matter concerning public grievances and that of corruption at the political level could not be looked into by it.

It was in 1966, that the Administrative Reforms Commission (ARC) of the Government of India in its interim report under the chairmanship of Morarji Desai favoured the idea of setting up the Ombudsman to deal with grievances as well as corruption.[23] It needs specific mention here as to why in India the Ombudsman was assigned the twin functions of dealing with the grievances of the people arising out of maladministration and fighting corruption at administrative and political levels. And here also, more emphasis was laid on the corruption-fighting role of the Ombudsman. It was, in a few words, the result of the existing social and political conditions in which serious concern was being shown from various quarters regarding the growing evil of corruption and need to check it.[24] This feeling has been found to be well-reflected during the debates of Lok Sabha in India, wherein member after member laid primary emphasis on the corruption-fighting role of the Ombudsman in India and the grievance-redressal aspect was, thus, given a secondary emphasis. Thus, not only that a peculiar feature of fighting corruption was added to the Ombudsman system in India, it also made the institution strikingly different from its European counterparts.

Lokpal Legislations

The ARC also submitted a draft bill, the Lokpal Bill 1966, for the consideration of the Government of India. It was on 9 May 1968, the Government of India introduced the Lokpal and Lokayukta Bill in the Lok Sabha. Though modelled on the Lokpal Bill 1966, the 1968 Bill made a major departure in the sense that whereas the 1966 Bill talked of one comprehensive scheme covering both the central and the state administration, the 1968 Bill confined itself to Central administration along with the Union Territories and left the states completely out of its purview. Perhaps this change was made due to changed political environment in the country after the fourth general election in 1967 in which Congress had lost power in many states. The Bill, after being referred to the Joint Select Committee (JSC) of both the Houses, was passed by the Lok Sabha in August 1969. While awaiting its consideration by the Rajya Sabha, the Bill evidently became one of the legislative casualties of the Congress split in 1969. Later on, it lapsed due to the subsequent dissolution of the Lok Sabha in December 1970.

Meanwhile, the ARC in its final report on the problem, in 1970, again emphasized the importance and the need for setting up the offices of the Lokpal and the Lokayukta. Containing certain modifications, a Bill with identical title was again introduced in August 1971, but this also lapsed with the dissolution of the fifth Lok Sabha on 18th January 1977.[25] A Lokpal Bill was again introduced by the first non-Congress (Janata government at the federal level in July, 1977). A typical product of the aftermath of the Emergency, this Bill was instituted to combat the problem posed by corruption at higher political levels. It proposed to alter the scheme of the Lokpal from the 1971 Bill. The fate of the Lokpal Bill 1977 was no better than the earlier Bills. Before it could be passed by the Lok Sabha, the House was dissolved on 22nd August 1979, and the Bill lapsed as a result of it. During the 1980-84 there was virtually no talk of establishing the office of the Lokpal at the federal level. As a result of renewed interest in the Ombudsman institution during the Prime Ministership of Rajiv Gandhi, the Lokpal Bill 1985 was introduced in the Lok Sabha on 26th August 1985. Once again, the Bill was referred to the JSC. After 40 months of consideration and constitution, the government withdrew the Bill in the first week of September 1988, ostensibly due to lack of consensus on some important provisions of the Bill. Other reasons for not proceeding with the Bill were, first, the passing of the Prevention of Corruption Act, 1988; and second, the setting up of a Directorate of Public Grievances in April, 1988, headed by an official of the level of Secretary.[26] In view of the above, the government felt "the need to re-examine the entire issue relating to the establishment of Lokpal, his powers, and jurisdiction." In 1989, the National Front government, headed by V.P. Singh, introduced the Lokpal Bill which also lapsed due to the defeat of the government on the floor of the Lok Sabha. During the term of P.V. Narasimha Rao, despite several pressures from the opposition, no Lokpal Bill was introduced. Only at the far end of the five-year term the Prime Minister gave assurance in the Rajya Sabha to introduce a bill to this effect, but nothing concrete came out of it.[27]

Recent Interest

In recent years, a lot of interest has been generated in the institution of Lokpal, primarily because the Ombudsman institution is viewed as a strong institutional bulwark against the hydra-headed monster of corruption in the country. With more and more disclosures in recent months of *hawala,* scams, scandals, and other corrupt practices adopted by the politicians and bureaucrats the case of a federal Ombudsman is steadily getting strengthened. The proof of this lies in the fact that almost all national political parties in their election manifestoes for 1996 parliamentary election promised to set up the institutions of Ombudsman at federal level. Both the short-lived

Atal Bihari Vajpayee government and the minority coalition government of the United Front headed by H.D. Deve Gowda pledged to institute the office of the Lokpal. Thus, having a Lokpal at the federal level is no longer a debatable point. What, however, is debatable is how genuine and sincere politicians are about implementing the idea.

Lokpal: Features

An overview of the various Lokpal legislations brings out the salient features of the Ombudsman institution in India and spells out its main provisions. The main features of the institution may be summarized as follows:

1. The status of Lokpal should be compared with the highest judicial functionary in the country.
2. He should be impartial, independent, non-controversial, and non-political so as to gain the confidence of all concerned.
3. He should be empowered to investigate into matters of alleged injustice, corruption, and favouritism indulged in by high functionaries.
4. He has the power to call for government documents providing information required in a case in hand from all concerned.
5. He cannot be easily removed by the government.
6. He has to maintain confidentiality in functioning and secrecy of information.
7. He has the powers of a court in a limited sense.
8. He should be approached directly by the people.
9. He has to annually present to parliament consolidated report about his functioning.
10. The institution is recommendatory in character.[28]

Having discussed the main features of the proposed federal Ombudsman in India, an attempt has been made to critically examine the main provision of the various Lokpal legislations in brief.

Appointment and Tenure

The Lokpal is to be appointed by the President of India in consultation with other important functionaries, like the Chief Justice of India. Consultation with the Leader of the Opposition in the Lok Sabha was provided for in 1968 and 1971 Bills, but was later on dropped in subsequent Bills of 1977, 1985, and 1989 to be substituted by the Speaker of the Lok Sabha and Chairman of Rajya Sabha. The earlier Bills did not prescribe any qualification for the Lokpal. That only a judge of the Supreme Court could be appointed to this position was prescribed in the 1985 and 1989 Bills. That the Lokpal is to hold office for a term of five years has been provided in all the Bills. The Bill of 1989 provided for a three-member Lokpal, one of them being designated as the chairman.

In order to discharge his responsibilities without fear or favour, the Lokpal has been debarred from becoming the Members of Parliament or Legislative Assembly; hold any office of trust or profit or carryon any business; could not be connected with any political party. He was ineligible for reappointment. He could be removed from the office by the President only on the grounds of misbehaviour or incapacity. The procedure for removal was the same as the one provided for the judges of the Supreme Court or a High Court.

Jurisdiction

The jurisdiction of the Lokpal has been perhaps the most controversial aspect in the whole debate on the Ombudsman system at federal level in India. As stated earlier, the ARC had suggested one comprehensive scheme covering both the Central and state administration. But, the Lokpal Bills introduced in the parliament from time to time related to Central administration only. The 1968 and 1971 Bills authorized the Lokpal to investigate any action taken by or with the approval of a minister (other than the Prime Minister) or a Secretary or any other public servant belonging to that class into alleged complaints of grievance or an allegation.

A grievance was claim by a person that he sustained injustice or undue hardship in consequence of "maladministration". Maladministration was defined as action taken in exercise of administrative function in any case.

1. Where such action or administrative procedure or practice governing such action was unreasonable, unjust, oppressive or improperly discriminatory; or
2. Where there had been negligence or undue delay in taking such action or the administrative procedure or practice governing such action involved undue delay.

An 'allegation' in relation to a public servant meant any affirmation that such public servant:

1. had abused his position as such to obtain any gain or favour to himself or to any other person or to cause undue harm or hardship to any other person;
2. was actuated in the discharge of his functions as such public servant by personal interest or improper corrupt motive;
3. was guilty of corruption or lack of integrity in his capacity as such public servant.

It may be understood that the term allegation was a euphemism for corruption which included political corruption as well. In 'allegation' an element of guilt is involved, whereas in 'maladministration' an element of administrative negligence is implied.

The Lokpal Bill, 1977, restricted the jurisdiction of the Lokpal to enquire into complaints of misconduct, again a euphemism for corruption, by union ministers (the Prime Minister not excluded), Members of Parliament and Chief Ministers, etc. The Bill excluded the civil servants from its purview, but included Members of Parliament.

The Lokpal Bill of 1985 excluded the Prime Minister and the Members of Parliament from its jurisdiction. It was applicable only to a small group of public functionaries which covered ministers, Ministers of State, Deputy Ministers, and parliamentary secretaries of the union. Similar to the Bill of 1985, the Bill of 1989 also covered only public functionaries. Grievances were excluded in both the Bills. The Bill of 1989, however, included the Prime Minister. Unlike the earlier Bill, the Lokpal Bills of 1985 and 1989 did not make any provision for *suo moto* investigations by the Lokpal.

Exemptions

There were certain matters which, however, were not subject to investigation by the Lokpal. They were, action taken in a matter affecting the relations or dealings between the Government of India and a foreign government or any international organization of governments; action taken under the Extradition Act, 1962, or the Foreigners Act, 1946; action taken for the purpose of investigating a crime or protection of the security of the state; action taken in the exercise of a court of law; action taken in matters arising out of a commercial contract with some exceptions; action relating to service matters; grant of honours and awards; exercise of discretion being absent to such an extent that no discretion was exercised at all; the entire judicial establishment was also outside the scope of enquiry by the Lokpal. The 1985 and 1989 Bills excluded any matter if the same had already been referred under Commissions of Enquiry Act, 1952, and if the Lokpal had any bias or the case was referred to him after expiry of five years from the date on which the offence was alleged to have been committed.

Provisions Regarding Complaints

In case of grievances only the person aggrieved had the right to move to the Lokpal, whereas in the case of allegations, any person, other than a public servant, could seek the help of the Lokpal. Thus, public servants were expressly prohibited from seeking redressal from the Lokpal organization. The complaints had to be lodged on a prescribed form and to be accompanied by such affidavits and fees as may be prescribed by rules under the different Bills. The Bills of 1977, 1985, and 1989 provided for ₹1,000 as a fee for registering complaints. This was done, perhaps, to discourage frivolous, false, and vexatious complaints.

Maintaining Confidentiality

The procedure for conducting an investigation by the Lokpal or the Lokayukta was to be such as was unexceptionable as well as appropriate.

The identity of the complainant and the identity of the public servant affected by the investigation was not to be disclosed to the press or the public before, during, or after the investigation.

Powers

As per the provisions of the Bills, the Lokpal could require any public servant or any person who, in their opinion, was able to furnish information or produce documents relevant to the investigation to furnish any such information or produce any such document. Any proceeding before the Lokpal was deemed to be a judicial proceeding within the meaning of Section 193 of the Indian Penal Code. The Lokpal was given powers to punish for contempt for showing willful disrespect to him. The Lokpal was required to submit a consolidated annual report which was required to be laid before the Parliament along with an explanatory memorandum. In the 1985 and 1989 Bills, the time limit of 'not later than 90 days' was stipulated for laying of the reports before each House of Parliament. Again, in the 1985 and 1989 Bills, the Lokpal was empowered to award punishment up to 3 years or fine up to ₹50,000 to anyone for making false complaints or giving false information before the Lokpal.

The Bills provided that if after the investigation, the Lokpal was satisfied that the action complained against resulted in injustice to the complainant or the allegations were substantiated as the case may be, he, by a report in writing, could recommend to the competent authority concerned the suitable course of action to be taken in such manner and within such time as may be specified in the report. Lokpal also had the power to issue special report if he was not satisfied with the action taken by the competent authority. But this provision was dropped in the 1989 Bill.

The various Lokpal Bills also provided for provisions relating to the conferment of additional functions to the Lokpal, his powers to delegate functions, etc.

Basic Issues

An analysis of the five abortive Lokpal Bills brings into sharper focus some of the basic issues which deserve serious consideration. These are, whether the Prime Minister should be included within the jurisdiction of the Lokpal? What should be the area of enquiry of the Lokpal? Should it include either the cases of grievances and allegations, or only either of the two?

Should we have a single or a multimember Lokpal? Should the Lokpal have the power of *suo motu* investigation of a case? Should there be a Parliamentary Select Committee to supervise and coordinate the activities of the Lokpal? In our view, the Prime Minister's office should be included within the purview of the Lokpal, especially in view of the charges of corruption levelled in recent years against some of the Prime Ministers. That both grievances and corruption cases should come under his jurisdiction. Looking into the size of the country and by putting both grievance and allegation cases under his charge our preference would be for a multi-member body of the Lokpal consisting of three persons. One of them being designated the Chief Lokpal to coordinate the activities in order to ensure uniformity in decision. All important cases, particularly those of allegations should be decided by the body as a whole.

Other Ombudsmen

The establishment of the federal Ombudsman still remains only a theoretical proposition. In the meanwhile, the first press Ombudsman in the person of former Chief Justice of India, Justice P.N. Bhagwati, was appointed as the Ombudsman of *The Times of India* on 7th January 1989, to create a forum for speedy solutions to readers' complaints and to ensure objectivity, accuracy, balance, and fairness in reporting and comments. As Justice Bhagwati himself has remarked, "it will not cover comment and editorializing unless it was unfair."[29] Any matter related to the financial transaction, such as claims arising out of financial damages has been kept outside the purview of the press Ombudsman.[30]

Some of the nationalized banks have also appointed their Ombudsmen. In addition, there is a growing demand 'to appoint Ombudsmen for public utility services and public sector undertakings to make them accountable to the people.'

Lokayukta in States

The Ombudsman functioning at the state level is known as Lokayukta.[31] While the federal-level Lokpal proposals were lapsing due to one reason or the other, many states, in the meanwhile, influenced by these proposals and the draft bill of the ARC, went ahead with their plans to enact legislations for establishing the office of the Lokayukta and Up-Lokayukta. The office of the Lokayukta now exists in Maharashtra (1971), Bihar (1973), Rajasthan (1973), Uttar Pradesh (1975),[32] Madhya Pradesh (1981), Andhra Pradesh (1983), Himachal Pradesh (1983), Karnataka (1985), Assam (1986), Gujarat (1986), and Punjab (1995). The Delhi government has passed Delhi Lokayukta and Up-Lokayukta Bill (1995) which is pending before the Central government for approval. The Kerala legislation, in our view, stands on a different footing. It can't be equated with Lokayukta legislation. The state of Orissa was the first to enact legislation in 1970, and also the first state to abolish the institution in 1993.

A study of the Lokayukta legislations brings out some very interesting facts and figures. It reflects that there is no uniformity in Lokayukta legislations. It also makes it clear that there are wide variations in respect of the qualifications, jurisdiction, and powers of the different Lokayukta and Up-Lokayuktas. As far as the qualifications of the Lokayukta is concerned, states, like Maharashtra, Bihar, and Rajasthan have not prescribed any specific qualification for the Lokayukta. On the other hand, states, like Anhdra Pradesh (AP), Madhya Pradesh (MP), Karnataka, Himachal Pradesh, Assam, Gujarat, and Uttar Pradesh specifically prescribe judicial background for Lokayukta. Similarly, the term of the Lokayukta varies from 3-6 years, but most of the state legislations stick to a 5 year term. States, like AP, Gujarat, MP and UP provide for security-money ranging from ₹1000-2500 as a necessary precondition for investigation by Lokayukta into cases of allegations/corruption. All states, however, do insist on filing of affidavits by the complainants.

Section 3(1) of the Lokayukta Acts in the states of Maharashtra, Rajasthan, Bihar, UP, HP and Assam provide for similar method of appointment, whereby the Lokayukta is to be appointed by the Governor of the state in consultation with the Chief Justice of the High Court and the Leader of the Opposition in the Assembly of the concerned state. In Karnataka, in addition to the above functionaries, the Presiding Officers and Leaders of Opposition in Karnataka legislatures are also to be consulted by the Governor. In AP, there is no provision of consultation with the Leader of the Opposition in the Assembly.

In some states, controversies regarding the appointment of the Lokayukta have also taken place, thereby underlying the need to protect the office from political controversies. The states are, Bihar, in 1973, during the appointment of the first Lokayukta of the state, S.V. Sohoni; AP in 1988, during the abortive attempt to appoint Justice R.N. Aggarwal as the second Lokayukta of the state; both the first and second Lokpal (as the institution was legally known) of Orissa, in 1983 and 1989, and that of Justice P.D. Kudal in Rajasthan in 1990.

There is a complete lack of uniformity on the question of covering authorities within the jurisdiction of the Lokayukta and Up-Lokayukta. The Chief Minister of the state has been covered under the Lokayukta legislation in the states of MP, HP, Karnataka, and Gujarat only. Similarly, legislators have been covered under HP, UP, AP, Assam, and Gujarat legislations. Ministers and high-ranking civil servants have been covered under all Acts. Most of the Acts include the authorities of local bodies, corporations established and owned or controlled by states, government companies, and societies, etc.

With an exception to the Lokayukta of Assam, HP and UP, all the other Lokayuktas have been given with *suo motu* power to initiate any investigation.

The Lokayukta in Maharashtra, Bihar, UP, Karnataka, and Assam have the powers to look into cases of both grievances and allegations concerning the actions of different functionaries placed under their jurisdiction. However, the Lokayukta in UP, MP, HP and Rajasthan can look into only against complaints concerning allegations. Like provisions in the Lokpal Bills, the Lokayukta legislations have also placed certain matters outside the jurisdiction of the Lokayukta.

Working Experience

The experience gained out of the functioning of the Lokayukta institution shows that a large number of complaints had to be rejected by the Lokayukta for want of jurisdiction, and also, because many of them were anonymous, pseudonymous, or trivial in nature. However, the number of such rejected cases has been going down in every year.

It has been observed that those departments that are intimately associated with public dealings, *e.g.*, public works, health, irrigation, civil supplies, municipalities, cooperative societies, etc., attracted large number of complaints in the office of the Lokayukta.

In some states, like Bihar, Orissa, and Maharashtra when the Lokayukta tried to investigate into the allegation cases against ministers and high-ranking civil servants, his experiences were far from happy, and, at times, frustrating also.

The working experience shows that delay, and at times inordinate delay in sending requisitioned papers by the government departments constituted the single and most irritating factor in conducting investigation by Lokayukta. The average delay ranged from 2-6 years. The situation became worse if it concerned a minister.

The cooperation from the complainants had also often been found to be very inadequate, except in the case of AP. Even when repeatedly asked to do so by the Lokayukta office, in a substantial number of cases, the complainants preferred not to comply and maintained silence.

The working also shows that the Lokayukta organization took up numerous and varied type of cases in different states, in which relief could be granted to the complainants. One such important area belonged to cases relating to non-payment of pension and other retirement benefits to government employees. The intervention of Lokayukta brought relief to very humble and low-paid public servants, like village school teachers, constables, peons, clerks, and various categories of retired non-gazetted public servants who had failed to get their claims settled even after running from pillar to post.

The functioning of the Lokayukta in checking corruption has not been very effective. But for that, the Lokayukta organization alone cannot be held solely responsible. Apart from structural and other deficiencies, a fact which needs to be stressed repeatedly while assessing the functioning of the Lokayukta is the socio-cultural milieu in which the Lokayukta organization has to function.

❑ Conclusion

The Ombudsman idea has continued to attract the attention in India for the past several decades. From time to time, it has occupied the centre stage of the national political agenda, but due to a number of factors and forces operating at the national level an Ombudsman at the federal level remained a dream until 2014. With more and more disclosures of political corruption in recent years and months, once again, the establishment of the Lokpal went on the top of the agenda of all the political parties.

The experience of the Lokayukta organization functioning at the level of states has not been similar in all the states. Nor are the Lokayukta legislations alike. The success of the Lokayukta has been at the lower levels of the administration and in remedying the grievances of the people and petty government servants. The organization has not been very effective in curbing corruption at higher levels of administration. Walter Gellhorn rightly remarks that the Ombudsman should not be seen as a "knight in shining armour" and a "possessor of a cure all." Lokayukta should not be painted as a "super-Chief Minister". He should be viewed with both his strength and weaknesses. For the Ombudsman institution to function successfully and effectively, the internal grievance-redressal and investigative mechanism of the government needs to be adequately streamlined and put under the unified command of the Ombudsman.

Notes and References

1. See Geoffrey Sawer, *Ombudsman,* Carlton, Melbourne University Press, 1968 (Second Edition), p. 6.
2. R.L. Narsimhan, "The Ombudsman Proposal: A Critique" in L.M. Singhvi (ed), *Law and Commonwealth,* Delhi, National, 1971, p. 24.
3. Bernard Frank, *Ombudsman Survey,* Pennsylvania, International Bar Association Ombudsman Committee, July 1975-June 30, 1975, p. 2.
4. See Niell Mac Dermot, "The Ombudsman Institution" in *The Review,* No. 21, International Commission of Jurists, Geneva, December 1978, p. 38.
5. V. Jagannadham and H.R Makhija, Citizen *Administration and Lokpal,* New Delhi, S. Chand & Co., 1969, p. 52.
6. Frank, n. 3, p. 133.
7. *Ibid.*
8. In Sweden and Finland, the Ombudsman enjoys the unparalleled power of criticizing the working of the courts and its personnel which includes not only procedural matters but also the decisions of the courts. See Frank Stacey, *Ombudsmen Compared,* Oxford, Clarendon, 1978, p. 5.
9. Even in the case of documents relating to national security the British Ombudsman has been entitled to all information relevant to his enquiry, but the minister-in-charge may impose a restriction that he shall not disclose in his report any matters whose disclosure would, in the opinion of the minister, "be prejudicial to the safety of the state or Contrary to the public interest." See Mac Dermot, n. 4, p. 41.
10. G.B. Sharma, "The Office of the Ombudsman in Nova Scotia Province: A Conceptual Empirical Analysis" in *Indian Journal of Public Administration,* Vol. XXIV, No. 4. (Oct-Dec. 1978), p. 1108.
11. In New Zealand, initially, some fee was charged from the complainants, but it has now been abolished. In India, in the state of A.P., *U.P.,* M.P., and Gujarat some amount of security-money is required.
12. Like the Ombudsman in some Canadian provinces.
13. Mac Dermot, n. 4, p. 34.
14. *Ibid.*, p. 38.

15. In Britain the parliamentary commissioner reports his findings first to the Member of Parliament concerned who had referred the matter to the Ombudsman for investigation. It is for the member concerned to disclose it to the press or not.
16. See Guy Powles, "Ombudsman and Human Rights Commission" in The *Review* no. 21. International Commission of jurists, Geneva, December 1978, p. 38.
17. Sawer, n. I, p. 49.
18. Walter Gellhorn, Ombudsman and Others: *Citizens' Protectors in Nine Countries.* Cambridge, Mass, Harvard University Press, 1967, p. 131.
19. Selwyn Ryan, "Trinidad and Tobago: Transition from Monarchy to Republic" in *The Parliamentarian,* London, July 1977, Vol. LVIII, No. 3, p. 159.
20. For details, see P.B. Gajendragadkar, "Role of Administration in a Democratic Welfare State. *The Indian Journal of Public Administration,* Vol. 9. No. 4, October-December, 1963.
21. For details, see *Report of the Administrative Reforms Committee,* Jaipur, Government of Rajasthan, 1963.
22. *The Hindustan Times,* New Delhi, 4th November 1963.
23. See *Interim Report of the Administrative Reforms Commission on Problems of Redress of Citizen's Grievances,* New Delhi, Government of India Press, 1967, pp. 19–25.
24. In the late fifties, demands for setting up commissions of enquiries began to be raised against some of the top-ranking politicians and civil servants on charges of corruption. C.D., Deshmukh, an ex-Finance Minister and the then Chairman of the University Grants Commission, was the first man to demand the setting up of a tribunal in 1959. The confirmation that corruption was increasing in public life came from D. Sanjivaiyya, one of the Congress Presidents, who is reported to have said that Congressmen who were paupers before independence had become millionaires. Hurling of charges against some of the ministers became almost daily affair and *ad hoc* enquiries had to be instituted in one or two cases. It became impossible any longer to brush off the demands for some kind of high-level permanent enquiring body.
25. It could not be, but striking that while the government found time to pass other laws and even substantive amendments to the constitution (42nd Amendment Act), it could not manage to pass this Bill. Probably, the Bill was not taken seriously by the ruling party which never gave it the priority it deserved.
26. *The Times of India,* New Delhi, 7th December 1988. For details regarding Directorate of Public Grievances, see *Ibid.,* 5th December 1988.
27. *The Times of India,* 1st March 1996.
28. Some of these features have also been discussed in Interim Report of ARC, No. 23, pp. 19–20, and also in Norman Lewis and S.S. Singh (eds.), *Ombudsmen: India and the World Community,* IIPA and British Council Division, High Commission, New Delhi, 1995, p. 6.
29. *The Hindustan Times,* New Delhi, 8th January 1989.
30. *The Times of India,* New Delhi, 8th January 1989.
31. The term Lokayukta or People's Procurator was for the first time suggested by L.M Singhvi in the Lok Sabha while moving a resolution on 22th April, 1964.
32. Legislation came into effect in 1977.

Bibliography

Dhawan, R.K., 1981, *Public Grievances and the Lckpal: A Study of the Administrative Machi1lery for Redressal of Public Grievances,* New Delhi, Allied.

Gellhorn, Walter, 1967, *Ombudsman and Others: Citizens' Protectors in Nine Countries,* Cambridge, Harward University Press.

Jain, M.P., 1970, *Lokpal Ombudsman in India,* Bombay, Academic.

Jha, Rajani Ranjan, 1990, *Lokayukta: The Indian Ombudsman,* Varanasi, Rishi, 1985. "The Lokayukta in Bihar: Expectations and Achievements (1973-84)." *The Ombudsman Journal,* No. 4, 1984-85, pp. 49–58.

——, 1991, "The Ombudsman in an Indian State: Andhra Pradesh" in Arun Chaturvedi (ed), *Indian Contribution* to *Political Science,* Jaipur, Printwell, pp. 159–181.

——, 1995, "Lokayukta in Uttar Pradesh" in Norman Lewis and S.S Singh (eds.), *Ombudsmen: India and World Community, New Delhi* and *HPA, British Council,* pp. 201–218.

Kotval, S.P., 1976, "Citizen Grievances and the Lokayukta, *Public Administrator,* Bombay, 1978. "The Lokpal Bill 1977," *Freedom First,* No. 312, Bombay.

Lewis, Norman and Singh, S.S., 1995, *Ombudsmen India and the World Community,* New Delhi, IIPA and British Council Division.

Mishra, T.S., 1986. *Lokayukta and Public Interest,* Patna, Secretariat Printing Press.

Monterio, J.B., 1966, *Corruption: Control of Maladministration,* Bombay, Manaktalas.

Rowat, D.C., (ed.), 1968, *The Ombudsman: Citizen's Defender,* London, George Allen and Unwin.

——, 1984, "The State Ombudsman in India," *Indian Journal of Public Administration,* 30(1) Jan-March, 1984, pp. 1–32.

——, *1985., The Ombudsman Plan,* London, University Press of America.

Saxena, D.R., 1967, *Ombudsman (Lokpal): Redress of Citizen Grievances,* Delhi, Deep & Deep.

Sawer, Geoffrey, 1968, *Ombudsmen,* Melbourne, Melbourne University Press.

Shukla, K.S. and Singh, S.S. 1988, *Lokayukta* (Ombudsman in India): A Socio-Legal Study, New Delhi, IIPA.

Singhvi, G.C., 1978, "The Lokayukta Institution: Rajasthan Experience," *Indian Journal of Public*

Administration, 24(4), Oct-Dec., pp. 1145–1158.

Sohoni, S.V., 1984, *The Ombudsman in India,* Ahmedabad, Harold Laski Institute.

——, 1990, "Lokpal of India-Some Aspects," *Janata,* 45(12), 5 May, pp. 13–14.

Stacey, Frank, 1978, *Ombudsman Compared,* Oxford, Clarendon.

Toor, N.S., 1993. "Ombudsman and Banks", *Tribune,* 25th October, p. 19.

Weeks, Kent M. 1973, *Ombudsman Around the World: A Comparative Chart,* Berkeley, University of California Press.

POST SCRIPT

After repeated abortive attempts for over four decades, the Parliament finally passed the Lokpal and Lokayuktas Act, 2013, in the wake of the India Against Corruption (IAC) movement launched in the spring of 2011 and the spectacular showing of the Aam Aadmi Party founded by Arwind Kejriwal in the Delhi Assembly elections in 2013. Both these organizations almost exclusively agitated for what they called a *Janlokpal* as the panacea for rampant corruption in politics and administration. The Act provides for the establishment of a body of Lokpal for the Union and Lokayuktas for states to inquire into allegations of corruption. The institution of Lokpal consists of a Chairperson who is or has been a judge of the Supreme Court or an eminent person who fulfills the eligibility specified in the Act. In addition, it consists of a maximum of eight members at least 50 per cent shall be 'judicial members' (*i.e.,* sitting or retired judges of the Supreme Court or present or past chief Justices of a High Court). The Lokpal will have formidable financial autonomy, superintence and control over inquiry and investigation, and powers of a civil court. It is also empowered to utilize services of officers of the Central and State governments. It can also order confiscation of assets, proceeds, and benefits procured by means of corruption in special circumstances.

The Act also enjoins every state to establish Lokayuktas, if they have not already done so, within a year from the date of the commencement of this union Act. The Lokpal Act extends to whole of India in central subjects, whereas the Lokayukta Acts will operate in respective state jurisdictions.

PROCESS

15

Election Commission and Electoral Process

Sushma Yadav

Elections are the most significant aspect of contemporary political systems, democratic or otherwise. For, they remain the first and foremost touchstone on the basis of which the parameter of representation and legitimacy of a system is to be judged. In fact, elections are complicated political processes which provide a link between the society and the polity and between the traditional social systems and evolving political structures. Therefore, the elections must be analyzed within the context of the complete political and social system. Besides being a formal act of collective decision, they involve a stream of connected antecedent and subsequent behaviour and a concatenation of thousands of events, significant and trivial. Nevertheless, elections perform different roles in different political systems. In some situations, they are central while in others they may be peripheral. They may contribute to political development in some, to political decay in others. They may sometimes be used as veiled disguises for authoritarianism, while in established democracies, they are the institutional procedures for system-maintenance and also the instruments for support-building, interest-aggregation, peaceful and orderly transfer of power, recruitment and training of leaders, and above all for an increasing democratization of the political system. Thus, the elections are devices for legitimacy, identification, integration, communication, political education, participation, socialization, mobilization, conflict-resolution, political choice, political control, and are inextricably linked with the distinctive characteristics, traditions, experiences, values, and goals of different political systems.

Broadly, election may be regarded as the procedure for authoritatively aggregating political preferences of the mass electorate. At a conceptual level, it may be defined more generally as "a form of procedure recognized by the rules of an organization, whereby all or some of the members of the organization choose a smaller number of persons or one person to hold office of authority in the organization."

Elections induct an element of accountability into a political system and make it possible for the citizens to exercise a genuine and meaningful degree of political choice and control. This, in turn, makes the system itself a democratic and effective instrument of governance. In short, Norman Palmer seems to be most apt when he observed, "Elections are particularly conspicuous and revealing aspect of most contemporary political systems. They highlight and dramatize a political system bringing its nature into sharp relief, and providing insights into other aspects of the system and the basic nature and actual functioning of the system as a whole. During an election, so to speak, a political system is on display, even though the features that are most obviously on display may be only a small part of the iceberg that lies beneath."

Gerald Pomper describes elections as "the great public ceremonies of American life." This is even truer in developing countries where elections are newer and often more exciting experiences. In India, for instance, the elections are massive spectacles mobilizing millions of people into the political process. They are, thus, not only great festivals providing entertainment and excitement for virtually the entire population but have also acquired what Albinski and Pettit have termed as "a sacramental or commemorative *aspect"* and have become a conspicuous symbol of nationhood and social purpose." This is true, as in the words of Morris-Jones and Biplab Dasgupta, "Elections in India provide the occasion for the widest degree of popular participation; they constitute the most important single arena for genuine competition between political groups: they are the principal agency through which recruitment to a significant part of the political elite is affected; and the skills and resources which they especially call forth figure prominently in political life in general. Elections in India can now be seen not merely as useful indicators but actually as the events through which the party system and hence, in a measure, the political system achieve their evolution."

The elections tend to be complex events in a developing democracy, like India since they involve individual and collective decisions and, thus, directly affect the total political and social process. Unlike most of the new states in the developing world, elections in India have been central, not peripheral to the system. They have, no doubt, been conditioned by the ancient, heterogeneous and basically traditional nature of the social system and the general environmental factors; they have also greatly influenced the nature and evolution of the entire political system termed as 'the immense transformational impact of our electoral system' by Imtiaz Ahmed.

Basic Constitutional Provisions

The provisions regarding franchise and elections are contained in Part XV of the constitution which consists of six articles (Articles 324-329). Article 324 provides for a single Central Election Commission to superintend, direct, and control all elections to Parliament and to the state legislatures and to the offices of President and Vice President. The article provides that the Election Commission shall consist of the Chief Election Commissioner (CEC) and such number of other Election Commissioners (ECs), if any, as the President may from time to time fix. It also provides for the appointment of Regional Commissioners at the time of general elections. The word "elections" under this Article, as interpreted by the Supreme Court in *Union of India vs. Association for Democratic Reforms & others* (2002), is used in a wide sense to include the entire process of election which consists of several stages and embraces many steps. The jurisdiction of the Election Commission is also wide enough to include all powers necessary for smooth conduct of elections. Article 325 lays down that there shall be a general electoral roll for every territorial constituency for election to either House of Parliament or of a state legislature. No person is ineligible for inclusion in any such roll on the ground only of religion, race, caste, or sex nor can anyone claim to be included in any special electoral roll for any such constituency on any such ground. Article 326 provides for adult suffrage as the basis for elections to the House of the People and the Legislative Assembly of every state, namely, a vote for every citizen not less than 18 years of age who is not, otherwise, disqualified under the law on the ground of non-residence, unsoundness of mind, crime or corrupt or illegal practice.

Article 327 vests legislative power in Parliament to make laws relating to all matters concerning elections to either House of Parliament or of a state legislature, including the preparation of electoral rolls, the delimitation of constituencies and all other matters "necessary for securing the due constitution of such House or Houses."

Article 328 confers similar powers on state legislatures to make laws relating to elections to the House or either House of legislature of the states, insofar as provision is not made on that behalf by Parliament by law.

Article 329 bars the jurisdiction of courts to enquire into the validity of laws regarding the delimitation of constituencies or the allotment of seats to such constituencies. It also lays down that no election may be called in question except through an election petition, presented to such authority and in such a manner as may be provided for by law.

Political commentators have hailed the provisions as "revolutionary, in the context of the Indian political and social environment. They envisioned an electoral system that would be quite different from any that had prevailed before." However, not many know that representative form of government existed in many parts of ancient India during the Vedic and post-Vedic period where every adult male had the right to vote and to be present in the general assembly which decided all public matter. Nevertheless, India underwent a change during the medieval period under the Muslim rule and later under the British East India Company rule when there was no democratic system of election at any level. It was only during the last years of British rule that elections were introduced on a limited scale, with a restricted franchise, based mainly on property and education, and with separate electorates for certain minority groups, especially the Muslims.

However, it was also during the last years of British rule that Indian National Congress had started demanding a democratic system based on universal direct suffrage, with no communal electorates. As early as 1931, the Congress adopted a resolution drafted by Jawaharlal Nehru emphasizing that the franchise shall be on the basis of universal adult suffrage. Thus, when the members of the Constituent Assembly considered the legislative provisions of the Draft constitution regarding elections, they agreed without much discussion or opposition on the desirability of electing members of the lower house of the central legislature by direct, universal suffrage, by a single vote system and mainly in single-member constituencies. The question of the reservation of seats for communal minorities was debated at greater length and eventually it was agreed that separate electorates for them should be abolished.

From the beginning, there was almost a consensus of opinion among the members of the Constituent Assembly on the issue that the right to vote should be treated as fundamental right of the citizen and that, in order to enable him to exercise this right freely, an independent machinery to control elections should be set up, free from local pressures and political influences. There was considerable discussion on these issues in the Fundamental Rights Sub-committee and the Minorities Sub-committee. However, discussion centered mainly on the question whether the chapter on fundamental rights was the proper place for laying down these matters which, in fact, pertained to electoral law. C. Rajagopalachari, P.R. Thakur, and B.R. Ambedkar differed in their opinion on this. Ultimately, a compromise solution suggested by G.B. Pant was accepted following which the Advisory Committee recommended that, instead of being included in the chapter on fundamental rights, the provision regarding the setting up of an independent Election Commission, along with the other two proposals regarding adult franchise and free and fair elections to be held periodically, should find a place in some other part of the constitution.

Similarly, while there was a complete unanimity on the need of having an independent Election Commission there was considerable discussion on the question whether there should be a central commission under union auspices or there must be separate provincial Election Commissions so that state government were not deprived of all power. K.M. Munshi, H.V. Pataskar, B.R. Ambedkar, Kuladhar Chaliha, and H.N. Kunzru differed in their opinion on the issue. Eventually a compromise formula was evolved that the power of the President to appoint the Chief Election Commissioner and other Election Commissioners would be subject to law made by Parliament and that the power of the President to make rule regarding the conditions of service and tenure of office of the Election Commissioners and the Regional Commissioners shall also be subject to law made by Parliament.

Besides the provisions embodied in Articles 324-329 of the constitution, the elections are conducted on the basis of two statutes, namely, the Representation of the People Act of 1950 and 1951, both shaped by B.R. Ambedkar, one of the principal architects of the constitution. The Act of 1950 embodies provisions regarding the delimitation of constituencies, allocation of seats, appointment of election officers and preparation and revision of electoral rolls, whereas the Act of 1951 deals with qualifications and disqualifications for membership of central and state legislatures, corrupt practices and electoral offences and also with the entire machinery and procedure for the conduct of elections. Both the Acts empower the central government to make rules thereunder. Two such important sets of rules are the Registration of Election Rules, 1960, and the Conduct of Election Rules, 1961.

One of the major revisions of the Representation of the People Act, 1951, were implemented in 1966, when a new machinery for disposal of election petitions was provided. The Act abolished Election Tribunals and empowered the High Courts to dispose of the petitions whose orders are final and no appeal could be filed against them, except by grant of special leave to appeal by the Supreme Court under Article 136 of the constitution.

During the emergency, the Election Laws (Amendment) Bill was rushed through the Lok Sabha and Rajya Sabha on 5th August 1975, and on the next day it received Presidential assent. It amended certain provision (especially, explanation to Sections 77 and 123) of the Representation of the People Act, 1951, in order to meet the challenge posed by the Allahabad High Court judgment which had set aside Indira Gandhi's election to the Lok Sabha. This judgment had disqualified her for a period of 6 years. Within 5 days, the constitution (Thirty-ninth Amendment) Bill was also rushed through the Parliament. The Act inserted Article 329(A) in the constitution containing special provision regarding elections to Parliament in case of Prime Minister and Speaker, and also put the Election Amendment Act in the Ninth Schedule which is immune to judicial scrutiny. In effect, Indira Gandhi succeeded in her appeal against the Allahabad High Court judgement due to amendment of the election law retrospectively in her favour. However, this Act was repeated by the constitution (Forty-fourth Amendment) Act, 1978.

Thereafter, Rule 90 of the Conduct of Election Rules, 1961, was amended to raise the ceilings on election expenditure from ₹35,000 to ₹1 lakh in 1964 and to ₹4,50,000 in 1979 in respect of a parliamentary constituency. Similarly, the limit of expenses in respect of elections to the legislative assembly of a state and Union territory has also been raised to ₹1,50,000 in 1994. Another major step in the direction of cleaning our public life was the enactment of the constitution (Fifty-second Amendment) Act, 1985, popularly known as the Anti-defection Law. This has been further modified and updated by the constitution (Ninety-first Amendment) Act, 2003. Besides, the Representation of People (Amendment) Act, 1996, the Representation of People (Amendment) Act, 2002 and the Election and other Related Laws (Amendment)

Bill, 2003 have sought to bring greater transparency and accountability into electoral process by making it mandatory for all contestants for both the Parliament and the Assembly elections to declare their assets and liabilities and also disclose their criminal antecedents.

❑ Electoral Machinery

Election Commission

The constitution, thus, provided for an Election Commission consisting of CEC and such number of other ECs, if any, as the President may from time to time fix. As is apparent, the constitution did not prescribe any specific qualifications, i.e., administrative, legal or judicial for eligibility to the post of the CEC nor did it lay down any procedure of his appointment. However, all the persons appointed to this high office have been illustrious in their own way. They include names, like Sukumar Sen, N.V.K. Sundaram, S.P. Sen Verma, Nagendra Singh, T. Swaminathan, S.L. Shakdhar, R.K. Trivedi, T.N. Seshan, J.M. Lyngdoh and T.S. Krishnamurthy. Except for S.P. Sen Verma who was a legal luminary and S.L. Shakdher who was the Secretary General of the Lok Sabha, others came from the Indian Administrative Service and had served in the highest positions before becoming the Chief Election Commissioner. Still, there have been doubts in the public mind that if the government keeps appointing retiring government officials, they may remain beholden to the government and may not function as independently as is expected. It was suggested by a committee that members of the Election Commission be appointed by the President on the advice of a committee consisting of the Prime Minister, the Leader of the Opposition (or a Member of Parliament selected by the opposition) in the Lok Sabha and the Chief Justice of India.

Regional Commissioners

Besides the Chief Election Commissioner and other Election Commissioners, there is also a provision under clause (4) for the appointment of Regional Commissioners,before each general election, to assist the Election Commission in carrying out the functions. Two such commissioners were appointed in 1951-52 with their headquarters at Bombay and Patna. However, the practice was replaced at the time of second general election with the appointment of Deputy Election Commissioners in 1956 which continues and has proved to be quite successful. The expansion of Election Commission was also recommended by the Joint Select Committee of the Lok Sabha on Electoral Reforms in 1972, and later, by the already mentioned Joint Parliamentary Committee on Electoral Reforms. Both the committees also recommended the appointment of Regional Commissioners for a more systematic conduct of elections.

The Election Commission discharges a number of very important functions, including the preparation, maintenance and revision of electoral rolls, the notifications, scrutiny, withdrawals and polling, registration of and recognition to political parties, allotment of election symbols, the appointment of a Chief Electoral Officer (a state government official) for each state, and Electoral Registration Officers and Returning Officers and Assistant Returning Officers for each assembly and parliamentary constituency, and the receiving of election petitions and the appointment of Election Tribunals to consider such petitions.

The Election Commission faces certain disadvantages at times as it has no power to recruit and regulate the conditions of service of its secretarial staff. It depends for its staff requirement for the preparation of electoral rolls and conduct of elections on the central and state governments. Realizing this, one of the Chief Election Commissioners, S.P. Sen Verma, had suggested to the government in 1970 that a permanent election organization/machinery independent of government at the centre and the states be set up in each state to ensure smooth and fair poll all over the country. It was pointed out that the estimated expenditure was trivial (just about ₹50 lakh annually), but it could create an enormous sense of confidence among people. The government, however, referred it to a parliamentary committee headed by former Law Minister A.K. Sen which met once on 27th December 1970, before the dissolution of the fourth Lok Sabha and that was the end. No action has been taken since to provide a permanent staff to the Election Commission.

However, a small permanent unit of electoral machinery headed by the Chief Electoral Officer (CEO) does exist in every state and union territory for carrying out works relating to election process. The CEO is nominated by the commission from the panel of names submitted by the state government and is normally a senior secretary to the government. He is assisted by a Joint or a Deputy Chief Electoral Officer who is appointed a full-time officer to attend to the election work although the post is yet not recognized by law. The recommendations of the Election Commission regarding strengthening of election machinery at state level had been considered by the Joint Committee of the Lok Sabha, most of them were approved also, but they are yet to be implemented.

At the district level, a District Election Officer (DEO) is provided for to supervise and co-ordinate the work of the Electoral Registration Officers (ERO) as well as Returning Officers. The ERO is supposed to prepare and revise the electoral roll in each constituency. However, in actual practice, no such officer has been appointed.

Although the Election Commission has acquired enormous respect and stature, there is need to augment the staff at the headquarters as well as at the state and district levels. It is not a simple task to hold regular elections based on universal adult suffrage in a country like ours with nearly 590 million electorate and nearly 5.5 lakhs of polling stations including those located "in sky high and snow-clad mountains in North, scattered tiny islands in South, thick forests in East and vast tracks in marshy and desert lands in West."

Seeing the vastness of the task, the government should seriously reconsider the plea of the Election Commission for creation of an independent election department or an independent secretariat which was not accepted by the 1972 parliamentary committee.

The success of electoral politics in India gets confirmed by the results of elections to the eleventh Lok Sabha, while women and minorities remain under-represented accounting for 6.5 per cent and 5 per cent, respectively, the number of backwards and agriculturists increased considerably going up to 23 per cent and 51.8 per cent, respectively. Thus, giving the Parliament a 'distinctly rural flavour' or 'an earthy touch' to be more apt. What is all the more significant is that more than 50 per cent of the members have entered the Lok Sabha for the first time. Another notable feature of the election results is the increasing rationalization of the Lok Sabha. Although the trend was discerned as early as in 1983-84 on the basis of first seven national elections, the results to the eleventh Lok Sabha establish it beyond doubt.

Elections are part of a larger political process which includes nominating procedures, campaigning, and the actual voting. In short, "all those means, whereby a person becomes a member of an elected assembly" can be termed as the 'electoral process' which operates in a still wider network of social and political institutions and largely accounts for the interesting phenomenon that the elections often operate very differently and serve different functions even when they seem to be similar in form and conduct.

W.J. Mackenzie has laid down four conditions for free elections and for the successful functioning of an electoral system, namely, an independent judiciary to interpret electoral law; an honest competent, non-partisan administration to conduct elections; a developed system of political parties, well enough organized to put their policies, traditions and teams of candidates before the electors as alternatives between which to choose; and a general acceptance throughout the political community of certain rather vague rules of the game, which "the struggle for power because of some unspoken sentiment that if the rules are not observed more or less faithfully, the game itself will disappear amid the wreckage of the whole system."

No developing country can claim to meet these conditions fully, however, India comes closest to meeting them in comparison to others. It can rightly boast of an independent judiciary and a non-partisan election administration despite certain aberrations. Although India cannot claim to have 'a developed system of political parties there is nonetheless a general acceptance of certain rules of the game' which has gained deeper roots with time. The eleventh national election (1996) confirms this. The electorate has more than trebled, the number of people seeking election is steadily on the rise, and a reasonable level of voter turnout has been maintained over the years which are considerably high based on the continuing belief that elections make a difference. After a detailed study of politicization and partisanship in India, Osgood Field comes to conclude: "... elections have become the principal mode of leadership selection at all levels; and ordinary citizens have been encouraged to become politically involved and to use the competitive process for their own benefit."

It is established that elections have acquired a central place in the Indian political system. Not only are they "more than just important political events" they have been a kind of national festival, or *tamasha,* a source of entertainment, education, and excitement for countless millions of people. The campaigns are lively and colourful marked with intense political debates, symbolic processions or *yatras* and increasing use of electronic technology; audio-cassettes, video-cassettes and Radio-TV broadcast by major political parties. Visual symbols acquire greater importance in India due to widespread illiteracy; as such voters identify the candidate with the help of the symbol allotted to him/her. Issues in form of slogans become critical at times, like '*garibi hatao*' (remove poverty) in 1971, '*Indira hatao*' (remove Indira) in 1977, '*Indira lao, desh bachao*' (bring Indira, save India) in 1980, corruption in terms of Bofors scandal in 1989, and *hawala* scam in 1996. Argument over ideology or policy-issues as such are debated during campaigns as all parties make almost similar promises/pledges to eradicate poverty and unemployment, combat corruption, preserve national unity, etc. Despite the common knowledge/belief that politicians are engaged in a battle over power as an end in itself or as a means to money, people acclaim the arrival of elections and celebrate them as momentous events. The wisdom of their judgment has left even the worst of critics dumb-founded and the election results confirm what Morris-Jones observed in the 1971 elections are one of the things Indians do well. Surprisingly, despite poverty and illiteracy the people have displayed maturity of judgment through their native intelligence and commonsense in choosing, and also changing the government according to their choice.

❑ Electoral Politics

The evidence found in election studies shows that the most powerful factor determining party choice is where religious, linguistic, and regional cleavages coincide as for example as with the Aakali Dal in Punjab. The combination of region and language comes after this as with the prominent parties in Tamil Nadu (DMK, AIADMK, and recently TMC), Telugu Desam in Andhra Pradesh, Asom Gana Parishad in Assam. With increased democratization/politicization, the political parties have tried to exploit the caste factor for election purpose which in turn, enables parts of some castes to get inducted into the political process and get mobilized to influence the political system. Myron Weiner noted this phenomenon as early as 1962,"... *as economic growth has occurred in India and political awareness has grown within political parties, ascriptive identifications are playing a prominent role and the major social institutions (with the exception of family and kinship units) have associations that articulate their interests: ... increasingly such groupings have had their political manifestations."*

The caste associations in India, began much before independence as agents of Sanskritization seeking to secure educational, service, and other facilities to raise the status of their caste in social hierarchy. But, their post-independence role has become much more important and complicated since now they combine the roles of "pressure groups in economic and political field as well as agents for the political mobilization of their respective castes." The caste associations have made people conscious of their rights and privileges. Their most important contribution lies in making the illiterate masses participate effectively in politics. Through this process, politicization of caste has reached a stage where not only is the caste regarded as one of the main issues for deciding in favour of a candidate by the voters, but caste is also one of the most variables in the distribution of election tickets and formation of ministries. Thus, the caste connections of leaders, command over their caste men and the ability to form coalitions of castes for the purpose of political gains came to play significant roles. Moreover, with the introduction of universal adult franchise, the backward castes became conscious of their potential power due to their sheer numerical size and mass-base. Initially, they were patronized by the upper-caste leaders who wanted to expand their power-base.

Lately, caste-solidarity has acquired tremendous importance. People tend to vote either for a party with which their caste or sub-caste is identified, or for a respected member of their caste standing for election irrespective of the party he/she belongs to. What Brass observed in 1965 in the context of a state is truly apt in national context in 1995-96, "The role of caste in elections is easily the most discussed aspect of contemporary Indian political behaviour." However, the interaction between caste and electoral politics/democratic politics has resulted in traditionalization of politics, on one hand, and politicization of caste, on the other hand. As Rajni Kothari observed, "The alleged casteism in politics is, thus, no more and no less than politicization of caste. By drawing the caste system into its web of organization, politics finds material for its articulation and moulds it into its own design. In making politics their sphere of activity, caste and kin groups, on the other hand, get a chance to assert their identity and to strive for positions." In the democratic process, politics has penetrated into the deepest recesses of village India. Political consciousness and participation have increased among all segments of the society awakening them to the power of their votes in determining the fate of political leaders. Thus, at times electoral process has been the route to social mobility as in the case of Yadavas in Bihar and MY (Muslim-Yadav) factor in Bihar and UP. Awakened to its political weight by force of numbers, the community has dominated the political scene in the states since the mid-1980s. The logic of electoral politics has also compelled the political parties to broaden their bases.

Thus, anti-Brahmin parties, like the DMK had to co-opt Brahmins to make their regional identity more inclusive while the upper caste and urban parties, like the BJP have had to reach out to the middle and lower castes and rural periphery to challenge the Congress dominance.

Dangers to the Electoral System

Nevertheless, the working of the Indian electoral system has witnessed considerable drawbacks and malpractices. One cannot ignore the discrepancy between the votes cast for a party and the seats it gains in parliament, the multiplicity of political parties, personality cult in party system, exploitation of caste and communal loyalties, role of muscle and money power, misuse of governmental machinery, fraudulent practices including booth-capturing, intimidation and impersonation have become increasingly prevalent with each succeeding election. Practices range from the physical capturing of booths and stuffing of ballot boxes to the organization of youth-wings of parties or goon squads who could target and terrorize particular communities before the poll to prevent them from casting their ballots. There have been allegations of ballot-box tampering also. Even the poll staff is either bribed into active connivance or intimidated into passive acquiescence. The menace of booth-capturing has been in vogue since the second general election of 1957, especially in Bihar where, according to the report of the Election Commission, "politicians and their supporters and workers belonging mainly to three dominant castes, to whatever party or parties they belong, take leading part in arranging or instigating booth-capturing by organized *goondas* and hoodlums in large numbers, with the result that in good number of cases, reports are received from the presiding officers and returning officers necessitating re-poll or fresh poll in the polling Stations." The phenomenon gradually spread over the country in different forms and dimensions. The fact that in 1989, 1991, 1996, 1998 and 2004 re-poll had been ordered in hundreds of polling stations, even in the Prime Minister's constituency, is a clear proof of the extent of violations of the norms. There is a positive side also that this also is a proof that there are enough honest officials who could be depended upon to report these violations to the Election Commission for a poll reorder.

The increasing need for the muscle power in elections necessitated more input of money too. Earlier, voters used to be bribed individually, and then it was found to be more convenient to buy musclemen who could ensure victory by capturing booths or intimidating voters rather than buying individual voters. This has led to progressive criminalization of politics and the emergence of politician-underworld nexus. Gradually, the criminals themselves have started contesting elections instead of letting out their talent to others. This can be gauged from the scale on which most of the high officials are changed with the change of a government. This is done to condition the bureaucracy to act in favour of the ruling party during elections.

The police department's intelligence-wing is used to collect information on political rivals. The state functionaries come handy in hiring crowds, intimidate targeted sections of voters, creating local tensions, conditioning staff for poll duties, enrolling additional voters or removing certain names from the voters' list, etc. They also, in turn, allow the bureaucracy to make some money so that they remain vulnerable. In the process, significant sections of bureaucracy get incorporated into what has often been called the politician-underworld-bureaucracy (PUB). In its efforts to cleanse the electoral process, the Election Commission under T.N. Seshan has put a ban on transfers and promotions after the elections are announced. Although revolutionary, the step can be of limited value as the final dispositions of the bureaucracy can and are usually made much in advance. Other practices of misuse have also been banned by the subsequent CECD under the Model Code of Conduct that has come to be more strictly insisted on and adhered to.

Role of Money

Electioneering tends to be an expensive exercise in modern democracies. In a vast country, like India, this is more so because the electoral constituency is usually very large both in terms of size and population. With mass illiteracy, a candidate is required to make extensive personal contacts with the voters which involve enormous expenditure. It comes to lakhs of rupees even for an assembly election. One important reason, besides many others, for the elections to have become so expensive in our times is the growing distance of political parties from the people. A politician of earlier days explains it as, "The elections were not as costly in 1952 as they have become today. Besides the higher value of the rupee all round, the political parties had field-cadres and organization networks and this, in turn, meant less expenditure to canvass for an election. That was an era when the ideals of service and sacrifice were very much in the air. Political leaders and workers did not expect much in return for their work in the elections. Many workers considered it unethical to work with a desire for reward and return. After a period of 10 years, the organizational structure of political parties began to crumble. Altogether a new machinery had to be organized for every election. Transport, publicity, and maintaining the campaigners involve a handsome amount in present days. Moreover, the desire to win an election at any cost, and the increasing reliance on muscle-power in elections have necessitated unbelievably enormous expenditures collected through dubious means, by the political parties and their candidates."

The gap between expenses incurred in an election and legally permitted is increasing with time. Ceilings on campaign expenses being absurdly low, and inflow of black money in the form of generous donations to the election funds of the political parties or powerful leaders has become an established norm. It is estimated that 90 per cent of all election funds comes from the business community in expectation, naturally, of special favours or patronage.

The scams involving crores of rupees from the financial institutions of the country is enough proof of the impact of money-power in the electoral system of India. It not only eliminates men and women of undoubted ability from electoral contest for want of financial support, but also promotes criminalization of politics.

Misuse of Governmental Machinery

There are a number of other ways in which the government power and machinery can be misused by the parties in power at the Centre and in the states. Some of those can be listed as follows:

1. Holding official functions attended by ministers during the election period;
2. Coverage of such function by the official radio or television;
3. Combining official tour of ministers with election work;
4. Use of government vehicles or aircraft by ministers for election purposes or during the election period;
5. During the election, advertisements of government achievements in newspapers at government expenses;
6. Use of jeeps, buses or other vehicles belonging to government and local bodies, public corporations and undertakings, for election work of any political party;
7. Use of Public Works Department (PWD) or government contractors for erecting rostrums for election meetings of ministers or their party;
8. Announcement of new government policies, making promises or starting new projects, grant of allowances or loans, waiving of interests on loans and increase in salary on the eve of election, or after the notification of election schedule, and
9. Transfer of government officers after the notification of election schedule.

Electoral Reforms: A Survey of Attempts Made

The need to reform the electoral machinery and electoral process was realized quite early in India and attempts in this regard have been made by opposition parties, various committees, and commissions appointed for the purpose, lawyers, jurists, and concerned scholars. First, such major concern for electoral reforms was discernible in 1971 when a Joint Parliamentary Committee on Amendments to Election Law was appointed in pursuance of a motion adopted in the Lok Sabha and concurred by the Rajya Sabha on 22 and 25th June 1975. Under the Chairmanship of Jagannath Rao, the committee submitted the report in 1972. The report was in two parts. Part I contained recommendations for amendment to the Representation of the People Act, 1950 and 1951, while Part II dealt with matters like voting-age, electoral system, etc. The reforms could be helpful in removing certain distortion but none could be, implemented.

In 1974, Jayaprakash Narayan as the President of the Citizens for Democracy (CFD) set up a committee under the chairmanship of Justice V.M. Tarkunde to study and report on a scheme for electoral reforms to combat various forms of corrupt practice including use of money-power, misuse of official machinery, disparity between the popular vote, and the number of seats under the present system of election, defects in existing law and administration, etc. This committee also known as the Tarkunde committee submitted its report in February 1975. On the basis of this report, Jayaprakash Narayan launched the first ever people's movement against corruption and for electoral reforms and presented the People's Charter to the presiding officers of both Houses of Parliament on 6th March 1975, after a massive demonstration. Urging the Parliament and assemblies to be "more responsive to popular aspirations", the charter demanded that "the unanimous recommendations of the Joint Parliamentary Committee on Electoral Reforms be implemented without delay."

However, emergency was proclaimed soon after and whatever amendments were made to the election laws went on distorting the system further instead of reforming it. After the 1977 election, Janata government was formed. For the first time that year, the national and state political parties were given time on radio and television to broadcast election messages during the state assembly elections. Besides passing the constitution (Forty-fourth Amendment) Act to remove distortions brought a cabinet sub-committee to consider proposals for electoral reforms. The committee was headed by the then Union Home Minister, Charan Singh. At the same time, the then CEC, S.L. Shakdhar, made significant suggestions on various issues ranging from election expenses to "booth-capturing." An agreement to reduce voting age from 21 to 18 years was also reached. But the Janata party government had to resign from office before it could initiate any electoral reform.

Another committee on electoral reforms was constituted by the National Front government under V.P. Singh in January 1990, after discussing various aspects of electoral reforms with the representatives of political parties in Parliament. Comprising MPs and experts and headed by the then Law Minister, Dinesh Goswami, the committee did laudable and prompt work and submitted its report in May, 1990 itself. On the basis of the proposals therein, the government introduced four bills in the Parliament to give effect to its recommendations. But the government had to resign on 7th November 1990, before these bills could be enacted.

A further attempt, in this regard, was made by the P.V. Narasimha Rao government which summoned a special session of the Parliament to get two bills. The constitution (Eighty-third) Amendment Bill, 1994, and the Representation of the People (Second Amendment) Bill, 1994, passed. However, the Bills were withdrawn before introduction.

The united front coalition succeeded in partially fulfilling its promise to the people to reform the electoral process in form of the

Representation of the People (Second Amendment) Bill on 25th July 1996, which was passed unanimously on the same day. The Bill has the following features:

1. Candidates will not be allowed to contest in more than two seats at a time.
2. Non-serious candidates will be eliminated from contesting parliamentary and assembly elections through a manifold increase in the security, from ₹500 to ₹5000.
3. Elections will not be countermanded because of the death of a candidate, in the case of a candidate of a recognized political party, the party will have the authority to nominate a replacement within seven days. No such replacement will be allowed in the case of an independent.
4. The campaign period is reduced from 21 days to 14 days.
5. Names in a ballot paper will be arranged in an order which would give priority to the candidates of recognized political parties. The same would be followed by the candidates of regional and other registered parties. The last category would be of independent candidates.
6. Fresh delimitation of Lok Sabha constituencies will be on the basis of the 1991 census report.
7. Penalties on officials put in charge of election work will be imposed for breach of official duty.

The reforms, though minimal to begin with, can prepare ground for more thorough and comprehensive overhauling of the system with a majority government in power.

❑ Agenda For Electoral Reforms

There is enough evidence to feel that comprehensive legislation on electoral reforms is required in India to remove obstacles in the way of free and fair polls to 'carry forward the process of democratization' and to establish a 'moral polity'. However, reforming the electoral process is too broad a subject to be confined to mere amendment of the election law and of the rules and procedures relating to the conduct of elections. It has to involve a multi-pronged effort towards cleansing public life. Nonetheless, one can start with the following agendas.

Change in the Electoral System

An electoral system must progressively democratize the representative arena. There is a glaring gap between the ratio of votes and seats in our present system where no single party has ever won a majority of votes in any of the Lok Sabha elections, but has been able to capture absolute majority of the legislative assemblies many times. Over the years, the system has come under severe criticism, especially from the non-Congress parties.

Therefore, opinions have been expressed to either change to a system of proportional representation with the list system or a combination of both the systems. While L.K. Advani and C.P. Bhambri advocated proportional representation way back in 1970, the Tarkunde Committee recommended a variant of the German system in 1975. Lately, S.L. Shakdhar and L.P. Singh have argued for a combined system of voting in which 50 per cent of the seats in the Lok Sabha and legislative assemblies would be filled by direct voting and the remaining on the basis of proportional representation. The Tarkunde committee had also given an innovative suggestion to combine the present system with a list system, *i.e.,* with declared elected directly, while the remaining seats may be filled from party lists according to the proportion of votes for each party with some relaxation for independents. Although, all systems have their drawbacks, one can always search 'the best' out of them by minimizing the pitfalls, enhancing the plus points and keeping in mind the requirement of the system as well as changes taking place with time.

Restructuring the Election Commission

One of the basic proposals of those advocating electoral reforms since long had been that of making Election Commission a multi-member body. The Tarkunde and Goswami committees advocated a regular three-member Election Commission for independent functioning. This seems to be the intention of the constitution makers too. Most of the CECs have opposed it on the ground that quick decisions are required in the fast-moving electoral affairs which may be impeded by different commissioners. With the 1993 constitution Amendment Act and the 1995 Supreme Court judgement, multi-member commission has come to stay. However, the manner in which the ECs were appointed and the provision of majority-decision under Article 324(A) raise the suspicion that the executive may, at any point, appoint as many ECs as would constitute a majority and would, thus, control the commission's decision. Therefore, a regular three-member EC with a fixed term of five years can be a more respectable solution. A statutory requirement of consulting the Chief Justice of India and the Leader of the Opposition prior to the appointment of the CEC and ECs can go a long way in ensuring a non-partisan character of the EC.

Their salary and service conditions should also be part of the constitution as it is in the case of other independent constitutional offices. A ban on all post-retirement appointments by the government will eliminate the tendency/possibility of the CEC trying to please the government.

Strengthening the Electoral Machinery

There is an imperative need to augment the present electoral machinery by: (1) setting up the secretariat of the Election Commission; (2) appointing Regional Commissioners with statutory recognition and powers to assist the EC; (3) appointing judicial officers as Chief Electoral Officers (CEOs) and

Returning Officers (ROs); and (4) empowering the EC with (1) an effective disciplinary control over the CEOs and ROs, and (2) with statutory powers to inquire into cases of misuse of official machinery and to reprimand those found guilty of such misuse.

Curbing the Influence of Money and Muscle Power

To get rid of the growing influence and show of money-power, the effort should be towards fixing reasonable ceiling on election expenses by law and strict enforcement of such law as was done during the 1996 elections like a legal requirement for every political party to publish annually an audited account of its income, mentioning the sources and the names of all donors whose contribution exceed ₹10,000 in a year and ultimately state-funding of elections (accepted and recommended by all the committees on electoral reforms).

To prevent increasing criminalization and violence there is an urgent need to implement the EC's proposal of keeping out persons with proven criminal record from electoral context, issue of photo identity proofs to voters, maintaining and updating electoral rolls with accuracy, progressive use of electronic voting machines, and statutory sanction for the Model Code of Conduct formulated by the EC. Gradually, ways must be found to implement the voters' right to recall as well as the right to reject candidates who fail to perform.

Ensuring Free and Fair Electoral Process

For administrative problems caused by multiplicity of candidates, dummy candidates should be discouraged, the practice of a candidate contesting simultaneously from more than one constituency should be banned, measures to ensure political parties' democratic functioning have to be undertaken, the existing law related to electoral offences needs to be strengthened in some respects, *e.g.*, increased penalty for impersonation, booth-capturing, carrying firearms or lethal weapons on polling day, and for officers on election-duty found guilty of acting for candidates or influencing voting; holding bye-elections within a specified period (may be six months) of a seat falling vacant must be made mandatory by the constitution; steps should be taken to ensure decisions on election-disputes and appeals within a stipulated period (6-12 months); reserved constituencies should be rotated in every election; the anti-defection law must be amended to balance the Speaker's unqualified powers in disqualifying elected members, the Central or state governments should function only as a caretaker government during election period and should include leaders of the opposition parties so as to avoid allegations of misuse of government-machinery and office.

In a representative democracy of India's size, the importance of political parties cannot be undermined. Therefore, not only should the political parties be clearly defined by law, but apart from the present registration with the

Election Commission for allocation of symbols, their registration must also be made obligatory under law. The firm stand taken by the CEC on the issue of running the party affairs in accordance with democratic norms, inclusion of all party expenditure on a candidate's election with his knowledge as expenditure to be accounted for by the candidate, making it essential for parties to file return of income for each assessment year in accordance with the Income Tax Act, appointment of 1500 election-expenditure-observers (during the 1996 election), the announcement of unilateral Model Code of Conduct, and the recent judgement of the Supreme Court on making parties accountable will go a long way in enforcing financial discipline.

More recently, the Election Commission's new initiatives and directives in terms of computerization of the Electoral rolls, introduction of photo-identity cards, use of Electronic Voting Machines, appointment of poll-observers to monitor polling across the country, close monitoring of postings and transfers of senior officials, not allowing politicians to inaugurate state projects and to seek time slots for regional parties in the government-run-electronic-media; the Supreme Court's repeated directives for declaration of educational qualifications, assets, liabilities and criminal antecedents by the candidates at the time of elections; latest parliamentary enactment ensuring greater transparency and accountability into election funding, restriction on public-financed government and campaigns all seeks to ensure a level playing field for the contestants as well as to make the election process free of unhealthy extraneous influences.

No doubt, the electoral process cannot be cleansed or perfected merely by a comprehensive legislation, as there are aspects of politics which cannot be dictated by law such as political culture, etc. Therefore, enlightened citizens who are prepared to uphold political norms and punish those who transgress them can be an effective instrument to implement norms of clean electoral politics. Strengthening the intermediary political and civil institutions, whose collapse has accelerated electoral malpractices, can also be helpful in removing the defects of electoral democratic process. A survey of the 'recent history of electoral reforms' clearly indicates the lack of political will for obvious reasons. In such a situation, the only alternative lies in people's initiative as Jayaprakash Narayan had rightly urged,"Let every citizen who realizes the paramount importance of a moral regeneration of our politics, lend a helping hand in whatever way possible to this process."

Notes and References

W.J.M. Mackenzie, "The Functions of Elections" in *International Encyclopedia of the Social Sciences,* edited by David L. Sills, The Macmillan Company & Free Press, 1968, Vol. 5, p. 2.

Norman D. Palmer, *Elections and Political Development: The South Asian Experience*. New Delhi, Vikas Publishing House Pvt. Ltd., 1976, p. 1.

Gerald M. Pomper, *Elections in America: Control and Influence in Democratic Politics*. New York, Dodd, Mead, 1968, p. ix.

Henry S. Albinski and Lawrence K. Pettit, *European Political Processes,* p. 117, Quoted in Palmer, *op. cit.,* p. 101.

W.H. Morris-Jones and B. Das Gupta, "India's Political Areas: Interim Report on an Ecological Investigation," *Asian Survey,* Vol. IX, June 1969, p. 399.

Imtiaz Ahmed, *et al.* 'Elections and Political Process: Studies in the Fifth Parliamentary Elections' (unpublished paper, issued by the Centre for the Study of Political Development, Jawaharlal Nehru University, New Delhi).

Norman D. Palmer, *op. cit.,* p. 151, K.M. Munshi called it 'the most striking feature of the constitution'. See K.M. Munshi, *Hindu Society at the Cross Roads,* Bombay, Asia Publishing House, 1955, pp. 63–64.

For details, see Max Muller (ed.), *Sacred Books of the East,* Vol. XVII and KP. Jayaswal. *Hindu Polity-A constitutional History of India in Hindu Times,* III Ed., pp. 12–16.

Verinder Grover, "Elections in India: A Short Historical Study" in Verinder Grover (ed.) *Elections and Politics in India,* New Delhi, Deep and Deep Publications, 1988, pp. 13–15.

B. PattabhiSitaramayya, *The History of Indian National Congress,* Bombay, Padma Publications Ltd., 1946, Vol. I, p. 464.

See for details, *Constituent Assembly Debates* (*CAD*), Vol. VI, pp. 210–250 and Vol. VIII, pp. 930–932.

For, details B. Shiva Rao, *The Framing of India's constitution,* New Delhi, IIPA, 1968, pp. 460–462.

For details, see *CAD,* Vol. VIII, pp. 900–950.

This suggestion was made by the Committee on Electoral Reforms appointed by Jayaprakash Narayan on behalf of the Citizens for Democracy in February 1975, also called the Tarkunde Committee. See also, Mahendra Prasad Singh, 'Jayaprakash Narayan on Parliamentary Democracy and Electoral Reforms in India: *Gandhi Marg,* Vol. I, No. 12, March 1980.

R.P. Bhatia, "Electoral Mechanism in India (1951-71): *The Indian Journal of Political Science,* Vol. 33, Jan-March, 1972, p. 36.

Lok Sabha, Joint Committee on Amendments to Election Law, Report, New Delhi, Lok Sabha Secretariat, pp. 1–2.

See *The Hindustan Times,* 1st February 1971.

Joint Committee on Amendment to Election Law, *Report, op. cit.,* Part 1, p. 15.

The Representation of Peoples Act, 1950, Section 134-AA (1).

Report of the Committee on Electoral Reforms (Chairman, Dinesh Goswami) Government of India, Ministry of Law and Justice, May 1990, p. 1.

India Today, 15th July 1996, pp. 37–47.

See for instance, Richard Sisson and William Vanderbok, "Mapping the Indian Electorate: Trends in Party Support in Seven National Elections,"*Asian Survey,* Vol. 23, October 1983, pp. 1140–1158 and "Mapping the Indian Electorate II: Patterns of Weakness in the Indian Party System,"*Asian Survey,* Vol. 24, Oct. 1984, pp. 1086–1097.

Encyclopaedia Britannica, Vol. VIII, p. 134.

W.J.M. Mackenzie, *Free Elections,* London, George Allen & Unwin, 1958, p. 14.

Ramashray Roy when he asserts about India that "as far as democratic institutions are concerned, they have acquired a high degree of acceptability and legitimacy" see his, *The Uncertain Verdict: A Study of the 1969 Elections in Four Indian States,* Berkeley, University of California Press, 1975, p. 281.

John Osgood Field, *Consolidating Democracy: Politicization and Partisanship in India,* New Delhi, Manohar, 1980, p. 327.

N.D. Palmer, *op. cit.,* 1976, p. 173.

W.H. Morris-Jones, "India Elects for Change and Stability", *Asian Survey,* Vol. XI, August, 1971, p. 739.

Myron Weiner, *The Politics of Scarcity: Public Pressure and Political Response in India,* Chicago, University of Chicago, 1962, pp. 37–38.

Roma Mitra, *Caste Polarization and Politics*, Patna, Syndicate Publication, 1992, p. 104. For detailed analysis of different ways by which caste interacts with political parties. See also, Y.B. Darnle, *Caste, Religion and Politics in India,* New Delhi, Oxford & IBH Publishing Co., 1982, pp. 57–60.

Paul R. Brass, *Factional Politics inan Indian State: The Congress Party in Uttar Pradesh,* Berkeley, University of California Press, 1965, p. 155.

Rajni Kothari, *Politics in India,* Boston, Little Browns & Co., 1970, p. 225.

Election Commission of India, *Report on the Fifth General Election in India,* 1971-72, New Delhi, p. 192.

"Power without Politics," *The Statesman,* Calcutta, 9th December 1984. Also, see for details, Jaytilk Guha Roy, "Electoral Violence and Role of Law and Order," *Indian Journal of Public Administration,* Vol. 37, Nos. July-September, 1999, pp. 383–391.

Krishna Kant, "Black Money and Electoral Reform," *Towards Fair and Free Election,* Delhi, Lok Niti Parishad, p. 46.

Satish C. Kalcati, "Poll and Corruption-One Inseparable from the Other", *The Statesman,* 13th September 1984.

Stanley A. Kochenek, *Bussiness and Politics in India,* Barkeley University of California Press, 1974, p. 232.

Ramakrishna Hegde, *Electorarl Reform: Lack of Political Will,* Banglore, Karnataka State Janta Party, 1987, p. 24

For the text of the charter, see R.K. Hegde, *op.cit.*, pp. 24–25.

For details, see S.L. Shakdhar, *Electoral Reforms for India*, Delhi, The Voter's Council and Ctizen's for Democracy,1980; and S.L. Shakdhar, 'Electoral Reforms', *Journal of Constitutional and Parliamentary Studies* , Vol. XVIII, Nos. 1-2, Jan-June, 1984, pp. 1–11.

Jayantilak Guha Roy, "Electoral Reforms", Theme Paper for the Thirty-Eight Annual Conference, IIPA, New Delhi, 1994, p. 13.

For comments on these Bills, see T.S. Sankaran, "Electoral Reforms: A Farce and an Oppurtunity", *Economic and Politcal Weekly*, July 2, 1994, pp. 1635–1637.

Jayaprakash Narayan, *Towards Free and Fair Elections,* Delhi, Lok Niti Parishad, 1975, p. 28.

16

The National Party System

Mahendra Prasad Singh

So far there is hardly any comprehensive scholarly analysis of the new Indian party system that emerged in the 1989 Lok Sabha elections and was maintained by the 1991, 1996, 1998, 1999, 2004, and 2009 Lok Sabha polls. We know that a new party system is now in operation in India. The old system which was earlier variously called the "Congress system" by Rajni Kothari, a "one-party dominant system" by W.H. Morris-Jones, A "predominant party system" by Giovanni Sartori, is no longer in existence.[1] It is a new party system. This new party system has to be adequately conceptualized and adequately analyzed. To begin with, We introduce the major phases of the evolution of the Indian party system after Independence. One can talk about at least six-party systems in India after Independence. The first phase may be called the "Congress system" in Rajni Kothari's terms and may be dated from 1952-69. This was a phase of one-party dominance, as only the Congress was voted time and again with an overwhelming parliamentary majority on plurality (not majority) of vote in democratically contested elections. It coincided with the Nehru premiership, the Shastri premiership and the premiership of Indira Gandhi. The second party system was a brief spell of multi-partisan configuration following the 1969 Congress split between the Indira faction and the Syndicate faction when the Indira Gandhi government was reduced to a minority status and survived with the support extended without formally joining the government by the leftist and some regional parties. The third party system may be called the Indira Congress system of one-party dominance. It may be dated from 1971-77. The fourth phase is the phase of bipartisan tendency. For the first time in India, a two-party system appeared and it was in existence from 1977-79 when only two parties, the Janata and the Congress accounted for over 80 per cent of both votes and seats. The fifth phase of the system may be called the

Indira Gandhi and Rajiv Gandhi phase of Congress restoration. It may be dated from 1980-89. The sixth is the phase of multi-party system. It formally took effect in the 1989 Lok Sabha elections. It had a very bumptious, unstable start, a very precarious existence for about a year. Then, a mid-term election was held. But the mid-term election in 1991 again brought about a "hung parliament". Now, today, of course, there is a large number of political parties in the system not only in numerical terms, but also in terms of systemic relevance. Indian elections, indeed, have always been multi-party elections. But the nature of the party system has varied over time. It has sometimes been a one-party dominant system, sometimes a two-party system, and so on. It is now a multi-party system. The two major parties or cluster of parties that today lend dynamics to the system, in addition, of course to a number of smaller parties, are the Congress and its allies (AIADMK, National Conference, and some other parties in the North-East India) in the United Progressive Alliance and the BJP and its allies, like the Akali Dal and a member of other smaller parties in the National Democratic Alliance.

Transitions in the Party System

India's transition from the one-party dominant system (very different from one-party system) or the 'Congress system' to the multi-party system has been slow, but steady. Broadly speaking, it has taken the country nearly four decades to decisively cross the threshold at the national level. India's political stability in the early decades after Independence has been generally described and explained either in terms of the one-party dominant system under the aegis of the INC or in terms of a delayed industrialization in the country, leading to an absence of the class formation and competition typical of industrial societies. The routinized Congress dominance of the early post-Independence decades rested on the laurels of the political hegemony built up during the anti-colonial nationalist movement whose bedrock was a bourgeois peasant alliance, albeit complicated by religious, linguistic and caste cleavages. Additionally, with the accession to power by the Congress, its political dominance was also buttressed by patronage and the extremely weak and fragmented opposition parties in divided India. These factors favourable to the Congress gradually diminished in efficacy. They were quite seriously eroded at the state level by the time of the 1967 general elections and at the Centre by 1977. The restored Congress dominance under Indira Gandhi was also eroded in the wake of the JP movement, the Emergency regime, and the 1977 Lok Sabha elections, which witnessed the formation of the first non-Congress government in New Delhi by the Janta Party, a centrist party, like Congress, but with a rural and 'other backward castes' (OBC) bias.

The premature fall of the Janata Party government led by Morarji Desai in 1979 paved the way for the return of India Gandhi's Congress in 1980. This held the fort until 1989 under Gandhi and, after her assassination, under her son Rajiv Gandhi. However, the restored Congress rule faced several challenges from electoral reverses in Assembly elections: in Karnataka and Andhra Pradesh in 1983, in Punjab in 1985, from state autonomy movements in Punjab and Assam, along with agitations over religious and linguistic issues that tended to turn secessionist with encouragement from foreign powers.

The Post-1989 Party System

The 1989 Lok Sabha election proved to be a decisive turning point when the Congress government initiated an era of coalition and minority governments in New Delhi. The endemic instability since 1989, nine governments in almost as many years, can at least formally be described as the failure of the party system for, on the surface, it would appear that a democratically disciplined party system has been the institutional mechanism through which parliamentary or parliamentary federal governments have attained and ensured political stability anywhere in the world. From this perspective, the lack of any serious thought or action on the part of the political class on the issue of electoral and party reforms would appear to be an inexplicable death wish.

The structural contours of the post-1989 Indian party system can be synoptically conceptualized and theorized in a manner akin to the model of Kautilya's theory of *rajamandala,* consisting of a series of concentric circles of friendly allies (*mitra*) and unfriendly adversaries (*ari*).[2] In the innermost circle of the post-Congress system are the two major pivot parties, the BJP and the INC, neither of them reaching the majority mark, but being the two largest single parties, together accounting for 49.09 per cent of votes and 60.65 per cent of seats in 1996. The comparable figures for the 1978 Lok Sabha elections are 51.35 per cent and 59.37 per cent respectively.

Until the 1996 Lok Sabha elections, there were three pivot parties at the core of the system. Besides the Congress and the BJP, there was the Janata Dal. The Janata Dal, however, has been so decimated through regional fragmentation and electoral reverses that the party that appeared to be the historic alternative to the Congress in 1977 remains only a pale shadow of its past and potential glory. The party has suffered a precipitous decline over the years. Its predecessor, the Janata party, bagged 41.2 per cent of votes and 54.42 per cent of seats in 1977. The corresponding figures for the Janata Dal were 18.70 per cent and 26.15 per cent in 1989, 15.20 per cent and 11.78 per cent in 1991, 3.24 per cent and 0.10 per cent in 1996, and 8.27 per cent in 1998. In 1999, its two splinters got 3.10 per cent and 3.90 per cent (JD-U) and 0.91 per cent and 0.20 per cent (JD-S) respectively. Since 1977, the Janata Party/Dals have been plagued by unending splintering and feuding, just like a *judayi* (separation)-prone peasant family in the rural-urban milieu. We now have the Samajvadi Janata Party, the Samajvadi Party, the Haryana Vikas Party, the Haryana Indian National Lok Dal, the Rashtriya Janata Dal,Janata Dal (United) which, despite its name, is just a rump in the house of mirrors that goes by the name of the Janata *parivar* (family) parties. Despite the souring of the Janata dream of offering itself as an alternative to Congess, the Janata Dal (along with some of its splinters) continued to be central to the National Front and United Front minority coalition governments in New Delhi between 1989-98. Both the National Front and the United Front included the Janata Dal and some major regional parties, like the Dravida Munnetra Kazhagam (DMK), the Telugu Desam Party (TDP), the Asom Gana Parisad (AGP), the National Conference, and the Tamil Maanila Congress. Indeed, besides these parties in the executive (cabinet) coalition of the National Front and the United Front, there were other parties in legislative coalitions extending support to the minority governments from the parliamentary floor without joining them.[3] This included parties as diverse as the Communist parties and the Hindu nationalist BJP in the case of the National Front, and the Congress in the case of the United Front. The Communist Party of India directly joined the United Front cabinets, but the Communist Party of India (Marxist) only joined the Co-ordination Committee of the ruling front and extended support to the government from the parliamentary floor on the strategic preference of not joining a coalition government in which it did not have a decisive voice.

The Janata Dal, thus, served as the pivot party for both the National Front and the United Front. However, the finest hour for the Janata (then Party rather than Dal) was in 1977 when it formed the first non-Congress government under Prime Minister Morarji Desai and Party President Chandra Shekhar with the blessings of its patriarch Jayaprakash Narayan. In 1989, when it headed the National Front government, it had lost its Hindu right Jan Singh constituent, but roped in the Communist parties whom Prime Minister V.P. Singh described as the Janata Dal's 'natural allies' who campaigned together, but did not join the government. Both the Communists and the BJP separately extended issue-based support to the government, but the latter withdrew support from it when the BJP's Somanath to Ayodhya *rathayatra* (chariot drive) was halted in Bihar with L.K. Advani's arrest. In the two Union Front governments headed by H.D. Deve Gowda and I.K. Gujral, the Communists moved even closer to the Janata Dal, with the CPI joining the cabinet itself and the CPI (M) joining the Steering Committee of the ruling front (but not the cabinet). Besides, the Congress extended issue-based support to both these governments from the parliamentary floor.

The National Front government was bedeviled by internal bickering, especially between Prime Minister V.P. Singh and Deputy Prime Minister Devi Lal. Personality clashes between the Prime Minister and the Deputy Prime Minister also developed ideological glosses over time: there were feuds over the impulsive implementation of reservations for OBCs (other than Scheduled Castes [SCs] and Scheduled Tribes [STs]) by V.P. Singh without any consultation with his colleagues. However, the immediate cause of the fall of the United Front government turned out to be the issue of communal mobilization by the BJP, the legislative ally of the government. The two successive United Front government managed their internal policy and personality differences remarkably well, thanks to the more amicable premierships of both Deve Gowda and I.K. Gujral (in comparison to the domineering and impulsive Singh) and mediation between the centrist Janata Dal, the leftist policy preferences of the Communists and regional susceptibilities of the state-based parties in the coalition by an active Steering Committee headed by the Prime Ministers and convened by the TDP Andhra Pradesh Chief Minister Chandrababu Naidu. What brought the two United Front governments down prematurely was the withdrawal of support to them by the Congress President Sitaram Kesri: first on the issue of the replacement of Deve Gowda by Gujral for the alleged insensitivities of the former to Congress party interests, which was grudgingly conceded; and then on the Congress Party's insistence on dropping DMK ministers from the government following the indictment of its leadership in the Jain Commission's interim report inquiring into Rajiv Gandhi's assassination. The United Front refused to yield to Congress pressure in the second instance. This, however, proved to be the undoing of the government. Kesri's plans for an alternative coalition government headed by the Congress and possibly supported by the United Front and others backfired, with the President finally ordering elections instead. The United Front proposal for a Coordination Committee with the Congress would probably have eased the tension. The Congress, true to its authoritarian style, preferred to give a free hand to its President, who, in turn, was unceremoniously asked by his partymen to make room for Sonia Gandhi, ignoring his pleas to let him relinquish office in a more regular way at an All India Congress Committee (AICC) session.

The failure of the Janata-led National and United Fronts by 1997 turned attention to two other pivot parties, the BJP and the Congress. From the outset in the post-Congress phase, however, both these parties suffered serious disabilities as rallying poles for alternative all-India governing coalitions: the Congress on account of its association with the authoritarian Emergency regime and its excesses, and the BJP from its alleged Hindu religious 'communalism' and the unwillingness of other mainline ('secular') parties to do business with it. Indeed, 'non-Congressism' had long been in gestation, and was, even before the Emergency, a trend in opposition politics. The three major watermarks of non-Congress opposition unity were: (1) non-Congress coalition governments in the aftermath of the 1967 General Elections; (2) the formation of the Janata Party and its victory in 1977; and (3) the rout of the Congress Party led by Rajiv Gandhi in the 1989 Lok Sabha election. On two of these occasions, 1967 and 1977, the non-Congress unity included the Hindu right but excluded the Communists. However, on the eve of the 1989 elections (and subsequently), the National Front and United Front increasingly tended to remain equidistant from both the Congress and the BJP. Indeed, the non-Congress sentiment came to be overshadowed to some extent by non-BJPism, for in the intervening period the BJP, with a more aggressive Hindutva platform, made rapid electoral headway: in the hung Parliaments of the 1990s it outpaced the Congress to become the largest single party, and thus a potential pivot party for putting together a probable coalition government.

In contrast to the Janata Party/Dal, the BJP and the Congress have been less naturally inclined to take to the politics of coalition governments. They first preferred to go it alone in search of the one-party dominance of the good old days. However, disappointed owing to repeated failures since 1989 in their preferred strategy, they finally opened up to the politics of coalition. However, their moves in this direction have often been hampered by the negative aura of 'non-Congressism' and 'non-BJPism'. Nonetheless, with the passage of time, the impact of the negative factors has been diminishing in inter-party relations.

The BJP's moment of coalitional power, as well as of impotence, came after the 1996 Lok Sabha elections when President, Shankar Dayal Sharma, invited its leader, Atal Behari Vajpayee, in the hung Lok Sabha, to form a coalition government and prove majority. The political 'untouchability' of the BJP, as also its pragmatism, were dramatically demonstrated when, after fruitlessly trying to muster a majority following the delivery of a fairly moderate Presidential address on behalf of the government to the opening joint session of the Parliament Vajpayee resigned in desperation after a valiant speech in the Lok Sabha at the end of the debate on the confidence motion. The Presidential address spelling out the policies of the BJP government, and before it the Prime Minister's broadcast to the nation, were more conciliatory than the 1996 election manifesto of the party. Several controversial items of the manifest, like the emphasis on construction of Ram temple in Ayodhya, a common civil code for all religious communities, and the repeal of Article 370 of the constitution regarding Jammu and Kashmir, were omitted in the later addresses. Moreover, the Prime Minister used his good offices to persuade the Shiv Sena-BJP Chief Minister of Maharshtra to restore the Shri Krishna Judicial Commission inquiring into the Bombay riots. This commission had been instituted by the previous Congress government, but disbanded by its successor.

It was this evident moderation, coupled with the fall (in quick succession) of the two United Front governments that were formed in the 11th Lok Sabha following the ignominious exit of Vajpayee, that brought about a sea change in the political scenario for the BJP on the eve of the mid-term 1998 Lok Sabha elections. In the months before the election there was an evident surge in favour of the BJP, both in the political class as well as among the public. A number of parties and prominent individuals, especially from the Congress, rushed to align with or join the BJP. In public opinion polls, Vajpayee moved ahead of other possible candidates for premiership, like Gujral, Deve Gowda, Jyoti Basu and Sonia Gandhi (although Sonia Gandhi quickly moved ahead of the rest, being next only to Vajpayee by the end of the 1998 campaign). This development in favour of the BJP was preceded by a consistent increase in its electoral and parliamentary strength. From the low of 7.40 per cent of votes and 0.37 per cent of seats, it had nowhere to go but up, yet it had remained chronically short of the majority mark: 11.50 per cent and 15.84 per cent in 1989, 20.10 per cent and 22.09 per cent in 1991, 20.29 per cent and 29.65 per cent in 1996, and 25.59 per cent and 33.52 per cent in 1998. In 1999, it more or less maintained its individual position with 23.75 per cent and 33.50 per cent, but improved the position of its National Democratic Alliance as never before.

The patterns of the realignment of parties with the BJP reveal two broad features, both geared towards overcoming two weaknesses in the pivot party's support base. The BJP has been historically deficient in recruiting leaders and in mobilizing voters from the regions beyond the Hindi heartland. It has also been a typically upper-caste, especially Brahmanical Hindu party. Its new allies mainly came from non-Hindi rimlands, that is, the AIADMK and its regional allies in Tamil Nadu, the Samata Party in Bihar, the INLD in Haryana, the BJP in Orissa, the Trinamool Cogress in West Bengal, Lok Shakti in Karnataka, and the Akali Dal in Punjab, among others. After the elections, at the time of the formation of the BJP-led coalition government, the Telugu Desam in Andhra Pradesh also deserted the United Front and moved closer to the BJP alliance to enable it to form a minority government in the hung Lok Sabha. However, it did not join the cabinet. The TDP MP, Balayogi, was elected the Lok Sabha Speaker. Besides, another feature of the new allies, at least of some like the Samata Party and the INLD is that they bring to its fold the support of middle-caste peasant leaders and voters. This is, in fact, in line with BJP's own new strategy of 'social engineering' a euphemism for political recruitment among OBCs and Dalits. The ideologue behind this is K.N. Govindacharya, one of the general secretaries of the party and a Brahman from Tamil Nadu. Its most prominent mascots are the former Uttar Pradesh Chief Minister Kalyan Singh and Union Minister Uma Bharti, both Lodhs, an OBC group, a Dalit leader from A.P. Bangaru Lakshman to top the OBC and Dalit vote banks. Though the Mandal applecart of the Janata Dal has largely upturned at the national level, its regional splinters in Uttar Pradesh and Bihar, the Samajvadi Party of Mulayam Singh Yadav and the Rashtriya Janata Dal of Laloo Prasad Yadav hold sizeable influence with the OBCs. Even in Karnataka, the BJP's recent electoral gains are at least partly attributable to its alliance with Lok Shakti, led by Rama Krishna Hegde, a former Janata Dal Brahman. In Gujrat, the BJP's strategy to 'Mandalize' itself suffered a setback owing to the desertion, in 1994, of the predominantly OBC faction led by Shankarsinh Baghela to form a regional party, the Rashtriya Janata Party, resulting in the fall of the BJP government there. In the latter part of the 1990s, a new national party, the Bahujan Samaj Party (BSP), led by the Dalit duo Kanshi Ram and Mayavati has risen to prominence. This has turned out to be free-floating coalition partner, alternately aligning and breaking with parties as diverse as Samajvadi Party, the BJP and the Congress, and has formed coalition governments in Uttar Pradesh, first with the Samajvadi Party and then with BJP. However, both attempts have been abortive due to caste contradictions, that is, OBCs versus Dalits in the former instance and castes versus Dalits in the latter.

The political alignments among parties since 1989 have broadly crystallized into a tripartite configuration: the two largest parties, the BJP and the Congress, and their respective allies represent the two poles, while the middle ground is held by the third force comprising the Janata Dal, the Left Front, and some regional parties. After the rise and fall of the BJP-led coalition government in the 12th Lok Sabha, some new alignments among the parties were evident. The most important changes included: the virtual disintegration of the United Front; the Left Front becoming more receptive to the Congress then to the Janata Dal; and the Samajvadi Party and RJD forming the Rashtriya Lok Mancha (RLM), though the two subsequently fell apart. These formations, along with the AIADMK led by Jayalalitha (deserting the BJP alliance) united to bring down the BJP-led coalition government in mid-April 1999. The BJP coalition tried to survive the vote of no-confidence by winning over the DMK and the INLD, the former from the ranks of the opposition and the latter a piqued ally of the ruling coalition, but this was insufficient to keep it afloat. However, those trying to topple the government attempted to form another government supported by Jayalalitha of AIADMK and others from outside. The RLM preferred a coalition government of all those who voted against the Vajpayee government during the confidence vote. The Left Front offered to lead a coalition government headed by West Bengal Chief Minister, Jyoti Basu (CPI-M), but the Congress (I) was lukewarm to the idea. Mulayam Singh Yadav of the Samajvadi Party voted the Congress proposition, although his RLM ally Laloo Prasad Yadav of the RJD broke ranks to support the Congress (I). The Congress torpedoed the other two alternatives. Barely a year after the 1998 mid-term elections, India faced another mid-term poll in 1999.

Within a month of this turmoil (by mid-May 1999), the Congress (I) itself faced a split. Three members of the Congress Working Committee, Sharad Pawar, P.A. Sangma and Tariq Anwar, questioned Sonia Gandhi's eligibility to be the Prime Minister on account of her foreign birth and suspected dual citizenship, as well as her evident political inexperience, although they welcomed her continuing as the party's President. Sonia Gandhi's mass appeal is unquestioned, though its extent remains to be tested again. In any case, the trio also suggested, pre-empting the critique of some opposition parties that the Congress (I) itself should propose in its election manifesto that, as in leading Western democracies, the Indian constitution ought to be amended to the effect that only an India-born citizen should be allowed to hold the highest political executive post in the government.

In a week-long melodrama, Sonia Gandhi resigned as Congress President, but was persuaded by loyalists to reconsider her decision. The three rebels were promptly expelled from the Congress, and subsequently formed a new party, the Rashtravadi (Nationalist) Congress Party, with promise of regional support in Maharashtra and the North-east, the home turfs of Pawar and Sangma. The former is a Maratha Hindu and the latter a tribal Christian with secular images and following. Pawar had been Chief Minister and Union Minister with considerable number of followers among the prosperous Maratha peasants in the sugar belt of Maharashtra. This independent power base was resented by Sonia loyalists who repeatedly tried to cut him down to size. Sangma, a former Chief Minister, acquired something of a national stature as the Speaker of the 11th Lok Sabha. Anwar, a Biharian Muslim, lacked evident mass support, but was expected to make some dent into the RJD Muslim vote bank in Bihar where Laloo Yadav thrived on the Yadav-Muslim vote bank in Bihar, but failed to groom any prominent Muslim leader in his party. Anwar was also expected to divert some of the then evident indications that the mood of the Muslim voter everywhere was to turn towards the Congress (I). This split in the Congress (I) could also help revive the dwindling hope of the Third Force, which was in disarray, as the Nationalist Congress Party made it clear that it intended to remain equidistant from both the Congress (I) and the BJP. It could also provide more comfortable company to former Congressmen in the All India Trinamool Congress, which had split from the Congress (I) in the recent past due to lack of internal democracy in the parent party. The TMC was then in the orbit of the Third Force, but its ally in Tamil Nadu, the DMK, moved closer to the BJP alliance around the time of the fall of the Vajpayee government. The TMC stayed with the BJP coalition, but often took a critical stance vis-a-vis the BJP in deference to its not negligible Muslim vote bank in West Bengal. As it happened, most of these prospects failed to materialize, except for a Congress-Nationalist Congress Party coalition government in Maharashtra in the aftermath of the 1999 elections.

Indian party politics has been getting messier by after day, without much indication of a polarization of political forces. The post-1989 party configuration appeared simultaneously to be a mix between Sartori's categories of multi-party systems of 'moderate' and 'polarized pluralism' with some tendency towards what he calls 'atomization'. While mainline parties have, over the years, tended to become moderate, especially in the crucible of coalition and minority governments, parties on the peripheries, especially those fuelled by ethnic and class militancy, exacerbate forces of polarization and atomization.

The parliamentary system of government and plurality (first-past-the-post) as a system of elections in single-member constituencies that are generally supposed to encourage the development of the two-party system have failed to produce the expected outcome in India. There was initially a one-party dominant system and there is now a highly regionalized and fragmented multi-party system, with only a brief interlude of a tendency towards a two-party system, during 1977-80 when only two parties, the Janata and the Congress, accounted for a sizeable of votes and seats. This tendency, however, did not turn into a trend. This is explained partly by the extreme social and regional diversity in India and the federal component of the government along with the parliamentary system, both initially held in check by the past momentum of the freedom struggle and the charismatic leadership of the Nehru-Gandhi dynasty. The upsurge of the forces of regionalism and ethnic particularism has engendered the trend of federalization in India's predominantly parliamentary regime, but with a very unstable headstart. National parties have tended to fragment, regional parties have tended to mushroom, and even smaller parties have acquired a vested interest in maintaining a separate existence due to the possibility of acquiring power disproportionate to size and of playing a balancing role in shaky coalition governments.

Neither the fall of the BJP-led government in 1998 nor the unstable track records of the Janata Party, or the National Front and United Front governments warrant the writing of an epitaph for the experiment in federal coalition/minority governments in India. For one, we seem to have got stuck with hung Parliaments that only countenance coalition dispensations. For another, stable coalition governments alternating in power in Kerala appear to be a fairly hopeful lighthouse to the ship of the aggregate federal Indian state from the high sea of uncertain governance. In terms of modem and traditional social and cultural divisions, Kerala is a miniature India, and shows the way to India today.

Why have not the federal coalitions attained the kind of cohesion and solidarity that is displayed by CPI (M)-led Left Democratic Front and the Congress-led United Democratic Front in Kerala? The reason seems to be the lack of will and ability of the political class to learn and generalize from the empirical experience and praxis. This is partially because politics has become the breeding ground for crooks and undesirable elements. A modem profession which originated in democratic and egalitarian patriotism and social service in India has turned into one underpinned by patronage, fiefs, personal pelf and power and plunder. Parties and coalitions in India display some instinct to swim or sink together only when in power. Both the Congress and the Janata Party/Dal disintegrated at the slightest hint of being in the political wilderness. Yet some new signs of coalitional solidarity are also apparent. The United Front preferred being voted out by the Congress (I) to abandoning the DMK in the wake of the Jain Commission Report on Rajiv Gandhi's assassination. Similarly, the BJP coalition refused to budge before the AIADMK insistence on making George Fernandes the scapegoat for the ineptly handled issue of the sacking of Admiral Vishnu Bhagwat.

Where did the Indian party system stand after the Lok Sabha mid-term polls in 2004? The system continued to be fragmented and heavily regionalized. There was no majority party in the Lok Sabha. The two largest parties, the BJP and the Congress, together accounted for 52.05 per cent of votes and 54.50 per cent of seats, but individually each was in a minority. The rest of the national or all-India parties, two Communist parties, two Janata Dals, and the BSP, were way down both in terms of votes and seats. Due to this seven-way fragmentation, the over 67 per cent of votes and seats commanded by national parties did not mean much.

Even if we discount smaller state and registered (unrecognized either as national or state) parties, there were 18 major state parties, together accounting for 26.93 per cent of votes and 29.10 per cent of seats. Within their own respective states, these regional parties were reasonably well-placed, but nationally they presented a picture of extreme political fragmentation and regionalization. However, in the context of coalition or minority governments at the Centre, state parties become crucial players as balancing forces in competing coalitions. Though this openness of the coalitional system to even smaller parties promotes integration of the political system through an accommodation of regional and ethnic forces, it also acts as a factor leading to unprincipled compromises and governmental instability and drift.

In terms of electoral and parliamentary groupings in 2004, the party system presented a two-fold division. There was the BJP-led NDA consisting of parties, like BJD, TDP, INLD, JD(U), Shiromani Akali Dal, Shiv Sena, Trinamool Congress, etc., which was in opposition; and there was the ruling United Progressive Alliance led by the Congress and consists of Lok Jantantrik Party, RJD and CPI.

The foregoing pattern of party fragmentation more or less continued in the 2009 Lok Sabha elections, although the situation slightly improved for the Congress-led UPA, which, again, formed the government. It consolidated itself considerably as its strength jumped from 215 seats in 2004 to 261 seats in 2009. The Congress improved its position from 145 seats to 201, thus making it less vulnerable to internal blackmail by coalition partners. BJP-led NDA went into further reverses, its representation going down from 186 to 159 seats. BJP's own tally went down from 138 to 121 seats. Parties outside these two alliances got their own seats reduced from 136 in 2004 to 124 in 2009.

As to the forthcoming Lok Sabha elections in 2014, the Congress-led UPA appears to be in precipitous decline, mired in unprecedented corruption, policy, paralysis, and unbearable inflation. The meteoric rise of the Aam Aadmi Party (AAP) in Delhi Assembly elections of 2013 has projected a vision of 'alternative politics' wedded to control corruption and criminalization in politics and intra-party democracy. It promises to make a national splash, but its impact beyond Delhi is still uncertain. Most of the regional parties outside the two competing coalitions are making repeated attempts to form a third front with the Left parties noting for a non-congress and non-BJP coalition with alternative policies. But these efforts have not yet yielded any front or a common Prime Ministerial candidate. The Congress too has stopped short of declaring the heir apparent Rahul Gandhi, Congress Vice President, its prime ministerial candidate; he is nominated as the head of only the congress campaign, with the UPA allies being in a state of disarray.

Reforms

The decade-long spell of governmental instability at the Centre has made it amply clear that urgent reforms are called for in the arenas of electoral, party and coalitional systems of governance. Even without the infrastructure of electoral reforms by a reluctant Parliament (under discussion since the 1970s), the activism of the Election Commission under T.N. Seshan and his successors has made a palpable difference in the conduct of elections in the 1990s. The judicial organ of the state as well as civic action on the part of some grassroots movements have also contributed to the limited transformation of the political atmosphere. However, pervasive and durable reforms can follow only from purposive political action. The proposals of the Election Commission appear to be rather limited and timid. Indeed, unless Parliament introduces substantial legislation, the Election Commission must make do with cosmetic changes in the party political processes. To be fair to the Election Commission even the limited reforms proposed by it often go unheeded by the governments in New Delhi and in state capitals. The Election Commission has recently gone on record to express its concern at frivolous party formation. But the measures proposed by it to remedy the situation are as ineffectual as the media and police campaign against children playing with Diwali crackers. The question that we need to pose seriously is whether any organization can be recognized as a party unless (besides contesting elections) it has: (1) a regularly elected organization at the national/state/grassroots levels; (2) a minimum number of enrolled members (not just voters); (3) transparency in funds and expenditure, with legally mandatory public auditing of accounts and filing of tax returns; (4) identifiable policies and programmes to be adhered to at least pending a mandate; and (5) a probability of survival as an organization beyond the period of its founders. Both Parliament and the Election Commission must grapple with the institution of the above concepts defining a party. Not many Indian parties neither the major ones at the centre of the ideological spectrum nor the category of new regional parties can fulfill all the above criteria. *Ad hoc* and personalized organizations are particularly typical of the post-Nehru Congress, the Janata Dal, the TDP, the HVP, the RJP, the BJD, and the RJD, to mention only parties of national and regional stature.

The Law Commission, in a comprehensive review of election-related laws, had recommended in 1999 a 25 per cent increase in Lok Sabha and Vidhan Sabha seats, with the new Lok Sabha seats (138 in number) to be filled through the list system on the panels of prospective legislators furnished to the Election Commission by political parties. In apportioning these seats, parties with less than 5 per cent of votes should be eliminated. Old territorial constituencies should also continue, but their number should stand frozen at 550 until the year 2025. If thus reconstituted, the Lok Sabha would have a total of 688 seats. This reform, in the view of the Law Commission, is necessary to rectify the anomaly arising out of the freezing of Lok Sabha seats since the 1971 Census. Moreover, the Law Commission also recommended bringing political parties within the purview of law by amending the Representation of People Act, 1951, requiring parties to constitute executive committees in every three years, with specific powers being granted to local party units in decision-making, and with elections by secret ballot within the party, as well as regular maintenance of accounts.

The practice of parliamentary federal politics in the era of coalition/minority governments has demonstrated that neither a highly-centralized party nor assortments of personalized state parties are appropriate structures of political ambition in the federal arena. We need to examine the type of experiments that the Canadians have made to democratize and federalize their national political parties. Canada, like India, is socially and regionally diverse. It has adopted a parliamentary federal constitution. The Canadians also elected their prime ministers, like in India, that is, through elected MPs belonging to the party in power. Early in the 20th century, however, they adopted the American practice of national party conventions to elect presidential candidates. The Canadian national parties hold a federal leadership convention to elect the leader who will lead the party concerned to the hosting and in the Parliament. This sets into motion a federal aggregation process in parties before, during and after the elections in the glare of nationwide visibility and debate. The difference between the American party conventions and their Canadian counterparts is that the delegates in the former vote *en bloc* as states, whereas those in the latter vote as individuals. The Canadian system is a good mix of parliamentary as well as federal principles. India will do well to emulate it. Given the centrality of parties in the electoral and legislative arenas in ensuring governmental stability in a parliamentary federal system, we may consider introducing this reform through a parliamentary legislation or through the Election Commission's power under Article 324 of the constitution.

Another weak link in coalitional governance in India has been a perfunctory approach to the Coordination or Steering Committee. A coalition government in a system like ours cannot be effectively managed by the cabinet alone. The pre-eminence of the cabinet cannot be formally questioned either in a one-party government or in a coalition cabinet. However, if the cabinet in a coalition situation is not to become a hopelessly divided house bereft of collective responsibility, the prime minister and his colleagues must learn to promote reconciliation of conflicting policies and ambitions in two forums, one outside Parliament and the other inside. These are the multi-party Coordination Committees of the governing coalition and the all-party Parliamentary Committees on the floors of the parliamentary chambers. Given the multi-layered nature of Indian coalitions, with some parties joining the cabinet while others extend support only from the parliamentary floor, the Parliamentary Committees may be used as additional *foci* of sharing power. This can be done by empowering these committees to summon documents and witnesses and to challenge the government on the parliamentary floor by changing the confidence convention in parts. The Coordination Committee also needs to be strengthened by imparting greater seriousness and regularity as a sounding board for policies in broad terms to be worked out in detail by the cabinet. This will avoid the embarrassment of the rolling back of cabinet/ministerial decisions, notorious for its frequency during the BJP-led coalition government. In ruling coalition's in New Delhi since 1989, the Coordination Committee of the United Front was *prima facie* more efficacious than its counterparts in the National Front and BJP coalitions. An indicator of the efficacy of the two United Front governments under H.D. Deve Gowda and I.K. Gujral, respectively, was the frequency of meetings and the ability to forestall crises which could have placed the continuance of the coalition governments in jeopardy. On the other hand, Coordination Committees of the National Front and the first BJP-led coalition governments failed to avert the major crises which posed serious problems for coalition maintenance, precipitated by the V.P. Singh-Devi Lal feud in the case of the National Front and the tantrums of the AIADMK supremo, Jayalalitha, in the case of the BJP-led alliance. However, the second BJP-Ied coalition government, the National Democratic Alliance formed in 1999, and the UPA government formed in 2004 has managed to develop a different style of conflict resolution at the top. The supreme leaders bilaterally negotiate with the partners, practically sidelining the Coordination Committee. The Congress-led United Progressive Alliance governments (2004-09 and 2009-14) also followed a similar style of top leaders addressing conflict resolution in a UPA council chaired by the Congress President Sonia Gandhi. She also headed a National Advisory Council on policy and legislation largely consisting of civil society members and activists. It created dual power centres led by the party President and the Prime Minister as the head of the government.

NOTES AND REFERENCES

1. The first post-Independence phase of the Indian party system has been termed the 'Congress system' by Rajni Kothari (Kothari 1970: ch. 5); the 'One-party dominant system' by W. H. Morris-Jones 1978: part 3); and the 'Predominant party system' by Giovanni Sartori (Sartori 1976: 192-216). This type of party system is defined in terms of one-party dominance with appreciable margin from contesting smaller parties in the system that legally coexist with the majority party without alternating in power for a considerably long time-at least for three successive elections according to Sartori. The potential of them forming the government some day is improbable but never impossible. Such party systems typically emerge in conditions of a national liberation struggle or of civil war, or in conditions of exceptional homogeneity in a state of a national liberation struggle or of civil war, or in conditions of exceptional homogeneity in a state of external or inter-regional polarisation. Such a party system has existed in contexts as diverse as post-Independence India and post-World War II Japan, and at various points in time in Canada (both nationally and provincially), Mexico, Uruguay, pre-proportional representation Switzerland, and Sweden.

   The one-party states in post-colonial Africa are, of course, in a different genre for they are basically authoritarian. Also different are the totalitarian one-party systems of the Communist and Fascist varieties.

2. The theory of *Rajamandala* in the *Arthashastra* is actually a theory of inter-state relations aimed at conquering the entire Indian subcontinent in antiquity. However, with suitable modifications it can be applied to analyzing inter-party relations in India today. Thirteen different kinds of relations are conceptualized between the *vijigsu* (conqueror) and his adversaries. To quote from the ancient text:
   "Every king has his own circle of allies. Since the conqueror, his enemy, the Middle King and the Neutral King are all independent actors, there are four circle. It must, however, be emphasized that the circle, of kings is not meant to be imagined geographically as a series of concentric circles, though they may be symbolically represented as such. The nomenclature defines relationships in a dynamic situation, which may create opportunities to some and expose others to danger." (Rangarajan 1987: 551-52)
   Also pertinent here is Maurice Duverger's observation: 'Solid and homogenous coalitions may give a multi-party system a close resemblance to a two-party system and make the opposition more coherent, more coherent, more moderate, and more distinct' (Duverger 1963: 418). Obviously, the politics of coalition governments in India at the national level has not yet attained this coherence and maturity.
3. 'Executive' coalitions are definitionally coterminus with the parties formally joining the cabinet, and with their members becoming ministers at various levels of the Council of Ministers. 'Legislative' coalitions are wider than cabinet coalitions, including parties that extend support to the government from the parliamentary floor without formally joining the cabinet. 'Federal' coalitions are defined as a group of parties that are part of the cabinet and/or legislative coalitions at the Centre as well as in some states.

Bibliography

Duverger, Maurice. 1963. *Political Parties: Their Organisation and Activity in the Modern State* (translated from the French by Babara and Robert North and with a foreword by D.W. Brogan). New York: John Wiley and Sons.

Election Commission of India. 1998. *Personal Communication*.

—, *2000. Statistical Report on General Elections,* 1999, to *the Thirteenth Lok Sabha,* Vol. I. New Delhi. *Indian Recorder,* 1999. Vol. VI. No. 45, 5-11, November.

Kothari, Rajni. 1970. *Politics in India*. Boston: Little Brown and Company.

Morris-Jones, W.H. 1978. *Politics Mainly Indian*. New Delhi: Orient Longman.

Republic of India. 2000. *Statistical Report on General. Elections,* 1999, to *the Thirteenth Lok Sabha:* Vol. I: *National and State Abstracts and Detailed Results*. New Delhi: Election Commission of India.

Rangarajan, N. 1987, *Kautilya's Arthashastra* (edited, translated, rearranged and with an introduction). New Delhi: Penguin Books.

Sartori, Giovanni. 1976. *Parties and Party Systems: A Framework for Analysis*. Cambridge: Cambridge University Press.

17

State Party Systems

Himanshu Roy

This paper analyses the nature of the contemporary party systems in different states of India, which have been inadequately discussed in the academic discourse. The focus of the study is on broad patterns of electoral and political processes rather than on the specificity of political configurations in each province. It argues that among the different factors (regionalism, religion and liberalization) that influence the voting behaviour of the electorate, the most important is the rise of Other Backward Castes [OBCs] who have facilitated the demise of the one-party dominant system and have helped in the growth of alternative party systems in different states. In other words, the states which witnessed the early emergence of the OBCs or the regions which had the *Ryotwari* system also witnessed the early demise of the Congress system and the regions which had the Zamindari system or late awakening among the OBCs witnessed the late demise of the Congress system. The paper arrives at the conclusion that there are three kinds of party systems operational in Indian states at this juncture that may further decline to two namely bi-party and bi-coalitional systems.

In the electoral history of independent India 1967, 1977 and 1989 are turning points that facilitated the growth of alternative party systems in different states and at the Centre. In 1967, the Congress system faced its first major crisis particularly in States. It lost in eight of the then sixteen States, but retained the Centre with a reduced majority. Since then the Congress began to gradually lose its electoral base in the States to be replaced by the non-Congress parties either purely regional in character or nominally national. In 1977, the Congress lost power even at the Centre [gaining only 154 seats] and in many states of North India. However, it retained power or won the elections in Karnataka, Andhra Pradesh, Kerala [where it leads a coalition of different political parties known as United Democratic Front (UDF)], Punjab, Tamil Nadu [under the leadership of All India Anna Dravida Munnetra Khazhagam (AIADMK)], etc., when assembly elections were conducted in 1977-78. In 1989, it once again it lost power at the Centre and in many states. This incremental change of ringing out the old and ringing in the new still continues. But these developments were not unilinear. There were ups and downs.

In the last twenty-eight years [1989 and after] in the electoral war of position, the BJP has acquired a vantage position *vis-a-vis* the Congress. From being confined to few pockets of North India, in the aftermath of Gandhi's assassination, it expanded organizationally into most States of India, though it did not win seats in every legislative assembly or in Lok Sabha from every state. Further, in coalition with other non-Congress parties or without it, BJP has managed to form governments in several States, and at federal level in New Delhi.

In the three decades from 1967, changes in the party systems, both at the Centre and in the States, may be described as a part of resolutive-compositive process. The old party system got dissolved and on its ruins emerged a new one. Of the old system, certain elements of the Nehruvian project like greater democratization of social structure, unity in diversity, focus on universalization of health and education, etc., were retained. The discrepancies that had crept into the old body-politic during the Indira-Rajiv regimes are being discarded either as part of self-purificatory measures or under the pressure of competitive politics. Issues like marginalization of party leaders and cadres *vis-a-vis* the minister of the same party in the government, concentration of administrative power into the hands of the ministers in the federal government vis-a-vis the ministers of the same party in the provincial governments, or the monopolization of power by top leaders vis-a-vis cadres and grassroots workers at party level are now on active political agenda for reforms. In fact, there is a pressure from below for greater decentralization of power both, in the provincial government and on the party units in their routine functioning. The local leaders and cadres in the parties and in the provincial governments are now vociferous in seeking autonomy in policy formulations, which concern local governance both at administrative and party levels. Thus, democracy within parties is an issue which is being discussed and demanded including transparency in party funding, its accounting and auditing and the likes. The directives from the Election Commission have played an affirmative role in such developments. And the parties, which are not adapting to the changing situation are breaking up. As a result, the resolutive-compositive process has led to three types of party systems in the States that may be described as follows: (1) Bi-party system, (2) Bi-coalitional system, and (3) multiple coalitional system.

In the bi-party system as it is operational in States like Gujarat, Delhi, Rajasthan, Himachal Pradesh, Madhya Pradesh, Andhra Pradesh, Assam, Orissa, Karnataka, Jammu and Kashmir, Punjab etc., its mainly the two parties which dominate the political and electoral proceedings and form the government. One of them is the Congress. The second party in the first five States is Bhartiya Janata Party (BJP). In the subsequent states, the other parties are Telugu Desham Party (TDP), Asom Gana Parishad (AGP),

Janata Dal (JD), Biju Janata Dal (BJD), National Conference (NC) and Akali Dal respectively. The dominance of two parties in different States as stated above, however, does not preclude the existence of other parties, either in the legislative assemblies or as electoral contestants. In short term, they may influence/facilitate the formation of the local governments or may be partners in it in exceptional cases. But, in the long run, they play only marginal roles. In Himachal Pradesh, for example, the Himachal Vikas Congress (HVC) in the last election formed a pre-poll alliance with the BJP 'and was partner in the government. It was a small provincial party with a limited influence in the province that facilitated the formation of the government at the time. But when it attempted to play larger role in recent election, the electorate rejected it. In Madhya Pradesh, similarly, the Bahujan Samaj Party (BSP) had pre-poll alliance/'friendly' contests/electoral understanding without any formal declaration, either with the BJP or with the Congress and won few seats in the legislative assembly. But it remains only a marginal party till date in Madhya Pradesh. Thus, in both the States, the HVC and the BSP are only fringe parties either as electoral partners or as partners in the government. Similarly, Peoples' Democratic Party (PDP) in Jammu and Kashmir, as the electoral history of Jammu and Kashmir, may remain a minor player in long run despite heading the government in partnership with the Congress which commands more legislative members than the PDP in the local assembly. There, it is the Congress and the National Conference who have the predominant political existence. The acquisition of pre-dominance by the PDP can only be possible when the Congress or the National Conference is marginalized. In Gujarat, the formation of Janata Party by Shankar Singh Baghela, after he broke away from the BJP, aimed as a third political force failed. Thus, in brief, smaller parties in these States who have influence only in few constituencies of their States in which they are located do not play any significant role. Only those local parties play predominant roles who command decisive influence all over the states in which they are located. In Punjab, Andhra Pradesh, Karnataka, Orissa and Assam, for example, it is the one local party out of many in each State, mainly confined to their States, which play the dominant role, along with the Congress as the other second party in the bi-party system. In recent years, the BJP has attempted to enter into these states' assemblies mainly riding piggy back on the State-based parties but it has not yet succeeded in displacing the Congress or the predominant local party. In such states, a marked feature of the party system is the electoral, organizational and political stability of the two predominant parties either as the ruling or the main opposition party, irrespective of revolts, factional quarrels and break-ups. The change in the nomenclature of the local unit of the predominant parties does not essentially change the character of the party system as it happened, for example, during Chief Minister Chimanbhai Patel's tenure in Gujarat. He broke away from the parent party [Janata Dal], changed the name of the State unit and converted it into a new party, Gujarat Janata Dal, mainly on the strength of the MLAs of Gujarat unit of Janata Dal. In Orissa and Karnataka, the local Janata Dal units acted almost similarly. Thus in spite of such problems and uniqueness in each State the States referred to above have bi-party system in governance.

In the second kind of party system operational in the States like Kerala, West Bengal, Maharashtra, Tamil Nadu, etc., a bi-coalitional pattern may be observed. The essential features of it are the existence of (1) two polarized political formations, each being led by two different parties, (2) constituents of each political formations have electoral understanding among themselves for jointly contesting elections or sharing seats and forming coalition government, when voted into power, and (3) each of the two coalition groups work on the basis of common minimum programme (CMP) irrespective of different ideological strands. In Kerala, for example, Left Democratic Front (LDF) and United Democratic Front (UDF) are led and dominated by the Communist party of India (Marxist) and the Congress respectively. In Tamil Nadu, it is the Dravida Munnetra Kazhagam (DMK) and the All India Anna Dravida Munnetra Kazhagam (AIADMK), which lead their coalition partners. In Maharashtra, the Shiv Sena-BJP coalition and the Congress-Nationalist Congress Party (NCP) coalition have dominated the political proceedings in past years. Both the coalitions have been led by the major parties-Shiv Sena and the Congress, who command largest numbers of legislators in the legislative assembly in their coalitions or are in prominent positions in the State either in terms of percentage of votes or in terms of their organizational strengths. In Bengal, it is the CPI(M) and the Trinamool Congress, which lead their respective political coalitions. But for all of these practical purposes, it is the one-party dominant system, which still prevails. The Congress, which dominated till 1960s, has been substituted by the CPI(M), which has the legislative strength to form the government at its own without the support of coalition partners in the Left Front (LF) who has run the government for more than 34 years since 1977. Technically, however, Bengal may be called as one-coalition dominant system. Here, Congress has been reduced to a minor party with no phoenixian quality. In recent years, nonetheless, both in parliamentary and assembly elections the coalition of Trinamool Congress along with the BJP, or the Congress and other smaller parties attempted to pose a serious electoral challenge to the Left Front (LF). The Trinamool Congress proposed a *mahajot,* (a grand electoral coalition) of non-LF parties, which the local unit of the Congress supported. But the opposition of the Central leadership of the Congress to this programme of *mahajot* checked the formation of a grand coalition of the opposition that provided a needed breather to the LF. It is believed that if the *mahajot* becomes operational, the LF, which wins because of the fragmented votes of the opposition, may lose elections. However, unless the *mahajot* becomes feasible and wins alternative space for itself, which remains vacant, Bengal today cannot be called a State where real bi-coalitional system exists as in the last 20 years no alternative coalition has occupied the governmental power.

One of the features of this (bi-coalitional) system is that smaller parties may shift their allegiance from one coalition to another but this does not affect the functioning of the system. A recent case in point (around 1999 Lok Sabha polls) was of Tamil Nadu, where the BJP, Tamil Rajiv Congress, etc., which were earlier in the coalition led by the AIADMK, shifted to the coalition led by the DMK. Or, in Bengal around the 2001, during Assembly election, the Trinamool Congress formed an alliance with the Congress and dumped the BJP with which it had earlier formed an alliance for the parliamentary elections. Governance in such system is smoothened through a coordination committee of the coalition partners, which resolves the internal contradictions among the parties that arise despite a common minimum programme. Later, Trinamool congress deserted the congress-led coalition as well.

A third category of the party system operational in States like Manipur, Meghalaya, Mizoram, Bihar, and Uttar Pradesh (UP), is multiple coalitions of parties, which exist along with many other major parties contesting the elections independent of any coalitions. The parties outside the coalitions may enter into limited electoral adjustments, 'friendly' contests or constituency specific understandings with one another. In this system, there are more than two important power contenders aiming to form the government but not powerful enough to do it at their own or dictate terms to smaller parties; neither powerful enough to electorally wipe them out as it happens in bi-party/coalitional systems. On the contrary, here the smaller parties are powerful enough to challenge the dominant contenders through their own coalitions. Or within a coalition if there exists a large party, they extract more number of constituencies in their favour for contest. The polarization of forces does take place and it primarily veers around/against the ruling coalition or with/against the dominant contestant. Yet, the forces are not so tightly polarized or there is no sharp division among them as it takes place in the bi-coalitional system. That is, in this system, once the election ends and result is declared reflecting hung assembly or simple majority for any coalition, reconfiguration of political forces begins afresh breaking all the preceding alignments that existed during the election period. In fact, even if a electoral coalition is placed in governmental power by the voters, the government may collapse within short duration far ahead of its scheduled term under different pulls and pressure leading to the beginning of another political! electoral permutation and combination. Only in rare cases, an electoral coalition or a coalition formed after election or a single party placed in power by voters have completed their tenure. In brief, in this system political forces are always in flux and every possible gamesmanship occurs except for dominant contestants forming coalitions among themselves. A brief presentation of the electoral contests of recent years may illustrate the point. To begin with, in Manipur, for the Assembly election 2000 there were three alliances: (1) United Front consisting of Mainpur State Congress Party and Federal Party, (2) Secular Democratic Front consisting of Congress, Mainpur People's Party, CPI, CPI(M), JD(S), Revolutionary Socialist Party; (3) Manipur Democratic Alliance consisting of BJP, Samata Party, Kuki National Assembly. Besides these three alliances, there were parties like Nationalist Congress Party (NCP), which contested the elections on its own. Similarly, in Bihar Assembly election 2005 there were four alliances: (1) RJD-led alliance of CPI and CPI(M), (2) NDA alliance of BJP and JD (U), (3) Congress and LJP alliance, and (4) CPI (ML) alliance. Earlier, in 2000, there were three alliances: (1) RJD-Ied alliance consisting of CPI(M), JD(S), Samajwadi Janata Party (SJP), (2) alliances of CPI and CPI(ML), and (3) BJP-Ied National Democratic Alliance (NDA) of JD(U) and Samata Party. Further, there were other parties like Congress, which contested the election alone. In 1995, JD and CPI were part of one alliance whereas BJP and Samata Party had contested the election separately independent of any alliance. However, in 1990, JD and BJP were part of one alliance. In Uttar Pradesh, in 1993, Samajwadi Party (SP) and BSP had formed an alliance whereas BJP, Congress and JD had contested the assembly election independently. Subsequently, BJP and BSP had formed alliance, and again parted ways and contested the last election independently. In Mizoram, in the last election, in 1998, there were two coalitions that contested the assembly election, namely, (1) Mizo National Front + Mizo People's Conference, and (2) Mizo National Front (Nationalist) + Citizens Common Forum. Besides, the Congress contested alone. Subsequently, in the recent election with slight modification the electoral/political polarization continued. Thus, due to electoral compulsion the parties keep on forming different number of coalitions with partners changing. Even electoral opponents may join hands in government formation. (A case in point is the role of the Congress and Rashtriya Janata Dal in Bihar who contested the Bihar Assembly election in 2000 as opponents but joined together to run the government). Or the parties split with a faction joining the government against the electoral stand of their parent parties. Splits in the BSP and Congress in UP are cases in point. The breakaway factions joined the BJP-Ied government. In Bihar, there are numerous such cases. But even in such political flux one characteristic can be noted, *i.e.,* irrespective of changing number of coalitions and number of parties contesting the elections, there are broad but sharp polarizations either in favour of or against the single largest party (in terms of organizational strength, mass support and spatial reach). In UP for example there is polarization in favour of or against the BJP. In Bihar, similarly, the polarization is either in favour of or against the RJD. And, in Meghalaya, Mizoram and Manipur it is the Congress which propels other parties for polarization. In such system, the parties/coalitions are evenly balanced and no political formation is in a decisively dominant position. Capture of governmental power, anyhow, is the guiding principle of praxis resulting in to opportunistic alliances, splits in parties, etc. The struggle for political survival is so intense that even in the matter of routine, everyday administrative functioning there are frequent bickerings among the alliance partners in the government that affects their overall governance adversely. Since there does not exist any Coordination Committee of parties in power which can smoothen their frictions the contentious issues are resolved through ad hoc decisions taken by the top leadership of the largest parties in power in consultation with the leadership of the smaller parties sharing power.

Both in the bi-party system and in the coalitional systems-bi-coalitional and multiple coalitional-electoral adjustments with minor parties are agreed upon to check splitting of votes and to create an impression in the public that the parties or coalitions are omni-sized and have omni presence in their concerned states with sure winnability in the elections. Splitting of votes among parties having common electoral base usually mars their chances of winning more number of seats. Even in electoral propaganda, they lost out as it. reflects lack of unity among their electoral base. An alliance of parties having common electoral base projects large size of the political formations representing diverse regions and sections of society, which provide benefit to the image making. It also projects the welfare of diverse kinds of people. To take benefit of such a situation, parties even in states like Assam, Orissa, Karnataka, and Andhra Pradesh where there is essentially a bi-party system, both the Congress and the major regional parties (AGP, BJD, JD and TDP) in the respective states form alliances with parties, which have marginal electoral support base. A closer look of the marginal partners, for example, the BJP in Andhra, Karnataka and Orissa or that of the CPI+CPM+UPP in Assam brings forth such facts as enumerated above. They have only minor political presence in such states and the alliances with bigger parties are intended to piggy ride in assemblies/ government or to expand their electoral organizational bases by projecting themselves as extension of larger parties, taking benefits of their networks, contacts, resources or manpower. On the other hand, larger parties like JP/ JD/BJD in Orissa, TDP in Andhra, AGP in Assam or JP/JD/Lok Shakti in Karnataka along with Congress in these states are formidable enough to form governments on their own strength. They form alliance to check the splitting of votes that may benefit their chief political rivals. In this system, the alliance partners may not necessarily join the government, they may not share each other's ideologies but work together on the basis of a Common Minimum Programme. The formation of alliance does not alter the nature of the bi-party system in these states or in Assam, Andhra, Orissa, Karnataka, etc. Even in other states where there are bi-or multi-coalitional systems the purpose of electoral alliance is the same.

Overall, this survey of the party systems in different states of India points out that there is a development towards political polarization that may turn the third category of party system, *i.e.,* multiple coalition, as discussed above, vacuous. Moreover, in the age of globalization and growing centralization of capital the party system, cannot remain undented. The mounting electoral expenses with only a few seats won by a party may not be viable in future. With the scale of economics tilting against such parties, they may become politically obsolete in course of time. And, in the changed social context and competitive political milieu where accountability and auditing by the people are in vogue, only the fittest may survive on the electoral firmament. Thus except for an aberration in Arunachal Pradesh, which still clings to the one-party dominant system with all its features, except for the caste being replaced by the tribe, the party systems in different States may have either bi-coalitional or bi-party system in future. Or, at least, irrespective of number of parties polarization among them may become sharper.

It is difficult to explain as to why some States have bi-party or bi-coalitional systems while others have other kinds of party systems. There are no definite reasons in such diverse society and for such systemic variations. Only some plausible arguments may be posited. One such important factor may be the political emergence of the OBCs as a force to be reckoned with, who have been generally considered as hostile to Congress. In the *ryotwari* areas of mainly South India, *e.g.,* Tamil Nadu, Kerala, etc., the OBCs arrived on the political horizon relatively earlier. Their individual political mobility was propelled by capitalism from below in agriculture, which was brought about by new revenue settlement in the early years of the nineteenth century in colonial India, (which was a caricature of the 1789 French model of development). It may be noted here that in France during the bourgeois revolutionary period of 1789 the peasants had seized the lands of the estates and appropriated them as their private property that was later on legalized. The landed intermediary strata of zamindars existing between the State and the peasants ceased to exist thenceforth. It was a self emancipatory process. The peasants were brought into direct relation with the state. In colonial South India, neither the British as the lead bourgeois party nor the peasantry as the revolutionary force played the same stellar roles as it had happened in France. Nonetheless, the new land settlement initiated a limited break from the past. Modern education further helped the peasants to compete for new spaces provided by colonial capitalism. In the zamindari areas of mainly North India, *e.g.,* in Bihar, UP, etc., the emergence of OBCs was facilitated by the land reform measures initiated in 1950s, which were formulated in instalments and implemented after years of courts' anglings and administrative circumvention.

Actually, it was the sheer raw power that decided the fate of land reforms in villages, at least, in the initial years. Later on, the economics of market and numerical power of the OBCs tilted the possession of land in their favour. Being in majority as OBCs, but not cohesive and united, they supported a number of parties that challenged the Congress in the electoral fray, but could not keep it out of power for long. The lack of opposition unity factor brought the Congress back into power. The OBCs, therefore, took many years to dethrone the Congress through painful forging of opposition unity. The rise of the OBCs in the *ryotwari* areas in combination with the power of their brethren in the post-zamindari areas led to the undermining of the electoral base of the Congress. In other words, Madras and Bombay Presidencies or the areas in the Calcutta presidency witnessing effective land reforms (West Bengal) were the weakest links in the chain of Congress system where it was broken first, giving rise to alternative party systems.

Further, with the expansion of industrial economy to hinterland, mechanization of agriculture and growth of agro-based industries there is an increasing differentiation among the peasantry. And more the differentiation, which was/has been facilitated by gradual economic liberalization over the year particularly beginning in small measures during Rajiv Gandhi's premiership, greater is the desperation among the peasantry to cling to old system and values. BJP and other non-Congress parties used this opportunity to catapult themselves to power.

'From all these developments, Muslims did not remain aloof. Majority of them spread over in rural areas, particularly in rice growing belts which are situated in river basins.' Some of them were benefitted from the commodification process but a large section was displaced and has been marginalized. Still having mired in poverty (the benefit of green revolution, which had occurred in wheat growing areas first, did not percolate to them much) and illiteracy (Muslim women are much below the Dalits in literacy), the Muslims are electorally appropriated by different parties in different States. Though not voting *en bloc*, they do influence considerable number of seats by their religious perceptions. Lack of modem education and rural economic development has placed them in a blind alley. Majority of Muslims being converts from the poor economic and caste strata, they perform mainly their traditional professional chores, which have been hit hardest by economic liberalization. In the economic milieu of searching for alternative livelihood, a section of them are attracted towards religious revivalism and fundamentalism.

Such social transformation particularly in the States undergoing post-zamindari transition felt the change in the nature of party system. The change being gradual and the zamindari areas, comprising approximately 60 per cent of the territory in the country, being too vast, it took almost two to three decades, depending upon the regions, for the OBCs to catapult not only the non-Congress parties in to power on a sustained basis but also their caste brethren in the hierarchies of these parties. Such socio-political transition however, as per the history of India's growth rate was relatively fast. Indira Gandhi, and for a brief period Rajiv Gandhi, had temporarily stalled the undermining of the Congress power through their deft electoral handling; but the gradual demise of the traditional landlords, particularly of the absentee variety, and the rise of "bullock capitalists" at the grass-roots level along with growth of the rich farmers at the upper echelon of rural hierarchy disjointed the class coalition of the bourgeoisie and the landlords that was reflected in the nature of the state during the Nehruvian period which was subsequently replaced by the absolute' dominance of the bourgeoisie, lacking till 1960s, under Indira's authoritarianism which was the measure required for facilitating the absolute dominance of the bourgeoisie. Her economic policy, like nationalization of major banks, was to facilitate the availability of large amount of capital, using the resources of the State, at the disposal of a weak bourgeoisie that was devoid of such benefit in the absence of big banks. Indira-Rajiv charisma and their deft electoral handling could not withhold the social transformation underway for long. Once the splitting of the OBCs votes was checked through some semblance of opposition unity in plurality of the first-past-the post system of election the Congress system, which was already undermined, collapsed. More or less, the Congress had never commanded the majority percentage of votes, with the voter turnout itself restricted to around 60 per cent on an average. The weakening of the Congress system also led to another interesting change. The legal demise of the zamindari system, already corroded by the market and electoral system, also led to the change in the roles of the political parties, which they had, hitherto, played. Now onwards, they confined themselves, gradually, to contesting the elections and forming the governments. Their commitment and roles in radical social transformation atrophied, which was subsequently taken care of by Non-Government Organizations (NGOs).

Apart from these socio-economic factors, the role of contemporary problems like river water disputes, religion, language, region-specific problems, caste-cultural identities, etc., did play important roles in electoral and party politics. During last ten years, their importance has increased. Further, the constituency-specific problems and the number of candidates contesting in a particular constituency ultimately decide the victory of a candidate. Growth in the percentage of vote of a candidate may not be the winning factor. A candidate with a less percentage of vote may win the election, depending upon the split in the opponents' votes. Thus, there are innumerable factors responsible for the victory of candidates of different political parties that determined the nature of party systems in Indian states.

It is believed that there has been growth of regionalism in the past forty years, which has moved in fast track in the last decade. Arguments are posited, to substantiate it, that State-based parties have recently proliferated in large numbers and they have successfully positioned themselves in governmental power replacing national parties, mainly the Congress. Even the BJP, which has emerged as a national party in the twenty years eclipsing the Congress, has been halted by the phenomenon of regionalism, which focuses on sons of the soil, local issues, and greater autonomy to the States. At surface, such arguments may seem plausible. But a deeper probe makes them untenable. A brief explanation to refute such beliefs is required here.

With the expansion of capitalism in agriculture and benefits of land reforms reaching out to the OBCs, SCs and STs, and their realization that the electoral politics can be commanded or influenced by their numerical strength, the pre-capitalist dominance of the upper castes, which had lingered on till 1960s, gradually declined. It was substituted by the new sets of political power holders (now known as Mandal elites along with dalits), backed by their constituencies, that dismantled the Congress system which was dominated by the upper castes. The fallout of the zamindari abolition combined with the benefits of *ryotwari* system hastened its decline. The neglect of emerging social aspirations of the OBCs, in particular by the Congress, played an equally important role in its gradual demise. The new rulers' political survival depended on nurturing local/rural aspirations. Their new political formations away from Congress, survived mainly at regional levels essentially as (1) an electoral protest of new social forces, mainly or OBCs, against the Congress system for its failure to cater to their local requirements, and (2) for decentralization of power and its accessibility at district and *talook* levels catering to their local needs. The grassroots perception never differentiated the 'regional' or 'national' parties. But people definitely vote for the parties that perform. Mainly belonging to the profession of cultivation and possessing traditional rural outlook, these castes, now dominant, required parties that were locally rooted like them and work for them. Unconscious of or indifferent to the image of regionalism, as created and sustained by the parties and leaders for their own political ambitions, the local population faces similar problems that are encountered by the populace of other constituencies all over India. They, simultaneously, face problems that are region, and constituency-specific as well. Solution of their problems, and not the dominance over others, is the need of the people: Behind voting regional parties into power, the intention is not exclusion from India but the solution of their problems of everyday existence. Recognition of identity was sought for self-governed development. It meant a desire to participate in their development in democratic governance. Separation just for its sake and false prestige has not been the part of their psyche. They have voted Congress or other 'national' parties back into power time and again. And they have rejected their 'regional' parties when the parties of the regions have failed to perform. Regionalism, thus in contemporary period, is only an electoral verbiage for the State-based parties and leaders bereft of any serious popular support for the separatist agenda. Or such leaders and parties use the verbiage of separation/regionalism to keep their electoral support intact or conceal their bad governance or attempt to cover up their failure of performance by blaming others. Growth of state-based parties reflects only the existence of unsolved problems. Indirectly, it creates pressure on the 'national' parties to take into account, seriously, the local needs of the people and solve their problems. In an economy, which has still to acquire developed capitalist structure, the competition for appropriating resources among different regions and segments of society is reflected in different images. Many of such images are false and are deliberately created to pressurize the resource distributing agencies. Regionalism is one such false image used for appropriating resources from the distributing agencies by a regional party from among the competing sections. The desire of a State government for an autonomous administrative functioning, away from the clutches of the Central government, need not be confused for regionalism. The proliferation of contemporary state-based parties contesting elections has no serious link with regionalism or separatist agenda. It is only a desire for autonomous administrative functioning. The growth of regionalism takes place when democratic governance and welfare measures elude a society. In India, flexible constitution, liberal democracy arid expanding capitalism provide enough space for social mobility that acts as countervailing force to regionalism. The demand for separation from India is sought by only those political organizations, which do not contest election, or by those who exist at political fringe at that point of time and use the verbiage of separation just to remain in existence.

The incremental change in the nature of party system in different states of India in the last forty years have resulted into coalition politics at the Centre and in States. The years 1977 and 1989 are marked as watersheds in such developments that heralded and culminated respectively into breaking the hegemony of the Congress and one-party dominant system, and substituted it with either bi-party system, bi-coalitional system, or polarized pluralism. There were many factors responsible for such changes. Growth of OBCs as "bullock capitalists" in the post-zamindari period, breakdown of the class coalition between bourgeoisie and landlords and its replacement by absolute dominance of the bourgeoisie, expansion of civil society, etc., were factors that affected the process of change. More importantly, the Congress represented a period of transition from political dominance of upper castes to their decline, from their land dominance in rural India to their urban-migration. It was the dominance, both actual and residual, that had lingered on from the days of pre-capitalist society. The beginning of the end of Congress system was also the end of vestiges of feudalism and expansion of rural capitalism at a faster pace. *Ryotwari* area had witnessed such socio-economic changes earlier hence, anti-Congress ideology in such States in the South India arrived earlier. When the benefits of Zamindari abolition coalesced with the benefits of the *ryotwari* system the Congress system was dismantled forever. It heralded the arrival of rural capitalism all over India at grassroots level, which politically energized the majority of rural population against Congress system.

The dismantling of the Congress system affected different regions and segments of population in different proportions. The non-fulfilment of the aspirations of the people under the Congress system threw up many local parties and leaders who promised a better life to their constituencies in the post-Congress system. It resulted in open display of caste, communal and regional cards for vote mobilization. Suiting to the local requirements of the rural population, who felt the sense of power, it became a necessity for the non-Congress parties to identify with the idioms of the rural world and, competitively, prove themselves, in verbiage, more faithful to the sons of the soil. But most of the parties got trapped in such political cocoons of being regional and local, which was a creation of their own, and could not expand beyond a limited vote bank, which proved detrimental to their expansion and graduating to governance on their own steam. They were consequently compelled to form coalition for governance or form alliances for electoral contest resulting into coalition politics of the day and polarization of political forces. Apart from acquiring the images of being regional, secular, religious or caste-oriented that suited these parties in the initial stage, in the aftermath of the Congress system, such labels are now turning into their fetters. Economic liberalization has posed another problem for their survival. It has hastened the process of differentiation among and uprooting of the rural population, thereby, eroding and changing the vote banks of different parties. It has also extended the law of market to the realm of political competition with more intensity. With large number of competitors for votes targeting same voters and the voters migrating to towns every year in a different socio-economic milieu, a number of parties may become extinct or get marginalized as the victory of candidates would become elusive due to splitting of votes among large number of candidates. The electoral expenses with lesser probability of electoral success shall deter a party from making bad ventures. Thus, the economy, acting as catalyst may, in future, help in further polarizing the political forces into limited number of blocks.

More or less, the diverse factors acting against a number of political parties, and the contemporary political trend already existing towards polarized formations, the nature of party systems in different States of India, where multiple coalitions exists today, may move towards bi-coalition or bi-party systems.

Notes and References

The data presented in this paper about the election results have been compiled from Butler, David, *et.al. India Decides:* New Delhi: Books & Things; Election Commission of India (2000). *Election in India: Major Events: New Initiatives 1996-2000*. New Delhi: Rana, M.S. (2000) *India Votes*. Delhi: B.R. Publishing Corporation.

Roy, Himanshu (1997), "Mandal Elite vs. Indian Democracy" in Singh, M.P. and Saxena, Rekha (eds.) *Political Science Annua11997*, New Delhi: Deep and Deep Publication.

This information was given by Professor Imtiaj Ahmed in a lecture at Academic Staff College, Jawaharlal Nehru University, New Delhi in 1999.

For the economic and political emergence of OBCs, see Rudolph, L.I. and Rudolph, S.H. (1987) *In Pursuit of Lakshmi: Political Economy of the Indian State*, New Delhi: Orient Longman.

For such view see Yadav, Yogendra, Kumar, Sanjay and Heath, Oliver (2000) "Regional Parties to the Fore", *Frontline*, March 17: 127-130.

See Balveer Arora's arguments in Frankel, Francine, Hasan, Zoya, Bhargava, Rajeev and Arora, Balveer (eds.) (2000) *Transforming India: Social and Political Dynamics of Democracy*, New Delhi: Oxford University Press.

For arguments on increasing federalization of India democracy mainly in matters of administrative governance, see Singh, Mahendra Prasad (1994) "Political Parties and Political Economy of Federalism: A Paradigm shift in Indian Politics", *Indian Journal of Social Science*, Vol. 7, New Delhi.

18

State Politics in India

Mahendra Prasad Singh

❑ INTRODUCTION

The study of provincial politics and native states in British India was an underdeveloped area. Native states,in any case, formed a backyard of the British Raj but politics, both constitutional and institutional, were largely eclipsed by the nationalist movement. In retrospect, constitutional reforms introduced in the first half of the 20th century in the British Indian provinces, by the imperial government of London, were significant in the early experiments of representative, responsible, and federal governance. Bolder moves structured in all these respects under the 1950 constitution, after India's independence, must be studied in this historical backdrop. There are certain missing information in studies of devolution of powers to the provincial governments under the Government of India Act. 1909 which can be observed in the studies of diarchy at the provincial level under the Government of India Act, 1919. and in the provincial autonomy of the first federal constitution in British India underthe Government of India Act, 1935.

Study of State politics, in independent India, also remained a rather under-cultivated field of enquiry which may be explained in terms of a number of reasons. Firstly, in the Nehru era there was a carryover of the nationalist ambience and fervor of the freedom struggle, and for this reason all that really mattered was the politics at the national level. Congress dominance at the Union as well as state levels submerged politics in the states under the overarching national patterns. Popular mass movements for the creation of unilingual states in various parts of the country during the 1950s and 1960s briefly brought federal and state politics to forefront, but once such demands were conceded, the leaders of these movements in Andhra Pradesh, Maharashtra and Gujarat tended to join or rejoin the Congress Party.

The overarching dominance of a single party was easily restored once again even in the areas of the linguistic regional agitations.

Secondly, the breaches in Congress dominance in the late 1960s and the late 1970s relatively lived for a short span of time after which Congress dominance was again restored. The emergence of states as important arenas of politics turned out to be rather brief episodes. The reigning eras of Pt. Jawaharlal Nehru, the first Prime Minister of independent India, Smt. Indira Gandhi, the third Prime Minister of independent India and Rajeev Gandhi, the sixth Prime Minister of independent India were characterized by a great deal of centralization or 'nationalization' of the Indian political system. State politics were then either a subsidiary arena or were appendage to national politics.

Thirdly, the distribution of powers and revenue resources in the Indian constitution is heavily skewed in favour of the centre. This feature greatly reduces the importance and effectiveness of the State Governments, and make them immensely dependent on federal mandatory and discretionary fiscal transfers under the constitution and shared-cost-centrally-sponsored schemes of development under the federal spending power. Notably the union and state jurisdictions are demarcated with at least some exclusive areas reserved for each order of government, but the constitution does not expressly prohibit the union government to spend its money even in exclusive state concerns.

Fourthly, even though the law and order is supposed to be an exclusive concern of State, there has been an enormous expansion in the central paramilitary police forces. The 42nd constitutional Amendment (1976) has made the deployment of armed forces and central paramilitary forces in aid of civil power in a state an exclusive union competence. Incidence of internal disturbances and terrorist activities by external and indigenous groups has resulted in a great deal of increase in the coercive power of governments and centralization in the political system. These developments tend to overshadow the State Governments and subordinate state politics to the imperatives of national politics, although the state governments are now very zealously guarding their turf against any new encroachments by the center.

It has presumably been for these reasons that the studies of politics in the states (as well as federalism with its focus on intergovernmental relations) have been less andalso sporadic over the years. The first major attempt in study of state politics was published in 1968 by Myron Weiner.[1] It made a selective study of only eight states: Uttar Pradesh., Madhya Pradesh, Maharashtra, Jammu and Kashmir, West Bengal, Rajasthan, Andhra Pradesh and Punjab. The focus was deliberately kept rather open-ended and wide, in view of the exploratory nature of the exercise, though the conceptual and theoretical concern reflected the dominant pre-occupation of the Western, especially American, scholarship of the time, emphasizing on the political aspects of modernization in relation to political and economic development.

Methodologically, Weiner made a significant point, which says "Each of the Indian states provides us with an unusual microcosm and macrocosm for studying processes of development: a microcosm since the states are constituent units of a larger system, and a macrocosm because the units are themselves so large that they can be studied as total systems.... The states share a common legal system, a common constitutional framework, a common administrative structure, a common international environment, but their internal political patterns vary considerably."[2]

Weiner set a great store by this methodological advantage that the factors that are held constant in this quasi-experimental research design cannot account for states' variable political patterns and must be looked for in historical, sociological, and political economy factors. The author's writing on the respective states tried to explain the varying patterns of state politics in terms of the social and economic factors, such as why West Bengal, Andhra Pradesh and Kerala had active communist movements while the others did not have why was the Central Congress party leadership able to impose a Chief Minister in Madhya Pradesh from outside but was not able to influence the choice of the Chief Minister in West Bengal and Madras, why was political participation high in Kerala, Madrasand Punjab, and low in Madhya Pradesh, Orissa, and Bihar why was factionalism in the ruling Congress party and fragmentation among the opposition parties more intense in some states than in others, why were some states more seriously afflicted by community tensions and violence than others, why did some states such as Punjab manage to register better economic development than others such as Uttar Pradesh. No overarching or systematic explanatory framework emerged from the separate state studies beyond the rather overstated methodological assumptions alluded to above, and the underlining of two crucial all pervasive factors of the dominant Congress party and the All India Services.

Myron Weiner, in his Editorial Introduction, candidly admitted that the volume is sought to measure political stability more than political performance. He also surmised that until then the states had not really played 'an innovative role in development. He went on to say: "Some powers constitutionally shared by the states and central government are exercised almost exclusively by the central government because of lack of interest or skill on the part of state leaders".[3] Under the veneer of political stability attributable to one-party dominance of the Indian National Congress, Weiner did point to the seeds of latent instability earlier. This was evident in the fact that even before the 1967 General Elections, in which the Congress lost in 9 out of 18 states, there were 5 states, Kerela, Madhya Pradesh, Orissa, Rajasthan and Andhra Pradesh, in which party competition was so intense that the Congress had failed in at least one of the 3 preceding General Elections to win a majority of seats and had either formed a Government with a plurality of seats or actually failed to form a Government at all.

The second and a more comprehensive academic foray (inclusive of 22 states alongwith a regional cluster of the North-Eastern states) in the field of state politics was made by a volume edited by Iqbal Narain in 1976.[4] Its antenna was conceptually and theoretically as wide as that of the Weiner volume and interpretations and conclusions were even less tangible. It made some interesting and impressionistic observations regarding the integration of the princely states into the Indian Union and the subsequent linguistic re-organization of the States, and raised the question, without really answering it, 'whether political remapping could result in organic political communities or whether the states or even their people continued to retain their pre-integration identities with their own sense of pride and prejudice.'[5] As to the style and idiom of politics, it hypothesized that the States were 'passing through a process of continuity and change which on the one hand symbolises in itself a gradual transition from tradition to modernity and on the other a syncretization of the two in a sort of modernization of tradition'.[6]

Since this volume was published during the wake of the restoration of the Congress party led by Indira Gandhi in the 1971 parliamentary and 1972 state assembly elections, following its traumatic defeat in 1967 followed by the great split in it in 1969, the editor could not help but raise the question whether the preceding debilitating events were just a short-lived deviant aberration. His answer was that "most of the contributors to the volume do not seem to subscribe to the viewpoint and they do not appear to be far wrong either."[7]

State politics in the 1970s and especially in the 1980s were revisited by a third significant volume covering seven states-Uttar Pradesh, Bihar, West Bengal, Kerala, Karnataka, Maharashtra and Gujarat-edited by John R. Wood in 1984.[8] It succinctly analyzed the political developments during the periods of Indira Gandhi's Congress' ascendance during the turbulent 1970s, the Janata Party's Government interlude during 1977-79 and the return the Indira Gandhi's Congress in 1980 in the trail of the premature fall of the Janata Party Government. Wood in his editorial Introduction and Roderick Church in the concluding chapter highlighted the three different tendencies and trends in quick succession foundationally altering the parameters of state politics during the period under review in this volume:

1. The attempt of Indira Gandhi to centralize and personalize political power in her imperious premiership dominating the Union and State Governments alike by dispensing with internal party democracy, stamping out any dissent, imposing Chief Ministers in Congress-ruled states handpicked by herself and destabilizing opposition-ruled States by partisan use of President's Rule in States, under article 356, to suppress an extra-parliamentary mass movement against authoritarianism and corruption in the Congress governments.
2. The pluralization and regionalization of politics under the Janata Party governments in New Delhi and the north Indian states elected in the wake of the defeat of the Congress party in the 1977 general elections.

3. The recapture of political power by the Congress party in 1980 under Indira Gandhi and revival of her centralizing drive in the party and the governments at the Union and the states but less forcefully this time than in the 1970s. For the '70s were very different from the 1980s. As Church aptly noted in his concluding observations that the party was almost continuously in crisis ever since Indira Gandhi came to power on account of the participatory political rise of the regionally and locally dominant middle peasant castes. She did badly in the 1967 and 1977 elections, both the times followed by splitting the party in 1969 and 1978 to get rid of the dissident factions tarring them as representatives for the vested interests seeking to perpetuate the status quo. On both the occasions, she confounded her critics and political observers by winning hands down in 1971 and 1980,as new elections approached in 1989 with signs of her losing power again. Church mused whether there would be other emergency and undemocratic constitutional amendments like those in the 1970s to avert the defeat.[9]

Church's concluding piece, in J.R. Wood (1984), postulated an interesting hypothesis that political participation crisis of the lower castes/classes may help to classify Indian states into a typology of political regimes comprising the following four types of states, as in the early 1980s:

1. Upper caste/class dominated Congress regimes in Bihar and Uttar Pradesh.
2. Lower castes/classes consequentially recruited into Congress regimes in Gujarat, Karnataka and Maharashtra.
3. Lower castes/classes strongly represented in non-Congress regimes in Kerala and West Bengal.
4. Competition between the Congress and a middle caste regional party, excluding lower castes/classes in Punjab.[10]

Atul Kohli in 1987 compared the differential effects of three different kinds of party regimes in three states on poverty alleviation policies and found significant variations among Karnataka under the Congress Chief Minister Devraj Urs, Uttar Pradesh ruled by a Janata Party coalition and West Bengal under the Left Front. The performance in terms of effectiveness in policy implementation was found to vary, in terms of Indian standards, from excellent in West Bengal, to good in Karnataka, and poor in U.P.[11]

Atul Kohli in a subsequent study focused on the growing crisis of governability in three states, i.e., slippage from political order to it's breakdown in Bihar, exit from breakdown to order in West Bengal and the growing turmoil in Gujarat, an otherwise relatively developed state. His explanation for these varying political trends was offered in terms of the decline of the social and political dominance of the landowning upper castes in the erstwhile Congress party, which was unable to incorporate the newly mobilized lower strata nor was any alternative party readily available to perform this task. Such a task could be accomplished only by a reformist party which simultaneously respected the rights of propertied groups, on one side, and ensure symbolic and real gains for the lower strata, on the other side. The Communist Party of India, Marxist led Left Front in West Bengal, managed to do it better during the period of this study, while Bihar and Gujarat were found groping for it with increasing levels of political conflict and violence.[12]

An exclusive study of left-wing State Governments in Kerala, West Bengal, and Tripura was undertaken by T. J. Nossiter and published in 1988.[13] By the time of this study the Indian communist movement and parties had come out from the orbit of the declining or disintegrating international communist movements and their national autonomy had become established. Indian communism had also made the switch to the thesis of peaceful transition to socialism in 1956-57. Yet the question remained as to what kind of communism had the Indian variant become-social democracy of early European vintage or Euro-communism of the more recent European politics. Nossiter found both interpretations offered in the literature, but seemed himself inclined to treat Indian communism in some ways sui generis or unique. Indian communism was constrained to adapt to the peculiar Indian socio-economic milieu and India's federal constitution and political system. Besides, the Indian communist parties seemed to have only adopted the practice of democracy as a strategy or tactics and not as an ideology or theory. In contrast to the communism in Europe, Indian communist parties never formally renounced the revolutionary path nor abandoned the dictatorship of proletariat in transition from socialism to communism.[14]

Regarding the Indian communists' attitude towards the use of governments, Nossiter delineated three phases of evolution:

1. The first communist government in Kerala during 1957-59 was cautiously optimistic but it was prematurely dismissed by Prime Minister Nehru;
2. The subsequent split in the united Communist Party of India in 1964 begetting the Communist Party of India (Marxist) and the rise of the ultra left, prompted the CPI(M) to adopt the Leninist strategy of simultaneous pursuit of administration and agitation; and
3. A via media between the first two strategies by forming Left Democratic Front or United Democratic Front Governments depending on what is feasible in a state and trying to do the best under the conditions knowing it fully well that communists are in office not in power.[15]

After a more or less objective analysis of the three left-wing governments that are different but not spectacularly successful in comparison with other state governments formed by non-communist parties, Nossiter's succinct assessment is the following: 'In terms of performance, the three unequivocal successes of some or all of the Marxist-led governments have been: land reform rural local government, and minimum needs programmes in food, health and education. Significantly, each area is, more or less, within the state governments' competence under the Indian constitution and each closely echoes the demands of the developing mass movement. To a considerable extent, formal and informal popular participation-land grabs, *panchayats* and *zilla parishads*, and local party committees and locally recruited officials-has done much to energize the implementation of legislation and executive orders. The record varies as between the states.[16]

In a mega two-volume study edited by Francin R. Frankel and M. S. A. Rao, published in 1989 and 1990 covering a larger number of states across India, the authors sought to analyze politics in the Indian states from the theoretical perspective of the interface between social dominance and state power which underpins the competition among the old as well as new social formations for the capture of the state power in modern India.[17] Frankel projected the trajectory of this process in terms of three broad phases:

1. The coalition and competition among the political and social elites during the British Raj in the colonial and nationalist arenas of politics.
2. The extension of this process among the newly emergent elite-based alliances of the period of Congress dominance over the 1950s to the 1970s.
3. The further extension of this process to the voters' alliances at the mass level with the deepening of electoral democracy heralded by the advent of the Janata Party/Dal in the post-Emergency period beginning with the late 1970s and beyond.

Frankel hypothesized: "As Brahmanical legitimacy weakened, the potentialities for conflict within society greatly expanded. Simultaneously, the forms which these conflicts assumed became more varied according to the situational context and the regional pattern of social organization."[18]

In Hindi-heartland, the Congress thrived on the electoral alliances among the elite castes of the Brahmanical social order, but the competition among these castes created openings for the subaltern castes and minorities who were co-opted to leadership positions as junior partners who would subsequently become leaders in their own right with the deepening of electoral completion with the gradual political rise of lower castes and formation of alliances spanning Backward and Forward castes and classes. In Rajasthan, the Congress electoral strategy counted on the urban educated middle classes and Jat and Rajput peasants to mobilize against the ex-Maharajas and former Jagirdars.[19]

To the northwest, in Punjab, the Congress contended against the Akali Dal factions agitating for a Sikh-majority, Punjabi Suba and Hindu-based Bharatiya Jan Sangh. The states of western and southern India were dominated by subregional or state-wide dominant cultivating middle castes such as the Reddys in Andhra Pradesh, Lingayats and Vokkaligas in Karnataka, Marathas in Maharashtra and Pattidars in Gujarat. The Congress made these castes it's mainstay with all in complex alliances with urban upper castes and classes as well as scheduled castes and tribes and Muslims.[20]

In the extremesouth and the east there were no exact equivalents of dominant castes of peasants and farmers. In Madras, later Tamil Nadu, the Congress first relied on the Brahmans and Vellalas in the hinterland of the capital city and on the notables of localized cultivating castes. In West Bengal, the urban *Bhadralok* Congress leaders mobilized the village-level *jotedars* (cultivators) and intermediary peasant castes. In Orissa, the Brahman-Karna middle class Congress leadership entered into electoral alliances with rich peasant Khandayats and scheduled castes and tribes.[21]

John Harris[22] made an elaborate classification of state political systems around the turn of the century on the basis of caste/class power and the nature of organization of the party/parties in power in those states. He then offered causal connection between political regimes across Indian States and policy formulation and performance under them, especially with regard to decentralization of power to lower caste/class groups and poverty alleviation (see Table 1). The Table is self-contained in terms of the

TABLE 1 Typology of Indian State Regimes

Category	Characteristics	States
A (i)	States with upper caste/class dominance persisted and Congress has remained strong in the context of a stable two-party system. [Traditional dominance rather than politics of accommodation vis-a-vis lower classes].	Madhya Pradesh, Orissa, Rajasthan
A (ii)	States in which upper caste/class dominance has been effectively challenged by middle castes/classes and Congress support has collapsed in the context of fractured and unstable party competition. [Both dominance and politics of accommodation have broken down].	Bihar, Uttar Pradesh
B	States with middle caste/class dominated regimes, where the Congress has been effectively challenged but has not collapsed, and there is fairly stable and mainly two-party competition. [The politics of accommodation vis-a-vis lower class interests have continued to work effectively, most effectively in Maharashtra and Karnataka and least effectively in Gujarat].	Andhra Pradesh, Gujarat, Karnataka, Maharashtra, Punjab
C	States in which lower castes/classes are more strongly represented in political regimes where the Congress lost its dominance at an early stage.	Kerala, Tamil Nadu, West Bengal

Notes: a. These states are classified as Mow income states.
b. AP and Karnataka are 'middle income states' and Punjab, Gujarat, and Maharashtra are 'high income states'.
c. These are 'middle income states'.
Source: John Harris (1999: 3371).

postulated relationship between the regime type and governmental policy performance. Harris concludes: "Where stable, relatively well institutionalized parties complete for their votes, the political system is likely to be more responsive to the needs and interests of poorer people, and more effective in bringing about poverty reduction."[23]

In a subsequent survey of research on the relationship between regime differences across Indian states and rural poverty reduction, Harris considered evidence and argument on both sides of the debate. He particularly took note of studies by Minhas, Jain, Tendulkar (1991), Datt, Ravallion (1998),Vyas and Bhargava (1995). The former analyzed trends in poverty alleviation in two phases, i.e., 1970-71 to 1983 and 1983 to 1987-88. They ranked the major states, taking into account both the changes in headcount ratio and absolute number of poor people across both the phases, as follows: 1. Andhra Pradesh 2. Kerala 3. West Bengal 4. Tamil Nadu 5. Madhya Pradesh 6. Uttar Pradesh 7. Haryana 8. Rajasthan 9. Bihar 10. Orissa 11. Maharashtra 12. Karnataka 13. Himachal Pradesh 14. Assam 15. Punjab 16. Gujarat 17. Jammu and Kashmir. Andhra Pradesh and Kerala registered reductions in both headcount ratio and absolute numbers in both the phases. The headcount ratio declined in the first phase than in the second in Andhra Pradesh, Kerala, Haryana and Rajasthan. Its decline was more in the second phase than in the first in West Bengal, Tamil Nadu, Madhya Pradesh and Uttar Pradesh. After declining in the first phase, it improved in the second phase in Orissa, Maharashtra, Karnataka, Himachal, Assam and Gujrat. Conversely, it marginally increased in the first phase but declined in Bihar in the second. Jammu and Kashmir registered increase in both the phases. Harris finds these variations rather erratic, but notes that what appears to be significant is that the second phase is marked by the launch of a more comprehensive poverty alleviation programme featuring Integrated Rural Development Programme aiming to put productive assets into the hands of the poor, the National Rural Employment Programme and the Public Distribution System to supply essential commodities at a lower price to the poor. This was largely in place in the first period as studied by Minhas and his collaborators. Vyas and Bhargava (1995) reported later, which supports the above interpretation, that poverty ratio decreased only by 3 per cent in the pre-poverty alleviation programme period (1970-71 to 1977-78), whereas its decline was to the tune of a per cent in the poverty alleviation programme period (1977-78 to 1987-88).[24]

In a comparative study of politics across India's states edited by Rob Jenkins,[25] the contributors have presented paired studies of some aspects of politics in the states along the dimensions of economic policy-making (Andhra Pradesh and Tamil Nadu by Loraine Kennedy, and West Bengal and Gujarat by Aseema Sinha); subaltern politicization (Bihar and Orissa by Sanjay Kumar, and Uttar Pradesh and Madhya Pradesh by Christophe Jaffrelot and Jasmine Zerinini-Brotel); civic engagement (cities in Uttar Pradesh and Kerala by Ashutosh Varsney, and Maharashtra and Rajasthan by Rob Jenkins); and political leadership (Andhra Pradesh and Karnataka by James Manor, and West Bengal and Tamil Nadu by Mukulika Banerjee). While the Telugu Desam Party's Chandrababu Naidu has implemented the neo-liberal economic reforms with greater commitment in Andhra Pradesh, the leaders of All India Anna Dravida Munnetra Kazhagam (AIADMK) and Dravida Munnetra Kazhagam (DMK) implemented the same policy with reluctance with the public posturing of distancing themselves from it in Tamil Nadu. Kennedy attributes this difference to the fact that Andhra Pradesh is less fragmented in its party system and comparatively less marked by politicization of the lower castes in comparison to Tamil Nadu.[26]

Aseema Sinha found that despite West Bengal being socially more peaceful and politically more stable, during the period, of study than Gujarat, the latter received twelve times more investment than the former. This difference is explained in terms of the prevalence of social democratic ideology in the eastern state and of the centrist or right-wing ideology in the western state. In addition, industrialization in West Bengal is concentrated around Kolkata where as more widely dispersed in Gujarat. This makes for a stronger support for neo-liberal doctrine in Gujarat than in West Bengal.[27]

On the dimension of subaltern politicization, the states of Bihar and Uttar Pradesh are considerably higher than that of Orissa and Maddhya Pradesh. This has significant different impact on the party systems of the two sets of states. The ascendant backward castes in Bihar managed to dislodge the earlier dominance of the Congress party by helping the rise of the Rashtriya Janata Dal (RJD) and the Janata Dal (United) (JD-U) in shifting alliances with upper castes, Muslims and scheduled castes. The same process is reflected in the decline of the Congress party in Uttar Pradesh, the failure of the Bharatiya Janata Party (BJP) beyond a certain point, and the strategic emergence of the Bahujan Samaj Party (BSP) with its core electoral base amongst the scheduled castes andthe Samajwadi Party with its mainstay among the backward middle peasant castes, both in alliance with other castes and communities. This kind of outcome is not found in Orissa. Sanjay Kumar explains it in terms of the fact that the Biju Janata Dal (BJD) which has replaced the previously dominant Congress party, is largely supported by the upper caste Karnas and Brahmans. There is no dominant backward caste in Orissa. The Khandayats have an ambiguous caste status and are ambivalent between the upper and lower castes. The scheduled tribes of the states, although sizeable, lack politicization and power. In Maddhya Pradesh, Zaffrelot and Zerinini-Brotel report, neither the backward castes nor the scheduled castes have been able to project parties of their own. The BJP and the Congress continue to run the show seeking to follow the electoral strategy of forging coalitions of extremes, i.e., upper castes and scheduled castes.[28]

On the dimension of civic engagement studied with reference to religious communal riots in selected cities of Uttar Pradesh and Kerala, Ashutosh Varsney comes up with the finding that the northern cities are more prone to riots and less able to expeditiously control them than the southern. This is on account of greater civic engagement, defined as inter-community contacts and reconciliation in contrast to mainly intra-community communication, in the South than in the North. Jenkins in his paired study of anti-corruption movements in two districts explain greater occurrence of such movements in these two districts rather than others, by the demographic fact of the cohesive community structure of one community structure of one particular caste in each of the two districts-Marathas in Ahmednagar in Maharashtra and Rawats in Rajsamand in Maharashtra. This type of community structure is conducive to the maintenance of cohesive social norms. It also precludes the political clash from degenerating into inter-caste conflicts. An additional factor that contributes to the above bahavioural pattern is that both the Marathas and Rawats have a sort of split personality resulting from their numerically large castes divided along caste-class nexus.[29]

On the dimension of political leadership, the contrasts are portrayed by James Manor between Karnataka and Andhra Pradesh and by Mukulika Banerjee between West Bengal and Tamil Nadu. Andhra Pradesh parties operate in a more socially divisive locale than the Karnataka parties. That may be the reason why the national party leadership found it more feasible to intervene in the less socially embedded parties in former state than in the latter which are rooted in their own respective regional political cultures and socio-economic settings. In Trinamool Congress, Mamata Banerjee's political leadership is more mass-oriented, kind of Didi-populism than the elitist *amma*-populism of All India Anna Dravida Munnetra Kazhagam's leaded by J. Jayalalitha.[30]

In a recent study of Indian politics with bifocal coverage of national as well as state politics, Atul Kohli has offered an intriguing typology of the states with (1) neo-patrimonial political tendencies, (2) developmental political tendencies and (3) social democratic political tendencies.[31] At the national 1evel, the major change over the last three decades highlighted by Kohli is the growing power of the corporate business class in the political economy and processes, the exclusionary spiral engendered by this narrowing state-business alliance, and the political challenge of incorporating the excluded groups and classes to ward off the revolutionary politics. In seeking to explore the regional diversities in this phase, Kohli gingerly formulates the three-fold typology referred to above. His caution is evident in his disclaimer that India is no Congo or Zimbabwe, on one hand, and in his admission that the postulated types are mixed with redeeming features or possibilities of change, on the other.

Neo-patrimonial states of the Hindi-heartland minus Haryana and plus Orissa are generally at the bottom of the physical economic and human development indicators. They lack purposive, public-spirited, cohesive and robust political parties animated by civic regional nationalism or organized class politics. Their parties are mostly based on patron-client networks rooted in ascription and personal loyalties of the minions to the leaders, who routinely channel public resources to personal and patronage ends. Their bureaucracy is often politicized and venal. And the electoral cycle is often a vicious circle of corruption and criminality. This neo-patrimonial type of state is portrayed in some detail in a case study of politics in Uttar Pradesh.[32]

Developmental states of India such as Gujarat and Maharashtra in the west, Haryana in the north and Punjab in the northwest are historically reasonably well-endowed with a sounder base of economic and human development, and in some cases an enterprising agricultural class or industrial entrepreneurial class, in modern times. The parties and political leadership in these states may not be entirely different from those in the bulk of the Hindi heartland, but they are imbued with nationalism or regionalism and with a larger public purpose. Their bureaucracies are not as politicized and venal as in the neo-patrimonial states. Personalization of political power is not entirely absent in these states, it is somewhat balanced by governmental and political institutionalization. In Kohli's words, "These states not only mirror the national-level trend in India toward prioritizing growth and supporting private capital but are also beginning to perform some of the functions that one associates with the developmental states of Asia".[33] The developmental state in India is illustrated with a case study of the BJP-ruled Gujarat.

Kohli takes Kerala and West Bengal as the clearest examples of social democratic states in India, though he also confusingly and questionably brings in the ambit of his discussion the states of south India as well. Kohli contends that social democratic states are characterized by mobilized lower middle and lower castes and classes through well-organized political parties, "who are in a position to implement modest redistribution, adding an egalitarian bias to the growth process". In Tamil Nadu, Andhra Pradesh and Karnataka similar socio-politcal mobilization is evident "insofar as Brahmanical in them was successfully challenged rather early on trouncing the power pyramid." However, the political parties in these states have mobilized the people on the basis of regional nationalism instead of class lines. Social egalitarian ethos is part of the political idiom but in the absence of class-based parties populist political leadership and parties have flourished. This model of state politics is illustrated by a case study of West Bengal.[34]

To my mind, Kohli would have done well to create a separate category for southern states as their indigenous anti-caste egalitarian political ideology is a far cry from either Marxism or democratic socialism or social democracy, all the three being different conceptual nuances.

Nevertheless, there has been paradigm shifts in the politics and political economy of India since the 1990s which have enhanced the role and autonomy of state governments, civil society and the market forces. The arena of state politics, in this process, has acquired an unprecedented importance. It might very well be said that state politics have really come into their own for the first time in the contemporary history and politics of India. Our study of state politics at this moment is very timely and topical.

❑ Analytical Framework

The analytical framework that we propose is developed in five components. The five overall factors are (1) democratization, (2) multicultural secularization, (3) federalization, (4) economic liberalization/privatization/globalization and (5) sustainable development and characterizing politics in India in general and its states in particular. Our attempt is to pinpoint the variations in the ways these processes and factors manifest themselves in different states of India. We raise the question as to whether these variables or factors at the state level that may be accountable for the differential ways in which the foregoing crucial processes and factors unfold in different states. We also seek to ascertain the varying state capabilities that facilitate or ensure democracy, good governance and economic development. The five crucial dimensions of politics and political economy delineated here and the explanatory factors that affect their variability from state to state are partly mutually interdependent and partly reinforcing or in some cases contradictory. The state-level variations highlighted in this analytical framework are the dependent variables or factors that are in search of explanation. The overarching factors identified above are causal or independent variables that help us explain state-level differentials in political and economic performance.

Democratization

Democratization refers to the process of increasing politicization of the masses in general and of subaltern classes or groups in particular through electoral mobilization and political participation. This process of democratization began to greatly affect the lower social orders by the late 1960s and has continued unabated since. Under the impact of this process, India's traditional and semi-feudal society is moving towards greater liberty and equality. Democratic politics tends to undermine caste and class differences and furthers the cause of political participation in elections based on universal adult franchise. Democracy is also imbued with the ideal of popular participation in the process of making a Government to the extent that it is practicable in a representative and republican democracy. Fundamental rights and directive principles of state policy provided in the constitution contain the ideals of a free and egalitarian civil society and state in India. The structures of governments outlined in the constitution at national and state levels are parliamentary federal and at the local level devolutionary. In addition, the 6th schedule of the constitution also makes special arrangements for autonomous district and regional councils within the tribal areas of of Assam, Meghalaya, Tripura and Mizoram. The 5th Schedule makes provisions for tribes advisory councils for administration and control of scheduled areas and scheduled tribes in other states of India. These advisory councils consist of members amongst whom nearly 3/4th (but not more than 20) must be the representatives of the scheduled tribes in the Legislative Assembly of the state. The 73rd and 74th constitutional amendments (1992-93), in pursuit of gender justice, ensure 33 per cent reservation for women in executive positions in Panchayats and Municipal Councils. In some states it is increased to 50 per cent, a move that is being contemplated by others as well.

The chapter on fundamental rights is one of the strongest in the universe of liberal democratic states in the world, with the possible exception of USA. The constitutional, legislative and judicial discourses on fundamental rights in India are very extensively and intensively elaborated. In the case law on the fundamental rights and directive principles of state policy, new dimensions have been created and added on to the rights and entitlements. The examples include the right to life, the right to live in human and healthy environment, the creation of the right to primary education to the children etc. The right to primary education was first created under case law and subsequently added on to part III of the constitution on fundamental rights by an amendment. An implementing parliamentary enactment also subsequently followed in 2010. Moreover, several new legal rights have been created under legislation, e.g. the right to information (2005), right to manual work in the rural employment sector in public works (Mahatma Gandhi National Rural Employment Guarantee Act. 2005), forest rights to people inhabiting in those tracts (2006). A legislation guaranteeing the right to food (June 2013) is also presently being proposed by the Congress-led United Progressive Alliance Government. Since 1993, we also have an activist National Human Rights Commission under a parliamentary statute. The mass media in India offers one of the most developed and independent democratic public spheres in the Third World, though the new trends of the menace of paid news, cross-media or multimedia oligarchic private corporate ownership patterns, political class floating their own media-all with serious consequences for editorial autonomy are causes for grave concern for the independence and integrity of the public sphere, crucial for deliberative democracy. Over bureaucratization has yielded place to a resurrected voluntary sector and non-governmental organizations, but these new developments are also not securely free from the menace of corruption and indirect bureaucratic colonization and control. Civil society vigour in India is more often seen in political and social movements than in the institutional domains.

Scheduled castes, scheduled tribes and other backward classes (OBCs) have been granted reservations in education and employment or legislative representation for specified time frames under the constitution and/or law. There are also schemes for their economic and financial empowerment by the Governments at Union and state levels. Rights of religious and linguistic minorities have also been guaranteed by the constitution, supplemented by enabling and entitling laws and policies by Union and state Governments. Yet these noble intentions of the makers of the constitution have been vitiated by vote bank politics and brute majoritarianism and minoritarianism. Some landmark, in Supreme Court judgements on reservations and obiter dicta on discrepant majority/minority status in the states and the nation at large, have implied that the crutch is tending to be used as a stick to beat the system within a self-defeating way so far as constitutionalism or rule of law is concerned.

Party system is the vital link between the civil society and the state. No representative democracy can survive without a democratically constituted party system and social and political movements. Most political parties in India lack internal organizational elections. Personalism and imamoral familism are the order of the day. The oldest national party of the country and practically all regional parties are particularly vulnerable to this malaise. Corruption and criminalization afflict practically all political formations.[35] The legitimacy of popular movements in the face of governments and administration lacking in integrity, transparency and accountability is unquestionable. However, not a few social and political movements are mounted in pursuit of sectarian and selfish interests in disregard of public interest.

Multicultural Secularization

'To take the tack of multicultural secularization', the meaning of this term is the process through which ethnic pluralities of a society are brought into the public sphere for interaction and civic action in a spirit of tolerance and mutual respect. Firstly multiculturalism goes beyond the abstracted liberal individualism and assumes that human beings are culturally embedded in the sense that they grow up and live within a culturally structured world and organize their lives and social relations in terms of a culturally derived system of meaning and significance. Secondly, multiculturalism believes 'that no culture is perfect and has a right to impose itself on others, and that cultures are best changed from within.' Thirdly, in a multicultural perspective every culture is internally plural and reflects a continuing conversation between it's different traditions and strands of thought. It is important to clarify the relationship between secularism and multiculturalism in the Indian context. In Indian political thought, to name only two leading representative thinkers of modern India, Jawaharlal Nehru and Mohandas Karamchand Gandhi espoused approaches to the relationship between religion and politics that may be dubbed (1) secularist premised on the complete separation between state and religion in the Western revolutionary sense as in France and USA (Nehru), and (2) multiculturalist in the traditional Indian sense of equal respect for all religions-*sarvadharmasamabhava* (Gandhi). The Indian constitutional theory of multicultural secularism is built on a judicious combination of both these perspectives. The major premise of the constitutional theory in this regard is liberal secularism in the sense that most of the fundamental rights guaranteed under the constitution make individuals as the bearers of universal rights enjoyed by all irrespective of ethnicity, gender, place of birth, etc. Yet some cultural rights of religious and linguistic minority communities are also guaranteed to enable them to preserve their culture language and script and to establish educational institutions with certain legal autonomies. Moreover, the state is prohibited to collect any taxes for the promotion of any particular religion. However, there is no will of separation between the state and religion as legislation for religious and social reforms is not prescribed, although after the initial spurt of religious reforms such as the Hindu reformist code, the state has, for all practical purposes, left the constitutional ideal of a common civil code in splendid isolation.

It is for the foregoing features of the Indian constitutional approach to religion and politics that I think that it can best be characterized as multicultural secularism. It draws attention to the question as to how democracy deals with the phenomenon of cultural diversity, whereas in political theory it was earlier thought that the universalist conception of citizenship was sufficient to deal with diverse categories of citizens in a society. It came to be later realized that different blind laws with universal scope were incapable of erasing deeply engrained socio-economic disparities and discriminations. For these conditions differentialist conceptions of citizenship came to be argued for recognition of difference and differential affirmative action for creating a leveled playing field. Will Kymlicka and Wayne Norman (1994) have talked about three kinds of provisions and policies to deal with multiple diversities and cumulative inequalities, i.e., "special representation rights (for disadvantaged groups), multicultural rights (for immigrants and religious groups), and self-government rights (for national minorities)."[36]

Federalization

Now, we come to the process of federalization that has gathered momentum since the 1980s, especially since the 1990s. The constitution of India combines parliamentary as well as federal features of Government. However, for about four decades after the commencement of the constitution the parliamentary features practically overshadowed the federal features due to one-party dominance of Congress and the charismatic and imposing leadership of Jawaharlal Nehru and Indira Gandhi, the first and the third Prime Minister. Federal features gradually gained ground over the 1980s, when non-Congress state governments were elected to power in one state after another and when Prime Minister Rajiv Gandhi signed regional and ethnic peace accords with Akali Dal in Punjab, Asom Gana Parishad in Assam, Mizo National Front in Mizoram and Tripura National Volunteers in Tripura. The 1989 Lok Sabha election, in particular, greatly accelerated the federalization process throughout the country, when a multiparty system with federal coalition/minority governments was ushered in at the national level. In the new party system regional parties have gained considerable power at the cost of national parties that have been diminished, fragmented or have been unable to grow beyond a certain threshold of power. Led by one of the national parties like the Janata Dal, Bharatiya Janata Dal or Indian National Congress, federal coalition governments have been particularly vulnerable to the making and breaking power of the regional parties. Whereas regional parties accounted for 8.10 per cent of votes and 6.95 per cent of parliamentary seats in the popularly elected house before the 1952 general election, their corresponding shares have gone up respectively to 14.39 per cent and 27.97 per cent in 2009 General Election.

The federal phase has witnessed an unprecedented increase in the autonomy and role of state governments. Toppling of State Governments by the wielders of central power for partisan political considerations has been considerably contained. A new grammar of presidential, prime ministerial and cabinet working has developed in the era of coalition and majority governments. The president has acquired greater maneuverability in the exercise of discretionary powers, the prime minister must contend with powerful ministerial colleagues representing various constituent parties in the coalition, and the cohesion and collective responsibility of the cabinet to the Lok Sabha have become fragmented and stretched to extra-parliamentary centers of regional power. However, there has been an enormous expansion of the power and activism of the judiciary.

Economic Liberalization

The take the tack of economic liberalization and globalization: the chipping at the Nehruvian mode of 'Indian socialism' began in the 1980s but a comprehensive package of reforms in this model of state-directed economic development was introduced in 1991 to deal with a severe balance of payment crisis and recurrent losses in most public sector undertakings. By the end of the decade, state economies also faced a serious fiscal deficit that also necessitated neo-liberal capitalist reforms. Both Union and State Governments gradually embraced policies of bureaucratic deregulation of the economy, disinvestment or privatization of public sector undertakings, and globalization.

These economic reforms have augmented the scope of the private sector and autonomy of State Governments. Like the Union Government, State Governments are now also vying with each other to attract private capital-national, multinational and global-multilateral-by offering better infrastructural facilities ('race to the top') or tax concessions and holidays ('race to the bottom'). India's annual rate of growth has considerably improved. The growth rate during the British colonial rule was a paltry 1.5 per cent. It was around 3 per cent in independent India before the 1980s. It moved up during the 1980s and jumped to upto 5 to 8 per cent since the neoliberal capitalist reforms of 1991. However, the problem with this development has been that it has been a jobless growth with negligible employment opportunities.

It also lacks in distributive justice and inclusiveness. It has engendered a dual economy comprising relatively small enclaves of affluence, on one hand, and vast areas of abject poverty and destitution, on the other.

In his study of neo-liberal economic reforms India; in relation to democracy, Rob Jenkins[37] made the point that the policy regime change was made by stealth, violating democratic norms as the matter was not duly discussed in electoral campaign or in Parliament. Business liberalism replaced political liberalism bypassing democracy, so to say. The point more directly relevant to our present discussion here is the argument that the federal political structure of the country contributed to the success of the reforms. For federal division, powers were made to serve as voltage transforming sub-stations of the national power grid. The reforms at the centre sought to win support for specific dimensions of the reformist policy package by various State Governments, including the communist-led Governments in West Bengal and Kerala by incentivizing them through fiscal and political measures advantageous to them. Centre-State conflicts were thus forestalled and inter-state rivalries were either played one against the other or diffused by federal power-sharing in minority and/or coalition Government at the centre. The reforms offered openings for all in the new political economy whose transition was made possible supposedly through democratic means—the avaricious political and bureaucratic elites, interest groups and pressure groups and demanding electorates. While hesitating to be definitive, Jenkins hinted at a new balance of political and economic forces and ultimately a new economic order and political policies.

Stephen Howes (2003)[38] focused on the problems of state level reforms directly in a study emanating from an international seminar organized by the India's States' Reforms Forum 2000. They argued that just as national level economic reforms were precipitated by a financial crisis of great magnitude in 1991, the state level reforms were pressed by a severe financial crisis in the States by the late 1990s. The relative uniformity of policies across the States prior to 1990s was in for a change by the end of the 1980s, both on account of political and economic transformations. Politically the party systems at national as well as state levels changed from Congress party's dominance to a variegated configuration of political power. The economic policy regime also changed from a socialistic welfare state in promise to one wedded to business liberalism. States found themselves on uncharted waters. States started to take leads in introducing reforms. The early straws in the wind came in the news of power sector privatization in Orissa, education guarantee scheme in Madhya Pradesh and organization of user-groups in management and distribution of canal irrigation water in Andhra Pradesh. The reforms spread to other states through contagion effect, increased quantum of state autonomy in the federal set-up and the sheer necessity of survival in the evolving Dravidian political economy. The states were forced to set their house in order both in terms of fiscal stability and better governance. Karnataka took the lead in 2002 to enact the first Fiscal Responsibility Act—an example soon followed by several states as well as the Union overnment. Other areas of reforms addressed were administrative reforms, including improving service delivery, curbing corruption and e-governance. Contributors to this study present informative overviews and case studies of numerous states, including the best practices from the West. The editors underline "the importance of seeing reforms at the state level as being about more than solving the state-level fiscal crisis, as urgent and deep as that crisis is. If the crisis is to be solved and if that solution is to mean anything to the people of India, far-reaching governance reforms will be needed to enable states to become agents of rapid economic, and indeed human development".[39]

How are the states faring since the above study? While we do not have a comprehensive systematic study focused on state-level economic reforms available, things are not all too bad at the state level today. India's GDP growth has slowed down in the last few years (averaging 7.7 per cent 2009-2012). States, especially the backward ones, have surged ahead. In the years 2009-2012, the fastest growing states were Uttarakhand and Bihar (12.5 per cent each), followed by Gujarat (10.3 per cent), Madhya Pradesh (9.9 per cent), Goa (9.8 per cent), Maharashtra (9.7 per cent) and Jharkhand (9.2 per cent). Chhattisgarh and Odisha slowed to 7.5 per cent after averaging nearly 10 per cent in the preceding five years, trailed by Rajasthan (7.3 per cent) and Uttar Pradesh (6.8 per cent). Poverty ratio has also declined generally, but the absolute numbers of the poor remained stationary.[40]

A supposed effect of economic reforms is the enhanced economic freedom in the political economy of the states. Table 2 gives quantitative data on the overall economic freedom ratings in the states in 2011.

Economic freedom index, in a nutshell, is constructed by adapting the methodology of the Economic Freedom of the World Report to the subnational Governments in India and thus taking into account only the areas where the stable governments have powers under the constitution to impact conditions and institutions: size of the Government-expenditures, taxes, and enterprises, legal structure and security of property rights, regulation of labour and business. After calculating index for each of these dimensions, the values are aggregated to make a composite or overall index.

The authors report that economic freedom in the Indian States has increased even though it has declined at the national level. The median value of this index in the states has improved from 0.38 in 2005 to 0.41 in 2011. The improvement in Gujarat is phenomenal from 0.46 to 0.64 and this state has jumped from the 5th position in 2005 to the 1st position in 2011. However, some other states have regressed, the worst performer being Jharkhand, from 0.40 to 0.31. Bihar has a mixed performance moving up from 0.25 to 0.29, but still comparatively stays at the bottom of the Table 2.[41]

TABLE 2 Overall Economic Freedom Ratings 2011

States	2005 Overall/ Rank	2009 Overall Rank	2011 Overall/ Rank
Gujarat	0.46/5	0.52	0.64/1
Tamil Nadu	0.57/1	0.59/1	0.57/2
Madhya Pradesh	0.49/2	0.42/6	0.56/3
Haryana	0.47/4	0.47/4	0.55/4
Himachal Pradesh	0.48/3	0.43/5	0.52/5
Andhra Pradesh	0.4/7	0.5 /3	0.51/6
Jammu and Kashmir	0.34/15	0.38/8	0.46/7
Rajasthan	0.37/12	0.4/7	0.43/8
Karnataka	0.36/13	0.34/13	0.42/9
Kerala	0.38/10	0.36/10	042/10
Chhattisgarh	0.33/16	0.33/15	0.41/11
Punjab	0.41/6	0.35/12	0.39/12
Maharashtra	0.4/9	0.36/10	0.39/13
Uttarakhand*	0.33/17	0.26/19	0.38/14
Assam	0.3/19	0.29/18	0.36/15
Uttar Pradesh	0.35/14	0.34/13	0.35/16
Orissa	0.37/11	0.31/17	0.34/17
West Bengal	0.31/18	0.33/15	0.32/18
Jharkhand	0.4/8	0.38/8	0.31/19
Bihar	0.25/20	0.23/20	0.29/20

Source'. Bibek Debroy
Note: * Formerly Uttaranchal.
Methological Note: Elaborated in the source in the text itself on pp. 4–5.

Sustainable Development

In addition to the foregoing political processes relevant to public policies and governance, a more recent concern that has become increasingly salient is sustainable development. The term 'sustainable development' was formulated by the United Nations Brundtland Commission, which defined it as "development that meets the needs of the present without compromising the ability of the future generations to meet their own needs."[42] In standard scientific opinion, we stand at a historical juncture when we face the danger of destroying earth's life-sustaining capacity. Our attempts at preservation of our local, national, regional and global ecosystems are incipient and ineffective, given our outmoded notions of living, political economy, national sovereignty and international law and organizations. The imperative of Green Governance at the local level with challenges to livelihood, the national level with those of resource conservation and global level with those of greenhouse warming and climate change require a paradigm shift in the way we relate to the natural environment. An alternative mode of economy, natural rights and commons-based governance is called for, which is predicated on a philosophically pragmatic architecture

TABLE 3 Environmental Law in India

General
1. The Environment (Protection) Act, 1986
2. The Public Liability Insurance Act, 1991
3. The Biological Diversity Act, 2002
4. The National Green Tribunal Act, 2010
Agricultural
5. The Protection of Plant Varieties and Farmers' Rights Act. 2001
Water
6. The Water (Prevention and Control of Pollution) Act, 1974
Air
7. The Air (Prevention and Control of Pollution) Act, 1981
Forest and Wild Life
8. The Indian Forest Act, 1927
9. The Wild Life (Protection) Act. 1972
10. The Forest (Conservation) Act, 1980
11. The Forest Dwellers (Recognition of Forest Rights) Act, 2006
Natural Disaster
12. The Disaster Management Act, 2005

of environmental law and public policy, and possibly even de-growth and demilitarization.

Major environmental issues, in India today, are degradation of agricultural land and urban habitat, deforestation and land erosion, loss of mangrove and coastal land inundation, pollution and threat to public health, loss of biodiversity, extinction of wild life, resource depletion and loss of ecological sustainability and threat to livelihood security for the poor. A glance at Table 3 gives an idea of belated governmental legislative response to the problem. Except for the Indian Forest Act, 1927 enacted by the Central Legislature during the British colonial rule and copiously amended and adapted by State Legislatures in the post-independence period, all the other laws are recent federal enactments dating back to the decades since the 1970s. A separate Union Ministry of Environment and Forests was itself first set up as late as in 1985. A transition from the colonial extractive to post-colonial conservational approach to ecology and environment has been very slow even at the federal level. The response has been even more tardy and inadequate in the states of the Indian Union. In fact, the constitutional amendments relating to water pollution and wild life protection fall within the state jurisdiction but the federal legislations were undertaken by the Indira Gandhi Congress Government by prompting some State Legislatures to authorize the Parliament under article 252 of the constitution to make laws on an entry in the State List under article 249 providing for an enabling resolution by the Rajya Sabha (representing the States) by a two-thirds resolution of the members present and voting that such a law is 'necessary or expedient in national interest'. Other State legislatures can adopt those laws subsequently, and they have done so. A parliamentary law under article 249 is provisional or temporary but a law under article 252 can be amended or replaced only by the Parliament. Subsequently, the 42nd constitutional amendment (1976) transferred forests and protection of wild animals and birds from the State List to the Union List in the constitution. The same amendment also enjoined the moral duty on the citizens and the federal and regional States to endeavour to protect and improve the environment and to safeguard the forests and wild life of the country (articles 48A and 51A-g). After the United Nations' conferences on the Human Environment held in Stockholm in June 1972 and on Environment and Development held in June 1992 in which India participated, it was realized that that a comprehensive framework of laws was necessary to cope with the daunting challenges to sustainable development. Under the constitutional and legal frameworks a number of Union and State autonomous statutory authorities, advisory councils, rules and notifications regarding environmental protection and ecological clearance of industrial, infrastructural, and governmental projects have been set up and framed. Some of these involve people's participation and consent at the local level. These laws often also establish original and appellate tribunals, subject to penultimate appeal to the National Green Tribunal or final appeal to the Supreme Court of India. The Supreme Court and the High Courts have been proactively engaged in addressing ecological concerns, often egged on by nongovernmental organizations and civil society movements through right to information and public interest litigation, on account of the failure of the executive and legislature and governmental agencies.

Ecological democratic or federal governance still awaits systematic empirical research worth its name in India. It appears that we still have a long way to go to have an effective Green Governance in place. The evolving policy formulation and implementation scenario have revealed growing tensions and conflicts along the axles of Union-State relations in the federal structure, political democracy and corporate capitalism, mass movements against industrial and infrastructural projects, federal regulatory authorities and Union ministries and the National Advisory Council of the United Progressive Alliance (UPA) chaired by Congress Party President Sonia Gandhi and the Congress-led UPA government headed by Prime Minister Manmohan Singh (2004-09 and 2009-2014).[43] This was amply borne out by the unprecedented monsoon mayhem in Uttarakhand in the third week of June in 2013[44] which found both the National and State Disaster Management Authorities mapping.

The Disaster Management Act, 2005, makes provision for the National Disaster Management Authority (NDMA) chaired by the Prime Minister and a detailed action plan involving the Union Government, State Governments, District Administration and the Local communities in drawing and implementing disaster management strategies. However, the NDMA is still to classify disasters and disaster-prone zones in the country and streamline responsibilities at various levels and participation of local communities.

❑ Variations in these Processes at State Level

The political processes' policies outlined above have unfolded in an uneven way and their effects have not been uniform across the states of India. Democratic transformation in some states has gone ahead in comparison to others. Some states still continue to be largely steeped in tradition propped up by the hangovers of caste and tribal structures and semi-feudal economy. Some states are much more mired in social and electoral violence and recurrent conflicts than others. Citizens of some states enjoy better democratic rights and economic empowerment than those in others.

The same can be said about the process of federalization. Quantum of federal autonomy existent in various states is markedly different. This is not only because of asymmetrical federal autonomy granted to the states of Jammu and Kashmir Nagaland, and Mizoram by the constitution itself under articles 370, 371A. and 371G. The rest of the states of the Indian Union are federated in a symmetrical way with uniform constitutional status yet federalization process is marked by considerable variations across the states.

Very few systematic and substantive scholarly studies of macro scope of democratization and federalization are available in the existing literature on state politics. The situation is a bit better with regard to economic liberalization and globalization. Since the early 1990s, when these processes were accelerated, there has been a tremendous increase in regional economic disparities amongst states. Even newspaper reports project a parallel development of two contrasting corridors of economic growth and radical class violence. The Blue Corridor spans Delhi-Gurgaon/Mumbai-Pune/Bangalore-Chennai on one hand and the Red Corridor stretching across the central tribal belt from the Indo-Nepalese border to the Deccan region on the other.

Social science studies also reveal that during August 1991 to March 2000 the states of Andhra Pradesh, Gujarat, Haryana, Karnataka, Kerala, Punjab and Tamil Nadu got proposals of private capital investment in the tune of 66.7 per cent as compared to only 27.4 per cent received by the states of Assam, Bihar, Madhya Pradesh, Orissa, Rajasthan, Uttar Pradesh and West Bengal. Differences in regard to Foreign Direct Investment (FDI) are even more glaring. In the phase of globalization, only five states-Andhra Pradesh, Gujarat, Karnataka, Maharashtra and Tamil Nadu-got a disproportionately large 75 per cent of the FDI invested in India.[45]

❑ Explanatory Factors for Variations across States

How do we explain the differentials among the states of India on the dimensions of democratization, multicultural secularization, federalization, globalization and sustainable development? For this purpose, we may employ an explanatory framework comprising the following five factors: (1) geography and history; (2) demography, culture and social capital; (3) political economy with foci on macro economic sectors and class structure; (4) patterns of state party systems and social and political movements; and (5) the quality of political leadership with appropriate motivation and skill.

Does history and geography matter? Are there any perceptible or measurable differences between the formerly British Indian provinces and native Indian states or etween the border states and inland states or between the coastal rimlands and the Hindi heartland? The studies bearing on these questions would naturally be expected by historians and geographers. So far, studies of this inter-disciplinary nature appear to be conspicuously lacking in the literature.

Similarly, some states have dominant castes and communities whereas others have more pluralist and fragmented social structures. Some states are parts of the cultural mainstream of classical Hindu civilization whereas others are more composite in terms of multicultural fabric. Some states are multicultural whereas others are marked by ethno-nationalist movements and even separatism. Some states are endowed with greater degree of social capital measurable in terms of the vigour of associational, cooperative and corporate organizations than others. How far these differences, if any, are consequential for patterns and trends in state politics across the country? As the review of literature in a preceding section above suggests, the studies so far have mainly focused on the interface between caste and community and politics, largely in a compartmentalized way, within a state without much attention to regional and national linkages, with the possible exception of the Northeastern states as a region.

Likewise, how significant are the differences in historical patterns of the British land tenure system divided in terms of the *zamindari*, the *ryotwari* and the *mahalwari* subsystems? It is same with tribal and non-tribal land holding systems. Similar questions arise with regard to differences among the states in terms of their class systems and sectoral composition of the state economy. The same is the situation with differences in material and human development indicators. Apart from some historical studies of the land tenure system , much of the work form our conceptual and theoretical perspective is yet awaited.

Moreover, there are marked differences among the states as to the patterns of their party systems and social movements. Some have developed one-party dominant systems with continued re-election of the same party consecutively for at least three terms (e.g., Delhi, Gujarat, etc.), while others have two-party systems (e.g., Andhra Pradesh, Madhya Pradesh, Himachal Pradesh, etc.) or a multi-party bi-coalitional system (e.g. Maharashtra, West Bengal, Kerala, etc.). Some states are more prone to the incidence of mass movements or sectarian movements than others. How consequential are these differences correlated with other dimensions of state politics?

Political scientists have given considerable attention to this dimension as the survey of research above and the chapters in this volume illustrate. We have constantly reminded our contributors to view politics in the larger socio-cultural and political economy contexts as well as deal suggestively with the local, state, regional and national political linkages.

Quality of political leadership at the state level is more difficult to conceptualize and operationalize in terms of measurable empirical referents or indicators. Yet there are some palpable differences, including some studies by scholars, of leadership styles of Digvijay Singh, Narendra Modi, Nitish KumarMayavati, Chandrababu Naidu, J. Jayalalitha. Mamata Banerjee, Sheila Dikshit. etc. Our survey of research, above in this Introduction and the chapters those follow this introduction, demonstrate this.

❑ The Varying State Capabilities

We have so far sought to describe and explain the patterns and trends of politics in the States of India in a general sort of way. Here we narrow our conceptual and theoretical focus to the crucial problem of state capability. This concept is defined as the ability of the Government to achieve the objectives it sets for itself. These objectives may be gleaned from the purposes of the social contract that brings a civil society and state in existence in the first place, namely, security of life, liberty and property on a universal and equitable basis. This is proposed as the first indicator of good governance. Other dimensions of goals of governments may be identified by scanning the constitution and laws, five-year plans, national policy statements, public policies, election manifestos, Governor's addresses to the state legislatures, budgets, legislative debates, Chief Ministers' and other intergovernmental conferences, etc. Since the paradigm shift to neo-liberal economic reforms in 1991, the State Chief Ministers and their Governments have acquired an enhanced role in state-level reforms with the diminished role of the State and public investment in the era of privatization and globalization, the State Governments must attract private capital-domestic and external-to ensure economic development. A bureaucratic state must yield space to a regulatory state. The host of independent regulatory commissions that have sprung up, especially since 1991, are still in their early stage of operation, and bristle with teething troubles. These problems mainly concern the question of their adequate autonomy from the executive, effective parliamentary accountability and insulation from the corporate capitalist sector.

The interventionist state[46] must transform itself into an autonomous and effective regulatory facilitator of development yet we must remember that even in this changed scenario in political economy of India, the constitutional mandate is for a democratic developmental state rather than just a developmental state in the mould of east Asian economies.

We propose to elaborate our concept of state capability in terms of good governance. Our index of good governance is operationalized by including the following indicators: accountability of Government to legislature and of administration to the people, human development, poverty alleviation, quality of regulatory regime for economy, rule of law and governmental stability. Performance of a state on these indicators may be measured by objective quantitative data wherever available, Or else, they may be assessed in terms of subjective intuitive judgment with some supportive qualitative evidence or argument. We must endeavour to go beyond mere description of the state of affairs explanations that carry persuasiveness.

It is pertinent to refer to a recent study of the quality of governance in major States of India by Sudipto Mundle.[47] Their index of governance is state-centric rather than straddling the interface between the governmental, civil society and market institutions-an aspect greatly emphasized in the neoliberal discourse emanating from the World Bank, International Monetary, Fund, World Trade Organization etc. While Constructing their index of governance on the three classical governmental institutions of the legislature, executive and judiciary, they measure governance performance on the dimension of a dualistic conceptual combination between authority (*danda)* and responsibility (*dharma*), using factual rather than perceptual data. They ranked 17 selected states variously using three different statistical analysis methods. We will selectively focus here on what they call the average of averages ranking. If we group their 17 ranked states into three broad categories–High, Medium and Low in terms of the quality of governance index-the picture that emerges can be viewed in the last two columns of Table 4.

In terms of actual data without any transformations applied to them, Andhra Pradesh, Punjab, Haryana, Tamil Nadu, Kerala and Gujarat (in that order) belong to the High performing States. The Medium level of performance is registered in Karnataka, Maharashtra, Rajasthan, Chhattisgarh, Orissa and Assam. The most Low' performing states are Uttar Pradesh, Madhya Pradesh, West Bengal, Bihar, and Jharkhand all except West Bengal is in the Hindi heartland. Notably, not all the 10 states in the Hindi belt are low performers, although not all of them figure in the study reported here.

The foregoing study also finds 'a positive but statistically weak correlation between the quality of governance in a State and it's rate of growth.' The authors go on to surmise that, "This is not surprising, because growth is presumably the collective outcome of several factors that are left out in a simple statistical correlation between quality of governance in astate and its rate of growth. Also growth may depend not so much on the quality of governance at a point in time, but the change in that quality over time".[48] Moreover, when the authors control for the effect of development on the quality of governance, it is found that some poorer states improve their rank on the index of governance. This implies that their governance' performance is much better than otherwise would be expected at their level of development.

The studies of state politics in the contemporary phase are too much preoccupied with the dimension of economic growth to the neglect of what is called above state capability in terms of a composite index of political,

TABLE 4 Governance Ranking of States

Rank	(a) Principal Component Analysis Ranking		Rank	(b) Modified Borda Ranking		Rank	(c) Average of Averages Ranking	
	Actual Data	Transformed Data		Actual Data	Transformed Data		Actual Data	Transformed Data
1	Punjab	Punjab (0)	1	Tamil Nadu	Punjab (+1)	1	Andhra Pradesh	Punjab (+1)
2	Haryana	Haryana (0)	2	Punjab	Tamil Nadu (–1)	2	Punjab	Andhra Pradesh (–1)
3	Andhra Pradesh	Andhra Pradesh (0)	3	Kerala	Kerala (0)	3	Haryana	Tamil Nadu (+1)
4	Gujarat	Tamil Nadu (+1)	4	Haryana	Karnataka (+4)	4	Tamil Nadu	Kerala (+D
5	Tamil Nadu	Rajasthan (+2)	5	Gujarat	Bihar (+12)	5	Kerala	Haryana (–2)
6	Maharashtra	Madhya Pradesh (+5)	6	Maharashtra	Maharashtra (0)	6	Gujarat	Karnataka (+1)
7	Rajasthan	Gujarat (–3)	7	Andhra Pradesh	Madhya Pradesh (+6)	7	Karnataka	Madhya Pradesh (+7)
8	Kerala	Karnataka (+1)	8	Karnataka	Andhra Pradesh (–0)	8	Maharashtra	Odisha (+3)
9	Karnataka	Maharashtra (–3)	9	Rajasthan	Haryana (5)	9	Rajasthan	Uttar Pradesh (+4)
10	Chhattisgarh	Odisha (+2)	10	Chhattisgarh	Uttar Pradesh (+2)	10	Chhattisgarh	Rajasthan (–1)
11	Madhya Pradesh	Chhattisgarh (–1)	11	West Bengal	Odisha (+3)	11	Odisha	Maharashtra (–3)
12	Odisha	Uttar Pradesh (+1)	12	Uttar Pradesh	West Bengal (–1)	12	Assam	Gujarat (–6)
13	Uttar Pradesh	Kerala (–5)	13	Madhya Pradesh	Gujarat (–8)	13	Uttar Pradesh	Bihar(+3)
14	Assam	Bihar (+2)	14	Odisha	Assam (+1)	14	Madhya Pradesh	Chhattisgarh (–4)
15	West Bengal	Assam (–1)	15	Assam	Rajasthan (–6)	15	West Bengal	Assam (–3)
16	Bihar	West Bengal (–1)	16	Jharkhand	Chhattisgarh (–6)	16	Bihar	West Bengal (–1)
17	Jharkhand	Jharkhand (0)	17	Bihar	Jharkhand (–1)	17	Jharkhand	Jharkhand (0)

Source : Sudipto Mundle

economic and human development indicators. Even in terms of economic development, the existing studies need to come to terms with the emerging realities in an integrated way leading to a coherent bigger picture. For example, Francine Frankel argues that sustained growth rates of approximately 6 per cent from the mid 1980s contributed to the emergence of a consumer class and development of some sort of a national market, including rural areas. It also produced an information technology revolution related to the expansion of the service sector developing much faster than industrial and agricultural sectors, yet both these developments were confined to certain classes and communities and regions. This development led directly to growth without redistribution and inclusion and precipitated the slide towards the two economies 'a smaller, yet sizeable affluent economy growing up in larger cities and spreading to self-contained islands of export-oriented, high technology parks', on one hand, and 'the larger predominantly agricultural economy, of landless, marginal and small farmers, many belonging to historically disadvantaged lower castes, minority religions, tribal groups and women,' on the other.[49] Frankel also demonstrates the definite trend of increase in inter-state disparities, with Maharashtra and Gujarat showing the potential of replicating East Asian levels of annual growth in the 1990s; with Rajasthan, Madhya Pradesh, Tamil Nadu and West Bengal growing above national average; with Bihar, Uttar Pradesh, Orissa and even richer states of Haryana and Punjab experiencing a decline in annual growth rates, and Rajasthan, Andhra Pradesh and Karnataka remaining more or less at the same level as in the 1980s.[50]

Yet by the end of the 1990s, we find a rather sudden transformation of the scenario of economic growth in Indian states, especially the supposedly backward states, often derisively called 'BIMARU states'. As India slows down in the wake of the economic recession in the US economy since 2008 and the nearly global recession in tandem since 2009, backward states of India move into a faster track of growth as already noted above. It is, however, important to bear in mind that there is still not much to write home about. For me , the acceleration in the growth rates are from a rather poor base while for another, it's sustainability cannot be taken for granted. We have still a long way to go.

Summing up, a study of state politics today is based on a classification of States by party or coalition in power would be a natural starting point but one must go beyond the descriptive plane to the explanatory and theoretical elevation and put these political configurations in their socio-cultural and political economy context. In terms of political parties in power today, Indian states are divisible into five broad classes:

1. Congress ruled states: Delhi, Rajasthan, Haryana, Assam, Andhra Pradesh, Uttarakhand, Manipur, Himachal Pradesh and Karnataka.
2. States under a coalition government of which the Congress is a part-United Progressive Alliance (UPA): Maharashtra (INC + Nationalist

Congress Party), Kerala (United Demoratic Front), West Bengal (until recently All India Trinamool Congress + INC which had replaced continuous Left Front government in the state since 1977 to 2012) and Jammu & Kashmir (J & K National Conference + INC).

3. BJP ruled states: Gujarat, Madhya Pradesh, Chhattisgarh, Himachal Pradesh, Karnataka and Goa.
4. States under a coalition Government of which BJP is a part-National Democratic alliance (NDA): Bihar (Janata Party United + BJP), Punjab (Shiromani Akali Dal + BJP until recently, June 2013 for seventeen years).

States ruled by regional parties-Orissa (Biju Janata Dal), Tamil Nadu (All India Anna Dravida Munnetra Kazhagam), Uttar Pradesh (Samajwadi Party) and several states of the Northeast.

Contextualizing these contingent political texts of regimes, public policies and governance into their socio-cultural and political economy contexts-historically and contemporarily are: the major paradigmatic and theoretical challenges of political analysis in the study of state politics in India. Coalition Governments in some States In India have been pre-poll in their formation while in some others opportunistic post-poll coalitions are cobbled together. The former are more durable than the latter, e.g., Kerala and West Bengal. Indeed pre-poll coalitions in some states have survived for decades and registered a longevity better than such pre-poll coalitions at the national level-a clear indicator of greater political maturity, ideological and policy compatibility and purposive governance and enviable models of development. Even in the run-up to the 2014 parliamentary elections at this writing (2013), the Gujarat model of development *a la* Narendra Modi and the Bihar model of development *a la* Nitish Kumar are figuring more frequently and saliently than the Congress-led United Progressive Alliance and the Bharatiya Janata Party-led National Democratic Alliance models!

Coalitions also often straddle the electoral, legislative and executive domain. This feature underscores the complexity of the phenomenon of coalition formation in India than elsewhere in the world Electoral adjustments to reduce the vagaries or plurality or first-past-the-post (FPTP) system of electoral representation is a preliminary step of interparty coalition formation in India. These electoral coalitions may or may not directly and fully extend to the legislative coalitions on the floor of the legislatures with parties extending support to a Government without joining it nor is there an exact overlap between the legislative coalition and the cabinet coalition. The electoral coalition is wider than the legislative coalition and the legislative coalition is wider than the executive coalition. These complexities lend a greater instability to coalitional configuration of the government and opposition in India than, say in European political systems. There, the coalitions are often formed pre-poll and have greater durability and therefore greater stability of policy frameworks and functional governance. Since coalitional governance is likely to continue at the federal level in India and in some States of the Indian Union, a reformist reappraisal of the current state of affairs by the political class would appear to be an imperative. There is no dearth of ideas for reforms from political analysts and constitutional commission appointed by the governments from time to time. Acute instability of the earlier years at both the Union and State levels is now behind us. There is still a long way to go to ensure a more purposive governance and political and economic development. Party system reforms and electoral reforms are, in fact, begged more generally, not only in the States and the Nation where coalitional governance has become a recurrent feature but also in the States where two-party systems and one-party dominant systems (say a state where the same party is voted back to power successively for at least three times) are the prevailing pattern.

Notes and References

1. Weiner. Myron, ed., *State Politics in India*, Princeton: Princeton University Press, 1968.
2. *Ibid.*, pp. 4–5.
3. *Ibid.*, p. 57.
4. Narain. Iqbal, ed., *State Politics in India*, Meerut: Meenakshi Prakashan, 1976. An earlier, less comprehensive, attempt was his edited work by the same title published by the same publisher in 1967.
5. Narain's edited title above published in 1976, p. xxii.
6. *Ibid.*, p. xl.
7. *Ibid.*, p. 597.
8. Wood. John R., ed., *State Politics in Contemporary India: Crisis or* Continuity? *Boulder & London: West view Press, 1984.*
9. *Ibid.*, pp. 233–34.
10. *Ibid.*, Chapter 9.
11. Kohli, Atul, *The State and Poverty India*, Cambridge: Cambridge University Press, 1987.
12. Kohli, Atul, *Democracy and Discontent. India's Growing Crisis of Governability,* Cambridge: Cambridge University Press, 1' 91, Part III.
13. Nossiter. T.J., *Marxist State Governments India: Polities*', *Economics and Society,* London and New York: Priner Publishers, 1988.
14. *Ibid.*, pp. 170–180.
15. *Ibid.*, pp. 180–186.
16. *Ibid.*, p. 184.
17. Frankel. Francis R. and M.S.A. Rao, eds., *Dominance and State Power in Modern India: Decline of a Social Order* 2 vols, New Delhi: Oxford University Press, 1991.
18. *Ibid.*, the quote at p. 12 of volume 1.
19. *Ibid.*, 'Conclusion' by Frankel.
20. *Ibid.*
21. *Ibid.*
22. Harris, John. 'Comparing Political Regimes Across Indian States: A Preliminary Essay', *Economic and Political Weekly,* Vol. 34. no. 48. 27th November 1999.
23. *Ibid.*, p. 3376.

24. Harris, John, 'How Much Difference Does Politics Make? Regime Differences Across Indian States and Rural Poverty Reduction', www.siteresources.worldbank.org/inpoverty/resources/WDR/Dfio-projectpapers.pdf, accessed on 6th June 2013.
25. Jenkins, Rob. ed., *Regional Reflections: Comparing Politics across India's States*. New Delhi: Oxford University Press, 2004.
26. *Ibid.,* Part I, Chapter 2.
27. *Ibid.,* Chapter 3. See also Aseema Sinha, *The Regional Roots of Developmental Politics in India: A Divided Leviathom,* New Delhi: Oxford University Press, 2005, for a fuller elaboration of her argument in an Indianest as well as comparative cross-national perspective.
28. *Ibid.,* Part II, Chapters 4 and 5.
29. *Ibid.,* Part III, Chapters 6 and 7.
30. *Ibid.,* Part IV. Chapters 8 and 9.
31. Kohli, Atul, *Poverty and Plenty in the New India,* Cambridge: Cambridge University Press, 2012.
32. *Ibid.,* pp. 160–178.
33. *Ibid.,* pp. 179–191. The quote from p. 155.
34. *Ibid.,* pp. 192–208. The quote from p. 158.
35. Since political parties have grown largely in the civil society in functional response to some structural needs of parliamentary democracy, they are not regulated by any comprehensive legislation or constitutional provisions, excepting incidental anti-defection tenth schedule of the constitution. Income Tax Act (1961), Companies Act (1956), Foreign Contributions (Regulation Act (1976), certain regulations of the Election Commission of India, and a recent ruling (June 2013) of the Central Information Commission under the Right to Information Act (2005). The National Commission for Review of the Working of constitution, chaired by Justice M.N Venkatachalaiah. has recommitted a comprehensive law regulating the organization, functioning, and financing of political parties in Chapter 4 of its report. Republic of India, *Report of the National Commission to 'Review the Working of the constitution,* http://lawmin.nic.in/ncrwc/finalreport/volume.htm.2002, accessed on 4th December 2002. See also Mahendra Prasad Singh, 'Elections and Party System in India: Federalization of the Party,' *Think India Quarterly*. Vol. 15, no. 1, January-March 2012, pp. 1–42.
36. Parekh, Bhikhu, 'What is Multiculturalism?' www.india-seminar.com/1999/484/484 per cent zoparekh.htm, accessed on 1st March 2011.
37. 'Citizenship', *Stanford Encyclopedia of Philosophy*, http://plato.stanford.edu/entries/citizenship, accessed on 1st March 2011.
38. Jenkins, Rob, *Democratic Politics and Economic Reforms in India*. Cambridge: Cambridge University Press, 1999.
39. Howes, Stephen, Ashok Lahiri, and Nicholas Stern, eds., *State-Level Reforms: Towards a More Effective Government*, New Delhi: Macmillan. 2003.
40. *Ibid.,* p. 22.
41. Swaminathan S.A. Aiyar, 'Backward States surge even as India slows down', http://articles.economictimes.com 2012-11-04, accessed on 20th June 2013.
42. Debroy, Bibek., Laveesh Bhandari, Swaminathan S. Anklesaria Aiyar. and Ashok Gulati, 'Economic Freedom Rankings for the States India. 2012. www.niticentral.com/wp-content/uploads/2012..., accessed on 6th June 2013.
43. United Nations, *Report of the World Commission on Environment and Development*, General Assembly Resolution 42/187, 11th December 1987.
44. *India Today*/Archive/Cover Story. 15th October 2012. http://indiatodav.intodav.in..., accessed on 18th June 2013.
45. *Economic and Political Weekly*, Vol. XLI, no. 35, 2nd September 2006.

46. Bagchi, Amaresh, and John Kurian, 'Regional Inequalities in India: Pre-and Post-Reform Trends and Challenges for Policy', in Jos Mooij. ed., *The Politics of Economic Reforms in India*, New Delhi: Sage Publications, 2005.
47. The concept of democratic developmental state in the comparative perspective has recently been theorized in which India seems to takes a pride of place. See Mark Robinson and Gordon White, eds., *The Democratic Developmental State: Political and Institutional Design*, New York and London: Oxford University Press, 1998.
48. Sudipto Mundle, Pinaki Chakraborty, Samik Chowdlhury, and Satadru Sikdar, 'The Quality of Governance: How' Indian States Have Performed?' *Economic and Political Weekly*, Vol. XLVII, no. 49, 8th December 2012. pp. 41–52.
49. *Ibid.*, p. 50.
50. Frankel. Francine R. *India's Political Economv 1947-2004,* New Delhi: Oxford University Press, 2005, 2nd edition. The passages in quote on p. 625.

19

Panchayati Raj

S.N. Mishra

The contemporary Indian society has been striving for establishing social, economic, and political justice through modernization of its political and administrative institutions. The rising expectations of people and the government's ideological commitment to economic development, democratic political ideals, and administrative decentralization are placing increasing demands on the public bureaucracy to implement socio-economic development programmes more effectively and with greater public participation. Due to this changing socio-political milieu, the local development bureaucracy is confronted with a formidable task of promoting economic development through democratic management, local autonomy, and the joint sharing of responsibilities with people's representatives.

The institutional expression of the policy of "democratic decentralization" in India is identified with "Panchayati Raj." The development needs and concern for democratization of the administrative mechanism determine the role of political and administrative institutions in the country. Any analytical study examining the role of these institutions, therefore, cannot escape the impact of social setting, local political dynamics, development goals, functional dimensions, structural process and relationships, popular support and governmental attitude towards the capacity and from the nature of responsibilities of these institutions. In a rapidly changing political environment, it is difficult to assess the actual contribution of these experiments to the theory of democratic management and control. However, the operational dynamics do present a number of challenging questions to normative as well as empirical democratic theory.

It is, therefore, desirable to identify some of the fundamental questions that will provide the basis for discussion in this paper. Related to the political consequences, the first basic question draws our attention to the problem of conceptual clarity. What does the concept of "decentralization" mean in Indian context? Is there any conflict between "democracy," "decentralization," and "development" as the three basic goals of decentralized democracy? Should the institution of democratic decentralization be treated purely as a "developmental mechanism" or a "power mechanism" providing a hierarchical chain of political offices through which the actual political power can be exercised? What type of relationship should these institutions have with the national or state political organization? Without any organization or party lines, can these institutions serve the function of interest aggregation and interest articulation reflecting the people's aspirations and demands?

Arising out of these questions, the chapter first deals with the conceptual underpinning of decentralization, for comprehending the substantive meaning and nature of democratic decentralization. It then deals with the normative aspects of democratic decentralization by analysing the desirable nature of decentralization in terms of basic unit of decentralization that could be administratively viable and also closer to the people. The chapter afterwards proves the efficacy of the experiment tried in this regard which raises certain questions at this stage, viz., do these patterns of decentralized democracy involve the decentralization of political or administrative powers or do they merely lead to the transfer of certain governmental functions to the local authorities? How far have the institutional organization and administrative arrangements been successful in promoting harmonious working relationships among the officials and elected members of political organs? Has there been adequate inter-institutional, inter-departmental coordination among the different components of the decentralized system to facilitate an effective planning and execution of development plans at the local level? Based on the analysis of all these aspects of the problem the paper finally puts forward, some observations in view of the 73rd constitutional Amendment Act, 1992, and the future challenges would have to be confronted by Panchayati Raj institutions in days to come.

Democratic Decentralization: The Conceptual Context

The real meaning and significance of democratic decentralization can be understood in the light of the prevailing social, economic, and political conditions that determine the purpose and pattern of democratic process. India has greater diversities in terms of culture, languages, caste groups, and economic stratification apart from authoritarian political tradition. Side by side the demands for eradication of proportion and require massive efforts. This challenging task emphasizes economic priorities and increasing public participation to fulfil the rising expectations of the vast masses. At the same time, aspiration aroused by political freedom requires a widening of the base for political participation. With a view to contain the forces of diversities, the emerging trend is tilting the balance towards decentralization. Thus, a true image of pattern of 'democratic decentralization,' both at conceptual and operational level, can better be visualized in contextual term where the objective and motivation of the political leadership provides a true perspective for understanding the process and problems of decentralization.

The concept of decentralization, as it applies to India, presents a different approach to the decentralization of political and administrative powers. Having its mixed goals of democracy, decentralization, and development, it refers to the programmes and tendencies which implies devolution of governmental power and responsibilities, decentralization of political institutions, development of local leadership and strengthening the efforts for economic modernization.

The Balwant Rai Mehta Report of 1957, however, repudiates the above conceptual development and holds the view that delegation of power does not divest the government of the ultimate responsibility for the actions of the authority to whom power is delegated, this authority is under the control of the government and is in every sense subordinate to it. Decentralization, on the other hand, is the process whereby the government divests itself completely of certain duties and responsibilities and devolves them on some other authority.

However, the real test is not decentralization of political agencies or institutions, but the effective decentralization of responsibilities, powers and prestige or status. Presumably, genuine decentralization involves a significant measure of either deconcentration and delegation or devolution, conferring of real powers on local authorities. Decentralization also implies clear understanding of socio-cultural and legal factors.

Thus, the pattern of decentralization as evolves in India involves both the delegation or de concentration and devolution or transfer of political and administrative powers. Thus, the degree of democratization and decentralization is determined by the politico-economic objective and the operational procedures designed to regulate the administrative mechanism.

Democratic Decentralization in India: The Genesis

Many efforts in India were made before independence, both by individuals and voluntary associations, for rural reconstruction by decentralizing the political and administrative powers. After independence, Community Development (CD) and National Extension Service (NES) programmes were launched in 1952 and 1953 respectively for the development of rural areas. But, they failed to achieve their development objectives. The review of the working of the CD and NES movement revealed that its attempt to evoke popular initiative was one of its least successful aspects. The proposal of the Planning Commission for the Second Five-Year Plan stressed the need for creating within the district a well-organized democratic structure of administration in which village panchayats would be organically linked with popular organization at a higher level. The proposal was subsequently taken up by the Study Team appointed by the Committee on Plan Projects. The team, presided over by Balwant Rai Mehta submitted an elaborate report in 1957.

The Mehta committee, realizing the importance of popular participation, recommended creation of institutions that were to be statutory, elective, comprehensive in duties and functions, equipped with necessary executive machinery, with adequate resources, and with enough autonomy and freedom. The creation of the Panchayati Raj in 1959, with the object of entrusting the authority and responsibility for rural development to rural people was hailed "not only as an innovation but also as a revolution."

The Mehta committee recommended a three-tier system for self-government at the grass-roots level. Subsequently, when the Panchayati Raj Institutions (PRIs) were introduced in early 60s, they were assigned three major tasks viz., developmental, administrative, and political. The Mehta committee had assigned greater importance to the developmental tasks but the three tasks mentioned above were supposed to maintain a mutual inter-relationship. However, non-devolution of sources of revenues proved to be the greatest stumbling block in performance of these assigned tasks. This led to the mounting pressure on the district-level bureaucracy; ultimately, it led to a hostile attitude of the bureaucracy towards these grass-roots institutions.

As these institutions took a shape, the Members of Legislative Assembly (MLAs), Members of Legislative Council (MLCs), and other politicians came to realize the strategic importance of PRIs and started looking at the representatives of PRIs as the political rivals. Therefore, they seemingly started a non-cooperation movement against these institutions. This inevitably led to a decline of these institutions. The performance and objectives of the PRIs were considerably diluted making them directionless. The declining political support coupled with indifferent attitude of local-level bureaucracy led to further diminution of the developmental and administrative role of the PRIs making the political role more prominent.

The basic philosophy behind the PRIs was to ensure People's participation in development programme, which was expected to unleash the arrested process of change and growth. However, these institutions failed to a great extent on both the fronts due to their non-performance. So much so that during the seventies it created an impression of a god that failed. Nevertheless, it had perceptible impact in terms of galvanizing the average citizen in rural India, and wherever it took its roots, it helped in narrowing the gap between the bureaucracy and the people. At the same time, it also succeeded in devising a development strategy for the people.

Towards a Fresh Look: Ashok Mehta Committee Report, 1977

After initial enthusiasm and promising performance, when PRIs began to decline rapidly, the Ashok Mehta committee was appointed in 1977 by Janata government for suggesting ways and means of reviving the PRIs.

The terms of reference of the Ashok Mehta committee encompassed all important aspects of the Panchayati Raj as is evident from its extensive 132 recommendations. Diagnosing the ills afflicting the PRIs, the committee pointed out that haphazard programmes, non-performance, rise of vested interests, lack of political will on the part of the central and state governments, lack of adequate financial resources, etc., have positively contributed to its decline. It also felt that the concept of Panchayati Raj itself got lost in the haze of conflicting interpretations. However, the committee hastened to add that failing was not peculiar to Panchyati Raj only. It was only symptomatic of the decline afflicting the entire body politic of the nation.

The major thrust of the Report pertained to decentralization: "the formulation of structural functions and the utilization of financial, administrative, and human resources in Panchayati Raj institutions should, in our opinion, be determined on the emerging functional necessity of management of rural development."

The committee's dominant thinking centres round the functional necessity for decentralization of administration. It was called a "new approach" towards Panchayati Raj. Without going into the details of the Report of the committee, let us look at the major recommendations of the committee and the model suggested by it. It suggests that Panchayati Raj should be viewed as a "government" in its own right at the grass roots level, which means a three-tier structure of federation, instead of two at present.

The Model

1. Being conscious of the operational realities of Panchayati Raj Institutions, the committee adopted a flexible approach to the problem and recommended a "two-tier" model of Panchayati Raj. Keeping in view the development necessities, the first point of decentralization below the state was suggested should be the district. Apart from being the basic units of devolution, the district-level should be treated as the unit of planning.
2. For the second-tier, the committee thought that in order to be a viable unit, the unit has to be bigger than the existing Panchayats. It, therefore, suggested the creation of "Mandal Panchayat" (which will be the implementing body) consisting of a cluster of villages covering a population of 15,000 to 20,000. The committee further felt that a Mandal Panchayat would alone be able to ensure a balance between technological requirements and possibilities of popular participation in decision-making.
3. The committee recommended direct election for both tiers, i.e., Zila Parishad and Mandal Panchayat with reservation of seats for Scheduled Castes and Scheduled Tribes in proportion to their population and women (two seats) who get the highest number of votes in Panchayati Raj elections.
4. It suggested to encourage committee system at both the levels.
5. MLAs and MPs should not be "insiders". However, the committee was of the opinion that a committee of the whole Zila Parishad may be constituted for planning purposes and MLAs and MPs should also be ex-officio members of this committee. Therefore, in the proposed system

of elections the directly elected component would be larger than the ex-officio and co-opted elements.

6. The committee categorically favoured the participation of political parties in Panchayati Raj. This was thought to impart distinct orientation towards programmes and would facilitate healthier linkages with the higher-level political processes. It would also help in providing constructive outlet to opposition parties at the state level who may chalk out their achievement at the district level. Moreover, direct elections coupled with programme based contest would offer greater scope to weaker sections for availing the opportunities offered by the political system.
7. The committee suggested that the Zila Parishad would be the first point of decentralization and the basic unit of Panchayati Raj endowed with a comprehensive range of developmental responsibilities. At the grassroots level, the Mandal Panchayat would be the hub of development activities.
8. In regard to the functions of Panchayati Raj institution, the committee felt that development being a dynamic process, functions could not remain static; periodic adjustment would be necessary to suit the changing requirements. As such, the committee recommended that all development functions relating to a district, which were being performed by the state government should be entrusted to Zila Parishad.
9. So far local level planning was concerned, the committee suggested that there should be a professionally qualified team at the district level for the preparation of district plans.
10. With a view to ensure social justice the committee favoured representation of Scheduled Castes/Scheduled Tribes on the basis of their population, and social justice committee with the Chairman from weaker sections of the society, it also suggested social audit system.
11. An important related recommendation was that all the staff with decentralized functions should be under the Zila Parishad. The Committee thus visualized a separate development administration giving decentralized functions along with a composite Zila Parishad secretariat.
12. Since all functions relating to implementation at the district level were to be transferred to Zila Parishad, the committee felt that the funds should also be transferred to Zila Parishad automatically. Administrative expenditure on the salaries and allowances of staff transferred to Zila Parishad should be borne by the government.

In sum, the committee's approach was that the pattern of administration should suit the decentralization of development functions. "A delectable comparison of administration is made with a women's dress. It has to drop well the body politic and has to fit with the contours."

CAARD Report (*Committee on Administrative Arrangements for Rural Development*): The committee which was constituted on 31st March 1985, had C.V.K. Rao as its Chairman. In the terms of reference of the committee, apart from other issues, one of the important matters was to study the role of Panchayati Raj bodies and their relationship with the proposed administrative set-up, and to make appropriate recommendations in this regard.

While examining the genesis and role of Panchayati Raj in historical perspective the committee looked into the factors which were responsible for decline in their status. The committee pointed out that decline in the status and authority of Panchayati Raj may be attributed to the reluctance of political leadership at state level to share power with district leadership.

With a view to activate the PRIs the committee gave several useful suggestions. District being the prime unit for overall planning and development, it suggested to strengthen Zila Parishad by introducing a system of sub-committees constituted on the basis of proportional representation. This would encourage and enhance the participatory democracy. Planning, plan-implementation, and monitoring of rural development programmes were suggested to be entrusted to the PRIs at the district and lower levels. It even talked of transferring some of the planning functions at the state level to the district level. In order to appreciate the ideals of participatory democracy, it envisaged the holding of the local elections regularly.

In regard to integration of rural development programmes, one of the suggestions of the committee was that Zila Parishad should be the apex body for the overall planning at the district level. It should be assisted by a District Planning Board (DPB) which should be an advisory expert body with a Planning Cell. The plan should be prepared by the DPB and sent to Zila Parishad for review and authentication. In the model all the rural development activities pertaining to the district should be covered under the purview of district body.

Phase of Hectic Activities (1985-92)

This is the period in which some serious thinking in favour of giving constitutional status to Panchayati Raj Institutions was given.

L.M. Singhvi, a noted constitutional lawyer and former the High Commissioner in U.K., in his report suggested that to provide viability to the villages, they be reorganized and Panchayati Raj institutions be viewed as institutions of self-government having complete say in development planning and implementation. The committee further observed that Panchayati Raj institutions must transcend the barriers of caste, religion, sex and disparities in wealth and surmount social disabilities and disadvantages. Apart from having a Panchayati Raj Judicial Tribunal, the committee also favoured giving constitutional recognition to Panchayati Raj.

Sarkaria Commission in its report recommended that to rectify the dysfunctioning of the local self-government bodies it was necessary to ensure by legal provisions analogous to this in Articles 172 and 174 of the constitution that elections to, the sessions of Zila Parishad and Municipal Corporation are held regularly, and these institutions do not remain superseded for long periods. The power of enaction of such a law vests under Entry 5, List II, exclusively in the state legislature.

Thungon Committee, in its report, apart from giving constitutional status to Panchayati Raj, suggested three-tier structure for these bodies and favoured the functioning to these institutions with the help of committees. Much emphasis was laid on decentralization of planning and problem of co-ordination. It also suggested reservation of seats for Scheduled Caste/Tribes as also for women. To provide financial viability to these institutions, the committee recommended for setting up of Finance Commission in every state, and, finally the committee suggested that a model Panchayati Raj Act be enacted by the central government to maintain uniformity.

The Congress Committee on Policy programmes headed by V.N. Gadgil looked into the matter and came out with following precise recommendations:

> "There should be three-tiers of Panchayati Raj at village, block and district levels respectively having elected representatives for a fixed term of five years and in case of dissolution, elections must take place within six months. constitutional status with details of role, authority and jurisdiction be given to these institutions. There should be provision of reservation for SCs/STs and women in the range of 30 respectively. Election by Central Election Commissioner and provision for State Finance Commission under Article 280 are some of the important recommendations. constitutional amendment to accommodate such provisions was also recommended by the committee."

Comparative Analysis of the 64th and 74th Constitutional Amendment Bills

In the light of the experience in the last forty years and in view of the shortcomings which have been noticed, it has been recognized that there is a need to enshrine in the constitution a chapter dealing with the Panchayats. The proposals contained in the constitution 64th and 74th Amendment Bills are important for the development of the Indian polity and a dispassionate analysis of the implication of the Bills is called for. Till date the Panchayats have not been able to develop as responsive people's bodies due to a variety of reasoned including absence of regular elections prolonged suppression, inadequate representation of weaker sections, insufficient devolution of power and lack of financial resources. Here we have examined the provisions of the Bills.

Gram Sabha

The 74th Amendment Bill has restored the pivotal role of Gram Sabhas. It has been recognized that it is the primary source of democratic power in a village. The Bill provides for a Gram Sabha which may exercise such powers at the village level as the legislature of state may by law provide. On the other, the 64th Bill does not mention about Gram Sabha.

Constitution of Panchayats

The 64th Amendment Bill makes it obligatory for all states to establish a three-tier system of panchayats at the village, intermediate, and district levels. However, states having a population of less than twenty lakhs, would not be obliged to establish panchayats at the intermediate level. Whereas the 74th Amendment Bill provides for a single-tier of panchayats at the village level to be constituted in every panchayats at other level or level.

Composition of Panchayats

According to the 64th Amendment Bill all the seats in a panchayat shall be filled by persons chosen by direct election from territorial constituencies in the area. However, the 74th Amendment Bill provides that all the seats in a panchayat at the village level and not less than 50 per cent of the seats in panchayat at any other level, if any, shall be filled by persons chosen by direct election from territorial constituencies in the panchayat area.

Reservation of Seats

Both the Bills provide for identical reservation of seats for the SC/ST candidates. They differ on the percentage of seats to be reserved for women candidates. The 64th Bill reserves as nearly as 30 per cent of the total seats to be filled by direct elections in every panchayat for women and allotted by notation to different constituencies in a panchayat. The 74th Amendment Bill provides that not less than 1/3rd of the total number of seats be filled by election in every panchayat shall be reserved for women and allotted by rotation to different constituencies in a panchayat.

According to the provisions of the 74th Amendment Bill, state legislature can reserve seats for Backward Classes in a panchayat.

Duration of Panchayats

Both the Bills provide for a duration (term) of five years for the panchayats. The election to constitute a panchayat when dissolved shall be held within a period of six months; the reconstituted panchayat small function for the remaining period that the dissolved panchayat would have continued.

Finance Commission

Finance Commission has been provided in both the Bills with a difference. The 64th Bill provides that the governor of a state shall constitute a Finance Commission to review the financial position of the panchayats and to make recommendations to the governor who shall cause every recommendation made by the Finance Commission together with an explanatory note thereon to be laid before the legislature of the state. On the other hand the 74th Bill states that there shall be a finance commission in every state to make recommendations to the government of the state and such recommendations shall be laid by the government of the state before the legislature of a state together with explanatory note.

Audit of Accounts

The 64th Bill provides for the form of audit of panchayat accounts. The bill states that the accounts of the panchayats shall be kept in such from as the government may, on the advice of the Comptroller and Auditor-General of India prescribe and the report shall be submitted to the governor of the state who shall cause them to be laid before the legislature of the state. Whereas the 74th Bill does not provide the form of manner of audit of panchayat accounts.

Conduct of Elections

According to the provisions of the 64th Bill the superintendence, duration, and control of the preparation of electoral rolls for, and the conduct of, all elections to the panchayats shall be vested in the Election Commission, whereas the 74th Bill states that the legislature of a state may make provisions with respect to all matters relating to, or in connection with, elections to the panchayats. It does not provide for an Elections Commission.

Disqualification of Members

The 74th Bill provides for the grounds on which a person shall be disqualified for being chosen as a member of the panchayat. This provision does not exist in the 64th Bill.

Interference of Courts

The 74th Bill provides that the validity of any law relating to the delimitation of seats of the allotment of seats to such constituencies shall not be called in question in any court. The 64th Bill does not bar the courts from interference.

Thus we can conclude that the 64th Amendment Bill had sought to strengthen centralization through holding PRI elections under the supervision of the Central Elections Commission, auditing of PRI accounts by the Comptroller and Auditor General. It has been apprehended that the Central government through governor as its representative intended to have control over Panchayati Raj.

On the other hand the 74th Amendment Bill does not intend the Centre's intervention in the areas connected with panchayats. Each state will appoint its own election commission to supervise elections. The finance commission will also be constituted by the states. Thus the federal structure of the constitution has been maintained and strengthened. Besides, the plenary legislative power of the state legislature under item five to State List of Seventh Schedule has been given due importance and respect in the interest of state autonomy.

Now the Seventy-third constitution Amendment Act, 1992, has added new dimension to the concept of Panchayati Raj by providing enough scope for direct election and for political parties to contest elections and to play effective role, and by giving it a constitutional status.

In the present scenario, the concept of Panchayati Raj has come to be accepted as an extension of democracy up to the village, and has found favour amongst politicians. It is often said that mere exercise of the right to elect representatives to the central and the state legislatures is not enough for the ordinary citizen. In other words, the concept of participation of the people should be considered as an ideological commitment and therefore what is needed is legislative and structural measures to give legitimacy to peoples' participation.

The 73rd Constitutional Amendment Act: Main Features

The constitutional (Seventy-Second) Amendment Bill was passed with near unanimity by the Lok Sabha on 2nd December 1992, and by the Rajya Sabha on 31st December 1993. After having been ratified by 17 state assemblies, this has emerged as the constitution (Seventy-third) Amendment Act, 1993, and carne into force from 24th April 1993. So this Amendment Act is the culmination of various proposals made by the earlier committees or subcommittees on Panchayati Raj bodies, and thus giving PRIs a viable shape. The salient features of the Act are as follows:

There shall be a Gram Sabha in each village exercising such powers and performing such functions at the village level as the legislature of a state may provide by law.

Panchayats shall be constituted in every state at the village, intermediate and district levels, thus bringing about uniformity in the Panchayati Raj structure. However, the state having a population not exceeding 20 lakh have given the option of not having any panchayat the intermediate level.

While the elections in respect of all the members to panchayats at all levels will be direct, the election in respect of the post of chairman at the intermediate and district level will be indirect. The mode of elections of chairman to the village level has been left to the state government to decide.

Reservation of seats for SC and STs have been provided in proportion to their population at each level. Not less than one-third of the total membership has been reserved for women and these seats may be allotted by rotation to different constituencies in a panchayat. Similar reservations have been made in respect of the office of the chairman also.

A uniform term of 5 years has been provided for the PRIs and in the event of supersession, elections to constitute the body should be completed before the expiry of 6 month from the date of dissolution.

The state legislatures have been given the power to authorize the panchayats to levy, collect, and appropriate suitable local taxes and also provided for making grants-in-aid to the panchayats from the consolidated fund of the concerned state.

A finance commission has to be constituted once in every five years to review the financial position of the panchayats and to make suitable recommendation to the state on the distribution of funds between the state and local bodies.

With a view to ensuring continuity it has provided in the Act that all the panchayats existing immediately before the commencement of this Amendment Act will continue till the expiry duration unless dissolved by a resolution to that effect passed by the state legislature concerned. The state legislatures should bring the necessary amendments to their panchayat Acts within a maximum period of one year from the commencement of this Amendment Act so as to conform to the provision contained in the constitution.

So far the Seventy-third constitution Amendment Act, 1992, has only provided the general guidelines for the effective and efficient PRIs in India. It granted the PRIs a constitutional status, some sort of a uniformity by making three-tier system a permanent feature, a regularity by making elections an imperative after the termination of the PRIs after every five years and the state Election Commission to conduct and supervise the election, more financial autonomy with the constitution of the state Finance Commission, etc. But, the major question still remains: how the various states are responding and at what speed they are implementing the Panchayati Raj as envisaged by the constitutional amendment.

It can be said that India is on the threshold of a historic political power to the grass roots with all the states completing the process of enacting fresh legislation on strengthening the PRIs on 23rd April 1994. As many as eleven states pushed through fresh legislation in 72 hours, some of them even in the early hours of 23rd April 1994 to beat the stipulated deadline of 23rd April 1994, the day panchayats became part of the Indian constitution. However, the 73rd constitutional Amendment Act is not applicable to Jammu and Kashmir, Mizoram, Nagaland, and certain Scheduled Area of the country. But mere legislative enactments do not ensure effectiveness and viability of the PRIs in the states. What is more important is their operationalization.

Thus the journey from the "Local Self-Government" idea of Lord Ripon to the "Institutions of Self-Government" concept in the 73rd constitutional amendment took more than a century. This evolution in our federal polity must be underlined.

The essential prerequisites for the Panchayati Raj Institution in order to function as institutions of self-government are: (1) clearly demarcated jurisdiction, (2) commensuration with responsibilities of adequate power and authority, (3) to manage the affairs of PRIs, necessary human and financial resources, and (4) within the federal structure functional autonomy. The new Panchayati Raj must be seen as "third tier of government" as the constitutional Amendment Act opens possibilities for fulfilling these conditions.

Issues Ahead

In regard to making Pnachayati Raj Institutions functional and effective, there are some scholars who have expressed serious doubts about the wisdom of a constitutional amendment. For example, Nirmal Mukharji raises issues like, (1) can a constitutional provision by itself be an adequate substitute for political will? (2) given the harsh realities of the states, would these statutes be implemented in letter and spirit or would they remain laws on paper only? and (3) is implementing decentralization below the state level through the most centralizing of all conceivable instruments-a constitutional amendment desirable? Beside Mukharji held the view that a constitutional amendment could well mean thrusting a uniform prescription on states which are widely disparate in administrative culture, in historical background, and in demographic size.

The arguments put forward by Mukharji may be valid. But there is no doubt that the constitutional amendment was highly desirable for creating vibrant grass-roots democratic institutions in the country. However, some issues relating to the amendment need to be emphasized here.

The uniform three-tier of PRIs for states having more than 20 lakh population has its own limitations so far structural differences are concerned. And so is the case of states and union territories having less than 20 lakh population. It would have been better had it been left to states' discretion. The constitution Amendment Bill, when introduced, had the provision for direct elections to the post of chairpersons at the village and intermediate level. At the district level it was left to the state legislature to decide. The Joint Committee of Parliament looked into this question, but advocated for the direct elections only at the village level. The Marxist members of the committee had objected to direct elections at any level. But in order to achieve unanimity they suggested that the issue of the election of the chairpersons at the village level may be left to the state legislatures. Without going into the plus and minus points of indirect or direct election, it may be said that direct elections to the post of chairpersons are more in conformity with the presidential form of government and indirect elections with the cabinet form of the government, the later one has been adopted in India.

A major lacuna in the act is the contradictory and inconsistent approach to the idea of Panchayati Raj being the institutions of self-government. The bill had rightly defined the panchayats as an institution of self-government but later, in defining the functions of these institutions, had narrowed them down to developmental functions, as in Article 243 (a) and (b). To our mind without policing (law and order) as a function at each level, no institution of self-government is worth the name. Since the idea of "district-government" or "third-tier of governance" has come into being, its important point is sadly missing. Nirmal Mukharji, in this regard, rightly suggests that this dilution of the concept of institutions of self-governance is flawed thinking and drafting.

The past experience suggests that wherever panchayats have not taken roots or they have been uprooted after brief spells of success, it has been observed that the MPs and MLAs have not been friendly to these institutions. Apart from being indifferent to local governments, they have also been hostile to these bodies. They do not like to see another centre of power emerging as a challenge, nor do they like to see one's existing powers being diluted. In an attempt to assuage their feeling and the pre-emptive of any mischief from them, the MPs and MLAs have been given membership and voting right in the panchayats in the Acts now passed. This will certainly undermine the panchayats which we aim to strengthen. Yet another disturbing feature for Panchayati Raj Institutions is the "MPs' and MLAs' Local Area Development Schemes." Many may not agree with our apprehension, but it is almost certain that these schemes will further strengthen the stronghold of MPs and MLAs over the local community and the basic concept of empowering the grass roots democratic institutions may be forfeited.

A crucial question not yet visible is, with the states being asked by the PRIs to give more powers and departments to them, when the centre devolve more powers to states. This question will have to be answered, if not today, then in the near future.

Reservation of one-third seats and chairpersons for women is a step towards silent revolution. It is our firm belief that a social transformation aimed at women could be achieved by Panchayati Raj institutions. But the task is beset with enormous difficulties for women.

Development of healthy convention in a democratic polity is of immense value. The British parliamentary system is an example of such values. In our society too we have to recognize them as the backbone of our society and polity. The countryside, city, and local government institutions below the state level in the USA have had a satisfactory existence for so many decades and one of the reasons assigned for their sustenance and success is the tradition of democracy that they have preserved with maximum care. However, in our country violation of conventions have been very high. In such context constitutions amendment may not have any meaning.

It is a sad affair for a democratic country like India that the basic ideology behind the Seventy-third Amendment to the constitution of India of making panchayat institutions of self-government had been largely ignored in the recent state legislations. What is required is that the legislators should cut across party lines and implement the laws in true spirit with the implicit purpose of transferring power to the people, and to plug the loopholes in the existing system, only when the tree-tiers of the constitution-the centre, the state, and the local bodies will function with regularity and efficiency, the federal nature of the constitution, the democratic nature of the polity will be preserved. Otherwise, the constitution will become very much distorted in its content as well as implementation. It can be said that the PRIs in India have since their inception, remained "down to earth" without ever taking roots. But the PRIs have survived without regularity in elections show their inbuilt strength and, perhaps, make them the only institutions that live on despite appalling conditions justifying their departure. So what is required is the "will" to make the PRIs a viable democratic institution on which the real democracy will thrive on.

It is notable that the PRIs are the primary institutions of democracy where people from village, block, and district could participate. Except for them none of the other institutions can have direct participation of the local people. Devolution of power has to start here, and this is also where people at local levels got into the mainstream of development as well as public affairs. The PRIs, especially the *Gram Sabhas,* make the concept of direct democracy like that of Greek city-states of Plato and Aristotle days feasible at the present and centuries to come. The *Gram Sabhas* have been designed to be the place where development issues should be discussed, development programme initiated, and beneficiaries of development schemes selected.

It may be added that the prospect of the PRIs would be on increase keeping in the pace of economic liberalization in India. In fact, they would become watchdog bodies to ensure proper implementation of the employment generation programmes like the Jawahar Rozgar Yojana (JRY), poverty alleviation and special programmes like Integrated Rural Development Program (IRDP), Training of Rural Youth for Self-Employment (TRYSEM) and other different Area Development Programmes like Drought Prone Areas Programme (DPAP), Desert Development Programme (DDP), etc. All schemes falling under Minimum Needs Programme (MNP) and several other programmes of this nature of local development work. In fact, the PRIs would play an important role in accelerating socio-economic development in the rural areas.

Thanks to the Amendment Act, the PRIs are going to be vested with a lot of power and money in the coming years. The enhancement of the outlay for rural development to ₹30,000 crore in the Eighth Plan assumes greater significance in the context of this Act. In addition, the panchayats are assured of a regular existence like any other democratic institutions enshrined in the constitution and they will also have adequate powers both administrative and financial for implementing the economic development programmes meant for people living in rural India.

It is quite encouraging that the states are to transfer 36 per cent of their total plan outlay to the sub state level planning bodies from 1994-95. Of the proposed 36 per cent outlay to be earmarked for micro-level planning, 30 per cent will go to sub-state planning bodies through lump-sum grants for expenditure on areas including rural water supply, roads, electricity, education, and any other local schemes. The list of 29 areas included in the Eleventh Schedule of the Act is flexible giving discretion to the PRIs to select schemes depending on local resources and problems. Five per cent of the state's plan outlay will be "united fund"-few transferred to district or village bodies to be utilized at their own discretion. The remaining one per cent will be for poverty alleviation and employment generation programmes which are to be planned and funded at the village level. For the proper implementation of these, the activities and functioning of the PRIs will have to be closely watched and monitored so that they do not overstep their limits and cause irreparable damage to those living in their jurisdiction. What is needed is a consensual and uniform approach of auditing.

It can be observed that the democratization of our pluralistic society cannot be ensured merely through legislative and administrative actions of the state. These enabling provisions will require massive mobilisational support and non-governmental organizations, academics, and professional bodies, political parties and other groups should involve themselves in exerting pressure to restore power to the place where it belongs. For the entire exercise of decentralization, people like school teachers, progressive farmers, social workers, and professionals should be involved. Above all, the PRIs elected representatives should also be trained in rising over their electoral rivalry. They should be made to understand that once the elections are over, the rivalry ends. In fact, elections to the PRIs must carry a look of *mela* (festival) to attract massive turnout.

To brighten the prospects of the PRIs in India, some suggestions made are as follows:

> The elected representatives of the panchayats should exercise superintendence and control over government officials, *i.e.,* serving the panchayats instead of playing a subordinate role.
>
> An inter-zila panchayat parishad should be constituted in every state with the Chief Minister as its chairman to thrash out legislative, financial, and administrative matters of the panchayats. The planning set-up at the zila level should be headed by the chairman of the zila-panchayat.
>
> The requirements of financial accountability should be designed and supervised by the CAG and the power of dissolution as well as accountability of lower level panchayat units rest with the next higher levels of panchayats and not with government officials in order to establish peer group accountability.
>
> A constitutional amendment for ensuring election to cooperatives is a must because a vibrant cooperative system is important for successful Panchayati Raj.

Here, we may raise the question: Do we seriously believe in success of Panchayati Raj Institutions or is it a mere paper exercise? It can be said that if the problems, both at macro-and micro-level are not solved, if the vested interest and the power brokers are not knocked out of the system, if a half-hearted, uncooked, unplanned exercise is being done for the democratic decentralization, if the financial autonomy conferred with accountability is not improved, we may land up in a situation, which a wise man once put it as "Honey, I shrunk from the Peoples' Participation". If the policy of the government in giving impetus to the Panchayati Raj movement is implemented faithfully and fully, it will surely bring about the political, social, and economic revolution which will not only strengthen the democratic character of our society, but will also prove a perennial source of throwing up energetic leadership which may change the entire face of the country and guide the destinies of the people most efficiently and effectively.

Peoples' Aspirations

In regard to peoples' aspirations two important questions arise, *viz.*, what are the peoples' aspirations? And how to get them fulfilled? As far as the first question is concerned, it may be said that peoples' aspirations include equity, *i.e.*, social justice, peoples' participation in decision-making, implementation, monitoring and evaluation, and sharing the benefit of change and development, representative character of grass-roots democratic institutions, protection of the interest of SCs/STs and other socially deprived sections/including women, maintenance of social harmony, removal of feuds and factions, sense of freedom and equality, etc.

In spite of the best efforts of the policy planners and implementing agencies, right from the CD programmes to the present day we have badly failed in meeting the peoples' aspirations due to the lack of popular participation. The past experience with PRIs also suggest that they had been incapable in harmonising local community, minimizing feuds and factional fightings and protecting collective interest. As such they badly failed in honouring peoples' wishes and aspirations. The political developments in rural areas as a result of electoral process also suggest that PRIs inadvertently set forth the process of parliamentary system at the grass-roots level on a wrong track and gradually made these institutions a shelter house for self-seekers and power seekers. The PRIs, in past, failed in setting a sound mechanism of communication, influence, and control from grass-roots level upwards. They also failed in institutionalizing peoples' will.

Further, they did not serve as an instrument of social and economic change. The concept of popular participation, defined in leadership term, also failed in delivering goods. The leadership, which emerged as a result of PR politics did not reflect the aspirations of the people and the question remained unanswered as to how to make both the structure and the leadership responsive to the needs of the people.

There are certain prerequisites for the survival of PRIs. They are as follows:

1. There should be commitment to the PR as a political value and the consequent political will to establish it;
2. It should not be forgotten that the effort to revitalize PR, in fact, is an attempt to reconstruct Indian polity by way of bringing so far deprived sections into the mainstream; and
3. PRIs should be treated as the single agency for development of the rural local levels.

Whatever had been the other reasons for the failure of these institutions, one that is glaring and on which there is unanimity among the scholars, is its inability to protect the interest of the weaker sections of our society. Since this did not happen, the political power at the grass-roots level was unevenly distributed. As a result the weaker sections were not only deprived of the development programmes but in most of the cases they were kept out of development process.

When the PRIs were introduced in late fifties and early sixties; peoples' hopes and aspirations were very high. In certain cases, the PR leadership had been alive to the hopes and aspirations of the people but in absence of adequate financial support and bureaucratic cooperation they found themselves in the state of helplessness. Moreover, whatever, development programmes for weaker sections and rural community were introduced they lacked proper planning and effective popular participation. They had been bureaucratic oriented implemented by local level bureaucracy and far from the hopes and aspirations of the local community. In absence of the real assessment of needs and requirement of local community, they gained routinized character.

As a corollary to the second question that arises is whether the 73rd constitutional Amendment Act will be able to meet the hopes and aspirations of the people? In answer to this it may be said that at least on paper it appears that PRIs will be in a position to meet the hopes and aspirations of the people. Our assumption is based on the fact that the very element of popular participation, which was missing till now, may be ensured by the present Act. As such periodic elections will provide local community enough opportunity to throw young, energetic, and action oriented leadership belonging to all sections of rural community. Reservation of seats for women, SCs and STs and Other Backward Classes (OBCs) will ensure their participation and effectiveness in decision-making. No doubt in initial years elite from the above mentioned category will dominate over the scene but the local community will be in a position to judge them on the basis of their performance. Enough care has been taken to make *Gram Sabha* an effective institution of grass roots democracy. If they are really made effective they can be in a position to remove the self-seekers and partisan elites by the instrument of vote of no-confidence. If it so happens, the Pareto's concept of circulation of elite will come true and there will be gradual and frequent shuffling and re-shuffling of PR leadership which may help in fulfilling the hopes and aspirations of the people. Since district and decentralized planning has been emphasised in 74th Consitutional Amendment Act and district planning councils have been constituted, it is hoped that a need based planning reflecting the hopes and aspirations of the people will be the usual feature. At the same time, they will not remain only on paper but effectively implemented as implementing agency will be the PRIs themselves. One may hope that the centrally sponsored developmental and employment generating programmes for the benefit of the local community will also be implemented effectively as they are supposed to be implemented under the direct supervision of PRIs. Even identification of beneficiaries is also to be done by them. These brightening provisions under the Act force us to be optimistic in regard to fulfilment of hopes and aspirations of the people. The constitution of State Finance Commission and provision for effective local tax administration in the Act also present a rosy picture about the financial health of PRIs. In past lack of financial resources made these institutions totally handicapped and did not allow them to fulfil the hopes and aspirations of the people.

Moreover, for the last few years there has been a sharp shift in the perception of rural people towards the change in developmental activities. Political and social awareness have also opened the eyes of so far deprived section of the rural society. However, any administrative innovation to bring about deliberate change in PRIs for better results cannot be effective unless devolution of power from the centre to states, state to districts, and districts to panchayat units is rationalized and exercised in true sense. Any talk of power to the people becomes meaningless unless power and political awareness is channelized in the right direction. The 73rd Consitutional Amendment Act further aims at reducing political and bureaucratic interference in rural development programmes. For this many states have redefined and redesigned the role of state bureaucracy in order to facilitate effective functioning of PRIs. It is felt that what Gandhi said in 1946 is going to materialize with the help of the 73rd constitutional Amendment Act. The statement of Gandhiji is as follows:

> "Independence must begin at the bottom. Thus every village will be a republic or panchayat having full powers. It follows, therefore, that every village has to be self-sustained and capable of managing its affairs even to the extent of defending itself against the whole world."

He further added:

> "In this structure composed of innumerable villages, there will be ever widening, never ascending circles. Life will be a pyramid with the apex sustained by the bottom. But it will be an oceanic circle whose centre will be the individual always ready to perish for the circle of villages, till at last the whole becomes one life composed

> of individual, never aggressive in their arrogance but even humble, sparing the majesty of the oceanic circle of which they are integral units. Therefore, the outermost circumference will not wield power to crush the inner circle but will give strength to all within and derive its own strength from it."

While supporting the idea of Mahatma Gandhi and the ideas of some of the revolutionaries of pre-independence era like Bhagat Singh, one may hope that peoples' movement can be launched to demand that the devolution of funds for development works in PR system should first come to *Gram Sabhas* on per capita basis. It would be the responsibility of *Gram Sabha* to decide its needs according to its priorities, how much to keep it for itself, how much to contribute for the intermediate level and how much for the district level panchayats. For example, a particular *Gram Sabha* may decide to have with floods rather than have an embankment. Initially, it would mean lengthy negotiated settlements between *Gram Sabhas* and panchayats at intermediate and district levels and, therefore, slow pace of progress. Then participation of beneficiary and a slow pace of progress are certainly better than the existing non-development and dependence paradigm. Moreover, the whole process, will be geared towards increasing the understanding and raising the consciousness of the masses and activating them.

Let us examine yet another possibility. Either a *Gram Sabha* could, in the interest of unemployed persons (who *ipso facto* are its members) ban the entry of some articles (such as toothpaste, bathing, and washing soaps, etc.) in its area either singly or in combination with the neighbouring *Gram Sabha,* in this process it could encourage village and household industries and generate employment. If such a phenomenon remains confined to a few pockets, it is likely to be ignored. But if it catches the imagination of the people and spreads to a large area, it will hurt the interests of multinationals foreign collaborators and their Indian lackeys, and, finally, the interests of neo-imperialism. Pressure will be mounted to suppress it for the sake of free market commitment. The Indian ruling class, in all probability, will succumb to the pressure. But, the problem is that all other institutions of the Panchayati Raj system can be superseded but not the *Gram Sabhas*. Their existence will always be legal and constitutional. How the struggle will proceed, what course it will take, when it will acquire a revolutionary character, all this will depend on the members of the *Gram Sabhas*. There may be many other possibilities depending on subjective and objective conditions prevailing in different *Gram Sabhas.* But one thing is certain, along with the struggle (whatever be its form) mass consciousness will increase. This is the lesson which history teaches us and increasing mass consciousness is the singular need of the hour.

Concluding Remarks

While concluding, one more question comes to our mind, which may be everybody's apprehension, as to what would be the fate of PRIs by AD 2020?

In regard to this apprehension we are quite optimistic about the future of PRIs as the units of grass-roots democracy. No doubt most of the successes of PRIs will depend upon the political will of the concerned state governments. However, making Panchayati Raj elections a regular phenomenon and giving them constitutional status may ensure their bright future. No doubt the elections at the state and Central level are the regular phenomenon but still we have not been able to take our democratic polity towards a bright future. However, this situation, to our mind, is not going to affect rural political system in a substantive manner; the rural masses are, of course, illiterate and ignorant but very sensitive and capable of taking suitable decisions in the larger interest of the community. Moreover, due to mandatory and periodic elections, this will be in a position to shuffle and reshuffle the leadership of PRIs making them to realize that only those leaders could stay who are committed, non-partisan and take care of development of the village community. Besides, it is our hope that *Gram Sabhas* are going to play a very decisive role in coming years as a result of growing consciousness among the rural masses. In such a way, we hope that by the end of AD 2020 the Panchayati Raj institutions may be deeply rooted in the rural community and become the real vehicle of change and development in the country side. The only danger which, we visualize, is from the side of the state government. This is because of the fact that the 73rd constitutional Amendment has provided latitude to the states to make suitable amendments in their Panchayati Raj Act as and when required and this process has perhaps, already started. And as such, if such negative approach of the state governments continues then it would be difficult to save the Panchayati Raj institutions from the callous attitude of the state governments. Even then, we are optimistic that future of Panchayati Raj looks bright and they shall be in a position to fulfil the hopes and aspirations of the people as the societal norms, social stratification and values are changing very fast as a result of democratic process in the country.

In regard to futuristic trends in Panchayati Raj politics, effectivity of *Gram Sabhas,* changing social relationships and emerging social movements, similar optimism has been expressed by many social scientists. For example, Rajni Kothari is of the opinion that as a system of managing the affairs of the society, the long experienced model of "top down" has failed. And it is against. this failure that the rise of new actors and levels, new forms of political expression and new definition of the content of grass-roots politics acquire significance.

Now the question is who and what are these new actors and definitions? There is, first, the resurgence of the "people" themselves, both in consciousness and in behaviour, asserting their democratic rights and challenging the established order, at local levels affecting the entire social and political order. There is, second, the emergence of a new class of mediators in the political process, generally called the activists-upper and middle class in their social origin but identifying themselves with the lower orders of society-the poor, the oppressed and the segregated, ranging from the untouchables and the destitute among the tribes and ethnic minorities all the way the victims of sexual, ethnic, ecological, and generational discriminations, atrocities and violence. It is in this background that we feel that the rural masses will rise to the occasion and help to see the future of Panchayati Raj Institutions bright, which could fulfil the hopes and aspiration of the people in years to come.

Notes and References

Henry Maddic, *Panchayati Raj: A Study of Rural Local Government in India*, London. Longman, 1970, p. 3. Norman D. Palmer describes it as the most exciting experiment in democratic decentralization in any developing country. See his, *The Indian Political System*, Boston, Houghton Mifflin, p. 104. A.H. Hanson and Janet Douglas considered Panchayati Raj as India's distinctive contribution to the theory and practice of local government. See *their, India's Democracy*, Delhi Vikas, 1982, p. 64.

L.C. Jain, "Future of Panchayats", *The Hindustan Times*, 4th October 1991.

B. Krishnamurthy, "About Panchayati Raj", *The Patriot*, 21st July 1993.

"15-Point Programmes for Panchayats", *The Hindu*, 21st August 1994.

"M.P. Panchayat Bill Passed", *The Statesman*, 31st December 1994.

The Economic Times, 2nd October 1993.

A. Imbanathan, "Panchayati Raj at the Crossroad", *The Deccan Herald*, 19th November 1993.

K.K. Sharma, "Finance for Panchayati Raj", *The Financial Express*, 13th September 1993.

S.N. Mishra and S.S. Singh, *Roads to Model Panchayati* Raj Mittal Publications, New Delhi, 1993.

T.N. Chaturvedi (ed.), *Panchayati Raj, IIPA*, New Delhi, 1991.

"My Vision of Village Swaraj", *Harijan*, 26th July 1992.

R.N. Jathar, *Evolution of P.R. in India*, Institute of Economic Research, Dharmar, 1964.

B.S. Bhargava, *Panchayati Raj System and Political Parties*, Ashish Publishing House, New Delhi, 1979.

H.D. Malviya, *Village Panchayats in India*, AICC, New Delhi, 1956.

Iqbal Narain *et. al., Panchayati Raj Administration: Old and New Challenge*. IIPA, New Delhi, 1979.

N.R. Inamdar, *Functioning of Village Panchayats*, Popular Prakashan, Bombay, 1970.

P.C. Mathur, *Political Dynamics of Panchayati Raj*, Konark Publishers, New Delhi, 1991.

L.C. Jain, *et.al., Grass without Roots*, Sage Publications, New Delhi, 1985. For the role political expediency has played in stifling the growth of PRIs, see Gorge Mathew, PR *from Legislation to Movement*, Concept Publishing Company, New Delhi, 1994.

Nirmal Mukharji, "The Alternative District Government" in M.L. Dantwala *et. al.*, (eds.), *Rural Development: The Indian Experience*, Oxford, IBH, New Delhi, 1986.

S.N. Mishra, *Participative Management and Rural Development*, Mittal Publications, New Delhi, 1992.

Chandra B.P. Singh, "Panchayati Raj: Power to the People" in *Third Concept*, March 1995.

Pradhan H. Prasad, "Panchayati Raj and People's Movement" in *Mainstream*, 4th March 1995.

Rajani Kothari, *Politics and the People: In Search of a Humane Governance*. Vol. II, New Horizons Press, New York, 1989.

20

Peasantry and Peasant Movements

Rajendra Singh

❑ Introduction

An attempt at presenting a working outline of peasant and peasant movements in India requires some initial clarificatory discussions on the conceptual meaning of peasant on the one hand, and on social movements, in general, and peasant movements in particular, on the other hand. R.K. Merton, an American sociologist, pointed out that in social sciences, "Too often, a single term has been used to symbolize different concept, just as the same concept has been symbolized by different terms". The people who make the conventional category of peasant, in the context of the contemporary rural scene in India, and elsewhere also, hardly constitute a relatively simple homogeneous rural scene in India, and elsewhere also, hardly constitute a relatively simple homogeneous and self-sufficient social entity. Consequent to the gigantic process of developmental changes in the countryside, the traditional notion of peasantry as a specific category of human population in history is under severe theoretic strain.

The objective life situations of the coastal population vary with those living in the mountains, and the life situation of the people living in mountains vary with the inhabitants of the plain regions. What are new are the emerging internal variations within any of the given three patterns of human settlements. Take for instance, the case of the peasantry of the plains. During the sixties decade of this century, scholars of the agrarian dynamics had made note of the emergence of 'model farmers' of Karnal (Haryana), the 'grape kings' of Maharashtra, and the mechanized farm and orchard owners of Bara Banki (Uttar Pradesh). The emergence of business-farmers with poultry farms, fruit, vegetable and spice producers, and even fisheries in the contemporary Indian countryside, mocks at the conventional textbook image of a peasant. In India, peasantry, if at all this term remains valid in its traditional meaning, now reflects an enormous internal variation in its economic practices, cultural styles, social organization, political aspirations, values, and behaviour. What are those objective social characters which help identifying 'peasants' as a distinct category of population? The question demands for a brief survey of the usage of this term in social sciences and the analysis of ground data which validates this concept.

The concepts of social and peasant movements, like the concept, 'peasant' also suffers from the surfeit of meaning. If one takes the pain of scrutinizing the senses, in which the conceptual phrases, 'social movements' and 'peasant movements' have frequently been used in the social science literature on the themes of collective mobilization and protest of people for and against some social values, the nebulous definitional character of these phrases could be made vivid. In the context of collective mobilization, we often come across conceptual terms, such as 'struggle', 'revolt', 'rebellion', 'uprising', 'insurgency', and even the use of the term revolution. These terms, otherwise carrying separate and distinct meanings from each other are found constituting semantic domains which often overlap upon each other and frequently get dissolved in each other. And the worst of all, anyone of them, or, all of them, tends to be treated as the serviceable synonym for social or peasant movements, depending on the nature of the context. The taxonomic and definitional meanings of these conceptual terms, in the theoretic discussions carry separate, specific and distinct meaning. Each of the above concepts is anchored to and is adduced from separate range of social data. The substantive status of the concept of social or peasant movements, therefore, requires a cautious analysis of this concept and its definition.

Finally, closely connected with the first two areas of referential or definitional problems suggested above, there also exists the problem of comparative methods of generalization and theory formulation about peasants and their movements. It is axiomatic that all peasant movements in social sciences are historical events and, therefore, their indexing and classification, comparison, and generalization are post-factum exercise in social science. The way peasants and peasant movements have historical dimension, they at the same time have and are embedded in social-space dimension also. Social movements emerge from and belong to a society in time and which has a territorial or spatial aspect.

How can the temporal and spatial coordinates of human society be combined and compared to provide for a theoretic ground for the comparative study of peasant and peasant movements in India? We shall briefly try to respond to these issues step by step, below. The purpose is to sensitize the situation of the conceptual confusion in the contemporary social science literature.

The Concept of Peasantry

"The systematic study of peasantry", writes Shanin "originated in Central and Eastern Europe", where search of national identity and the emerging political consciousness not only impelled the Westernizing political elites to face the question of the poor, but the social scientists also turned their attention to peasants. After sketching the various traditions and usages of the peasants as a social entity as reflected in the writings of scholars ranging from Krober (1948), Redfield (1956) to Durkheim (1960) via Vasil Chakov (1891) and Chayanov (1925), Shanin arrives at identifying four basic facets of peasants and peasant societies. These ideal-typical facets are:

Peasant Family Farm as the Basic Unit of Multi-dimensional Social Organization

Family and farm constitute the fulcrum of social and economic life. Around these two, all other aspects of social life tend to be organized. Family labour is the only labour on the farm. The farm produces only to suffice for the family consumption and payment of duties to the "holder of political and economic power". The role of market and profit-making is as much ruled out as the impulse for capital accumulation and economic investment for further multiplication of capital. The image of peasantry is based on the fusion of not only family and the farm reflecting the merger of 'social' with the 'economic', but also on the relative insularity of peasant society. Its relative social immobility steeps the peasant society deep in the past and traditions weight heavily on it.

Land Husbandry as the Means of Livelihood Directly Providing the Major Part of the Consumption Needs

Traditional peasants farming involves low level of task and tool specialization. Whatever task training is required, it is learnt at the family level. Conception of peasant family is relatively autonomous. Its basic fortune is seen to be in nature: famine, flood, and drought, or in a timely and sufficient rain. Peasant does not look at nature from the perspective of an artist, poet or a natural scientist, instead, in the peasants' eyes nature stands as the controller of bread and life. Nature carries an overtone of an enormous utility value for the peasant. For the peasant, nature is hardly an object of romanticist concept of beauty and aesthetics. Most of the learning takes place within the family. The elders of the family educate the younger generation on these matters.

Presence of a Specific Traditional Culture Related to the Way of Life of the Small Communities

The system of values and norms are highly community-based. These are primary in nature. They derive their legitimacy and authority from the past standard and precedents. Peasant culture carries a specific meaning in terms of its simplicity, homogeneity and uniformity of values, rules and regulations in the community. Peasant culture, therefore, generates and sustains conformist behaviour among its members and groups. Most of the peasant societies are repetitive societies and reflect perpetration through replication. Social mobility and change are relatively slow. The archetypal image of peasant society is of the 'non-changing' society.

Underdog Status—The Domination of Peasantry by Outsiders

This aspect of peasantry refers to its subordinate position in the society. Peasantry as a social entity has been distant from the sources and seats of power and authority. Peasant's social, political, and economic subjection is linked with the exploitative practices of the superlords who imposed exactions in the form of rent, tax, and interest on the peasant. It may be pointed out that it is perhaps this type of subordinate existence of the peasant that led scholars to assign passivity, apathy, and a sense of resignation to the peasant, who could not muster courage to protest against exploitation. Karl Marx, the failed god of class revolution, too, sneered at the peasant and dubbed them as 'sack of potatoes'.

In essence, Shanin's definition of peasantry would refer to the following: The peasantry consists of small agricultural producers who, with the help of simple equipment and the labour of their families produce mainly for their own consumption and for the fulfilment of the obligation to the holders of political and economic power of the time.

The summation of the above four facets of the attributes of peasant and peasant society reflected in the above definition highlights more of the empirical life-situation of pre-modern rural folk, especially of Central and Eastern Europe. This definition mayor may not hold true and speak for the rural folk of modern and modernizing societies of the contemporary world. Prof. A.R. Desai aptly observes that such a construction of peasant and peasant society does not clearly:

> "Reveal the qualitative impact and differentiation that takes place in the agrarian arena, as a result of capitalistic system through an expansion of the market, changed objection of production, commercialization, introduction of capitalist type of private property in land resulting in the vital process of differentiation within the agrarian population resulting in the emergence of rich, middle, and poor peasants, a massive process of pauperization and proletarianization creating a qualitatively new category of agricultural proletariat...."

The emerging country-town nexus, introduction of capitalistic mode of agricultural production, market relation, increased mobility of rural population and communication, and above all, the active participation of the rural population in the sharing and shaping of the power of the state-are some of the general processes operating in most of the Asiatic rural societies. These processes foretell the doom of the image for the idealized rural folk and the pristine simplicity of the village life. Have the contemporary villages of India retained their villageness? Are there peasant communities in the Indian countryside? Answer to such questions by the sheer force of academic inertia, generally, would be in the affirmative, but is always in negation to the version of peasantry outlined by Shanin. Villageness of the North-Indian villages, as depicted in Munshi Prem Chand's novels or the image of peasantry of the 19th century Tzarist Russia portrayed in the novels of Maxim Gorky or in the description and analysis of A.Y. Chayanov's theory of family farm economy, by and large, seems to be the social realities of the past.

The concepts of the *'gemeinschaft'* and 'mechanical solidarity' articulated by F. Toennies (1955) and Emile Durkheim (1960), respectively, to characterize the relatively undifferentiated, simple, and homogeneous communities approximating closely to the traditional conception of peasant society hardly hold true to the current social data of the countryside. Daniel Throners' *The Shaping of the Modern India (1980)* attests to the fact of the total or near eclipse of the conventional version of the rural or peasant communities.

On account of the accelerated social structural differentiation, mobility, and change in the system of power and economy, Indian scholars of peasant and peasant movement, instead of applying the concept of peasant and peasant society to the community aspect of the rural population, tried to 'sample-out' peasant from the differentiated, hierarchical, and inequalitarian structure of the changing rural society. This tendency is observed in the writings of a number of Indian scholars.

Following the principle of *exclusion* and *inclusion,* I have tried to construct the working concept of peasant by first, excluding the following two sections of the rural society:

1. The erstwhile rent and tax collecting class of the *ex-rajas, talukdars,* and *zamindars* who were, generally, related to the peasant because of land ownership rather than by productive relation.
2. The class of traders who live mainly by trading rural commodities rather than keeping direct involvement in land and agriculture.

The local equivalent of the term 'peasant' is *kisan* and *khetihar mazdoor* in Uttar Pradesh.

Residually, I arrive at the following categories of agrarian population as suggestive of constituting the peasantry in North India. These are:

1. All the ex-tenant cultivators who held subordinate land proprietary right before the abolition of *zamindari* systems in Uttar Pradesh.
2. All the *khetihar mazdoor* (agricultural labourers) who have either too small land holding or no land at all and have to work on other's land or on daily wage.

3. The village artisans who get a share in the agricultural crop on the basis of the local norms of *jajmani* system.
4. Finally, the category of *peasant/kisan* includes all the pauperized and proletarianized section of *zaminadars* and *talukdars* who have suffered a loss of land ownership abolition of *zamindari system* in several states.

It is noteworthy that all the above indices for exclusion or inclusion in the category of peasant are only suggestive in nature. These categories of rural population are subjected to rapid change. In fact, with the loss of peasant as a specific type of social formation, that is, *peasant community* or *peasant society,* search of peasantry in the highly differentiated, hierarchical, economically unequal setting of current rural scene, where markets, banks, post-offices, doctors, telegraph, etc., are now in a state of rapid expansion. These days, peasantry, in India, is a metaphor; it is not a social reality of the contemporary rural society.

Structure of Social Movement

Since peasant movement, in this article, is treated as a specific type of the generic concept of social movement, let us first, elucidate the concept of social movement. While it is a generally accepted fact by the scholars that social movements refer to the data of social change, there is no need to separate the fact of the concept of social change from those of the movements. In this respect, the following contrasting points can be made explicit for comprehension of the concept of social movement:

1. Social change is ubiquitous, universal, and all embracing facet of social realities; social movement is not a universal and overreaching concept. Social movement in its manifest expression could be of a sudden, dramatic, and episodic nature.
2. The birth, maturation, reutilization, and even the failure and end of a social movement can be described in the same way we describe the biography of a person. While social movements have a career in history and society, social change, on the other hand, cannot be described in the terms of a temporal limit of a biography or a "career". Like the concept of time, the notion of change is an ontological continuum.
3. Social change may or may not be the causes and the consequences of a deliberate and conscious effort of an organized collective social activism of the people. On the other hand, all social movements signify and express a relatively well-structured activism of the people which is deliberately and consciously organized.
4. Finally, every social moment carry a critical core, that is, some values, norms and even social practices prevalent in a society. At the beginning

of the movement, these are considered as oppressive, unjust, and unethical. Therefore, these are unacceptable to a group of people. On the later stage, struggle takes place for overthrowing and rejection with allegation of unjust and unoppressive values, norms, and practices. The social movements revolve around conflicts. These always remain in negation 'to' and 'for' something. A social change, unlike a social movement, may or may not carry a critical core in it.

Despite an optimum degree of overlap of the concept of the social change on the concept of social movement, the above four areas of differences are helpful in articulating a separate domain of social movement studies as a special field of social science theorization research.

Defining Social Movements

After completion of the task of bifurcating the concept of social movement from the broad and generic concept of social change, we now proceed to present an elucidation and analysis of the concept of social movements. In this process a ground for a similar exercise of peasant movement is prepared.

It may be recognized right at the outset that the conceptual roots of social movement studies lie deep in the classical tradition of 'crowd' and 'group mind' studies of Lebon Tarde, McDouggal, etc., in social psychology, and in the study of 'herd behaviour' of animals at the time of peace and crisis and also in the Brinton's (1938) study of *Anatomy of Revolution,* and in many such works. The study of 'collective behaviour' as a domain of social science inquiry provided direct context for the emergence of social movement studies in social sciences. In addition, one can also see a shift in the theoretical emphasis and explanation of the concept of society and its relation with the *individual* and groups from an *organacist-functional* perspective to that of dialectical and *oppositional perspective.*

The rather simple and preliminary attempt to situate the concept of social movement at a point in the theoretic evolution of conceptualizing group behaviour is only suggestive and is presented to give a peep in the antecedents of this concept.

Heberle defines social movement as "collective attempts to reach a visualized goal, especially a change in certain social institution. He treats social movement as constituted in social collectivity. Heberle, further separates movements from "social trends", 'tendencies' and 'cultural changes' which are merely "the aggregate effect of many individual actions". Finally, he observes social movements as groups in the process of becoming organized. He states, "The main criterion of social movement is that it aims to bring about fundamental changes in the social order". Wilkinson (1971) defines social movement as "a deliberate collective endeavour, to promote change in any direction and by any means not excluding violence, illegality, revolution or withdrawal, into utopian community", it "must evince a minimal degree or organization, though it may range from a loose, informal or partial level of organization to a highly-institutionalized and bureaucratized movement and the corporate group". Wilkinson further states "A social movement's commitment to change and the *raison d'eire* of its organization are founded upon the conscious volition, normative commitment to the movement's, aims or beliefs, and active participation on the part of the followers or members". Before we identify some of the unique and general features of social movements reflected in the definitions of Heberle and Wilkinson, it is worthwhile to present a more inclusive, clear, and systematic definition given by Turner and Killian. They defined social movement as "a collectivity acting with some continuity to promote or resist a change in the society or group of which it is a part".

We can derive the following basic and consistent features of social movements.

1. The existence of a system of shared values, objective, and aspirations collectively cherished by a section of population of society or group. These values may function sometimes as myths and utopias and attain enormous ability to mobilize the adherents of the movement.
2. The shared values and objectives must be sustained and reinforced by a justificatory or 'rationalizing' system of *ideology*. According to Killian, in the context of social movement, ideology consists of typically four parts: (1) a version or a vision of history emphasizing the fact that goals of movements are in tune with tradition of society; (2) a projected wishful image of future or an imagery of paradise-attainable after the success of the movement. For an instance, during the freedom struggle movement in India, the idea of *Ram Rajya* was frequently used to portray the wishful image of Indian society after the independence; (3) the acute urgency for the success of the movement is dramatized by inculcating the fear of misery among the followers if the movement fails; and (4) the conception of "martyrs and heroes" as opposed to the villains or Judas of the movement. Suffering and dying for the cause of the movement is exalted. These four aspects of ideology generate an intense and heightened emotive action in the behaviour of the participants, who constitute the mobilization force of social movements.
3. A collective sense of membership of and participation. The membership notion infuses in the participants a sense of 'identity' with the other participants. The participants feel being on the "same boat" and develop a strong sense of belongingness with the members of the collectivity. The 'we-ness' of those who are part of the collectivity as opposed to those who make up the opponents or adversary group emerges from such a notion of membership of the collectivity. The fusion of the dispersed

individuals into a "solidarity group" of the collectivity as a solid human entity upholds the ideology of the movement and struggles for the realization of the collective goals. It is this fusion of the individual into the collectivity that gives the idea of the initiatives and of what Eric Hoffer (1951) calls the "brotherhood" of the "true believers."

4. A system of shared norms about the behaviour and action of the members of the group. The rules and regulations of the group not only define the general orientation of the members towards their own group, but also towards those who belong to the other groups. The "other group" may represent the opposition or the adversary group. The commonly agreed upon system of norms may range from an amorphous (often in the beginning of the movements) ad-hoc rules to a system of elaborate and stable rule of conduct.
5. The structure of the collectivity, that is, the group which is mobilizing itself to achieve certain values has to develop: (1) a division of members into leadership and followership and then, into other sub-groups, depending upon the requirement of the movement. The leader behaves as the 'torch-bearer' and shows the "correct-path" to the followers. He is often a populist demagogue, who promises earth to the participants, defines the tactics, and the strategies of the movement; (2) a system of communication which links the participants with the leaders. The communication methods may include, in the relatively less literate societies, the use of sound-making drums, symbols, songs along with oral transfer of commands, and the messages. Among the literate societies, however, written communication is generally in use. Modern means of communication with an advance technology is being used by the contemporary leaders of various movements taking place around the world.

After having analyzed the concept of social movement and its basic salient features, we now proceed to focus our attention to examine the nature of peasant movements, in general, and the Indian peasant movements, in particular. A few contextual points ought to be made explicit at the outset. Some aspects of social movement, such as the problem of their classification, their genesis and impact on social structure at large have been deferred at the present in favour of taking up these issues after the nature of peasant movements have been analyzed.

At present, to repeat again, it would be helpful to note that peasant movements are a specific type of movements of the *generic* concept of social movement. The specificity of peasant movement is highlighted by the fact that it, generally, arises and revolves around the question of *land control* and demands for *ownership of land* and share in *land produce*, including control over and share in natural resources, such as water and *forest timber*. Second, in the social science literature, peasant movement is generally referred to as, *agrarian movement, land struggle, rural protest* and *uprisings*. We are going to employ these significant conceptual terms to describe peasant movements, though the phrase "agrarian movement" could have been empirically more authentic in comparison to "peasant movement". Here, on account of the paucity of space, it is sufficient to recognize the existence of a theoretic tension (as suggested earlier in this chapter) in respect of the relevance of the continued use of the term 'peasantry', even though its supportive empirical base seems almost eroded.

Further, in order to situate the theoretic status of peasantry as the largest segment of human population in the intellectual tradition of social science thinking and also to point out the way these tradition treated peasantry as either as passive or active agents of social, economic, and political changes, including the peasant's potential to bring about radical and revolutionary overthrow of the social system of a time, we shall present a brief account of the classical Marxist and neo-Marxist views on peasantry. By classical Marxism, I refer to the writings of Marx.

Peasant and Peasant Movement in the Marxist Tradition

For Karl Marx, the agents of the eventual revolutionary overthrow of the capitalist order of society did not reside in the countryside; they were not the soil-bound tillers of patches of land. Instead, it were the city-based industry and factory workers (i.e., the proletariat), who, after dissolving all the social and emotive bonds that enmeshed the peasant in the countryside with false contentment, were to establish the socialist order of classless society. It were these urban industry and factory-based workers who, according to Marx, were the heroes of history and it was on to them that Marx hitched the destiny of history, that is, the promise of equality among men not in heaven, but on the earth.

One of the greatest minds of the 19th and 20th centuries, Marx was also one of the prominent utopians of the period. The other two who could be ranked parallel to Marx in terms of their intellectual impact on the modern man are Charles Darwin and Sigmund Freud.

Marx sneered at the peasants for the absence of revolutionary potential in them and dubbed them as a sack of potatoes. Writing about the French peasantry Marx states:

> "The small-holding peasants form a vast mass, the members of which live in similar conditions, but without entering into manifold relations with one another. Their mode of production isolates them from one another instead of bringing them into mutual intercourse. Their field of production, the small-holding, admits of no division of labour in its cultivation, no application of science, and therefore, no diversity of development, no variety of talent, no wealth of social relationships. Each individual peasant family is almost self-sufficient; it itself directly produces the major part of its consumption and thus acquires its means of life more through exchange with nature than in intercourse with society.

> A small holding, peasant and his family; alongside them, another small-holding, another peasant and another family. A few score of these make up a village, and a few score of villages make up a Department. In this way, the great mass of the French nation is formed by simple addition of homologous magnitudes, much as potatoes in a sack form a sack of potatoes".

On account of the nature of their objective existence, Marx found the peasant totally incapable of forming a "class".

"They are consequently incapable of enforcing their class interests in their own name, whether through a parliament or through a convention. They cannot represent themselves, they must be represented. Their representative must at the same time appear as their master, as an authority over them, as an unlimited governmental power that protects them against the other classes and sends them rain and sunshine from above".

This passive and resigned majority section of human population making the peasantry in Marx's own writings is visible only in its event lessness and as an insignificant social data of history. In the stride of such thinking that Marx presents, the famous, but the most contemptuous portrayal of peasantry of the Indian village communities, he states:

"We must not forget the barbarian egotism which, concentrating on some miserable patch of land, had quietly witnessed the ruins of empires, the perpetration of unspeakable cruelties, the massacre of the population of large towns, with no other consideration bestowed upon them than of natural events, itself the helpless prey of any aggressor who designed to notice it at all. We must not forget that this undignified, stagnant, and vegetative life, that this, passive sort of existence, evoked on the other part in contradiction, wild, aimless un-bounded forces of destruction, and rendered murder a religious rite in Hindustan" (*New York Daily Tribune:* 25th June 1853).

The citation of the two rather large passages from Marx's writings on nature and role or (non-role) of peasantry in history are amply suggestive. In Marx's materialistic paradigm of society and history, of classes, class struggles and class revolution, peasantry is conceived as a useless social appendage devoid of an ability to stand on its own feet, speak its own language, articulate its own problems and issues or even to look at its own image in the mirror of an objective life-situation of an utter sub-ordination to and consequently, of its exploitation by the superior power of their lords and masters. This faceless social entity in Marx's thesis of class revolution is a non-entity.

Marx, however, could not recognize the ability of the peasant to organize, identify the situation of exploitation, hold the class responsible for its misery, and finally, its ability to give a lethal blow to the system of exploitation. Not only Marx, but his followers of different shades and varieties, together referred as the neo-Marxists, however, did recognize the peasant's potential for organizing, mobilizing, and revolting against the oppressions of the masters and the lords. This urgent and fighting face of the peasantry is reflected in the writings of Lenin (1970), Mao (1954), Fanon (1974), etc. In the case of the Indian scholars of neo-Marxist tradition, P. Sundarayya (1972) and Sunil Sen (1971) are two bright examples.

In relation to the peasantry and to the peasant's potential for revolt and rebellion, the major theoretic departure of the neo-Marxists from Marx is seen around three crucial modifications of the classical Marxist thesis. We summarize these modifications as follows:

1. In the ideological writings of the neo-Marxists, peasantry attains the status of a class; it is found capable of possessing "class consciousness". The successful role of peasant in the Russian and Chinese revolutions, under the leadership of Lenin and Mao, respectively, validates the neo-Marxist conception of peasantry as a revolutionary class.
2. By assigning the class-status to the peasants, the neo-Marxists retrieved the peasants from their projected perennial passivity and as such, from their perceived image of historical insignificance in the making of society and history contrary to the way Marx had perceived and projected the peasants.
3. Finally, the neo-Marxists transformed the classical Marxist science of political economy into an ideology of mobilization, protest, and revolt. The neo-Marxism catalyzed the peasantry's potential to revolt against and reject the system of injustice and exploitation. No wonder that most of the peasant wars of the 20th century reflected the impact of the revolutionary ideology of neo-Marxism in peasant mobilization across different societies. In India, Naxalism and its continued mobilization of peasants in some parts of the country, affirms the points noted here. The departure of the neo-Marxists from the classical Marxism in respect to the peasants, therefore, was a great theoretic departure. This was a great ideology also.

The assertive appearance of angry peasants on the agrarian backdrop of protest and conflict against the perpetuation of a grossly inequalitarian and exploitative rural social order was and continues to be backed and supported by the neo-Marxist ideological conceptions. No wonder that many of the peasant uprisings took place in the 20th century India, including the peasant uprising in Telengana (1946-51), Tebhaga in Bengal (1946-47), and Naxalbari revolts which began in 1967 and continues to be a force to reckon with are illustrations of the mobilizing potential of the neo-Marxist ideology.

After studying the peasant in the Marxist thought, let us briefly discuss the issue of peasant movements.

Structure of Peasant Movements

Shanin writes, "The last few years have seen a somewhat paradoxical rediscovery of the peasant. In our rapidly expanding world, the character, livelihood, and fate of massive majorities in most explosive areas have come to be seen as one of the most crucial issues of our time". The ability of peasant to organize, identify people, and principles of society responsible for the sub-ordination and exploitation, and further, to name the 'enemy', to heap blame on and hold them responsible for the peasants' abject life-situation, and to demand for a remedy in the various parts of the world have been studied by scholars. In India, there are references to peasant uprising during the Mughal era.

Historically, it is noted that the incidences of peasant revolt increased with the increasing rate of peasant politicization. The frequency of peasant uprisings in the various parts of the Indian society seems to be denser around and after India's Independence in 1947 than the past. The revolt of the peasantry in Telengana during 1946-51 (Sundarayya, 1972; Dhanagare, 1983: 180-212; Ranga Rao, 1984; 149-68), Tebhaga in Bengal during 1946-47, Naxalbari which began in Bengal in 1967 and spread over other parts of the country, Nijai *bol* of 1946 and land-grab movements of 1970 and numerous other reportings on peasant uprisings give support to our observations. Let us now attempt at defining peasant movements.

Defining Peasant Movement

Treating 'social movement' and 'peasant movement' as synonym for each other, Kathleen Gough examines and discusses social movements among the peasantry. She defines social movement as "the attempt of a group to effect change in the face of resistance", and peasants as people, "who engage in agricultural or other related production with primitive means and surrender part of their produce or its equivalent to the landlords or to the agent of the state". Social movement of peasants, therefore, according to Gough, refers to those movements, which: (1) involved peasants as the sole or main force; (2) are class struggles against those who exact surplus from the peasants; and (3) as the result the peasants undertake or are provoked to armed struggle in the course of their career". Though peasant movements are an expression of a rather broad and generic concept of social movements, yet there is a need to introduce some classificatory system to separate peasant movements from the general domain of social movement studies. Clarity of concept is the hallmark of the clarity in the comprehension of the social reality.

For Dhanagare, 'peasant movement' and 'agrarian movement' are blanket terms which refer to "all kinds of collective attempts of the different strata of the peasantry either to change the system, which they (the peasant) felt was exploitative, or to seek redress for a particular grievance without necessarily aiming at overthrowing the system. Dhanagare treats 'peasants' movement' and 'agrarian movement' as two interchangeable concepts. We have suggested earlier that the term 'peasant' came into use to capture the empirical social reality of the pre-revolutionary Russian rural life or of the life-style of the Central and Eastern Europe's traditional rural folk. It may be emphasized that peasants and *peasantness* was seen (as we have discussed earlier) in terms of its being a relatively simple, *undifferentiated, homogeneous* and *self-suficient* community. The movement, when one introduces the notions of "strata", as Dhanagare does, the conceptual meaning of the term peasant tends to suffer an erosion of its traditional meaning.

In order to avoid such difficulties, I tried to define peasant movement as "a relatively organized and continuous collective action involving violence or the threat of violence, for securing more share in the control or ownership of land and its produce and to abolish injustices which have arisen thereof and which involves *kisans* and *khetihar mazdoors*. (Singh, 1984:96). The term 'peasant' in the above definition has been avoided. The conceptual uneasiness in the use of the term 'peasant movement' on various counts is reflected in the writings of a number of scholars. A.R. Desai categorically states "the term 'agrarian' represents a larger category of humanity than the term 'peasant'...". A similar echo is sounded by Ghanshyam Shah who states, "We use the term peasantry in a broad sense, for convenience rather that out of conviction to cover a large number of studies. In fact, our preference is to avoid the term 'peasant' which is not very useful in the analysis of agrarian relationship in the subcontinent".

The theoretic tensions and ambivalence in the usages of conceptual terms, such as 'peasant movement' and 'agrarian movement' or 'struggle' suggest of the rapid social structural dynamics in the Indian countryside. Before the abolition of the class of the intermediaries, the systems of *zamindari, talukdari, jagirdari* types of superior proprietary tenures in land, the division of rural population in the unmistakably neat categories of landlord, on the one hand, and the underdog tenants, the exploited rural poor, on the other, was clear and vivid. The decline of the ex-landlords, the rise of middle class/caste cultivating ex-tenant and, further, the penetration of modern agricultural technology, market system and the emphasis on capital formation, and its further investment in agricultural and various other developmental factors operating in countryside, including the rise of territorial cultivating caste, groupings, such as those of the Jats in western Uttar Pradesh, Rajasthan and Haryana, and the Ahirs (Yadavas) and Kurmis cultivating castes of Eastern Uttar Pradesh and Bihar have introduced hierarchies and heterogeneities in the rural society.

Let us elucidate some of the relevant aspects of peasant movements with an illustrative case of my own field study of land-grab movement that took place in Basti district of East Uttar Pradesh in 1970. This study was based on the recording of data during the course of the operation of the movement in Basti district. Structure of this movement is presented in its natural components.

❑ The Case of Land-Grab Movement

Agrarian Structure and the Genesis of the Movement

Like any social movement, peasant movements, generally begins from the contradictions inherent in the structure of land relationship in the countryside. Basti district has a total area of 2821 sq miles and its 95.5 per cent of population living in 7653 villages. About 91 per cent of its population is engaged in agriculture. During the colonial phase, 14.4 per cent of population of the two upper castes, that is, the Rajputs and Brahmans, owned and controlled as much as 64 per cent of the land of the district as opposed to 63 middle and lower castes with as much as 86.6 per cent of population owing only 36 per cent of the land.

The Ahirs and the Kurmis with 11.83 per cent and 8.71 per cent of the total district population, on account of the Land Settlement Acts of 1883 and 1889, had become *pukhetadars* and *dakhilkars* (*i.e.*, occupancy tenants) or received permanent under-proprietary right on land. These two castes, together, possessed four per cent of the agricultural land. In addition, they also cultivated land under temporary ownership granted by the *zamindars*. With large family size, absence of taboo on manual labour, lower economic consumption, and high agricultural production, these two castes could save more economic surplus and, at the time of the abolition of the *zamindari system* in 1954. They had attained sufficient economic strength to purchase more land from the upper castes.

The lower and exterior castes, especially the Harijans with 21.6 per cent of the total Hindu population of the district had just 29 acres of land under their possession.

The laudable aim behind the *zamindari* abolition policy of the state of Uttar Pradesh was that its implementation on the *zamindars* held land holdings beyond the stipulated ceiling of the *zamindari* Abolition Act would release the surplus to be distributed among the landless and those who had grossly uneconomic small land-holdings. This aim could not be realized. The *zamindar's* defensive response was more effective in defeating the very purpose of the *Zamindari* Abolition Act than the efficiency of the state to implement it. The *zamindars* resorted to the use of following methods to defeat the objectives of *Zamindari* Abolition Act:

1. Fictitious land transfer in the name of distant relatives and loyal ex-tenants;
2. Transfer of land in the name of trusts, like schools, temples, and *pathshalas* (esoteric educational institutions) of which the landlord himself became the controller of the property;
3. Conversion of agricultural land in orchard and grooves, dairy, and cooperative farms on which ceiling limits were not applied initially;
4. Transfer of land in the name of any tenant and taking loan from government or bank by mortgaging the land on behalf of such a tenant; and
5. Fictitious partition and divorce in the family.

The land retained under (a), (b), (c), and (e) were of the temporary nature. Subsequently, a large-scale legal sale of land took place in Basti district. The main purchasers were, generally, the ascendant castes of Kurmis and Ahirs who, on account of: (1) large family size, absence of taboo on manual labour, abundance of domestic labour-power, with low rate of economic investment on agriculture, reaping richer harvest, less costly life-style, etc., and (2) their opportunity, which again, on account of their large family size, allow some members of the family to migrate to cities, like Bombay, Calcutta, and Kanpur to earn money and send that back to the village home, had helped these two castes in accumulating and furthering their economic power by purchasing more land from the declining *zamindars*. In this process, other factors, in addition to these pointed above, such as the cultural notions of the upper-castes about land also helped the Kurmis and Ahirs to increase the size of their land-holdings.

The shape of the emerging agrarian scene during the late sixties of this century was characterized by the emergence of a conservative caste peasantry as a force in the countryside who reaped the harvest of the land reform policies of the state. This ascending class of the middle-class caste population after becoming richer and secure began to socially mingle with their ex-masters, the Rajputs and Brahmans than with lower and exterior castes and classes in the society. Consequently, they also began distancing themselves from the lower and exterior castes. The lower and exterior castes, especially the Harijans were left behind and they could not improve their life situation of poverty, deprivation, and neglect. It was these people, who were psychologically ready to put a struggle for securing social justice in the countryside.

The left-oriented political parties, like CPI, CPI (M), and SSP, not only provided ideological backing to the uprising, they, in fact, also began educating the small cultivators in the art and value of agitation and revolt. The cultivators were introduced with notions of 'party', organization', membership', 'rights', and 'demands'. The political socialization of the peasant, generally, becomes effective if the injustice exists and is allowed to persist in the system of land-relationship. This is exactly what happened.

The lower exterior castes who had failed to get benefits from the land policies of the state, under the leadership of the left, started occupying land not only of the upper-caste landlords, but also of the middle caste cultivators. Under the leadership of the left political parties, many attempts, in some cases, involving violence, were made by an ideologically active lower and exterior caste members, forcefully occupying the land of the bigger landholders. Their mobilization, communication, and strategy of the revolt were defined by the left leadership.

Land-grab movement suffered a failure on account of the absence of local leadership, lesser numbers of the fighting collectivity, and the introduction of sectarian factor in the movement. Even though, this movement did not immediately bring about any changes in the agrarian system of Basti district, it introduced a "consciousness" about the political value of protest and revolt as a weapon for seeking social justice in society.

The rather over-simplified summary of the relevant aspects of land-grab movement presented above, could be, with some variations, the biography of many peasant movement in India. Some movements, such as those of Telengana, Tebhaga, and the Naxalbari had have greater and far wide impact on the state and society than the other, such as the one depicted above, which had died with lesser impact on social structure.

After having presented an illustrative case of a peasant movement, let us now do some exercise in the problems of the classification of social movement and present an introduction to the notion of "new movements".

❑ Classification of Movement and The "New Movements"

Problem of Classification

Scientific inquiry is characterized by its emphasis on empirical rationality and causal explanation of phenomenon. Codification and classification are attempts at systematizing phenomenon and make them amenable for the scientific inquiry. In fact, all definitions of phenomenon imply and contain within them some principles of classification. The basic principles used in developing a system of classification are: (1) the principle of resemblance, and (2) the principle of difference. In what ways concept of social change differs from the concept of social movement? In the earlier section of this article, we have attempted for separating the concept of social change from that of the movement. And, if one follows the way, they have been separated, one would note the way these two principles, *i.e.,* the resemblances and differences principles have been used as tools for classification.

In the study of social movement, the problem of classification is more acute. Suiting the theoretic or ideological preferences of the scholar, the same movement has, in the writing of one scholar, been characterized as peasant movement and in the other as a sectarian one.

While it is simple to refer tribal uprisings as 'tribal movement' or women's protest against gender discrimination as "women's movement", it is far more difficult to separate reformative, restorative or revivalist movements from the other types of social movements, including the tribal and women's movements. This problem can be made more vivid and explicit with an illustration taken from Kathleen Gough's system of classification of peasant uprisings. Taking goal, ideology, and method of organization, Gough develops a five-fold type of peasant movements in India during the colonial period. These five types of peasant movements are: (1) restorative rebellion, (2) religious movements, (3) social banditry, (4) terrorist vengeance, and (5) mass insurrection.

How could *raja* Chait Singh's revolt (1778-81) against the British be referred to as peasant uprising? And, if the subject population of the *raja* rallied behind their master in the present context, *raja* Chait Singh, the peasantry was not fighting for its own interest but for the interest of the master. *Raja's* and *zamindar's* struggles can hardly be referred to as peasant movements. Similar classificatory distortions can be identified in other types of Gough's classification of peasant uprising. In order to avoid such pitfalls, we developed a set of three different indicators to help classifying different types of social movements. These indicators are:

1. Identifying the foci of protest and conflict. This indicator relates to the issue of locating the axial factors, such as land and its produce, communal, religious, cultural, gender, ethnic, ecological around which a collectivity of protesting group comes into being.
2. Identifying the membership and participation of different sections of community, including gender groups. This indicator helps us in narrowing down to the specific sections of population who share the foci of the mobilizing collectivity.
3. Identifying the target group or institution, caste, class against which or whom a movement is launched. Aided with the guiding principles of resemblance and difference, the above three indices provide a dependable classificatory scheme for the classification of different types of social movements. Further, each type, with the application of the same scheme, can render simple, concrete, and specific sub-types of the movements. Our concern on the question of the classification of social reality, especially social movements, has been on account of the fact, that classification of phenomenon, in many instances, amount to the near comprehension of the same and is a front door that leads to the proper scientific understanding of the reality.

After having discussion on the various aspects of social and peasant movements and having done some elementary exercises on the problem of classification of social movements, it is worthwhile to present the essential details about those social movements which are being referred to as 'new movements' at the end of this article. On account of constraint, we shall only present the theoretic context and expression of these movements.

The New Movements: Many expressions of the new social movements are not new (Frank and Fuentes, 1987-1503)

The dominant theoretic articulation expressed in the new movements, is that they are, generally, non-class movements. New movements do not have a class core. The new movements symbolize the post-modernist intellectual and emotive outburst of an age which has come to discover that pinning an unbounded faith and optimism on the hitherto-force man redeeming magical potency of science and rationality, modernism and industrialism, bureaucracy and other apparatuses of modern society are hopeless and misleading. Scholars (Touraine, 1987a, 1987b; Touraine, Wieviorka, and Dubet, 1992; Cohen, 1985:663-716; Melucci, 1985:789-816; and Eder, 1985:869-89) lay emphasis on non-class movements which are, generally, social mobilization in search of identity, social and cultural roots; to fight alienation and sickness which are the product of modernism and industrialism, to resist ecological destruction and pollution produced by economic enterprises. The feminism, anti-racism, and struggles for the safeguard of human rights and civic liberty are the best examples of the new movements.

The new movements are the product of a shift in the modern thinking from the model of functionalism and the materialistic paradigm of Marxism, industrialism, economic imperialism, etc., to a new paradigm of human and individual dignity. In India, new movements signify movements of the farmers for a bargain with the state; Chipko movement of Himalaya for the restoration and safeguard of ecological balance and many more movements around gender discrimination, civil rights, ethnic issues, and also on the questions of forests and dams.

In the emerging system of contemporary communicative global social order, many aspects of the new movements, such as "saving the planet", ecology, pollution, civic rights, universalize the human concerns and have a tendency to transform the native man into an universal man. And it is in this direction that the future role of the new movement lies.

❑ Conclusion

This article has attempted to present an outline of peasant and peasant movements in India. It aimed at situating the conception of peasant movements in the centre of the emerging tensions between the theoretical constructions and their empirical roots and meanings in society. It made effort to demonstrate how conceptions, like 'peasantry', 'change', 'movements', in the social science texts, swing between the poles of an utter empirical vacuity and empty theoretical resonances. Like the historicity of feudalism, peasantry was the expression of a specific phase of history. It did exist as a 'social type'. The uncritical acceptance of its continued presence in the contemporary phase of the Indian countryside which is the scene of dramatic social transformations, this article suggests, is an exercise in academic ritualism.

The concept of social movement is linked with the concept of society. If society is seen as a process, it emerges as an entity defined by change. This article attempted at separating the foci of social change from the foci of social movements. The peasant movements are presented as a specific form of social movements. These make an effort to examine Marxist paradigm of collective mobilization and social movements. In order to present a holistic account of the contemporary discussion on social movements, the present article includes a brief discussion onthe theoretic background of the conception of the new social movements. Our overall aim has been to present a bird's-eye-view of peasant and peasant movements. It aims to sensitize the scholar to the issues relating to the need of critically re-examining some of the conceptions and meanings of peasant and peasant mobilizations in India. We believe that the empirical rationality, coupled with sensitivity to social data, alone can add further progress in this field of social science inquiry in the domain of movement studies in India.

Notes and References

H. Blumer, 1957. 'Collective Behaviour', J.B. Giteer (ed.) *Review of Sociology,* New York, Wiley.

C. Brinton, 1938, *The Anatomy of Revolution,* New York, Norton.

Chayanov, A.Y., 1925, 1966, *The Theory of Peasant Economy,* Homewood, Illinois, Irwin Press.

Cohen, Jean L., 1988, 'Strategy of Identity, New Theoretical Paradigms and Contemporary Social Movement'. *Social Research,* Vol. 52, No. 4, pp. 663–716.

Dasgupta, B., 1974, *The Naxalite Movement,* Delhi, Allied Publishers.

Desai, A.R. (ed.), 1979, *Peasant Struggles in India,* Delhi, Oxford University Press.

Desai, A.R., 1986, *Agrarian Struggle in India After Independence,* Delhi, Oxford University Press.

Dhanagare, D.N., 1983, *Peasant Movements in India, 1920-1950,* Delhi, Oxford University Press.

Dumont, Rene, 1965, *Lands Alive,* New York.

Dumant, Rene, 1969, *The Hungry Future,* London, Andre Deutsch.

Dumont, Rene, 1973, *Socialism and Development,* London, Andre Deutsch.

Durkheim, Emile, 1960, *The Division of Labour in Society,* New York, The Free Press.

Eder, Klans, 1985, 'The New Social Movements, Moral Crusade, Political Pressure Groups or Social Movements?' *Social Research,* Vol. 52, No. 4, pp. 869–890.

Fanon, Frantz, 1974, *The Wretched of the Earth,* Hormonds worth, Middlesex, Penguin Books Ltd.

Gough, Kathleen, 1979, 'Indian Peasant Uprisings', A.R. (ed.), *Peasant Struggles in India,* Delhi, Oxford University Press.

Guha, Ramachandra, 1989, *The Unquietwoods: Ecological Change and Peasant Resistance in the Himalayas,* Delhi, Oxford University Press.

Gurr, Ted, R., 1970, *Why Men Rebel?* Princeton, N.J., Princeton University Press.

Habib, Irfan, 1963, *The Agrarian System of Mughal India,* Bombay, Asia Publishing House.

Heberle, Rudolf, 1951, *Social Movements: An Introduction* to *Political Sociology,* New York, Appleton Century Crafts.

Hoffer, E., 1951, *The True Believer,* New York, Mentor Books.

Karna, M.N. (ed.), 1989, *Peasant and Peasant Protest in India*. New Delhi, Intellectual Publishing House.

Killian, L.M., 1968, 'Social Movement', E.L. Faris (ed.). *Handbook of Sociology,* Chicago, Rand McNally and Company.

Kothari, Rajni, 1987, 'Human Rights: A Movement in Search of a Theory', *Lokayan Bulletin,* 4-5, (Sept.), pp.24–27.

Krober, A.L., 1948, *Anthropology,* New York, Harcourt.

Landsberger, H.A., 1974, *Rural Protext: Peasant Movement and Social Change,* New York, Macmillan.

Lenin, V.I., 1970, *Selected Works,* Vol. II, Moscow, Progress Publishers.

Mao, Tse-Tung, 1954, *Selected Words of Mao Tse-Tung,* Vol. I, New Delhi, Orient Longman.

Marx, Karl & Engels, E., 1950, *Selected Works,* Moscow, Foreign Languages Publishing House.

Marx, Karl, 1853, *New York Daily Tribune,* June 25.

Melucei, Alberto, 1985, The Symbolic Challenge of Contemporary Movement', *Social Research,* Vol. 52, No.4, pp. 789–816.

Merton, R.K., 1963, *Social Theory and Social Structure,* New York, The Free Press of Glencoe.

Mukherji, Partha N., 1984, 'Naxalbari Movement and Peasant Revolt in North Bengal', M.S.A. Rao (ed), *Social Movement in India,* New Delhi, Manohar.

Nadkarni, M.N., 1987, *Farmers' Movements in India,* New Delhi, Allied Publishers.

Natarajan, L., 1953., *Peasant Uprising in India:* 1850-1900, Bombay, People Publishing House.

Nehru, Jawarharlal, 1945, *Glimpses of World History,* London, Lindsay Drummond.

Ornvedt, Gail, 1988, 'New Movements', *Seminar,* No. 352, pp. 39–45.

Oommen, T.K., 1985, *From Mobilization to Institutionalization: The Dynamics of Agrarian Movement in 20th Century Kerala,* Bombay, Popular Prakashan.

Ranga, N.G., 1949, *Revolutionary Peasants,* New Delhi, Arit Book Co.

Redfield, R, 1956, *Peasant Society and Culture,* Chicago, University of Chicago Press.

Rude, George, 1964, *The Crowd in History: A Study of Popular Disturbances in France and England: 1730*-1849, New York, John Wiley and Sons.

Sen, Sunil, 1971, *Agrarian Struggle in Bengal;* 1946-47. New Delhi, People's Publishing House.

Shah, Ghanshyam, 1990, *Social Movement in India,* New Delhi, Sage Publications Pvt. Ltd.

Shanin, T. (ed.), 1971, *Peasant and Peasant Societies,* Harmondworth, Penguin.

Siddiqui, M.H., 1978, *Agrarian Unrest in North India,* New Delhi, Vikas.

Singh, Rajendra, 1980, 'Culture of Inequality', *Seminar,* No. 255, pp. 15–17.

Singh, Rajendra, 1982, 'Land, Caste and Power in Uttar Pradesh: 1775-1970', Gail Omvedt (ed.). *Land, Caste and Politics in Indian States,* Delhi, Authors'Guild.

Singh, Rajendra, 1984, 'Peasant Movement in Uttar Pradesh', M.S.A Rao (ed.). *Social Movements in India,* New Delhi, Manohar.

Singh, Rajendra, 1986, 'Agrarian Social Structure and Peasant Unrest: A Study of Land Grab Movement in District Basti', A.R. Desai (ed.), *Agrarian Struggle in India After Independence,* Delhi, Oxford University Press.

Singh, Rajendra, 1989, 'Caste Factors in Rural Revolt: A Study in Emerging Agrarian Contradictions in Uttar Pradesh', M.N. Kama (ed.). *Peasant and Peasant Protest in India,* New Delhi, Intellectual Publishing House.

Smelser, Neil, 1963, *The Theory of Collective Behaviour,* New York, Free Press.

Sorel, G., 1950, *Reflection on Violence,* Glencoe, III, Free Press.

Surana, P., 1983, *Social Movements and Social Structure,* Delhi, Manohar.

Thorner, Daniel, 1980, *The Shaping of Modern India,* Delhi, Allied Publishers.

Toennies, F., 1955, *Community and Association,* London, Routledge and Kegan Paul.

Touraine, Alain, 1987, 'Social Movements, Participation and Protest', *Scandinavian Political Studies,* Vol. 10, No. 3, pp. 207–222.

Touraine, Alain, Vieviorka, Michel and Dubel, Francois, 1987, *The Workers' Movement,* Cambridge, Cambridge University Press.

Touraine, Alain, 1992, 'Beyond Social Movements?' *Theory, Culture and Society,* Vol. 9, No. 1, Feb, pp. 125–47.

Trotter, W., 1925, *Instinct of Herd in Peace and War,* London, Macmillan.

Turner, R.H., and Killian, L.M., 1957, *The Collective Behaviour*, Englewood Cliffs, N.Y., Prentice-Hall.

Turner, R.H., 1968, 'Collective Behaviour', E.L. Faris (ed.), *Handbook of Sociology*. Chicago, Rand McMally and Company.

Wolf, Eric, 1971, *Peasant Wars of the Twentieth Century,* London, Faber and Faber.

Wilkinson, Paul, 1971, *Social Movements,* London, Pall Mall.

Wilson, John, 1973, *Introduction to Social Movement,* New York, Basic Books.

21

Trade Union Movements

Sharit K. Bhowmik

Trade unions are unique organizations in many ways. They are formed mainly for protecting the interests of workers or employees against those who would harm them. These could be the employers, the state or any agency identified as such. In this sense, trade unions could be considered as opposition organizations. Most trade unions broadly centre on this basic objective. Secondly, trade unions are a product of industrialization. They were born out of the industrial revolution and, as such, had no connections with any pre-industrial form of social organization. Thirdly, the most important features of trade unions are that theory did not play bigger role in their initial formation. In other words, there are no theoretical roots to the origins of trade unions. Their growth was a spontaneous, healthy process which grew out of the needs of common people. The result is not a neat and tidy pattern, but something which is complex and overlapping. Hence, in order to understand the nature of trade unions and has to go back to their origins. In this chapter, we will deal with the features of trade unions in India, and in doing so we will begin with the origin and growth of trade unions and then discuss the problems of trade unionism in the country.

Trade unions had their origins in England and they were a result of the industrial revolution. In the early stages, they were formed to regulate competition among the workers. The industrial revolution had impoverished the British peasantry and artisans who were then forced to flock to the industrial townships in different parts of England. These people provided cheap labour for the factory owners. The factories were damp, dark unhealthy places, and the hours of work were long and the work was tedious. The wages which the workers get were very low and in most cases the entire family had to work to make both ends meet. Since the number of unemployed was large, there was constant competition between low-paid workers and job seekers. If a worker was unwilling to work at a particular wage the employer could find several others who would be willing to work for even less. This competition for jobs depressed the wage-rates and provided total power to the employers.[1] Friedrich Engels wrote in 1848 that this was the worst side of the present state of things in its effects upon the workers, the sharpest weapon against the proletariat in the hands of the bourgeoisie.[2]

Workers tried to overcome this competition by forming associations. They did so in the face of stiff opposition from the employers. In fact, trade unions were a result of these spontaneous attempts of workers to end competition.

At first, these associations carried out their activities underground as legal status was not given to them. They were able to organize a few strikes. In most cases, violent outbursts against intolerable conditions were observed. However, their growth was inhibited because of secrecy. It was only in 1824 when the British parliament granted the right to free association that trade unions could finally take off. As a result, "these combinations were soon spread all over England and attained great power."[3]

By and large, unity achieved through trade unions gave the workers a feeling of confidence resulting from collective action. It also provided better awareness. Trade unions strove to remove competition among the workers and changed the conflict between individuals within the class to the conflict between classes. Indeed, one of the most important contributions of trade unions has been that they made workers realize that the supremacy of their employers lay in the disunity of the workers.

Origins of Trade Unions in India

Factory production started in India in the early 1860s. During that time, the objective was to export the manufactured goods to markets in Britain. To facilitate export, factories were set up in the port towns of Calcutta and Bombay. Cotton-textile mills were set up in Bombay and jute mills in Calcutta. Later, factories were set up in Madras too. One of the reasons for the setting up of industries was that costs of production were much lower in India as labour was available at very cheap rate. A few decades earlier, in 1839, tea plantations were encouraged in Assam. The workers, in these tea gardens, were tribal people from Central India who had been brought to the plantations as indentured labour. The tea produced in these gardens was again mainly for consumption in Britain.

The existence of a large pool of cheap labour in India was mainly due to two reasons. First, the indigenous economy had been devastated with the introduction of colonial rule by the East India Company a hundred years earlier. During this period, the local crafts were replaced by cheaper imports of factory produced goods from England. This led to the complete rout of artisans in the country. The agriculturists, too, were no better of as in many parts of the country they were forced to cultivate cash-crops which were needed as raw materials for the factories in England, and give up cultivating food crops. Alongside, there was higher taxation on the cultivators through the new types of land-settlement and land-revenue imposed by the colonial rulers. As a result, there was a general impoverishment of the rural population. These people served as pools of cheap labour when the factories were set up in India.

The other reason for cheap labour was that at the initial stages of industrialization the colonial government, by any means, did not try to regulate working conditions or wages. The workers were unorganized and the industrialists were able to make them work long hours at low wages. Women and children were worst affected in this system as their wages were even lower.

The miserable plight of the textile-workers, especially the children working in the mills, in Bombay, caused concern among some of the social workers there. One of them was S.S. Bengalee, a philanthropist and social reformer. He tried to convince the government to pass some regulations protecting children in the factories. He even drafted a bill on this subject and sought the help of his friends in England to influence the government to pass it. Meanwhile, the mill-owners in Lancashire were unhappy over the state of affairs, because they faced competition from the cheaper Indian goods. They, too, tried to influence the government to impose regulations on the conditions of labour in India. Their move was not out of concern for the conditions of the Indian factory workers, but more, because such regulations would lead to increase in cost of production of the Indian goods.

These pressures led the government to pass the first Factories Act in 1881. This Act reduced the working time of child labourers to nine hours a day. Ten years later, in 1891, the second Factories Act was passed which reduced working time of children to seven hours and of women to eleven hours a day. A half hour recess was allowed for workers to take their meals. At the same time, there was no move to regulate the working hours of males. The employers accepted the provisions of the Act, but since there were no regulations on wages, they resorted to paying women and children less for the reduced time. This, in fact, increased the burden on the male-workers as they had to work longer hours to make up for the loss in the family income. Working hours of male-workers were regulated only after the third Factories Act was passed in 1911. This Act laid down that their working hours should not exceed twelve hours in a day.

During this period, there was uneven development of industries since they were mainly set up for export purpose. Industries were largely concentrated in the three port-towns and they manufactured mainly cotton-textiles and jute. The Census of 1911 showed that there were 524,000 persons employed in factories and plantations in India. Of these, around 400,000 were in tea plantations and jute mills. The total number of workers in the secondary and tertiary sectors totaled around 800,000.

Though trade unions had not yet emerged on the industrial scene, the workers did not always accept their fate meekly. There were frequent protests and strikes to highlight their miserable conditions. But these actions were more spontaneous in nature. Some leaders of the nationalist movement, too, tried to draw the workers into the mainstream protest against the

British rule. The most striking manifestation of this was observed in 1906 when Lokmanya Bal Gangadhar Tilak, a nationalist leader and a long-time friend of the textile-workers, was arrested by the colonial government. The mill-workers of Bombay came out on the streets to protest and suspended work for six days.

In spite of the growing discontent among the workers and their frequent outbursts, they were yet to unionize themselves. There were attempts to form organizations among the workers, especially in Bombay, by social reformers, but these were more in the nature of mutual aid societies. The most prominent of these was the Bombay Millhands Association formed by N.M. Lokhandey, the editor of a Marathi newspaper in Bombay. Lokhandey had been working among mill-workers and he tried to focus on their grievances. This association was formed in 1980 and Lokhandey was made a member of the second Factories Commission. It was on the recommendation of this commission that the second Factories Act was passed in 1891.

Industries in India expanded at a rapid rate during the First World War (1914-18) which led to the expansion of the working class. Moreover, this gave an opportunity for the existing factory-workers to be promoted to the ranks of skilled workers and supervisors, positions which formerly were held by Europeans.[4] Hence, changes occurred in the composition of the working class, which was mainly composed of unskilled workers. The inclusion of skilled and literate workers provided conditions for initiating the trade union movement.

Beginnings of Trade Unions in India

Though the war had led to expansion of industries in India; it also brought a lot of misery for the poor. There were food-scarcity and inflation. This condition mainly impacted on the working class as wages remained low. This led to large-scale labour unrest in all the towns where industries existed. The workers in Bombay and Calcutta were, especially extremists while expressing their grievances. The textile-mills of Bombay witnessed a wave of strikes. In the months of September and October in 1917 alone, more than thirty strikes were called. Strikes became even more frequent in 1919. The workers in Calcutta went on a long strike in protest against reduced wages. In Madras, the workers of Buchingham and Carnatic Mills (Binnys) struck work for increased wages. Textile-workers in Ahmedabad struck work and demanded a fifty per cent wage increase. Their movement resulted in Mahatma Gandhi's involvement in the labour movement and the formation of the Textile Labour Association which was also known as Majoor Mahajan. These strikes were all centred on the demand for increased wages. There was a regular pattern in these strikes. Workers in one factory would demand increase in wages, and if this was granted workers in other factories in the vicinity would put up similar demands and go on strike if the management refused to concede. Workers followed this trend because by that time there was no trade union movement which would have coordinated their demands on a common united platform.

The year 1918 witnessed the birth of the first trade union. The Madras Labour Union was formed in April and was led by B.P. Wadia, a social worker, who had been organizing the workers of Buchingham and Caranatic Mills. It is necessary to make a clarification here. Some researchers on the labour movement mentioned N.M. Lokhandey as the founder of the trade union movement as he had established the Bombay Millhands Association in 1890. However, this association and the similar ones set up after it were basically mutual aid societies. They had been formed by philanthropists and attempted to aid the poverty-stricken mill-workers. They had no memberships nor did they collect any subscriptions from the workers. Moreover, they did not organize the workers to protest against their employers. Instead, these philanthropists tried to use their personal influence to convince the government of the need for legislation to protect the workers. This is based on the views of two labour historians, namely, Revri and Sen. The Madras Labour Union was different even though its founder, B.P. Wadia, was a philanthropist. It had an elected leadership, it maintained records of its members and collected subscriptions from them. It also tried to seek recognition from the managements as the bargaining agent of the workers (this was never given to them though).

During the same year, but a few months later, Mahatma Gandhi founded the Majoor Mahajan in Ahmedabad. This union, which is till now the largest union of textile-workers in that city, had several unique features. Since August 1917, the mill owners of the city were paying a bonus of about 70 per cent of wages to compensate for the rising costs. In January 1918, they stopped the bonus and this created bitterness among the workers. They demanded that they be given at least 50 per cent dearness allowance as compensation and when the employers refused they struck work. The workers sought Gandhiji's intervention. He agreed to negotiate with the millowners provided the workers scaled down their demand to 35 per cent. The millowners were willing to pay only 20 per cent and they declared a lock-out when the workers refused to accept this. Gandhiji then went on a fast to pressurize the owners. Finally, the owners agreed to arbitration and in the end the workers received 27.5 per cent. After this incident, Gandhiji decided to form the 'Majoor Mahajan' which was based on his ideals of trusteeship. The union sought to protect the interests of labour through cooperation rather than confrontation with the employers. It enlisted the support of the employers and other wealthy people in running welfare and educational programmes for the workers. In doing so, it developed close links with the employers and at times even supported them in the Municipal elections.[5] This union had little or no influence outside the textile-workers in Ahmedabad, and it did not seek affiliation with any trade union federation.

In 1919, the International Labour Organization (ILO) was formed. Britain and its colonies became its members. In order to have a labour representative in the ILO, it was necessary to have a national centre of trade unions. At the same time, some of the nationalist leaders including Bal Gangadhar Tilak and Lala Lajpat Rai had been active among workers and peasants in trying to draw them into the anti-colonial struggle. These leaders evolved a plan for starting a national trade union centre. In October 1920, the All India Trade Union Congress (AITUC) was formed in Bombay. Tilak, one of its architects, had unfortunately, died only a few months earlier. The first president of the AITUC was Lala Lajpat Rai. In his presidential address, he emphasized three basic ideals of the working class movements, i.e., class consciousness, international proletarian outlook, and the place of nationalism in the class outlook.[6] However, a section of the Congress did not seem favourable to the formation of the AITUC. This was because there were several industrialists in the movement who felt that though the organization would be a front against colonialism, it could also challenge the interests of capital. Lala Lajpat Rai, a few months after his election, resigned from the post of President of the AITUC. It was believed that he was pressurized to resign.

After the AITUC was formed, the colonial government became more cautious in dealing with labour. It attempted to grant workers some concessions in order to contain unrest. In 1922, it passed the fourth Factories Act which reduced the working day to 10 hours and in 1926 the Trade Unions Act was passed. This Act provided for registration of trade unions and proposed some regulations. By the mid-1920s, the AITUC had nearly 200 unions affiliated to and its membership stood at around 250,000.

Splits in the Movement

As the AITUC was a broad-based organization involving diverse ideologies, it soon started being pulled apart by the different streams. The two main ideological groups in the organization were the communists led by S.A. Dange and M.N. Roy and the moderates, like N.M. Joshi and V.V. Giri. There were differences over the objectives of the AITUC. The moderates were eager to use the organization to get representation at the ILO (N.M. Joshi had been appointed by the government as the labour representative at the ILO). While the communists were interested in focusing on the problems of the working class, the moderates also had no objection in co-operating with any government body to solve problems of the labour class. There was another group, namely, the nationalists. They were in favour of the AITUC opposing the colonial government. Initially, there were several areas of agreement between the nationalists and the communists and the two groups were collectively known as the Left. In 1929, the colonial government appointed the Royal Commission on Labour in India under the chairmanship of Lord Whitley. The moderates were in favour of supporting this commission, whereas the communists and the nationalist leaders in the AITUC wanted to boycott it. The latter managed to pass a resolution to this effect upon which the moderate leaders in the Executive Council including

V.V. Giri, N.M. Joshi, Dewan Chamanlal, and others resigned and decided to form a rival organization. Jawaharlal Nehru, who was then president of the AITUC, made the following comment in this autobiography: "The left-wing was in favour of a boycott of the Commission, the right-wing in favour of co-operation, and the personal factor came in, as some of the right-wing leaders were offered membership of the Commission. My sympathies were with the left. It seemed absurd to co-operate with official commissions when we are carrying on, or going to carryon, a direct action struggle."[7]

Apart from seeking representation in the Royal Commission on Labour (N.M. Joshi and Dewan Chamanlal were appointed members), there were other issues of affiliation which led to the split. The Left was keen to affiliate the AITUC to the Pan-Pacific Trade Union Centre and to the League Against Imperialism (Nehru was an active member of the League). The moderates on the other hand wanted to participate in the ILO and develop close links with the British Trade Union Congress. Since these issues could not be resolved the moderates broke away and formed the Indian Trade Union Federations in 1930 and took with them around 50 of the affiliated unions. V.V. Giri was the leader of this federation. In 1931, another split took place in the AITUC. This time the split happened because of differences between the communists and the nationalists. The Congress was on the verge of launching the civil disobedience movement and the nationalist leaders in the AITUC wanted to involve it in the movement. The communists opposed this move because they believed that the nationalist movement was controlled by the bourgeoisie, hence the working class should retain its distinct identity by distancing itself from the movement. Thus, in the Calcutta session of the AITUC in 1931, which was held under the Presidentship of Subhash Chandra Bose, the communists split to form the Red Trade Union Congress.

The splits in the trade union movement affected it badly. There was a sharp fall in membership and the working-class which was reeling under the effects of the Great Depression of 1930 were the worst sufferers. The communists realized their mistake and rejoined the AITUC in 1934. The Second World War had begun in 1939 and India was unilaterally pulled into the war. The government promulgated the Defence of India Rules which prevented strikes or any form of militant trade union activity. At the same time, as in the First World War, there were shortages of essential commodities, rise in prices, and a freeze on wages. In 1940, the leaders of the Indian Trade Union Federation too decided that the workers had paid a heavy price for the splits and they decided to merge their organization to the AITUC. This unity continued till the dawn of independence when the trade union started splitting even further.

The Post-Independence Period

During the last few years of British rule several Congress leaders of the AITUC were imprisoned and the communists managed to take complete control of the organization. Unable to gain a foothold in the organization after their release from jail these leaders decided to form another trade union centre. Thus, the Indian National Trade Union Congress (INTUC) was formed in May 1947, a few months before independence. After independence when the Congress came to rule the country the INTUC became the most important federation because of government backing. Its ideology was close to the Gandhian view of co-operation rather than confrontation with the employers and it was opposed to any alliance with the communist-led AITUC. The AITUC had since then become the trade union front of the communists while the INTUC was identified as a Congress front. Since this time onwards the trade union movement has been increasingly split on the lines of the political parties. It seems the rule now that a political party must also have its trade union front. Thus, when political parties split their trade union fronts also split.

In 1948, the Congress Socialists who had remained with the AITUC decided to form a new political party called 'the Praja Socialist Party'. Subsequently, their groups in the AITUC broke away to form the Hind Mazdoor Panchayat with the hope that it would be able to draw the non-communist and non-Congress trade unions into its fold. This was partly realized when the Royist, Indian Federation of Labour merged with it to form the Hind Mazdoor Sabha (HMS). In 1949, however, the members of the Revolutionary Socialist Party (a Marxist group with influence mainly in West Bengal) decided to break away from the HMS, because it was under the control of the socialists. They formed their own federation called 'the United Trade Union Congress (UTUC)'. In 1952, the Bharatiya Jan Sangh, a political party having a Hindu fundamentalist background, was formed and in 1955. It initiated another trade union centre known as the Bharatiya Mazdoor Sangh. In 1965, another socialist party called 'the Samyukta Socialist Party' was formed and its most important trade union leader, George Fernandes, broke away from the HMS to form another Hind Mazdoor Panchayat. However, till 1970 the three major national centres in the country were the INTUC, the AITUC, and the HMS.

The split in the communist party into the Communist Party of India and the CPI (Marxist) split the AITUC in 1970. The CPI(M) formed in that year the Centre of Indian Trade Unions (CITU) and took away a large section of unions with it. The UTUC, too, was split on political lines between the RSP and the Socialist Unity Centre of India.

We can see from the above that the trade union movement became increasingly split on the lines of political parties since the country became free. Another feature developed in the late 1960s, namely,unions of regional parties. The DMK in Tamil Nadu started its trade union centre and later when the AIADMK split from it, they started their own trade union wing. The year 1967 saw the birth of the Shiv Sena in Bombay. In its early phase the Sena was a pro-Maharashtrian and anti-South Indian front. It soon set up its own labour wing called 'Bharatiya Kamgar Sena'. It was widely believed then that the Shiv Sena had the backing of the big industrial houses in the Bombay-Pune belt to combat the strong influence of the communists and socialists in the labour unions. It managed to do this fairly successfully and by the mid-1970s, its trade union wing became the largest union in Bombay. The challenge to the Sena's supremacy came in 1977 from a fiery INTUC leader, Dr. Datta Samant.

Though a medical doctor by profession, Samant, got involved in trade union activities during the late 1960s when he started organizing the low-paid stone-quarry workers in the north-eastern part of Bombay. Later, he was approached by workers from other industries in that area for help in forming unions. In doing so, Samant came in conflict with the Shiv Sena which was by then controlling the labour belt. He encouraged the workers to oppose the Sena's domination in a militant manner. This led to several clashes between the supporters of the Senaand Samant, and in most cases Samant emerged victorious. In 1972, Samant was elected as an MLA from Kurla on a Congress ticket. When the emergency was declared in mid-1975, Samant refused to tone down his militant approach and he encouraged his union members to strike work whenever necessary. The government arrested him and jailed him till the emergency was lifted in 1977. Samant was the only Congress MLA in the country to have been imprisoned. After his release, his popularity increased even further. By the end of the 1970s, he became the most important trade union leader in the Bombay-Pune industrial belt. He left the Congress and the INTUC in 1978 and became an independent union leader, and thus setting a new trend in the trade union movement- that of independent unions.

Independent Unions

In our discussion so far, we have seen that the trade union movement in India, especially after independence, has had strong links with political parties. These parties have formed their own trade union federations, which was led to the proliferation of trade unions. This has led to frequent inter-union rivalries with the result conflict between unions are at times stronger than conflicts between unions and the employers. This trend has to a large extent harmed the interests of the working class.

At the same time there has been a trend, since the 1960s of independent unions. These are unions which are not directly affiliated to a federation or to any political party. One of the earliest major unions of this type is the Engineering Mazdoor Sabha of Bombay. This union is led by a veteran trade union leader, R.J. Mehta. It is one of the largest unions in the metropolitan covering workers in the engineering, chemicals, printing, and allied industries. Dr. Datta Samant's activities have been discussed above. He started a number of unions covering different industries. These are, Association of Engineering Workers, Mumbai General Kamgar Union, Maharashtra Girni Kamgar Union, among others. The last named union (Maharashtra

Mill Workers Union) was formed in 1981. It received unprecedented support of the textile-mill workers of Bombay. In the same year, in October, the union led the largest and longest strike of textile workers in the city. The strike was a massive failure and half the mill workers lost their jobs. The total workforce before the strike was 250,000. After the strike, that lasted 18 months, the workforce was reduced to 125,000. Though Samant's popularity as a trade leader has reduced considerably, he continued to be a formidable force in the trade union movement in Bombay till he was murdered in 1996.

There were two independent union leaders who came into prominence during the late 1970s. These were Shankar Guha Neogi who organized the contract workers in the iron-ore mines of Dalli Rajhara near Bhilai in Madhya Pradesh into a formidable union, and A.K. Roy who organized the coal-mine workers in the Dhanbad-Jharia belt of Bihar. The workers, in both these cases, joined the unions because they felt that the traditional trade union federations operating in the areas were not sensitive to their problems. In Dalli Rajhara, the trade union federations (INTUC and AITUC) were more concerned with the problems of the workers in the organized sector, namely, the permanent and better-paid workers of the Bhilai Steel Plant. The problems of casual workers were largely ignored. Neogy's union, therefore, got overwhelming support from these workers and other workers employed in small and medium-scale industries in the region. Unfortunately, Neogy fell victim to his success. He was brutally murdered in 1990 in Bhilai. It is suspected that some of the industrialists were responsible.

A.K. Roy's union has a similar support-base, namely, the contract and casual labour in coal-mines. In addition, a large number of local tribal mine-workers have lent him support as these people too have been bypassed by the trade union federations operating there.

In Ahmedabad, Ela Bhat, a leader in the Majoor Mahajan broke away to form the Self-Employed Women's Association (SEWA) when she found that the union was not sensitive to the problem of women workers in the unorganized sector. This union became independent in 1982. Within a short span it emerged as the largest trade union in Gujarat. By 2004, its membership grew to over 700,000 and was spread in four states, Gujarat, M.P., Kerala and Bihar.

There are several other cases of independent unions in different parts of the country. In almost all cases, they have come up, namely, because the existing trade union federations have been unable to meet the expectations of the workers. The concerned workers have then tried to seek alternatives for improving their bargaining conditions with their employers. The main feature of these unions is that they are more often than not centred on a particular leader. This can be a problem because, in most cases, the policies of the union are determined by the leader alone. Nonetheless, the emergence of these unions expose the weakness of the traditional trade union federations.

There are also other types of independent unions which are different from the ones discussed here. In traditional industries, such as textiles, jute, mines, and plantations, we find trade union organizations revolved around industries rather than enterprises. In modern industries, with better educated and skilled workers, we find a tendency of trade unions based on enterprises. One can find this trend in the enterprises employing skilled and better paid workers in cities, like Bombay, Bangalore, Hyderabad, and Pune. In most cases, these enterprises have internal unions, the leadership of which is elected by the workers. In many cases these unions are not affiliated to any central federation though individuals, in the leadership, may have personal loyalties to them. The need for a single internal union comes up precisely because workers in these enterprises want to have a single bargaining agency.

Since the problems of the trade union movement in India seems to be linked to the problem of political parties, let us briefly discuss the relationship between unions and politics.

Trade Unions and Politics

The proliferation of trade unions on political lines is believed to have harmed the interests of the working class. The logic of a trade union is based on the dictum, 'in unity lies strength'. Workers join a trade union mainly because they realize that individually they are helpless. In the early stages of industrialization we have seen that workers formed associations because they were unable to protect their interests in any other manner. Therefore, this basis of unity and strength can be weakened if workers are fragmented into a number of unions based on diverse or conflicting ideologies. Moreover, involvement of trade unions in politics can divert workers to issues which are not immediate to the problems relating to their employment and working conditions. It can, therefore, be argued that since the basic objectives of trade unions is to protect the interests of the workers vis-a-vis their employers, politics can cause more harm than good. However, before we come to any conclusion let us examine whether the delinking of trade union from politics is possible, and if so, desirable.

First of all, in civil society it is difficult for any person or group to remain aloof from politics. The state influences every aspect of our lives. It passes laws to regulate behaviour between individuals and between groups. The entire framework for industrial relations is made legal through the laws passed by the state. Therefore, when trade unions want to defend the rights of workers they have to not only protect them against their employers, but also try to influence the state to pass laws for protection. In this respect, the involvement of trade unions in politics is not only desirable, but also necessary.

If we look at the trade union movement all over the world, and especially in the developed countries, we will find that it has strong links with politics and political parties. Let us begin with Britain, where trade unions helped forming the Labour Party after they realized that their interests could be served only if they had their own political party. It began at the turn of the century with the famous Taff Vale case. The workers of Taff Vale Rail Company went on strike when some of their basic demands were not met. The company then sued the trade union for breach of employment contract. In 1901, when the case went to the House of Lords, it passed a judgement upholding the management's claim. This decision rendered almost any form of union action illegal. Trade unions then realized that without political intervention their actions would be fruitless. They, therefore, started moving politically and, finally, in 1906 the government passed an Act which immunized trade unions from charges of conspiracy or breach of contract.

In other countries, too, the links between trade unions and political parties are explicit. In France the largest trade union federation (CGT) has strong links with the Communist Party while another federation, CFDT, is linked with the Socialist Party. Similarly, in Germany and Italy trade union federations are supporters of either the Communist or Social Democratic parties. In fact, in most countries in Western Europe which have communist parties and socialist or social democratic parties at least two trade union federations exist. Invariably, one will support the communists, and the other, the socialists. In most cases, the unions help mobilize electoral support for the party concerned and also make contributions to the party funds.

We can, hence, see that links between hade unions and political parties are not unique to India alone. In fact, the USA and Japan could be perhaps the only two countries where unions do not have direct links with political parties. Both countries have only single trade union federations-AFL-CIO in the USA and SOHOYO in Japan. Even so, these federations are not totally apolitical as they lend support to some candidates or political parties during the elections. The AFL-CIO has supported some of the candidates of the Democratic Party in the presidential elections and the SOHOYO has given support to the communist, socialist and liberal candidates.

The influence of trade unions on political parties can have positive features for the working class. One can observe this in some of the European countries which have socialist governments backed by the unions. When these parties are voted to power, they pass legislation granting greater security to workers. In Britain, when the Labour Party was ruling in the 1970s, it passed a number of legislations relating to security of employment, unemployment insurance, and regulations concerning termination of employment. Most of these laws were later rescinded by the Tories after they came into power. Similar legislations were passed by socialist or social democrat governments in Italy, France, West Germany, Denmark, Sweden, Norway, and Finland. In addition, in France the government of the Socialist Party has included the right to strike in the country's constitution. In Norway, the government passed a law which makes it mandatory for employers to consult the unions before introducing labour saving technology. On the other hand, in the USA, though the workers are supposed to be the highest paid in the world, they do not have the same security of employment as in the above mentioned European countries. There are no laws guaranteeing permanency of employment even if a worker has put in several years of service. A worker's job guarantee depends on the willingness of his employee or the ability of his union to protect him. This is in spite of there being a single unified trade union federation. This is mainly because the labour movement there has not been able to intervene in politics effectively.

We can, therefore, see that the link between trade unions and political parties are not necessarily detrimental to the interests of workers. However, we have a somewhat different situation in India. Here fragmentation of unions takes place on the basis of narrow party lines. The unions receive divided when political parties split resulting in a large number of unions competing for support from the same group of members. In the countries as mentioned above, political parties do not split as easily as in India. Moreover, even if they do split, the union does not follow suit. For example, the Labour Party in Britain split in the late 1970s when a group broke away to form the Social Democratic Party (SOP). Some of the constituent unions of the Trade Unions Congress supported the SOP, but they did not break away to form another federation.

Almost all the major unions in India have admitted at some point of time that the prevalent form of multi-unionism is the major drawback of the trade union movement. Yet nothing much has been done by them to rectify the situation. A recent example will illustrate the gap between slogans for unity and practice. In its general conference of 1989, the AITUC leadership gave a call for merger of all trade union federations (except the BMS) into a single federation. This they maintained could be possible only if the federations delinked themselves from their parent political parties. To prove their seriousness, the president and the general secretary of the AITUC resigned since they were secretariat member and general secretary of the Communist Party of India. Though most of the trade union federations appreciated AITUC's stand, but only one of them came forward to accept the offer. This was the HMS which, a year earlier, had made a similar appeal. It was then decided by the leadership of the two organizations that they would merge into a single centre. Soon after this, talks between the two centres began. It was even declared that after the merger this federation would rank as the largest in the world in membership. However, nothing concrete has emerged till 2005. This perhaps shows the lack of seriousness in such proposals.

Recognition of Trade Unions

Fragmentation is not the only problem plaguing the trade union movement. In fact, much of this chaotic and unwieldy situation is caused by the legal structure, or lack of it, in regulating trade unions.

Perhaps the most shocking aspect of the legal system regulating industrial relations is that till now there is no law providing for compulsory recognition of trade unions in an enterprise. The decision is left to the management. In the absence of any mechanism for compulsory recognition, it is possible for unions with miniscule membership to vie for recognition. Managements, too, find it convenient to recognize more than one union to promote the divide and rule policy for workers. The Trade Unions Act of 1926 which exists till now unchanged provides for registration of any union having ten or more members in an enterprise. Verification of union membership is left to the Registrar of Trade Unions and it is rarely done. Unions are asked to voluntarily submit their membership figures and it is often found that after adding the figures submitted by each union the total exceeds the actual number of workers.

The Industrial Disputes Act of 1947, which provides the basis of the industrial relations system, allows state-appointed labour officers to mediate in disputes between labour and management. Any union, irrespective of its membership, can bring up a dispute before the conciliating officer and seek redressal. This makes it possible for several unions to exist simultaneously without being recognized.

There have been occasional attempts to change the situation, but none of these have borne fruits so far. In 1947, an amendment to the Trade Unions Act was placed which provided for the right to organize and for compulsory recognition of trade unions, but it was never passed. In 1952, the then labour minister V.V. Giri tried to frame an Act for recognition of trade unions and for voluntary collective bargaining with minimal government interference, but was unsuccessful. He, ultimately, resigned in protest. The opposition was mainly from the ruling Congress Party. The INTUC leaders felt that such a law benefit the communist (AITUC) and socialist (HMS) unions as they were strong. More recently, in 1989, labour minister, Ram Vilas Paswan, framed a bill for remodelling industrial relations. This was the most widely agreed upon document by all the unions, but before it could be introduced in the Parliament, the government had to resign.

Compulsory recognition of trade unions as the bargaining agencies could bring about some order in the present trade union situation. Though most of the unions agree on principle to the recognition of the majority union in the enterprise, there are sharp differences on how this majority can be established. Unions, like AITUC, CITU, and HMS are strong advocates of the use of voting through secret ballot to decide the issue. The INTUC is equally strong in opposing this measure. It advocates recognition through verification of membership and has been arguing that voting would bring politics and corruption to the workplace. The prevalence of these two divergent views has, in fact, prevented the introduction of any law providing for compulsory recognition of trade unions. However, it should be noted that while discussing the draft of the Industrial Relations Bill of 1989, the INTUC finally agreed to accept the secret ballot to decide on the majority union. This had then raised hopes that the problem would be finally solved. Therefore, as things stand now, unless the government decides to change the existing industrial relations laws the working class will be plagued with the problem of fragmentation through multi-unionism.

Current Trends in Trade Unionism

The expansion of the industrial base in India since 1950s and industrial growth using modern technology has given rise to a new section of educated and skilled workers. The social and educational backgrounds of workers engaged in large-scale heavy industries and the hi-tech industries are significantly different from those of the traditional workers engaged in the older industries, like textiles, jute, and plantations. These workers are less dependent on the outside leaders for managing their trade unions. The unions, too, as noted earlier, tend to be enterprise-based rather than industry-based. This makes it easier for internal leaders to control their unions. In most large public sector industries the union leadership at the enterprise level comprises almost exclusively of the employees, though at the industry level these unions may be affiliated to one of the trade union federations which are dominated by outside leaders. The distinction here is that at the industry level outside leaders may be required to conduct negotiations along with the inside leaders whereas at the enterprise level the workers themselves are capable of managing their affairs. This is quite different from unions in the textile industry in Bombay, the jute industry in Calcutta, and tea plantation in West Bengal and Assam where outside leaders are required to negotiate at the enterprise level or in several cases even at the shop floor.

Apart from the development of internal trade union leadership which is undoubtedly a healthy trend, there are some new trends in employment which have had their effects on the growth of trade unions. During the past two decades or so, two distinct trends have emerged in industrial employments which have had adverse effects on the development of the organized labour.

First, permanent employment has decreased in most of the industries. A part of this may be due to the adoption of labour-saving technologies. But, it has been observed that even in industries where such technologies have not been applied employment has fallen. A recent publication[8] containing studies on employment and unionization in twelve industries shows that employment has declined in absolute terms in all industries, even while these industries have grown as indicated by volume of production. If facts, as these studies indicate, there is an attempt to scale down permanent employment by replacing permanent workers by temporary, contract or casual labour. An unfortunate manifestation is that the reduction of permanent workers is more often the result of legal enactments and facilities gained by the workers through their trade union action. The employers find that casual or contract labour is cheaper and easier to control.

Secondly, the fall in permanent employment is due to ancillarization or the putting-out system adopted by many industries. This means that a large part of the manufacturing is contracted out to smaller industries. The cost of production falls because labour wages in the small-scale sector is much lower. This has resulted in the growth of the informal or unorganized sector. Since most of these units operate with low capital and small number of employees they do not come under the purview of the industrial or labour legislations. Hence their costs are further reduced. The unfortunate aspects of this process are that these workers are rarely unionized. The larger trade union organizations prefer to concentrate on the organized sector.[9]

The growing ranks of unprotected contract and casual labour without organized industry and in the unorganized sector are a result of the high level or unemployment in the wider society. The employers have no doubt taken advantage of the availability of large pools of cheap labour. However, they could not have adopted this strategy of cutting labour costs were it not for the insularity of the trade union movement. Unionized workers in the organized sector are able to get higher pay and more benefits. This increases costs for the employers hence in order to cut costs employers hire casual or contract labour. As these people are not unionized their wages are low and they can be hired or fired at will which gives the employers greater control over them. The contrast between permanent workers and casual workers would not have been so glaring had the latter been unionized. The unions of Shankar Guha Neogi, A.K. Roy, and Ela Bhat discussed earlier, have been successful in providing a great deal of protection to casual and contract labour in their respective areas of operation. The larger federations could have helped to ensure that workers elsewhere, too, get some protection in their employment and, fair wages. In the present state of affairs, casualization without union protection has gone so far as to threaten the interests of permanent workers and, of course, their unions as employers find it convenient to replace permanent workers by casual workers. By bringing them into the union-fold the unions could be in a position to regulate the competition for jobs which would have benefited the working class in general. We have discussed in the beginning while tracing the origins of trade unions that competition for jobs among workers in England actually worsened their conditions. In such a situation labour is the loser and the benefits go to the employers.

Reduction in costs due to casualization or the putting-out system does not necessarily result in lowering of prices of manufactured goods. In fact, we can often find that industries which resort to casualization or the putting-out system are those which produce expensive goods. For example, most of the large companies manufacturing clothes, hosiery, shoes, toiletry (soap, tooth paste, cosmetics, etc.) get a large part of their output through contracting out to small industries. Though costs are considerably reduced because of this, the prices of these goods do not fall. In fact, they show a tendency to rise. Thus, casualization and putting-out help neither the workers nor the consumer. The main beneficiaries are the employers who are able to amass high profits. Hence, in the present context, growth of casualization leads to greater inequalities within the industrial sector, and it threatens to take away from the permanent workers the gains they have made by organizing themselves into trade unions. This, in fact, is the greatest challenge to the trade union movement today.

Globalization and economic liberalization have raised new issues. In general, the trend towards informal work has increased and jobs in the organized sector have declined. At the same time, new types of employment have been created. At the lower level, employment has been created in logistics services, cable TV, private security, hotels,restaurants, etc. At the higher level, there are employment opportunities in the information and communication technology sector. Educated youths are finding jobs in call centres and other forms of Business Process Outsourcing (BPO). All these jobs are not unionized and neither are there any legal regulations. Hence, the trade union movement faces the challenge of unionization of these new workers. The International Labour Organization (ILO) has raised this issue in its annual report of 2001.[10]

Concluding Observations

We have observed that the birth of the trade union movement in India has been an arduous process. There was severe opposition from the employers who had the backing of the colonial government. At the same time, the trade union movement has been to a large extent responsible for securing the basic rights of the workers and giving them dignity. The contribution of trade unions in developing a militant yet disciplined workforce cannot be denied. The necessity of the movement is far greater in the present phase as workers are losing their jobs and there is an increase in the number of cheaply available, unprotected labour. Trade unions can protect the interests of the various sections of the working class and influence the state to pass remedial legislation. However, to do so, trade unions have to, first, set their own house in order. A highly-fragmented trade union movement split on narrow political divisions can hardly be expected to protect employment as unions are too busy fighting each other. Compulsory recognition of trade unions is necessary to help reduce the prevalent inter-union rivalries. The Trade Union Act needs to be changed to ensure that only genuine unions with proper membership can be recognized. Industrial relations laws need to be modified to ensure that there is no unnecessary interference from the government. A decline in the trade union movement will help no one. Even employers have to realize that trade unions help to institutionalize industrial conflicts and solve them within the legal framework. Indeed, without trade unions there would be greater chaos in industry.

Notes and References

1. A. Flanders, *Trade Unions,* London, Faber and Faber, 1970. p. 1. This book is a good introduction to trade unions.
2. F. Engels, *The Conditions of the Working Class in England in 1848.* Moscow, Progress Publishers, 1973, p. 115. This is a classic ethnographic study on the English working class.
3. *Ibid.*, p. 252.
4. R.K. Mukherji, *The Indian Working Class,* Bombay, Popular Prakashan, 1955, p. 240. An excellent study of the early history of industrial labour.
5. C. Revri, *The Indian Trade Union Movement-An Outline History 1880-1947,* Delhi, Orient Longman, 1972, p. 75. This book gives a detailed history of labour movement till independence.
6. S.A. Dange, *Outlines of the Indian Trade Union Movement,* Delhi, People's Publishing House, 1973, p. 10. This booklet contains a lucid history of the AITUC.
7. Jawaharlal Nehru, *Autobiography,* Delhi, National Book Trust, 1955, pp. 198–99.
8. Sarath Davala (ed.), *Employment and Unionisation in Indian Industry,* Delhi, Friedrich Ebert Foundation, 1992. An important source book on the subject.
9. Sen, Sukomal, *The Working Class of India,* Calcutta, K. P. Bagchi, 1979.
10. ILO (International Labour Organization), *World Employment Report 2001: Working in Information and Communication Technology Sector,* Geneva, ILO, 2002.

Note: The name of Bombay has been changed to Mumbai from 1996.

22

Women's Movement in India: Issues and Perspectives

Pushpa Bali

The end of the Second World War and the retreat of imperialism in the twentieth century led to the increased demand and awareness of the human rights all over the world. The changes that followed the two world wars created atmosphere and built structures which emphasized the end of inequalities in the social order so that liberty, equality, and democracy could flourish. The quest for genuine equality has also laid greater emphasis on the collective rights of the vast majority of disadvantaged groups, such as women who constitute roughly 50 per cent of the total population. The twentieth century promoted the cause of gender justice by internationalizing struggles for equality by women all over the world. The new world order and the institutions, which emerged, promoted the debates on women's rights and genuine gender equality so that it become meaningful. The International Women's Decade initiated women's struggle against subordination, freedom, self-determination, equality and justice. The debate found expression in the form of various movements in the developed as well as developing countries. In fact, in developing countries, like India, women's movement was apart of the national movement against imperialism which emerged after the independence.

Women's Movement in India (WMI) emerged as a part of social reform movement in the early nineteenth century. This was the period when rights and wrongs to women became major issues. Early attempts to reform the conditions of women were led by men who came under Western influence, and tried to reform the society, started campaign against caste, polygamy, theism, adulatory, *purda*, child-marriage, and *sati*. They considered those outdated. They also took up fight against the issues which affected women, particularly widows, who were so ill-treated, that the only viable option for them was either to become *sati* or be driven to accept prostitution. They initiated campaign for education of women which was non-existent at that time. The initial efforts for the upliftment of women was led by men. There were no independent movements of women for women and by women. It is a debatable issue "whether their main rationale for the upliftment of women was the production of companionable wives and enlightened mothers, the strengthening of the family structure or simply humanitarian feelings for inhuman and unjust atrocities". Be it what may, but one cannot deny the fact that for the first time it was realized that it is not the destiny of women to be illiterate and suffer. Society has a key role in their education and enlightenment. Social reform movement set in process, and as a result of it, many educated women, who were either wives, sisters or daughters and others who were beneficiaries of education, initiated by them, and joined the movement. By the early twentieth century, women's own autonomous organizations began to emerge. However, by the 1930s, after the mass participation of women in non-cooperation and civil disobedience movements led by Gandhi, WMI entered into the second phase.

During the second phase, there was a serious debate in the WMI regarding the rights of women. The supporters of pragmatic reforms demanded reservations for women, keeping in mind the real status of women in society, particularly in rural backward areas. But the women who were active in the national movement opposed any kind of reservations and demanded adult franchise, gender equality as the constitutional rights, and the like. There were occasional clashes between the two, but both agreed to work for social reforms and welfare of women. It was because of the active participation of women in the anti-imperialist struggle that the fundamental rights resolution of the Indian National Congress in 1931 in Karachi emphasized freedom, equality and justice for women which was later on incorporated in the constitution of India and hailed as a landmark, so far as rights of women are considered.

During the early years in the WMI, it was more or less taken for granted that the difference between the two sexes are such that they affect their roles, desires, and aims, so they should be treated differently and reared differently. Early nineteenth century reformers argued that these differences from men made them socially useful (as mothers), hence, proper care for their well-being was also socially necessary. Later on, when more and more women joined their own organizations though the difference between the two sexes was again stressed, emphasis was also laid on women's right to speech, education, equality, and emancipation.

❑ Constitutional and Legal Rights

The constitution of India is one of the most progressive documents so far as the legal rights of the women are concerned. The constitution makes no discrimination on the basis of sex and provides equal rights to all citizens irrespective of sex. It not only prohibits the state from discrimination against any citizen on the ground of sex, but also empowers the state to make special provisions for the well-being of the women.

Article 15 specially prohibits gender discrimination and provides "prohibition of discrimination on grounds of sex or place of birth". At the same time, Article 15(3) gives positive power to the state to make special provisions for women and children. Article 16(2)(1) provides equal opportunities to all citizens in matters of public employment and Article 16(2) categorically prohibits discrimination on the basis of sex in respect of any employment or office under the state.

Besides the fundamental rights, the constitution of India has made special provisions for women under the Directive Principles of State Policy, particularly in Articles 38, 39, 42 and 44. Article 38(2) states that "the state shall, in particular, strive to minimize the inequalities and endeavour to eliminate inequalities in status facilities and opportunities." Article 39(a) specifically provides "that the citizens, men and women equally, have the right to adequate means to livelihood." Article 39(d), again, categorically states "that there is equal pay for equal work for both men and women." Article 39(d) further lays down "that the health and strength of workers, men and women and the tender age of children are not abused and the citizens are not forced by economic necessity to enter a vocation unsuited to their age or strength." The constitution under Article 42 made specific provisions "for just and humane conditions of work and for maternity relief." Article 44 provides for "uniform civil code for citizens throughout the territory of India."

The constitution of India and the various provisions can be considered as a landmark as far as legal rights of women and gender equality is concerned, but it has raised a pertinent question: Can law bring social change? Can there be genuine equality among unequals? The ruling elite and the society overlooked the socio-economic backwardness of the women in the process of constitution making. It had adverse impact on the women which constituted one of the major segments of the disadvantaged group. Gender equality through constitutionally guaranteed remained a pious legal dream of the constitution-makers for quite some time.

Women activism in the post-independence era gave way to the building up of the institutions and structures. Though the government started *Mahila Mandals* and various reform programmes, many women were disillusioned by the half-hearted measures adopted by the government in the post-independence era, particularly on the issue of Hindu Code Bill. Even the plans for enacting a uniform civil code for all communities was shelved. It remains a distant dream even today. The WMI was more fragmented during that era than before, because of the elimination of the common enemy, the British Raj, which had great unifying impact on all segments of the WMI. Political divisions among the movement became more important than before because the WMI had never "identified their enemy on gender basis, partly due to the exigencies of colonialism and partly due to the complexities of the Indian culture in which gender relations has not been clearly distinguished as in the west." Moreover, many women Congress activists of the pre-independence era were now part of the government, so they could not take active part in the movement against their own party. Hence, there was a lull in the WMI, with the exception of one or two movements which were parts of their larger movements of that time but also raised women issues.

The first political movement which took place immediately after independence was the Telengana peasant movement in Andhra Pradesh (1948-50). It was a movement led by CPI in which about 2500 villages were liberated. It was basically an agrarian movement in which thousands of women participated along with the men but, besides the agrarian issues, it also paid attention to women's issues, such as "wife-beating, making it known that they would chastise the offenders," though "the attitude towards women remained one of benevolent paternalism."

In the early sixties, another movement, named, *Chipko Andolan* took place in Uttarakhand under the leadership of Sarvodaya leader Vinoba Bhave against degradation of forests. Women in large number participated in this movement. The movement also took up the issue of increasing consumption of alcohol, which the women considered the major cause of their suffering. Meera Behan and Sarla Behan, the two disciples of Mahatma Gandhi, were active in this movement. The movement focussed attention on action against the manufacturers and sellers of alcohol, but not the consumers who are the main cause of the problem.

❑ Contemporary Women's Movement

Contemporary WMI, which started in the seventies and eighties, was very different from the earlier movements and is influenced by two factors. First, the WMI which emerged in the seventies was greatly influenced by powerful women movement in the USA which ignited a world-wide debate and protest by women for their emancipation and rights. This influenced the women in India, particularly the urban educated elite classes. There was abundant feminist literature available in the universities, colleges and shops. At the same time, there was huge growth of Indian literature on socio-economic and socio-cultural issues focussing on women. But this was limited to the urban areas. Though the international events influenced WMI, the Indian movement had basically emerged due to the widespread disillusionment of women at the grass roots level with the process and model of development, which failed to eliminate poverty, discrimination, and injustice to the women. By the 1970s, there was widespread disillusionment among women groups with the process of development, and the attitude has gradually started shifting to confrontation. In fact, contemporary WMI has emerged out of radical confrontationist movements of the time.

Four movements played a crucial role in the consolidation of the WMI at the grassroots level.

Shahada Movement

Shahada is a Bhil *adivasi* settlement in Dhulloia district of Maharashtra. Many young Sarvodaya workers started the Shramik Sangathan to help the *adivasis* suffering due to drought and famine. These organizations took a more militant approach, initiated land-grab, demanded minimum wages, and held women *shivirs* (camps). Women played active role in mobilizing the masses. As militancy developed in the movement, women issues also began to be raised along with the wider issues. Women applied their consciousness to the question of their oppression on the basis of gender. The movement shortly led to the anti-alcohol agitation, because many men after consuming alcohol beat their wives. Women *shivirs* were organized to discuss and help each other to eradicate this evil which is one of the main causes of their oppression. The Shahada movement started as a protest movement against landlords turned into a movement against the sale and consumption of alcohol and attack on wife-beaters. It was an indirect protest against violence in the family, which had so far been held as a private matter of the family. Shahada movement, in a way, challenged some aspects of patriarchy.

SEWA

The first attempt to organize a women's trade union was made in Ahmedabad by a Gandhian socialist leader, Ella Bhatt, attached to the women wing of Textile Labour Association (TLA). She formed the Self-employed Women Association in 1972 to organize the women working in various trades in the informal sector. They all suffered due to extremely low wages, poor working conditions, and lack of training, harassment by the authorities or middlemen and police. The aim of the SEWA was to improve their working conditions, provide technical and economic assistance, help them to sell their products at better prices by collective bargaining and improve their economic status. The SEWA helped the women to become economically self-sufficient to give them freedom from exploitation by assurance of regular work arid access to opportunities for development. Thus, the SEWA helped the poor working women to improve their economic status and become self-sufficient, because economic dependence is one of the major reasons of their exploitation by men.

Anti-Price-Rise Front

The conditions of famine and drought affected the urban areas in Maharashtra, which led to the rising prices and black-marketing. Mrinal Gore of the Socialist Party and Ahilya Rangekar of CPI(M) formed the United Front,

Anti-Price-Rise Front, to mobilize the women in the cities against inflation. It became a mass movement demanding price-control and proper distribution of essential commodities at fair prices. The women groups also raided the premises of the black-marketers. It was a mass movement of urban housewives against economic hardships affecting their daily life.

Nav Nirman Samiti

After Maharashtra, the movement soon spread to Gujarat. Known as Nav Nirman Samiti, it was initially a student protest against rising prices of the essential commodities and political disorder. Later, it turned into a massive movement when middle-class women joined it. Women participated in these movements because rise in the price of essential commodities had adversely affected their daily life. Hoarding and black-marketing activities had caused added more hardship to the plight of the common people. The Anti-Price-Rise Front and Nav Nirman Samiti indirectly helped in crystallizing women's identity as a group.

In the same year, in Andhra Pradesh, the first feminist group formed the Progressive Organization of Women (POW). This group stressed on the existence of gender-based oppression and motivated women against it. The manifesto of this group emphasized on the concept of equality between men and women in every walk of life. According to them, the two primary structures of exploitation are gender-based division of labour on the biological basis and the culture which provides justification to such division.

The year 1975 witnessed a sudden development in the feminist movements. It was also declared as the International Women's Year by the United Nations. The declaration also focussed on the various activities. Influenced by the POW, the progressive women in Pune formed the *Purogami Stree Sangathan,* and in Bombay they founded *Stree Mukti Sangathan*. Lal Nishan Party, a splinter group of the CPI, brought out a special issue on women. Socialists organized a conference on *devdasis* and Muslim women. Several government and semi-government organizations celebrated the I.W.Y. in their own ways. In Hyderabad, radical women students of the POW organized campaign against sexual harassment, dowry, bride-burning. Social issues,such as dowry, bride-burning, violence, and sexual harassment of the women were debated all over India.

The proclamation of Emergency in 1975, and the suspension of civil liberties led to the suspension of the WMI. But, with the ascending of Janata Party to power in 1977, the movement was revived. In the later seventies and early eighties, the WMI was mainly dominated by urban groups though similar movements were going on in certain rural areas, such as Telengana in Hyderabad, where an incident of kidnapping of a woman and murder of her husband by a local landlord led to a chain of events ended with development and demand for independent women's organizations in the area because women felt that "Women organization affiliated to political parties (even in socialist countries) have become mere appendages of those parties Women's organizations should guard against such a danger, but without isolating themselves from the masses and from the revolutionary movement."

By the 1980s, women groups were active all over India. They organized poster-exhibitions, meetings, study circles and activists' meetings to debate on issues related to women and started campaigns against them. A forum against rape was formed against the Supreme Court's judgement in the Mathura rape case. The third phase of the WMI is also concerned with woman's control over her body. It debated issues including women's health, violence, rape, wife-battering, divorce, right to maintenance, child custody, etc. They are also concerned not only with the enactment of legislation in favour of women, but also with amendments to the existing anti-women laws. The WMI is equally concerned about the proper implementation of the existing laws concerning women and their rights. WMI in its current phase is not only concerned with education of the women, but equally concerned about standard education, textbooks having women-oriented content in the proper perspective. Many universities have opened women studies and development centres, introduced women-oriented education programmes. Women Development Centres are conducting academic researches on women-related issues. The WMI, in this decade, is concerned with equality which is genuine. They not want reservations alone, but proper share in all material resources, means of production, education, and in decision-making process. The progressive WMI is the outcome of changing social, economic, and political reality.

The WMI is an ongoing process. It started as a protest against negative outlook towards women and their problems. It moved on to the second phase where they denied biological explanation of existing disparities between the two sexes, then to the third phase where men and women are equal. In the early nineteenth century, it started with humanitarian concerns for the suffering of women, and the need for reform. By the twentieth century, the emphasis has shifted to stressing women's right to be treated as useful members of society. By the late twentieth century, it has moved to women's right to self-determination.

The WMI demonstrated a variety of ideologies in it. Each group has its own perception and theories. According to the Left groups [Left is a wide term including so many groups such as CPI, CPI(M), Maoist groups], the primary reason for women's subordination is their economic dependence on men and exploitation in the capitalist system of production and the feudal structure, and the culture of the society. The classless, stateless society will eventually liberate the women from such subjugation.

The socialist groups (*e.g.,* Samajwadi Mahila Samaj) and Congress-oriented AIWC explain women's exploitation and her unequal status in terms of social traditions, religious practices, materialistic, and consumerist attitude of society. Following the Gandhi an ideology they urge women to develop their own inner strength, use rational persuasion for strength.

The newly-formed radical youth and feminist groups perceive the women problems, such as violence as the manifestation of unequal relationship of men and women because of patriarchy. According to them, the domination and exploitation of women's labour, fertility, and sexuality are caused by men's exploitation of women. So, the man-woman relationship has to be changed. Unless there is genuine equality between the two sexes, women cannot be liberated.

Women in India have been deprived of their rights, for long. They were forced to suffer deprivation by the society in silence. The women's movement in India is the reassertion of their rights as equal in the political economic process. It is the manifestation of their desire to live with dignity in society, but this has directly challenged the old feudal, conservative values and structures based on patriarchy.

Women's movement has mounted a great pressure on the government. Responding to this pressure is a formidable task for the government. A democratically elected government cannot overlook these issues. So, how to maintain a balance between conservative feudal forces and radical forces in a democratic society is a challenge for the government. Women's movement has played a dual role in this process, confronting/demanding and petitioning the state on one hand and advocating, collaborating with and briefing it on the other. Quite often, the women's groups have succeeded in seeking positive legislation's in their favour. In 1991, the government set up National and State Commissions for women to monitor the women-oriented programmes of the government. Various political parties, too, are quick to realize the importance of women as voters and have set up their women's wings. Within the women's movement, there are so many diversities, dissensions, ideological differences which affect their perception of the women and issues related with them. It is natural for a plural, multi-culture, multilingual, multi-religious democratic society, and this is the strength of the movement. Any social movement in such a diverse society, is bound to have different views. Moreover, the problems of the rural women are different from those of the urban women. Similarly, the problems of dalit, tribal, poor, illiterate, working-women are bound to be different from the urban, literate, working women or urban elite women. Even the culture and religion have their own cultural and religious biases which may adversely affect the women's belonging to them. Certain issues may be crucial for a particular women group, but may not be of the same importance for others. Hence, the women's movement in India, is bound to have cleavages. Despite these differences, there are certain issues which are of equal importance for the women in general. *Towards Equality*, the report of the Committee on Status of Woman appointed by the Government of India in 1974, highlighted certain key issues which are crucial for gender equality in India. The Committee expressed serious doubts about the process of modernization which had ignored the real difference and exaggerated the influence of culture, religion, and social values on gender roles. It is clearly reflected by study of the role of women in economic life where they are shown as consumers and reproductive beings and not as producers. There is accelerated decline in the sex-ratio, increasing gap in life expectancy, mortality, and economic participation. Even demographic trends have supported these facts. The government failed to fulfil the constitutional-legal mandate. Women's organizations demand real equality.

❑ Issues before the Women's Movement

There are so many issues before the women's movement and their organizations in a culturally and economically diverse society like ours. Some issues are local, some are issues before a particular community or section of society. There are certain issues which can be identified as the key issues affecting women all over India, and are the main causes of the marginalization of women and key to gender equality. Each one of them is so crucial that it requires thorough in-depth study to understand its true impact. These issues are:

Violence

Violence is one of the major issues before the movement since the time of its inception. In general, it is a coercive mechanism to inflict one's will over another, to assert one's own power. A hierarchical social structure,like ours, has violence in-built in it. The intensity of violence exercised by the dominant group to subjugate the subordinate group differs from place-to-place and time-to-time. Violence is often perpetuated through the institutions of state, community, family, and the society at large. Any demand or efforts to change it, is interpreted as a revolt against the institutions of the society. Quite often, the women's movements have protested against such violence and demanded legislation against it. The women's movements have taken up issues, like domestic violence, dowry-deaths, rape, female infanticide, amniocentesis tests for sex determination, burning of widows, lynching women on suspicion of witchcraft and forcing them into prostitution. A new kind of violence is inflicted upon women's body by conducting different types of medical tests (particularly for family planning), without realizing the side effect on their health. For medical research, female body is used as guinea pigs.

Despite laws and women's movements, there is a sharp increase in the number of cases of violence against women. In recent years, there have been many cases of stripping, individual and gangrape, humiliation inflicted on *Dalits* as well as other women. Often this is attributed to the media and its activism to project such cases, but the fact is that in so many cases, it is due to the backlash of the feudal conservative structures of society which want to reinforce their subjugation through coercion, humiliation, and violence. On one side, the movement for women's rights is strengthened, on the other side, there is an increase in social acceptance of violence and its use for personal and political benefit. Although the government has enacted legislations, but these laws are full of lacunae or they have been implemented half-heartedly due to the patriarchal and feudal values of the law-enforcement agencies.

Fundamentalism and Communalism

Fundamentalism and communalism is another major issue before the women's movements in India. The wave of fundamentalist upsurge sweeping across the world has adverse impact on women's movements abroad and in India in particular. The complex structure of the Indian society, economic constraints before the state and political opportunism have provided enough breathing space to communalism. Religion plays a dominant role in the life of individuals in our society. Though the constitution proclaims India as a secular state, political opportunism has led to the revival of religious fundamentalism in the last few years. Often, the political parties play religion as a trump card to gain the support of the particular community. Religious, ethnic or cultural fundamentalism is opposed to gender equality and dignity. The year 1985 marked a shift in the Indian politics. For lack of effective leadership and the need for the support of the various groups, the government and various political parties adopted policies and played the communal card for their own benefits. In May 1986, the government totally surrendered to the Muslim fundamentalists on the issue of Muslim women's right to maintenance in case of divorce, under Section 125 of the Criminal Procedure Code, a secular law open to all communities. It was a total surrender by the government to the Islamic fundamentalism and was opposed by the women's organizations, irrespective of religion. Even the progressive and educated section of the Muslim community was opposed to it.

In 1992, the demolition of the 500-year-old Babri Masjid in Ayodhaya by Hindu fundamentalists sparked off violence and riots in several parts of the country. Women were the most vulnerable targets of the communal frenzy. Because of the patriarchal ideology of the family and community honour, women were subjected to rape and humiliation in order to demoralize them. There have been many riots in India, but the riots after the mosque-demolition witnessed the worst kind of sexual perversities inflicted upon the women, particularly women from the minority community.

Since women are deeply attached to religion, the various fundamentalist groups are floating new kind of religious women's organizations, like Durga Vahini, Matri Shakti, which focus on the role of the mother, defender of the faith, protector of the social and cultural values of society and, thus, maintain the status quo. Quite often, the religious platform is used for propagating fundamentalism. The illiterate and religious women in the rural and urban areas are the main target of communal fundamentalism. There is a greater need for the reinterpretation of religion as a progressive social force because the power of the fundamentalist resulted from all-male religious hierarchies which excluded women from interpretation of scriptures. Moreover, the women's movements also have to start a dialogue with other women's organizations, cutting across the barriers of religion, education, and space, bring them to the mainstream of women's movement, and save them from the clutches of fundamentalists.

❑ Women and Economic Issues

Impoverishment of the majority of women in the economy is one of the vital issues of concern for the movement as well as academics. The committee on Status of Women in India, for the first time, raised the issue to examine the relationship between macro-economic changes and the women's status. The focus on the economic themes by the women's studies in the National Conference helped the academics to conduct serious research on this issue. Moreover, some organizations of poor women in the informal sector (*e.g.*, Self-employed Women's Association, Annapurna) were doing excellent work at the grassroots level for the upliftment of women through economic development and empowerment. In fact, their record is much better than the government. In 1977, the new government decided to review various development policies, and started search for alternative strategies for the development to check the marginalization of women, particularly poor women in the development process. It was during that time, because of the combined efforts of women members of Parliament belonging to various political parties and pressure of the active women's groups, that Planning Commission included a chapter on "Women and Development in the Sixth Five-Year Plan." Henceforth, all government programmes will focus on women, as a separate category, acknowledging government's inability to achieve gender equality, the plan clearly stated that without economic independence, equal access to education, skill-training and family planning services, constitutional guarantees of equality remain a myth. Henceforth, all anti-poverty programmes were directed to include women as target. In case of distribution of assets by government, it will provide joint ownership to husband and wife, will also give priority to families headed by women. Women's groups have consistently demanded for genuine land reforms. The late Prime Minister Rajiv Gandhi, in the last years of his prime ministership hosted the second NAM conference on "Women and Development" and also initiated debate on the new Panchayati Raj Bill which proposed to give greater power to women. It was implemented after 73rd constitutional Amendment Act in 1991 and reserved 33 per cent seats for women in local bodies. In 1991, the government also set up the National Commission and State Commissions for women to serve as watchdog bodies, monitoring the implementation of pro-women policies.

Today, the Indian women feel that the Structural Adjustment Programmes (SAP) have adverse impact on the women and children. First, it has removed the regulatory aspects of the state in the mixed economy and replaced it with globalization and open market. The opening up of the market has allowed the multinational corporations to enter the Indian market, leaving women and deprived groups at their mercy. At present, 94 per cent of the women are part of the informal sector. When the future of informal sector itself is in question one can imagine the plight of women employed in it. Second, steep rise in prices due to SAP has badly hit the women and children. The per capita intake of cereals have dropped in the past two years causing serious health concerns. Third, as a result of SAP, traditional industries, like coir, cashew, tobacco, khadi, fishing, which generally employ women are severely affected and, thus, cause further impoverishment of women in the rural areas.

Contemporary women's movement in India covers a large canvas. It includes many organizations in its fold and many ideologies and viewpoints on the various issues. They may differ in their understanding of class gender and the origin of women's oppression, but they all share a common belief that women are an oppressed section of the society. Even at the time of the Beijing conference, held in September 1995, besides the official delegation and the paper, seven Indian leading women's organizations which had the support of over a hundred welfare organizations, released their alternative paper titled, "Towards Beijing: Perspective from the Indian Women's Movement", which criticized the governmental paper and some of the policies directed towards women, which they placed in the conference along with the official paper. Almost an equal number of Non-Governmental Organizations (NGOs) also participated and presented their papers, criticizing the governmental policies concerning women, their health and family planning.

Due to the pressure from the women's groups, the government has enacted several new legislations; amended many of the existing laws. But, it raised one very important question to ponder, whether law can bring social change. Despite the government enacting or amending legislations in favour of women, these legislations and efforts are half-baked, full of lacunae, could not be implemented effectively due to over bureaucratization at the government level, patriarchal values and hierarchies, and vested interests of law-enforcement agencies. Even serious crimes, like rape or dowry-deaths at times are difficult to register, leave aside the question of punishing the guilty. Even their interpretations and judgement are at times much influenced by the prevailing social and cultural prejudices. The case of Bhanwari Devi, a social worker in Rajasthan and the judgement of District and Sessions Court, Jaipur, is an eye-opener.

Gender equality remains a utopia unless the values of those who interpret and implement the laws are changed. We have to bring a social change in the outlook of the society. It is essential that women have more access and participation in the decision-making at all levels. This can only be possible by literacy, social awareness, and economic empowerment of the women. Gender equality and social justice have yet to tread a long way. "Today, the WMI has created an ethos and environment, it has put forward a hope and a future which every woman can claim and gain strength from so she may work out in her own way, her struggle for a better life and society."

Notes and References

All India Women's Conference, *Indian Women in the 1980s: Development Perspectives,* All India Women Conference, 1980.

Government of India, *Towards Equality:* Report *of the Committee on Status of Women in India,* Government of India, 1974.

Bibekanand Das and LN. Dash, The *Feminine Gender,* New Delhi, Manak Publications Pvt. Ltd., 1995.

Hem Lata Swaroop and Sarojani Bisaria (ed.), *Women. Politics and Religion,* A.C. Brothers. Etawah, 1991.

Jean Grimshaw, *Feminist Philosophers: Women's Perspective on Philosophical Traditions,* Sussex, Harvester Press, 1986.

K. Murali Manohar (ed.), *Women Status and Development in India, Society for Women's Studies and Development,* Warangal, 1983.

Nandita Gandhi and Nandita Shah, *The Issues at Stake:* Theory *and Practice in the Contemporary Women's Movement in India,* New Delhi, Kali for Women, 1992.

Radha Kumar, *The History of Doing: An Illustrated Account of Movements for Women's* Rights and Feminism in India 1800-1990, New Delhi, Kali for Women, 1993.

Kum Kum Sangari and Sudesh Vaid (ed.), *Recasting Women. Essays in Colonial History of India,* New Delhi, Kali for Women, 1989.

Subrata Mukherjee and Susheela Ramaswamy (eds.), *Women in the Past, Present and Future,* New Delhi, Deep and Deep Publications, 1996.

Susheela Kaushik (ed.), "History Politics and Theory", *Teaching Politics,* Delhi, 1988.

Tanika Sarkar and Urvashi Butalia, *Women and the Hindu Rights: A Collection of Essays,* New Delhi, Kali for Women, 1995.

Flavia Agnes, "Women's Movement within a Secular Framework", *Economic and Political Weekly,* Vol. XXIX, No. 19, 7th May 1994.

Indu Agnihotri and Veena Mazumdar, "Women Movement in India. 1970-90: Changing Political Discourse", *Economic and Political Weekly,* Vol. XXX, No. 29, 22nd July 1995.

Supriya Akerkar, "Theory and Practice of Women's Movement in India", *Economic and Political Weekly,* Vol. XXX, No. 17, 29th April 1995. *The Hindustan Times,* Year Page, Delhi edition, 31st August 1995, p. 14.

23

Communalism

Bibekbrata Sarkar

More than fifty-seven years after independence, communalism continues to divide the Indian people and waste their human potential, defying all potential and administrative measures, and scholarly concern and analyses. As in the case of several other problems of Indian polity, any attempt to understand the complexity of communalism and its hold on the Indian psyche require taking a look into the politics of nationalism during the pre-independence days. Two theories were frequently offered as explanation of communalism in pre-independence India: (1) the British policy of divide and rule, and (2) deliberate economic underdevelopment. These theories have not lost their currency completely even today.[1] Uneven capitalist growth can offer only part of the explanation of the existence of communal mentality and communal violence today as well as in the past. Communalism has always been too complex a phenomenon to be explained solely in terms of an economic situation. If uneven economic and social development prepared the ground for communalism, as Asghar Ali contends, then the Sikhs who are economically well off than other communities of India, would not have succumbed to it as they did in the eighties. The colonial policy of divide and rule became effective in India and elsewhere, not so much by creating divisions among the people by accentuating the cleavages that already existed. The British colonial government provided monetary incentives and a variety of other forms of encouragement to nurture the growth of any potentially divisive factor could be developed to drive a wedge into the solidarity of the nationalist forces, including religion, caste, and tribal loyalties. In this connection, this is important to remember that every state is interested in keeping the forces opposed to it divided as an overall strategy of survival, though it need not, however, amount to encouragement of communalism.

At this point, it is necessary to clarify certain issues. Much of the confusion associated with the discussion of communalism arises from the initial assumption that communalism is a given (or natural) category of thought and action in India. Communalism as one of the stereotypes of Indian reality was abstracted from the local history and politics of strife between communities[2] by colonial historians and creators of its justifying discourse. Religion is one of the elements in the make-up of a community, not necessarily its qualifying characteristics. But colonial stereotypes made it appear so. The colonial reading of India's past as one of perpetual disharmony between 'religious' communities was, thus, an amalgam of colonial political necessity and deliberate misinterpretations of India's history and political tradition.

The colonial authorities were, indeed, quick to resort to the strategy of dividing the political opposition to its rule. As long as such opposition was sporadic, spontaneous, and was limited to small areas, they could use strong arm tactics. But sustained political opposition, like the nationalist movement, required a longer term strategy. To this end, they turned their attention soon enough, that is, much before the onset of mass movements. In the early phase of British rule, they followed a policy of systematic enfeeblement of the Muslims as they were the ruling authority in North India. The revenue system brought about by the British authorities accorded a lot of prominence to the money-lenders, who were overwhelmingly Hindus. The expropriation of Muslim peasantry in Punjab and Bengal reached serious proportions. The Muslims were excluded from the army and government service. The introduction of English as official language compounded the difficulties for the Muslims and further restricted their opportunities. A hundred years of British rule almost completely emasculated the Muslims, identified by the British as a religious community hostile to the British.[3]

As Indians, mostly Hindus in this case, began to set up associations to express political, economic or social demands in different parts of India in the 1870s, followed soon by a move to establish an all-India organization, the British strategy changed. The overt attitude of hostility to Muslims was changed to one of patronage. In 1877, Sir Syed Ahmed Khan founded the Mohammedan College at Aligarh for the purpose of introducing English education among the Muslims. Under the influence of British teachers of the college, Sir Syed finally turned away from cooperation with the nationalist movement which was slowly developing with the establishment of the Congress in 1885. At this stage, the British authorities were trying their best to direct the growth of consciousness among the Muslims along the line of district and suspicion towards the Congress, identifying the latter as a Hindu organization. True, at this time only a small number of Hindu leaders and fewer Muslim leaders were involved in this exercise. The majority of people were away from the scene of action: Syed Ahmed Khan started the Muslim Education Conference which had its annual sessions at the same time as the sessions of the Congress. Surendranath Banerjee regretted: "We were straining every nerve to secure the cooperation of our Mohammedan fellow countrymen...".[4] In 1893, the Mohammedan Anglo-Oriental Defence Association was started with British encouragement. One of its objectives was to "protect the political rights of the Muslims."[5]

The reforms of 1909 introduced separate electorate for the Muslims. But the ground was prepared by the colonial bureaucracy with meticulous care. Following Lord Curzon's idea of Council of Princes to checkmate the Congress, Minto suggested the idea to Morley, the Secretary of State for India. Morley replied,"Be sure that before long, the Mohammedans will throw in their lot with the Congressman against you...."[6] Minto took the hint and proceeded to put it into effect. Col. Dunlop Smith, Private Secretary to the Viceroy, wrote to the Principal of the Aligarh College intimating the readiness on the part of the Viceroy to receive a deputation of the Muslims.[7] Under the prodding of the Principal, the Secretary of the college Nawab Mohsin-ul-Mulk constituted a 35-member strong deputation led by Aga Khan, which met the Viceroy on 1 October 1906, and claimed special representation for the Muslim community.[8] The Viceroy agreed to the demand and said, "You justly claim that your position should be estimated not only on your numerical strength, but in respect to the political importance of your community...."[9]

It is not surprising that the Viceroy regarded it as a "very eventful day", and an "epoch in the Indian history."[10] Perhaps, more to the point were the words of an official who communicated with Morley, the Secretary of State, in the following manner:

> "I must send Your Excellency a line to say that a very, very big thing has happened to-day. A work of statesmanship that will affect India and Indian history for many a long year. It is nothing less than the pulling back of sixty-two millions of people from joining the ranks of the seditious opposition."[11]

The All India Muslim League was established in 1906. The Morley-Minto Reforms (1909) put the seal of official approval on the doctrine of minority representation on the basis of the concept of religious communities. It was a pernicious doctrine, and Mohammad Ali admitted as much when he said, "... certain Anglo-Indian officials sowed discord between the Hindu and Mohammedan communities by showing special favours to the Muslims."[12]

Thus, the stage was set by the British for a number of Muslim leaders having substantial economic standing to advance the politics of separate interests, separate representation on grounds of being a 'minority religious' community, thereby seeking to legitimize non-cooperation with the Congress and the nationalist movement led by it. To be sure, the masses of Muslims were yet unaffected by such ideas. For, these Muslim leaders with no mass following worth the name could not possibly bring the Muslim people to their side unless there were opportunities in the shape of conducive situations to influence Muslim public opinion in the desired direction. The Congress, however, laid itself bare, perhaps unwittingly to the charges of presenting precisely such opportunities in the thirties and forties. Not that the Muslim League was not intransigent. But evidently it was the

Congress which wanted to secure the cooperation of the Muslims in the nationalist struggle. And so, by implication the responsibility for ensuring Muslim cooperation devolved on the Congress. This is not to say that British "divide and rule" policy was responsible for the communal problem and the partition of India. Such stratagem is to be expected, and the strategy to counter it should have been carefully thought out be the nationalist leadership. This is what appeared to be absent in the early phase of the nationalist movement when contrary developments within and outside the movement were not adequately censured. Despite strongly criticizing the Morley-Minto Reforms at the Lahore session of 1909 for making 'unjust' distinction between Muslims and non-Muslims, the Congress, in effect, accepted the concept of minorities and separate electorate. This became evident, later, when the Congress entered into agreements and pacts with the League.

Towards the end of the nineteenth century, Tilak used religious appeal for political mobilization. In the early years of the twentieth century, religious language and imagery were extensively used by extremist Congressmen, revolutionary terrorists and the leaders of the Swadeshi movement in Bengal, where the anti-partition agitation was gathering momentum. It is very likely that such widespread use of religion for political purposes prompted Muslim leaders to feel that Muslim interests would suffer unless the same is done to boost Muslim identity.

The Congress strategy for securing cooperation and participation of the Muslims in the nationalist movement was one of unity from above, that is, pacts and agreements with the leaders. The discussion between the leaders almost invariably focussed not on "protection" and "safeguards", but on guarantee of jobs for the "lower-middle class and the urban intelligentsia."[13] The inability of the Congress to approach the Muslim masses to develop their consciousness along secular, democratic, and anti-imperialist lines[14] was the most glaring deficiency in the Congress strategy. The momentous years between 1927-29 offered unusual opportunities for arriving at a creative understanding between the two communities. In the Muslim League session at Calcutta in 1927, Jinnah offered to negotiate with the Congress on the question of framing a constitution for India on certain conditions "under which the League might forego" its claim to separate electorates.[15] The demand for parity of status was one of these conditions which was atleast worth a discussion. Another opportunity came next year (1928) when the Nehru Report was discussed. Jinnah asked for 33 per cent of the seats to be reserved for Muslims at the centre (instead of the 25 per cent given) and statutory majority in Punjab and Bengal. The latter was not easy to accept, but 33 per cent of seats could have been accommodated as part of a deal. The Round Table conferences were a disappointment for Gandhi, and for Jinnah as well who wanted a friendly atmosphere for discussion. The end of the eventful decade of the thirties witnessed another important opportunity slip by. In the 1937 elections, the Congress made a better showing than the League for which the results were pathetic. In spite of feelers from the

League, the Congress quite firmly refused to give reasonable accommodation to the League in ministry-making. Such a decision appeared rational, but completely lacked foresight. In retrospect, it proved to be a serious mistake. For, that was the real parting of ways between the League and the Congress. Why is it that so many moves to solve the communal problem at the political level failed in the pre-independence period. Several questions comes up when one examines the sequence of events, the formal or informal remarks and statements by important leaders on both sides. The League was not a mass organization at the time. The Congress formed ministries, but some gestures could have been made to avoid antagonizing the League in U.P. where it was tied up with *Zamindari* interests. Alternatively, 'socially radical measures' and Muslim mass-contact programmes should have been vigorously pursued. It will be true to say that for the Congress in the late thirties it could have been a counsel of despair. The search for a political community was given up in the quest for political power.[16]

Partition and communal holocaust connected with it left a deep dent in people's mind on both sides of the border and belied all hopes of a peaceful co-existence of the two major communities. A variety of developments in the post-independence period added to the proliferation and diversity to the communal problem. The political system in India has rapidly undergone several important changes, especially after the mid-sixties. These are systematic devaluation of institutional functioning and increasing centralization of state power and social intervention. Politics appear to be almost entirely devoid of ideals and values, and has instead become a question of elections squabbles regarding sharing of seats, coalitions, compromises and facile rationalization. Communication links between civil society and the political society have worn themselves thin, as growing inequality, conspicuous consumption, and the inability to the state to even soften the blows of poverty, unemployment, and falling standards of living have prompted more and more groups, communities and individuals to take to a variety of forms of protest. In such a situation, communalism of different forms is bound to thrive. Communalism is not so much an ideology as a device, an escape, a means of attaining almost invariably non-secular goals,[17] a form of propaganda and control. It could equally be an exercise in 'authoritarian populism'. Scholars have commented on the spurt in popular religiosity in the form of festivals which sometimes last for many days, something that hardly even happened before.[18] Popular religiosity has lately received a big boost in the concept of *Hindutva* and the massive propaganda it received in the politico-religious campaigns of the Bharatiya Janata Party. A dedicated secular activist has pointed out that communalism is a 'universal phenomenon' though he has not told us when the assertion of communal identity becomes dangerous. Among some of the most disturbing and problematic aspects of communalism and communal violence are the involvement of large number of people who do not fall into the category of the deprived or the wounded, and the typical pattern of response that they exhibit. It is as though frequent repetition has created a structure of though and action in the minds of men which takes care to cause such incidents repeatedly over time.

Today communal violence has become more widespread and complex than ever before. Close to six decades after independence, we do not seem to have progressed far in the direction of controlling incidents of communal violence. It has assumed new forms, become larger in scale and brutal in character. Communalism has become part of organized, modern politics. Communalism has twin aspects of being exclusive in outlook and full of antagonism for others who do not share the same religious beliefs. A person with communal consciousness is one who attempts to present his own religious community as the only relevant category for understanding the world around it and acting to safeguard or advance interests projected by him and those who share his perceptions. Politics and other social relations will naturally come within the ambit of such perceptions. Rasheeduddin Khan says that "communalism is a perversion of religion from a moral order to a temporal arrangement of contemporary convenience from a faith into a constituency, from a strategy of living into a tactics of politics".[19]

Communal outlook gains ground among co-religionists when an exaggerated or imaginary fear of other communities is promoted.

Today communalism has become more widespread and complex than ever before. More than half-a-century after independence, it seems, as though, we have given up all hopes of bringing about a solution to this intractable problem.

The attainment of freedom solved none of those problems, the roots of which lay in the pre-independence period. Communalism is one of them. An analysis of communalism, under colonial administration, shows it up as a predominantly political and economic maneuver. It was not the clash of religion or culture that provided the motive force behind communal politics, but protection of the material interests of the landholder rich, lower-middle class, and urban intelligentsia. As Moin Sharir put it, "Thus, certain classes within a community, and not the whole community, had a vested interest in communalism".[20] The Muslim League had no mass following worth the name until 1937. The Congress approach to national unity was also flawed. It preferred unity from the top, and whenever Muslim mass contact was considered more desirable, the effort put behind it was not vigorous as there were communal elements within the Congress and there were pressures from Hindu communal parties, like the Hindu Mahasabha.

Communalism continued to thrive in independent India. The state declared itself as secular, but society was not secular. Wherever secularism has worked successfully, it has done so because society is secular. The state has provided constitutional safeguards, political parties have made promises and public discourse has been full of rhetorical exhortations, but the incidence of communal violence has not diminished. The reasons are many and varied. One of the sections of population consisting rural and urban small capitalists, traders, and businessmen is prone to communal thinking. A large chunk of money and electoral support for communal parties come from this section. These people have little hope of graduating to big-time capitalists; they are inconvenienced by governmental regulations, price-control, labour-legislation, trade unionism, human rights and child labour restrictions, and interventions by the judicial decisions. Many of them were refugees who suffered as a result of partition and the riots that followed. Their political priorities are a government and a party that is particularly sympathetic to their economic interests and gives them a more or less free-hand in running their business. A significant portion of the Indian middle-class also has similar background, and support communal parties. Together, they along with a sizable number of the economically depressed sections (including the urban underclass and those grown-up people who have come to the cities and towns in search of a living) are situated in a grey area where tradition and modernity meet in a curious, complex amalgam.

Political parties and the so-called non-political 'cultural' organizations promote communal sentiments or deliberately pursue a communal strategy as part of build-up for elections or for consolidation and creation of an effective social base. For this purpose, false propaganda, communal interpretations of actions, and engineering of situations that could lead to a communal flare-up are often resorted to by political parties. There are parties and organizations which are almost openly communal or present veiled version of it. Whenever communalism is resorted to as part of a political strategy, the goal is creation of a constituency and capture of political power, at any level, local or national. But, there is another purpose for which sometimes communal politics is resorted to mostly in a covert way. The larger framework to which this kind of communal incitement belongs is 'authoritarian populism'. Since the latter half of the seventies as sections of population began losing faith in government intentions and ability to remove poverty or to redistribute income in any meaningful way, a variety of groups and organizations sprung up representing disillusionment, discontent as well as a search for new ways of exerting pressure, and spreading a more broad-based awareness of the human situation. It is in these directions that new political theory is moving. But socio-economic mobilization of organized or not-so-organized kinds which took to protesting and demonstrating met with not only ruthless suppression by state authority, but also the phenomenon of authoritarian populism. A feature of this style of politics is the widespread use of rhetoric by the state for popular mobilization, usually the economically marginal and poor, for the purposes of gaining their support and at the same time controlling them. Sometimes communal fracas of different degrees form part of this politics, more so when society is multi-ethnic, multi-religious as in India. This can always go with selective suppression of protest demonstrations and flare-ups within the society. Authoritarian populism not only helps a certain kind of capitalist development particularly where indigenous capitalism is weak, but also encourages authoritarian decision-making by the state. The upsurge in Hindu nationalism since 1980 was a case in point, although much of its fruits, in terms of electoral gains, were later cornered by the Bharatiya Janata Party.

Muslims face a different set of problems. M.R.A. Baig points out, "partition left the Muslims without their acknowledged leadership, the Muslim League, separate electorate, and leading professional men."[21] The gap is filled by communally-oriented leadership who are more keen on keeping their hold on the masses than in clarifying matters or leading them towards acquiring modern education and skills for significant improvement of their economic position. As long as Muslims stay away from modernization, they will continue to be dominated by traditional elites among them, whereas the modern Muslim elites will find it extremely difficult to exercise influence or build a following among them. The traditional or revivalist leadership keep the poor Muslims in "mental mohallas"[22] from which they have to get out and take advantage of the many opportunities that exist. Education, including training in particular vocations, setting up of business enterprise, the habit of thrift and, generally, cultivating a desire to do well and go forward rather than staying put in a medieval ambience. Zafar Imam writes, "... Within the present limitations of the socio-economic and political structure of contemporary India, there is hardly any social base existing for such modernization of the Indian Muslim Society."[23] This was perhaps true for the Muslims seen as a community in 1970. But opportunities, and to an extent social awareness, have increased since then. If necessary reforms cannot be agreed upon by the community, individual enterprise also can be effective. This will help a more useful modern approach to replace the medieval outlook within which a large number of poor Muslim peasants and urban workers are confined. Abad Ahmad emphasizes, "educational and economic upliftment, and an environment of security and trust" to be provided for paving the way to modernization.[24] Liberal Muslims in politics, education or in other occupations would, hopefully, show more initiative, and earn acceptance within the community to be able to influence others. This can be done by social service and participating in, competitive democratic politics more vigorously.

At the same time, Hindus can take the initiative to change the image of the 'other community' held by them, and liberal Muslims can reciprocate. To a considerable extent, it is this image that tends to generate communal thinking when the incitement is present. But Hindus and Muslims will have to generate the thrust from within themselves.

There is little doubt that communal sentiments are propagated in a variety of forms. Religious ideas are packaged for mass consumption, and religion is being commercialized.[25] Festivals, television serials, some apparently innocuous state ceremonies, and above all, political discourse do by intent and, sometimes, inadvertently create suspicion and distrust which foster communal thinking. Democratic citizens' organizations should exert pressure on the government and political parties, while national debates, inducement to modernization and political participation can also act as long-term correctives.

Notes and References

1. Moin Shakir, *State and Politics in Contemporary India,* Delhi, 1986, p. 164. Also, Asghar Ali Engineer, *Communalism and Communal Violence in India,* New Delhi, 1989.
2. Cf. Gyanendra Pandey, *The Construction of Communalism in Colonial North India,* Delhi, 1992.
3. V.P.S. Raghuvanshi, *Indian Nationalist Movement and Thought,* Agra, 1959, pp. 60–61.
4. Surendranath Banerjee, *A Nation in Making,* cited in Raghuvanshi, *op. cit.,* p. 63.
5. Mehta and Patwardhan, *The Communal Triangle in India,* cited in Raghuvanshi, *op. cit.,* p. 64.
6. Mary, Countess of Minto, *India: Minto and Morley, 1905-10,* cited in Raghuvanshi, *op. cit.,* p. 106.
7. Mehta and Patwardhan, *op. cit.,* cited in Raghuvanshi, *op. cit.,* p. 107.
8. Raghuvanshi, *op. cit.,* p. 107.
9. *Ibid.,* p. 107.
10. *Ibid.,* p. 107.
11. *Ibid.,* pp. 107–8.
12. *Ibid.,* p. 108.
13. Moin Shakir, *op. cit.,* p. 164. Also, Bipan Chandra, *Nationalism and Colonialism in Modern India,* New Delhi, 1979, pp. 253--54.
14. Bipan Chandra, *op. cit.,* p. 255.
15. Hiren Mukherjee, *Recalling India's Struggle for Freedom,* Delhi, 1983, p. 118.
16. B.B. Sarkar, *Nationalism and Marxism in India: Quest for People and Power, 1920-40,* Delhi, 1990, p. 129.
17. Moin Shakir, *op. cit.;* Asghar Ali Engineer, *op. cit.*
18. See Bipan Chandra, *op. cit.;* Rajni Kothari, *State Against Democracy,* Delhi, 1988.
19. Rasheeduddin Khan, 'Communalism and Secularism in Indian Polity', *Mail1stream,* 28 February 1987.
20. Moin Shakir, *State and Politics in Contemporary India, op. cit.*
21. M.R.A. Baig, 'Enlightened Communalism', *Seminar,* No. 125, January 1970, p. 13.
22. *Ibid.,* p. 14.
23. ZafarImam, 'Modernization', *Seminar,* No. 125, January 1970, p. 17.
24. Abid Ahmad, 'Economic Participation', *Seminar,* No. 125, January 1970, p. 28.
25. Rajni Kothari, *State Against Democracy: In Search of Humane Governance,* Delhi, 1988, p. 250.

24

Secularism: The Search for a Theory

Bibekbrata Sarkar

In recent times, we have witnessed a polarization of political debate between communalism and secularism in India. While the discourse on communalism has already reached intensity and sways that demands startled attention, the case for secularism has so far lacked the necessary momentum. Conflicting interpretation of India's culture, political legacy and history are being pressed into service to strengthen the case of both communalism and secularism. There seems to be no doubt that in the near future new controversies will develop around the aspects of India's nationalist past. Two points need to be mentioned here in connection with secularism and nationalist politics. When Gandhi became the supreme leader of the Indian National Congress in 1920, one of his most important priorities was to unite the diverse population of India into one political community in order to be in a position to challenge effectively the modern political framework set up by the colonial government, as well as to simultaneously lay the foundations of a future Indian polity. The Congress was made the model of a miniature political community. It offered a platform and a political context with nationalism as its ideological mooring within which a variety of political groups could meet and work together for a common political goal without having to merge their independent identities. To this end, the Gandhian Congress allowed everyone a membership of more than one organization, and negotiated with the leadership of other representatives organizations outside the Congress, like the Muslim League, the Hindu Mahasabha, the Scheduled Castes Federation, etc. However, as the decade of the thirties advanced, it became increasingly clear that the desired unity of the anti-colonial struggle was already impaired by exclusive, contending mobilizations on the basis of religion, caste, and tribe. Communalism emerged as the single-most important factor disrupting the formation of an effectively unified political community of all Indians.

To advocate secular stance under such circumstances was, therefore, only natural for a party, like the Congress. But, though secularism remained at a policy level and was an article of faith for some of the most popular Congress leaders, it never became the subject matter of a popular discourse. Secular ideas and values did not become the focal point of the Congress Party's nationalist preaching.

In the colonial period, there was an absence of a "secular" disclosure per se simply because 'nationalist' discourse was thought of as all-encompassing, and it was believed that it included in it "secular" discourse as well. It was also felt that the 'nationalist' discourse was capable enough to neutralize communal appeal. Hence, the absence of a separate secular discourse from the Congress. Communists also assumed that Marxism could take care of communalism through its stress on class struggle. The Socialists, however, thought that communalism should be tackled specifically at the political level. In recent times, the old "nationalist" discourse has lost its legitimacy and, hence, the capacity to counter "communal discourse". This is mainly due to:

1. Loss of legitimacy of "nationalist elites".
2. Fading memory of both partition and nationalism.
3. Crisis of political institutions leading to breakdown of channels of communication in the political arena which defines the political community. This has inevitably led to the growing appeal of sectarian politics at the grassroots level.
4. The old idea of nationalism itself is facing problems. An attempt has been made in recent times by the BharatiyaJanata Party and its allied organizations to redefine nationalism in terms of '*Hindutva*'. On the other hand, the Congress, which continues to regard itself as the heir to the heritage of the freedom struggle, has not yet tried to formulate an alternative view of nationalism under changed circumstances. The emotional and idealistic fervour of the freedom struggle is no longer present to lend strength and credence to the nationalist ideas of those days.

As a result of the growing inability of old nationalism to counter the new communal discourse, a need has been felt even by the ruling elites to put together a secular discourse even though secularism is a principle and policy of the Indian state. This discourse and the public language used by the Congress party now is no more than a condemnation of communalism. It is not a coherent thesis on the political credentials of secularism. It is at best a secular discourse by proxy.

In India, secularism could not come as a result of historic struggles as in the West, but was introduced as a principle of state policy for a heterogeneous society. Secularism could have drawn sustenance from the religious, universalist, rationalist, and humanist works of eminent Indians, like Raja Rammohan Roy, Akshay Kumar Dutta, the early writings of Syed Ahmed Khan, Swami Vivekananda, and others. These 'cultural-ideological' movements were directed against certain aspects of the traditional social structure, like caste, religion, marriage, family, education, language as well as colonial culture and westernization.[1]

Before any of these trends could bring about significant advances towards the development of a secular consciousness, new political urgencies came to the forefront. The rise of mass movements and modern politics brought with it the desire on the part of interested groups to arrive at political equations of accommodation and maximum advantage in the emerging political scenario. There was parallel or 'counter-mobilization' on the planks of religion, caste, ethnicity or cultural distinctiveness of Hindus, Muslims, Scheduled Castes, and the tribals to increase respective bargaining power with the Congress and the British government. Such primordial appeals were highly emotive and 'identity-defining'. The prodding of the colonial government was a major factor in bringing into existence forces and claims that divide nationalist ranks. The desire to protect religious identity and integrity as well as the desire to resist colonial cultural onslaught sharpened the emphasis on sectarian mobilization thus marginalizing the rationalist and universalist traditions of the 19th century socio-cultural movements.[2] At the same time, both Nationalists and Marxists tended to ignore the cultural components of politics, political movements, and consciousness. Consequently, the masses that joined the anti-colonial struggle were socially and culturally grounded in non-secular or anti-secular values.

Even though Gandhi's political programmes included cultural movements, like removal of untouchability and temple entry of the Harijans, these were seen as extensions of his Hindu religious outlook. Gandhi's religious symbolism, singing of devotional songs at meetings, the concept of 'ashram' life and non-violence rather firmly implanted his image as the supreme leader of the Hindu nationalist movement designed to establish Hindu political domination over Muslims and domination of the upper castes over scheduled castes and the tribal population. It was apparently a convenient excuse to ignore Gandhi's secular credentials as a political leader, as an individual, and the concept of secularism he represented. In a sense, it was the biggest failure of the anti-colonial struggle.

Gandhi was a religious man and his secularism flowed from the belief that all religions are paths to the 'supreme being' and 'truth' and so claim to equal respect and treatment by all, including the state. This was a view that pleads for the religious amity or a high degree of mutual toleration in a multi-religious society. At the same time, there is demarcation of distinct social groups on the basis of religion.

Jawaharlal Nehru, the chief architect of India's secular state politics after 1947, was more outspoken and less misunderstood than Gandhi. Nehru's efforts at curbing communalism and helping the growth of a secular temper in India was more rationalist, modernist, and extensive than those of perhaps any other leader. In a decade and a half, during which he led the country and shaped its politics, Nehru created the discourse, framed policies and directed its administration to spread the ideas of a secular society and politics indirectly. In the process, no doubt, he was also consciously preparing the ground for the acceptance as well as smooth functioning of the Nehruvian mode which he had set before the country. Nehru tirelessly campaigned against communalism, casteism, and sectarianism of every kind and urged people to inculcate scientific temper and a modern outlook. His exhortations were path-breaking and undoubtedly valuable, but not an unmixed success. One of the reasons is that it is not easy for people to give up a pattern of confined thought when that is perceived to constitute the basis of social identity and consciousness of a person. This does not show the futility of discourse, but highlights the need for a more appropriate public language backed up with action to make it more effective. True, these are aspects of the social structure that are hard to change. But selective aspects can be reformed, or their rigorous impact can be considerably diminished through a combination of discourse and action. This has happened in the past. Even when movements for reform failed, they still become and remain a cause to champion. One of the surely unintended offshoots of the Nehruvian policy of protecting the sensitivities of religious minorities was to strengthen a tendency on their part to remain an exclusive group with a conceptually distinct and, therefore, separate, religio-cultural entity of their own.

Since the conflicting demands of religious, caste, and tribal groups for a share in the emerging power equation of post-freedom India could not be amicably settled within a framework of common understanding during the colonial days, the sectarian political scene. For a while, however, these lay submerged under the surging tide of expectations following independence.

By the end of the sixties, as the euphoria of independence gave way to despair because of sharp economic disparities, traditional caste, linguistic, religious, regional, tribal clan and kinship loyalties re-emerged with a vengeance to put pressure on the state for a share in the fruits of development threatening to disrupt all that was still in the pressure of being built with expectation and hope, like national integration, political democracy, economic welfare, and the reduction of socio-economic disparities.

As the pressure on the system increased, the levels of commitment and sincerity dwindled. Representative and pluralist democracy gave way to populism, emotional demagoguery, and increased repression by the state at all levels. The inability or unwillingness on the part of the state to tackle the sharpening distribution crisis prompted more and more people to move out of the ambit of institutional functioning and organize for independent action for redressal of grievances. Such action took place on varying scales and at different levels of society. Although the root cause is almost always economic, they manifest themselves in different ways, increasingly eroding the credibility and reach of the state. In such circumstances, institutions become largely dysfunctional and the state's legitimacy is sharply compromised, especially as one moves into the countryside where money, caste, class, patronage as well as poverty and desperation are most easily translated into violence, and yet, as long as the situation continues, institutions can neither be renewed or replaced by new ones, forcing the state to resort more and more to problem-solving devices as well as trying to divert people's attention in a variety of ways.

Rebuilding of institutions and reinforcing institutional functioning require redefinition of social goals and matching discourse to familiarize people with new goals which can instil hope and bring back a reasonable degree of social peace, the terrain on which institutions can function.

The legacy of mutual suspicion and rivalry, as mentioned above, prevented the emergence of a unified political consciousness in those days when the settings was that of anti-colonial struggle in which every group was interested. As a result, we were left with a social consciousness which was itself fragmented in terms of beliefs and rivalries of locality, customs, caste, and creed.

After independence and with the onset of parliamentary democracy, the type of political consciousness that emerged was not more than the extension of this fragmented social consciousness inherited from the past. Consequently, a distinct political consciousness, which is identifiable separately from social consciousness, is hard to find.

That makes politics in India a vehicle of conflicting primordial loyalties in this country. Another contributory factor is the uneven development of the civil society in India. Crass commercialism thrives in friendly cooperation with semi-feudal attitudes and structures. The natural consequences of this state of unevenly developed civil society are:

1. The absence of a civic code of behaviour, and
2. The blurring of the distinction between the priorities of the private and the public spheres often resulting in a spelling-over of one into another.

Our code of behaviour primarily consists of the norms we are taught to practice within the nuclear and the extended family. But as soon as we go out into the larger world where the family norms are no longer applicable, we are at a loss to decide as to what should be the norms for the public sphere of life. This kind of a confused response to the impersonality and competitiveness of the larger society (i.e., public life) frequently creates anarchic situations.[3] In the West, secularization of social relations helped to stabilize social mobilization in favour of modernization. There could be, however, difference of opinion on the desirability of modernization on western lines.

Culture theorists have opposed the western version of secularism on the basis of certain arguments that need to be carefully examined. Ashis Nandy explains that secularism as known to a westerner means that religious tolerance can come only from devaluation of religion in public life and from the freeing of politics from religion.[4] We propose a qualified acceptance of the second part of the above statement. The qualifications to bear in mind will be made to explicit later. As far as the first part is concerned, lets draw attention to the fact that in the West and elsewhere in the world, liberation theology is not only making waves in the civil society, but is certainly contributing to the linking up of religion with public affairs. There are other efforts also by religious personalities to take active interest in matters of public concern.[5] In recent times, such activities have been most prominent in Nicaragua, Brazil, and parts of Africa. Nandy feels that secularism stops all "dialogues between the public and the private within a person, and between politics and culture", and that "culture is frozen in time."[6] Since there is a proposing of secularization of the political community,[7] and not of the entire civil society, there is no need to stop all dialogues. But, even if there is secularization of the whole society as in the West, it is difficult to accept that the creative world of the private person would cease to interact with the larger reality outside. Again, the Indian concept of secularization expects the Indian state to follow secular policies, and it has not so far tried seriously to secularize the society. It has also not banished religion and ethnicity from society,[8] Nandy says that nation-states are by definition "suspicious nature."[9] In fact, culture is being extensively used in support of nation-states today. Nandy's assertion that official secularism attempts to limit the democratic process by truncating the personality of the citizen[10] does not appear to be well-founded. A look at the spate of religious and ethnic mobilizations in India, today, should dispel any such idea. As long as religion is allowed to influence the symbols and language of political interaction, it should be expected that a political leader or an ordinary citizen who is not secular and does not share the morals of Gandhi will use religion for maneuvering public sentiments in his preferred manner.

T.N. Madan argues "in the prevailing circumstances, secularism in South Asia as a generally shared credo of life is impossible, as a basis for state action impracticable, and as a blueprint for the foreseeable future impotent."[11] From the above, one could get the impression that both Madan and Nandy have taken their assertions as unalterable facts. People in India are perhaps not as intensely religious in their everyday behaviour as implied above. Religious and cultural tolerance are evident in popular culture as it is in the market-place.

It may be useful here to put the problem in the form of a specific question. Are we obliged by nature, habit of thinking, or conviction to allow emotive manipulation of large numbers of people in the name of religion, ethnicity or culture? Such mobilization is frequently used to secure political goals. So, if our reply to the question posed above is negative, then secularization of the language and symbols of politics constituting all forms of communication is a necessity. Unlike in the West, where secularism as a principle of state policy and as a way of life came about as the result of historical struggles, in India secularization of the political sphere will have to be brought about by designed, without intervention in other areas of civil society. This is possible if state-policy does not discriminate between religions, and is combined with a sustained discourse.

Among those who have recently expressed their views on secularism, Badrinath Chaturvedi says that "contesting polarities" of the kind that religion and secularism represent are alien to the Indian mind.[12] He proposes a version of secularism which is based on India's '*dharmic*' tradition, beginning with a "secular analysis of everyday experience" to "draw our attention to the transcendent reality that manifests itself through everyday life". This, in his opinion, will end the alienation of Indians from their own heritage.[13] The problem with such prescriptions is not the concept of '*Dharma*' which is materialist and consists of philosophical generalizations drawn from everyday experience, but the acceptability of a Hindu concept by other religious communities.

That, in a way, poses the problem. Civil society in India is rapidly coming under the pressure of exclusive mobilizations, religious, ethnic, and tribal groups are not only organizing themselves on sectarian lines, but are also assuming increasingly militant postures. A situation like this does not come up all of a sudden. Over the years, nationalism of pre-independence vintage has become completely devoid of its force and appeal. The Nehruvian as well as the post-Nehruvian promises of making a significant dent in the disparity of income is no longer regarded as a target to be achieved in the foreseeable future. The sustained decay and devaluation of established procedures have deprived the ordinary citizen of much of the sense of certainty, and dependence on the force of law. All these, together, have helped to bring to the forefront movements and mobilizations based on primordial loyalties, popular, and democratic struggles reflecting a variety of grievances. This leads to the breakdown of the social and political community, of the consent manufacturing processes within the civil society, which, in turn, leads to the absence of decisive majority for any political party, to coalition governments, and crises of governability. The commotion in the civil society and the eventual breakdown of the channels of regular communication among social groups and of social groups with the power canters is made particularly complex and intractable when primordial loyalties assume dominance. Hence, the need for secularization of the political community.[14]

NOTES AND REFERENCES

1. K.M. Panikkar, *Culture and Consequences in Modem India,* PPH, New Delhi, 1990, p. 35.
2. See Bipin Chandra, *et.al., India's Struggle for Independence,* 1857–1947, Penguin Books, 1989, p. 90.
3. Public Language is found in Indian Media, official writing and intellectual expressions and include term like casteism, communalism, parochialism, provincialism, obscurantism with of course neagative cannotaion.

4. Ashis Nandy, "An Anti-Secularist Manifesto", *Seminar,* No. 34, October 1985, p. 14.
5. The Vatican has officially admitted that a section of the clergy is "closely involved in social activism" BBC broadcast, *World Newsweek,* dated 11th October, 1992.
6. Ashis Nandy, *op. cit.,* 1985, p. 15.
7. *Ibid.,* p. 16.
8. *Ibid.,* p. 14.
9. *Ibid.,* p. 15.
10. *Ibid.,* p. 17.
11. T.N. Madan. "Secularism in its Place", *The Journal of Asian Studies,* Vol. 46, No. 4, 1987, p. 748.
12. Badrinath Chaturvedi, "Dharma is not Religion: Misconception has to be Removed", *The Times of India,* New Delhi, 20th January, 1980, p. 8; Badrinath Chaturvedi, "The Quest for India's Secular Identity," *The Times of India,* New Delhi, 28th February, 1990, p. 9.
13. Badrinath Chaturvedi, "The Quest for India's Secular Identity," *The Times of India,* New Delhi, 28 Februay, 1990, p. 9.
14. A political community is formed when citizens are linked with one another and with the political authority in terms of political interests as well as through the use of common public language.

25

Regionalism

Manju Subhash

A state is a political entity. It provides a forceful identity to its citizens. In predominantly monolingual and monocultural societies, a state was formed around unitary symbols, one language, one religion, one culture, and in its extreme manifestation, one party and one leader. In a dominant monolingual, monocultural nation-state, different dominant groups seek national identity in their terms. Multiplicity and variation are the key concepts in a pluricultural state. In such a state, recognition and management of diverse identities is a challenge before the politicians and political scientists.

India's fundamental integrative ethos and its self-identity have been drawn from a social reality that is composed of great diversity and plurality, running across which there are certain major cultural streams, and a cultural elite that shape and interpret these streams. Until recently, up to the growth of the national movement and founding of the Indian Republic, what held Indians together was the basic identity of being a civilization tied together by a set of values, by a set of cultural norms, and by an interpreting elite first within the broad stream of *Hinduism,* which, itself had an extremely plural framework and, then through a multicultural, multiethnic, and ultimately multi-national society, which we are now.[1]

Today, all over the world, specific ethnic, linguistic and religious groups are seeking specific regional identities. *The International Encyclopedia of Social Sciences* defines a region "as a homogeneous area with physical characteristics, distinct from the rest of the country". Notwithstanding this definition, anthropologists think of region in terms of culture and seek to relate specific cultures to specific geographic environments.

Regionalism refers to amalgamation of states into geographical, cultural, economic or administrative regions, and to resemblances in politics and policies among such states. Regionalism is portrayed as the effort to meet an area's needs in such a way as to integrate the area into the national culture and economy.[2]

Regions and regionalism are relative to the context or the parameters within which they are referred to and/or meaningfully operative. The social boundaries of a region are more often than not elusive as regions are seldom homogeneous social groupings, differences within a region may be more significant than superficial similarities or traits. However, a combination of cultural and physical characteristics makes one area distinctive in some measure from another area.[3]

Differences in population characteristics or attitudes alone do not necessarily lead to regionalism. It is only when these differences are specifically recognized as a differentiating feature from other regions that they can produce, reinforce or sustain regionalism. In other words, regionalism has a political dimension that involves a consciousness of kind, a collective identity, and a defence of territorial interests. Regionalism involves the politicization of regional concerns and the articulation of regional commitments.[4] Januzzi argues that regional identities are shaped not only by shared language, culture and political consciousness, but also by economic variables.[5]

India has remained multi-lingual and multi-cultural from time immemorial. It has remained so, because variation is accepted and differences are respected making conflict and conciliation a continuous process. Regionalism is rooted in India's cultural and linguistic diversity. In fact, much of India's known history is regional in-between sub-continental empires. Since independence in 1947, cultural politics whether in the demand for linguistic states or in the controversy over Hindi as the national language, or in the nativism of the "sons of the soil" have deepened regional identities confirming Paul Brass that, despite periodic appearances to the contrary, the long-term tendency in India is towards pluralism, regionalism and decentralization. The politics of revivalism and sub-nationalism has created a dilemma for the state.[6]

Projected in geographic terms, it is at the state level both an ethnic and an economic phenomenon. It is an expression of heightened political consciousness, expanding participation and increasing competition for scarce resources. Economic grievances expressed in charge of unfairness, discrimination or centre's neglect may be fused with cultural anxiety over language status and ethnic balance. It is this fusion that gives regionalism its potency. Language and culture, like religion, are at the core of an individual's identity and when politicized take a potentially virulent form.[7]

The regional, sub-regional movements based on language, religion, ethnicity or culture, combine popular grievances from below with elements of manipulation from the above. The leadership of such regional movements seeks to institutionalize its own political authority. These movements are expressed as secessionist, communal, often nativist and parochial. There was a time when people fought for their country. In the next phase, people fought for their party. In the current phase of Indian politics, the predominant mood is to fight for individual's interest. Such regional movements seem to have been very powerful when economic issues are fused with cultural grievances, may be due to the hangover of communal killings and the partition; over-reaction of the leaders and government authorities led to the intensification of regional sentiments and its fallout agitations.

There are several models available for understanding the regional movements based on language, ethnicity, and nativist demands. More situation-specific demands have been developed. Some of the important models for analyzing the regional movements are discussed here.

A new state can be said to be passing through a process of reduction of its primordial sentiments to that of civil order. This transfer of sovereignty from a colonial power to an independent state is more than a mere shift. It is a transformation of the whole pattern of political life, a metamorphosis of subjects into citizens.[8]

The primordialists, therefore, have culture as their major asset. To them, ethnic identities are not 'chosen', but are 'given', *i.e.,* these identities proceed inexorably from the cultural past. Looked this way, they perceive ethnicity as ineluctable and immutable.[9]

The emphasis laid by the primordialists on certain attachments in the cultural sphere as part of personality-formation and development which persist with them through life, consciously, is well taken. There is no doubt that such affiliations provide the impetus and impulses for social and political mobilization. By necessary implication, these assumptions, in the form of cultural attachments tend to change. For among the various components of such a cultural core, one may assume preeminence at a time, but may be supervened by another as the focal point of group identity assertion.

Furthermore, the premise of primordial ties being particularistic, they are perceived as potential road-blocks in the process of national cohesion. It is also argued that since ethnic attachments pertain to the 'non-rational' domain of human personality they lead to social turbulence and violence and, thereby, tend to be dysfunctional in the development processes of the civil society.[10]

The primordialist view limits ethnicity to actual primordial ties. But some of these ties can be changed or acquired. For instance, sectarian and even linguistic affiliation can be changed during the life-time of an individual and can form the basis of ethnic identity. Secondly, even the 'ascriptive' identity of caste can also be acquired through appropriate mythologies, if it is founded on military power, and legitimized by priests. Thirdly, it is incorrect to argue that ethnic identities and boundaries remain fixed. On the contrary, they wax and wane according to situational contexts. Further, the mere presence of ethnic ties does not necessarily mean that they are ethnic formations. The latter are the result of political action.[11]

India is beset with virtually the entire range of primordial conflicts, and superimposed complexities. It has to be so. India, the vast and various labyrinths of religious, linguistic, racial, tribal, and caste allegiances is developing a many-sided political form. One peels off Punjabi linguism and finds Sikh religious communalism; scratches Tamil regionalism and finds anti-Brahman racialism; views Bengali cultural arrogance from a slightly different angle and sees Greater Bengal patriotism. No general and uniform political solution to the problem of primordial discontent seems possible in such situations, only a loose assemblage of diverse, locally adapted, *ad hoc* solutions, related to one another only incidentally and pragmatically. The policies suitable for the tribal dissidence of the Naga are not generalizable to the caste-based disaffection of peasant landlords in Andhra. The Central government's stance toward Orissa princes cannot be taken towards Gujarati industrialists. The problem of Hindu fundamentalism in Uttar Pradesh, the heart-land of Indic culture, takes a rather different form in Dravadian Mysore. So far as primordial issues are concerned, Indian civil politics amounts to a disconnected series of attempts to make the temporary endure.[12]

The rise of regionalism and of divisive forces is no more a phenomenon confined to the North-East or North-West. It has spread in every direction. The regional movements in the post-Independence India may be characterized as a response to the imposition of alien process of nation-building in the frame of a single political community. The process was supposed to erode all the so-called primordial identities and build up a single national community. Influenced by political modernization, the Indian elites also did put faith in this version of nation building. The civilizational base of our nation and pluralist identities were considered incongruent with the modernizing set-up. Soon, the rise of linguistic state demands and popular movements based on religious-ethnic demands exposed the Western notions. A tough dealing with these agitations was of no avail, most of the demands had to be acceded.[13] As the regional interest has become more powerful than the national outlook, sub-regional feelings have become even powerful than a regional outlook. The uneven economic development had led to increased inter-state and intra-state disparity resulting in a qualitative transformation of the Indian politics. The direction and process of transformation depends upon the ability of the regional movements and parties.[14] Regional movements are growing and have ascended to power in many states. Confirming that, though primordial groups and loyalties are traditional and predate even colonial rule, primordial discontents are also movements based on these frustration and are very often the result of independence and subsequent efforts at nation-building. Modern technology and knowledge have increased mobilizing potential of primordial loyalties faster than that of the political parties and other modern institutions. In political sphere, the processes of modernization are identified with secularization, participatory democracy, structural differentiation and replacement of ascriptive loyalties to the rulers by achieved loyalties on the basis of elections or other mechanisms of participation,[15] which, within a democratic framework, create a sense of self-awareness for identities based on region. The ethnic groups acquire an added importance as they fill a vacuum created by the decline of institutions.

Improvements in communications and transportation tend also to increase the cultural awareness of the minorities by making their members more aware of the distinctions between themselves and others. The ethnic conflict within the more industrialized, multi-ethnic states of Europe and North America seriously challenges the contention that modernization dissipates ethnicity,[16] which has been characterized as the new spectre haunting the power elites of our times, variously expressing itself as an assertion of cultures, of communal upsurges, revival of religious voices, and movements of marginalized peoples, regions, and nationalities.[17]

Modernization tends to create awareness of separate identities, and the situation calls for considerable ingenuity in the development of new patterns of federal association. The secessionist demands in the Naga region are being managed by the establishment of an independent Naga state known as Nagaland and the adoption of a flexible attitude in New Delhi towards the "Naga rebels" which has resulted in dissensions and divisions among the rebels. In Assam, the aspirations of the tribal party, the All Party Hill Leaders Conference (APHLC), have been accommodated by the establishment of a new kind of arrangement; a "subfederation" within the state of Assam with considerable internal autonomy and access to resources. Another constitutional innovation was tried earlier with respect to giving special status to Jammu and Kashmir.[18]

Impact of Modernization on Ethnicity

The process of modernization and development are caught up in the dialectics of their own dynamics, combating ethnic loyalty on the one hand and stimulating ethnic consciousness on the other. Consequently, whatever the level of the development of the state, ethnic conflicts need to be viewed as parts of an ongoing process which have to be coped with and managed, but cannot be resolved once for all except through the total assimilation or elimination of a particular group.

Modernization does not require the extinction of tradition. On the contrary, as Lucian Pye has put it, we must consider "what mixture, or rather fusion, of traditional and modern patterns will lead to national development. The effective operation of the society depends upon whether the traditional patterns of behaviour tend to reinforce and give greater substance and charity to the modern superstructure or whether they tend to undermine and disrupt the superstructure."[19] Once this general proposition is made, we must think in terms not of replacement, but of fusional structures.

There is another group of scholars. They are Marxist in approach and seek to examine regional phenomenon in the post-colonial third world countries, essentially in the light of the problem of nationalities and the path of development the country has treaded. The Marxists argue that primordial loyalties which constitute some of the key sources of regionalism rooted in pre-capitalist relations of production. In the post-colonial third world countries, capitalism coexists with feudalism. This forms the breeding ground of primordial loyalties.[20]

Karl W. Deutsch suggests that six dynamic factors that appear to determine the rate of assimilation. These are: (1) degree of similarity of communication habits; (2) the level of learning capacity on the one side and the teaching capacity on the other; (3) the frequency of contacts; (4) the material rewards and penalties; (5) the values and desires of groups; and, (4) the existence of any social and political symbols and/or actual barriers to assimilation. On the basis of these considerations, it would seem that relatively few of the ethnic conflicts in the currently developing world are likely to be resolved by assimilation, while the elimination of a particular group can only be genocidal and, therefore, an affront to human values and dignity.

In modernization theory, and in the Western scholar's concept of development, ethnic sentiment has been branded as primordial which would disappear in the course of development. But as ethnic factors came up to pose a challenge to the state, and the state development programmes held responsible for the marginalization of ethnic groups came to be attacked; modernization theory received a conceptual jolt. The new concepts as ethnicity, ethno-development, and ethno-politics have captured the stage of social science by surprise. These so-called primordial affiliations, far from being eroded, have set the tenor of politics in many third world countries including India.[21]

The model on which India is set is one of modernization of an ancient and highly-plural society in the context of an open polity[22] with unevenness of economic development in different parts of the country as one of the most dramatic contributory causes of regionalism in India.

❑ What Causes Regionalism in India?

The dynamic approach to regionalism views regions as not just different territories with different names and characteristics, but as units that must be understood in relation to one another. By analyzing how regions relate to one another within a country, we understand more clearly how power is distributed throughout that society. Regional characteristics can serve merely as benign descriptions unless people within explanations can be identified to understand the process of transformation of regional characteristics into a more political form of regional awareness which is the essence of regionalism.[23] These are:

1. Uneven development
2. Fear of losing cultural identity
3. Political domination
4. Personal and selfish motives of politicians

The two types of problem which India face: (1) to uplift the backward areas, and (2) check the unplanned growth of metropolitan centres.

Forces interacting between these two are to be regulated by region-specific judicial policy measures and, consequently, regional concepts are bound to be followed. The national planning is to be placed in the framework of regional planning.[24]

The Indian society, for all intents and purposes, has adopted a capitalist path of development. This path was preferred by the Indian bourgeoisie which took control over the state. It has encouraged the development of capitalist relations.[25] With the mechanization of farming industry and introduction of HYV (high-yielding varieties), chemical fertilizers, cooperative credit, and dependence on power-oriented water resources, agriculture is becoming more and more a capital and labour-intensive industry. This improved phenomena infield-produce resulting from these shifts in cultivation (popularly called, 'Green Revolution') has created a privileged class of rich farmers on the one hand and a pauperized stratum[26] of marginal farmers, landless peasants, and migratory labourers on the other hand.[27]

The uneven development of capitalism led to regional concentration of industrial development. The unmitigated sharpening of contradictions of capitalist economy has led to the growth of monopolies, concentration of wealth in fewer hands, and a slow pace of development on one side, and an increase in wage-erosion, unemployment, poverty, and crime on the other. The gap between expectation and achievement for a large mass of the population is increasingly widening. The state has tried to take the economy out of the woods from time to time by resorting to measures, like nationalization of financing institutions, devaluation of currency, borrowing and deficit budgeting. The maladies ingrained in the path of development, however, have defied all these remedial steps.[28] All of these changes took place in the context of heightened expectations regarding governmental performance in bolstering India's economy following Gandhi's *Garibi Hatao* (eradicate poverty) campaign in 1970-71. The costly Indo-Pakistan war over Bangladesh, however, and a series of droughts and floods in several states in 1971, 1972 and 1973, gradually undermined the economic gains of the late 1960s. International inflation accentuated by the oil emergency of 1973, added to rising prices in India and created a desperate situation for huge number of population living below the poverty line. In brief, increasing political centralization combined with failures in governmental planning led inexorably to a crisis of confidence and charges of mismanagement.[29] The growing contradictions of capitalist economy have obliged the state to play a more positive role in the crisis management. It has necessitated centralization of power at the governmental and the party levels on the one hand and unleashed a hostile regional reaction on the other. Hence, the failure of planning developed economic imbalances between states, regions, and sub-regions.

There are also inter-state migrations of labour which gave rise to the 'sons of soil movements' for restricting employment to local residents. The agrarian bourgeoisie, generally, welcomes migrant rural labour as it helps to push wage-rate down. Most of the sons of soil movements have been urban-based.

Many political issues have emerged because planning brought over centralization and the planning process failed to effectively deal with regional imbalances and, especially backward regions of the country. Regional assertions have emerged because of a feeling of deprivation and backwardness of some of the regions in India. Hence, regional political parties are demanding restructuring of the federal divisions of powers, especially transfer of financial resources from the centre to the states.

Regional imbalances are producing both prosperity and poverty between regions. Within the regions, they are also giving rise to the birth of two classes, rich and poor. Punjab, with the proud record of the highest per capita income during the sixties as a result of Green Revolution in India, represents a peculiar case of regionalism with heavy communal overtones. It also resulted in uneven development in different regions of the state. The fruits of the Green Revolution in the 1960s led to the rise of the regional bourgeoisie. The regional political parties and formations which came to prominence in 1967 represented the interests of the locally placed ruling class groups like the landlords and the *kulaks* in Punjab, Haryana, Western U.P., etc., or non-big-bourgeoisie in Tamil Nadu. The uneven development has not only increased disparity between the states, but also among different sections and regions within the state. Green Revolution created new areas of influence and strengthened the economic and political powers of the *kulaks*. Landless labourers, menial servants, and what is perhaps best categorized as a lumpen proletariat in urban areas, are neither significantly mobilized nor relatively economically improved as compared with the past because Green Revolution has been grabbed by just 20 per cent of Jat rich farmers who own more than 60 per cent of the total land.[30] It is this group of prosperous peasants who sought commanding positions in the Akali Dal as they were keen to match their economic muscle with political power. The Akali leadership which represented primarily the rich agrarian interests of the state took recourse to a rapidly religious path. It involves a combination of economic, cultural, and religious issues and at its core, the identity of the Sikh community.

A significant dimension of the contradiction born of the Green Revolution was the creation of new "cultures of deprivation."[31] Large numbers of Scheduled Castes and rural proletariat of the Sikh community felt alienated not only from the Akali Dal which was identified with the rich farmers who were Jats, but also from established Sikh institutions. To many among the socially and economically oppressed, it came to be identified as the religion of the oppressor, Jats who with 20 per cent of the Sikh population owned 60 per cent of land. Non-Jat Sikhs, such as the approximately 20 per cent of the Sikh population who are Scheduled Castes, tend to be anti-Jat and comprise an important element of the Congress party support base. Politically, economically, and numerically, Jats and after 1966, Jats Sikhs are most often the singlemost important group at the village level. In Punjab, the separatist identity has been strong among the Jat Sikhs, whereas non-Jats and Harijans are less involved in this sense of identity.

While the Green Revolution did not cause 'poverty' in Punjab, those who were not full participants in economic progress were placed in a position of at least "relative deprivation" as they perceived it.

The rural poor, though divided in various social, linguistic, and religious groups, share a common inferior status and a common experience of oppression and exploitation by rich farmers and state machinery. The rural poor who constitute the vast majority have at different times resorted to collective action and protest to express their aspirations and discontent against injustice perpetrated by the dominant class and the state which does not always protect their rights.

Jannuzi writes that political extremism in Punjab nurtured by Sant Jarnail Singh Bhindranwale, drew support in the early 1980s mainly from sections of the rural poor who had indeed been bypassed by the Green Revolution and whose interests did not coincide with the land-owning Jat Sikhs who have dominated the leadership of the Akali Dal.[32]

After the two partitions in 1947 and 1966, respectively, members from the displaced Sikh community were constantly searching for a homeland where they could be in a dominant position. It is considered as the root cause for regionalism in Punjab. It is rooted in the persistent struggle for authority between the ruling party at the centre and state government. They had a concern with the governance style of Indira Gandhi. It is also associated, paradoxically, with the Punjab's spectacular economic success after the mid-sixties. The economic success and political turmoil in Punjab are inextricably linked to the increasing expectations of the people mounting pressure on any government irrespective of its capacities and willingness to respond to pressure.

Here, it is important to recognize that both the assertion of a regional identity and its assimilation into a larger national identity have been essentially political coalitional processes.

Several cultural, historical, and political facts which reflected regional feelings in Jammu and Ladakh, consciousness of regional identity was not really sharp before independence. Internal communal tensions and cultural and political pulls from neighbouring Punjab inhabited the growth of this consciousness in Jammu. In the case of Ladakh, Tibet's spiritual and cultural domination dwarfed its personality.[33]

Regional divergence was widening by the controversy over the Centre-State relations. While Kashmiris demanded maximum autonomy for the state, regional urges of Jammu and Ladakh were articulated in the demand for maximum integration of the state with the Indian union.[34]

The fact, is that right from 26 October 1947, political power, decision-making, administration at higher levels, better deals in matters relating to employment, locations of prestigious institutions, and factories and funds for development have become the privileges of Kashmir alone with the people of Jammu and Ladakh becoming a hostage to the fickle leadership of the valley.

The regional identity of Jammu found its first effective though partial expression in the forum of the *Praja Parishad*, which was a coalition of hurt regional pride, protest against arbitrary rule, urge for share in power and democratic expression, a sense of insecurity about the future of the state, dispossessed feudal, and vested interests and Hindu communal sentiments. The coalition was articulated in the slogan of 'full accession' and abrogation of Article 370 which guarantees a special status for the state within India.

It is true that the people of Jammu, Kashmir, and Ladakh are belonging to different world views, social customs, and culture which are based on conflicting ideas and conceptions. They derive their inspiration from different historical sources. To keep together such people under a single state must lead to a growing discontent and ultimate destruction of any system that may be so built for the government of such a state.

The bifurcation of the state would be beneficial not only for the people of Jammu, Kashmir, and Ladakh, but for the whole of India. It would remove the suspicions generated in the minds of Kashmiris about regional and communal aspirations of the people of Jammu and Ladakh. The Kashmiris will be able to seek a future for them. They are bound to realize that they can find their real identity in democratic India rather than joining Pakistan or by acquiring independence.

It may be argued that Punjab, Assam, and Jammu and Kashmir are special cases because of their unique geographical locations, peculiar communal issues, and critical roles in preserving India's military security. There is no doubt that their internal politics and Centre-State relationships are extraordinarily vexed at present. But, in a very real sense all of the Indian states are special cases, each possessing particular historical, geographic, cultural or economic conditions which give rise to idiosyncratic problems of governance. Over half of the Indian states have sensitive international borders, and most have distinctive minorities whether communal, linguistic, tribal or regional. Virtually, every state lays claims to a special cultural heritage and most can mount a case for being "neglected" or "maltreated" by New Delhi.[35]

Regionalism may also manifest in the form of a movement for special privileges to the sons of the soil' against outsiders. The city of Mumbai is known for wide variety of linguistic, religious, and cultural communities. A political party, named, Shiv Sena, has demanded that outsiders will not be given employments to this city. The Shiv Sena has been particularly hostile to the Tamil migrants for grabbing the mid-range jobs sought by the local Marathi-speaking population.[36]

When an entire state is crowded with migrants, as in the case of Assam, it leads to a situation of cumulative domination, enveloping all aspects of life, the economic domination of Marwari and Punjabi capitalists, the cultural, educational, and occupational domination by the Bengali Hindu middle class, the domination of the rural economy through agricultural colonization by Bengali Muslims, from Bangladesh, and the Nepali-Hindu peasantry, leading to a 'loss of nerve' among the native population. In this content, clearly, there are two types of ethnic groups, that is, the illegal foreign immigrants and the Indian citizens who migrated to the state in search of better economic opportunities.[37]

In the south Indian city of Bangaluru, a political party, named, Kannada Chaluvaligars, emerged in the late sixties, and demanded restrictions against Tamil, Malayali, and Telugu migrants to the city. It is also demanding that preference in employment shouldbe given to the local Kannada-speaking population.

In Chaotanagpur, a native tribal population, a poor illiterate and predominantly rural people have been overwhelmed by waves of migrants who have settled in their region over the past century.

On each of these instances, anti-migrant sentiment took a highly-organized political form; in four of the five cases (Assam is the only exception) opposition parties ran in nativist platforms calling for employment preferences for the sons of the soil. In several of these states, there has been a substantial violence against the migrant communities. In other states, nativism has taken a less organized and, generally, a less virulent form, but it has been present. Meghalaya has adopted a residential permit bill that requires that persons from outside the state have to obtain a permit from the government even to stay in the state for more than four months. In Kerala, an agitation at a factory demanding that jobs be provided for local people resulted in police firing to disperse the crowd when it set fire to a factory. In West Bengal, the state assembly passed a law stipulating that anyone living in the state for ten years should be treated as a 'son of the soil' entitled to preferential treatment in employment. In Tamil Nadu, where people speak of '*mannin mainder*' (Tamil for 'sons of the soil'), the state government retaliated against Maharashtra's anti-Tamil policy by sending employers a replica of the Maharashtra Government's order on job reservations though this proved to be largely a political gesture in a state where skilled local labour and the local middle class compete effectively against migrants.

Hence, in India, the nativist reaction is not only to foreign migrants, but to socalled "foreigners" from other parts of the country itself. Nativism in India is fundamentally a protectionist movement whose tariff walls and domicile regulation for employment and whose middle-class population is like an infant industry seeking protection against competitive foreign imports.

Generally, a movement has a class base and intends to alter the existing social order and power structures or influence policy decisions and distribution of resources at the national or regional level where it takes place.[38]

The so called "regional" movements in India are actually political movements by ethnic groups to create or govern states organized around an explicit ethnic identity. For this reason, the Akali Dal (and what was more broadly known as the Punjabi Suba movement) demanded the creation of a Punjabi-speaking state; in Assam's hill areas, various tribal parties agitated for the creation of the tribal state of Meghalaya; and the Samyukta Maharashtra Samiti demanded for the creation of a Marathi-speaking state. Thereafter, other ethnically-defined (mainly linguistically) states were created, regional sentiments persisted and deepened. In each state, the governing party expressed regional sentiments persisted and deepened. In each state, the governing party expressed regional sentiments in clashes with the central government or with neighbouring states. Moreover, regional, but particularly linguistic sentiment affected state government policies concerning the choice of language in education and administration, and the adoption of a variety of cultural policies.[39]

The number games in the politics of Punjab and Assam bear examples in which significance of economic factors have been put to a secondary position. The movements in both the states agitated for enforcing ethno-linguistic majority. Indeed, economic factors as the outsiders, domination in service and industry, the lack of employment opportunities for the educated, etc., were responsible for the 'sons of the soil' sentiment in Assam. But, instead of fighting for the economic demands, Bengali language and the Bengali as a whole were taken as symbols of domination and exploitation. In Punjab also, the sentimental wound (of neglect/non-recognition of religious demands, script) was the effective input for mobilizing the popular emotion. The divided, uncertain linguistic composition in Assam and Punjab could by no means assure them of their identity and security.[40]

Hence, the regional identity, its formation, expression, and assertion have been a very complicated phenomenon. Economic regionalism or movements mainly based on economic issues, remain less explosive phenomenon than campaigns based on socio-cultural issues,[41] *e.g.*, the age-long dispute between Maharashtra and Karnataka over the piece of land in Belgaum, the recent fight over Chandigarh. Even the genuine economic issues and development demands, *viz.*, the ethno-religious idioms used in the movements have been channelized on ethnic lines giving rise to ethno-regionalism.

The Bodos claim to be the oldest tribal or ethnic group, largely inhabiting the northern bank of the Brahmputra and the two districts of Nilanchal and Laulung on the southern bank. The origins of the Bodo movement can be traced to the passage of Official Language Bill in 1960 which led to the assertion of separate tribal cultures by the All Party Hill Leaders' Conference, the Mizo Hill Districts Council and the Plains Tribals Council of Assam (PTCA). The PTCA, the precursor of the present-day All Bodo Students' Union (ABSU) and the Bodo People's Action Committee (BPAC), first articulated a larger version of the Bodoland demand under the name of Udayachal. In 1987, the leadership of the Bodo movement passed into the hands of the ABSU-BPAC combine.

Apart from ethnic factors, complex economic forces played a part in the origin of the Bodo movement. The major ones were the problem of land alienation, poverty, indebtedness, unemployment, and the lack of capital formation. The excessive pressure on land has pushed agriculture down to a marginal or below subsistence level. At the same time, vacant fallen land has been grabbed by outsiders, leading to economic stagnation and a consequent feeling of deprivation on the part of the Bodos.

Another long-drawn movement in the Eastern region was the Jharkhand movement. The Jharkhand area, known as Chotanagpur plateau, includes a cultural region comprising 16 contiguous districts in the states of Bihar, Madhya Pradesh, Orrisa, and West Bengal. Later, the demand for the proposed state included 21 districts. The prominent tribes living in these areas are Santal, Oraon, Munda, Ho, Birhor, Asur, Gond, Kheria, Bhumij, Mahali, Kurmi, etc. The region has the richest deposits of the mineral wealth, although it accounts for 2.5 per cent of the total geographical area of the country; more than 25 per cent mineral activities are carried on in this region.[42] The Bihar portion of the proposed Jharkhand area provides the country 100 per cent of cooper, 58.5 per cent of mica, 85 per cent of Kyanite, 44.5 per cent of coal, 22.4 per cent of iron.[43] The development and industrialization process has rarely benefited Jharkhand, or the indigenous people. Rather, dispossession and forced migration have remained chronic among them. The movement based on ethnic and regional economic demands, has always been loaded with split and division on ethnic and religious lines. The Jharkhand movement had long progressed from ethnicity to regionalism. The basic component or issue on which the so called Jharkhand identity came up is all about exploitation by the *dikus* (outsiders).[44] There are two types of *dikus,* those from outside the state of Bihar, i.e., Bengalis, Marwaris, etc., and those from within Bihar. Once again, the degree of legitimacy of the ethnic groups vary, those from outside the state being the object of virulent attack by those who lead the Jharkhand movement, its aim being carving out a separate homeland for the people of the region.[45]

Similarly, Uttarakhand, a region comprising eight hill districts of north western U.P., namely, Almora, Nainital, Pithoragarh, Dehradun, Uttarkasi, Tehri Garhwhal, Pauri, and Chamoli districts, also passed through a turbulent phase of crisis. An imbalanced process of economic development has resulted in distortions in the socio-economic structure of the region. A low level of urbanization, illiteracy, and the wide prevalence of unemployment is forcing the work force to migrate and making the families survive on what is called the "Money Order Economy". Migration is gigantic and in many villages the entire population has moved out except the old and very young.[46]

The lack of political consciousness is another factor which has left the region dormant for four decades. In fact, almost the entire Himalayas are now revolting against the prevalent static systems, which left the people in a state of extreme poverty. The utter disregard for socio-economic, political, and cultural aspirations of the people in such areas has now led to spontaneous movements of people at the grassroots level with mass participation including that of women, considered politically the most ignorant segments of our social strata.[47]

The seeds of awakening among the masses were sown by the Chipko movement which inspired similar forms of grassroots movements with Gandhian style of protest in other parts of the country. It reflected the anger of the common people against ruthless exploitation and attack on the precious natural resources and heritage of the region. Nearly 11 months ago, an agitation was launched by students of this region following the announcement of 27 per cent reservation by the state government for Other Backward Castes (OBCs) in addition to the existing 23 per cent reservation should bear a relationship to the OBC population here is estimated at two per cent making a 27 per cent reservations altogether unjustified.

The Gorkhaland agitation in West Bengal got momentum only in 1986, on the issues of Indo-Nepal Treaty, inclusion of Nepalese language in the Eighth Schedule and other sundry economic factors and a separate state for the Gorkhas to be called Gorkhaland, affecting the sub-division of Darjeeling, Kalimpong, and Kurseong in the Darjeeling district of West Bengal. This agitation was organized by the Gorkhaland National Liberation Front (GNLF) led by Subhas Ghising. From time to time, the movement also adopted violent method boycotted national festivals, like the Republic Day and the Independence Day celebrations, organized strikes which frequently turned violent and took a heavy toll on people and material.

The main thrust was on assertion of India Nepalese identity through citizenship demand. In the Ghorkhaland Accord (1988) enacting the establishment of Gorkha Hill Development Council, none of the two main issues were touched upon.

The process of state formation has since Independence taken place for reasons of strategic security or administrative efficiency, but most frequently to accommodate a primordial demand. The centre in virtually every instance created states in response to pressure exerted by primordial groups that had the most to gain by acquiring statehood. But it was usually manipulative as the centre sought to outbid the primordialists and to ensure the installations of a state government that would support or at least not undermine national unity.[48]

Rise of Regional Elites

The question is why are the state governments dissatisfied with the present federal arrangements in India?

Two things have changed the complexion of Indian politics. First, the all-India-party system has collapsed. All-India parties with an all-India perspective have been reduced to regional levels. Politically the Central government has ceased to be pre-eminent vis-a-vis state governments. The constitutional arrangements make the Central government pre-eminent, but the swift changes in the fortunes of political parties have robbed the centre of its leadership role. Second, rich strata in every state have emerged politically powerful whether it is the rich peasant class or its allies, the local level industrialists. The rich peasants and the local industrialists in Tamil Nadu or Andhra Pradesh or Karnataka want more resources and power for their state governments. Since the local rich have political influence only in their state, more resources for their state governments will bring more advantage will bring more advantage to the local power elite.

Because of their power and inter-relatedness with other elites, the economic elite is able to lobby for central and regional policies that support its benefit from the re-colonization of Indian society as agents for the central elite.

The regional elites attempt to marshal the powers of the region through the political machinery of the region. Within a national state, regional units struggle against each other for development, and it is the economic and political elite in each region that are frequently at the centre of the heightened competition and struggle between regions.

Regionalism has become equated with provincialism because the local economic and political elite use the province to challenge federal control, and to promote local development.

The Akali Dal in Punjab is a party of rich peasants and hence its demand for more powers for the state government. Local elites have become politically assertive and political power should bring economic benefits. This is the goal of local elite. Decentralizes are representatives of local power elite and centralizers of an all India elite.

Rising regional aspirants are a political and economic reality of India. The devolution of financial resources should seem credible to the twenty-five states of India. The country's complex economic problems cannot be resolved without national planning and this demands an effective central government.

Regional, chauvinism or 'sons of the soil' movements reveal important tendencies in Indian politics, but in dealing with them a distinction should be made between wood and the trees.

Federal-provincial hostiles and confrontations reflect the interest of the regional elite, and long-standing popular sentiment may even be manipulated in order to create regional solidarity.[49]

❑ Conclusion

On the whole, the economy, both in its agricultural and industrial sectors, is becoming more national in character, drawing all regions into an interactive web of mutual dependency. Power and water supply systems serve inter-state regions, and a national system of rail and transport carries agricultural produce and industrial goods across the whole of India. Labour migration and employment opportunities for the middle class have given India's major cities ethnic diversity. An all-India managerial elite, in government services and in private business, draws expertise from every region. The emergence of a national system of communication, the reach of newspapers, radio, cinema, and television has nurtured the growth of national consciousness, the sense of being Indian, and it penetrates to all, but the most isolated villages, linking the centre with the periphery, the rulers with the ruled, in (at least ideally) a two-way flow of information. But greater interdependence sharpens consciousness of regional disparities and intensifies the struggle among states to protect and advance their interests. Greater national integration, ironically, may deepen rather that alleviate stress on the federal system.[50]

Notes and References

1. Rajni Kothari, *Politics and the People: III Search for a Humane India,* Vol. II, Ajanta Publications, 1989, p. 480.
2. Roger Gibbins, *Regionalism: Territorial Politics in Canada and United States,* Butterworth and Co. Canada, 1982, p. 4.
3. Harry H. Hillar, *Canadian Society. A. Macro Analysis,* 1991, p. 9.
4. *Ibid.*, p. 10.
5. Paul Wallace (ed.), *Region and Nation in India,* New Delhi: Oxford and IBH for American Institute of Indian Studies, 1985, p. 14.
6. Paul R. Brasa, "Pluralism, Regionalism and Decentralising Tendencies in Contemporary Indian politics", In A. Jayaratnam Wilson and Dennis Dalton (eds.), *The States of South Asia: Problems of National Integration,* The University Press of Hawaii, Honolulu, 1982.
7. Robert L. Hardgrave. "The North-East, the Punjab and the Regionalisation of Indian politics", *Asian Survey,* Vol. XXllI, (Nov. 1983), p. 1173.
8. Clifford Geertz (ed.), *Old Societies and New States: The Quest of Modernity in Asia and Africa,* Amerind Publishing Co. Pvt. Ltd. New Delhi, 1971, p. 119.
9. M.S.A. Rao and Franchine R. Frankil (eds.), *Dominance and State Power in Modern India,* Vol. I, Oxford University Press, p. 38.
10. Paul R. Brass, "Elite Groups, Symbol Manipulation and Ethnic Identity among the Muslims of South Asia", in David Taylor and Malcolm Yapp (eds.), *Political Identity in South Asia,* Curzon Press, London, 1981, pp. 35–43.
11. *Supra,*n.9,p.38.
12. *Supra,*n.9,p.139.
13. Sajal Basu, *Regional Movements, Politics of Language, Ethnicity Identity,* Indian Institute of Advanced Studies, Simla (1992), p. 105.
14. Surinder Suri, "Shift in Indian Policies: Strong Regions and Weak Centre". *The Times of India,* 8th April 1987.
15. C.P. Bhambhri. "Contemporary Framework of Comparative Politics: A Critique", *The Indian Journal of Political Science,* Vol. XXXVI, No. 4, 1957, p. 425.
16. Walker Cooner, "National Building or Nation Destroying", *World Politics,* 1972, pp. 319–55.
17. Rajni Kothari, "Ethnicity" in Kumar. David and Santasilam Kadirgamar (eds.), *Ethnicity, Identity, Conflict and Crisis,* Areena Press, Hong Kong, 1989, p. 15.
18. Rajni Kothari, *Politics in India,* Orient Longman, 1970, p. 332.
19. S.N. Eisenstadt, "Initial Institutional Pattern of Political Modernisation", *Civilisation,* 19th March 1962, pp. 461–74.

20. P.K. Dutta, *Politics of Region and Religion in India,* Uppal Publishing House, 1991, p. 18.
21. *Supra,* n. 13, pp. 47–48.
22. Rajni Kothari, *Politics in India,* Little, Brown and Co., Boston, 1970, p. 12
23. *Supra,* n. 3, p. 10.
24. B.L. Dhakar, "Regional Trends in India". *The Modern Review,* March 1975, p. 225.
25. Ranjit Sau, *India's Economic Development,* Orient Longman, New Delhi, 1981, pp. 21–32.
26. *Ibid.*
27. *Ibid.*
28. K. Mathew-Kurien, "Class Character of Indian State" in K. Mathew-Kurien (ed.), *India: State and Society,* Orient Longman, Bombay, 1975, pp. 144–65.
29. John R. Wood, "Extra Parliamentary Opposition in India: An Analysis of Populist Agitations in Gujarat and Bihar", *Pacific Affairs,* 1975, pp. 313–34.
30. H.K. Puri, "Socio-Political Bases of Akali Agitation", *Economic and Political Weekly,* 22nd January 1983, p. 116.
31. Mark Juergensmeyer, "Culture of Deprivation: Three Case Studies in Punjab", *Economic and Political Weekly,* Vol. XVI, Nos. 7 & 8, pp. 253–62.
32. F. Thomasson Januzi, *India in Transition,* Orient Longman, 1989, p. 33.
33. Balraj Puri, "The Era of Sheikh Mohd. Abdullah", *The Economic and Political Weekly,* February 1983, p. 188.
34. *Ibid.,* p. 189.
35. John R. Wood (ed.), *State Politics in Contemporary India: Crisis or Continuity?* p. 6.
36. Myron Weiner, *Sons of the Soil,* Oxford University Press, 1978, p. 266.
37. T.K. Oommen. "Problems of Identity", *The Times of India,* May 1983.
38. *Supra.* n. 35, p. 268.
39. *Ibid.,* p. 295.
40. *Ibid.*
41. P.C. Mathur, "Regionalism in India: An Essay in Dimensionsalisation of State Politics in India", in Rama Kant (ed.), *Regionalism in South Asia,* Jaipur (1983), p. 37.
42. Mathew Areeparampil, *Tribes in India: Victims of Development,* p. 2.
43. *Jharkhand Andolon, Ki o'Keno?* Jharkhand Co-ordination Committee, Calcutta, 1988, p. 2.
44. *Supra,* n. 13, p. 56.
45. *Supra,* n. 36.
46. *Supra,* n. 7.
47. B.D. Pande, "Uttarakhand, case for a state", *The Hindustan Times,* 14th February 1995.
48. Bhupal Singh, "The Political Economy of Uttarakhand", *The Hindustan Times,* 9th February 1995.
49. John R. Wood, *Supra,* n. 35, p. 7.
50. C.P. Bharnbhri, 'Challenges to Indians Federalism', *The Financial Express,* 11th September 1990.

26

Social Structure and Democratic Process: Perspectives, Problems, and Trends

Satish Kumar Jha

❑ Backdrop

Democracy is a political arrangement in which the people and the government together create a civil society and build a common future. It is nothing but a 'tryst with destiny'. Hence, democracy is predicated on the essential equality of fellow citizens. When India started its political journey after the attainment of the independence, the biggest challenge which stared in its face was to find a form that could fit between its social diversity, characterized by structural hierarchies, and democratic processes and institutions. The founding fathers took up this challenge with optimism and hoped that the institutions of democratic government would exert a dissolving influence on the hierarchical social structure and would lay the foundation for democratic governance. This assumption was not implausible. The logic of industrial development and democratic citizenship, which India had adopted, were both to work as a combined logic of individuation, dissolving primordial identities like caste, and religion. The powerful discourse of modern citizenship enshrined in our constitution, while creating a tie between individual and state, was to break down all intermediate affiliations of identity and loyalty.[1] Over and above this, a particular type of democratic strategy, which implies treatment of each individual as individual citizen and not as a community, was given a place of prominence in Indian constitution.

Thus, the long and the short of political agenda adopted at the time of independence was to create a civil society. The goals permeating the entire discuss on social and economic development testify it. This is, however, not surprising as democratic system, conceived in Western liberal sense, definitely demands a civil society in which interpersonal relationships are informed not by primary communitarian ties but by secondary associations and impersonal rule of law based on secular principles. As noted by Austin, several members of the Constituent Assembly affirmed optimistically that the values and institutions of liberal democracy would transform India's tradition bound social structure. Sarvepalli Radhakrishnan said that modern parliamentary democracy would bring about a socio-economic revolution or, in other words; a fundamental change in the structure of Indian society. Another member of the Constituent Assembly, K. Santharam, wrote that new constitution was meant to help India get out of medievalism based on birth, religion, custom and community, etc., and reconstruct her social structure on modern foundations of law, individual merit, and secular education.[2] Such a vision about future Indian society and polity was anchored in a democratic theory, which believed in a functional reciprocity between democracy and liberal outlook and its social order, i.e., capitalism. Alexis de Tocqueville, in his celebrated *Democracy in America,* also argues at length that democratic institutions and values have to take root, there must be social and material equality, something found in capitalist American society.[3] An essential part of this theory of historical change is the belief that capitalist growth fosters democracy. And these in turn, it is assumed, reinforce secularization and conversion of identities based on primacy of communities to those based on primacy of individuals. However, there were some strands of thought in the Constituent Assembly which were not in favour of replicating Western democratic institutions and the premises on which they are based. It was frequently argued that these institutions and ideas could not be separated from the societies which they had originally evolved.[4] "India, it was argued, had an entirely different social order not suited for parliamentary institutions and would do better to search for its own traditions for institutions more in consonance with its culture."[5] But these arguments were largely ignored in the Constituent Assembly; the persons who mattered were wedded to the ideal of democracy as understood and practised in Western countries.[6]

Structure and Process

The Indian democratic process was inaugurated in an ironical situation. Democracy was being sought to be institutionalized and was to be practised in a highly unequal society, compelling Ambedkar to remark that "we are going to enter into a life of contradictions. In politics we will have equality and in social and economic rights we will have inequality. We must remove this contradiction at the earliest possible moment or else those who suffer from inequality will blow up the structure of political democracy."[7] The situation under which we started, i.e., democracy being put into practice despite having widespread poverty and inequality, was then likely to become the central contradiction of the society. It was not realized that the lack of economic-cultural content could become an impediment in the realization of its potential. Further, as it is well known that institutions of liberal democracy are premised on the existence of a highly individuated society; on the assumption that when people act in their political world, they would see their interests as individuals; and group interests would be merely the transient combinations of such individual interests. But, contrary to this, the ordinary people in Indian society lived according to the social principles which were fundamentally opposed to individualism. Contextually, they acted according to the membership of their groups like castes, religion, language, etc. Hence, when the bourgeois segments of Indian society coexisting with semi-feudal class relations, amidst abject poverty and illiteracy while surviving on communitarian culture, adopted modern liberal democratic process, it came both as surprise to the political observers all over the world. It was quite logical to believe, at that time, that either the logic of modern politics would disaggregate social communities or the strength of community existence would disrupt the functioning of modern democracy.[8] The political scientists, though mostly Western, were initially quite skeptical about the fate of Indian democracy. There was a tone of finality in their assessment that liberal democratic institutions, transplanted on a traditional social structure, would collapse like a house of cards.

In the early and mid-fifties, Western scholars of politics were wondering about the future of Indian political system. In 1961, Norman Palmer wrote that the Indian political structure is still in process of becoming and its final shape is still not clear as one might first assume. The Indianization of politics is still going on. Morris-Jones, on the other hand, advised Western students to be on guard while studying Indian political institutions.[9] But very soon it became apparent that some fundamental transformation was occurring in the actual functioning of democratic institutions and practices in which adjustments were being made which reflected indigenous cultural and behavioural patterns without any conscious modelling of the traditions.[10] Since these democratic models and institutions were located in a different kind of historically constituted social structure, it was discovered that their trajectories were bearing only faint resemblance to the tracks of Western history. Further, the success story of Indian democracy started not only exploding the 'development-democracy reciprocity' thesis, but also started questioning the rationale behind the 'tradition-modernity' dichotomy, compelling Morris-Jones, who had once alerted Western observers to be on guard while analysing the Indian experiment, to write that the Western parliamentary institutions were quite compatible with the traditional Indian social structure. Thus, came a new shift in the approach of political scientists analysing Indian democratic process. According to this new approach, the entire 'tradition-modernity' dichotomy was reconciled under the rubric of 'modernization of tradition' or 'traditionalization of modernity.'[11]

L. Rudolph and S.H. Rudolph, Rajni Kothari and few others were pioneers in heralding a new perspective in analysing the functioning of Indian democracy in a traditional social structure.[12] Their thesis went like this: Since there was no well-developed interest group, pressure group, and other supportive agencies of democratic institutions in a traditional, underdeveloped society like India, the traditional structure of caste, through its caste associations, played crucial role in inducting/bringing the people in the network of democratic process. This way, India's traditional socio-cultural sphere, instead of being hindrance to, served as a suitable under-structure of democratic political institutions. Rajni Kothari also pointed out a paradoxical and, at the same time, a puzzling fact that electoral politics, instead of diluting caste, seemed to reinforce it thereby changing the electoral practices; the caste altered the functioning of the democratic system reflecting an interesting process of the adaptability of tradition to modernity.[13] Apart from the existence of compatibility between caste structure and democratic process, there were other cleavages emanating from the social structure in India, *viz.,* religion, ethnicity, tribal identity, etc., which made adjustments in the new setting to the extent that it appeared that norms of democratic politics had acquired a semblance of acceptability among people, and this novel Indian experiment was alive and kicking.[14]

For the first twenty years after independence, political events seemed to follow obediently this framework. But after Nehru's death, particularly after 1967 general election, there started a reversal of relationship between the state and the civil society, on the one side, and the social structure and the structure of traditional ideology, on the other.[15] According to Kothari, this threw the balance between the traditional civil society and the modern state into jeopardy, moving away from the earlier 'fit' between social diversity and democratic institutions to a growing lack of fit between the two.[16] Consequently, the poorer and the socially marginalized sections, according to Kothari, including the ethnic and religious minorities, started seeking out their future on the basis of their identities and their numbers. This led to a mobilization based on caste, sub-caste tribe, ethno-regional, and other such identities.[17] Kaviraj, however, calls it the birth of a 'democratic society'. Using the Tocquevillian distinction, he pithily observes that "in the first two decades after independence, India seemed to operate a 'democratic government' in the absence of a 'democratic society'."[18] Commenting further on the unfolding scenario, Kaviraj writes: "As long as popular pressure on politics did not break the mould of a highly formal, restrained, 'civilized', elite politics, as long as the ordinary and the poor were content to address their grievances through the format of the system rather than alter that format itself, democratic civilities were maintained with impeccable form: elections were punctual, peaceful, orderly. Parliamentary procedures, despite their legal awareness, were understood and maintained. The courts ruled meticulously. Ministers resigned assuming responsibility for mistakes committed by their bureaucracies."[19] But interestingly, as soon as the masses started coming at the centre-stage and began questioning the existing terms of democratic discourse, the Indian state and its democratic institutions ran into series of crises, leading to a whole host of undemocratic measures like centralism, authoritarianism, populism, etc. These undemocratic thrusts of Indian state, however, were soon countered and challenged by series of democratic upsurges emanating from civil society, viz., farmers movements, women's movements, ecological movements, movements for regional and cultural autonomy, etc.

But this so called new democratic upsurge which originated from the fledgling democratic society basically came as a result of disenchantment with both institutional democratic process as well as its governing ideology. Rajni Kothari explains this disillusionment in these words: "The long held assumption was that as the project of nation-building sets under way, the democratic rights are extended to the people, as the development process also gets under way and more and more people and communities benefit from it and all the sources of poverty, unemployment, and human misery are eliminated.... people will enter into new relationship of a more secular and political kind. These assumptions have been belied."[20] According to Kothari, there are two reasons for this: (1) the very agenda of democratic nation-building and social transformation has not been carried through, and (2) the Indian reality is proving too complex and ridden with deep divisions and paradoxes which are proving unamenable to traditional analysis and ideological interpretation.[21] He further adds that after showing a lot of patience and forbearance, the people are losing faith in the existing set-up and are coming to the conclusion that they might have to fend for themselves. This however, according to Kothari, is not to be regretted for the essence of the democratic process is that people come into their own and not wait endlessly for the state or the political parties to make things better for them.[22]

Problems and Trends

Thus, as discontent and disillusionment have grown, the epicentre of the democratic process has moved from an almost exclusive preoccupation with parties and elections to deeper currents at work in the civil society. The period of erosion of parliamentary parties, federal institutions decline of the authority of state and of national political leadership, has also seen the rise of new actors on the stage along with new forms of political expression and new definition of the politics.[23]

In other words, one can say that the articulation of new found consciousness within the civil society has started getting channelized through a new politics, popularly called the New Social Movements. These new social movements should be seen as further and fuller extension of democratic process, though their means seem to be different from that of the preceding period. According to Kothari precisely at a time when the party system is losing credibility and party leaders are themselves closing and contracting political spaces, new institutional spaces are opening up by way of regional upsurges and movements for cultural autonomy, ecological movement, women's movement, etc.[24] For Kothari, it is from this comprehensive response, to a situation of shrinking spaces and closed options, launched from the variety of vantage points of an 'alternative movement' that the democratic process is likely to find its new bearings and new springs of sustenance over time.[25] Nonetheless, as Kothari himself observes: "Nearly all new social movements have emerged as corrective to new maladies—environmental degradation, violation of the status of women, destruction of tribal cultures, and the undermining of human rights—none of which are by themselves transformative of the social order."[26] Further, one should not lose sight of the fact that these vibrant democratic waves, unleashed in recent years in form of new social movements, are also riddled with problems and contradictions. Interestingly, some of the problems which are arising these days are from the same structural base which is also responsible for the birth of these alternative movements. Kothari too is sometimes not so optimistic about the trends in the social movements. He calls them as "being too fragmented, reactive, *adhocism*, providing no comprehensive framework of basic social change." He writes that "their being anti-this or-that (anti-West, anti-capitalist, anti-development, etc.) does not make them any more coherent, any more relevant to the oppressed and peripheralized communities."[27] In his opinion, it is against this growing irrelevance of various grassroots movements that 'New Dalit Movement' is emerging.[28] But when Kothari talks of New Dalit Movement as something which can plug holes in the democratic politics of new social movements, he seems, once again, to be pinning hope on caste system for secularizing and democratizing the society and the politics. Though, this time, it is true, he anchors his argument on altogether different premise. In his opinion, at present juncture, social justice in form of Dalit upsurge is becoming the primary agenda of the democratic process in India. But Kothari wonders whether "a more equal and just society creating a democratic polity or democratization of larger sections of the people (will}... proceed to create a more just and egalitarian society?" In his opinion, this issue, first raised in the pre-independence discourse on social reform and political rights, has now been revived in the course of the Dalit movement.[29]

But one has to be careful in stating the democratic potential of this upsurge. It is true that these movements are releasing new untapped democratic possibilities of the civil society. But there is a limit beyond which the democratizing capacity of these movements cannot be stretched. As one should not forget that in contemporary India, communalism, fundamentalism, and casteism, which constitute a danger to democratic polity, emanate from the same structural base which is being relied upon to rekindle new democratic hope. Thus, it ultimately boils down to a question, which reminds one of a puzzle with which both Toequeville and Mill had once to grapple with, i.e., how can a democratic society defend itself from its own democratic process.[30] But in any case, it is not certain which way the new democratic discourse will move. But there can be no two opinions about the fact that the 'mass society' has dawned in India which, apart from other things has eroded the Nehruvian statecraft considerably which was designed to accommodate the elites and not the masses of the society. The chances of realization of the goals of 'liberation discourse' prevalent during the national movement would depend on how much the recent democratic upsurge succeed in democratizing the Nehruvian statecraft and transcending it.

NOTES AND REFERENCES

1. Sudipta Kaviraj (ed.), *Politics in India,* Delhi, Oxford University Press, 1997, p. 8.
2. Thomas Pantham, *Political Theories and Social Reconstruction,* New Delhi, Sage Publications, 1995, p. 27.
3. There is a general consensus among the political theorists of the West that democratic institutions can be fully functional only in capitalist society, C.B. Macpherson traces the origin of liberal democracy with the rise of capitalism in the West. See his, *Life and Times of Liberal Democracy.*
4. S. Kaviraj, *op. cit.,* p. 14. Recent researches, however, question the compatibility between capitalism and democracy. It is argued that capitalism could develop in its early stages precisely because of the absence of universal suffrage. In Indian context, Ashutosh Varshney feels that democracy predated industrialization, which has provided the rural rich with an electoral veto to obstruct agrarian reforms, which were meant to support capitalist growth. Recently, N. Palkhivata's remark, that India is the only democracy which started with universal adult franchise and hence is suffering with endless problems, only supports this apprehension.
5. Paul R. Brass, *The Politics of India since Independence,* Cambridge: Cambridge University Press, 1992, p. 13. Gandhi and Gandhians along with J.P. were quite vehement about indigenous democratic institutions.
6. Chetakar Jha, *Indian Government and Politics: A Political Commentary,* Patna: Novelty & Co., 1960, p. 6.
7. A.S. Narang, *Indian Government and Politics,* New Delhi, Gitanjali Publishing House, 1996, p. 7S.
8. S. Kaviraj, *op. cit.,* p. 39.
9. S. K. Chaube, "Studies on the Constitution and Government of India: A Methodological Survey" in *Teaching Politics,* Vol. 1 & 2, 1978, p. 4.
10. P.R. Brass, *op. cit.,* p. 14.
11. S. K. Chaube, *op. cit.,* p. 12.
12. L.I. Rudolph and S.H. Rudolph, *The Modernity of Tradition: Political Development in India,* Delhi: Orient Longman, 1987; Rajni Kothari, *Politics in India,* New Delhi, Orient Longman, 1970.
13. Kaviraj, *op. cit.,* p. 31. M.N. Srinivas, a leading Indian sociologist, had long argued that with dawn of electoral politics caste would get new lease of life.
14. It is not to deny that there was no ethnic, tribal, and communal problems in India. But what is being stated is that they were not going outside the purview of democratic politics. Secessionist politics of north-eastern region was only an aberrant case.

15. S. Kaviraj, "On the Crisis of Political Institutions in India" in *Contributions to Indian Sociology* (N.5.), Vol. 19, No. 2, July-Dec., 1984, p. 233.
16. R. Kothari, "Caste, Communalism, and Democratic Process" in P. Bidwal, H. Mukhia, A. Vanaik (ed.), *Religion, Religiosity and Communalism,* Delhi, Manohar, 1996, p. 143.
17. *Ibid.,* p. 143.
18. For Tocqueville, democratic society is one in which the defence for the cultural and social habits of traditional upper classes has broken down, where ordinary people, despite poverty, cultural deprivation, do not hesitate to act politically on their ideas. See S. Kaviraj, *op. cit.,* p. 14.
19. *Ibid.,* p. 14.
20. R. Kothari, "Rise of the Dalits and the Renewed Debate on Caste" in Partha Chatterjee: (ed.), *State and Politics in India,* Delhi: Oxford University Press, 1997, p. 440.
21. *Ibid.,* p. 440.
22. *Ibid.*
23. R. Kothari. "Interpreting Indian Politics: A Personal Statement" in Upendra Baxi and B. Parekh (ed.), *Crisis and Change in Contemporary India,* New Delhi, Sage Publications, 1995, p: 165.
24. *Ibid.,* p. 149.
25. *Ibid.,* p. 166.
26. *Ibid.*
27. Kothari, in Bidwai, et. al., *op. cit.,* p. 149.
28. *Ibid.,* p.149.
29. R. Kothari, "Towards a People's Democracy" in *Biblio,* Vol. II, Nos. 7-8, July-August, 1997, p. 11.
30. S. Kaviraj, *op. cit.,* p. 33.

POLICY

27

Agrarian Policies and Their Impact

Shubha Pandey

It is well known that the structure of production preceding independence was colonial, geared to subserve the interests of the former "mother country", England. Under the British, India did develop a stable and strong government but very little effort was made to promote the economic development of India. In addition, the Indian economy was primarily an agricultural and plantation economy, producing and exporting agricultural commodities and raw materials, mainly to Great Britain. Even here, the techniques used were primitive and Indian agriculture presented a picture of backwardness in the international perspective.

One of the most important effects of the British rule in India was the growth of a new land system in India. In the early period of the East India Company's rule, the Company directors were keen on securing the largest possible revenue. This policy was marked by excessive extraction from peasants. Land revenue was a principal source of finance for the Company administration in India and it also satisfied the Company directors in England with larger returns every year from their conquest of India.

In order to bring about stability in agriculture, the British introduced land settlement in 1793. In Bengal and neighbouring areas 'permanent settlement' was introduced. The land raised the status of revenue collectors to that of private landlords. This was called the *zamindari* system and the *zamindar* was required to deposit an enhanced land revenue to the state. Later, the British extended the settlement to other states and created *zamindars* there too but they changed over to 'temporary settlement' under which land revenue could be re-assessed after a period ranging between 25-40 years in different states.

Another land system, which was introduced in Bombay and Madras and subsequently extended to north-eastern and north-western India, was the *ryotwari* settlement under which each peasant holding a plot of land was recognized as the owner-cultivator and made directly responsible to the state for the annual payment of land revenue.

But in both the systems, the land rent fixed were excessive and both the systems were instrumental in the destruction of the organic village community based on who was more interested in squeezing higher land rents that in real agricultural progress. Excessive pressures of population resulting in high demand for land helped the *zamindars* to charge exorbitant rent and numerous other exactions from tenant-cultivators. The result of the whole change in tenant system led to the emergence of a new system of exploitation in agriculture.

But a noteworthy change took place during the years 1850-1947 which gave impetus to the commercialization of agriculture. It aimed at the production of crops for sale rather than for family consumption. This was a deliberate policy worked up under pressure from British manufacturer, industrialist and merchant to acquire more and more of new raw materials for the British industries. By the middle of the nineteenth century, Industrial Revolution had been completed in England. There was tremendous demand for raw materials, especially, cotton, jute, sugarcane, groundnuts for the British industries. By offering a higher bait of market price, the peasants were induced to substitute commercial crops for food crops as the former were paying more than the latter. Consequently, the peasants shifted to industrial crops and in some districts, the movement for the commercial crops became so strong that the peasants started buying grain for their domestic needs. This led to a fall in the production of food and consequently this period is marked by the occurrence of most terrible famines in the economic history of India.

This new land system and the commercialization of Indian agriculture produced very adverse economic consequences on the Indian economy. These influences created "built-in-depressions" in agriculture and were responsible for the occurrence of famines in India.

The partition of the country in 1947 which accompanied political independence broke up the union of two complementary economies of India and Pakistan, created severe problems relating to the sources of raw materials, and upset the whole economic structure of the country. All the factors led to the economic chaos superimposed on the fundamental problems of the poverty of masses.[1]

Under these circumstances, the task before the political elites of Indian National Congress, which took the 'driver's seat in the nation's journey for its tryst with destiny', was to initiate, rather, continue the task of revamping the economic and the economic structure, mainly if not completely, dependent upon agriculture. The daunting task before the state, therefore, was to turn the wheels of agrarian reforms in such a way, that the existing semi-feudal production relations or colonial mode of production[2] which was superimposed on the Asiatic mode of production, could be transformed in such a way that it acted as a catalyst in 'building a socialistic pattern of society'.[3] But what happened after that remains tangibly dichotomous to the original proposition before and after independence. Much gap has been created between the radical commitments embodying populist ideology and the policies implemented.

In the formative years, the policy of the ruling Congress party was guided, rhetorically speaking, with the objective of achieving a 'socialistic pattern of society', for the benefit against all exploitations. In November 1954, Jawaharlal Nehru pressed the National Development Council to adopt this policy as the economy's goal after declaring: "the picture I have in mind is definitely and absolutely a socialist picture of society". He, of course, said: "I'm not using the word in dogmatic sense, but in the sense of meaning largely that the means of production should be socially owned and controlled". In January 1955, the Indian National Congress at its Avadi session (1955), and Nagpur session (1959) passed almost the same resolution. The Indian Parliament, too, 'adopted the goal of a socialist pattern' in December 1955. But, later, it became apparent that the ruling party was not in favour of outright rejection of an economic system based on private enterprise; rather it promoted an important role for the state in securing social justice and economic growth within the context of a capitalist economy. This dualism between the means and the end found its place because the ruling elites wanted to carry India along with an independent capitalist path of development with the assumption that to promote the much needed industrial growth, agricultural productivity had to be boosted up. A move had also to be made towards an effort to penetrate the rural areas with a view to creating an integrated national market. For this, the pre-capitalist relation in the countryside, aided and abetted by imperialism had to be dissolved. Thus, the socio-economic reforms were born out of an ideological concept of removing feudalism for the smooth development of capitalism.[4]

The problem, however, which came as a serious challenge before the state was related to productive forces and production relations in Indian agriculture. Productive forces in Indian agriculture at the time of independence were very backward. As relating to production relations, 40 to 45 per cent of the cultivated land under the direct control of the semi-feudal system of *zamindari*. In the region of *ryotwari,* the influence of moneylenders was visible. Moreover, with the passage of time, the whole hierarchy of parasitic elements was formed who appropriated the surplus produce. Daniel Thorner, therefore enumerates the following structure in rural society: (1) landlord; (2) permanent tenant (75-100 years); (3) protected tenant (6 and more years); (4) share-cropper; and (5) agriculture labourers. So the semi- feudal system had its components of (1) extensive spread of share cropping; (2) permanent indebtedness of small peasants; (3) lack of indebtedness of small peasants; (4) lack of access of small peasants to the rural market; (5) static production function with a low potential for internal growth. Moreover, more than half of the land-holdings were very small.

Obviously, therefore, must of the peasantry lived under slavery conditions or found work in the bigger holdings. At the same time, however, approximately 2/3 of the land area was held by economically viable holders. So, it is said that though India at the time of Independence was a land of small peasants, it was not a country of small holdings.

The Indian leadership decided to tackle the agrarian problem on the basis of the recommendations made by Kumarappa Committee of the Indian Congress which gave its report in 1949. It propounded the slogan 'land to the tiller'. The committee's recommendations included:

1. Eradicating the quasi-feudal social relations and economic institutions that dominated rural India;
2. Redistributing land to actual cultivators;
3. Providing various government-funded 'community developed' services in an effort to promote the development of a 'progressive peasant';
4. Increaing the production of food grains; and
5. Commuting of rent from kind to cash.

Owing to the commitment to democracy the recommendations, therefore, excluded the nationalization or compulsory collectivization of land on the Soviet or Chinese model. But neither could the free market approach or the North American model be adopted, under which invariably and inexorably, the small landholders would have been left on the streets. However, the whole programme seemed to reflect the interests of the development of capitalist relations based on peasant proprietorship.

❑ Agricultural Policy and Land Returns

Over the years, the policies of the agricultural sector have gone through the following distinct phases:

First Phase

The First phase, or the agricultural strategy of the Nehru era laid emphasis on advancing social justice and equity among agricultural producers and increasing agricultural production without diverting resources from the priority goal of the creation of basic and heavy industry. This was to be done mainly through agrarian legislations. As a result, since 1950, following laws were enacted in various states.

Abolition of Intermediaries

The *zamindari* system was first to go under these reforms. However, there were few hurdles in this regard, such as, (1) the problem of achieving a centralized control and direction because the entire field of agriculture was state subject; (2) the problem of bringing the actual owners of lands into the direct relationship with the state; and (3) the problem relating to compensation. A number of court cases, therefore occurred between the state and the intermediaries,[5] and, finally, Article 81 of the constitution had to be amended before land reform legislation could proceed further.[6]

Despite these problems the *zamindari* system was abolished and about twenty million peasants more or less liberated from feudal oppression. But, at the same time, they were also permitted to retain considerable resources as "land for personal cultivation". Ironically, therefore, instead of transferring land to tillers, the *zamidars* were given the status of tillers of soil.

Moreover the colossal amount of compensation already paid in cash to the exintermediaries formed an important component of the capital which was later invested in profit-oriented intensive activities like rice mills, refrigeration centres, etc. Thus, the policies helped them in attaining a new social status of rural entrepreneurs. In practice, therefore, the spread of capitalist production was seen as a sort of a basis for the programme. And, the reason for this may be seen in the understanding of Indian bourgeoisie that without the creation of the upper class peasantry in the village it would be in isolation. Therefore, there was an attempt to decisively push the landlords who remained after the reforms towards capitalist development. Commenting upon this aspect of the reforms, G.S. Kotovsky observes:

> "The main result of the agrarian was a relative betterment of the atmosphere in the village (as compared to the colonial period), which was achieved as a result of clearing the drag of the upper tier of the feudals and bringing big masses of tenants in direct relationship with the state. In this was expressed the wider influence of reforms on the growth of peasant capitalism".[7]

Rudolph and Rudolph also came to the conclusion that:

> "the abolition of intermediaries transformed agrarian relations by shifting the locus of rural power from feudal landlords to market-oriented independent cultivators". Further, they add that "marginal tenants, dwarf holders, and agricultural labourers did not benefit from intermediary abolition. Change occurred at the top and near the top of the agrarian pyramid."[8]

Tenancy Reforms

Tenancy reforms were intended to abolish tenancy by conferring the right of ownership in land on those who cultivate it on lease, and on share-croppers in respect of getting them due share or benefit of produce from cultivation of lease in land. The real objective, however, behind tenancy reform was to promote social justice through growth. But, these reforms practically did not yield any significant result because of the enforcement of laws: (1) structural forces and (2) the existence of legal flaws in tenancy acts.

The first may be explained in terms of the normative structure of tenancy reforms (which is equally true of the other agrarian policies) in the context of the share of landowning class of the rural population in the political power structure of rural India. The large farm-owing class of the rural population has a distinct place and a major share in power-structure of the country has been a powerful institutional force to reckon with. It creates a built-in-leakage at the level of policy formulation as well as implementation which acts as a formidable anti-land reform hurdle. Again, the existence of legal flaws in tenancy acts show the influence of vested interests in the policy structure to work for a dilution or subversion of the policies.

Land Ceiling

The land reform policy in India envisaged that beyond a certain specific limit, all lands belonging to the landlords would be taken over by the states and allocated to small proprietors or else to landless labourers. The idea of an upper as well as lower limit for individual farming could be traced in the recommendations of the Congress Agrarian Reforms Committee. Ironically, however, the First Five-Year Plan did not support the idea on the basis of the conviction that it would lead to small and uneconomic holding which is the root cause of many difficulties in the way of agricultural holdings.[9] Factually, however, it was not until the middle of the 1960s that serious attempt was made to bring in laws limiting landed property. Since then, the states have passed special legislation related with ceilings on holding from time to time. However, due to several factors, such, for example, as the lack of requisite political will, the apathy of administrative machinery, the apathy of the poor peasants, tenants, and landed labourers to press the government from below for distributive justice, and the deliberate built-in legal flaws, etc., it could not attain the desired objective.

But long before the ceiling was established, there was a chain reaction of fictive transfer of land. The magnitude of the landed property was reduced by its nominal hand-over to other members of the family or relations. As a result, there were no radical changes in agrarian structure. Till today less than one million hectares of land has been redistributed. But here it must be noted that, though this measure did not change the structure of land use, it facilitated the creation of a climate which made it difficult to consolidate landed property.

Community Development

The concept of community was introduced in the early 1950s keeping in mind two basic objectives. First of all, the bureaucracy inherited from the British were attuned to realize functions of law and order and collection of taxes. It therefore, naturally could not mobilize the people for implementation of various reforms. There was also a need for developing village life in the process of land reforms. The basic purpose, however, was on the creation of a liaison between the government and people and also in explaining to people that the government is an agent for bettering economic and social life. As Rudolph and Rudolph observed: "Nehru and the planners seem to have thought the introduction of an additional layer of administration... the community development programme initiated in 1952 and supplemented by non-official leadership would be able to inspire, organize, and manage the collective transformation of Indian agriculture." The concrete elements of the programme included: (1) securing mass participation in development programmes; (2) giving government subsidies and technical aid to the villages; (3) decentralization of power with the objective of democratization of the village community; and (4) introduction of a complex approach to the question of village renaissance.[10]

Cooperative Farming

The community development programme was followed by the concept of cooperative farming, especially after the Nagpur session of Indian National Congress in 1955. The proposal was opposed as a basis for mandatory legislation by advocates of peasant proprietorship like Charan Singh in their paranoia against collective farming. The idea behind the concept was to achieve productivity via cooperative joint farming in which farmers were to retain their property rights and to get a share from the net produce in proportion to their land. However, this concept, too, could not produce the desired result as it was sabotaged by a built-in structure to suit the interests of big farmers in two ways. First of all, they divided their large holdings among relatives or even among fictitious individuals, and then pooled them together, thus avoiding the possible dispossession of land. Further, they got preferential treatment from the government particularly with regard to large, long-term loans for capital investment because they only had the assets required for getting credit assistance. Therefore, this concept also could not make a frontal attack on the existing inegalitarian economic structure.[11] Commenting upon its operational drawbacks Gunnar Myrdal vehemently condemned the misuse of cooperative farming to subserve the ends of rural aristocracy:

> "Many urban landowners, in particularly, regard this system as a convenient device for converting share-croppers into wage-labourers, and, hence, a means whereby absentee owners of even relatively small pieces of land can-without giving up their absenteeism-reap gains from agricultural modernization that are unobtainable when land is cultivated by share croppers. They can count on receiving the benefits of the preferential treatment and subsidies offered to cooperatives by governmental agencies. It seems probable that their advantages are a major part of the explanation why absentel landowners can be found to support the cooperative farming idea. But, there are other reasons as well. Among them, the

fact that land pooling in cooperatives was expected to protect them against land reform measures, as cooperative farms are usually exempt."[12]

Thus, in the name of cooperatives, actually joint stock farming was to be encouraged a concomitant of capitalist agriculture.

Second Phase

This phase can be termed as an era of technological determinism/green revolution. Strictly speaking, this phase of agricultural development cannot be analysed as land reform measures, rather as an agrarian strategy which was committed to increase the agricultural production for self-reliance through new technological inputs, and increased investment in agriculture. It had two important dimensions: on the one hand, it was symbolic of the failure of the aim of land reform measures to bring about structural change in order to increase agricultural productivity; on the other hand, it was a cumulative consequence of the land reform measures, *viz*., the abolition of *zamindari* having led to the birth of rich peasants and introduced of capitalist growth in agriculture.

Moreover, the new strategy grew out of a series of independently caused but conjuncturally related events: the death in May 1964 of Prime Minister Jawaharlal Nehru, the primary advocate of the industrial strategy, and his replacement by Lal Bahadur Shastri, more a country than a city man; the 1965 Indo-Pakistan and Vietnam wars that led the United States President "Lyndon Johnson to put Indian food supplies on a short and arbitrary tether; World Bank and United States bargaining with the Government of India that linked increased investment in agricultural programmes… to the availability of increased foreign aid for planned investment and for meeting balance of payment problems; disappointment with the capacity of the industrial strategy to address the problem of rural poverty by generating large increase in employment; and the timing of scientific and technological breakthrough, particularly the adaptation to Indian conditions of new high-yielding varieties of seeds, such as dwarf wheat, initially bred in Mexico." Thus, confronted with the above-mentioned circumstances, the government shifted emphasis from institutional change to the technological upgrading of agriculture.[13]

The new approach was exemplified by the Intensive Agricultural Districts Programme (IADP) adopted in the 1960s which sought to concentrate efforts to increase productivity by the greater use of fertilizers, pesticides, high-yielding variety seeds, technical assistance, etc., in one pilot district in each of the Indian states with assured water supply: There was a hope that these districts would, with the passage of time, become poles of growth from which gradually impulses of development would be spread to other regions of the country.

The programmes launched during this stage were explicitly designed to allocate scarce agriculture resources to better-off regions and better off farmers capable of producing marketable surpluses in all-out effort to increase output with little regard for distributional consequences. At the same time, the farmers producing marketable surpluses had been assured of incentives prices so that they made the surpluses available for meeting the urgent needs of the urban population.

The major achievement of the new strategy is the boost in the production of major cereals, *viz.,* wheat and rice. Though part of this increase can be attributed to an extension of the agricultural area, the yield per acre rose as well to another record high of approximately 100 per cent.

But the gains of this Green Revolution has implied certain costs in economic, social and political. Benefiting mainly the better-off farmers, this development has accentuated the growing inequality in the rural sector, This is also true in the case of Ludhiana, which, most of the time is cited as a sample of success of the Green Revolution. Studies by Franchine R. Prankel[14] show that even in Ludhiana, where 80 per cent of landholder hold farms of less than 8 acres, the bottom 20 per cent, i.e., those with holdings of 10 acres or less, have experienced a serious relative deterioration in their economic position for want of sufficient capital. The bulk of credit from all sources went only to potentially viable and credit-worthy farmers who formed a very small minority. From this study of Green Revolution, V.K.R.V. Rao concluded:

> "It is now well known that so-called Green Revolution which helped the country to raise its foodgrains has also accompanied by a widening of the range of inequality in rural incomes, the loss of their status as tenants by a number of small farmers, and the emergence of social and economic tension in the countryside.... The challenge which India agriculture faces is not only of production problems. We should not forget the human and social implication of agricultural development."[15]

In the socio-political sphere, the Green Revolution opened up a Pandora's box—its very success had produced a number of new problems which were far more subtle and difficult than those faced during the development of new technology. The most disturbing phenomenon was a loss of peace in rural India. Unlike the traditional village-based conflicts between factions within dominant landowning groups, which involved localized symbols of power and prestige, the new conflicts emerged along class lines. The manifestations of these conflicts took several forms, *viz.,* Gandhian satyagraha, land-grab marches, forceful seizure of harvested crops, unionized demands for higher wages and at times physical annihilation of big landowners (*e.g.,* the Naxalbari movement of 1967); these specific forms varied depending on the objective situation.

From an analysis of the socio-economic relationships that developed with the introduction of new technology, one may conclude that, for the success of Green Revolution and its spread without social tension, it would be advisable-rather it is absolutely necessary-to make a frontal attack on semi-feudal land-relations. In other words, genuine land reforms must go hand in hand with technological improvement to bring the benefits of the Green Revolution from the social point of view.

Third Phase

During this phase, the reforms were based on basic needs and income redistribution approach. This approach was to outcome of two basic considerations of compulsions, political and economic. As far as the political aspect is concerned, Indira Gandhi (who had succeeded Lal Bahadur Shastri as Prime Minister after his sudden death in 1966) took a leftist ideological and policy position to outwit both the opposition parties as well as the breakaway Congress group. Thus, she tried to spread the message among the masses that she was the only champion of the masses of the poor whereas her opponents were for the propertied and privileged sections of the society. And, this political compulsion, which led her to use the rhetoric of *garibi hatao* paid her rich dividends in the form of absolute majority for her party in the midterm parliamentary elections on March 1971.

As far as economic compulsions for the adoption of the new approach are concerned, the fact remains that by the end of the 1970s hectic discussions and seminars went on in India and abroad around the priorities of development. The Nehru-Mahalanobis model of the Indian strategy of development came under fire since it was not in a position to solve the basic economic questions which stood before the Indian people. Poverty grew and unemployment was not liquidated. Thus, the solution proposed by the economists in India as well as the International Labour Organization at the conference on employment (1976), which was also supported by the agencies like International Bank for Reconstruction and Development and the Organization of Economic Cooperation and Development came to be known as the Basic Needs Strategy. This concept emphasizes the satisfaction of basic needs as a final aim of development and creation of employment as a means for the satisfaction of basic needs. So, the emphasis of the policy was to direct investment for seeing improvement in quality of life. The strategy, therefore, was to concentrate on the following points:

1. An appreciable increase in employment and consequently income of groups of people who in statistical terms were identified as poor.
2. Increase in investment in traditional agriculture and removal of bottlenecks in it through the democratization of credit and financial institutions.
3. Securing the main consumer goods for the whole of the population.
4. Reduction in inequality between various groups of population in the distribution of goods and services.

This policy was operationalized by generating two policy streams. First of all, the Central government increased *ad hoc* transfer payments to the state governments for famine and drought relief. Secondly, it seems that anticipating the future change in policy by the Janata government, programmes were launched which were specifically targeted to employment and creation for poor constituencies. These included Small Farmers Development Agency (SFDA), Marginal Farmers and Agricultural Labourers' Scheme (MFALS), the Drought Prone Areas Programme, Rajasthan's *Antyodaya* Programme, Maharashtra's Employment Guarantee Scheme, and the Centre's Food for Work Programme, etc. The objective of these programmes, therefore, ranged from short-term (*e.g.*, the politically hinged emergency relief measures) to long-term (*e.g.*, the creation of production assets and skills). The objective, however, was to lift increasing numbers above the poverty line and to enhance rather than waste the productive capacities of the poor.

Rural employment and increased investment in agriculture were to succeed after previous strategic during the Janata rule. In. fact, it was the continuation of its preceding strategy except that instead of using populist rhetoric, it decided to attack poverty primarily through generating employment opportunities and by providing productive assets to the rural poor. This was to be achieved through enhanced investment in those agricultural activities which would be pro-rich peasants. Therefore, it was intended to polarize, rather than harmonize, the interests of agrarian classes and interests. Though in 1980, the Janata government was replaced by the Congress (I), it did not make any significant shift in the programmes. In fact, it continued with the same agricultural programmes but without their labels.

The agrarian strategy after the fall of the Janata government came to be called 'integrated agrarian development'. Under this programme the strategy and methodology of a faster development of productive forces were based on:

1. Increasing production and productivity in agriculture and connected sectors;
2. Increase in the income of lower state of the population through the development of primary, secondary, and tertiary sectors;
3. Increase in the necessary amount of credit so as to support rural poor;
4. Support through the market for rural poor so as to ensure them against exploitation during exchange;
5. Minimum needs and closer contacts between science and production.

The objective, therefore, of the agrarian programme was to:

1. Speed up the tempo of implementation of land reforms;
2. Expand the horizons of new technology for a majority of peasants, regions, and crops, and also increasing attention towards supplying the means of production:
3. Transform agriculture;
4. Expand the scientific area of land on the basis of ecology, energy, economy, and conservation;

5. Support the interests of the producers and consumers with the help of measures in the field of production and distribution in an integrated form; and
6. Struggle with rural employment under a national programme of agricultural employment.

This was intended to help those strata of the rural poor who in general depend on selling their labour-power, and, hence, are condemned to poverty-stricken existence.

However, the above objectives and strategies, which more or less had been the hallmark of agrarian policies during the last decades, clearly reflect that, in essence, the talk is about new agrarian strategy which foresees no fundamental measures in the field of production-relations. But, it must also be noticed that there was some appreciable shift on the problems of landless agricultural workers and marginal holdings. The strategy, basically, has two lines of attack. This is, first, the continuation of the attempts to increase the horizons of modem agriculture with emphasis on techno-economic methods, and, secondly, an attempt to some extent to tone down the inevitable social problems with the help of such half-measures as the programme of rural employment, etc.

Fourth Phase

Since the early nineties, the agrarian policies witnessed the introduction of economic reforms by placing greater reliance on the market for allocation of resources, emphasizing private initiative and encouraging domestic and global competition. These reforms aimed at setting the stage for gradual liberalization, first as a part of stabilization policy, which was important to correct the distortions in key economic areas and secondly to bring in structural adjustments. The type of policy changes suggested and implemented with the adoption of NEP 1991 (though not wholeheartedly) include removing restrictions on the movement of agricultural commodities, reforms in domestic trade and stocking policies, liberalization of trade in agricultural commodities, abolition of quantitative restrictions and substitution whichever necessary, by export and import tariffs revamping public distribution system and gradual removal of input subsidies.

The most striking feature of this phase reflected in the announcement of a New Agrarian Policy on July 28 2000, which aims to attain, over the next two decades:

1. A growth rate of 4 per cent per anum in the agriculture sector.
2. Growth that is based on efficient use of resources and conserves our soil, water and bio-diversity.
3. Growth with equity, i.e., growth which is widespread across regions and farmer; growth that is demand driven and caters to domestic market mad maximizes benefits from export pf agricultural products in the face

of the challenges arising from economic liberalization and globalization; and

4. Growth that is sustainable technologically environmentally and economically.

The main feature of the National Agriculture Policy is as under.

5. Privatization of agriculture and price protection of farmers in the post-QR (Quantitative Restrictions) regime would be the part of government's strategy to synergize agricultural growth. The focus of the new policy is on the efficient use of resources and technology; adequate availability of credit to farmers and protecting them from seasonal and price fluctuation.
6. Private sector participation would be promoted through contract training and land leasing arrangements to allow accelerated technology transfer, capital inflow, assured markets for crop productions especially of oil seeds, cotton and horticultural crops.
7. Private sector investment in agriculture would be encouraged, particularly in areas like agricultural research, human resource development, post-harvest management and marketing.
8. In view of dismantling of QRs (Quantitative Restrictions) on imports as per WTO agreement on agriculture the policy recommended formulation of commoditywise strategies and arrangements to protect farmers from the adverse impact of undue price fluctuation in the world market and promote exports.
9. Government would enlarge coverage of future markets to minimize the wide fluctuations in commodity prices as also for hedging their risk. The policy hopes to achieve sustainable development of agriculture, create gainful employment and raise standards of living.
10. The policy envisages evolving a "National Livestock Breeding Strategy" to meet the requirement of milk, meat, egg and livestock and to enhance the role of draught animals as a source of energy for farming operations.
11. Plant varieties would be protected through a legislation to encourage research and breeding of new varieties. Development of animal husbandry, poultry, dairy and agriculture would receive top priority.
12. High priority would be accorded to evolve new allocation-specific and economically viable improved varieties of farm and horticulture crops, livestock species and aquaculture market would be liberalized.
13. The restrictions on the movement of agricultural commodities throughout the country would be progressively dismantled. The structure of taxes on foodgrains and other commercial crops would be reviewed.
14. The excise duty on materials such as farm machinery and implements and fertilizers used as inputs in agricultural production, post-harvest storage and processing would be reviewed.

15. Appropriate measures would be adopted to ensure that agriculture, by and large, remained outside the regulatory and tax collection system.
16. Rural electrification would be given high priority as a prime move for agricultural development.
17. The use of new and renewable sources of energy for irrigation and other agricultural purposes would be encouraged.
18. Progressive institutionalization of rural and credit farm would be continued for providing timely and adequate credit to farmers.
19. Endeavour would be made to provide package insurance policy for farmers, right from sowing of crops to post-harvest operations including market fluctuations in the prices of agricultural produce.

Fifth Phase: WTO and Agriculture

The World Trade Organization, the successor of General Agreement on Tariffs and Trade (GATT) is a multilateral trade body encompassing rules and disciplines for an orderly world trading system. The initiative towards the formation of GATT and International Trade Organisation (ITO) came during World War II, primarily from the USA. The original idea was to create an ITO, with GATT to be part of it. A draft chapter for an ITO was to be concluded during the late 1940s. Owing to resistance from the US Senate, the ITO never saw the light of the day. Instead, a Protocol of Provisional Application was signed in late 1946 by 23 original members, which became effective on 1 January 1948, ushering in the GATT.

The Government of India signed the Uruguay Round of GATT treaty at Marracas (Morocco) on 15 April 1994 and became a member of World Trade Organization (WTO) without putting up the required resistance for better terms on which India should enter such an agreement. It is directly related to the new economic policy that it adopted for the past few years. In fact, the government had prepared the background of accepting this treaty by implementing many fiscal measures called for under GATT, 1944. To be more specific, the so-called structural adjustment programme of 1991, under the influence of IMF and World Bank, was nothing but an exercise to culminate with the accession to WTO.

The new WTO accord is a momentous and historic achievement because it is believed to funnel $200 billion to $300 billion a year into world income through an increase in trade, i.e., more than one per cent of world GNP, over 10 years from 1995. World trade in 1992 was $7.5 trillion and at the same time world GNP was $22.5 trillion. It is believed that the agreement will infuse dynamism into the global economy through boosting exports by $200 billion to $300 billion in a year, which has considerable implications for India's export. At present, India's share in the world trade is around 0.5 per cent and it is expected that there will be an increase of $1.25 billion to $1.5 billion more over a period of next 10 years starting from 1995. It is for this reason that among the developing countries this package agreement has evoked both enthusiasm and anxiety.

The WTO treaty proposes to phase out what is called trade distortions in agriculture and liberalize trade in agricultural commodities. The basic idea of the WTO was to embody the results of tariff negotiations including some general protective clauses which would prevent evasion of tariff commitments. The tariff concessions are linked to non-discrimination through the principle of most-favoured nation treatment. The non-discrimination provides a basis for equal treatment for all contracting parties irrespective of the level of their economic growth. The WTO is a code of rules for international trade as well as a global forum for discussion on world trade matters. More importantly, it dispute settlement mechanism provides a basis for settlement of commercial disputes.

The long-term objectives in the process of reform of trade in agriculture, as spelled out is Punta Del Estate declaration in agriculture is to establish a fair and market-oriented agricultural trading system and to militate reform process through negotiations of the commitment of farm support and disciplines. As is well known, the agricultural sector has been creating grave concern for developing countries as most of the agricultural export is developed the world, in particular. The European Union were subject to variable levels under the common agricultural policy.

Broadly, two types of subsidies are given to agriculture. One is product-specific and the other non-product specific. While product-specific relates to specific terms like tobacco, sugarcane, wheat, etc., non-product-specific subsidies are given to agricultural inputs like water, seeds, fertilizers, agricultural credit, pesticides, etc. The final act stipulates that non-product-specific subsidies will be cut by 10 per cent of that total value of agricultural production.

However, as the costs of subsidies rise, the only way India can continue to remain under this cover is by unilaterally reducing subsidies. Thus the substantial reduction in subsidies that have come about already during the last few years was due to such compulsions of the treaty.

Another important but detrimental effect of WTO on our agricultural sector is related to its provision of market access. (Article 4, Clause 1). Under this provision, irrespective of whether the country requires to import an agricultural product or not, at least 4 per cent of its domestic consumption must constitute its imports.

Those who subscribe to the government view that those percentages are too small to adversely affect our interest should also take into account the following: First of all, only around 20 per cent of our production is marketable surplus. A four per cent of total means, 1/5th of this, which can play havoc with the prices. Secondly, in the base-years of 1986-88, our wheat production was around 50 million tonnes. A four per cent of this is two million tonnes. If this is to be imported on the basis of the difference between the domestic and the imported price of wheat in 1993, then it would amount to a loss of ₹3340 crore in one year. In 1993 the Government of India imported wheat at the rate of ₹517 per quintal, while the domestic procurement price was ₹350 per quintal. This is only for one product. The cumulative effect of all agricultural products would lead to colossal loss, and that too in foreign exchange.

A careful analysis of the provisions of the WTO treaty would reveal that the main impact of this on our agricultural production will be directed more towards the expectations of exports, it is bound to affect the choice of crops that individual farmers will produce. There will be an increasing tendency, therefore, to shift from food grains to cash crops, thus reducing the overall foodgrain production. In countries like India where huge increases in production are required to meet the food needs of a vast majority of our population, such a shift will reduce the availability of food grains for domestic consumption. Moreover, if the government has to maintain even a pretence of a public distribution system, which is fast eroding due to the consequences of the new economic policies, this would have to be done through the import of foodgrains. Further, under the WTO provisions, there are some conditions of the quality of food security in developing countries. Apart from conditions like "transparency" and "nutritional" requirements, these stipulate that the government can hold food-stocks and distribute them only on the condition that the difference between the procurement prices and international market-price, and difference between the issue price through ration-shops and international market-prices are added to the Aggregate Measurement of Support (AMS). AMS is the basis on which 10 per cent cover of subsidy operates. It the AMS crosses 10 per cent of the value of agricultural production, then we cannot continue the existing subsidies. Therefore, in order to remain within the 10 per cent cover, the government expenditure on the public distribution system will have to be drastically restricted.

The overall result of the provisions of the WTO, therefore, would be that the changes in cropping pattern in cash crop may benefit the individual strata of the rich peasant for a temporary period but would be detrimental to the country's overall food security. A classic example is the current soaring of sugar prices. One of the reasons is the shift away from sugarcane cultivation, resulting in sugar prices rising to a phenomenal ₹20 per kg. Import of sugar became necessary benefiting the MNCs and draining out the foreign exchange. Many foodgrains surplus economies which followed such policies in the past have ended up being importers of food grains to meet the basic requirements. In India, too many economists lament the cumulative effect of the new economic policies and the WTO would lead to a shift in the cropping pattern, a fall in food production and revival the spectre of famine-like situation in the country.

To sum up, we may conclude that no doubt the results of various policies and programmes of the government have been considerable, particularly in the realm of production, but at the same time, it remains an open secret that the fruits of growth have not trickled down to the poorer sections of rural India. And, there is a consensus among the intellectuals that the discontent of the disadvantaged is nearing some kind of ignition point. The old tranquilizers have worn off. Thus, the situation is becoming alarming and the need of the hour is not to disapprove our failure to achieve the desired goals, but to re-think and re-shape our priorities, otherwise it may be too late to keep away the imminent catastrophe, both social and political.

Notes and References

1. "As a result of partition, the Indus valley irrigation system in large measure was ceded to Pakistan. India received 77 per cent of the territory and only 69 per cent of the irrigated area of British India. Also, important centres of production of cotton and jute went to Pakistan". G.N. Seetharam, *Strategy and Tactics of India's Agricultural Development: The Role of the State,* Delhi, Ajanta Publications, 1984, p. 17.
2. The specific impact of colonialism on the mode of production in agrarian economies of erstwhile colonies is called the 'colonial mode of production'. Here the appropriation has feudal characteristics and there is closer integration with imperialist countries. Feudalism is at the service of imperialism: in this context it is important to take note of the role of intermediaries between the cultivator and the imperialist state. See Hamza Alvi, 'India and Colonial Mode of Production', *Economic and Political Weekly,* Vol. X, Special Number (August 1975).
3. See Maurice Goldier, 'The Notion of the Asiatic mode of production in Marx and Engels'. *Enquiry,* Vol. II, No. 2 (1960). The Asiatic mode of production is distinguished from feudal mode of production, though it has several features of feudal mode of production.
4. G.N. Seetharam, *op. cti.,* p. 21; see also, Lloyd I. Rudolph and Susanne Hoeber Rudolph, *In Pursuit of Lakshmi: The Political Economy of the Indian State,* Bombay: Orient Longman, p. 314.
5. A detailed study of the court cases has been made by H.C.L. Neerullat, *Land and the constitution of India,* New York, 1970.
6. G.S. Kotovsky, *Agrarian Reforms in India, quoted in Seetharam, op. cit.,* pp. 24–25.
7. Rudolph and Rudolph, *op. cit.,* p. 315.
8. India, Planning Commission, *First Five-year Plan,* 1951, p. 184.
9. Rudolph and Rudolph *op. cit.,* p. 317.
10. Seetharam, *op. cit.,* p. 27.
11. Gunar Myrdal, *Asian Drama,* Vol. II, p. 1350.
12. Rudolph and Rudolph, *op. cit.,* pp. 319–320.
13. Francine R. Frankel, *India's Green Revolution: Economic Gains and Political Costs,* Princeton University Press, 1971, p. 4.
14. V.K.R.V. Rao, 'New Challenges before Indian Agriculture', *Panse Memorial Lecture* (April 1974). Quoted in R. Datt and K.P.M. Sundharam, *The Indian Economy,* New Delhi: S. Chand and Company, 1993, p. 507.
15. Rudolph and Rudolph, *op. cit.,* pp. 328–329.

28

Industrial Policy

Kamal A. Mitra Chenoy

For an ex-colonial country like India, industrialization was a matter of priority. It has generally been argued that India's industrial policy has been extraordinarily restrictive of the private sector, particularly in big business. It is a common belief that the economic policy regime during the Nehruvian period with its 'socialistic orientation' severely hampered industrial development, in general, and that of the private sector, in particular. In this chapter, we shall subject this perception to critical scrutiny.

❑ Industrial Policy: The Early Years

Swadeshi or self-reliance was a major theme of Congress policy during the national movement. Towards this direction, there was a substantial discussion in the AICC set up National Planning Committee about a substantial role for the state in the development of Indian industry.[1] Leading industrialists including J.R.D. Tata, G.D. Birla, and Shri Ram published, in 1944, a comprehensive 15 year plan for industrialization, popularly known as the Bombay Plan, which called for the state to play a major role in the economy, especially in areas where large quantities of capital were required and returns were likely to be delayed and low.[2] The British government in its own Industrial Policy Statement of April 1945 proposed that "basic industries of national importance" could be nationalized.[3]

There was thus a substantial national consequence for the state's intervention and regulation of industrialization, though emphasis varied, sometimes drastically, based on divergent political orientations.[4] Consequently, the AICC's Economic Programme Committee (EPC) headed by Jawaharlal Nehru emphasized the role of the state in its report submitted in the late January 1948. The EPC advocated the reservation of the major area of economic activity for the state including (1) new undertakings in defence, key and public utility industries; (2) units defined as 'monopolies' serving more than one province; (3) banking and insurance; and (4) large-scale units producing/manufacturing food articles, clothing and consumer goods, and competing against the cottage and small-scale sectors. Privately-owned undertakings in these reserved areas were to be taken over within five years. The EPC also categorically proposed that "the place of foreign capital should be examined so as to ensure that the economic controls remain with the nationals of the country:"[5]

These radical recommendations were vigorously opposed by business lobbies spearheaded by the Association of Chambers of Commerce and Industry of India (ASSOCHAM) and the Federation of India Chambers of Commerce and Industry (FICCI), as well as by conservative forces inside and outside the ruling Congress party. Since the industrial policy proposals would have led to the nationalization and curbing of the industrial, trading, and banking concerns of big business, their representatives in FICCI and ASSOCHAM as well as the foreign private capital interests represented in the latter, opposed them vigorously despite their different attitudes about the rights' of foreign capital vis-a-vis Indian capital.[6] As a consequence of the pressures exerted by these forces, coupled with the relative weakness of radical forces, the Industrial Policy Statement which followed substantially reduced the role of the state and took a more sympathetic position towards foreign capital.

The April 1948 Industrial Policy Statement exclusively reserved only three industries: arms and ammunition, atomic energy, and railway transport for the state. New undertakings in six other industries: coal, iron and steel, aircraft manufacture, shipbuilding, manufacture of telephone, telegraph and wireless apparatus excluding radio receiving sets, and mineral oils, were also exclusively reserved for the state, except when it found it "necessary to secure the cooperation of private enterprise". The proposed five-year period in the EPC report for the takeover of private units operating in reserved areas was not extended to ten years, but it was further stated that this takeover itself would be reviewed at the end of that period. The Statement acknowledges "that participation of foreign capital and enterprise ... will be of value to the rapid industrialization of the country", and toned down the earlier emphasis on majority Indian ownership and control.[7]

Significantly, big business circles including FICCI and the big business-owned financial press welcomed the new policy despite some apprehensions.[8] But others like K.T. Shah, who had served as member-secretary of the National Planning Committee (NPC) were very critical. Shah felt that the recommendations of the NPC which had been chaired by Nehru himself, about the role of the state, had been substantially diluted. He claimed the new policy left "the total industry ... in the hands of the capitalists" and characterized it as "a charter of exploitation for the vested interests."[9]

On 6th April 1949, an official statement on Foreign Investment in India was made in which the earlier policy of regulation of foreign capital was significantly changed. Foreign investors were explicitly assured that their investments would be treated on par with local enterprise and they would even be permitted to retain control of a concern "in the national interest."[10] Big business' were divided. While ASSOCHAM welcomed the new policy, FICer opposed. But even its prominent leader G.D. Birla openly supported the policy. In any event, severe economic constraints which compounded insufficient domestic investment forced the government to turn to foreign capital, though its leaders sought to reassure business circles.[11]

Ironically, from this period till early 1955, the major sections of Indian big business opposed foreign capital reminding the Congress of its *Swadeshi* principles. At its 1953, annual meeting, FICCI actually adopted a *"Swadeshi* resolution". In its correspondence with the government, FICCI claimed that foreign capital had created difficulties for indigenous industries and, therefore, urged that foreign capital should not be permitted to adversely affect parallel Indian industry."[12] Thus, the trilateral relationship between the government, foreign capital, and a large section of Indian big business changed. Whereas in the first phase, FICCI wanted restrictions of foreign capital, in later years it, together with ASSOCHAM, wanted the government to further liberalize the entry of foreign capital. The 1956 Industrial Policy Resolution The Indian state's welcome to foreign capital did not result in a significant fresh foreign investment. The shift towards a Mahalanobis strategy in which the state played a major role in industrialization which was encapsulated in the Second Plan and which shaped the 1956 Industrial Policy Resolution, was largely a consequence of a number of political and economic factors, of which the West's refusal to provide the necessary support was a major one.[13] The ideological climate had also changed with the Congress adopting a "socialistic pattern" of society as its goal in its Avadi session in January 1955.

This resolution of, April 1956, provided the formal framework of the state-directed industrialization that followed. All subsequent Industrial Policy Statements have further defined industrial policy without formally superseding this original document. It divided industries into three broad categories. The first group of 17 "basic and strategic" industries was listed in Schedule A for further exclusive development by the state, except in exceptional circumstances when the support of the private sector could be enlisted. The second group of 12 industries was listed in Schedule B which was to be progressively state-owned and in which the state was generally to take the initiative in setting up new undertakings. But the private sector was to have the opportunity to develop in this field also. The remaining industries were left open to the private sector, though the state was free to enter that area, too, "when the needs of planning so require."[14]

The resolution dropped the earlier takeover clause, relating to private sector units functioning in reserved areas, and its flexibility was welcomed even by big business circles. G.D. Somani and a prominent businessman welcomed the new policy in the Lok Sabha as did most businessmen and the financial press. As the Birla-owned *Eastern Economist* put it, "There is nothing which should terrify private enterprise in this socialism". On the other hand, the CPI was critical of the resolution for not going far enough in extending the role of the public sector and nationalizing the private sector.[15]

However, the foreign exchange crisis of 1957 led to a pro-private sector interpretation of this resolution. There were also foreign pressures for a change in industrial policy. In September 1956, the World Bank President Eugene Black had written to the Finance Minister T.T. Krishnamachari that it wanted India to give "private enterprise, both Indian and foreign, every encouragement to make its maximum contribution to the development of the economy, particularly in the industrial field ... We would have to consider the pace and scale of our further loan-operation in India from time to time ... Taking into consideration the economic policies pursued by your government."[16] The government rejected the World Bank pressure but from the second half of 1957 onwards, reserved Schedule A and B industries were thrown open to the private sector, including foreign capital. On the other hand, a massive Soviet offer to set up a public sector pharmaceutical industry was rejected in favour of MNCs like Merck and Bayer.

In May 1961, the government in its statement on "the role of foreign capital in India's economic development", provided an "illustrative" list of 26 industries in which foreign capital would "ordinarily" be permitted to invest. Many of these were Schedule A and B industries. It was also explicitly stated that "exceptions" could be made for entry into Schedule A industries "in the public interest", and further clarified that Indian majority shareholding was not necessary in "on merits" cases.[17]

In September 1963, the government set up the "Industries Development Procedures Committee', popularly known as the Swaminathan Committee after its chairperson. Significantly, of the Five non-official members of the 10-man committee, four were leaders of FICCI, including its president Bharat Ram, and one from ASSOCHAM, its president A.R. Foster. Thus, all the non-official members were representatives of Indian and foreign big business. As a consequence of the Swaminathan Committee's recommendations, the government agreed in June 1964 to give "priority treatment" in licensing eight industries, a number of which were Schedule B industries.

The Swaminathan Committee was reconstituted in August 1965, with the new presidents of FICCI and ASSOCHAM replacing the earlier incumbents. In its recommendations of February 1966, the committee concluded "that generally speaking, industries which do not involve the import of capital goods or raw materials should be exempted from the licensing provisions."[18] As Bhagwati and Desai, in their generally pro-private sector study of industrialization and trade policies have noted, "From an economic view-point, this criterion made no sense ... as it took into account only the direct foreign exchange requirements and ignored other foreign exchange repercussions."[19] One the basis of these recommendations, the government in May 1966 delicensed 11 industries, a large number of which were in

Schedules A and B including iron and steel, castings and forgings, iron and steel structurals, and cement. In July more industries were delicensed, and in November 1966, 23 more items were delicensed.

Though the economic strategy enunciated by the Second and Third Plans was for the state or public sector to capture the "commanding heights of the economy", the actual implementation of the industrial policy was quite different. The ILPIC Report showed that during the Second and Third Plan periods, i.e., from 1956 to 1966, in the Schedule A industries the following proportion of licences were issued to the private sector including foreign capital: iron and steel, 42 out of a total of 46; heavy castings and forgings of iron and steel, 306 out of 312; heavy plant and machinery required for iron and steel, etc., 103 out of 106; heavy electrical plants, 58 out of 61; coal and lignite, 344 out of 390; aircraft, tow out of four; mineral oils, seven out of 10; shipbuilding, all 12; and telephones, telegraph and wireless apparatus, 17 out of 20. In Schedule B industries a similar pattern prevailed: in machine tools, 226 licences to the private sector out of a total of 235; ferro-alloys and tool steels, 58 out of 62; basic and intermediate products required by chemical industries, 184 out of 199; plastics, antibiotics, and other essential drugs, 334 out of 335; fertilizers, 42 out of 54; synthetic rubber, all three; aluminium, all 46; and other non-ferrous metals, all 87.[20]

This extensive private sector entry into areas generally reserved for the public sector was enabled by public sector funding. Of the medium and long-term loan assistance sanctioned by public financial institutions between 1956 and 1966, 52.6 per cent was to the large industrial sector (defined as business groups with assets of Rs. five crores or more in 1964). As the ILPIC Report summed up, "the licensing system provides considerable scope for a favour to be granted and ... these favours mostly are secured by firms belonging to the Large Industrial Sector."?[21]

As a consequence of this liberalization of industrial policy, the volume of foreign investments in the manufacturing sector increased from ₹70.7 crore in June 1948 to ₹630.9 crore by March 1967. It should be noted that these figures are for the book values of the investment, thus an underestimate of the actual market value.[22]

The liberalization of industrial policy that took place in this period, particularly, in 1956-66, was undoubtedly also, to some extent, a result of external pressures. Pressures from the World Bank, IMF, and the Aid India Consortium which culminated in the devaluation of the rupee in June 1966, must have contributed to the pro-private sector shifts in this period. The Congress regime which was able to put up some resistance to World Bank pressure in 1956, succumbed to it is 1966. By this stage, compared to 1956 the collaboration between Indian big business and foreign capital had deepened, the Congress had a new, relatively weak Prime Minister in Indira Gandhi, and these factors combined with the difficult domestic economic situation in 1965-66, was probably decisive in the shift in economic policy, both the deregulation and the virtual discarding of the policy of import substitution.[23]

❑ Further Relaxations in Industrial Policy

The changes in industrial policy were accompanied by a decline in public investment which manifested itself in lower growth rates in the Indian economy as a whole. The growth rate in the manufacturing sector that had increased in the fifties and sixties, declined thereafter despite the continued liberalization of industrial policy.[24]

The virtual dereservation of Schedule A and B industries was given an official sanction in industrial policy decisions taken on 18, February 1970, seventeen industries, which were specifically stated to exclude the reserved industries were specified as "core" and heavy industries in which Indian and foreign big business were normally expected to invest. A number of these industries were in fact Schedule A and B industries.[25] The same year saw the coming into force of the Monopolies and Restrictive Trade Practices (MRTP) Act, which was supposed to curb monopolistic practices. Though an MRTP Commission was set up, references to it under the Act were to be made by the government, and its clauses were sufficiently diffused so as not to significantly hamper big business growth.[26]

By February 1973, further additions were made to the 'core' sector list with the Appendix I industries totalling 19 and including those earlier reserved for the public sector. The Foreign Exchange Regulation Act (FERA) was enacted with the explicit objective of conserving and properly utilizing foreign exchange. It did not explicitly refer to the regulation of foreign capital. Under FERA companies with more than 40 per cent foreign equity would require permission from the Reserve Bank of India to continue their activities. Foreign companies were to be allowed to retain upto 74 per cent of equity only if they brought in sophisticated technology and/or exported substantially, but this was given liberally even in low technology areas.[27]

The result of the operation of the MRTP and PERA Acts was the continued growth of large Indian and FERA companies. Of the top 100 largest private sector companies, the assets of the FERA companies increased from a 28.05 per cent share in 1967-68 to 30.93 per cent in 1977-78; in absolute terms the increase was from ₹760.72 crore to ₹1938.18 crore, i.e., by 141.64 per cent. During the same period, the share of large Indian companies decreases from 71.94 per cent to 69.07 per cent, though their assets increase from ₹1950.61 crore to ₹4101.67 crore, i.e., by 100.43 per cent.[28] The Sachar Committee (the high-powered committee on companies and MRTP Acts) noted that only some 9.5 per cent of the effective applications received by government under Sections 21, 22, and 23 of the MRTP Act (pertaining to increased production by MRTP companies) between 1st June 1970 and 31st December 1977, were referred to the MRTP Commission. The Central government approved 74 per cent of the applications.

Between 1969 and 1975, the total assets of the top twenty business groups registered under the MRTP Act increased by 83.7 per cent. The Sachar Committee, whose members included leading industrialists like D.C. Kothari (ex-President, FICCI) and Keshub Mahindra (ex-President, ASSOCHAM), acknowledged that "these figures ... show that the Act has not stifled the growth of the economy. The central government has been quite liberal in allowing expansion or the setting up of new undertaking(s) (by the MRTP groups)."[29]

The Janata Party government that came to power continued these liberalized policies. On 31st December 1977, Industrial Policy Statement dropped the goal of a socialistic pattern barely a year after the 42nd constitutional amendment had enshrined socialism in the preamble. It further liberalized the investment procedures for foreign capital, dropped the price preference for the public sector, increased the areas for private investment, and reduced the reservations for the samall-scale sector.[30]

❑ Liberalizations in the 1980s

Mrs. Gandhi's government on her return to power in January 1980 further liberalized industrial policy. In February, Vice-President Hidyatullah criticized India's earlier industrial policy and called for an open entry of MNCs into the country. In May a more liberal approach towards FERA was announced allowing MNCs to retain higher levels of equity than earlier agreed upon. On 23rd July another Industrial Policy Statement, again formally based on the earlier 1956 Industrial Policy Resolution, was announced. This one, too, like its predecessor dropped all references to the socialist goal. The role of the public sector was explicitly reduced to 'building the pillars of the infrastructure' in contrast to its earlier role of capturing lithe commanding heights. Undertakings in all Appendix I industries were permitted *"automatic"* expansion upto 25 per cent of licensed capacity.[31]

The negotiations for the IMF loan in 1981 led to further pressures for liberalization.[32] In April 1982, this "automatic" expansion was further liberalized to permit industrial units to claim higher capacity upto an additional one-third over the highest production achieved in any of the five years ending 1981-82, as the basis for a further expansion of another 25 per cent. For MRTP/FERA companies this provision was restricted to Appendix I items. In 1984, this expansion was one again permitted. The effect of these successive amendments to the original "automatic" capacity expansion scheme was to regularize illegally created excess capacities (i.e., capacities in excess of those licensed), thus rewarding those who had violated industrial policy. Moreover, the cumulative effect of these expansions rendered "substantial expansion" (SE) licences wholly unnecessary since undertakings were permitted to virtually double their production.

After the return of the Congress (I) government in October 1984, further concessions were made. In December 1984, the licensing procedures for

MRTP companies were streamlined. Starting from January 1985, a "broad-banding" scheme was extended to a large number of industries. Broadbanding was originally introduced in machine tools industry in July 1983, which permitted manufacturers full flexibility to produce items similar to those for which they had a licence. In 1985, this scheme allowed entrepreneurs in a large number of industries including those in Schedules A and B to diversify their production. Though earlier relaxations, permitting diversification, had reduced the necessity for "New Article" (NA) licences under the Industries Act, the broadbanding scheme rendered these licences unnecessary.[33]

The 1985-86 Budget increased the asset limit for registration under the MRTP Act from ₹20 crore to ₹100 crore. Twenty-five broad groups of industries were also delicensed.[34] These included industries listed in Schedules A and B. Though this liberalization was not to extend to MRTP and FERA companies, since a large number of big business or foreign-controlled companies were not registered under the MRTP and FERA Acts, they were able to avail of these concessions. Furthermore, the exemption limit for the purposes of licensing was continuously increased from ₹5 lakh in 1951 to ₹5 crore from April 1983.

From 1985, the process of liberalization accelerated. Petroleum and natural gas exploitation (a Schedule A industry) was opened to foreign investors, even by reversing decisions taken by an earlier Congress (I) government, e.g., in the HBJ pipeline case. In the Assam accord that year between the government and AASU, it was stated that the proposed refinery in Assam would be set up in the private sector. The electronics policy announced in March explicitly welcomed the entry of FERA companies into the industry. The bulk of the industry was put outside the purview of the anti-monopoly sections of the MRTP Act, a substantial portion was delicensed, and the import of technology was freely permitted. Understandably, these changes were welcomed by the large private sector.[35]

In June the same year, the new textile policy virtually abolished the distinction between the mill, powerloom, and handloom sectors, as well as removing the distinction between natural and synthetic fibre for licensing purposes. Thus, the remaining constraints on the growth of the mills were virtually removed, the manufacture of polyester fibre and filament was virtually delicensed (and their excise duties sharply reduced), and by treating all sectors at par, the protection for the smaller powerloom and handloom sectors was in effect jettisoned. The policy statement promised to eliminate, phase out or at least "modify" all controls.

As a consequence of such policy changes, the number of foreign collaborations increased sharply from 526 in 1980 (then a record) to 740 in 1984, with a significant proportion of these in the public sector.

Throughout the latter part of the eighties, the liberalization process continued with the same speed. More industries including those in Schedules A and B were delicensed, industries earlier reserved for the public sector or the small-scale sector were thrown open to the MRTP and FERA companies.

The MRTP Act and FERA were further liberalized, and industrial licensing provisions were further relaxed. All this was done in pursuit of the official objective of maximizing growth, exports and foreign investment, by reducing unnecessary controls. Despite resistance by the Left parties and lobbies of smaller business, the liberalization process continued unabated.

❑ Industrial Policy Changes Since 1991

The Union Budget for 1991-92 further accentuated the liberalization process. Concessions in industrial licensing policy had preceded it, but them Finance Minister Manmohan Singh announced some major concessions which were further amplified in the Industrial Policy Statement of 24 July 1991. Like the earlier statements, this one also claimed to be based on the 1956 Industrial Policy Resolution. But it made far-reaching changes in industrial policy. Instead of the 17 Schedule A and 12 Schedule B industries earlier reserved for the public sector, only eight industries listed in Annexure I were reserved for the public sector. Yet, though 'mineral oils' was one of these reserved industries, petroleum (other than crude), and its distillation was one of the 18 industries listed in Annexure II for which licensing was still required. Similarly, coal and lignite were common to both lists, effectively dereserving them at the outset. All other industries were delicensed including MRTP and FERA companies subject to their being 25 km from the standard urban area limits of cities with populations exceeding 10 lakh according to the 1991 Census.

Thirty-four groups of industries including a number of them earlier reserved for the public sector like metallurgical industries, boilers and steam generating plants, electrical equipment, telecommunication equipment, transportation, industrial machinery, agricultural machinery, industrial instruments, inorganic fertilizers and chemicals were listed for automatic approval of foreign technology agreements and for investment by companies with 51 per cent foreign equity. Thus, basic and strategic industries that Nehru and his contemporaries believed should, because of the adoption of the socialistic pattern of society as the national objective, as well as the need for planned and rapid development, to be in the public sector,[36] were to be automatically handed over to Indian big business and the MNCs.

While sharply diminishing the role of the public sector, the new policy statement also promised the disinvestment of equity share capital in "selected (public sector) enterprises". It also stated that "chronically sick" public enterprises would be referred to the Board for Industrial and Financial Reconstruction (as a prelude to their closure or privatization). But, the public enterprises were in that period increasingly subject to reduced budgetary support which often caused their sickness. Further, the shift towards foreign capital had led to a sharp fall in the demand for public sector products, making them less viable. On the other hand, in 1990-91 the term-lending financial institutions lent ₹19, 385 crores to the private corporate sector, while the latter realized only ₹4, 130 crore from capital issues. Since the promoters share was only a fraction of the latter figure, this indicates the extent of public funding of the private sector.

Critics, including those in Parliament, argued that the concessions in the budget and in the Industrial Policy Statement were geared to the conditionalities of the IMP-World Bank and part of the structural adjustment programme (SAP). Ironically, similar SAP-oriented policies had been sharply criticized by Manrnohan Singh himself when he was Secretary-General of the South Commission.[37] But industrialists, Indian and foreign, and their lobbies like FICCI, ASSOCHAM, and CII (Confederations of Indian Industry), welcomed these changes and asked for further concessions. Since then most of the multilateral financial institutions have recognized that the industrial policy and other economic policy changes starting in 1991 were part of the structural reform process.[38]

In August 1991, a substantial expansion of an existing unit and the production of new articles was allowed without a licence. Procedures for foreign technology agreements including hiring of foreign technicians were simplified, so that permission was automatic subject to some conditions. While the investment limit (value of plant and machinery) for registration as small-scale sector units had been raised to ₹60 lakhs, and that of ancillary and export-oriented units to ₹75 lakhs in April, the limit for tiny enterprises was more than doubled from ₹2 lakhs to ₹5 lakhs. Procedures for foreign investment were also simplified. One-time additional imports of capital goods or balancing equipment for broadbanding and capacity enhancement were also allowed.

In October 1991, foreign imports, subject to certain conditions was automatically approved. In December, the amount of foreign exchange available for industrial units for import of technology and capital under the Technical Development Fund Scheme every financial year, was increased from Rs. three crores to Rs. five crores. The list of industries in Annexure III (which listed industries for automatic approvals of foreign technology agreements and for approvals for 51 per cent foreign equity) was expanded that month and again in June 1992.

In May 1992, foreign brandnames/trademarks were allowed in the domestic market. This was followed by foreign companies being allowed to increase their equity share to 51 per cent at share prices determined by the shareholders, without any prior government approval. In July, the earlier conditions imposed on industrial approvals including export obligations, financial management of MRTP/FERA companies, foreign exchange neutrality and prohibiting access to domestic financial institutions, obligations to set up joint sector units by State Industrial Development Corporations in association with private promoters, captive use of certain items of manufacture, and the prohibition of merchant sales, were all withdrawn.

In April 1993, the Cabinet Committee on Economic Affairs decided to remove automobiles, white goods, and leather from Annexure II, the list for compulsory licensing. Later the same year, it was decided to guarantee foreign investors in the power sector a minimum return of 16 per cent in dollar terms. This unprecedented profit guarantee, it is estimated, would triple the unit cost of electricity. As critics have pointed out, substantially less generous terms would have made public sector power companies economically viable. MNCs, including those with no prior experience of oil exploration, were invited to invest in proven oil-bearing areas already explored by the ONGC. According to one commentator, the estimated profit in one oilfield would be 278 per cent over five years. Consequently, MNCs would profiteer while the ONGC is starved of funds for capital investment.[39]

The Joint Parliamentary Committee (JPC) inquiry into the stock scam has indicted the foreign banks as being responsible in large measure for the illegal speculation in the stock market and has unanimously recommended punitive action against them.[40] As some of the Opposition members of the JPC have pointed out, the stock scam is a consequence of the deregulation and liberalization of the economy. The unprecedented statement by the British High Commissioner in India that Dr. Manmohan Singh's continuation in office as then finance minister despite his resignation is necessary for the economic reform process, and the absence of any official protest over this foreign interference in India's internal affairs, is indicative of the influence India's creditors now have. The removal of G.V. Ramakrishan from the chairpersonship of the Securities Exchange Board of India (SEBI), apparently in response to pressures from stockbrokers, appears to be the latest instance of how an honest officer seeking to protect public interest can be removed by forces unleashed by the current liberalization process.

❑ Disquiet in Indian Business

In late September 1993, a group of 12 leading industrialists including Keshub Mahindra, Rahul Bajaj, Hari Shankar Singhania, and B.K. Modi met in Bombay to pressurize the government to create "a level playing field" that would enable Indian industry to compete on equal terms with foreign companies. Rahul Bajaj, a leader of this group which has come to be known as the Bombay Club, put business fears very picturesquely; "For 45 years the government tied our hands behind our backs. Now they want to throw us to the wolves". Vijay Kalantri, President of the All India Manufacturers Organisation (AIMO) warned that the drive to attract foreign capital was turning Indian entrepreneurs into mere traders, who would be "permanently saluting multinational corporations."[41]

D.H. Pai Panandiker, a former Secretary-General of FICCI, summarized the Bombay Club's grievances which were later supported by FICCI[42] He noted that in a one year period till September-October 1993, 34 MNCs had increased their equity shares to 51 per cent. Of these only corn products paid more than the market price; the rest acquired these shares "at hefty discounts", a fact that Pai Panandiker found "amazing". According to him

"Colgate-Palmolive (bought) at 92 per cent discount, ABB 87 per cent, Bata India 84 per cent. Indian Shaving Products at 82 per cent ..." On the other hand, of the Indian companies only the Vyasa Bank matched the MNCs discount norms. Indian Rayon, Nahar Spinning, and Punjab Concast, according to him, got discounts of approximately 45 per cent.

Pai Panandiker noted that Indian companies could not obtain finances from the banks against their shares as collateral, and that the Companies Act restricted inter-company investment. Like the Bombay Club members, he pointed out that customs duties were higher on raw materials and components than on the final commodity, thereby discriminating against domestic production in favour of jmports. Public sector pricing policies were also making raw materials dearer than imports. He also alleged dumping of goods by foreign countries, especially China. Thus, Pai Panandiker concluded, "the playing field in tilted against Indian companies which, with many of the restrictions still intact, have to fight world giants."[43]

Barua and Varma have calculated that Colgate-Palmolive by buying 11.3 million shares at ₹60 each when the market price was ₹700 (i.e., at a discount of ₹640), made profits amounting to ₹723.2 crore or $231.05 million.[44] Since influential segments of big business were so distressed, Dr. Manmohan Singh was constrained to admit that Indian companies were too small compared to the MNCs and that their requirement for help to grow was legitimate.[45]

As the process of structural reform and the liberalization industrial policy continues, the contradiction between MNCs, on the one hand, and sections of Indian big business, and medium and small business, on the other, are likely to sharpen. At that stage, the political pressure on government against some of the industrial and other economic policy changes will mount. However, in view of the economic stranglehold of foreign creditors including multilateral financial institutions are likely to (unofficial estimates put India's external debt at over $95 billion), any substantial change in industrial policy will not be easy.

❑ MNCs and the Indian Economy

The actual performance of the MNCs have disapproved the assumptions of government policy. MNCs have avoided significantly supplementing domestic capital. For instance, Chaudhuri found that in the case of the then 50 largest MNC affiliates in India, only 5.3 per cent of the growth during 1956-75 was financed by foreign sources.[46] Similarly, Kumar and Chenoy found that the eight leading MNCs affiliate in the drug industry financed only 13.51 per cent of the total equity capital.[47] Union Carbide India Ltd. (UCIL) raised as much as 72.4 per cent of its equity through bonus issues, even though its parent company held 50.9 per cent of its equity.[48]

MNC investment has also been justified on grounds of foreign exchange earnings through exports. An RBI study found that the operations of foreign subsidiaries between 1964-65 and 1969-70 resulted in a net outflow of ₹684 crore of foreign exchange. The study also revealed that wholly and majority-owned foreign firms had a larger negative trade balance than firms with only minority foreign participation.[49] UCIL's net foreign exchange deficit was ₹6.81 crore in 1981, rose to ₹9.51 crore in 1982, and jumped to ₹16.62 crore in 1983.[50]

A major justification for foreign investment is that it brings in modern and sophisticated technology. But this is not quite the case. In the first place, any technology transfer through MNCs is a 'private' transfer, from the parent MNC to its affiliate or collaborator. Secondly, as the National Committee on Science and Technology has found: "The price one pays for foreign technology (either as a lump sum or a continuing combination of royalties, divided repatriations, technical fees, etc.) is not in any way 'fixed' by (the) market for such a technology. The market is a monopolistic one and the price of technology is a matter of bargaining between the potential supplier and his client."[51]

Thirdly, few MNC affiliates significantly invest in research and development to develop the indigenous infrastructure for imported technology, or to indigenize the same. Out of the 118 foreign subsidiaries in India in 1980, only 32 had research establishments recognized by the government. And of these, only 11 applied for any patents in 1978-82.[52]

Fourthly, the technology transferred is often hazardous as the Bhopal gas tragedy of December 1984 starkly demonstrated. The leakage of 45 tonnes of MIC from the plant, which caused thousands of deaths and affected the health of lakhs, was the consequence of the transfer of obsolete and ill-designed plant equipment, as well as an extremely dangerous production process not used anywhere else in the world, including in Union Carbide's other plants. While other plants producing MIC-based pesticides used up MIC continuously during the production process, UCIL chose to store upto 60 tonnes of this extremely poisonous and unstable chemical. The safety equipment was grossly inadequate and this was known to Union Carbide since at least 1982.[53] Another MNC, Johns-Manville Corporation, at one time the largest asbestos producing company in the USA, produced 50,000 tonnes of asbestos cement pipes and sheets annually in its affiliate Shree Digvijay Cement Company's Ahmedabad plant. Since asbestos dust inhalation is known to cause various types of cancer, its production dropped markedly in advanced countries like the USA and Sweden in the 1980s. But because of domestic pressures, MNCs have taken to transferring hazardous or polluting processes to the Third World.[54] The World Bank's chief economic adviser Lawrence Summers issued a memo (since withdrawn) advocating the transfer of environmentally polluting industries to the Third World, on the grounds that these countries have areas less polluted than those in the west.

MNCs have been known to produce commodities banned in their home country. For instance, in the drugs and pharmaceutical industry MNC affiliates have exported or produced locally in India drugs banned in their own country, by making full use of the weak regulations, which over the last decade have been further dismantled.[55] All this is not to say that MNCs should not be allowed entry into economies such as India, but only to highlight the need for transparent regulations to ensure that these companies do not flout the national interest in their quest for profits.

❑ Conclusion

These examinations of the evolution of industrial policy in India has shown that economic policies were neither socialist nor anti-big business at any stage. During the Nehruvian period, from 1947-64, private sector including big business and foreign investors were accommodated, even at the cost of deviating from stated policy objectives. A major pro-big business and pro-foreign capital shift began in the late sixties after the 1966 devaluation of the rupee and increased in the seventies. The pace of liberalization and deregulation further accelerated in the early period of the Rajiv Gandhi regime. Thus, the popular contention that the industrial policy was very restrictive of a large enterprise is not borne out. Facts indicate the virtual opposite: the industrial policy frame discriminated in favour of large industry, both Indian and foreign.

The structural adjustment programme (SAP) process initiated by the P.V. Narasimha Rao government and identified with Finance Minister Dr. Manmohan Singh since 1991 and now Prime Minister is, therefore, only a culmination of an earlier trend. It is, however, clear that this open door policy is markedly different from the Nehruvian policy, as the denationalization of the petroleum and gas industry, among others, highlights. For reasons of political legitimation recent policy announcements (like the 1991 Industrial Policy Statement) have claimed a Nehruvian heritage, but this is mere political rhetoric.

Yet the major decisions underlying the formulation and implementation of industrial policy at all stages were basically political. These reflected the ruling regimes' political choices, which in turn were influenced by the then prevalent political balance of forces. Future developments in industrial policy will also reflect the political realities, both national and international, of the time.

Notes and References

1. The arrest of the Congress leadership in 1942 and their preoccupation with the national movement did not allow the National Planning Committee (NPC) sufficient opportunity to bring out a final consolidated report. But reports of various sub-committees brought out by the NPC's Secretary K.T. Shah provide sufficient indication of the dominant thinking in nationalist circles. See for instance, *Report*

of the Planning Advisory Board, New Delhi, 1947; K.T. Shah. *National Planning: Principles and Administration,* Bombay, Vora, 1947.

2. P. Thakurdas, J.R.D. Tata, G.D. Birla, *et. al., A Plan of Economic Development for India,* Bombay, The Commercial Printing Press, 1944.
3. While Indian big business organized in the Federation of Indian Chambers of Commerce and Industry (FICCI) did not dispute the need for major state intervention, they were critical of the proposed controls on industry, anti-monopoly measures and the latitude towards private foreign capital. In any case they felt these decisions should be taken by an independent Indian government. See Kamal A. Mitra Chenoy, *Industrial Policy and Big Business in India: A Case Study of FICCI,* 1947-1966, unpublished Ph.D. thesis, Jawaharlal Nehru University, New Delhi, May 1983, (henceforth Chenoy, 1983), pp. 229–233. The text of the policy is quoted in Sharad S. Marathe, *Regulation and Development: India's Policy Experience of Controls over Industry,* New Delhi, Sage, 1986, p. 36 ff.
4. The authors of the Bombay Plan wanted the state to hand over control of state-run industries to big business after a certain period. But because of the economic burdens caused by the proposed quantum of deficit financing, "Practically every aspect of economic life will have to be so rigorously controlled by government that individual liberty and freedom of enterprise will suffer a temporary eclipse". Cf. Chenoy, 1983, pp. 219–225. Left nationalists had a much more radical approach, Cf. *ibid.,* & R. Palme Dutt, *India Today,* Calcutta, Manisha, 1970, the first Indian edition was published in 1947.
5. "Report of the Economic Programme Committee," reprinted in *Young India,* Special Independence Day number 1972, Vol. 2, Nos. 34-40. 0 101-0103.
6. For the then different representative character of ASSOCHAM and FICCI, see Stanley A. Kochanek, *Business and Politics in India,* Berkeley, University of California Press, 1974.
7. "6th April 1948 Industrial Policy Statement", *Constituent Assembly Debates, Legislative,* Vol. III, Part II, 1948, pp. 3293–3297.
8. Kamal A. Mitra Chenoy, "Indian and foreign Private Capital: Competition and Collaboration", *Social Science Probings,* March 1987, Vol. 4, No. 1, pp. 77–78, Henceforth Chenoy, 1987.
9. *Constituent Assembly Debates. Legislative, op. cit.,* pp. 3402–3405.
10. Michael Kidron, *Foreign Investments in India,* London: Oxford University Press, 1965, pp. 100–101.
11. *Ibid.,* pp. 97–98: Chenoy, 1987, p. 80; Kamal A. Mitra Chenoy, "Industrial Policy and Multinationals in India", *Social Scientist,* March 1985, Vol. 13, No. 3, pp. 19–17, Henceforth Chenoy, 1985.
12. Chenoy, 1985, p. 17
13. Kidron, *op. cit.,* pp. 133–136. A quite different reading of industrial policy is given in Jagdish N. Bhyagwati & Padma Desai, *India: Planning for Industrialization and Trade Policies since* 1951, London: Oxford University Press, 1970; and in Isher J. Ahluwalia, *Industrial Growth in India: Stagnation since the mid 60s.* Delhi, Oxford University Press, 1985.
14. Lok Sabha Secretariat, *National Industrial Policy,* New Delhi, 1985, Appendix II.
15. Chenoy, 1987, p. 83; *Eastern Economist,* 4th May 1956; A.K. Gopalan's (CPI MP) speech, *Lok Sabha Debates,* Vol. V, Part 2, 25th May 1956, col. 9424.
16. Quoted in the ITT Annual Report for 1963. See also Ranajit Das Gupta, *Problems of Economic Transition: Indian Case Study,* Calcutta, National, 1970, pp. 71–72.
17. India, Ministry of Industries, *Final Report of the Industries Development Procedures,* Delhi, Manager of Publications, 1964.
18. India, Ministry of Industry, "Final Report of the reconstituted Industries Development Procedures Committee", February 1966, mimeo.

19. Bhagwati and Desai, *op. cit.*, p. 478.
20. India, Ministry of Industrial Development, Internal Trade and Company Affairs, *Report of the Industrial Licensing Policy Inquiry Committee,* New Delhi: Manager of Publications, 1969, Main Report & Vols. I-IV.
21. *Ibid.*, Main Report, p. 74
22. *Reserve Bank of India Bulletin,* August 1969, p. 1150.
23. Studies that have examined these shifts in economic policy have generally not studied the role of Western pressures as a causative factor. See for example Bhagwati and Desi. *op. cit.*, Chapter 22; Jagdish N. Bhagwati and T.N. Srinivasan, *Foreign Trade Regimes and Economic Development: India,* New York: National Bureau of Economic Research, 1976, Chapters 8, 10 and 11: and Cheryl Payer. The *Debt Trap: The International Monetary Fund and the Third World,* New York & London: Monthly Review Press. 1974, Chapter 8. Payer is, however, aware that the IMF and the World Bank pressurize debtor governments of reduce or discard state controls over the private sector in their economies. *ibid.*, Chapter 10.
24. A.K Bagchi & Nirmala Bannerjee (eds.) *Change and Choice in Indian Industry.* Calcutta: K P. Bagchi, 1981; Prabhat Patnaik. "Market Question and Capitalist Development in India", *Economic and Political Weekly,* Annual, August 1984, pp. 1251–1260: KN. Raj "Some Observations on Economc Growth in India over the period 1952-53 to 1982-83", *Economc and Political Weekly,* 13th October 1984, pp. 1801–1804.
25. Chenoy, 1987, pp. 483–484.
26. S.K. Goyal, *Monopoly Capital and Public Policy,* New Delhi, Allied, 1979.
27. Sudip Chaudhuri, "FERA: Appearance and Reality", *Economic and Political Weekly,* 21st April 1979, p. 739 ff.: Nagesh Kumar, "Regulating Multinational Monopolies in India", *ibid.*, 29th May 1982, p. 909ff.
28. S.K Goyal, "Some Aspects of the Multinational Corporations in India", Indian Institute of Public Administration, New Delhi, December 1980, mimeo.
29. K.N. Kabra, KM. Chenoy, *et. al.*, "Recent Trends in Economic Policies and Planning in India", *Social Science Probings,* December 1985, Vol. 2. No. 4, pp. 459–499. (henceforth Kabra, Chenoy, *et. al.*, 1985).
30. S.K. Goyal, K.S., Chalapati Rao, and Nagesh Kumar, *Small-Scale Sector and Big Business,* New Delhi, Indian Institute of Public Administration, 1984.
31. India, Ministry of Industry, Department of Industrial Development, *Statement on Indusrial Policy.* Delhi, 1980.
32. The confidential IMF documents on India's loan were published in abridged form in N. Ram's dispatches in the *Hindu,* October 17-21, 1981. See also the white paper published by the Government of West Bengal on the IMF loan.
33. Kabra and Chenoy, *et. al.*, 1985, pp. 459–499.
34. *Ibid.*
35. *Financial Express,* 25th March 1985.
36. 1956 Industrial Policy Resolution cited in Lok Sabha Secretariat, *op. cit.*, para. 6.
37. Kamal A. Mitra Chenoy, "Industrial Policy Statement 1991: Privatizing India", *Mainstream,* 3rd August 1991, pp. 2–3, 32–33; K.N. Kabra, "From a Statist to a Corporatist Framework", *ibii.*, pp. 5–6, 34-35; N. Bhattacharya, "Tailored to suit Fund-bank Interests"; *Ibid.*, pp. 7–8, 28 Statement issued by the Conventian in Defence of Economic Sovereignty sponsored by the Left Parties in New Delhi on 19th July 1991, reprinted in *ibid.*, pp. 29–31.
38. For instance, the *Asian Development Outlook* 1993, Manila Asian Development Bank, April 1993, refers "to a major program(me) of structural reform initiated in July 1991. (p. 139).
39. Praful Bidwai, "The Big Pertroleum Scam", *The Times of India,* New Delhi. 13th January 1994, P: 8.

40. *Business India,* January 3-16, 1994, pp. 59–67.
41. Jefferson Penberthy and Anita Pratap, "Running Scared", *Time,* January 10, 1994, p. 28.
42. Rakesh Khar, "Delhi backs Bombay Industrialists demand for level playing field", *The Economic Times,* New Delhi, 7th November 1993, p. 1; & Rakesh Khar, "FICCI joins Bombay Club in seeking level playing field", *ibid.*, 14th December 1993, p. 24.
43. D.H. Pai Panandiker, "Level Playing Field", in ASSOCHAM, *Direct Taxation; Some Legal and Administrative Problems and Certain Specific Policy Issues".* New Delhi, n.d. (1993), pp. 45–52.
44. S.K. Barua and J.R. Varma, "Multinational companies strike gold", *The Economic Times,* New Delhi, 11th Novemebr 1993, pp. 1–4.
45. "Bombay Club's apprehensions legitimate: PM", *The Economic Times,* New Delhi, 16th November. 1993. p. 1.
46. Sudip Chaudhuri, "Financing of Growth of Transnational Corporations in India", *Economic and Political Weekly,* 18th August 1979, pp. 1431–1435.
47. Nagesh Kumar and Kamal Mitra Chenoy. "Multinationals and Self-Reliance: A Case Study of the Drugs and Pharmaceutical Industry", *Social Scieniisi,* No. 107, April 1982, pp. 13–34.
48. Calculated from information in the *Bombay Stock Exchange Directory.*
49. *Reserve Bank of India Bulleting,* June 1974, pp. 1040–1083.
50. Calculated from Union Carbide India Ltd. *Annual Reports, 1981-1983.*
51. India, Department of Science and Technology, Indian National Committee on Science and Technology, *An Approach to the Science and Technology Plan,* Delhi 1973, p. 28.
52. Calculated from India, Ministry of Law, Justice and Company Affairs, *Directory of Joint Stock Companies in India 1980,* New Delhi: Manager of Publications, 1980, Vol. II; and India, Department of Science and Technology, *Directory of R* & D *Units.* Quoted in S.P. Verma, Anil Nauriya, Kamal Mitra Chenoy, *et. al., Political Dimensions of Multinational Corporations in India,* a report under the Indo-Dutch Programme on Alternatives in Development, New Delhi: Indian Institute of Public Administration, August 1983, mimeo., p. 54.
53. Delhi Science Forum. *Bhopal Gas Tragedy,* New Delhi, Delhi Science Forum, 1985.
54. Barry Castleman, "The Double standard in Industrial Hazards", *Multinational Monitor,* Vol. 5, No. 9, September 1984, pp. 5–6.
55. Kumar and Chenoy, *op. cit.,* and Nagesh Kumar and Kamal Mitra Chenoy, "Multinationals in Less Developed Countries: A Case Study of Drug Multinationals in India", *Internationales Asienforum* (FRG). Vol. 14, Nos. 2/3, September 1983, pp. 175–194.

29

Political Economy of Employment Planning

Kamal Nayan Kabra

Planning, by its very nature, is a goal-oriented activity or rather a means for purposively operating, regulating, guiding, and controlling various specified activities. In socio-economic sphere, the inevitable inter-connectedness of various activities enlarges the scope and range of planning activities to encompass at least the totality of the relatively more closely inter-connected activities. Another source for enlarging the scope of planning are the inter-connections among the objectives of planning, their complementarities, trade-offs, and inter-faces. It is these features of the planning process which even without invoking its context and objectives, make planning—its methodology, principal-agent relationships, strategic decisions, decision-criteria, policies, programmes and implementation mechanisms and procedures—areas of intense political debates and conflicts. These debates are political because of their participants, be they theorists, technocrats, planocrats, politicians, social activists, businessmen, or workers, take their positions on the basis of their values, world-view, interests, and aspirations. No pure objective theoretical analysis or transcendental national interest or general principles of universal humanism in their abstract, quintessential form guide the course of these debates which inevitably turn into political conflicts using every possible fora and means. It is on account of such a character of the planning process and the catholicity of its applicability and relevance that no single social-science discipline by means of its pure and exclusive theoretical apparatus can do justice to the complex tasks of plan formulation, implementation, evaluation, and further refinement of the principles of planning.

Thus, planning is a subject which necessitates an integrated social-science approach. As a part of such an approach, it becomes essential to go into the political economy of any major objective of planning in order to move towards grasping elements of its actual traverse.

This approach becomes especially relevant and necessary in order to understand the fluctuating fortunes of the objective of attaining full employment which has, in one form or another, remained a constant accompaniment of India's successive Five-Year Plan and finds a prominent place in the election manifestos of various political parties.

In this paper an attempt has been made in the following section to consider the changing views and approaches of the planners (i.e., the official planning agency) to the question of ensuring employment opportunities to all the able-bodied and willing individuals (the principle 'he who does not work, neither shall eat' does not seem to have found acceptance in India). Following this, we will put forward some political economy hypotheses concerning the treatment accorded to the employment objective in Indian Planning.

Gainful productive work which steadily ensures means of maintenance and a reproduction to all the able-bodied adult, i.e., mechanisms which really, effectively, and symbiotically incorporate them in the economy, is still not considered a feasible proposition in the short-run at both mainstream academic and certain political levels, notwithstanding its undoubted desirability and significance. The Eighth Plan of the National Front government proposed to make a U-turn from the past insofar the place of employment objective in Indian planning is concerned (Manifesto of National Front, 1989; Planning Commission, 1990, para 3, 4, 6, and 14). It proposed to reject the trickle-down and indirect approach and work directly for employment, poverty alleviation, and equity (Planning Commission, March 1990).

Important theoretical and empirical issues as also questions of political and ideological stances are involved in these two diametrically opposed positions on the relative place, content, time-frame, and possibilities of the full-employment in development planning in countries like India. With a view to clarify some of the issues involved in this controversy, it is proposed to analyse and examine the evolution of the thinking of Indian planners over successive five-year plans on the strategy, priority, policies, and programmes concerning employment generation.

A retrospect of this kind throws helpful light on the present controversy regarding the feasibility and methods of attaining full employment as a guaranteed right say, over a medium term, with provision for compensation like unemployment allowance for those who fail to find such regular and secure work and with a level of productivity at least marginally higher than the currently obtaining level.

Having accepted employment generation as an important objective of planning, holding that "development is, in a sense, but another name for employment opportunities" the Indian planners tended, right from the First Plan, to adopt a rather cautious approach to the content of employment and its relative priority *vis-a-vis* output growth, capital accumulation, and technical efficiency. It was held that there were limited possibilities of increasing both real and money incomes in the short-run for the newly employed if inflationary pressures and a fall in the real income of those already employed has to be prevented. The gigantic size of the problem in terms of the backlog of unemployment, rising numbers, and low existing levels of productivity, the constraints on increasing capital-formation and technological advancement seem to have exercised considerable influence on the time-frame and methods for increasing employment. These factors argued in favour of the direct use of manpower for capital-formation without making a draft on the community's savings-a task for which the critical bottleneck appeared essentially as one of the organizations.

Quite different from the mobilization of idle manpower for building up social economic infrastructure was the problem of fuller employment at a higher real income. This was considered in a way, the quintessence of employment objective because in India the problem was mainly of under-employment which was considered "another facet of low productivity." It was maintained that under-employment, or low productivity is "due to a shortage of capital equipment and technical skills" and shortage of land. The task, therefore, was to utilize manpower for productive purposes so as to increase the volume of goods and services available in the country and to raise living standards all round. It is clear that this perspective makes the task of increasing employment distinguishable from that of increasing national income. Thus, the task was that of "increasing the productivity of labour so that larger employment can be provided at rising levels of real income. This is obviously linked to the whole question of capital accumulation and technical efficiency".

One may recall that similar role to capital accumulation has been assigned by the planners for development as such. It means fuller employment and economic development were treated as almost identical long-term tasks. However, one important aspect of complementarity visualized was that over a longer time period inadequate growth of one would exercise a check on the progress of the other. The idea seems to be that growth of employment without commensurate growth in output and productivity may lead to inflation and shortage of investible resources. A contrary process may invite complications owing to inadequate demand. Thus, the plan largely equated the problem of employment and development in a, long-term perspective.

The key proposition of this reasoning was that the processes of employment generation can get into swing 'only as capital-formation goes up'. Capital-formation leads to increase in national output and this involves an increased demand for labour, "especially if care is taken to adopt labour-intensive processes to the maximum extent possible". This is the classic statement of the basic trickle-down or pull-up approach under which investment-bred increases with income increase directly and indirectly with the demand for labour in order to enable the low-productivity under-employed population to share the fruits of growth. The planners implicitly recognized that, left to themselves, these processes may involve capital-intensive and labour-displacing technologies and hence the specific policy-guidelines, were explicitly enunciated. One, conscious adoption of labour-intensive technologies without compromising on efficiency. Second, in traditional large employment generating industries, replacement, and modernization should take care not to create technological unemployment.

Among the structural aspects of employment, greater need for employment in the industrial sector, particularly in small-scale and cottage-industries, and remoteness of the stage when tertiary sector employment would be able to absorb a growing proportion of the labour-force were recognized. It was maintained that changes in the occupational pattern are not ends of development but are "a corollary of development". Under this perspective, non-agricultural employment was to grow in stages as labour-absorption prospects in manufacturing sector were limited, particularly in view of the emphasis "on expanding producer-goods industries". In sum, it can be said that a conscious decision to approach the problem of unemployment and underemployment indirectly and in a long-term perspective was taken on the basis of a clearly spelled out process of reasoning. It is possible on this basis to spot out the missing links in the chain of arguments and subject this reasoning to a closer scrutiny, particularly in terms of the political economy of development.

The approach to the employment objectives evolved as a part of the development strategy devised in the First Plan document continued, in its essentials, right upto the Eighth Plan period with some modifications, refinements, fine-tuning, and in certain respects, greater degree of realism in some sectoral, regional, and programmatic aspects. In the following, we briefly examine the employment perspective and policies evolved as a part of different plans.

The Second Five-Year Plan recognized the poor performance on the employment front, leading to increase in the backlog of unemployment and under-employment. It happened during a plan which exceeded its output growth target. Even then the planners did not question, even in passing, the basic approach of indirectly dealing with unemployment and under-employment through capital-formation and technical efficiency as "the objective is increasing employment at rising levels of incomes." It maintained that "employment is implicit in and follows investment" and that "the volume of employment grows only as the supply of tools and equipment on the one hand and of the wage-goods on which the incomes of the newly employed come to be spent is expanded."

It is worth noting that along with "tools and equipment", there is an explicit mention of wage-goods as important determinants of the volume of employment. This should be viewed against the fact that the Second Five-Year Plan introduced the model of relatively higher priority for the capital-goods sector along with a plea to increase, the role of cottage and small-industries for augmenting the supply of consumers' goods. However, the thinking on employment continued to be dominated by the critical role of investment, labour productivity, the importance of the use of machinery, and new techniques for higher productivity. Making an empirical statement that the problem of endemic unemployment is not acutest in machine-using high productivity countries, it was argued that low productivity leads to low incomes, which in term inhibit the supply of "currently needed consumer goods and keeps down the size of the markets". Thus, the size of the market was made to impinge mainly on the level of productivity and not on the volume of employment. This may well be regarded as a preference for the market-deepening approach over the market-widening approach. In this restatement of the vicious circles tautology, the starting point is assigned to low productivity.

In fact, the link between rising investment and high productivity was visualized so strongly that even the case for labour-intensive methods of production was qualified because, for obtaining increases in employment "at rising levels of income" increased investment for the production of tools and equipment was considered necessary. This, in turn, required surpluses for investment and hence "it is nonetheless true that labour-saving devices in particular are often a necessary condition for increasing employment opportunities in the system as a whole" owing to their presumed contribution to reinvestible surpluses.

The plan went on to analyse the question of choice of techniques and its impact on the availability of surpluses considered crucial for long-term growth and full employment. In this analysis a distinction was made between "surplus generated" and "surplus available." Despite comparatively low surplus per person 'generated' by labour-intensive techniques, the surplus available may become larger if one took into account "the social and economic costs of maintaining those who would otherwise remain unemployed." This reasoning is true in the context of displacement of labour caused by capital-intensive techniques. One finds for the first time a reference to the 'social and economic costs' of unemployment, though without any practical results.

It may be mentioned that this dichotomy between low per worker surplus and larger total surplus has been recognized quite cogently by Kurt Mandelbaum and simply on the basis of the size of 'surplus' manpower involved at a relatively low level of productivity without bringing in the consideration of social and economic costs of maintenance of the unemployement and under-employeds.

The implications of this realization had the potential of changing the perspective of employment policy and plan priorities. But the availability of larger total surplus by means of labour-intensive methods was considered difficult to realize owing to "organizational" problems involved in its mobilization owing to a large number of small units involved.

Mobilization of surpluses from the propertied, well-to-do group is very difficult because of their political clout and the power they wield in all spheres, even though their number is very small. This is clear from, widely admitted low elasticity of direct taxes and exponential growth of tax evasions and black economy. The manner in which indirect taxes cover the goods of mass consumption and contribute many a times more revenue than that contributed by the direct taxes (presumably meant to mobilize the surplus accruing to the propertied and the high-pay employees) (*Long-term Fiscal Policy,* 1985) shows that the euphemism of organizational problems cannot be taken seriously, particularly a factor like "a large number of small units" from whom surplus has to be mobilized.

In addition to the above, the Second Plan gave attention to break up the problem in terms of "sectors, regions, and classes" and evolved specific policy and programmatic guidelines. Its thinking on the sectoral pattern of employment became crystallized around the position that shift of workforce away from agriculture and towards mining and modern small and large industry and transport, construction, and communications is inevitably involved in the very process of development. Therefore, it opted for the policy of keeping further labour-absorption in agriculture to the minimum. One wonders if it was this perspective which made the planners deny the employment friendly implications of redistribution of land among the landless.

One can say, with the benefit of hindsight, that the implications of this view for broad based agricultural growth, particularly in the international comparative context of rates, labour-absorption in countries similar to India, have not been helpful. Further, these Second Plan formulations regarding the pattern of occupational structure came in for rude repudiation in the reality as seen in the form of structural retrogression India experienced.

From the point of analysis, the Second Plan advanced one proposition of great insight which one can see as a preview of later theories in which the phenomenon of under employment was reformulated in the guise of 'informal sector' work. The plan maintained that with development-leading to larger demand for labour in the tertiary sector "many types of work which at present get done within the household become distinct commercial services. In this way develop a large number of small business and trades offering opportunities for independent work." One wishes in this line of reasoning to have been pursued further for its policy implications. The questions of employment, income-earning opportunities and levels of productivity viewed jointly with costs of production and levels of living have to be seen in their organizational-institutional context for devising appropriate policies and the content and strategy of development.

The experience of Second Plan led to further disillusionment regarding the capacity of investment, increased the supply of tools and equipment, high productivity techniques, and faster growth to make a dent into the problems of unemployment. The Third Plan projections uncovered addition of three million persons to the backing of unemployment and underemployment (*Third Five Year Plan*). Instead of inviting a review of the basic approach to the question of employment, the suggestion of starting fire-fighting tactical moves in the form of rural public works programme with some emphasis on programmes of rural industrialization by means of a strengthened economic infrastructure and industrial estates may be regarded as the distinct contribution of the Third Plan to employment planning.

By taking local conditions into account, the rural public works programmes were intended to bring about increased agricultural production, especially in relatively backward areas. The plan emphasized the area-approach in order to respect to the needs of specific occupational and skills groups.

The basic formulations in the plans remained unshaken in its commitment to the inherited approach, notwithstanding the empirical demonstration to the effect that "in industry, increase in investment and capacity does not lead to a proportionate growth of employment because new processes, especially in large-scale manufacture, generally have to be based on high productivity techniques." The conclusion which has been dawned upon the planners from the lack of a necessary positive elasticity of employment with respect to increased investment in industrial capacity was to go in for a balancing exercise "by a deliberate effort in other fields (non-industrial fields-KNK) to employ techniques which will be more labour-intensive and will save capital resources, specially foreign exchange." It is clear that the approach was to leave the choice of techniques in industries unaffected. Additionally, it was implicit that not only the policy of treating employment as a by-product of capital accumulation and growth of output should be continued but the choice of techniques need not to be integrated with questions of the pattern of income-distribution and choice of product-mix. One can see how selective choice of variable of analysis affect and is affected by powerful non-academic, broader social forces.

Against this background, the Fourth Plan sought to explicitly link "social justice and equity" and improvement of the condition of the common man and the weaker sections to "provision of employment and education" (*Fourth Five Year Plan*). It may be regarded as giving recognition to the importance of what has come to be called 'human capital'. The trade-off between restriction of modern (high-productivity capital-intensive) sector and increasing "employment and income opportunities for people employed in traditional industries" was recognized. However, the die remained cast in favour of the long-run, indirect, employment-benefits perspective, even though it was recognized that the short-run output growth-centred approach worsens the distribution of income and wealth as it "necessitates the concentration of effort in areas and on classes of people who already have the capacity to respond to growth opportunities."

Despite somewhat more strident reiteration of the interests of equity and. the welfare of the weaker sections, and the need for detailed specific and also local planning and implementation nothing really substantially different in terms of understanding, policies or programmes could emerge in the Fourth Plan formulations.

It was the plan when the need for lower level, micro planning in a multi-level planning framework was explicitly articulated, yielding a richer concept of district planning. Little wonder, therefore, that the inadequacies of the results obtained through rural-works programme were traced to the fact that "it was not integrated into local development planning." It argued a strong case for the local plans to take into account local needs for creating employment opportunities."

Following on the heels of a prolonged recession in industry and the switch-over to the Green Revolution strategy of agricultural development, the Fourth Plan faced quite a few difficult tasks. The organized manufacturing sector, primarily preservation of the private sector, came nowhere near the plan expectations regarding generation of employment opportunities. Therefore, the plan stressed the role of public sector investment in industry and infrastructure for making good the shortfalls. For dealing with the consequences of the 'betting on the strong' strategy initiated by the Green Revolution package, especially target-group oriented programmes like SFDA, IRDP, NREP, etc., were expected to open new possibilities of employment generation.

By this time, ILO has entered into the Third World employment scenario with its special programmes. The high point of these efforts was an attempt to come to grips with many aspects of low productivity, income differentials, and worsening situation in these respects. It was felt that the traditional concepts like underemployment and disguised unemployment were full of conceptual-theoretical inadequacies and turned out to be of little help in relieving these problems. The Fourth Plan formulations took explicit note of these strings and sought to redefine the concept of labourforce in the light of the preponderance of "self-employment and production within the household enterprises." These realizations beckoned to all the trappings of what came to be called the 'informal sector'. However, these realizations could change neither the basic indirect, long-term approach to fuller employment nor specific employment expanding policies, in term of inter- and intra-sectoral and regional and micro-level planning making use of and strengthening the informal work opportunities. It could not introduce any more realistic and effective thrust towards greater labour-intensity in the choice of techniques.

Hence claiming that the Fourth Plan development strategy has been "broadly in conformity with" the ILO approach, it went on to reiterate the old position that "emphasis has equally been placed on productive employment on a sufficiently high level of efficiency." It may also be noted that in the wake of the severe drought of the mid-1960s, the plan revitted the rural-works programme to 40 chronically drought-prone areas with a view to provide "unemployment relief in such areas." In the form of Maharashtra's Employment Guarantee Programme and Gujarat's scheme of 'Right to Work', the rural-works programmes acquired a new dimension towards the creation of such work-opportunities on a regular basis, though their integration under a local level plan and movement towards a living-wage remained far cries. Since these programmes were not regular in the sense of location, projects, and on-going employment to an identifiable group of persons, they offered only an opportunity for relief and were at best semi-productive.

The Fifth Plan built on the understanding and insights evolved by the Fourth Plan, particularly with respect to local level planning, especially for agriculture and unregistered sector in a multi-level fanning framework by proposing to strengthen planning machinery both at the states and local levels as a part of a comprehensive area approach (*Fifth Five-Year Plan,* 19-21). It was recognized that employment in various household industries had worsened and hence there was need for "regeneration of employment in the unregistered sector through an appropriate policy framework."

The Fifth Plan also continued its adherence to the basic approach adopted since the beginning of planning. The Fifth Plan adopted a redistributive agenda regarding consumption expenditure. Possibly reflecting this concern and reversing the position taken earlier, the Fifth Plan proposed to link rural employment to "augmenting agricultural productivity and rigorously implementing land reforms" in order to build a "productive small-farmer base by means of tenancy reform."

The Sixth Five-Year Plan assessed the progress of employment generation under the plans and noted that the backlog of unemployment has increased. However, the task was taken to be the same as has been understood so far, *viz.*, "to generate more employment without affecting adversely the growth in production" (Sixth Five-Year Plan, 19-22).

At the basic strategy and policy-level, the Sixth Plan marked no departure from what has been under operation so far. Its main point was an attempt at more precise estimates of chronic, seasonal, and part-time unemployment on the basis of NSS data. On this basis, a more detailed and disaggregated data-base was created for undertaking many special programmes like NRF, IRDP, TRYSEM, Dairy Development Programmes, minimum needs programmes, programmes by SFDA as also special programmes for women, tribals, unorganized urban poor, and programmes for desert and drought-prone areas.

Since organized sector subscribe only about 18 per cent of the increase in labour-force and public sector employment, too, could not be expanded, the planners opined that "policy-measures should be guided for self-employment ventures." Carrying forward the ILO inspired Fourth Plan approach towards the informal sector, it was postulated that some special measures for helping urban self-employed belonging to the informal sector will be undertaken mainly by way of training and credit-facilities. Since decentralized special target group-employment projects mostly as centrally-sponsored programmes, were the main thrust possibly owing to limited employment impact of growth-oriented planning and policies, at the district level a nodal employment agency, District Manpower Planning and Employment Generation Council was to be set up in each district, which will *interalia,* prepare district 'employment budget' encourage group self-employment and will assess 'employment impact' of development and modernization projects.

It can be seen that owing to actually observed limited effectiveness in obtaining adequate employment impact through the investment, growth, and modernization based basic plan strategy, a series of special, target-group-oriented and *ad-hoc* programmes for providing relief and employment for a limited period to a large number of rural and urban poor became important supplementary, fire-fighting elements of the planned approach to the employment objective. The physical assets, income flows, inter-sectoral and macro-balances, and productivity aspects of these employment projects were downplayed compared to their purchasing-power disbursement intention. One may well say that in effect and, to the extent such programmes could be successfully and honestly implemented, they may be considered a watered down and indirect 'social security' programme to a greater extent than full-blooded employment programme. However, the employment target in terms of standard person-years by means of special programmes can provide, at best, *ad-hoc,* irregular income-earning opportunities. This kind of work cannot be equated with regular, secure employment in viable public, private or cooperative sector economic activities. It involves essentially a budgetary transfer.

The Seventh Plan continued the same approach of growth plus supplementary special programmes, with somewhat larger financial allocations and attempted fine-tuning in terms of specific categories of labour-force, sectorally and regionally, for achieving the employment objective of planning. It went on to state that "the growth of the economy should have the capacity to absorb the backlog of unemployment, underemployment, and a proportion of additions to the labour-force. To meet this end, supplemental programmes should have to be incorporated for specific targets-groups/areas for employment creation, income generation and poverty alleviation" (Seventh Five-Year Plan).

Among the specific nuances attached to the basic approach of 'more of the same' with attempts to realize the advantages of learning by doing, notable advances were marked in areas of informal sector, involving self-employment (both in modern and rural areas) with a view to evolve a policy package for the informal sector, especially regarding the welfare and the working and living conditions of unorganized labour. After the First Plan, for the first time, the question of wage-policy was explicitly raised again though without yielding anything like wage-policy. Among the special target groups bonded, child and women labour and educated unemployed came in for specific attention.

Recent emphasis on electronics, automobiles, and other sunrise industries was considered especially favourable to the employment of educated manpower. It was maintained that "objective of employment generation should not mean the adoption of static technology." Like the Sixth Plan, latest NSS data and projections regarding the size of the labour force, its age composition, employment status, and likely magnitude of remainder of unemployment were worked out and the need for developing "a proper linkage of economic planning with manpower and educational planning" was recognized.

We have seen that the abortive Janata Dal Plan's approach paper (*Towards Social Transformations*) made declarations regarding a basic overhaul of the approach to employment planning. However, with the change of government, the Eighth Plan (1992-97) returned to the former basic position on the employment objective, though at the level of rhetory, there were some strident references to the need to ensure adequate growth of employment to achieve full employment by the turn of the century (*Eighth Five Year Plan*, 1992-97). An important departure in this plan was the enunciation of the focus of the plan which, *inter alia*, mentioned the creation of a *social security net* through employment generation. Apparently, it might be meant for dealing with the recessionary effects of the stabilization programme initiated to tackle the acute fiscal and external payment crises. The plan suggested a target of creation of some 10 million jobs per year; on an average, employment for some 22 thousand persons a day. It implied an employment growth rate of 2. per cent to 2.8 per cent per annum. The dismal performance in terms of employment during the earlier plans was recognized but without working out any change in the Seventh Plan framework.

Given the context of Structural Adjustment Programme (SAP) initiated in 1991, the prospects of a decline in growth rate and employment and an increase in unemployment for the first two–three years were recognized. Given this IMF-World Bank dictated perspective, and noting the absence of a wage policy, "excessive regulation of conditions of employment making labour adjustment highly difficult" was blamed for "restructuring employment expansion". Credit policy too came in for flak on the same count. Hence, placing reliance on the market-forces on giving employment-friendly results, a plea was made "to reduce the overall degree of protection to labour." Since only a small part of the workforce has some kind of protection of employment a reduction in the protection available to a small number was deemed to contribute to social security for an overwhelming majority of workers with "completely insecure and unprotected conditions in the unrecognized sector." If this is not so, the only other reason for the reduction in the overall degree of protection to organized labour may be equality in sharing adversity-a policy of removing privileges not available to a majority. The major hassle with this approach is that it runs counter to the overall tenure of SAP, which is more of the same, of betting on the strong by improving incentives, rewards, and opportunities. The plan's detailed sectoral work on specific sectors seemed to lack co-ordination and regard for conditions for realising the sectoral potential. For instance, it is maintained that "fisheries can grow as fast as 7 per cent per annum because about 2/3 of the marine and inland potential is unexploited." What is missing squarely is the consideration of potential demand and domestic affordability of fish at the prevailing price and income levels.

In sum, the Eighth Plan and subsequently other Plans are basically a reiteration of an approach which has shown scanty results so far. This is understandable in the sense that the role, scope, and methodology of the plan have changed in directions which are hardly employment-friendly rather than overcoming the limitation of over-centralized initiative, bureaucratic, economistic, paternalistic, one-dimensional, growth-oriented planning, it has blamed the plan failures on being excessively statist and hence has advocated a policy of rolling-back the state. Naturally, employment, a part and parcel of the process of the empowerment of the people so that they make use of the state, markets and the plans for their indigenous, integrated set of objectives, has to take backseat. The apparent emphasis on employment seems to be based on misleading and inappropriate concepts, theories, and policies.

After nearly five and a half decades and in spite of considerable expansion, strengthening, diversification, and acquisition of resistance by the Indian economy, neither employment in the conventional sense, nor active and rewarding participation in the community's efforts to produce and distribute the means of livelihood in a sustainable manner has become available to a rather large number of Indians. We have seen the traverse of the employment question over the successive plans, which has neither been marked for its fruit-bearing or light-bearing character. We have travelled a great deal basically in order to remain where we were, except for the lost opportunities, its immense human and social cost, particularly for the generations of the unemployed who have receded in the past. As a simple but telling indicator of the failure on the employment front, it may be noted that our agricultural-labourers' households, who constitute 23 per cent of the total, get less than 180 days of employment in a year at wages which are generally lower than the statutory minimum and with working conditions reminiscent of the feudal era. Creating opportunities for every participant in healthy economic life, described generally as creating near full employment (*i.e.*, making the labour-market a sellers' one) was treated as presently non-feasible and hence long-term objective during the 1950s. The same pleas are repeated presently when we are reaching the end of the century. In fact, the Eighth Five-Year Plan has placed the Structural Adjustment Programme (SAP) as the focus of the plan which is treated as superior to the plan objectives (*Eighth Five-Year* Plan, 1992). However, in keeping with the tradition of vexing eloquent on various 'desirable' objectives, the Eighth Plan reiterates the employment objective as well. But it has been demonstrated convincingly and accepted even by the votaries of the SAP that its immediate recessionary thrust would cause a net reduction in organized sector employment with similar repercussions in the unorganized/informal sector (*Alternative Economic Survey*, 1992). To put it straight, a plan with a focus on the implementation of SAP with negative employment implications cannot contribute to the attainment of fuller employment opportunities for its labour-force, howsoever, strident its articulation of the employment objective. There are other indications of how employment generation is finding a relatively low priority with the economic 'reformers' of the 1990s. Exit policy and deregulation of the labour-market have become dominant concerns in order to make India attractive to foreign investors. The main point of exit policy is to grant the management the freedom to 'fire' the entire workforce of the enterprise without any public regulation and scrutiny on the basis of its own decisions. In effect, this policy stance means that output growth, foreign exchange earning, modernization competitiveness, etc., are the prime concerns of the day and for this purpose, even if existing employment has to be sacrificed, let alone the question of creating additional employment avenues, the policy-makers will not hesitate to adopt such a course.

It is also clear that employment or avenues of meaningful, productive participants in the economic activities is something which matters to those who have no other means for it to save their labour. If for a certain length of time such a person fails to acquire access to means of meaningful participation or a scheme of social security, her/his supply price comes down or she/he is forced to adopt some informal 'survival' activity. This is an outcome which favours those who have under their direct command means of entering the circuit of economic activities as owners-controllers of the means of production and employers of the labour-power.

One need not labour the obvious class and social groups implications of the relative priority assigned to employment vis-a-vis other objectives in any highly differentiated society like ours. The very fact that employment effects of output growth were treated as important elements of the 'trickle-down' process and became the key means for the 'pull-up' exercises mounted by the public agencies highlights the social bias of those who accept a 'development' strategy incorporating 'trickle-down' or 'pull-up' mechanism for helping the poor by means of betting on the strong.

The politics of Indian planning failed to make the employment issue—despite its live-wire nature-an arena of active purposive socio-political conflicts and sustained popular struggles over plan-priorities, and popular mobilization programmes, policies, projects, technological and location-choices or short-run and medium-run macro-economic policies or the management of industrial relations. Partly, this became so owing to stated and declared concern for employment which was common between the ruling and the opposition parties. The sick industrial units were not allowed to close down, and quite a few were, in fact, taken-over, with a view, *inter alia,* to protect the existing employment avenues under trade union pressure. After the mid-1960s, massive absolute-size, special semi-productive employment programmes were taken up in rural India. The village and small-scale industries with the relatively higher rate of labour-absorption were given a special dispensation. As a result, a certain degree of operationally and credibility was acquired by the concern for employment, at least by way of special sectoral programmes and as a fire-fighting operation. Even the issue of reservations for the OBCs in public employment is related to preferential sharing of scarce job. These postures and taken steps helped generate some appropriate political responses and made for the survival of the essential window-dressing character of the stated employment-orientation.

Many people were duly impressed by the fact that thousands of crores of rupees were spent under the plans for creating millions of man-days of employment year-after-year. That effective employment remained a far cry and the overall impact of all the policies and plans taken together continued to increase the backlog of employment at the beginning of each new plan did not seem to have had so much visible impact on popular perception as the much advertised massive schemes of employment generation. Like the value of many much-touted democratic rights made available equally to everyone by the constitution (an instance of a type of democratic deceit) the employment rhetory and programmes tended to create among the literates, elites, and opinion leaders, a certain sense of complacency over the employment issue, particularly in view of the population explosion which contributed exponentially to the reserve army of labour and was treated as the villain of the piece-making unemployment an intractable problem for which they blamed the unrestrained and irresponsible reproductive behaviour of the poor themselves.

The frustration welling up among the unemployed youth, particularly those who either acquired some education or were school drop-outs was characterized by various political formations and socio-economic and political practices in such a diverse set of diversionary methods that nothing basic, far-going and really effective need to be conceded to these powerful, vocal potential centres of protest and worse. A telling and tragic instance of such an approach is the priority given to job-reservation for the OBC by the National Front government towards the end of the 1980s over its own promise of granting the right to work. Despite some indisputable merit of the reservation policy, its capacity to confer tangible benefits to the OBCs is rather limited (*The Third Concepts, 1989*).

The ruling party and other parties espousing similar interests and causes which are not serious about real employment-growth as a major correlate of development, recruited some vocal sections of the unemployed youth into the political arena as their storm troopers through the ubiquitous power-brokers, in the electoral and non-electoral politics, making them share the crumbs from the rent and clout which became available to them as a result of the commercialization, and criminalization of politics. The growing non-democratic, oligarchic, self-perpetuating, and self-selecting nature of the political parties and their leadership with excessive top-downism, in which political investment of billions of rupees of ill-gotten wealth and the adoption of campaigns for marketing of leaders, with advantage of pedigree as additional non-competitive advantage, created from the centre down to the villages and hamlets a class of political, lumpenized youths as brokers, vote banks, and *mastaans.* Those who could not find place in these found their way into various regional, ethnic, sectional, and communal political formations and movements with varying degrees of open and concealed militancy. Some political parties complemented these tactics and devices by occasional, sporadic movements demanding right to work, unemployment insurance, vocationalization of education, etc., with highly visible forms of one-shot agitation like *morchas, bandhs, gheraos,* and *jail-bharos.*

Some of the youth and students' wings of various political parties made these agitations, confined largely to their cadres, a hardy annual. These 'movements' and agitations hardly touched the really weak, unorganized, illiterate, and uncared-for youth, particularly from the rural and tribal areas. They could not conceive of integrating employment-oriented struggles with the overall policy-struggles over development issues. In fact, these activities cannot be sustained without grass-roots, direct, self-help programmes, for improving earnings and access to public goods. It is clear that heightened awareness of rights and possibilities which strengthen the will and capacity to struggle and define avenues of policy and programmatic reforms are related to the contexts, needs, and aspirations of people seeking a place under the sun. The youth wings of various political parties, even those of the left, have neglected these issues and adopted highly, sporadic actions which betray their highly centralized, non-empathic, alienated character-the politics from above which treats these constituencies basically as scaffoldings to 'power'.

Some beginnings in the form of presently fragmented micro-level NGOs shows a new avenue of hope and regeneration, though some black-sheep mar this scene as well.

There have been attempts to make planning a decentralized and participative exercise in order to make it a vehicle for the fulfilment of people's needs and aspirations. There can hardly be anything other than employment (not necessarily wage-employment) which can be a closet reflection of the needs and aspirations of the really marginalized. Thus, attempts to make Indian planning a multi-level exercise by instituting democratic decentralization and district level-planning should have acquired special orientation towards active manpower planning for full employment. However, larger socio-economic political and administrative factors saw to it that neither such a devolution of power nor granting of primacy to employment creation became really effective. Many studies of district planning and of Panchayati

Raj institutions lend support to these views. Thus, the new constitutional provisions for strengthening local institutions may not be able to do much for employment generation.

It has been argued that without changing the socio-economic power at the village level, grassroots democracy may remain a chimera. For this to happen, a thorough programme of land deconcentration and redistribution is essential. Land reforms are also a direct contribution to employment objective, as land provides/supplements productive work. So are land-augmenting techniques like irrigation, electrification of rural areas, etc., or rural industrialization and non-farm employment. But, given the present power-balance and its sway, land reforms are unlikely to be implemented through conventional administrative-legislative measures. It means in the near future, the employment question is unlikely to acquire primacy in our political economy as it stands today. In fact, signs of growing incorporation and the increased clout of the MNCs and G-7, as reflected in the SAP of the 1990s, has replaced employment generation and expansion r of the domestic market by exit policy, National Renewal Fund, preparation of a National Rehabilitation and Resettlement Plan, increasing adoption of product-mix and technologies of the MNCs which by their very nature tend to be labour-saving and loss of employment opportunities. Thus, one finds that the policy orientation during the 1990s is the same with which we started out during the 1950s: investment and output growth with accent on modem technology, through a combination of trickle-down, pull-up and social security cover, will over time create gainful employment opportunities. There is little reason, therefore, to expect a better deal on the employment front. With degeneration of politics and a sharp drop in the quelling of governance, one sees little reason to be surprised at such a turn of development.

Notes and References

GOI, Planning Commission, (1953), *First Five-Year Plan,* New Delhi.

GOI, Planning Commission, (1956), *Second Five-Year Plan,* New Delhi.

GOI, Planning Commission, (1962), *Third Five-Year* Plan, New Delhi.

GOI, Planning Commission, (1970), *Fourth Five-Year Plan,* New Delhi.

GOl, Planning Commission, (1976), *Fifth Five-Year Plan,* New Delhi.

GOI, Planning Commission, (1981), *Sixth Five-Year Plan,* New Delhi.

GOl, Planning Commission, (1985), *Seventh Five-Year Plan,* New Delhi.

GOI, (1973), *Report of the Committee on Unemployment,* New Delhi, Chairman, B. Bhagwati.

T.N. Srinivasan and P.K. Bardhan (1974), *Poverty and Income Distribution in India,* Calcutta, Statistical Publishing Society.

J.H. Adler, (1972), "The World Bank's Concept of Development", in J. Bhagwati and Eckans (ed.), Development and Planning.

J. Mouly and E. Costa, (1974), *Employment Policies in Developing Countries: A Comparative Analysis,* London, George Alien and Unwin.

K. Mandelbaum, (1955), *The Industrialisation of Backward Areas,* Oxford, Basil Blackwell.

Manmohan Singh, (1986), *The Quest for Equity in Development,* Pune, Gokhale Institute of Politics and Economics.

Rajkrishna, (1980), "The Economic Development of India", in *Scientific American,* September, pp. 166–178.

C.H. Rao, (1977), "Why our Employment Plans Fail?", in *Economic Times",* 30th September p. 5

Tarlok Singh, (1977), *"Organising the Rural Poor",* in *Janata,* 20th October.

Calmcross and Purl (ed.), "Management of the Indian Economy: A View in Retrospect," in *Employment, Income Distribution and Development stratetgy,* London, Macmillan, pp. 225–238.

M. Olson, (1982), *The Rise and Decline of Nations: Economic Growth Stagflation and Some Rigidities,* New Haven, Yale University Press.

K. Bhardwaj, (1989), *Paradigms in Development Theory: A Plea for a Labourist Approach,* D'Souza Honour Lecture, Indian Economic Association, Trivandrum (Mimeo),

A. Webster, (1984), *Introduction to the Sociology of Development,* Hampshire, Macmillan.

Mahbub Haq, (1976), *The Poverty Curtain,* New York, Columbia University Press.

C.T. Kurien, (1978), *Poverty, Planning and Social Transformation,* New Delhi, Allied Publishers.

O. Lange, (1960), "Some Problems Concerning Economic Planning in Underdeveloped Countries" in *Essays on Economic Planning,* Bombay, Asia Publishing House.

P.C. Mahalanoblis, (1961), *Talks on Planning,* Bombay, Asia Publishing House.

C. Bettlehelm, (1961), *Some Basic Planning Problems,* Bombay. Asia Publishing House.

C. Bettleheim, (1959), *Studies in the Theory of Planning,* Bombay, Asia Publishing House.

H.J. Duller, (1982), *Development Technology,* London, PKP.

F. Stewart and P. Streeten, (1971), "Conflict between Output and Employment Objectives in developing countries," In *Oxford Economic Papers,* Vol. 23, No. 2, pp. 145–168.

E.F. Schumachv, (n.d), *Social and Economic Problems: Calling for the Development of Intermediate Technology,* London.

Mahbub Haq, (1971), "Employment in the 1970's: A New Perspective", in *International Development Review,* Vol. 13, pp. 9–13.

L. Lefeber, (1967), "Regional Allocation of Resources in India," in PN. Rosenstain Rodan * (ed), *Pricing and Fiscal Policies,* Alien and Unwin.

G. Rosen, (1985), 'Western Economists and Eastern Societies: Agents of Change, " in *South Asia: 1950–1970,* New Delhi, OUP.

P.C. Mahalanobis, (1961), *Talks on Planning,* Bombay, Asia Publishing House.

National Front, (1989), *Manifesto of the National Front,* New Delhi.

Approach to Eighth Five-Year Plan, Draft, in *Financial Express,* 1990, New Delhi.

GOI, Department of Economic Affairs (1985), *Long-Term Fiscal Policy,* New Delhi.

A. Booth and Sundram, (1954), *Labour Absorption in Agriculture,* Delhi, OUP.

S.L. Shetty, (1978), "Structural Retrogression In Indian Economy," in *Economic and Political Weekly,* Annual No., March.

ILO, (1973), *Employment Incomes and Equality: A Strategy for Increasing Employment in Kenya,* Geneva.

C. Hanurnantha Rao and others, (1989), "14 per cent Growth Rate Required for Poverty Eradication," *Financial Express,* 26th August, 1989.

O. Lange, (1960), "Some Problems Concerning Economic Planning in Underdeveloped Countries," in *Essays on Economic Planning,* Asia Publishing House, p. 36.

GOI, Planning Commission, (1992), *Eighth Five-Year Plan,* New Delhi.

Public Interest Research Group, (1992), *Alternative Economic Survey,* Delhi.

K.N. Kabra, (1992), *Eighth Plan's Development Perspective: Economic Analysis and Policy Group,* mimeos IIPA, New Delhi.

GOl, Planning Commission, (1990), *Towards Social Transformation*, Approach to Eighth Five-Year Plan.

K.N. Kabra, (1990), "Debate on Reservation Policy," in *Third Concept (guested)*, October, New Delhi.

K.N. Kabra, (1978), *Planning Process in a District*, HPA, New Delhi.

Mahipal Singh, (1993), "Land Reforms: Key to Panchayatl Raj," *Times of India*, 20th July.

K.N. Kabra, (1981), "Concentration in Industrial Sector: Achilles' Heel of Land Reforms", *IFDA Dossier*, (Geneva) July-Sept. No. 22.

GOl, Ministry of Finance, (1993), *Economic Reforms: Two Years After and the Task Ahead*, New Delhi.

30

Science and Technology Policy

Subir Verma

❑ Science, Technology, and Development

Originating in the ambits of tremendous optimism about the western model of liberal democratic industrial modernity in the aftermath of the Second World War, development studies an extremely heterogeneous and inter-disciplinary had asserted the mutually beneficial nature of the relationship between the developed and the developing world and the possibility of transference of theoretical knowledge from the former to the latter.[1] Such an ideological support system, posited on the intellectual genius of the western socio-technological knowledge, had justified the transplantation of western culture, institutions and technology for the social, economic, and political changes in the developing countries. Accordingly, development of the underdeveloped countries had implicated their transition in a unilinear and teleological fashion from the ideal-typical pattern variables of tradition to those of western-style modernity, as epitomized by the USA. Thus conceived, development had involved not simply a process/stages of change but also a progressive transformation towards a goal. And this development, stylized as modernization, couched within which was westernization, had to be brought about by the modernizing elites.[2]

This tyrannization of historical possibilities, encapsulated in the ruling motif of development, had been succinctly captured by Jawaharlal Nehru, independent India's first Prime Minister: "Politics led me to economics and this led me inevitably to science and the scientific approach to all our problems and to life itself. It was science alone that could solve these problems of hunger and poverty, of insanitation and illiteracy, of superstition and deadening custom and tradition, of vast resources running waste, of a rich country inhabited by starving people."[3] Immanent in this instrumentalist notion of science had been the need for rapid industrialization poised on indigenous, scientific, and technological capacity as the lynchpin of development and the transmutation of the governing culture and values, institutions and processes on the test of scientific temper, and hence rationalization and secularization.

Four and a half decades of planning for scientific and technological development, India far from extracting the benefits of the scientific and technological revolution still faces inequity, injustice, and dependency. In the present dispensation of the deification of the market expressing the globalization and homogenization of the production and consumption systems, an evaluation of the science and technology policies, isolated as critical inputs in development, becomes therefore imperative.

❑ History—The Seeds of the Future Design

There was an urgency inspiring the Nehruvian call for a total renaissance of India. Under the British rule, India was not only bypassed by the industrial revolution but instead was de-industrialized and de-developed. Under the imperial scheme of things, not much thought was given to the application of science and technology in the economic development of India, forsaken as an agricultural colony. Consequently, because of a narrow policy, a vast technological gap appeared between the elites, fostered on British created opportunities exploited through the brazen adoption of English culture and striving to add political power to traditional priestly, commercial, and literary power, and the masses whose life-work was yet to be permeated with science and who pathetically lacked in scientific attitude, as also between India as a whole and the developed countries of the West.[4] Add to this, the fact that on the eve of independence, India was caught in the horrendous thores of partition and an equally abysmal poverty seen in low production and narrow productivity base.[5] Planned efforts towards correction and reconstruction was purportedly to be built upon developing the scientific and technological capability of the effulgent nation.

These imperatives notwithstanding, the seeds of the direction that the Indian society was required to undertake a planned industrial society integral to which was to be industrial research was sown in the pre-independence period itself.

In fact, the process of institutionalization of Western science in India, even though it was to subserve the needs of colonial presence and penetration, had commenced with the establishment of the Asiatic Society of Bengal in 1784 and its lineages of Great Surveys and Learned Societies.[6] However, the first efforts towards original research and its application began as a reaction to the pronounced literary bias of the modem education based on Macaulay'S Minutes and Wood's Despatch and with the formation of the Indian Association for the cultivation of science and the University College of Science. But, then, the systematic exposition of the envisaged order emerged only in the Indian Industrial Commission which was set up in 1916 in the vortex of the first world war's articulation of the needs of Indian industries. Here the discourses had crystallized at three levels: (1) the need to transform India from an agricultural to an industrial way of life with the colonial state as a pedagogue and a sponsor of organizations; (2) the role of science in mediating the transition from plantocracy to technocracy; and (3) the relationship of science and technology with the industrial process.[7]

While the recommendations of the Holland Commission fell victim to the logistics of war, by 1942 the cutting off of imports and the need to develop India as a supply base for the eastern theatre of World War II once again brought home the necessity of shifting the research emphasis from agriculture and medicine to import substitution. Support from the scientific organizations and scientists for this had already crystallized with the Meghnad Saha's Science and Culture Group orchestration of the need for planned industrialization underpinned by scienticized technology, institutionalized through industrial research, and guided by scientists and technocrats, informed with statistical inputs.[8] Fortified by the political support that had come forth in the form of Nehru's message "the future belongs to science and those who make friends with science and seek its help for advancement of humanity,"[9] the British Indian government constituted the Board of Scientific and Industrial Research (1940), the Council of Scientific and Industrial Research (1942), the Industrial Utilization Bureau, the Hill Commission, and upon its recommendations, the Department of Planning and Development. The Resolution on Industrial Policy, the setting up of the Planning Commission and the founding of the National Physical Laboratory and the National Chemical Laboratory with India's independence, belong to the same historical genre.

Science and Technology Policy Making 1947-84

The making of science policy in the first decade after independence was the outcome of the active, personal, and professional relationship of Nehru, Bhatnagar, and Bhabha. As such there was a lack of systematic institutionalized process of decision-making and a pernicious susceptibility to the constituency method based bargaining among interested agencies and groups. The result was a concentration on CSIR for industrial research and on nuclear energy establishments to the obvious neglect of such key sectors as agriculture, medicine, and even defence as larger priorities for India in the making of science and technology.[10]

On the other hand, state organization of research acquired further urgency given the absence of any sizeable base or industrial infrastructure and therefore of any economic reasons/demands of industry for industrial research. And so the First Five-Year Plan had expressed the need for creating and consolidating scientific arid technological infrastructure and its coupling with new social, economic, and political objectives. This had devolved on the policy makers the objectives of building a chain of research institutes and laboratories and of creating a stock of scientific and technical manpower.

By the Second Five-Year Plan, the irresistible march of rapid industrialization was recognized as the catalyst for social transformation. Formally recasted thus, it presaged a big push to the economic structure with considerable emphasis on investment goods sector to the short-term detriment of the consumer goods industries. The demands on science and technology arraigned itself to the programme for rapid industrialization through a massive import-substitution effort with the major emphasis on developing the basic and heavy industry.

On the supply side came the Science Policy Resolution. Introduced in the Parliament in 1958, this Magna Carta of the science of India proclaimed the philosophical commitment and objectives of the government. It expressed the intention to obtain all the benefits that can accrue from the acquisition and application of scientific research in terms of developing indigenous science and technology base, reducing the gap between the advanced and the backward countries and national participation in the march of human civilization. In programmatic terms, it exposited the aims for efforts to foster, promote and sustain the cultivation of science and scientific research, to ensure adequate supply and training of scientists and to provide conducive environment-material compensation, freedom, status and involvement in decision-making for facilitating creativity.[11]

Beyond this outlining of noble intentions, the resolution remained silent about the modalities to relate the work of the scientists to the productive system. Indeed it revealed Nehru's almost magical belief in the efficacy of science, that there is a direct and an automatic correlation between scientific research and the beneficial impact on the production process. Such an assumed linkage poised on science-based big push not only obviated the seed for a well documented, rational, and coherent technology policy but also, by implication, created structures devoid of any functions, means divorced from ends. Science became a consumption item.

This was no mere gainsaying, given the fact that it is not the science policy but the technology policy which is more closely related to the socio-economic development of a nation. For, in an era of industrialized science and scienticized technology, the process of innovation for higher productivity and speed and rate of manufacturing capital and consumer goods required research and development as an immediate take-off from the scientific invention. More than the scientific research, therefore, the development of indigenous capabilities in technology and their utilization are influenced by policies relating to import of technology and the strategies adopted for industrial growth. Seen thus, Nehru did have a technology policy. For, the official policy of technology import for producing heavy iron and steel, chemicals and machine making was implicitly a recognition of the Japanese model of industrialization. And yet in the absence of vigorous domestic Research and Development (R&D) it was flawed.

In any case, when it was considered premature to place demands on science and technology to contribute to specific development problems either in industry or agriculture and when the immediate shortage of food grains and consumer goods were met through imports and the modernization of industry was based on foreign technology and investment, the science and technology policies of the period was never integrated with the national economic policies. Besides, there was no rational policy for science or even guiding principles of decision-making on the magnitude and distribution of funds for scientific research. Indeed, the fundings were decided more by the absorptive capacity of the agencies and institutions concerned than by the considerations of the economic or social importance of the fields, or by the most fundamental question "What is this science for? Above all, the absence of an agency to promote indigenous technology debilitated any determined effort to utilize technological capabilities already developed in the country."[12]

All These Led Broadly to Two Related Consequences

1. Despite the creation of a sufficient R&D and an economic infrastructure, the hiatus between science and technology, laboratory and industry, and therefore between the supply and demand of the national scientific and technical manpower resulted into wasteful, reckless, and repetitive imports, forced savings for resource mobilization, fewer employment opportunities in highly capital intensive framework in which consumer durables or immediate payoffs to the public works was postponed. And as the high-cost economic regime shaded into one suffering from foreign exchange constraint, which was itself used to decide the technological policy,[13] and therefore the one in which the desire to have rapid industrialization put locally produced technology to a discount, especially when the resources for investment into R&D was available the application and commercial exploitation of a small proportion of the scientific results achieved attracted considerable public attention.
2. As a result of the above, the scientific scene in the late sixties presented an arena of intense controversy, the appointment of the committee after committees, questioning "introspection, discussions in and outside the press and the Parliament and in scientific forums on the strategy, organization, and planning of science and industrial R&D."[14]

The Indira era is noteworthy for the efforts to relate technology policy with economic development, social change, self-sufficiency, and self-reliance.[15] Science and technology policy making became a public affair, participatory for the scientific community and institutionalized as a whole. The setting up of National Council of Science and Technology in 1971 was an important step towards systematic planning of science and technology for development.[16] Its endeavour must be seen in the context of the demand for safeguards against fluctuations in agricultural production, steep hike in the prices of major import items thereby constraining debt-servicing in an era of uncertain foreign aid.

In 1973 the NCST produced the policy document entitled II An approach to science and technology policy. This document is significant, not only, for demonstrating that the scientific and technological efforts must be planned and geared to concrete socio-economic goals, but also, because it is the first official acknowledgment that the framework of our various scientific and industrial policies so far had a predilection to imported technology and even to turnkey-jobs-a predilection that has encouraged irrelevant needs and high cost and undermined self-reliance. To that effect it emphasized:

1. The need to develop indigenous science and technology capacity by training people for the understanding and absorption of imported technology and by giving incentives in terms of reassuring enhancements of productive capacity beyond the formally licensed level to industries affecting technological improvements.
2. The utilization of a mix of imported and indigenous scientific and technological resources in which the indigenous component will increase.
3. Increasing the bargaining power of the country in the International Technology Market that is monopolistic and in which technology is tied up with aid.

Overall, the Approach Paper lacked an understanding of the essential elements of the socio-economic context that perpetuates the import of technology and the altered context that will oppose this process. Even while momentously castigating import-substitution by one to one indigenous substitute for entrenching a consumption pattern dominated by the metropolitan sector, it failed to suggest any *alternative consumption piJllem* and the modus-operandi for its actualization. Implicit was also the failure to perceive clearly and state explicitly as to what were the objectives of self-reliance and national development.

The result was that the scientific and technological capability remained deficient. Thus (1) in large areas of economic activity relatively obsolete, cost-ineffective technology continued to be applied, and the pace of technological innovation and absorption of available technology remained unimpressive; (2) calculated risk-taking and development of risk reduction through systematic application of indigenous science and technology remained weak; and (3) financial support for science and technology activities and linkages between the various sectors and policies conducive to the use of indigenous efforts remained insufficient.[17]

By 1980 acute inflationary pressure was generated by the setbacks in such critical sectors as power, coal, steel, and railway, the steep rise in petroleum prices, low capacity utilization in several industries, inadequate utilization of irrigation potential and lower yields per acre in agriculture. The Sixth Five-Year Plan had therefore aimed at (1) rapid increase in economic growth rate by improving the efficiency in the use of resources and higher productivity; (2) strengthening inputs of upgraded technology for modernization; and (3) speedy development of indigenous sources of energy conservation and use.

This was the setting for the Technology Policy Statement announced in the 70th session of Indian Science Congress Association at Tirupati in January, 1983. It proclaimed that the use and development of technology must relate to people's aspirations, technological self-reliance, local needs, and, finally, to development based on our culture and personality. This context would then govern the choice of technology which would be evaluated on the touchstone of four E's. (energy, efficiency, employment and Environment).

All this did not rule out the import of technology, particularly when it talked about its acquisition, adaptation, and upgradation appropriate to national priorities and resources. However, such imports were not to be normally permitted where indigenous technology was adequately developed and the onus would be on the seeker of foreign technology to demonstrate its necessity while concomitantly contributing to adequate, R&D for its subsequent absorption, adaptation and upgradation.

On the other hand, the indigenous technological capability was to be encouraged by enhancing traditional skills and capabilities, upgrading to prevent obsolescence, providing fiscal incentives, strengthening design engineering and consultancy services and offering incentives for setting up in-house R&D units in the country.

The goal of the technology policy was self-reliance that neither meant autarky nor even self-sufficiency; instead it was redefined to mean "self-reliance of judgement"[18] in making a technological choice.

In sum, science and technology policy as it evolved through plans and related policies were geared towards the following objectives and goals:

1. Creation of infrastructure for research;
2. Promotion of basic research;
3. Research and development for import-substitution and export-promotion;
4. Self-reliance, self-sufficiency and national security;
5. Science for the resolution of social and economic problems and hence for the people.

Indigenous Scientific and Technological Capability

Now the scientific and technological capability of a developing nation is governed by the dialectics of imported technology and domestic R&D for its local adaptation, improvement and innovation and even export in the spectrum of technology dependence-independence continuum. Woven in this context are also the themes of self-reliance and self-sufficiency operational as they are in (1) reductions of imports and (2) import-substitution and utilization of indigenous technology.

But then the import of technology,[19] discernible in the rate of approvals of foreign collaboration, has continued unabated. Herein the policies on technology-import, as K.K. Subrahmanian has pointed out, has traversed through three phases: (1) period of liberalization until the mid-60s when the rate of approval per annum increased from about 35 until 1955 to 104 during the Second Plan period and touched 365 in the heyday of the Third Plan. This was in the era of sterling balance and the official thinking that the foreign exchange cost of the projects would be met by the capital-inflow part of the package. (2) Period of regulation since then and until the mid/late 70s when it remained at the low level of 204 per annum in the context of foreign exchange crisis and illustrative lists of areas, basis and conditions for such imports. This was the period of FERA and licensing. (3) Period of relaxation since then with the rate of foreign collaboration approvals in the course of modernization of capital equipment in the Indian industry rising up to 504 per annum.[20]

The direct impact of technology imports has been the remorseless outflow of foreign exchange on account of servicing and on the country's balance of payment, more adversely in the case of foreign direct investment (remittances of profits and dividends) than in the case of licensing (lump sum payments, royalties, and technical fees). Underpinning it, and even more deleterious, has been its indirect consequences. Insofar as such imports are tied up with certain regulatory clauses-sources of supplies and raw materials, restrictive clauses, purchase of raw materials, tampering with designs and original specifications, it subverted the local technological capacity for their diffusion, adaptation, and assimilation. All this not only led to repetitive, wasteful and indiscriminate imports with the increasing import-dependence as a logical fallout but also in as much as the foreign collaborators inserted clauses restricting the exports of the importing firms or discouraged it through a demand for higher royalties on export-turnover, it had a stifling impact on foreign exchange earnings as another debilitating social cost.

On the other hand, the very import-substitution and utilization of indigenous technology, a question of domestic R&D system, subsisted under a series of constraints.

Organizationally, the mammoth infrastructure and stock of scientific and technical manpower not withstanding, R&D in India has been delinked from the production process.[21] While in the advanced industrial countries, R&D projects actually originate from the production problems and the future projections of the corporate body and is either self-financed or government-sponsored-thereby generating technological competence, spin-offs, and even financial self-sufficiency-in India, the obverse has been true. The main expenditure on R&D has been borne by the Central government (about 74 per cent) and has been concentrated in the public industrial research laboratories. This reversal of role between the government and the private corporate sector has had its own debilitating consequences:

1. Given the lack of market research about the expected rate of return, active life-cycle and predictability of the degree of utilization of the process know-how, the innovation chain has largely remained incomplete.
2. Technologies so produced were marketed at an under developed stage and bench scale, without any pilot plant test and trial demonstration for large-scale manufacture. The private and even public corporate sector had therefore no economic reasons to buy it especially when post-purchase developmental consultancy, because of the geographical segregation of the laboratory and the industrial location, was inefficient.
3. The very selection of the research projects and technology were made on national and social consideration as against the private and profit considerations of the private sector and evaluation of the public sector performance.
4. The inhouse R&D in private sector became and has remained so, a mere window dressing fashioned to extract advantages of government incentives in terms of taxes, licensing, and subsidies. For, not only has their share in the expenditure on R&D and the corpus of personnel engaged therein been abysmal, but interestingly 70 per cent of the R&D personnel so engaged had graduate, diploma or even lower qualifications implying that most of them were engaged in routine duties of quality-control or testing and not so much on product and process R&D. Besides, these companies which had foreign collaborations were even less active in setting up R&D divisions, perhaps owing to the availability of newer technology from their parent bodies. Finally, the R&D activity in the subsidiaries was confined merely to minor product modification, raw material substitutes, etc.[22]

Besides, apart from the profile of R&D in the private corporate sector providing another angle for the explanation of the role-swapping between the government and the private sector along with all its deleterious outcome, has been the fact that the very industrial research in India subsisted within the context of the development of under-development. According to Shiv Vishwanathan, this internationally is an institutional system of obsolescence and has imposed literal death on a whole series of primary products (fibres, dyes, etc.) and the development and utilization of indigenous technology in the context of maintaining the comparative advantage of the developing countries.[23]

Finally, at the level of policy, the government frequently permitted collaborations and technology-imports irrespective of their application in the local environment, the efficiency of the local alternatives and the need to develop indigenous technology. While this proctivity of the government to go for market solutions to its needs is partially explainable in terms of its foregoing organizational constraints, the level of expenditure on R&D as one per cent of GNP (0.9 per cent)—meagre in terms of international comparisons of structurally competitive economics—and confused policy signals to the CSIR, it sufficiently dampened the indigenous initiative to create, duplicate or even imitate the developed technology.[24]

It is in this backdrop that the science and technology policy under the paradigmatic imprimatur of liberalization and structural adjustment and its concomitant underpinnings—the new industrial policy and trade policy-must be understood and evaluated.

Science and Technology Policy-Making Since 1984

In the emergent dynamics of the fiscal crisis of the state, hemmed in with the balance of payment crisis, industrial recession, negative growth rate and bounding inflation, the panacea by the Indian policy-makers, since the mid-eighties and more especially in the nineties, have been seen in the greater integration of India with the global economy. The resultant economic liberalization measures, deregulation and privatization under the dispensation of modernization plans and structural adjustment policies are all designated to welcome foreign investment and technological collaborations. The objective is to open up the inward-looking industrial/technology system to market-forces and global competition in which the acquired modern technology with the attendent marketing expertise and modern managerial techniques will inject technological dynamism, increase productivity, produce qualitatively superior goods at internationally competitive prices, increase exports and expand the production-base. The implication of all this in terms of the trends visible so far on the scientific and technological capability of the country has been very grave. These are the following:

1. The whole of India's production structure based on high technology is being brought under the ambits of joint ownership and management of Indian and foreign business interests. Given the setting where foreign equity participation has been raised to 51 per cent, where NRIs have been allowed 100 per cent equity participation with full benefits of repatriation of capital and income accruing thereof, in high priority industries, and where foreign collaboration agreements spiralled from an average 702 in early 1980 to 4000 in 1989, the trans-national corporations are now in a position to dictate the kind of technology to be introduced, its management and its transfer. In as much as the clause of export-obligation and technology-transfer have been jettisoned, their R&D efforts are being confined to only locating and adopting locally available materials to substitute some of the imported ones because of the pressure to reduce foreign exchange purchases. India is not only being turned into a provider of a large and growing market but also a dumping ground for obsolescent technology selling under foreign brand names which would finance the R&D efforts of the TNCs for the production and marketing of technologically superior products elsewhere.
2. There is being, in fact can be, no genuine absorption, adaptation, and development of indigenous technology under such a policy framework

where technology import is encouraged in the name of accelerating growth and modernisation of Indian industry. Indeed, there can be no genuine transfer of technology (it would be only of know-how and not of know-why) unless the imported technology is supplemented with internal R&D efforts for adaptive changes (mastering the manufacturing capability) as well as innovations for developing new processes and products (design capability). But then, as K.K. Subrahmanian has shown in his analysis of the electronics industry, economic liberalism, insofar as the incentive-structures of the market is biased towards continuous technology-imports for maximizing short-term gains, has distorted technology-behaviour of the firms in the direction of indifferent internal learning (R&D), albeit raising the firm's technological level on the basis of continued dependence on technology-imports and attainment of higher levels of productivity and output-growth.[25]

This technological backwardness would be even more entrenched given the envisaged role of the CSIR and the approach of the government as inscribed in the next Five-Year Plan.

Now the fourth review committee of the CSIR, while condemning the tendency to re-invent the wheel by placing disproportionate emphasis in terms of work on known' products and known process of the CSIR, had called upon the latter to move towards greater orientation to long-term research projects. It thus divested the CSIR of short-term technology-utilization linked to foreseeable economic returns and consigned the generation, absorption, adaptation of industrial technology to in-house R&D establishments of the industries-both public and private.[26] It was this lack of linkages with the demand from the production system and continued foreign assistance in basic engineering activities/product design and consultancy, that the Eighth Five-Year Plan has cited as the major constraints in the promotion of indigenous technology.[27] This becomes especially glaring when the Indian industries, according to it, needed a technological thrust for modernization and self-reliance. Inasmuch as it has pointed out that globalization of business and of R&D have been noteworthy developments in the fast-changing world and foresees "meaningful partnership in the international plane in the areas of mutual global interest... on the anvil,"[28] the resultant consequence would tantamount to technological colonialism in which Indian R&D and Indian industries would act not even as junior partners but as petty rentiers.

The High-Yielding Variety Technology

What is instructive here is that all this is being done to bring about an industrialization traversing through an export-growth that has to be rapid enough to carry India into the 21st century. This is the theme that looks into the future, sanctions high growth-rates, seeks to generate investible surplus through demands derived from a consumerist culture, keeps the people numbed by the consumerist culture and technological fixes and is founded upon an agriculture as a bargain sector charged with producing cheap foodgrains to galvanize the wheels of industrialization of a society informed by an urban industrial vision.

It was this rationale that underlay the introduction of the HYV (high-yielding variety) technology under the aegis of USAID, the Ford, and the Rockefeller foundations, and their institutional and peer group ideological linkages with their funded agricultural research centres in India. Although its impact in terms of rate of growth and sufficiency in foodgrains production had dramatically ushered in the green. revolution in India, the fact that technology-transfer presupposed an intimate knowledge of localized conditions-soils, climates, cropping systems and harvesting, processing and consumption patterns—it has disoriented the national research capacity. Thus one had seen research exclusively on the HYV package-high carbohydrate seeds, plant-breeding and genetics, the climatic zones and areas of assured water supply where they could be grown, and fertilizer-sensitive plants that could be protected from diseases only by chemicals. Concomitantly, there has been neglect of researches in a number of other fields—the pulses and oilseeds, non-irrigated areas and dry farming practices, soil and water conservation practices suited to the tropical conditions, on the biological means of disease-prevention as opposed to chemical pesticides, suitable cropping-patterns dealing in alternate water-supply with nitrogen plants that could reduce dependency on chemical fertilizers.[29]

Such a form of agricultural technology is becoming increasingly non-sustainable. Thus there has been a general squeeze on the micro-nutrients of the soil-copper, iron, manganese, molybdenum, and zinc along with the use of chemical fertilizers depleting the carbon-nitrogen-ratio in the soil and the use of pesticide affecting photosynthesis adversely. There has been the lowering of the ground water table because of tubewell and droughts. Finally, it has impacted on the nutrition quality of the masses, increasingly fed on the chemically stained food products on the one hand and protein deficient food items on the other (no pulses, oilseeds, etc.)[30]

Pattern of Development

The impact on the pattern of development in India has been extremely disarticulatory. It has spawned metropolitan enclaves of production and consumption, where the depression of wage-income growth by the use of capital-intensive technology have provided multiplied surplus to the dominant alliance of propertied classes to feed themselves on luxurious consumption that is internationally determined and where satisfaction of new artificial needs through an elaborate build-up have denuded potential investment for growth.

Besides, insofar as the success of the Green Revolution had been postulated only under certain optimum conditions-optimal irrigation, intensive use of fertilizers, monoculture (for the rational use of machinery and agricultural implements) and pest-control through chemical pesticides (also requiring monoculture), it has ushered in localized enclaves of capitalist farming in India. In this resultant disarticulation of the extant social organization, one sees both regional disparities and interpersonal inequality, accentuated further by the use of high-cost inputs-HYV seeds, fertilizers, tractors, harvesters, and tubewell-purchasable only by the rich farmers on the one side, with the growing unemployment and under-employment and increasing casualization and proletarianization of the small and poor farmers, sharecroppers and agricultural labourers.

More importantly, the bypassing of the local science and technology system has brought about a debilitation of the domestic R&D. It has choked off the masses from the production system especially when the large traditional sector is informed by empirical knowledge and has no institutional back up to improve productivity and its competitive ability.

❑ Conclusion

Thus far from ushering in socialism and self-reliant development, the science and technology policies have harvested inequity, injustice, and neocolonial dependency. And yet, such was logically incumbent upon certain historical and structural factors.

Historically, it was the very development strategy to which the Third World regimes were hooked upon. The impact of imperialism and colonialism, while causing deindustrialization and de-development, had also led to an imperialism of categories[31] in terms of examining a non-western concept and tyrannization of historical possibility, under-driven by an internalist model of technological development, implying that the technological futures of the non-west is the one in the west and that everything in the non-west is refractory, traditional and hence a barrier to the development, seen as modernization, as westernization. This gave way to the transfer of technology and the thesis. of technological leapfrogging, of the Listian strategy of technological development in which the 19th century Germany and the 20th century Japan were the models.

But such a strategy was basically flawed in that wherever it had succeeded it was founded upon (1) strong state, (2) dominance of capital over labour, (3) compensating nationalism leading to aggressive nationalism, and (4) fit between the structure and values encapsulated in the technologies of the supplier and buyer countries. But in a state that was ostensibly wedded to socialism and self-reliance and drew its legitimacy and autonomy from that, such a cultural environment for technological change was simply not there.

For, the very nature of the Indian state provided for a structural straitjacket. The reigning dispensation of the dominant alliance of propertied classes-industrial big bourgeoisie under the commanding heights of the metropolitan capital, rich peasants-landlords in the ambit of failed land reforms policy and the capitalist restructuring of the rural social organization of production, and urban middle class\professionals seduced by the mindset of luxurious consumption of goods selling under foreign brand-name—influenced the pork-barrel nature to the political process. It effectively throttled the capacity, autonomy, and support for the developmental actions of the state, especially when both the industrialization through dependency based upon the technology-transfer, and export-promotion industrialization posited on trade, as has taken place in Japan and the Asian NICs, had rendered the adoption of certain critical policies imperative.

On the other hand, the forces of technological dynamism were blunted by the lack of organizational capacity for producing new products through the use of high technology and developed an indigenous capacity to assimilate and efficiently utilize such a technology. Given the feudal, monopolistic, and oligopolistic nature of the international technology-market, the high direct and indirect cost of the local technological capacity, the persistent predilection to the import of technology pushed India into a neo-colonial form of dependency.

The signing of the WTO has further paved the way for the invasion of the foreign capital, foreign trading monopolies and services, and foreign technologies (both product and process). On the anvil is not merely the subversion of the motifs of self-reliance, competitiveness and development of indigenous technological capability. But also and more importantly, when seen in the context of the rolling back of the state before the new presiding deity-the market-underdriven by the global alliance of capitalist class with their hanger-ons and rentiers, the very incorporation of the traditional masses, the very India into the global system of control, hegemony, exploitation and repression.

Notes and References

1. The resolution of the major economic problems of industrial society-poverty, unemployment, and inequalities seen in technical sense and their reduction by growing technological expertise, the failure of Fascism in the war, the disrepute of the Stalinist version of Marxism and the expanding and prosperous character of the America-led world capitalist economy was the basis of this optimism and even complacency. See A.R. Higgott, *Political Development Theory,* London etc., 1983, p. 16.
2. D. Lerner, *Passing Away of Traditional Societies,* New York, 1965, pp. 43–75.; S. N. Eisenstadt, *Modernization Protest and Change,* Englewood Cliffs, 1966, pp. 1–15.; Samuel Huntington, *Political Order in Changing Societies,* New Haven, 1968, pp. 32–35.; Edward *Shilis, The* Intellectuals *and Powers,* Chicago, 1972, p. 361.
3. Jawaharlal Nehru, Message sent on the occasion of the Silver Jubilee Session of the Indian Science Congress Association, Calcutta, 3rd January 1938.
4. For the impact of British rule on the growth and nature of science and technology in India, see Claude Álvares, *Homo-Faber: Technology and Culture in China, India and the West 1500 to the Present Day,* New Delhi, 1979; and Susantha Goonathilake, *Aborted Discovery Science and Creativity in the Third World,* London, 1984.

5. In the first half of the 20th century, the growth rate at aggregate real output was less than 2 per cent per annum and per capita output less than 1/2 per cent p.a. Industries, essentially agro-based, employed less than a tenth of labour force, and as the population multiplied, foodcrop production shrunk. See Amiya Kumar Bagchi, *The* Political *Economy of Underdevelopment,* Cambridge etc, 1982; Anupam Sen, *Industrialization and Class Formation in India,* London etc, 1982.
6. Setting up of the Trignometrical Survey of India (1800), Royal Botanical Garden (1788), Botanical Survey of India (1889), Geological Survey of India (1851), Indian Marine Survey (1877), Indian Coastal Survey (1875), Meteorological Observatory (1792), Agricultural Society of India (1820), and Bombay Natural Society (1848), were among the Learned Societies indirectly associated with the raw material needs of the new international division of labour.
7. For an excellent exposition on this, see Shiv Vishawanathan, *Organizing for Science,* Delhi etc, 1985, pp. 39–96.
8. *Ibid.*, p. 105.
9. Jawaharlal Nehru, Message sent on the occasion of the Silver Jubilee Session of the Indian Science Congress Association, Calcutta, 3rd January 1938.
10. See Baldev Raj Nayyar, *India's Quest for Technological Independence-Policy Formulation and Policy Change,* New Delhi, 1983, pp. 275–282.
11. Government of India, *Scientific Policy Resolution* No 131/CF/57, New Delhi, 4th March 1958.
12. National Council of Science and Technology, *An Approach to the Science and Technology Plan,* January 1979, second section (1).
13. Nayyar asserts that for some three decades India had no technology policy. Instead there was a foreign exchange policy where every application for foreign collaboration for technology was tested on the touchstone of foreign exchange outflow. Baldev Raj Nayyar, *op. cit.*, pp. 190–191.
14. In 1965, the first CSIR and Industry get-together was organized to re-orient research programmes of the laboratories so that they have a direct relationship with the industrial and economic plans of the country. Even the Third Review Committee suggested that the programmes of research were to be focussed on applied level with the related basic research to be pursued in the context of well-defined projects. See *Proceedings of the First Get-together of Research and Industry,* December, 20-21, 1965, New Delhi, 1966; and *Report of the Third Review Committee of the* CSIR, 1964.
15. To Indira Gandhi, self-reliance assumed special salience. In 1967 she pointed out that "The experience of the past year has underlined the danger of agricultural stagnation and dependence on foreign aid and know-how especially in the vital fields of industry and defence". While science was an instrument of change and modernization, technology was the key to independence, "for it was the failure to advance technologically which made Asia and Africa dependent and poverty stricken". Insofar growth and self-reliance cannot be sustained on borrowed, even adapted technology, she reiterated her endeavour to rationalize and relate science and technology system more closely with the process of planning and development. See Indira Gandhi, *"Science and Social Change",* Inaugural address at a Round Table on Science and Technology, 7th September 1967, in *Selected Speeches of Indira Gandhi,* January 1966-August 1969, New Delhi, 1971, pp. 190–191: "India and the Space Age", speech at Thumba Rocket Centre, 2nd February 1968, *op. cit.*, p. 204; Managers for a Developing Society', address at I.Z.M, Ahmedabad, 13th April 1968, *op. cit.*, pp. 208-210.
16. In 1969, the Indian National Congress passed a resolution on Science and Technology. It proclaimed the achievement of Scientific Policy Resolution within the quickest possible time as the basic policy of the country and demanded that the government devote 1 per cent of the GNP to R&D, prepare a short-term and long-term

comprehensive plan for science and technology. In 1970, the Third conference of scientists, technologists and educationists, organized under the auspices of the committee on Science and Technology, recommended the formation of NCST to formulate science plan and to establish firm links with the Planning Commission and thus with the national economic plans.

17. Planning Commission, *Report of the Working group on Science and Technology for the Sixth Plan (1980-85),* New Delhi, December 1980.
18. P. S. Shanker and R N. Sharma, 'Technology Policy in Relation to Industrial and Science Policies of India', *Journal of Scientific and Industrial Research*, Vol. 42, February 1983, p. 58.
19. Technology imports can be through two modes: (1) formal or disembodied form in which the technology transfer contracts requires specific government approval; (2) informal or embodied in capital goods, technical skills, scientific and technical literature. It can be through either foreign direct investment (FDI) package consisting of capital entrepreneurship, management, technology etc., or licensing specific resources like proprietary process/product technology etc.
20. See KK Subrahmanian, Technology Imports. Regulation Reduces Cost', *Economic and Political Weekly,* Vol. XXI No. 32, pp. 1412–1413.
21. The oft-repeated third largest stock of S&T manpower is fallacious. The manpower includes graduates and even diploma holders. Quite revealingly, India has 3.76 scientists, engineers, and technicians per 1000 of population as against 186.27 in Canada, 112.77 in Japan and 72.41 in Germany. Of these only 0.22 per thousand were engaged in R&D activities in India as compared to 3.32 in Canada, 6.01 in Japan, and 4.68 in Germany. And 78 per cent of these personnel were in the institutional sector with 22 per cent only involved in the Industrial sector. See Government of India, Ministry of S&T, DST, New Delhi, R&D statistics 1992-93.
22. For a fuller discussion on these aspects: See Baldev Singh, 'Research & Development In Industry', *Economic & Political Weekly,* Vol. XXII, No. 34, pp. 1431–1434.
23. While the destruction of the market for mica was taking place in the industrial research laboratories in the west in terms of specifying new standards, mechanized mica processing and synthetic mica substitutes in India no efforts were made to find new uses for mica and thus to create demand. Shiv Vishwanathan, *op. cit.,* pp. 227–236.
24. Illustrative studies on select idustries—fertilizers, telephone, electronics, tractors, combine-harvesters, automobiles, auto-ancillaries, LCD watches etc.—dot the annals of *Economic and Political Weekly* and the *Social Scientists.*
25. There is a stagnation in R&D efforts of the private sector as indicated by the decline of the R&D expenditure as a percentage of sales turnover of firms in the private sector and the growth trends in expenditure on in-house R&D, See: K.K. Subrahamanian, *op. cit.,* pp. M87–M92. Kewal Ram in his study of the petro-chemical industry in India points out the very low R&D base in Indian firms as vital in the lack of diffusion and innovative development of technology that were imported. See: Kewal Ram, 'Technology Transfer and Indigenous Technology-Petro-chemical Industry in India', *Economic and Political Weekly,* Vol. XXV, No. 21, pp. M75–84. Besides, several foreign technology suppliers have highlighted the fact that Indian firms search for low technology package that squeezed out the know-why content of the technology transferred and concentrate their R&D on its adaptation and indigenization thereby constricting innovative technical change. The restrictive government policies and the uncompetitive industrial milieu does not fully explain this attitude of Indian firms for short-term profits and monopolist advantage to the determinant of long-term technological capability Is now amply borne out. See *Economic and Political Weekly,* Special Number, Vol. XX, Nos. 45, 46 & 47, pp. 1975–2094.

26. Baldev Singh, 'Perspective Before the CSIR', *Economic and Political Weekly,* Vol. XXH, No. 17, p. 442.
27. Government of India, *Eighth Five-Year Plan* (1992-97), New Delhi, p. 442.
28. *Ibid*., p. 439.
29. See for fuller discussion Dinesh Abrol, 'American-Involvement in Indian Agricultural Research', *Social Scientist,* Vol. 11, No. 10, pp. 8–21.
30. B. Bowonder, *The Myth and Reality of HYV in Indian Agriculture. Development and Change,* Vol. 12, 1981. pp. 293–313.
31. The politico-philosophical underpinnings in the theory of development and ideology of progress in the third world ruling regime, as of India, remained unquestioned simply because of the western secular—materialist eschatology, a cultural dominance resulting from their political dominance riding on the motor of imperialistic wars and economic dominance through colonial and neo-colonial exploitation. It was embossed in the discourses on political development, economic growth, scientific and technological policies. All these had been not because the world was divided between developed and underdeveloped, modem and traditional but simply between dominant and dependent powers. See Claude Alvares, *op. cit.,* pp. 20–34; also see Ashis Nandy (ed.). *Science, Hegemony and Violence: A Requim for Modernity,* Delhi. 1988; Uberoi, J.P.S., *Science and Culture,* Delhi, 1978 and *Theory of an Alternative Science,* Delhi School of Economics, Delhi.

31

Terrorism, Public Order, and Human Rights

Jaytilak Guha Roy

The struggle to preserve, protect, and promote human rights is as old as human civilization. Sadly, even more than six decades after the United Nations proclamation of the Universal Declaration of Human Rights (10, December 1948), the struggle for human rights not merely continues but becomes intense too. Every day, in country after country, human rights are now being violated, irrespective of whether a country is developed or developing, whether it is governed by a totalitarian or a democratic regime. To quote Martin Ennals, former General Secretary of the Amnesty International:

> Each violation of human rights, wherever it occurs, is a threat to the welfare and dignity of the entire human family. The protection of human rights, therefore, is a worldwide responsibility which transcends all racial, ideological, and geographical boundaries.[1]

❑ Genesis and Growth of Terrorism in India

British Period

India has a long history associated with terrorism. During the British rule, the revolutionary freedom fighters were labelled as terrorists. They had either martyrdom or suffered imprisonment for the emancipation of their motherland from bondage, and were, therefore, loved and respected by their compatriots. Moreover, unlike the present-day terrorists, the freedom fighters of British India did not indulge in indiscriminate violence against common Englishmen, but resorted to violence only against their adversaries or exploiters, such as the English bureaucrats, judges, police officials, and their native associates. The sixteen-year-old martyr Khudiram, for instance, repented when he came to know after his arrest that he and his associate had killed Mr and Mrs Kennedy instead of Mr Kingsford, the then District and Sessions Judge of Muzaffarpur, whom they actually wanted to kill. Yet, as Chari has observed forthrightly, "Freedom fighters could be seen as rebels, extremists, or separationists, and national liberation movements could be described as insurrections depending on perceptions and whether the question is addressed by those who question the regime in power or are sympathetic to the regime in power."[2]

Post-Independence Scenario

The transformation of our polity from *rajtantra* to *prajatantra* could not restrain violence. On the contrary, the bankruptcy of our political leadership of the post-independence era has resulted in a phenomenal rise in gangsterism and mafia rule in the political process, increasing role of money and muscle powers in the electoral process, and glaring distortions in the notion of an impartial law-enforcement machinery. No wonder, the developmental exercises by such bankrupt political leadership have generally increased the hiatus between haves and have-nots and ultimately given rise to socio-economic inequalities, regional disparities, and the problems of identity-crisis and national integration. Over and above, growing unemployment and frustrations of youths, all pervasive corruption, evils of consumerism, cancerous growth of casteism and communalism, ethnic, linguistic and regional conflicts, scourge of insurgency and terrorism, desperate onslaughts by the Naxalites, threats from separatist, secessionist, and disruptive forces and various other problems of a turbulent society as ours have made the world's largest democracy extremely difficult to survive. Thus, the problem of terrorism and its growth in independent India have to be understood in the broader context of our socio-political milieu.

The peasants' movement in Telangana led by the communists in the late forties marked the beginning of a new era of terrorism in independent India. During this movement in 1946-50, 659 persons were killed, 347 houses burnt, and 470 attacks were made on police and armed forces by the terrorists. On the other side, 400 terrorists were killed and 8000 arrested in police action.[3]

The second phase of terrorism in free India started in 1967 in the form of Naxalite violence. Inspired by the Maoist tactics of guerrilla warfare, the Naxalites unleashed a reign of terror in West Bengal and other parts of India for nearly five years in between 1767-72. In West Bengal alone, 1711 persons including 153 policemen were killed by the terrorists, while 384 terrorists were killed and 6000 interned under such "draconian laws" as the Prevention of Violent Activities Act and the Maintenance of Internal Security Act (MISA) between 1969 and 1972.[4]

The march of terrorism in India took an extreme turn in the early eighties with the rejuvenation of Khalistan movement in Punjab under the leadership of Bhindranwale. Many of us have forgotten today that the thesis "Sikhs are a nation", and the slogan of Khalistan was first inspired and encouraged by the theoreticians of the British imperialism to weaken India and her freedom movement in the same way as were the thesis of "Muslims are a separate nation" and the slogan of Pakistan.[5] External factors apart, various internal forces and factors including heightening of the feeling of relative deprivation were responsible for the rejuvenation of the Khalistan movement in Punjab. What is still more distressing, the success of green revolution could not quench the feeling of relative deprivation, but rather resulted in its further acceleration. Nevertheless, the problem of terrorism in Punjab, as in Kashmir, was more a creation of religio-political forces than anything else. To quote Surendra Nath, a former Governor of Punjab, "For a long time a certain section of the religio-political leadership in Punjab has been articulating the perceived injustice with Sikh community which has led to serious disorientation among the Sikh youths and a large number of them now think that a separate sovereign state is the answer to Sikh aspirations."[6]

In Kashmir, too, the same strategy was adopted, by the religio-political forces to arouse religious animosities among the ignorant civilians. As H.N. Singhal, a retired Major-General has observed forthrightly, "It is argued that the three million Muslims of the valley have been alienated and no longer want to be part of India. We used to hear the same argument from the prophets of doom about Sikhs in Punjab. With the establishment of peace and recourse to the democratic process normalcy prevails there. Similarly, in Kashmir alienation is temporary since independent Kashmir have voted eight times as Indians, during a period when Pakistan was reeling under military dictators of various hues. The free will of the Kashmiri's has been exploited by fundamentalist's propaganda."[7]

The recent incidents in Kashmir, however, reveal that militancy has taken a virulent turn in that state due to Pakistan-sponsored trans-border terrorism. The 1994-95 annual report of the Government of India's Ministry of External Affairs noted that "in addition to training, equipping, funding, and guiding militants, Pakistan has stepped up its trans-border terrorism.[8] By injecting mercenaries from other countries into the Valley, especially Afghan and Sudanese mercenaries. Consequently, the level of cruelty and perversity has only been on the rise. The type of torture and brutality inflicted on victims and frequency of beheading, hanging, and rape of innocent women "far surpasses that in either Punjab or the North East."[9] Even the holy shrine of Charer-e-sharif, which is a symbol of secular Islam taught by Sufi saint Nooruddin Noorani (Light of the Faith), also known as Nand Rishi, had been burnt into ashes by these pro-Pakistan militants on the holy day of Idu'l Zuha on 11th May 1995."

Nuclear terrorism or terrorist access to nuclear weapons may pose an unprecedented threat to our national security in near future. The 1994-95 report of the Ministry of External Affairs noted further that Pakistan has continued to "pursue its nuclear weapons-oriented programmers, its clandestine procurement of material for this purpose and its acquisition of sophisticated weapons and arms technology far beyond its legitimate defence requirements."[10] Of late, some American Senators have also expressed their concern for the Pakistan's endeavour to increase its nuclear-weapon storage.

There are reasons, therefore, to assume that in near future militants and foreign mercenaries operating in the valley would have access to nuclear weapons through Pakistan.

❑ Terrorism and Public Order

In *Kartar Singh v. State of Punjab*[11] 1994, the Supreme Court observed that terrorism and public order are conceptually different "not only in ideology and philosophy but also in causes, the manner of its commission, and the effect or result of such activity. Public order, as the Court has elucidated further, is well understood and fully comprehended as a problem associated with law and order. Terrorism is a new crime far serious in nature, graver in impact and highly dangerous in consequence. One pertains to law and order problem whereas the other may be political in nature coupled with the unjustified use of force threatening security and integrity of the state." Whatever be the conceptual difference, it hardly needs to be emphasized that the law enforcing authorities have to observe the rule of law while dealing with public disorders of any nature. The observance of rule of law is, in fact, the basic requirement of a civilized society. Violations of human rights by the authority of the state are, therefore, detrimental not only to the rule of law but also to the very existence of a civilized society. Unfortunately, such violations are quite common in India, the holy land of Buddha, Ashoka or Gandhi. But before we discuss this problem, it is necessary to explain briefly what human rights really mean.

❑ Conceptualization of Human Rights

Since the concept of human rights is "an idea with a history, an idea that changes in both content and social function,"[12] there is still immense disagreement as to the meaning and contents of human rights. Without getting involved in such conceptual controversies, human rights may be said to be those rights which are essential for the dignified and decent human existence as well as for the adequate development of human personality. To speak more broadly, human rights are those "fundamental rights to which every man and woman inhabiting any part of the world should be deemed entitled by virtue of having been born a human being."[13]

Human rights, thus, conceived, constitute two categories of rights: (1) rights which are essential for the dignified and decent human existence, *viz.*, the right to have basic human needs like food, shelter, clothing and health, and the right to work; and (2) rights which are essential for the adequate development of human personality, such as, the right to education, the right to freedom of culture, the right to freedom of speech and expression, and the right to free movement.

Human rights, therefore, no longer imply merely civil and political liberties for the individual, conceived some kind of protection or safeguard against state power by the classical as well as contemporary western liberal scholars from John Stuart Mill to John Rawls. The bearers of human rights in contemporary societies, and more particularly in developing societies, must have an implicit right to be and remain human.[14] They must have some autonomy of choice in planning their own survival. They must not have merely the right to life, but rather the right to subsistence, this is, in fact, the new trend in human rights thinking which results in growing recognition of the idea that economic and social rights are a prerequisite of the enjoyment of civil and political rights. However, for our present discussion, we are concerned only with human rights as a safeguard against state power.

❑ State Violations of Human Rights

Certain countries have now waged a relentless propaganda war in various international forum against India for alleged violation of human rights by police and armed forces in Jammu and Kashmir, although their own records of human rights are not at all satisfactory. In one of these countries, barbaric, and inhuman punishments under the religious laws are still in existence, violating all standard norms of human dignity including the Universal Declaration of Human Rights. This is by no means enough for our complacency. We should not deny that violations of human rights by the state apparatus have been taking place in India, and more so in Jammu and Kashmir, because of certain practical problems and evil necessities, so common for any democratic system of governance. These are, briefly, as follows:

1. Just as totalitarianism is an ideal condition for the growth of state terrorism, political democracy is an ideal system for the growth of anti-state terrorism. In a parliamentary democracy such as ours, liberal laws and lenient criminal justice system make punishment difficult, sometimes impossible. This is more so when a reign of terror is let loose by terrorist groups.
2. The terrorists in the valley, as elsewhere, have successfully and surreptitiously provoked the state to use indiscriminate mass-violence and have thereby been able to win sympathy, though temporarily, from the community.
3. Our law enforcement agencies often had to operate under the constraints of the dilemma so common for a democratic state, since "under-action would expose it as vulnerable while over-action and indiscriminate repression would bring out the loss of popular support and legitimacy."[15]

4. Lack of community-support and co-operation and also a lack of faith in the existing judicial system have often provoked the police and armed forces to use wrong and repressive methods.
5. In Punjab, Kashmir, and the North-East, a large number of police and security personnel have been killed by the terrorists and militants during the last several years. Such killings often had provoked the forces to retaliate.
6. In a developing country such as ours, there is bound to have a wide variation in the perception of human rights issues and the concern for human rights not only in respect of functionaries of the judiciary and the police but also within the force itself. For, the educational, cultural, and family backgrounds of a policeman at a lower level are altogether different from an officer at the higher level. As one Indian observer has observed very poignantly: "Applying western standards to developing countries which have inherited the police, judicial, and jail systems from their colonial rules are apparently fraught with some risks."[16]

The above facts and arguments have been put forth to appraise the ground realities and real-life situations in the terrorist-ridden Kashmir and other parts of India, rather than to justify or condone violations of human rights by policies and security personnel. In fact, the vast majority of the people of India are of the view that human rights violations need to be condemned and halted, whoever the perpetrators-whether they are centres of political, economic, military power or terrorists. The former Chief Justice of India, Justice P.N. Bhagwati, has, therefore, said that "it would be wrong to look at the problem only from one side", and advocated "a fair and even-handed approach". He is firmly opposed to allowing any fact-finding mission to visit Kashmir or any part of India. As he says very poignantly, "India should stoutly resist any such move as this would amount to interference in India's internal affairs by foreign elements". However, this does not mean that we should allow the situation in Kashmir or elsewhere to drift. On the contrary, he says, "We must set right our internal affairs by our own moral authority and strength."[17] In fact, some monitoring mechanisms have since been evolved in India, the world's largest democracy, through judicial activism, free press, and human rights bodies which provide checks and balances on state terrorism.

❑ Judicial Activism

The Human Rights Committee (HRC) of the United Nations while examining the second periodic India's report (submitted on 12th July 1989), welcomed the important role the Supreme Court played in defending human rights. Several members of this Committee had evinced great interest in Public Interest Litigation (PIL) and asked how it was being used to protect such rights. This is indeed, a great compliment for the apex court of India, because the HRC is a prestigious international body of 18 experts from a wide range of legal systems which forms the treaty body established under the International Covenant on Civil and Political Rights to supervise implementation of the Covenant.[18]

As a matter of fact, the Supreme Court of India have made commendable innovative exercises, in the process of adjudication of PIL, to evolve new remedies, devise new procedures, and invent new reliefs for the protection of human rights. As part of this enthusiastic judicial movement, the Supreme Court not only liberalised the traditional rule of *locus standi* in order to liberate itself from the "shackles of procedural limitations", but also attempted to provide judicial remedies even *suo moto,* as in Asiad[19] and Salal Hydro Electric Project.[20] Judicial activism in India, therefore, is not confined to police brutalities and excesses, but rather extends to covends to cover any violation of human rights by any public authority.

Of late, the Supreme Court has made another landmark innovative exercise in *Sabeli v. Commissioner of Police,*[21] 1989 Delhi. The Delhi Administration was directed to pay ₹75, 000 as damage to the parents of a child who died in police custody because of beating and assault by police officers. The Delhi Administration was further directed to take appropriate steps to recover the amount or part thereof from the officer or officers who would be found responsible. This is a glaring instance of our judicial innovation in the area of public law. For, under the common law system which is operative in our country, the concept of individual accountability does not exist. Our Supreme Court has, in fact, borrowed this concept from the continental law system operative in France and innovatively applied it in our legal system to ensure accountability of individual public functionary for abuse of authority or violation of human rights. Following the footsteps of the apex court, the High Courts are also increasingly applying this concept of individual accountability for protection of human rights.

❑ Role of Free Press

In India, radio and television are yet to be liberated from governmental control. Nevertheless, India is fortunate to have a very powerful free press which contributes considerably to the protection of human rights. It is, indeed, due to the free press that most of the state violations of human rights have been brought to the notice of the voluntary activists, parliamentarians, jurists, and all those who are concerned with preservation and protection of these sacred rights. On a number of occasions, voluntary actions, parliamentary debates or judicial activism were based on the press reports.

Let us consider, for instance, a recent case of police excesses in which the Punjab police were involved in tattooing the four alleged female pickpockets on their foreheads while they were in illegal police custody in Amritsar. This gruesome act was initially reported in the local and national newspapers, and then, referred to the Punjab and Haryana High Court which ordered a CBI inquiry into the case and directed the state government of

Punjab to pay ₹50000 as interim compensation to each woman. The former Director, Research and Medical Education, and ex-head of the Department of Plastic Surgery, Rajendra Hospital, Patiala, Dr. K.S. Thind, was asked by the court to supervise the treatment and conduct plastic surgery to remove the marks.[22] This single most instance is more than enough perhaps to appraise the role of free press in India as the protector of human rights.

❑ CONCERN OF HUMAN RIGHTS GROUPS

The human rights movement in India, in its present shape, owes its origin to "the political milieu of the national emergency imposed by Indira Gandhi for about eighteen months between 1975 and 1977."[23] The movement is yet to gain adequate numerical strength. However, the quantitative shortcoming is somewhat compensated by the quality and dedication of its activities cadre, consisting of students, teachers, scientists, etc. "In a sense the division within the movement on the question of priorities", says an eminent civil rights activist, Ray, "has enabled a better optimization of the benefits of the thinly-spread movement based on ideological proclivities and availability of talent in each of the organizations-between sixty and seventy-spread in the various parts of the country, and, in many instances, leaving scope for coordinated joint action when desirable and possible."[24] A glaring instance of such joint action is the report on the 1984 anti-Sikh riots in Delhi, "Who are the Guilty", brought out by the joint investigating team of the People's Union for Democratic Rights (PUDR) and the People's Union for Civil Liberties (PUCL). A number of other organizations, *viz.*, Committee for the Protection of Democratic Rights (Bombay), Andhra Pradesh Civil Liberties Committee (Hyderabad), and Association for the Protection of Democratic Rights (Punjab) are active in defending the democratic rights of such social groups as the tribals, the "untouchables", unorganized labour in urban areas, women children and ethnic minorities, who are either not conscious of their rights or incapable of defending them against violation.

The human rights activities in India are criticized by the state authority and also by some eminent personalities like Justice P.N. Bhagwati for their concern with violations by the state authority only. As Justice Bhagwati has observed very poignantly, "When terrorists kill innocent persons, they are definitely violating human rights and they must be condemned. I do not agree with human rights activists who condemn only violations by security forces. Otherwise, terrorists will derive strength from these activists and make capital out of their criticism."[25] But Justice H.R. Khanna belongs to the group which feels that issue of human rights arises only when the official apparatus of the state does something violative of these rights. Violations by the terrorists cannot be treated in the same manner. However, about the state action against terrorists, Justice Khanna says, "No one takes exception to dealing firmly against militants within the domain of the law."[26]

❑ GOVERNMENTAL RESPONSE

The Government of India has already constituted the National Human Rights Commission (NHRC) under the chairmanship of Justice Ranganath Mishra. The composition, functions, and powers of NHRC have been clearly enumerated in the protection of Human Rights Act, 1993. Under this historic legislation, the NHRC has been given certain powers including the power to appoint its own investigation staff to probe violation of human rights.

Despite these powers, the NHRC is nothing more than a recommendatory body. It cannot take any penal action against a public servant for violation of human rights by misusing or abusing his authority. The Act also provides for constitution of State Human Rights Commissions. Since the NHRC has started its functions not long ago, it is too early to evaluate its performance. It is expected that the state governments will soon constitute HRC in their respective state. Despite the limitation of powers, these statutory bodies can play a significant role as protectors of human rights depending upon the attitude, approach and dynamism of the persons who would be involved with them.

❑ CONCLUDING OBSERVATIONS

Our foregoing discussion centres round the problem of terrorism in India and its consequent impact on human rights. Violations of human rights by our state apparatus have been discussed from a realistic perspective with a focus on Indian socio-political realities. The concluding part of the discussion highlights the various monitoring mechanisms that have been evolved in India to provide necessary checks and balance on state-terrorism. However, these mechanisms need to be strenghtened further to preserve, protect and promote human rights and democratic values in the world's largest democracy.

NOTES AND REFERENCES

1. Martin Ennals, "The Struggle for Human Rights", in A.R. Desai (ed.) *Violation of Human Rights in India,* Vol. I, Bombay, Popular Prakashan, 1986, p. 3.
2. P.R. Chari, "Etiology of Terrorism": Its Indian and Regional Portents" in S.C Tiwari (ed.), *Terrorism in India,* Delhi, South Asia Publishers, 1990, p. 34.
3. B.K. Tripathi, "Terrorist Challenges in Punjab" in S.C Tiwari (ed)., *op. cit.,* pp. 152–153.
4. *Ibid.,* p. 153.
5. Satyapal Dang, "Terrorism in India" in S.C. Tiwari (ed.), *op. cit.,* p. 116
6. *The Hindustan Times,* 29th December 1991.
7. H.N. Singhal, "Human Rights Trap", *The Hindustan Times,* 26th April 1994.
8. *The Times of India,* 4th April 1995.
9. *The Times of India,* 2nd June 1994
10. *Supra,* n. 8.

11. (1994), 3 see *569.*
12. Eugene Kamenka and A.E. Tay (eds.), *Human Rights,* London, Edward Arnold, 1978, Introduction by Kamendka, p. vi.
13. S.C Kashyap, *Human Rights and Parliament,* Delhi, Metropolitan, 1978, p. 2.
14. For further details, see Upendra Baxi, "From Human Rights to the Rights to be Human: Some Heresies", in Upendra Baxi, *et al.* (eds.), *Rights to be Human,* Delhi Lancer International, 1978, pp. 185–200.
15. S.K. Ghosh, *Social Order* in *India,* Delhi, Ashish, 1990, p. 109.
16. S. Kirpekar, "Forcing the Issue", *The Times of India,* 7th November 1993.
17. Quoted by Kirpekar, *Ibid.*
18. As on 31st January 1993, 112 States had ratified or acceded to the Covenant; India did so on 10th April 1979. Under Article 40 of the Covenant, State Parties commit themselves to submit a report on the measures they have taken to give effect to the rights recognized in the Convenient. One of the tasks of the HRC is to examine these reports. For further details, see Amnesty International, *Index: ASA 20-05*-93, March 1993.
19. *PUDR vs. Union of India, AIR,* 1982 SC. 1473.
20. *Labourers Working on Salal Hydro-Electric Project vs. State of Jammu and Kashmir, AIR,* 1984, SC, 177.
21. *AIR,* 1990, SC, 513.
22. *The Pioneer,* 22nd April 1994.
23. For Further details, see A.N. Ray, "Civil Rights Movement and Social Struggle in India", *Economic and Political Weekly,* 12th June 1986, pp. 1202–05.
24. *Ibid.,* p. 1204.
25. Quoted by Kipekar, *Supra,* n. 16.
26. *Ibid.*

32

Environment: A Matter of Survival

Ashish Kothari

In the middle of 1995, two very different events signaled the arrival of the environment debate squarely into the centre of Indian society and polity. The first was the announcement, by the Tehri Garhwal district authorities, prohibiting the entry of Medha Patkar and other members of the Narmada Bachao Andolan into the district. Their stated reason was that they feared violence between the supporters of the controversial Tehri Dam and those who opposed it; environmentalist Sunderlal Bahuguna was then in the middle of a fast seeking stoppage of the construction on the dam. In reality, of course, the Government was simply scared that the agitation against the dam would greatly intensify if the Narmada Bachao Andolan was allowed there.

The second event, rather on a different note, was the publication of articles on environment in the front page of several issues of *Employment News,* the official organ for such news brought out by the Government of India. The fact that a magazine devoted to employment thought the subject to be important enough was an indication enough that the old division between economy and environment had been officially demolished.

The intricate and inextricable link between economy and environment is a recent realization for formal economists, but has always been recognized and practiced by rural populations. After all, humans survive not by money, markets and televisions, but by fresh air, fresh water, productive food-growing land and biological resources. Take these away, and humanity would perish within minutes, regardless of how robust the stock markets are. The most powerful economy is ultimately based on these elements and even the most sophisticated technologies cannot recreate them, if destroyed.

This paper addresses four basic issues:

1. The kind and extent of major environmental problems;
2. The impacts of these problems, especially on vulnerable human populations and other species;
3. The causes of these problems, both fundamental and proximate;
4. The solutions, including those already being implemented and those proposed or needed.

The basic propositions put forward here, corresponding to the above four issues, are:

1. In India, the environmental crisis is already here, causing enormous disruption of lives and livelihoods, threatening the collapse of its entire life-support system.
2. Environmental problems affect different parts of our population differently, the main brunt being borne by poor and dispriviledged classes of humans and by non-human species.
3. Thee problems have only their proximate causes in factors like population growth, poverty, consumerism resource mismanagement and technological inappropriateness. More fundamentally, the environmental crisis is rooted deep in the social, economic and political structure, more specifically in the relation to inequality between different classes and generations of humans and between humans and other species.
4. Solutions to these problems therefore cannot be technological, managerial or demographic, but has to be more crucially, socio-political and ethical. While governmental structures are addressing the issue mainly at the former, superficial level, people's movement and sensitive intellectuals are raising the more fundamental issues and are coming up with viable alternatives.

Dimensions of the Environmental Crisis in India

As agriculturists, fisher folk, forest dwellers and pastoralists, the majority of Indians are still *directly* dependent on nature-soil, biodiversity and water-bodies for their survival and livelihood. For these people, other natural environment is not merely a thing of beauty and joy, but the very basis of day to day survival. Farmers, constituting 70 per cent of our workforce, would be helpless without productive land, which in turn is dependent on forests for soil conservation and nutrients. Fisher folks, another several million, would be rendered jobless and hungry without productive fisheries, which can only survive in healthy rivers and seas. Forest-dwelling tribes would be deprived of not only their livelihood, source (bamboo, *tendu patta,* cane etc.), but also of a substantial input of nutrition from wild fruits, tubers and animals, in turn dependent on intact forest ecosystems. And so on is the case, for the millions of crafts persons, nomads and other 'ecosystems people' who eke out a living from, and whose cultures and psyches are intimately associated with, the natural world.

In the last few decades a massive attack has taken place on this natural resource base with severe impacts on the majority of the Indian population.

There are many dimensions to this crisis, some more frightening than the other; take *land,* perhaps our most threatened resource. The Union Ministry of Agriculture admitted in 1980 that out of a total landmass of 328 million hectares in India, as many as 175 million hectares or 53 per cent of the total area, are suffering from various levels of degradation. A major portion of this, about 150 million hectares, is seriously eroded by water and wind. The soil lost thus would be worth several hundreds of crores rupees and one estimate puts the nutrient at greater loss than the total fertilizer product in India. Even surface irrigation, designed to give a boost to land productivity, has actually degraded land over vast areas. Water logging and sanitization threatens the loss of over 10 million hectares of agricultural land. Indeed almost 60 per cent of our total cultivated area, out of 140 million hectares, is facing degradation.

One major cause for land degradation is deforestation, which is a serious problem in itself. The dimensions of *forest* destruction in India in the last few decades are staggering. Precise estimates of forest cover are not available for the period prior to the 1970s, but rough calculations suggest that at the time of Independence, possibly about 30 per cent of India was covered by forests. Latest satellite imagery and interpretation by the Forest Survey of India indicate that by the early 1905, the cover was down to about 19 per cent. This too is an exaggeration of sorts, for dense forests (above 40 per cent canopy cover) were measured at less than 12 per cent of the Indian landmass.

Water, too, is equally threatened. Deforestation and land mismanagement have caused severe hydrological imbalances resulting in acute water shortages all over India. This is added to by rampant over exploitation of ground-water reserves in many areas; to check which still no regulations are there. To top it all, pollution from towns and cities, industries and Green Revolution fields (pesticides and fertilizers) has rendered much of the remaining water unfit for direct use. Over 70 per cent of surface water in India is seriously polluted today. *The Economic Survey of 1995* admitted that 90 per cent of water in India's 241 Class II towns was polluted. Over two decades of pollution control and sewage treatment have not substantially improved the situation, as rapid urbanization continues to outpace official pollution control efforts. Recent surveys suggest that over 50 per cent of industries may still be disgorging effluents above the prescribed standards. Deadly industrial wastes like arsenic, mercury, nitrates and fluoride flow unchecked into rivers and lakes, thus increasing pesticide and fertilizer inflows from fields are contaminating water sources.

To add to water pollution are various other kinds of pollutants. The *air* in most of our cities is filthy with average levels of suspended particulate matter in the four metropolitan cities is over 360 micrograms per cubic meter, while the World Health Organization has stipulated a safety level of 150 mg/m. Oxides of sulphur and nitrogen, hydrocarbons, lead, carbon monoxide and other hazardous gases are emitted in tones from industrial chimneys and auto-vehicular exhaust. Noise too is becoming a serious menace, the average level in many cities having crossed 70 decibels, and certain congested areas recording over 90 decibels for the better part of the day. Millions of workers are being exposed to highly unhealthy occupational environments, full of dust, heat, noise, dirt, gases and dangerous machinery.

To add to the hazards are the mushrooming chemical industries and nuclear power plants, both of which have shown a terrible safety record in India. The Bhopal disaster was only the most visible sign of the dangers posed; smaller 'accidents' like Bhopal are happening all over India all the time, killing or maiming workers and the surrounding population in smaller numbers. Though no major accident has so far taken place in the growing number of nuclear facilities in India, the possibility is certainly not remote. Despite a veil of secrecy around the nuclear programme, it is well-known that most of India's nuclear power plants have been plagued by minor reactor accidents with the Rajashtan Atomic Power Plant which has perhaps the most radioactively contaminated interior in the world. The number of time-bombs amidst us is steadily, rapidly increasing, not only in the form of large hazardous industries but also tiny, unnoticeable pollutants like *pesticides* which continue to accumulate in our bodies until they reach a level high enough to cause cancer. Indians, today, have the highest pesticide residues in their body fat in the world while foodstuffs in several major cities have regularly shown residues much higher than the prescribed tolerance levels.

❑ The Impacts

Impacts on Humans: The Poor are Worst Hit

The localized and national effects of environmental damage in India are becoming increasingly clear. Loss of topsoil, water logging and sanitization and shortages of water and biomass have caused serious decline in agricultural productivity in many areas, a decline which can only be temporarily offset by pumping in artificial stimulants like chemical fertilizers. The prospect for food security is bleak when we are facing the loss of over half our crop-producing land.

While environmental degradation ultimately affects everyone, the immediate and most severe impacts are felt by the poor.

Land degradation directly hits farmers, lowering agricultural productivity. Big farmers can afford to compensate this loss by putting in artificial stimulants like fertilizers, but for marginal farmers it is a rapidly losing battle. Deforestation directly affects those for whom the forests are the main means of survival tribes. Tribes are displaced and rendered unemployed as the bamboo that they used to make houses, baskets and various articles for sales, are sucked away by a nearby paper mill. Villagers have become increasingly marginalized and impoverished as their sources of firewood, fodder and minor forest produce get destroyed and they have to buy these things at an ever-increasing prices. Indirectly, too, deforestation hits the poor. The widespread and debilitating droughts which have struck India in the last few years are in many cases greatly intensified by forest destruction, and thus have obvious negative repercussions on the rural poor; even where severe drought does not occur, streams and other water sources get drier and drier, making the once-simple act of obtaining water more and more difficult. As an ironical contrast to this, millions of people are rendered homeless and jobless by the increasing fury of deforestation induced floods. Poverty in these cases is a direct outcome of environmental destruction.

Pollution, too, affects the poor more. Perhaps over 70 per cent of the diseases in India (in terms of number of people affected) are caused by polluted water. These diseases hit the poor more than the rich for three reasons:

1. They are often forced to live in more polluted surroundings (like urban slums).
2. They are, due to their low nutritional status and general ill-health, more susceptible to pollution-caused diseases.
3. They are also the ones who have least access to or can least afford medical treatment.

This triple-edged sword affects the vast majority of India's population. Apart from the human suffering, there is enormous economic loss too. An estimate puts the number of workdays lost, due to diseases caused by water pollution, at 73 million annually. This is added to by an increasing number of illnesses caused by air and noise pollution, and injuries resulting from exposure to hazardous chemicals and processes. Again, it is the poor who are worst hit-annually, hundreds of thousands of industrial workers, especially contractual labours, fall prey to environmentally degraded working conditions; agricultural labours, the poorest rural strata, are most exposed to the dangers of threshers and pesticides.

It is also becoming increasingly apparent that women are generally more affected than men. In most cases they are the ones who do chores like collecting firewood, fodder and water, and as these get harder and harder to get due to deforestation, the drudgery of their life increases. Women in several parts of India now walk over 10 km daily just to obtain these necessities, often traversing treacherous mountainous terrain. All over India women of poor households cook in ill-ventilated kitchens, inhaling up to 40 times the volume of suspended particles considered safe by the World Health Organization, or an amount of cancer-causing benzopyrene equivalent to smoking 20 packs of cigarettes in just a few hours. Being of lower nutritional status than men, *e.g.*, with a very high prevalence of anemia, women are also more susceptible to such pollution. Also in this extra-susceptible category are, of course, small children and old people.

Impacts on Other Species

Some 130, 000 wild plants and animals have been recorded within the country, with possibly twice or thrice more remaining to be discovered, and with micro-organic life being as yet virtually unknown. However, a combination of habitat destruction, over-exploitation, poisoning and the introduction of exotics has endangered a large part of this biological diversity. Unfortunately, status surveys of all but a handful of species are still not available. Conservative estimates suggest that at least 10 per cent of India's recorded wild flora and 20 per cent of its mammals are on the threatened list. Many of these would now be categorized as "critical", *i.e.,* on the verge of extinction.

In fact, no-one can say for sure how many species we have already lost. Amongst mammals, the Cheetah/*Acinonyx jubatus,* and amongst birds, the Pinkheaded duck-*Rhodonessa caryophyllacea,* the Mountain *quail/Ophrysia superciliosa* and the Forest spotted owlet/*Athene blewitti,* are extinct Indian species, about which much has been written. Not so well-known are plants like *Hubbardia heptaneuron,* which disappeared when a hydro-electricity dam was built upstream of its riverside habitat. Indeed, there are likely to be hundreds, perhaps thousands of other species which are gone forever, unsung and unrecorded either because they were not "glamorous" enough, or because we simply did not know that they existed. This is, of course, a major ethical tragedy; but it is also a major loss to the majority of India's population, which depends on biodiversity for food, drink, medicine, objects for ritual use and other needs.

These needs have also been badly hit by the erosion in India's domesticated biodiversity. This region is recognized as one of the world's major centers of crop and livestock origin and diversity; to take just one example, there were till not so long back, at least 50,000 to 60,000 varieties of rice being grown by Indian farmers. The Green Revolution, with its emphasis on high-yielding varieties, has homogenized agriculture so much that much of this genetic diversity no longer exists in the farmers' fields. Several indigenous livestock breeds are also seriously endangered, due to state-sponsored programmes of hybridization with exotics. Unfortunately, no overall estimate is available about the level of genetic erosion which has taken palace in crops and livestock, but the loss is considerable. Since the modern agriculture depends on this genetic diversity for new characteristics, the Green Revolution process is a bit like building the roof of a house by taking material from the foundation.

The Causes of the Environmental Crisis

To a casual observer, the causes of environmental problems in India are obvious enough: too much population, poverty, consumerism by small elite, outmoded technology and corruption. These are, however, only the proximate or surface causes. The view that such demographic, technological or managerial factors are the roots of the environmental crisis just does not hold water if one looks closely enough. Population growth, the needs of the poor, mismanagement and inappropriate technologies add to the pressures on our environment, but they are not the origin of the crisis-indeed, they are all themselves a result of another factor which lies at the bottom of environmental problems, which is the socio-political structure of our society.

An average American consumes 40 times more resources than an average Somali. A similar ratio is probably seen in the Indian context, if one compares the resource consumption of upper class urban dweller with that of an average villager. The American population with its profligate consumerism is far more destructive of the earth's environment, than a much larger Asian population; similarly, the richest 5 per cent of Indian society probably causes much more ecological damage than the poorest 25 per cent. Clearly, it is not mere numbers which are critical, but rather *who* consumes *what* and *how much*. This in turn is dependent on relations of power, on *who* decides what is to be done with an area's natural resources. In this context, the most important aspect is the relations of inequality between people on the one hand, and between humans and other species on the other.

Fundamentally, it is these relations of inequality which catalyze environmental destruction. Three main forms of inequity can be distinguished in this context:

1. *Intra-generational inequality:* Hierarchical relations between classes, castes, races, communities, countries and the sexes, within one generation, can create conditions for environmental destruction. Those in power are able to dictate the use of natural resources to suit their own needs, regardless of its consequences on others.
2. *Inter-generational inequality:* Entire generations of human beings as yet unborn, who will be depending on the same natural resources we are currently using, have no voice in decisions taken regarding these resources. Humanity is clearly over-exploiting the earth's natural gifts-water, topsoil, minerals, forests, fossil fuels etc-eating into their 'stocks' at a rate which is likely to leave little for future generations. What we are likely to leave for them in massive quantities, on the other hand, are toxic wastes, barren wastelands, polluted waterway and a handful of pest species which have thrived on human wastes.
3. *Inter-species inequality:* Humanity shares the earth with a mind-boggling diversity of life-forms, perhaps up to 30 million plants, animals and microbial species. This extraordinary explosion of biological diversity is not merely a source of wonder, but acts as a fundamental bedrock of human' existence as air, water and land Simply because we have the right. We have considered it our right to colonize most of the earth's land surface and increasingly even its aquatic habitats. Never before in evolutionary history has one species achieved such destructive dominance with over one-fourth of all plants and animal species condemned to extinction within the next few decades due to the human hand. The inequality between humans and other species is the most pervasive of all inequalities; and its consequences are the most tragic.

A clear understanding of the origin of the environmental crisis in these relations of inequality can be gained by taking some examples from India. Deforestation in the subcontinent has been generally attributed to the rapid rise in population during this century. However, its roots lie elsewhere, as is evident from several keenly documented historical accounts which have recently emerged. The 'nationalization' and take-over of India's forests by the British colonial government in the last century was primarily meant to establish control over a valuable resource. It was then that large-scale forestry operation started. Unfortunately, this centralized control was continued after Independence, and a systematic process of exploiting forests for commercial uses was intensified. This also forced local communities into over-using the remaining 'Village Forests' which were in their control. This over-use for growing local populations was intensified because, with their basic livelihood resources being taken over by the State; they often had to cut and sell wood for making a livelihood, and so was built up a situation in which both rich and poor, both the powerful and the powerless indulged in environmental destruction. This situation remains prevalent even today.

To take an even more specific example, bamboo forests in many parts of India have been nearly wiped out by paper mills. It is an indication of the anti-poor character of government policies that these mills were till recently given bamboo at prices far below the market price while tribes, who once obtained free bamboo for their livelihood from the forests now destroyed by the mills, had now to buy it in the market. For instance, till not so long ago, paper mills in Karnataka were paying ₹15 per ton of bamboo while the poor could purchase it only at ₹1200 per ton. As pressure from industries and urban consumers continues to grow, the poor have to depend on lesser and lesser forest area for their essential needs of fuel, fodder and shelter, forcing them to destroy their own resource base.

Millions of hectares of land go under mining or urban growth or other such 'development' projects because those who benefit from these projects,mostly urban consumers, industrialists, contractors, politicians, and the like, have greater control over land than the farmers and pastoralists depending on that land. The worst cases of pollution are found inside factories, because workers have little power in industrial decision-making and little scope for moving to another job. Big industrialists, on the other hand, continue to cause pollution because they have influence over local politics or money to pay the nominal penalties imposed on them. Agricultural labours who conduct hazardous operations like pesticide spraying are mostly from the lowest economic class as well as lowest social rank (caste). Slum dwellers live in sub-human conditions because they do not form an influential lobby in urban planning and cannot afford to buy adequate land. Domestic air pollution by smoky wood or coal stoves has till recently been completely ignored by energy policy makers because women have little say in a male dominated society.

Development and Environment

India's entire development process has been distorted by the structure of inequality outlined above. Adapted almost wholesale from the west and characterized by unrestricted, large-scale industrialization, urbanization, consumerism and materialism, today's path towards 'progress' is quite evidently causing severe environmental destruction and resource depletion. It is a process which greatly benefits a small section of Indian society, has some "trickle-down" effects on a somewhat larger section, but almost completely leaves out another large section that becomes more and more impoverished. Millions of people are today worse off than they were when our modem 'development' process was started. Tribess have been alienated from their land and forests, nomadic communities have had their pasture lands taken away by mega projects; marginal peasants and the landless have become economically even more insecure. Between 20 and 30 million people have been displaced by development projects, rendered refugees in a desperate search for shelter and jobs, because they had no say in the development planning of the country. For these people "development or destruction" is not a mere cliché, it is a burning question.

The process of liberalization and 'structural adjustment' which India embarked upon in the 1990s, has only served to further intensify the environmental and social crisis outlined above. There are at least four aspects to this:

1. The drive towards an export-led model of growth is rapidly sacrificing natural resources to earn foreign exchange, as especially seen in the fisheries and mining sectors.
2. The move towards liberalization is resulting in an atmosphere of a free-for-all, with industries increasingly ignoring environmental standards, and State Governments sacrificing natural habitats, including their own wildlife protected areas, to make way for commercial enterprises.
3. The directive to reduce Government's expenditure was resulting in cuts in social and environmental sectors. This was leading to a reduction in programmes for the conservation and regeneration of natural resources.
4. Opening up of the economy was bringing in companies with a notorious track record on environment (including pesticide manufacturers who had almost wound up in their parent countries), and wasteful consumer goods and toxics which were adding to the country's garbage and health problems.

The debate on one of the economic policies of the 1990s has also highlighted another vital aspect of the environmental crisis: the role of international organizations and relations. Many like inequities within the country have fueled the crisis; those between countries have also resulted in considerable environmental degradation. The most visible was during the colonial era, when colonies were looted of their natural resources by

European powers. Several forms of 'neo-colonialism' continue this loot today: unequal trade regimes forcing southern countries to over-exploit their resources to compete in the international market, financial debt burdens which countries try to get rid off by selling off their forests and fish and minerals, foreign aid from multilateral and bilateral donors (notably the World Bank) which primarily finance environmentally destructive development projects and aid packages (notably of the IMF) like structural adjustment which drive macro-economic policies further towards unsustainable and inequitable resource use.

❑ Towards Solution

People's Efforts

The scale and depth of people's response to the growing environmental crisis in India is quite impressive. Literally thousands of citizens' groups have sprung up in the last two decades or so, forcing their voices into the process of decision-making even where the State has not wanted to hear them. Two broad categories of groups (and individuals) can be recognized here-those who challenge and oppose environmentally destructive activities and those who carry out regenerative work or build up alternatives to these activities. Of course, neither of these roles is more important than the other and many groups and individuals are playing both.

Challenges to the destruction of India's environment are as old as the destruction itself. As an example, in many parts of India there was severe, though usually localized, resistance to the attempts by the British colonialists to take over forests for commercial exploitation. An even earlier case of resistance to tree-felling is cited from Rajasthan in western India. Over three centuries back, a king's orders to cut several hundred trees was challenged by members of the Bishnoi community, a sect which broke off from mainstream Hinduism to live a life in harmony with the environment. Two of their central tenets were: never cut a live tree and never kill an animal. The king's orders were therefore blasphemy to them; they expressed their resistance by hugging the trees slated for cutting. Several Bishnois lost their lives to the King's axe men that day, until in sheer shame the monarch was forced to call the operation off.

Several more recent examples of such successful resistance can be given. In the 1970s, a major World Bank funded project, to replace a massive area of natural mixed forests in Central India by industrial pine plantations, was abandoned after strong local tribal opposition. A move to hand over several thousand hectares of common land to a private industry in Karnataka (South India) was contested and won in court, backed by considerable local mobilization. The National Fisher folk Federation has managed to stop destructive trawling off of parts of the India coast, and to enforce seasonal fishing restrictions in marine waters. Several major dams have been stopped before or during planning stages by popular local opposition: these include Both Ghat, Bhopalpatnam and Ichampalli in Madhya Pradesh, Silent Valley in Kerala, Vishnuprayag in Uttar Pradesh and others.

The currently ongoing agitation by the Narmada Bachao Andolan against the Sardar Sarovar (Narmada) Project has redefined the contours of the environment development debate all over the world, and shown that even as powerful and agency as the World Bank can be successfully challenged. The Andolan has combined massive grassroots mobilization with incisive critiques of the Project, and generated support amongst a large range of people: scientists, trade unionists, human rights activists, environmentalists, students, even bureaucrats and politicians. Considerable media attention has ensured that Narmada has become almost a household word, symbolizing the current conflict between elitist development and the sustainability of resource use. This has not been restricted to India; perhaps all over the world, the Narmada debate has become a cause célèbre, prompting hundreds of organizations in other countries to direct their attacks at the destructive policies of the World Bank, and forcing the Bank to withdraw from the Project.

The social roots of the environmental crisis are clearly recognized by popular movements like Narmada. They have, therefore, opposed certain measures which are touted as environmental protection by the State but which in reality are both anti poor and short-sighted from the conservation point of view. In the early 1980s a blatantly anti-forest dweller Forest Act drafted by the Central Government had to be dropped due to nationwide mobilization by tribal, human rights, and environmental groups; a similar draft in the early 1990s has also encountered widespread resistance. Increasingly, top-down wildlife protection steps in the country's national parks and sanctuaries are being challenged on human rights rounds, with the assertion that human and wildlife interests have to be reconciled in any biodiversity conservation attempts. Trade unions are joining hands with some sensitive environmental groups to resolve the apparent conflict between environmental protection and employment, a conflict which has become exacerbated by overzealous environmentalists calling for closure of industries and mines without addressing the resulting problems of workers unemployment. At an international level, groups are becoming wary of the environmental conditionality being put by several countries (*e.g.*, the recent ban on import of certain Indian textiles by Germany), trying to distinguish between those which are genuinely inspired by consumer concern and those which are disguised attempts at protectionism. As the environmental rhetoric is increasingly picked up by governments and agencies like the World Bank, whose basic developmental thrust remains destructive and iniquitous, the environmental movement has to carefully dissociate itself and voice more sensitive concerns.

It is not a far step from such opposition and resistance, to regeneration and the creation of alternatives. Here too, citizens' efforts in India are many and diverse. The famous Chipkoo movement in the Himalaya has not only successfully resisted deforestation in several areas, but also shown that community forestation with indigenous species can be enormously successful. Attempts at reviving traditional or developing new methods of ecological farming are now widespread. Farmers and citizens' groups have shown that adequate levels of diversified crop production without the use of synthetic chemicals is possible and economically viable, and are increasingly networking amongst themselves to build an effective lobby. A group of energy experts in Bangalore has developed alternative energy scenarios for several states, which would be far less resource-depleting and environmentally destructive than the current energy generation models. Assisted by engineers and hydrologists with a pro-people bent of mind, communities in diverse ecological zones, including the driest arid areas of western India, have shown that watershed management and simple rainwater harvesting techniques can achieve, at much less ecological, social, and financial costs, what big dams cannot. Ralegan Siddhi, Sukhomajri, Jardhar, Seed, Baliraga, etc., are just some of the villages across the country which have reversed ecological degradation and shown alternative developmental models.

Social equity and decision-making, by as many of the members of the village as possible, have been essential features of these efforts. For instance, water scarcity in the arid tracts of Maharashtra has been tackled by *Pani Panchayats*, an innovative structure of decision-making in which villagers ensure the equitable distribution of irrigation water. Van Panchayats in the Himalayan foothills are attempting the same with forest resources.

The clear lesson from the dynamics of both environmental destruction and environmental reconstruction in India is that people-local communities everywhere have to be involved in any kind of natural resource management. That is a lesson that even the Indian State is beginning to learn.

Governmental Efforts

Early efforts by the Government of independent India to address the environmental issue were restricted to enacting laws and setting up bureaucracies for enforcement. Official policies and programmes have come a long way since then, though for the major part, an essentially top-down approach continues to permeate. In the last two decades or so, the State has responded to the environmental challenge by a series of steps:

1. *Creation of a central agency charged with the protection of environment:* Earlier a department, and upgraded in 1980 to a full-fledged Ministry of Environment and Forests, this agency handles environmental clearances for development projects, drafts or revises relevant laws, undertakes centrally funded environmental restoration projects, and so on. Most states also now have a separate ministry in charge of environmental affairs, or merge this portfolio with science and technology and have a separate ministry handling forests and wildlife management.

2. *Framing environmental policies:* Essentially statements of intent, several policies or policy statements relating to natural resources have been framed by the state. These include forests, water, pollution and wildlife. An overall conservation policy statement was framed and put forward in the early 1990s, stating the Government's view of the relationship between development and environment.
3. *Enactment of environmental legislation:* A large number of acts are now in operation in India, dealing with forest management and conservation, wildlife conservation, water and air pollution, and other environmental aspects. An overall Environmental Protection Act was passed in 1986, covering clearances for development projects and there general environmental measures. After considerable pressure, citizens' groups have managed to gain *locus standi* under all the major acts, except the Forest Act of 1927.
4. *Formulating and funding environmental programmes:* Several major schemes for forestation, pollution control, wildlife conservation, environmental awareness and other environmental work have been launched in the last two decades. These include the massive National Wastelands Development Plan, the Ambitions project to clean up the river Ganga and the creation of one of the world's largest networks of national parks and sanctuaries. The country's largest single environmental education effort, the National Environmental Awareness Campaign, is also sponsored by the Ministry of Environment and Forests.
5. *Creation of institutional mechanisms to implement laws and programmes:* The Forest Department was one of the earliest agencies created by the State to centrally manage a natural resource, dating back to the last century. More recently, wildlife wings (within the Forest Department), central and state pollution control boards, a National Wasteland Development Board and various other agencies at the national, regional and state level have been set up.

In all the above steps, two major lacunas remain-the lack of any fundamental change in India's overall development thrust and the absence of public involvement. As a result, many well-meaning efforts (*e.g.*, at forestation) have, at best, been only partial success, and at worst, ended up adversely affecting the poor. As an example, social forestry in places has emphasized industrially useful species like Eucalyptus, not only failing to meet the stated aims of providing fuel and fodder needs to the poor, but even causing labour displacement and damage to soils. In the unchanged scenario of inequality, and capital-intensive development, the greed of industry will prevail over the needs of the poor.

Changes are coming, though slowly. The concept of joint management of forests, with controls being exercised by the Forest Department and local village committees together, is catching on after some successful experiences in West Bengal. Increasingly, the Government is opening up with information, consulting independent people in official plans and programmes, and in other ways involving citizens. However, a national level policy on environment should contain the following key elements:

1. A fundamental vision that could form the overall context for the specific parts of the *National Environmental Policy (NEP):* What is our view of where we want to be, sayig 25 years from now? Do we want a world in which everyone has a right to and easy access to fresh water, fresh air, healthy food, productive lives and so on? Do we envisage moving towards a governance model in which people who are living amidst natural resources have a central say in deciding about these resources? Do we respect the right of other species to survive? We need a bold vision for the future, in a national document of this sort.
2. An alternative model (or models) of development, that puts the natural environment *and people at the centre:* The draft NEP does not challenge the fundamental nature of the current model of 'development', even though it is now widely recognized that this model is at the heart of environmental destruction. This model makes a holy cow of unlimited 'economic growth' (instead of more holistic human welfare and well- being), and in the process treats nature (and people) as a commodity, does not recognize nature as the basis of all human activities and relies on essentially technological solution to problems that are more fundamentally social or political in nature (e.g., increasing food production through artificial inputs when the real problem is not quantum of food produced but the unequal control over its production and distribution). The draft does talk about 'mainstreaming' environment into economic planning, but without fundamentally challenging the model of development (including in its 'globalization' form and the wasteful consumerism that it perpetuates), this would amount to some minor tinkering. What is needed is at least a vision that puts nature and overall human well-being (cultural, spiritual, material, intellectual) at the centre of a process of development, and from which would emanate the core principles and strategies for ecologically sustainable development models.
3. *A national (and local/state) land/water use plan:* An overall long-term plan for the use of India's land and water resources, has been a dire necessity for decades. Many governments have promised it, but none has yet been bold enough to develop one. With a new Government with a fresh mandate in place, this is a great opportunity to move towards a long-term policy and plan for how we look at the country's land and water resources in an integrated manner. This would include mapping out, from local to national levels, areas that for ecological and cultural/ social reasons should be off-limits to any kind of land use change (the draft NEP does talk about areas of "incomparable value", but does not place such area into an overall land/water use plan).
4. *A model for governance of natural resources:* At various places the draft NEP implies that the current way of governing our natural resources has

failed. But it does not, from this diagnosis, come out with a bold new alternative. At various places it talks of decentralization of 'partnerships' amongst various parts of society, and of specific elements like public access to information, ut what is needed is an overall vision of how natural resources will be governed, who at what stage should be taking the decisions will be governed ad how will current institutions of governance change. As mentioned above, the draft asserts the doctrine of "Public Trust" in which the State does not own the resources, but holds them in trust for the public. Unfortunately, this bold principle is not followed up to its logical conclusion, which would be to vest far greater powers in village and urban communities, and to work out a decision-making structure that emantes from this basic ground-level of governance.

5. A holistic view of our relationship with nature and natural resources, which includes *cultural, spiritua, and material dimensions:* Other than the material, all other dimensions are missing from the draft NEP. This is strange, given that these dimensions have been such an integral part of all Indian traditions, such a core part of how we have related to nature. The draft displays an extremely human-centered, materialist view of the environment which is seriously inappropriate for the Indian context.
6. *Assertion of the fundamental human right to a healthy environment:* The draft NEP lays emphasis on the critical role of the natural environment in human economic activity. It does not however, assert that a healthy environment (including access to fresh air, clean water, healthy food and natural surrounds) is or should be a fundamental human right. Such a right is increasingly being recognized in many countries, and in international circles, and India too should be at the forefront of asserting it.

POST SCRIPT

A set of laws have been enacted by the Parliament, mostly new but one dating back to the 'British Raj' namely the Indian Forest Act, 1927, subsequently amended by various State legislatives since the commencement of the 1950 constitution. The more recent laws include the Wild Life Protection Act, 1972; the Water Prevention and Control of Pollution Act, 1974; the Forest Conservation Act, 1980; the Air Prevention and Control of Pollution Act, 1974; the Environment Protection Act, 1986; The Public Liability Insurance Act, 1991; the schedules tribes and other traditional Forest Dwellers Recognition of Forest Rights Act, 2006; and the National Green Tribunal Act, 2010.

The real impetus for bringing about a well-developed framework came after the U.N. conference on Human Environment Stockholm, 1972 in which India participated. Another milestone in this direction was the upgradation of the Department dealing with these matters in the Government of India into the Ministry of Environment and Forests (MoEFs) in 1985.

The MoEFs have laid down the requirements and procedure for seeking environmental clearance for undertaking any new project or expansion or modernization of any existing industry or project under the Forest Conservation Act, 1980. In case of the following site specific projects, i.e., mining, thermal power stations, hydro-power/major irrigation and flood control projects, parts and harbours, and prospecting and exploration of major minerals in areas above 500 ha. The project authorities will intimate the location of the project to the Union overnment in the MoEFs while initiating any investigations and surveys. The ministry will convey a decision regarding suitability or otherwise of the project site within a maximum period of 30 days. If the sanction is given, it shall be valid for a period of five years for commencing the construction operation or mining.

The reports submitted with applications shall be evaluated and assessed by the Impact Assessment Agency (IAA) of the MoFEs. If deemed necessary it may consult a committee of experts, having a composition as specified in schedule I!I of the Act.

What Lies Ahead?

There is still a long way to go before local communities can be center-stage in decision-making, as they should be; and just as long a way to go before the development process can become truly environment-friendly. While the environmental movement has thrown up a series of exciting and viable alternatives to the current development model, there is an urgent need to merge these into some sort of a holistic ideology and strategy. Answers to the following questions are still being groped for: what sort of national and local political structure would be most responsive to environmental concerns, especially given that these concerns are highly diverse and site-specific? What kind of political ideology or ideologies are relevant? What does it specifically mean to say social equity in this connection and how does one achieve it is situations of extreme inequities, as prevalent today? What is the right mix of traditional and modern technologies which can help achieve sustainability, by being sensitive to local ecological and social conditions? What is the role of traditional political, social, technological and ideological systems in the context of today's changing world? How does one resist the forces of materialism sweeping the country, especially in the age of powerful mass media?

These and other issues present crucial areas of research and action in the years to come, as the environmental movement (if one can call a widely disparate set of people and groups and ideologies that) works it's way towards answers. One thing is certain: if answers are to emerge, if we are to achieve some sort of lasting peace with the earth, they will come from this movement and not from the economists and political ideologies which have so far only headed us towards mass suicide.

BIBLIOGRAPHY

Books

Agarwal, A. and Narain, S., 1989, *Towards Green Villages,* Centre for Science and Environment, New Delhi.

Agarwal, A. and Narain, S., 1992, *Towards A Green World,* Centre for Science and Environment, New Delhi.

Anderson, R. and Huber, W., 1988, *Hour of the Fox: Tropical Forests.* The World Bank and Indigenous People in Central India, Vis tar Publication, New Delhi.

Bandopadhyay, I., *et al.,* 1985, *India's Environment: Crisis and Responses,* Natraj Publishers, Dehra Dun.

Banwari, 1992, *Pancavati: Indian Approach to Environment,* Shri Vinayaka Publications, Delhi.

Centre for Science and Environment, *The State of India's Environment: Second Citizens' Report 1984-85.*

Fernandes, W. (ed.), 1992, *National Development and Tribal Deprivation,* Indian Social Institute. New Delhi.

Gadgil, M. and Guha, R., 1992, *This Fissured Land,* Oxfrod University Press, New Delhi. Ganguly and Thukral, 1992, *Big Dams, Displced People,* Sage Publications, New Delhi.

Guha, R., 1991, *Unquiet Woods: Ecological Change and Peasant Resistance in the Himalayas,* Oxford University Press, New Delhi.

Guha, R. (ed.), 1995, *Social Ecology: A Reader,* Oxford University Press, New Delhi.

Hiremath, S.R., Kanwalli, S. and Kulkarni, S. (ed.), 1994, *All About Draft Forest Bill and Forest Lands,* Samaj Parivartana Samudaya, Dharwad.

Kothari, A., 1995, *Conserving Life: Implications of the Biodiversity Convention for India,* Kalpavriksh, New Delhi.

Nadkarni, M.Y. *et. al.,* 1989, *The Political Economy of Forest Use and Management,* Public Interest Research Group, *Structural Adjustment: Who Really Pays?,* New Delhi.

Sen. Orijit, 1994, *River of Stories,* Kalpavriksh, New Delhi.

Singh, c., 1986, *Common Property and Common Poverty: India's Forests, Forest-dwellers, and the Law,* Oxford University Press, New Delhi.

Shiva, V., 1988, *Staying Alive,* New Delhi, Kali for Women.

Shiva, V, 1991, *The Violence of the Green Revolution,* Third World Network, Malaysia.

Shiva, V *et al.,* 1991, *Ecology and The Politics of Survival.*

Singh, G., Anklesaria, K. and Gonsalves, C. (ed.), 1993, *The Environmental Activists' Handbook: Statutes, Judgments, Srategies,* Colin Gonsalves, Bombay.

Viegas, P. and Menon, G., 1988, *Impact of Environmental Degradation on People,* Indian Social Institute, New Delhi.

World Resources Institute, *World Resources* 1994-95, Oxford University Press, New York.

Magazines/Periodicals

Down to Earth, Centre of Environmental Communications, New Delhi.

Ecologist Asia, c/o Sanctuary Magazine, Bombay.

Hindu Survey of Environment, *The Hindu,* Madras.

Lokayan Bulletin, Lokayan, New Delhi.

Sanctuary Asia, Bombay.

Third World Resurgence, Third World Network, Malaysia.

Special number on 'Environment and Administration', *Indian Journal of Public Administration,* Vol. XXXV No. 3, July-September 1989.

Special number on 'Sustatinable Development', *Indian Journal of Public Administration,* Vol. XXXIX, No. 3, July-September 1993.

Special Issue on 'The Indigenous Vision: Peoples of India, Attitudes to the Environment', *India* International Centre Quartely, 1992.

33

Emerging Trends in India's Foreign Policy: Challenges and Prospects

Sanju Gupta

A nation's foreign policy is primarily designed to promote its dominant class' interests. However, depending on the resources and the vision of the leadership, it may also aspire for national interests and a global role in search of market and resources by pursuing global interests of peace and development for the hegemony of the ruling classes in the existing world order. The foreign policy of India, ever since its inception, has been an amalgamation of class interests with global objectives. The moving spirit behind this policy has been the concept of Non-Alignment. This all-weather concept was an outcome, not only of our rich cultural and philosophical heritage, but it also reflected the consensual mode of domestic politics of the dominant classes in the post-independence era. This posture was a logical response to the Cold War.

The Cold War and its ideological baggage now appear to be a part of post-war history. Fundamental changes have taken place in international politics in the past two decades. The Soviet Union disintegrated and with its fragmentation, the world entered into the post-cold war era. The plethoric nature of change that occurred was further complicated by the multi-dimensional character of international regime transformations.[1] The twin processes of globalization and localization have been sweeping across national frontiers. Issues of global concern in the form of peace, disarmament, human development, environment, human rights & democratization dominate the global agenda. Coupled with these changes at the macro level, there have been progressive convulsions at the micro level, within the Indian state. In this changing global and local milieu, new challenges and possibilities have emerged before our vast entity of civilization.

India, like many developing countries, has tried to adjust her foreign policy according to the needs and priorities of the post-cold war world order. There have been numerous challenges and opportunities, and the survival and sustenance has been an adventurism at the maximization of opportunities. To what extent has India shown dynamism and flexibility, so as to cope up with these challenges? What are the evolving patterns of foreign conduct?

This chapter is an attempt at delineating the emerging contours of the post-post-Cold War world and an insight into the preparedness of India, to face the changed global political architecture. However, before attempting an exploration on the transformations through the 1990s, well into the new millennium, it would be apt to briefly discuss the foundational base and basic premise of India's foreign policy.

❑ Origins of India's Foreign Policy-Basic Principles and Objectives

As the Second World War ended and India's independence became a reality, Indians took note of emerging political impulses and strategic orientations in international politics. Several factors were instrumental in shaping the foreign policy. Perceptions of the Indian leadership were deeply influenced by the freedom struggle of India against colonialism. Indian leaders viewed the world through the prism of the political, economic and ideological contradictions, which resulted in two world wars. They were convinced that political contradictions and inequalities could not be confined or compartmentalized in order to prevent tendencies of competition, conflict and violence affecting the entire international community.[2] They were also convinced that international harmony, peace and stability could be achieved through a process of reasoning together; and also the that fact that if foreign relations were to contribute to peace and well being of the international community, then that had to be responsive to the profound aspirations of the common people.

The consequence of Nehruvian approach was a widely shared feeling that India had a catalytic role to play in establishing a moral and just world. It was believed that India should take initiatives to eradicate imperialism and all forms of discrimination. The disintegration of the alliance between the "democratic" and "progressive" forces and the emergence of the Cold War,[3] led by the US and the erstwhile USSR, were disappointments to India. Indian leadership was apprehensive about India becoming subject to extraneous influences, if nations were to take sides in this ideological confrontation. Nehru's assessment was that India should keep away from Cold War politics and should remain committed to its own democratic terms of reference for national consolidation.[4] This approach evolved into Non-Alignment became the guiding principle of India's foreign policy, and ultimately found manifestation in the creation of the Non-Aligned Movement.

These approaches have constituted the core of India's foreign policy. Over the years, successive governments have adhered to the basic premise laid down in the foundational years following independence. However, geo-political realities do not remain constant.

While the international system is constantly an evolving one, factors of time and space affect the nature of change. Furthermore, forces of global change continuously interact with domestic ingredients. It is true that though the driving force of India's foreign policy remained unchanged, yet the changing equations of the international system and complexities of sub-continental security called for the orientation. The War that lasted for well over four decades, ended with the disintegration of the Soviet Union in 1989. This ushered in the so-called New World Order. This post-cold war world was characterized by the end of bipolarism, the emergence of the uni-cum-multipolar worlds and the emergence of gee-economics as the primary factor governing politics among states.[5] India's first security concern was to cope with a more complex and competitive international situation. New political relationship had to be established with diversified economic and technological links. As the decade of 1990s has proved, the structured equations and antagonisms of the Cold War were perhaps easier to deal with, than the uncertainties, which the world faces today. Unprecedented changes and challenges confront the nation-states in the new millennium.

❑ Changing Contours of The World—The Rising Challenges

The dawn of the new millennium did not bring disarmament or usher in the widely expected era of stability, cooperative security and wider prosperity; rather, it engendered fresh political, technological and economic rivalries and unveiled new destructive capacities. Trade conflict among powerful states, external interventions in "internal wars" and UN's eroding ability to promote global security have given rise to economic protectionism, aggressive commercial diplomacy, ethnic militancy, nationalism and coercive unilateralism. The advent of the information age and the consequent revolution in military affairs have enhanced the role of technology in combat, deterrence and conflict prevention. The world therefore presents a scenario that continues to be in a state of flux. It would be proper to examine some dimensions of the emerging geo-strategic landscape.

Redefining Security: Towards a Paradigmatic Shift

The concept of security has undergone sea-changes in recent years. A number of significant questions have been raised. These include-What are the dimensions of national security? Can security be defined exclusively in state-centric terms? Are the states more threatened from within than from outside? What are the linkages between the internal and external threats? The realist and neo-realist school of thought, for a long time, provided a state-centric analysis of security. Herein, the Sovereign State was the unit of analysis, the State's behaviour was assumed as rational and the nature of the international system as anarchic.[6] This paradigm informed that an 'anarchic' world order predisposes the construction of a hierarchy between nation and states. An optimization of military power was concomitant with this model, to assure maximum security to the state against external threats.

In this scheme, national security was equated with expansion of military capabilities, acquisition of weapon systems to counter the adversary, quest for nuclear weapons and so on. Though these beliefs were adequate during the Cold War, they are totally inadequate to discover the dilemmas of national security in the post-cold war era.[7] There is now shift from strategic (national) to security studies, having both trans-national and international ramifications. National security, today, is being examined in a broader context including non-military threats and domestic security issues. There is growing consensus that security should comprise political, ethnic, social, economic, environmental, communal and religious strife that embrace the civil society and the citizen. This shift has now reversed the priorities of security studies, away from the earlier central strategic questions, to the emerging security predicament of the third world.

The Third World has been confronting internal security challenges emanating from ethnic conflict, sectarian crises, racial tensions, imbalances of socio-economic development, rising population and the increasing degradation of the environment.[8] The cumulative effect of such pressures led many third world regimes to seek refuge in building huge military establishments. Though the objective was "state security", what they actually achieved was "regime security". The Indian security perspectives, rooted in the geo-strategic context of South Asia, have been a reflection of these third world realities which have been characterized by external challenges to its integrity, as well as the external threats to its sovereign boundaries.

Security studies in India will have to reckon with the arguments on economic and political security.[9] Indian security analysts need to take into account the limits of military and nuclear weapons' power. There is need to shift the focus to a larger holistic meaning of security.

Globalization: The World as a Global Village

The process of globalization, with its obvious implications for foreign policy and defense interests of any nation, remains the subject of an intense debate across the world. The discussion is focused on whether it is good or bad; whether it is a bonding or unsettling factor; whether it fosters prosperity and freedom or allows the dominant players to exploit the market of the weaker players.[10] The world nevertheless has become a part and parcel of globalization, either by choice or by the force of events. Many see globalization as a primarily economic phenomenon, involving the increasing interaction or integration of national economic systems through the growth in international trade, investment and capital flows. One can also point to a rapid increase in cross-border social, cultural and technological exchange as part of this phenomenon. Sociologists like Anthony Giddens defines globalization as decoupling of space and time, emphasizing that with instantaneous communications, knowledge and culture can be shared around the world simultaneously.[11] The left critics of globalization have defined the phenomenon differently. They present it as a worldwide drive towards a globalized economic system, dominated by supranational corporate trade and banking institutions that are not accountable to democratic processes or national governments.

Globalization has led to a sharp rise in the volume of world trade. The free flow of finance capital is another major plank of economic globalization. Communication technology has made it possible to conduct financial transactions across the world. One of the benefits, which globalization has provided to poor countries, can be found in the new employment opportunities it offers. This is owing to the setting up of multinationals in various countries. Many governments have created special export processing zones in order to attract multinationals, and to encourage domestic industries to produce more for the international market. Larger than many host nations, these multinationals are often in a powerful position to dictate terms. A consequence of this growing corporate power can be seen clearly in relation to their foreign investment role. At its best, investment by a foreign company can provide jobs; stimulate growth and offer developing countries the access to key technology and skills. At its worst, these multinationals just exploit the cheap labour or natural resources.[12]

In terms of communications, globalization has been possible through the growth of computer network, telecom, electronic media etc. The military sphere has seen the advent of global weaponry. Intercontinental ballistic missiles and spy satellite for instance, have in certain respects, turned the world into a single realm of battle. Thus globalization has been transpiring through the proliferation and growth of companies, associations and regulatory agencies that operate as trans-border networks. It was assumed that the 'globalization' and 'liberalization' process would lead to a drastic altering and reshaping the role of the state in economic management.[13] While it is true that market forces today are shaping economic decisions, it would be an over simplification to assume that the State would have a small or secondary role to play. In developing countries like India, where the State has a primary responsibility in providing basic services, it would be unrealistic to think in terms of a shrinking role for the state.[14] The primary task of economic diplomacy in such countries has to be alert and alive to the changes that are underway in the international economic scenario, so as to react to them and recommend policy courses appropriate to the evolving situation.

US Adventurism Vs The World: Resisting Hegemony

Two events of the early 21st century-the 9/11 terrorist attacks on America and the American attempt at regime change in Iraq through the use of force-are major landmarks in contemporary international relations. These events ushered in a new era, an era that marks the end of the post-cold war era and the beginning of a new, post-cold war era.[15] Two important developments deserve mention here, first, the unfolding of a new unipolar movement in all its fury and vigour; second, the uncertain future faced by the alliance system the US has built in Asia and Europe. As early as 1991, in the wake of the Gulf crisis (Iraqi aggression of Kuwait), America displayed a foreign policy aiming towards a leadership role. According to the American leadership, the unipolar world which had emerged as a result of a victory in the Cold War, following the decline of the Soviet Union, has added to the American responsibility to help structure the new world order.

Critics alleged that this was a scramble for an alternative rationale for US interventionism in the post-cold war and was sought to be advanced by articulating the need for American role in a world-wide movement for democracy. With the emerging contours of the world in the early 1990's still being debated, a school of thought argued that it was unrealistic to announce the world as unipolar. The argument was supported by citing the cases of Russia consciously expanding its relations with China, the increasingly interdependent character of the world, recognizing multi polarity of the international system and the rise of regional powers in Asia, Africa and Latin America. With Europe integrating into a European Union, NAFTA creating an immense trading bloc and APEC attempting to integrate economies across the Pacific, it was believed that the world can at best be described as an uni-cum-multipolar world. This was a world with potential emerging new power centers, though the dominant power variables was still at the command of the US. These deliberations on post Cold War and post 9/11 world were jolted mid-stream, when in March 2003' the US invaded, conquered and occupied Iraq. The reason why was this war imposed, remains a mystery.[16] Clearly,it was not just because Saddam Hussain was unwilling to disclose and destroy his alleged weapons of mass destruction (WMDs). Was it all about the control of Iraqi oil? Was the objective guided at regime change or primarily regime ouster? Is the world now irrevocably unipolar or will the process towards multi-polarism be hastened? With numerous such questions looming large, it is clear that the "Operation Iraqi Freedom" has shaken the dynamics of world politics.[17] It has also sharpened the debate between supporters of American unilateralism and the urgency of restoring principles of multilateralism.

The recent American action relate to the consolidation of the so called 'neoconservative' view of the world in Washington. This is the form of neoimperialism, which represents a potential American role in the world that is at once progressive and assertive.[18] The Bush administration had outlined this goal in its National Security Strategy (NSS) released in September 2002. The thinking embodied in the NSS war articulated in the Project for the New American Century (PNAC), which provides for pre-emptive military strikes by the LIS against perceived enemies. It is true that the 9/11 terrorist attack on the World Trade Towers in the US, shook the world and American alike. American could have used this momentum to rejoin the rest of the world by proclaiming that it is with the countries, hurt by similar indiscriminate attacks. Instead, America Americanized the tragedy by visualizing it as an opening to flex its muscles and impose American presence on the world.[19] The US led unipolar movement is well in to the second decade and it is unlikely that this status will change in the next few decades.

Technology, Weapons and Transnational Crime: The Challenge of Unconventional Conflicts

The Cold War coincided in time with the nuclear age, the space age, the affluent society, the post-colonial age and the conflict interdependence of advanced industrial economies. These coincidences brought forth the following changes:

- The technological revolution through which we are living.
- Alterations in the relative weight of power factors as conventionally calculated by states.
- The importance of transnational activities and non-state participants in international relations.[20]

Among many dramatic changes in 20th century technology some of the most spectacular developments have taken place in communication and information. Drawing on the knowledge of electronic and space age, these technologies have reduced distances and penetrated secrecy. In a world with millions of fax machines and personal computers, with direct access to the internet, information flows faster and freer among people and across natural or man-made boundaries. The commercial, cultural, economic, educational, intellectual, military, moral and political repercussions of this are so enormous that the world is still grappling with them.[21] The rapid flow and incredible proliferation of information means that advantage in any field viz., stock brokering, public education, military intelligence, marketing popular entertainment etc., will go to those who have access to the most useful information, and to those who can disseminate this information the fastest to the largest audience. Political authorities are finding it more and more difficult to control or censure the flow of information.

Technological forces are playing a greater role in shaping geopolitics than at any time in history.[22] Technology is being primarily employed to gain military and economic advantage over competitors. High-tech defence systems are relying more and more on commercial technologies. On-going research and development activities suggest that new mass-extermination technologies could emerge in the decades ahead. A new revolution in military affairs (RMA) has already emerged on the horizon. The RMA process, ensuing from the information age, rests on three developments in military technologies that have serious implication for national security in developing countries:

- The first is the conceptualization and automation of the battlefields; this enhances the ability of countries, armies, commanders and individual weapons to gather, process and use information. This development is proceeding towards a fully automated battle-field.
- The second trend is the development of post-nuclear weapcnry.
- The third is the development of non-lethal weaponry comprising precision-guided munitions that temporarily stun adversaries. These weapons are expected to prove handy for fighting terrorist and quelling civil unrest.[23]

It is increasingly apparent that the era of global and large-scale inter-state conflict that distinguished much in the 19th and 20th centuries, is passing. Though mankind has lived under a shadow of a nuclear holocaust, the probabilities of the nuclear war are lower than ever before. On the other hand, phenomenon of sub-conventional war, transnational militancy and terrorism has been on the rise. One of the main reasons for this has been to proliferation and diffusion of small arms and light weapon across the world.[24] The basic problem is not that there are sophisticated small arms and light weapons but that the weapons developed and designed for use by the military forces of the state have diffused to non-state actors.

There are symbolic linkages between commercial interest in developed countries dealing with drug traffic, organized crime and arms traffic and the ethno-nationalist upsurge in various developing countries. The present trend of expanding international terrorism is helped by the increased availability of the latest technology to terrorist groups. The extent and reach of terrorism has posed serious threats to world peace.[25] The international community therefore will have to cooperate in sharing timely intelligence about the movements and plans of terrorist groups; and take action against professional mercenary groups which are selling expertise, arms and explosives to them.

Foreign Policy Responses—Indian Efforts at a Pragmatic Reorientation

The changes in the international security environment and the power structure, in the past one and a half decades, have been so revolutionary that most of the foreign policy and strategic establishments including those in India, are still trying to comprehend their emerging contours. India's foreign policy had to respond to three significant challenges:

1. The task of resolving the contradiction inherent in consolidating itself as a pluralistic nation-state through the more difficult, more gradual and rational processes of democracy.

2. The task of resolving the contradictions between its sense of self and self-importance, in contrast with the way that the rest of the world perceives India, in terms of its economic and military strengths and strategic motivations.
3. The task of reconciling the moral vision on the basis of which we wish the international order to be structured, with the non-moral requirements of real 'politik'.[26]

While meeting the fundamental national interests and adhering to moral terms of reference, India tried to achieve these objectives and has emerged as a responsible and mature country in the world. The events of post 1989 world brought forth new equations and new priorities. India's defence and security experts started gearing up for addressing to the new issues generated by the external events. Deliberations began as to how India could best plan and prepare for the future and how it could position itself to make the most of the changing configurations of global power. As India enters the 21st century many new pragmatic trends have been discernible.

Responding to Economic Challenges: Economization of Foreign Policy

We live in an era in which world trade is expanding at a faster pace than world output, capital flows are overwhelming, daily transactions in foreign exchange are rapidly increasing. The WTO regime is endeavoring to continuously expand the scope of multilateralism, not only in the trade of goods and services, but also in the area of investment. The spectacular progress of information technology has transformed the world financial markets into virtually a single entity. In such a rapid globalizing environment, India cannot keep itself aloof and alienated. Recognizing the crucial link between globalization and economic growth India is revitalizing its efforts to get the best out of the inevitable process of globalization.

In India critical actions like government deregulation, the advent and spread of new information technologies and the gradual opening up of financial market have together played crucial roles. India vigorously adopted liberalization, privatization, marketization and modernization through the 1990's. It was clear that the inability to compete economically in the capitalist world system cannot be compensated by any other power resource. India has identified foreign investment promotions as an important strategy in achieving the objectives of increasing industrial production and creating employment opportunities. A relevant aspect of all these investment related activities are the presence of a large number of transnational and other foreign companies in India. The prevention of the abuse of monopoly power by the MNCs and a reasonably long time, for creating a level playing field to ensure the sustenance of the national firms, is very vital issues in India today.[27]

As India enlarges its share of world trade, its voice in world councils will also gather weight. To this effect India is trying to build up new trade relations and strengthen the existing ones. One such endeavour has been the look-east policy in which South-East Asia, especially ASEAN, has been identified as central to India's policy in Asia-Pacific region. A two pronged approach has been adopted, consisting of efforts at increasing economic interaction (trade, investment, science and technology, tourism etc.) and forging defence links with several countries of this region.[28] As a result of the growing understanding between India and the ASEAN countries, India has been accepted as the full dialogue partner of ASEAN in 1995. Similarly, the launching of the Indian Ocean Rim Association for Regional Cooperation (IOR-ARC) is historic for India, as it brings together the countries of Asia, Africa, and Australia. The formation of this trading bloc among the countries of Indian Ocean Rim will provide market access to India's exports. Though India has vital stake in the evolution of SAARC as a full-fledged economic grouping; at the same time, there are attempts at seeking association with European Union (EU) and the Asia Pacific Economic Cooperation (APEC).

A primary task of our economic diplomacy has been the moulding of economic strength, vitality and ability to adopt and adjust to changing scenarios and to further our national efforts with the aim of making India economically strong and less vulnerable to international pressures.

Good Neighbourliness: Forging Regional Cooperation in South Asia

Geographical proximity, common language, common culture and inheritance of common physical and institutional infrastructure are the unique characteristics of the South Asian region. By definition, South Asia includes seven states-Bangladesh, Bhutan, India, Maldives, Nepal, Pakistan and Sri Lanka. However, there has been very little in common between the threat perceptions and security outlooks of India and the other South Asian states.[29] India's largest size in South Asia is accountable for this. Almost all the neighbouring countries suffer from an identity crisis vis-a-vis India. Therefore India's relations with its neighbours have been characterised by a big brother-small neighbour syndrome. In an attempt to strengthen their defences against India, the states of South Asia, especially Pakistan, have invited external powers into the region. One of the challenging tasks of India's foreign policy has been the generation of trust and mutual confidence with its South Asian neighbours.

The most significant development in the subcontinent during the 1990s has been an increased emphasis by India on good 'neighbourly' policies. At the heart of this policy were the efforts of the former Prime Minister I.K. Gujral and his so-called 'Gujral doctrine.'[30] This was a policy of giving unilateral concessions to neighbours and promoting people-to-people contact. Treaties were signed with Nepal, Bangladesh and Sri Lanka, as part of this doctrine. In the post-cold war era, three major factors have helped push India into developing a new policy towards the neighbours. First has been the economic imperative. As India and her neighbours launched themselves on the path of economic reform and globalization, the importance of economic cooperation became obvious to most of them. Second was the political imperative. There was a growing recognition in India that aspirations for a global political role would remain unrealized, so long as India was engrossed in regional conflicts. Third has been the balance of power imperative.[31] The smaller neighbours have allowed external powers to checkmate India within the subcontinent. Changing this negative balance of power dynamic called for an initiative based not on absolute symmetry, but on facilitating the development of common interests with each of the smaller neighbours.

India has looked up to SAARC as one of the greatest confidence building measures in South Asia. Its initiatives have been held hostage to political problems and misunderstandings between its members. But that is no reason why avenues of cooperation in trade and commerce, education and culture, sharing resources such as power and water, should not be exploited actively. India has been a persistent supporter of economic cooperation through SAARC. It is India's firm belief that by building common markets and facilitating exchange of human and natural resources, a climate of trust between member countries can become a reality.[32] Political and security problems would then become much easier to resolve.

Indo-Pak Relations: Efforts at Building Confidence

Throughout the last decade India was severely tested in dealing with a newly aggressive Pakistan.[33] It sought to cope with Pakistan in the radically changed context that brought nuclear weapons into the bilateral equation and increased Pakistan's ability to intervene in the disputed State of Jammu & Kashmir, through what has now come to be called cross-border terrorism. The history of INDO-PAK relations since 1990 is a history of ups and downs. From a limited conventional war to many summits that struggled to define a new framework of peace, the canvas has been full. In the ever-volatile environment of the South Asian neighbours, the nuclear dimension was added in May 1998. Both India and Pakistan entered the group of nuclear weapons states. Pakistan may well have restored the strategic balance in South Asia, but in doing so, it embarked on a nuclear weapon race. The logic on either side where the deterrence capacity of nuclearization, wherein the chances of war between India and Pakistan would reduce. However in mid 1999 a limited border conflict erupted in the 150 Km sector of the Line of Control (LOC) in the Kargil area of Kashmir. India accused Pakistan of violating the LOC agreements. Pakistan replied that the infiltrators where the Mujahideens, over which Islamabad had little control. The Kargil episode has raised a question mark on the distinct limits to nuclear power and deterrence. This demonstrates to India, that such low intensity conflicts will be the shape of crises, which are likely to confront the neighbours in this century.[34]

With the congress led Government taking over in 2004, efforts began towards a creative approach to the Kashmir issue. This was in the form of the various confidence-building measures, which the BJP led Government (Lahore declaration, Agra summit, Bus diplomacy) had initiated and the new Government endeavoured to take further. Among the proposals were nuclear CBMs like Indian Pakistan to notify each other before flight testing of ballistic missiles, all captured fishermen to be released, India's suggestion of Kashmiris to be allowed to visit the religious shrines in POK and India's proposal to setting up border trading points for Kashmiris in the LOC.[35] In June 2004 however, the Indian intelligence agencies reported streams of highly trained militants crossing the border. There was photographic evidence that the militant training camps have become active again in the interiors of POK.[36]

Regardless of the negotiating stances of the parties concerned it has to be acknowledged that both the countries have some fundamental objective. While India wants cessation of all violent and terrorist acts, Pakistan considers the acquisition of Jammu & Kashmir as an unfinished agenda of partition. While India and a section of people of Kashmir are convinced that a final solution can be brought through political negotiations, Pakistani militant groups believe in continuing Jihad. Therefore, India cannot unilaterally succeed in building an atmosphere of peace and confidence. Efforts are needed from both the sides.

Cultivating the Big Powers: Relation with America, China and Russia

Whe India found itself on the losing side of the Cold War at the turn of 1990s, she quickly set about the task of reorienting her relation with the great powers. Although the US has been the focus of foreign policy in the 1990s, there have also been efforts at revitalizing relations with powers like Russia, Western Europe, China and Japan. This was owing to the pragmatic approach of maximizing the room for maneuver in the world.

With such objective India is set about building alliances and reviving functional cooperation with Russia. The density of Indo-Soviet economic relationship during the Cold War and the new importance of Russia as the provider of important advanced civilian technologies in the space and atomic sectors made it imperative to build a special relationship with Russia. The recent visit of Russian president Vladimir Putin stands out as a landmark. A new vista of bilateral cooperation has opened up in diverse fields of defence, high-tech, energy security etc. Similarity of views on issues such as role of the UN, international terrorism and combating trends towards unipolarity in world affairs, were reiterated. A significant advance is the formalizing of Russia's, India's and China's trilateral initiative of mutual consultation and coordinated action.[37] This subject was figured for the first time in the Indo-Russian joint declaration.

Another important Indian relationship that had undergone significant political change after the Cold War is the one with China. The Sino-Indian normalization picked up momentum in the late 1980s and has now become a genuine rapprochement. It is true that since the 1962 border war, a number of factors appeared to limit the possibilities for improved Sino-Indian relations. These included the unsettled boundary issue, the Indian fears of the rising position of China and the special relationship between Pakistan and China. It was apparent that China was sustaining support for nuclear and missile programmes of Pakistan. There has been increased political cooperation of China and Indian neighbours to balance India within the subcontinent. Despite these obstacles, since 1980s effort at normalization began in the real earnest. Border talks, the setting up of Joint Working Groups on the boundary question, border trade and numerous agreements for economic cooperation and technology transfer were signed.

The dramatic event of India conducting nuclear tests in May 1998 changed the climate of confidence building. This was especially because China was described by India as a major security threat. Fortunately for India, China's initial reactions did not last for long. China has gradually accepted India's potential as a rising nuclear and economic power. This new thinking was evident in China's attitude of neutrality in the Indo-Pakistan conflict in Kargil in 1999.[38] The changing dynamics of the global and Asian situation has created opportunities for strengthening Sino-Indian relations in the new millennium.

Throughout the last decade of the 20th century, redefining the relationship with the United States has emerged as the principal objective Indian policy. There is agreement that substantive engagement of the US is a critical national goal. The 1980s and early 1990s saw divergence of US and India on security issues like the signing of NPT, CTBT, demilitarization of the Indian Ocean and American military assistance to Pakistan. The United States adopted policies of denial of dual-use technologies to the non-adherents of nuclear weapon regimes.[39] Nevertheless, even during these years the rising potential of Indian economic advance was not missed by America. India's indigenous efforts at technological and military development, India's mastering of critical strategy technologies such as guidance and control systems, navigation systems, ballistic missile programmes, convinced the US that India cannot be ignored or side lined in order to favour Pakistan.

The beginning of strategic partnership became evident in trade ties, economic cooperation and joint army exercises as well as joint naval exercises in the Indian Ocean. The issue of nuclear proliferation still presented a divide. When India joined the nuclear club in May 1998 America's initial reaction was an angered response in the form of economic sanctions. Gradually however, the US is showing a better understanding of Indian capabilities. In the nuclear reality of weaponized deterrence in South Asia, America can moderate the situation by maintaining equilibrium between India and Pakistan and restoring new tests and deployment.

Post-9/11 and post-Iraq, the world has moved into an era marked by end of alliances but beginning of new strategic relationships. Asia today presents enormous opportunities as well as challenges to the US.[40] If the US is the largest economy in the world today; the next three largest economic powers belong to Asia-China, Japan and India. These developments are likely to further enhance India's significance in American policy calculations. The Asian regional agenda is going to be dominated by issues such as ballistic missile defence, American shift of strategic focus from Europe to Asia, future of multilateral institutions etc. Hence the Asia-Pacific region has emerged as a prime area of US concern. This will have direct implications for India. It makes a lot of strategic sense for Washington to befriend India,[41] as there is no direct clash of interest after the nuclear issues have been removed. India's credentials as a responsible power especially with regard to WMD capabilities and India being on the forefront of fighting terrorism, all leads to a greater congruence of interests between America and India.[42]

India Enters the Nuclear Club

Indian threat perceptions have for long time revolved around Pakistan and China. China became a nuclear power in 1964. Pakistan has all along remained important in the strategic game plan of America as well as China. Increasing US and Chinese assistance to Pakistan in the fields of defence and missile technology, as well as nuclear know how, have been apparent. Since 1995, pro-nuclearists started putting forth their logic of deteriorating security environment of India. In the post-Cold War world, nuclear deterrence according to them provided a new rationale of security. Moreover India had rejected the NPT and CTBT on the grounds that they were partial and half hearted measures of arms control and a means of perpetuating nuclear hegemony of a selective few. In this backdrop, India conducted Pokhran II test and crossed the nuclear Rubicon (May 1998). Pakistan did not take long to equal-up. The pro-nuclearists supported the logic of greater security and sufficient deterrence against all possible threats.

The anti-bomb lobby in India feels that the costs of nuclear deployment are much too high.[43] Mere possession of the bomb according to them does not constitute deterrence. Credible deterrence requires the construction and maintenance of a retaliatory second strike capability. This includes the availability of delivery vehicles that can hit the targets designated for punishment. It also entails survivability of a retaliatory force, which includes the spreading out of nuclear weapons, early warning and an effective system of command and control. This would entail enormous expenditure and burden on the Indian state. Technologically, moreover, India is yet not prepared to venture into the construction of the post-nuclear structures. The futility of the deterrence logic has also been put forward. It is stated that though chances of an open nuclear or large scale conventional warfare have been reduced, the chances of limited probe (small wars like Kargil) and controlled pressure (cross-border infiltration, terrorism, vicious political propaganda etc) have increased.

The national security and advisory board has proposed a Nuclear Doctrine for India. The doctrine commits India to a No-First Use of nuclear weapons, a credible minimum (deterrent) retaliatory capability, as well as India's continued commitment to total nuclear disarmament. Newer trends in global economic interdependence and terrorist threats stemming from non-state actors have made it obvious that a nuclear-armed India cannot deter cross-border terrorism.[44] Therefore India's nuclear policy must be viewed in the broader international context. India is likely to remain a nuclear-weapon power, until the other nuclear weapon states agree to comprehensive nuclear disarmament.

❑ The Road Ahead

Despite a high level of economic interdependence and the revolutionary technological changes introduced by the information age, the international system depicts the typical characteristics of the sovereign state system. Global politics in this state-centered power driven system clearly works to the advantages of the powerful. With major states assertively promoting their interests and national security considerations overshadowing collective security interests, power and force are going to stay at the heart of international relations. Regardless of the claims for an emerging equitable and fair economic order, the international economic relations are going to be dominated by the industrially and technologically advanced countries. Their aim would be to create a globalized free market economy and to acquire access and control over raw material and natural resources of the world.[45]

These are the broad trends that India's foreign policy would have to deal with well into the 21st century. There is a need for establishing a pattern of relations with important emerging power centers of the world and fashioning a foreign economic policy, which would ensure the necessary financial technological and foreign trade inputs to meet India's developmental needs. The emerging world order has in no way changed the validity and relevance of the Non-Alignment, namely, independence of judgment and action in international affairs. The argument, made in certain circles that with the end of Cold War India should give up Non-Alignment, shows little understanding either inthe meaning of Non-Alignment or of the world situation. The Non-Aligned movement stands committed to securing a restructuring of international economic relations with a view to make these fair and equitable to all.[46]

Today India finds itself in a highly competitive, risky and lethal global strategic environment. There is a need to address the challenges posed by unconventional conflicts. Indirect wars such as covert or proxy wars are gaining ascendancy. Terrorism is another threat, which makes it imperative to develop instrumentalities to curb this transnational crime with the help of pro-active and inert-active diplomacy, both at the regional and global levels. India can take initiative in forging international cooperation against terrorism and use the SAARC forum to combat the problem.

India has begun to experiment with the politics of balance of power in a complex world. This involves efforts to build special relationships at the bilateral levels with most of the major powers. Further, while it remains hesitant about military alliances it might not be averse to become a part of *ad-hoc* coalitions aimed at specific security objectives in the Indian Ocean region and Asia. India will have to exert itself in the Asia-Pacific to help manage its security dilemma. The ASEAN Regional Forum (ARF) is the most important and active kernel of a cooperative security system for the Asia-Pacific. India must insist on its presence in the forum and to articulate an agenda for cooperation in the extended region. India is also a part of the global ecology. The reduction of the ozone layer, atmospheric warming, the rise of Ocean levels and the depletion of the great rain forests could devastate the planet. The greatest challenge, therefore, is sustainable development. Surely this will require a cooperative and coordinated effort across national boundaries.

India has reiterated its unrelenting faith in the United Nations as a prominent institution of multilateralism. No single nation or group of nations can expect to find a solution to the world's problems. With the American intervention in Iraq in March 2003, the political functions of the UN came under heaviest siege. However, the world is still left with innumerable 'Problems without Passport'[47] threats such as weapons of mass destruction, contagious diseases, chronic starvation, human rights abuse etc. These global challenges can be addressed by the world organization alone. India, therefore, realizes the need for stressing the reform and structuring of the United Nations. With the expansion of permanent membership of the Security Council being suggested, India has also staked her claim.

India with the help of other nations must begin on a thorough going technologically feasible and financially affordable plan that will make nuclear abolition operationally believable. It is necessary, therefore, to go beyond the formulaic stand on nuclear weapons. These emerging trends outline a world where there are more opportunities for rising powers, to play more relevant and independent role. India's current reality and future potential, endows it with a global importance that can grow over the years. India should, therefore, endeavour to develop on these lines in the decades ahead.

Notes and References

1. Shanta Nedungadi Vanna, "India's Foreign Policy in an era of Change", in S.K. Chaube and Susheela Kaushik eds., *Indian Democracy at the Turn of Century*, New Delhi, Kalinga Publishers and Distributors, 1999, p. 281.

2. J.N. Dixit, *Across Borders: Fifty Years of India's Foreign Policy,* New Delhi: Picus Books, 1998, p. 15.
3. The Post-Second World War period saw the emergence of the Soviet Union and the United States of America as major powers on the world scene. They came to be known as "Super Powers" and the ensuing conflict between them was termed as the: Cold War".
4. J.N. Dixit, *op. cit.,* p. 19.
5. The post-cold war world seemed to be a situation wherein the dominant power variables were undoubtedly at the command of the US, however new potential powers were also emerging.
6. For a detailed analysis of the changing meaning of security, see P.R. Chari ed., *Perspectives on National Security in South Asia—In Search of a New Paradigm,* New Delhi, Manohar Publishers, 1999.
7. *Ibid.,* p. 419.
8. For analysis of the shifting paradigms on security, see Navnita Chandra Behera, *State, People and Security the South Asian Context,* New Delhi, Har-Anand Publication, 2002.
9. Brahma Chellaney; "Challenges to India's National Security in the New Millennium", in Brahma Chellaney ed., *Securing India's Future in the New Millennium,* New Delhi, Orient Longman Ltd., 1999, p. 540.
10. *Ibid.,* p. 588.
11. V.T. Patil and D. Gopal, *Politics of Globalisation,* Delhi, Authors Press, 2002, p. 2.
12. *Ibid.,* p. 17.
13. A.N. Ram, "Challenges to India's Economic Diplomacy", in Nancy Jetly ed., *India's Foreign Policy: Challenges and Prospects,* New Delhi, Vikas Publishing House Pvt. Ltd., 1999, p. 117.
14. *Ibid.*
15. G.V.E. Naidu, "US and the Asia-Pacific: Future of the Alliance System and Regional Security", *Strategic Analysis,* Vol. 27, No. 4, Oct-Dec. 2003, p. 516.
16. An excellent analysis of the possible reasons for which America invaded Iraq has been presented in Chandra Muzaffar, "Hegemonic Terror", *Seminar,* No. 527, July 2003, pp. 22–32.
17. Siddharth Varadarajan presents detailed insights into the issues raised by the war in Iraq, in his article, "Eight Theses on the War in Iraq", *Seminar,* No. 527, July 2003, pp. 46–50.
18. C. Raja Mohan, "United States and the World", *World Focus,* Vol. 24, Nos. 4-5, April-May 2003, PA.
19. Goenawan Moharnad, "The War on Iraq", *Seminar,* July 2003, p. 20. Also see Madeleine K Albright, "Bridges, Bombs or Blusters", *Foreign Affairs,* Sep-Oct. 2003, p. 2.
20. Surjit Mansingh, "Realising India's Potential as a Global Player: Essential Tasks at Hand", in Lalit Mansingh etc. ed., *India's Foreign Policy: Agenda for the 21st Century,* Vol. 1, Delhi, Konark Publishers, 1997, p. 43.
21. *Ibid.,* p. 44.
22. For an excellent account of rapid technological advance and the emerging challenges to state security, see KP.s. Gill, "Technology, Terror, and a Thoughtless State", in K P. S. Gill and Ajai Sahni ed., *Terror and Containmcnt=Perspeciioes of India's International Security,* New Delhi, Gyan Publishing House, 2001, pp. 186–210.
23. P.R. Chari, *op. cit.*
24. Tara Kartha, *"Tools of Terror: Light Weapons and India's Security,* New Delhi, Knowledge World, 1999, p. 3.
25. Veena Ravikumar, "Clobalisation and Terrorism; The Case of Iraq", *U.S.I. Journal,* Jul-Sept. 2004, pp. 387–395.
26. J.N. Dixit, *op.cit.*

27. Mahendra P. Lama, "Globalization and India: Issues and Challenges", in B.E. Upreti, Mohan Lal Sharma and S. N. Kaushik, *India's Foreign Policy-Emerging Challenges and Paradigm,* Vol. 1, Delhi, Kalinga Publications, 2003, p. 175.
28. Sanju Gupta, "India's Foreign Policy: Continuity and Change", in Meera Verma, Mrinal Mehta, Rumki Basu, eds., *Essays on Indian Government and Politics: A Continuing Re-view,* New Delhi, Jawahar Publishers and Distributors, 2004, p. 375.
29. For a detailed discussion of India's position and policies in South Asia, see Sanju Gupta, "South Asian Security: The Asymmetry Syndrome", Unpublished M. Phil. Dissertation submitted to The Department of Political Science, University of Delhi, 1994.
30. Refer Jagmohan Meher, "The Gujral Doctrine: South Asia in a New Context", *Third Concept,* Oct.-Nov. 1997, pp. 21–22.
31. C. Raja Mohan, "India's Security Challenges", in Nancy Jetly ed., *op. cit.,* p. 56.
32. Backgrounder on National Seminar on "Historical Perspectives of SAARC and Prospects of South Asian Economic Union", 23rd July 2004, India International Centre, New Delhi.
33. C. Raja Mohan, *Crossing the Rubicon:* The *Shapina of India's New Foreian Policy,* New Delhi, Penguin Books, 2003, p. XVI.
34.]yotirmoy Banerjee, "From Fokhran to Ras Koh: Technical Strategic and Political Implications", in Ahindyo Majumdar ed., *Nuclear India into the New Millennium,* New Delhi, Lancers Books, 2000, p. 39.
35. Indrani Bagchi, "Now for the Tough Part", *India Today,* 12th July 2004, pp. 36–37.
36. Raj Chen gappa, "General Mischief", *India Today,* 13th September 2004, p. 4l.
37. M.K. Dhar, "A New Phase in Indo-Russian Relations", *Nation and World,* 1st January 2005, p. 9.
38. Swaran Singh, "Pakistan Factor in Sino-Indian Ties: From Pokhran to Kargil", in Anindyo Majumdar ed., *op.cit.,* p. 193.
39. W, Lawrence, S. Prabhakar, "Strategic Dimensions of India-US Relations", in N.K. jha ed., *India's Foreign Policy in a Changing World-Essays* in Honour of Prof. Bimal Prasad, New Delhi, South Asian Publication, 2000, p. 72.
40. G.V.C Naidu, *op. cit.,* p. 519.
41. *Ibid.,* p. 528.
42. A Thanikodi, "Indo-US Relations-An era of Maturity and Understanding", *Third Concept,* Dec. 2004, p. 9.
43. Kanti Bajpal, "The Fallacy on an Indian Deterrent", in Amitabh Mattoo ed., *India's Nuclear Deterrent: Pokhran II and Beyond,* New Delhi, Har Anand Publications, 1999, p. 160.
44. Raju G.C Thomas, "Whither Nuclear India?", in D.R. Sardesai and Raju G.C Thomas ed., *Nuclear India in the* 21'/ *Century.* (New York, Palgrave-Mac Millan, 2002) p. 4.
45. J.N. Dixit, *op. cit.,* p. 391.
46. Views expressed by Prof. M.S. Rajan at a lecture delivered during a workshop conducted by the Deptt., of Political Science, University of Delhi, October 1996.
47. C.S.R. Murthy, "India and the United Nations after the end of the Cold War, in N.K. Jha, *op. cit.,* and also, see Shashi Tharoor, "Why America Still Needs the UN", *Foreign Affairs,* Sep-Oct. 2003, p. 67.

34

Reservation Policy in India

Madhu Jha

The recent country-wide debate and discussion and the proceedings in the Parliament, with the introduction of Women Reservation Bill, has once again brought the concept of reservation in Indian politics into limelight. The issue of reservation, however, is not an alien concept to the India Society. In fact, it has been in operation prior to our independence.

After so many years of its implementation, the reservation policy has reached a stage where both its supporters and critics are unhappy about it. The former are unhappy because it has not created a noticeable impact on the social and economic conditions of the Scheduled Castes (SCs) and Scheduled Tribes (STs), majority of whom still continue to be socially isolated, illiterate and poor. Its critics complain that in matters of employment, promotions and admissions, reservations have been stretched too far at the cost of merit and equity giving rise to frustration and alienation among the unreserved category.

The direct outcome of this policy was supposed to be more equitable distribution of economic resources and a worthwhile sharing of power at different levels in the running of the state affairs. But in reality, what has actually happened is that this policy has been exploited by various pressure groups and vested interests within and outside the beneficiary castes and tribes. Extension of reservations to the Other Backward Classes (OBCs) and demand for reservation for the Dalits, Christians,Muslims and women are a few examples of the opening up of the Pandora's box. The constitution of India is the whole crux of the problem from which emanates the reservation policies. The constitution is based on the class philosophy of the bourgeoisie which is not supra historical, eternal and ideal to be accepted by all, and for all the time.[1] The reservation policies became more and more the tools for electoral gain rather than a system for delivering the goods for economic and educational upliftment of the poor.

The policies did provide economic and political opportunities for individual mobility. A section of the untouchables and tribes who were at the fringe of the Indian societies moved out of their social position and became part of the privileged class of the system. They were incorporated into the exploitative system. Reservation Policies, thus, widened the support base of the system and made it more durable.[2]

Marxists have also provided a philosophical basis to the existing reservation policy. They view the 'reservation policy' as a safety measure which the Government uses in order to sustain its own existence. Instead of undertaking a series of welfare measures required to solve the problems of unemployment, illiteracy and poverty especially prevalent amongst the minority groups in India, the Indian state chose the easier way out. It began giving special assistance in the name of reservation to these communities in order to appease them.

The Concept of Reservation

A caste-ridden Indian society, which never had the opportunity to be organized on the basis of equity even in the formal sense, needs to be structured in a way leading to the goal of social equality. The caste system is not rooted only in economic inequality; hence a decisive social change towards social equality cannot be left to economic functions alone. Justice demands fair distribution of authority, income and status. Marc Galanter characterizes Indian society as a "compartmental society",[3] within which a vast number of groups maintain distinct and diverse styles of life. The need to integrate the ethnic groups, minorities and other socially and culturally localized groups made the constitution makers opt for providing constitutional safeguards to these sections of the society in the form of reservation or protective discrimination. According to Justice K. Subba Rao, in a limited sense, the right to social justice may be defined as the right of the weak, aged, destitute, women and children and other under privileged persons, to be protected by State against the ruthless competition of life. It is a bundle of right: in one sense it is carved out of other's rights and in another sense, it is a preserver of other's rights.[4]

Equality before law is the most precious democratic right of an Indian citizen. However, by merely ensuring quality of opportunity to all citizens in respect of educational and employment opportunity, we may be ignoring the special problems of some backward sections of our society who have suffered from social, cultural, educational and economic deprivations for hundreds of years. It is a well-known dictum that there is equality only among equals. To equate unequal is to perpetuate inequality. When we allow weak and strong to compete on an equal footing, we are loading the dice in favour of the strong. As a matter of fact, unless adventitious aids are given to the under privileged people, it would be impossible to suggest that they have equal opportunities with the more advanced people. It is the real justification for the demand of social justice that the under privileged citizens should be given a preferential treatment.

History of Reservation Policy

An analysis of the history of 'reservation', as a means of promoting equality of opportunity, will be useful in providing an insight regarding the debate over the intended beneficiaries of the protective discrimination and the conflicting pulls and pressures, both social and political, necessitating preferential policies.

The Scheduled Castes consist of the groups that are considered to be unapproachable and untouchables according to the Hindu social order. The functioning of this unit of Hindu social order was made according to the syntax of purity and pollution, devising a social economic framework with a religious and political sanction behind it. SCs are spatially segregated in the villages and towns and are engaged in occupations with negative prestige and had no role in the power structure of the local community. Hence they demanded to be brought into the mainstream and to be given the power to decide for their upliftment.

The case of tribes have an altogether different history. Tribal insurgencies that intermittently challenged the state, eventually led the colonial rulers to accept them as a distinct social and political category. They were either quarantined in specific areas or were granted some patriarchal protective measure, but there were no reservation or any similar special provisions in the State services or in education. At the provincial level, in addition to castes and tribes, other socially identifiable collectives also came to be recognized. The origin of present day "OBCs" is located here. Two Indian states, Mysore and Travancore Cochin, took the lead along with two British Presidencies-Madras and Bombay-in this regard. Most of these OBCs came under the rubric of "Depressed Classes", a category that originally came into official parlance with the introduction of Montague-Chelmsford reforms in 1919.

The era of emancipation of untouchables began with the advent of the British rule and major spokesman like Dr. Ambedkar and Mahatma Gandhi; but, it would not be entirely correct to conceive that reservation is a British legacy. The advent of the British rule on the other hand, with the consolidation of political regimes and introduction of the Western oriented education system, produced many structural disturbances in the Indian caste structure.

Brahmins being the literate caste responded quickly to the western education and entered in big numbers to governmental services and professions. The emphasis of British rule upon the egalitarian system of justice with new ideas of equality of opportunity impressed the Brahmins. Although later, the distributive aspects of justice appealed to non-literate caste on the ground that these values were totally inconsistent with the gap between different castes. It gave rise to social reform movements aimed at eliminating caste disabilities, abolition of sati, upliftment of depressed classes etc.

It can be noted that Provincial Governments in India were also implementing special programmes for the welfare of the depressed classes. The first such step was taken by Madras Government with the framing of grants in aid code in 1885 to regulate financial and educational institutions, providing special facilities to the students of the depressed classes.[5] Subsequently in 1921, acting on a resolution passed by the State Legislative Council, Madras Government took steps for higher representations of non-Brahmins in Government services.

On the basis of representations received from the depressed communities in 1918, the Maharaja of Mysore had appointed a committee under the Chairmanship of Sir L.C. Miller, the then Chief Justice of Mysore to recommend steps for adequate representations of non-Brahmins in the services of the State. On the basis of the Report of the Committee, the Government of Mysore issued orders in 1921 extending special facilities to the depressed communities with regard to education and recruitment in State Services. Earlier, Census Report of 1910 had divided the Hindus into three categories (1) Hindus, (2) Animists and Tribes and (3) the Depressed Classes or Untouchables. Giving separate importance to untouchables acquired a new political dimension. Later, the Government of India Act 1919 provided for communal representations for Muslims, Sikhs, Anglo Indians, Christians, Depressed classes, etc. Similar communal reservation was provided by the Government of India Act 1935. The purpose of such reservation was to pacify different sections of minorities in India, especially the Muslims and to consolidate their positions.

The Round Table Conference held in 1930 marked the beginning of the claims of the untouchables in the area of the devolution of the political power from the British rulers to the Indian natives. In the Second Round Table Conference in 1931, Gandhi refused to consider both the separate electorates for the depressed classes as well as any form of special representation involving reserved seats. On the other hand, Ambedkar wanted future constitution to give some means such as equal citizenship, fundamental rights for equality before law and possession of equal civil rights and abolition of disabilities arising out of untouchability, representation of depressed classes in the cabinet. After the Third Round Table Conference in 1932, Communal Award was declared under which the depressed classes were given seats that were to be filled up by sections from special constituencies in which they alone could vote. However, Gandhi's displeasure ended in Pact, which provided for reservation of seats in the Provincial and in Central Legislature for the depressed classes through Joint electorates. It also declared about the representation of these classes in the public service. The numbers of seats, reserved for the depressed classes, were increased to equal to their proportion of population.

Making of the Constitution

On 13th December 1946, Jawaharlal Nehru, moved a resolution, which was in the nature of a pledge, a statement of policy and an introduction to the philosophy underlying the Indian constitution. Clause 5 of the resolution stated, 'wherein shall be guaranteed and secured to all the people of India Justice, social, economic and political, equality of status of opportunity and before the law, freedom of thought and expression, belief, faith, worship, vocation, association and action subject to law and public morality', Clause 6 provides, 'Wherein adequate safeguards shall be provided for minorities, tribal areas and depressed and other backward classes'.[6] Notwithstanding the above resolution, a controversy was gaining ground for sometime between Muslim League and Congress party over the question of job reservation for Muslim minorities. Nehru opposed such demand not only for Muslims but for any other minority group. In pursuance of the suggestion of the Cabinet Mission Plan an advisory committee on the Fundamental Rights and Minorities was set up by the Constituent Assembly containing due representation of all minorities in India. In the Advisory Committee, special demands for reservation of posts for their communities were made by Sikhs and Anglo Indians. Ambedkar made a very strong case for Schedule Castes. The Sub-Committee on minorities submitted its report to the Advisory Committee with Sardar Patel as its Chairman. Patel showed opposition to any proposal for reservation in services for any minority community. The Committee recommended that there should be some part of the constitution or the Schedule to keep view the claims of all minorities in making appointments to public services consistently with the maintenance of efficiency in administration.

The constitution straight away accorded specific recognition to both SCs and STs (Arts. 341 and 342) and made corresponding guarantees in the form of reservations in legislatures (Arts. 330 and 332), claims in services and posts (Art. 335) and in other forms (Arts. 17, 338 and 339). Their interests are also to guide the Directive Principles of State policy (Arts. 38 and 46).

The Constituent Assembly accepted community based classification for the purpose of preferential treatment only in case of the Anglo-Indian community (Arts. 331, 333, 336 and 338), but categorically rejected religious minorities as a separate category. However, it guaranteed certain safeguards in relation to freedom and practice of religion (Arts. 25, 26, 27 and 28), protection of their interests (Art. 29) and their educational institutions (Art. 30). The constitution accorded recognition to gender based discrimination in case of 'special provisions' (Art. 1513). Except in case of some Scheduled Areas, the State of Jammu and Kashmir and other cases, the constitution did not explicitly recognize any region-based classification, especially for the purposes of preferential treatment.

Thus, when it comes to preferential treatment of groups of people who otherwise face discrimination in our society, the constitution left many uncovered areas in an explicit fashion except in the case of SCs and STs. However, the makers of the constitution were aware of the need for such facilities to other similar groups, otherwise the promise of equality would make no sense in an inherently iniquitous society. It is in this context that the expression-backward class of citizens or socially and educationally backward classes of citizens-should be understood.

It is to be noted here that the reservation policy included in the constitution in 1950 was based on certain assumptions. Firstly, it is not a permanent way of bringing the deprived sections of the society into the mainstream of Indian society on the basis of equalilty, freedom, dignity, self respect and power. A time limit of 10 years was set in the constitution in 1950, with the hope that the government would implement the policy sincerely. Secondly, it was anticipated that with this policy the power and the creative energies of the tate and the individuals in India will be deployed towards bringing out structural changes such as medical reforms, basic educational reforms, efforts to return to India's cultural and civilizational roots and for building up of a political and economic democracy in tune with the needs of the country. Thirdly, the majority of the members of the Constituent Assembly endorsed the policy as a continuing social duty and as an expression of atonement on their part for the inhuman exploitation of the untouchables.

What emerged ultimately was an unequivocal constitutional policy providing for reservation of appointment and posts for the backward classes including the schedule castes and tribes. One thing is clear from the above analysis that the underlying purpose of compensatory discrimination was to counter balance the disadvantages suffered by certain classes for past wrongs suffered by them because of unequal social structure of the Indian society.

Provision for Reservation Under the Indian Constitution

It was on 26th November 1949, that the draft constitution of India provided for such preferential treatment in the form of reservation to the SCs and STs and recognized the need of the OBCs to be protected by the state. The Indian constitution clearly says that justice is not only political but economic and social as well. Equality is not only of opportunity but also of status.

The constitution specifically bars the State from discriminating against any citizen of India on grounds of religion, race, caste, sex and place of birth or any of them. Article 29(2) also guarantees protection to educational institutions on grounds of religion, race, caste and language or any of them. The first amendment of the constitution incorporating clause (4) to Article 15, empowers the State to make special provisions for the advancement of any socially and educationally backward class of citizens or for the SCs and STs. Article 16(4) incorporated in the constitution shall not prevent the State from making any provision for the reservation who in the opinion of State are not adequately represented is the services under the state. The law of protective discrimination also finds its place in Article 29(2) which says that nothing is this Article shall prevent the State from making any special provision for the advancement of any socially and educationally backward class of citizens or for SCs and STs. Article 46 also contains similar provision.

Reservation for Schedule Castes and Schedule Tribes

The constitution provides for 15 per cent reservation of seats for the SCs and 7½ per cent for STs in services and legislatures. This has been adopted for ensuring their participation in proportion to their population in the country. Articles 16(4) and 335 of the constitution ensure their participation in administration. Articles 330, 332 and 334 of the constitution provide for reservation of seats in Parliament and State Legislatures for the SCs and STs in proportion to the percentage of their population in their respective States and Union Territories. 'Schedule Castes' is an official euphemism for untouchables. Untouchablity, as the two faced monster of Hindu social institution, is a social stigma making them economically poor, educationally backward and culturally low. It is the caste system coupled with the pernicious system of untouchablity that confounded the class conflict by making social mobility next to impossible.

The constitution abolished untouchability and made the practice of untouchablity in any form forbidden on 29th November 1948. The social realities that existed forced the founding fathers of the constitution to give recognition to the untouchable communities as the SCs. This transition from the untouchable communities to the recognition of the SCs under the schedules has come to stay because of the constitutional abolition of untouchability. The term 'SC' is defined under Article 366 (24) read with Article 341 of the constitution[7] "366 (24) 'SCs' means such castes, races or tribes or parts of or groups within such castes, races or tribes as are deemed under Article 341 to be SCs for the purposes of this constitution." The provision that has been made under Article 341 runs as the President, (may with respect to any State or Union Territory) and where it is a State after consultation with the Governor, thereof, by a Public notification, specify the castes, races or tribes or parts of or groups within castes, races or tribes which shall, for the purposes of this constitution, be deemed to be SCs in relation to that State (or Union Territory, as the case may *be*). The most important point to be noted in connection with the meaning of the terms SCs is that the list of SCs has the legislative status. In exercise of the powers conferred by Clause (1) of the Article 341 of the constitution, the President issued the constitution (SCs) Order in 1950 for the purpose of reservation to the SCs. The statistical figures of the SCs listed in the Schedule in 1935, 1950, 1956, 1976 establishes beyond doubt that the number of SCs is not fixed but changeable.[8]

The preferential treatment is meant to bring about social transformation from uplifting the lowest of the low. When the purpose of establishing the social democracy is achieved and equality is established and inequality is totally eliminated, then not only the disabilities suffered by the SCs would hopefully disappear but even the utility and the purpose of the schedule listing the SCs would disappear. SCs have indeed gained more under political influence (though one is not sure about their power) in State and Centre-level politics. The massive occupational mobility in general, taking place since independence, has had some significant bearing upon the status of SCs as well.

STs, on the other hand, have a different meaning. The term tribe generally means an ethnic group geographically isolated or semi isolated, identified with one particular territory and having distinct social, economic and cultural traditions and practices, kinship ties, common territory, one language, joint ownership, one political organization which have all been referred to as the main characteristics of a tribe. Under these, certain tribes have been specified as the STs and only they have been given special treatment or facilities envisaged under the constitution.

The attitude of the British towards the tribes initially was paternalistic and protective but the compulsion of situation forced them to send their engineers and contractors and civil and military officials of all ranks, the traders and shopkeepers into all these inaccessible regions of the interior frontiers. Thus a money economy was introduced among the tribal communities. Along with this land hunger of the non-British vested interests worried the tribes. This affected their agriculture, their hunting and fishing rights.

The friction between tribes and non-tribes was limited to a restricted scale due to British policy of exclusion of tribal areas. The isolation of tribes from the main currents of Indian life helped them in preserving their traditions but at the same time it hindered the growth of competence in them to face growing competition in a wider society. The rapidly increasing interference and exploitation resulted in clashes and bloody uprising like Santhal rebellion (1855), Birsa movement (1895), Kandh rising (1837-56) etc.[9] This led to reforms in the administration of the tribal areas by the British. Some of the areas were made non-regulatory areas and were exempted from the operation of general law.

The constitution carried forward this dual treatment of tribal areas and tribal people in a set of provisions for their protection and advancement, for more elaborate than the provisions, for the other categories of backward classes. Article 16(4) and 335 of the constitution ensures their participation in administration. As per Article 16(4), the State shall make reservation for appointments or posts in favour of any backward class of citizens which is not adequately represented in the services under the State. Article 335 provides that the claims of SCs and STs shall be taken into consideration consistently with the maintenance of efficiency of administration in the making of appointments to services and posts. Articles 330, 332 and 334 of the constitution provides for reservation of seats in Parliament and State Legislatures for the SCs and STs, in proportion to the percentage of their population in their respective States and Union Territories.

Even after seven decades of independence, it is sad to note that the representation of SCs and ST s in various departments and public sector enterprises in Government of India has not reached the prescribed level of reservation.[10] Their representation has never gone beyond 7 per cent. National Commission for SCs and STs has been recommending in its various reports that the Government need to make all special efforts to fill up this short fall by taking such steps as special training and coaching for SCs and STs, passing of Central Legislation to enforce reservation in Government services, public sector enterprises, banks, etc.

There is also the problem of an elite class that has emerged in the midst of SCs and STs whose social base and numerical strength is larger than ever before. This is putting pressure for conformity to integrative principles of new Indian society.

Reservation for the OBCs

On 7th August 1990, the National Front Government announced its decision of reserving 27 per cent of posts for other backward classes under the Central Government and public undertakings. With this declaration the reservation policy that was hither to confined to SCs and STs got extended to OBCs as well.

The constitution is the solicitor about the welfare of the backward classes of the society while expertly providing for the reservations of posts in the country's public administration for sections of such classes namely, the SCs and the Sts. It makes a general mention of similar promotional measure for what it calls "OBCs".[11]

The constitution provided for the recognition of socially and educationally backward classes. Article 340 provided for the appointment of a Commission to investigate the conditions of the backward classes. On receipt of the report of the Commission thus appointed, the President may, by order specify OBCs under Article 338(3) of the constitution. Preferential treatment to the OBCs is to be covered under an egalitarian framework. While on one hand equality before law and prohibition of discrimination on grounds of religion, race, caste, sex or place of birth, equality of opportunity in matters of public employment and equality in cultural and educational rights are guaranteed as Fundamental Rights under article 14, 15 (1 and 2), 29(2) respectively, on the other hand, Article 46 included in the Directive Principles of State Policy enjoins upon the State to 'promote with special care the educational and economic interests of the weaker sections of the people'.

The apparent contradiction between the Fundamental Rights and the Directive Principles of the State Policy came out shortly after the commencement of the constitution through a pair of Supreme Court decisions in April 1951. In the case of State of Madras *vis* Chapakraman Dorajian, the Supreme Court struck down reservation in educational institutions in Madras and by implications barred all preferential treatment outside the areas of government employment for all groups other than the SCs and STs. These decisions caused a political furor in South India and occasioned the prompt addition of clause 4 to Article 15 of the constitution. It reads: "Nothing in this Article or in clause (2) of Article 29 shall prevent the State from making special provision for the advancement of any socially and educationally backward classes of citizens or for the SCs and STs."

Before going into the question of determination of the backward classes, it is necessary to appraise oneself about the historical usage of the term.

The term "Backward" is contextual. In one sense, it implies the presence of a forward or advanced counter part of the same entity. In another sense, in social realm, it may mean the presence of disadvantaged and advantaged sections in mutual interaction. However, in whatever sense the term 'backward' is used, it implies presence of inequality. Marc Galanter has traced the use of the term 'backward class' since the last part of the 19th Century.[12] According to him, the term was also meant as illiterate or indigent classes entitled to allowances for study in elementary schools. In 1928, the Hartog Committee defined "Backward Classes" in their glossary as 'castes or classes which are educationally backward'. They include the depressed classes, aboriginal hill tribes and criminal tribes. In 1930, the State Committee in Bombay recommended that the term 'depressed classes' should be used in the sense of untouchables. They also proposed that the wider groups should be called 'backward classes' which should be sub-divided into 'Depressed Classes (Untouchables), Aboriginals and the hill tribes, and other backward classes (including wandering tribes)'. The committee noted that the groups then currently called backward classes should be renamed 'intermediate classes'.[13] Simon commission refers to intermediate castes but makes no mention of backward classes. The objective resolution of Constituent Assembly, moved by Jawaharlal Nehru on December 1946, called for adequate safeguards to be made for OBCs along with general other categories of population.

There are many judicial pronouncements, which have interpreted the use of the term 'class' in a general sense with reference to the socially and educationally backward classes. The most important judgement which has been influencing judicial thinking is that between Balaji vs. State of Mysore, wherein the constitution held that caste, poverty, occupations, place of habitation were some relevant factors for determining backwardness.

The President of India, under Article 341 of the constitution is empowered to specify the castes, races or tribes or parts of or groups within castes, races or tribes, which shall be deemed to be scheduled castes by notification. Under Article 342, he may, by public notification, specify the tribes or tribal communities or parts of or groups within it which shall be, deemed to be STs. There is no such parallel article of the constitution for the backward classes. In fact no uniform nomenclature has been used in the constitution to devote backward classes, e.g., Article 15, (4) and 340 use the expression 'socially and economically backward classes'. Article 16(4) uses 'backward classes' whereas in Article 46, the terms used is 'weaker sections of the people'. As such it is one of the difficult problems to define the backward classes for the purpose of the constitution.

It is the state responsibility to take effective steps for the upliftment of backward classes of citizens socially, educationally and economically. Backwardness may be measured in terms of low level of income, the extent of illiteracy and the low standard of life demonstrated by living conditions.

Many communities desire to be characterized as backward because of the facilities of admissions and services which are available to such classes and thus they bring all their political influence to bear upon the Government for being recognized as backward. The danger is that the State may abuse its power and permit such reservation of seats to the socially and educationally backward classes, which may not be justified.

Central Backward Classes Commissions

The First Backward Classes Commission: On 29th January 1953, the President appointed the 1st Backward Classes Commission, by virtue of the power entrusted to him under Article 310 of the constitution, under the chairmanship of Kaka Saheb Kalelkar. The Commission was entrusted the task of determining the criteria for listing OBCs, investigating their conditions and recommending measures for their upliftment.

Kalelkar Commission prepared a list of 2399 backward castes or communities from the entire country and made use of criteria such as inadequate or no representation in joint service and commerce, lack of educational advancement, low social position in society, etc. The Commission recommended reservation of 70 per cent of seats in all technical and professional institutions for qualified students in all government services and local bodies for OBCs.

However, the report disclosed a considerable divergence of opinion among its members and the Commission failed to specify any easily discernible objective test to define 'backwardness'. Moreover, it seemed that caste was the chief basis of enumeration and preparation of the list of backward classes. The Central Government could not accept such criterion.

The Second Backward Classes Commission: On 20th December 1978, then Prime Minister, Morarji Desai announced in the Lok Sabha that under provision of Article 340 of the constitution, the Government has set up a commission to probe the conditions of socially and educationally backward classes with B.P. Mandal as Chairman. The Commission made use of 11 indicators under the three headings; social, economic and educational, to identify the degree of backwardness and granted them certain weightings in order to determine the OBCs.[14] The Commission submitted its report on 31st December 1980, and identified 3,743 OBCs. The failure of the Commission to clearly formulate the criteria for identification of Socially and Educationally Backward Classes (SEBC) has led to absurdities. For instance, one of the most literate upper caste, which is also highly represented in services and politics, the Bengali Kayasths, have been listed as SEBC in Assam, the Patnaik (surname mostly used by high caste Oriyas) are SEBC in Bihar. The Rajput in Karnataka has been similarly listed. The Bengalis as a whole are listed as SEBC in Madhya Pradesh. One can find many such entries in the Mandal Commission as undeserving. They would be able to take advantage of the privileges conferred by the Government as per the recommendations of the Commission and further enhance their position in the rural power structure.[15]

The Report of the Mandal Commission held that since the SCs and STs which constituted 22.5 per cent of the country's population had been given 22.5 per cent reservation in Government and public sector jobs, the OBCs who constituted 52.1 per cent of the population should be given reservation accordingly. Keeping in view the Supreme Court's judgment in Balaji *vis* State of Mysore and Devadasan *vis* Government of India that reservation of more than 50 per cent of the vacancies would be volatile of Article IS (1) of the constitution and also in view of the fact that SCs and STs were already having reservation of 22.5 per cent, Mandal Commission recommended 27 per cent of reservation for the SEBC listed by them. Reservation should apply to promotions and unfilled reserved quota should be carried forward for 3 years before being unreserved. After the formal presentation of the report of the Mandal Commission in the Parliament in 1982, the Report was shelved down by the Government led by Mrs. Indira Gandhi.

It was the National Front Government led by V.P. Singh, which chose to make the report public and to extend reservation benefit to the OBCs. In the year 1990, V.P. Singh announced in the Parliament the decision represented the first phase of the implementation of the report of the Mandal Commission.[16]

The report caught national attention and it was discussed widely and autopsied in the national press. The announcement triggered massive and widespread protest. There was large-scale violence in Bihar, Uttar Pradesh, Himachal Pradesh, Haryana, Punjab and Karnataka. About 100 persons were killed in police firing. Government property including railway, postal and telephone installations, State transport, State buses suffered extensive damage. The most tragic aspect of the agitation was the wave of attempts at suicides, mostly by students.

The Prime Minister and his close ministerial colleagues sought to justify the Government's decision as having meant to ensure social justice to the SEBCs and hence there would be no question of withdrawing his decision. It is perhaps not without significance that V.P. Singh decided to begin implementing the Mandal Commission's recommendations by reserving 27 per cent of the Central Government and Central public sector jobs for the OBCs; he had not initiate any developmental steps like literacy drives, special educational measures, assistance to become entrepreneurs, professionals, etc, prescribed to overcome the social, educational and other backwardness of the OBCs., nor did he begin the measures like land reform. People hence could not be blamed if they felt that the then Prime Minister's intention was to win over the support of the more powerful, advanced and rich among the OBCs. This intention was further suggested by his refusal to modify the proposed 27 per cent reservation by introducing an economic criterion or implement the Karpoori Thakur formulae on reservation which set apart a percentage of the jobs reserved for OBCs exclusively for weaker castes amongst them.[17]

In an article in the *Indian Express,* Neerja Chaudhaury mentioned three factors which according to her influenced the timing of V.P. Singh's decision on 27 per cent reservation.[18] The first was the rally staged in Delhi on 9th August 1990 by Devi Lal, Deputy Prime Minister and Minister of Agriculture, to prove his strength in the wake of his removal from the Union Cabinet, on 1st August. By announcing his decision, V.P. Singh wanted to win away the backward castes from Devi Lal and delink them from the Jats who constituted the power base of Devi Lal. The second factor was the Janata Dal's answer to the Vishwa Hindu Parishad's and Bhartiya Janata Party's movement for building a Ram temple at the site of what they considered to be the birth place of Ram after relocating the Babri Mosque that had been constructed there. The third factor was V.P Singh's desire to convey his readiness to go for a midterm poll and thereby take on his adversaries in the party. Thus it becomes clear that the decision to extend reservation for the OBCs was a politically motivated one and there were many criticisms labelled against it.

L.K. Naik, one of the members of the Mandal Commission has stressed on the need to identify the better off among the backward classes to prevent them from covering all the benefits of reservation in a note of dissent to the Mandal Commission. It also needs to be pointed out that the Commission made use of archaic methods of taking population figures as the guidelines to determine the quantum of reservation. Basically the Commission used the cover of the 1931 census to ignore the upward mobility that had taken place in many cases from 1931-1980.[19]

While dealing with reservation in the Public services, the constitution of India wants the claims of the target sections of society to be taken into consideration consistently with the maintenance of efficiency in administration. Of late, the efficiency of Public administration is getting ignored and by passed in the quest for vote. The immediate future is likely to see a further extension of reservation facilities to new groups. This trend is bound to lead to a backlash of the Gujarat style. When the Congress Chief Minister, Madhav Singh Solanki announced in early January 1985, that the reserved quota for the backward castes in universities and government employment in Gujarat would be raised from 10 to 20 per cent, it unleashed large scale riots in the State by the anti reservationist groups.[20]

The country is still fumbling with the implementation of 27.5 per cent reservations for SCs and STs. The hefty addition of 27 per cent reservation for OBCs is sure to place an enormous strain on the social system, unless lessons are learnt from the past and it is made sure that the maximum benefits are not covered by the more powerful castes. It is important to evolve a package that would help to identify the real needy among the backward classes. Everyone should feel justified in asking for a meaningful implementation which is not just symbolical but actually assists the impoverished sections of the OBCs and thereby uphold the sanctity of a "welfare oriented constitution".

Issue of Reservation for Women in the Legislature

It has now been over two decades of tremendous excitements and disappointment for the women rights activists. Starting with the President's address to the 11th Lok Sabha on 24th May 1996, where the promise to give 33.3 per cent reservation for women in the National Legislature was included, the women in India have been looking keenly forward for the all important legislation that will guarantee them seats at the political decision making levels of National Parliament and State Legislatures. It seems that the last half of the century was a painful period during which our educated, urban women were reinventing the wheel before learning the lessons the Dalits could have taught them; that despite India becoming a democracy, a feudal and false mythology of inferiority grounded on gender and in caste was used, time and again, to keep women away from the political mainstream. So the latest demand for 33 per cent reservation for women is a natural organic development of the events over the last 50 years.

It does not require much research or data to establish that, judged by any major economic or social or other relevant indicator, women as a category are not only literally the 'weaker' sex but clearly a disempowered section. Comprising approximately half of the population, the female-male sex ratio has steadily improved to 940 females for 1000 males, as per 2011 census. Despite great stride in reduction of literacy since independence, female illiteracy continues to outstrip male illiteracy.[21] The last 52 years of competitive politics under the existing system have failed to give more than a token representation to women in the highest political decision making. Since decisions at the policy making level effect women lives and have a significant impact on them, it is important that more women occupy decision making positions. Right now, women's representation in the last 16 Lok Sabhas stands at 12.2 per cent.

India is the largest democracy of the world. Democracy as we know is not just about mainstream politics. It is also about the values that guide our personal, financial and social existence. Various notions connected to democracy are rights, power and participation. Women constitute half the population of the country and therefore the issue of political empowerment of women needs re-interpretations, reanalysis and redefinition. Political empowerment simply means the right to be in the decision making process and this has eluded women in India, making gender equality a dream in our country. Professor Dahl has truly pointed out that equality and popular consent are perhaps the most important social values underlying pluralist democracy.[22]

Political equality is one of the defining characteristics of democracy. We simply cannot talk of a democratic system without qualification if any significant part of the adult citizenry is deprived of full political rights, at best we can speak of a 'limited' democracy in such cases. The basic argument for political equality is of course that any social group with limited political rights or none is always at a serious disadvantage-not only in political matters but also in economic, social and cultural affairs. For lacking political power, it will be in no position to defend its interests against politically more powerful groups. Access to power to democracy in India means mainly taking part in the electoral processes. In any modern political system, election occupies the most central place. According to Prof. Susheela Kaushik, the nature, periodicity and rate of the participation of people in the elections can be reviewed as the touchstone for the representative character of the democracy itself indicates the health and strength of democracy.[23]

Trend of women's representation in the last 64 years:

Participation in the Lok Sabha Elections:[24]

Election Year	Total No. of Seats	Seats Contested by Women	Seats won by Women	Percentage of Women Members
1952	499	51	22	4.40
1957	500	70	27	5.40
1962	503	68	34	6.70
1967	523	66	31	5.90
1971	521	86	22	4.20
1977	544	70	19	3.40
1980	544	142	28	5.14
1984	544	159	44	8.10
1989	517	189	27	5.30
1991	544	325	39	7.16
1996	544	491	39	7.18
1998	543	274	43	7.9
1999	543	274	48	8.8
2004	543	355	45	8.35
2009	543	556	59	10.87
2014	543	668	61	12.15

Women's presence in the top decision making committees.[25]

Party	Committee	No. of Women	Total Member	Percentage of Women
CPI (M)	Politburo	0	15	0
	Central Committee	5	70	7
CPI	Secretariat	0	9	0
	National Executive	3	31	10
	National Council	67	125	5
Janata Dal	Political Affairs	0	15	0
	Parliamentary Board	0	15	0
	National Executive	11	75	15
United Front	Steering Committee	0	15–17	0
B.S.P.	Parliamentary Board	10	9	11
	Election Committee	2	17	12
Congress	Working Committee	2	19	11

A study of the above tables makes it immediately apparent that political parties have generally given less importance to women issues in terms of ideology, either as priority in their electoral manifesto or in terms of the number and importance of the position that women occupies in individual political parties. Women are not even seen as a vote bank to be approached and canvassed, as it is expected that once the men are mobilized women will merely endorse their choice of party and candidate. Such kind of expectations emanate due to a long historical background of women's subdued role in the society.[26]

Debate on Reservation for Women in India

From the beginning, the women's movement was divided on the issue of reservation of seats for women.[27] One wing of the movement labeled 'moderate' was more willing to accept certain features of the proposals of the colonial Government such as reservation, nomination, co-option and wifehood qualification for women voters. The other wing represented a difference in approach to women's question. The Women's Indian Association (WIA), All India Women's Conference (AIWC) and National Council for Women in India (NCWI) were steadfast in their demand for fundamental rights and universal adult franchise.

In 1931, Jawaharlal Nehru, succeeded in setting the concepts of 'equal obligations and equal rights', into the Fundamental Rights Resolution of the Karachi Congress. In 1939, a women's sub-committee was appointed under the National Planning Committee of the All India Congress Committee to examine the role of Indian women and to make recommendations on their behalf. The members of the sub-committee endorsed the 1931 Fundamental Rights Resolution made at the Karachi Session of the Congress and rejected reservation of seats for women.

In independent India, the debate on reservation was kicked off by the Report of the Committee on the Status of Women in India (CSWI) in 1974. The Report brought to the notice that despite being given equal rights under the constitution, and the right to vote under a system of universal adult franchise, the number of women in State and National legislatures had been dwindling in the past 50 years. The Report recorded arguments in favour of reservation of seats for women voiced by experts in the field and representatives of women in groups. To do justice to women who constitute practically half the population, reservation of seats appeared to be the only solution. Both the government and political parties viewed the problems of women from the view of social welfare.

However, the declaration of the year 1975 by United Nations as International Women's Year and the next ten years—1976 to 1985 as the International Women's decade shifted the emphasis from women's welfare to women's development and later on to women's empowerment, women's participation at the grassroots level and 33 per cent reservation for them at that level.

Democracy and development, in order to be successful, needs maximum participation of people at the ground level. Panchayati Raj is an important political innovation and a vital conduct in independent India for popular participation and democratic development. Panchayati Raj Institutions, the grassroots unit of self-government have been proclaimed as the vehicle of socio economic transformation in India. Empowerment of women for effective participation at various levels in Panchayati Raj Institutions has been discussed and debated in different forms particularly from 1957 onwards. First concrete measure to give constitutional sanction to it was taken by late Rajiv Gandhi's Government by introducing the 64th Amendment Bill. The Bill aimed to reform the Panchayati Raj Institution by bringing changes in their power structure and functions. The bill was defeated by a small margin in the Rajya Sabha. However, Narsimha Rao's Government became successful in enacting the constitution 73rd and 74th Amendment Acts in December 1992, which included various provisions for strengthening Panchayats at all levels. The Act is extremely important for political empowerment of women. Not less than 1/3rd of the total membership of Panchayati Raj bodies has been reserved for women. These reserve seats would be allotted by rotation to different constituencies in a Panchayat. The chief idea behind such a move was to enable more women to enter the political stream and create a 'critical mass' of women leaders.

Reservation under Panchayati Raj for rural women is in a state of flux at present and the women are not adequately empowered to play an effective role because of social, economic and political factors.[28] So far elections for Panchayats have been held in most of the states like Rajasthan, Haryana, Orissa, West Bengal, Andhra Pradesh etc. More than one million women have become part of the political set up. Study undertaken on elected representatives of 67 Panchayats at Mhow Block of Indore District during training programmes revealed that women out numbered men in attendance, expression and their concern for the deprived and depressed.[29] Similar findings have been made in states like Haryana and Maharashtra. However, the result of reservation policy at the Panchayati Raj level has yet to be consolidated and studied. Whether it has revitalized the democratic functioning of these bodies or not, only time will tell. What we can say, is that it has surely helped them enter into the decision making process and provided opportunity for deciding priorities pertaining to the real needs of the community.

Women Reservation Bill: The next logical step, after the 73rd and 74th Amendment Bills, was naturally its extension to the State Assemblies and the Parliament. The constitution Amendment Bill, 1996 as it is called, provided not less than *1/3rd* seats to be reserved for women in the Lok Sabha and Legislative Assemblies.[30] The proposed Bill cannot be said to trench upon any of those fundamental principles of India's policy: Article 14 of the Indian constitution which forbids discrimination clearly permits classification into different groups and classes as long as the classification is reasonable. Article 15(1) categorically prohibits discrimination on grounds of religion, sex, caste, birth, etc., but Article 15(3) declares that "Nothing in this Article shall prevent the State from making any special provision for women and children". Article 16 further focuses on the specific subject of equality in public and state employment. The other relevant constitutional provisions are those in part IX and part IXA of our constitution which contains Articles 143A to 243G which deals with the structure and content of our instruments and institutions of local self-government like Panchayats and Municipalities, which were inserted by 73rd constitutional Amendment of 1992.

The Bill in the midst of Controversy: Ever since its inception in September 1996, the Women Reservation Bill has gone through several controversies. This is in spite of the fact that all the major national parties had unambiguously supported *1/3rd* reservations for women in Parliament and State Assemblies in their election manifestoes during the 1996 general elections. The debate that followed in the Parliament on the day the Bill was introduced (13th September 1996) exposed certain doubts about the "unanimity in the House about the Bill."[31] The Bill had to be deferred for the time being and got referred to a Joint Select Committee of Parliament. The main argument for holding the Bill was that it should ensure representation for other Backward Class women otherwise women from the upper caste sections will cover the seats.

The Joint Select Committee although accepted few amendments in the Bill like instead of not less 1/3rd the amendment was as near to 1/3rd, but it could not accept the provision of reservation for women belonging to the OBCs. This amendment had been tabled by Nitish Kumar, Ram Kripal Yadav and P.N. Shivam. The Bill could not be introduced in the Winter session of the parliament again due to the anti-Bill sentiments. On 13th July 1998, when the Bill was to be introduced, the opponents of the contentious Women Reservation Bill physically prevented the Law Minister from introducing it in the Lok Sabha.[32] The Bill was shuttled on the plea that it did not guarantee for Muslims and OBC women. The controversial Bill was again introduced on 1st December 1998 amidst several adjournments, complete pandemonium and loud protests by those opposing the Bill[33] such as Rastriya Loktantrik Morcha and BSP. Janta Dal had decided to move an amendment seeking reservations for minorities SCs and STs in the Reservation Bill. Even in December 1999, the Bill got shelved down due to lack of consensus among the various political parties.

If we take an objective look at the issue of women reservation, we can definitely say that it is unfortunate that Indian women, who had participated so actively during our freedom struggle, have now to fight for their own freedom, freedom from patriarchy. Reservation though may be considered by few to be a retrograde step from equality conferred by the constitution, but then it has been used as the last straw, a means that would help them to enter public spheres. 73rd and 74th Amendments did not raise any controversy. The resentment over the Bill only conforms to the facts that men wish to preserve their position of power and do not wish to share them with the other half of the population. It has to be noted that women are not a minority group. Where the marginalization of certain castes and classes have been reorganized, efforts to redress these sections of women has completely been ignored. Women are not a community, they are a category, and hence the rationale for their demand of reservations should be seen from a different perspective. Of course, claims of creating a Zenana Dabba,[34] coterie of elitist women, coming up as proxy candidates cannot be discounted altogether. Nevertheless, reservation in Legislature for women shall help in building up a 'critical mass' so that a change in the nature of policy formulations can be expected. Democracies have to be made real after all.

To conclude, it needs to be noted that, when judged by reservation policy's own objectives and the values and goals that underlie it, its performance on all counts is much below any reasonable expectation. Even after half a century of preferential treatment, only negligible number of the SC, ST and OBC officers can be found in class I positions of the Government services. For of all the class I officers on the rolls of the central government in 1979, only 5.68 per cent belonged to the SCs and STs taken together and were 4.69 per cent came from the OBC category.[35] Provision of reservations is not enough. For reservations to improve the life chances of the socially disadvantaged significantly, other components of the policy will have to show a much higher operational efficiency. The low rate of utilization, for instance, is indicative of the poor performance of the entire policy for utilization is essentially a function, not of availability of benefits but to the capacity of the potential beneficiaries to receive the benefits.[36]

It should be remembered that reservations are part of a much larger policy package. It comprises a series of legislations, ameliorative programmes and preferential schemes designed to benefit the weaker sections of the society. Hence there is no need of rejecting preferential politics for pragmatic and utilitarian considerations. Reservations, along with other measures of protection and upliftment of the weaker sections of society, should be viewed as an instrument of a larger social policy of the State addressed to a long-term goal of creating a civil society through extending effective citizenship rights to the vast sections of the population, who have been historically deprived and marginalized.

Notes and References

1. Himanshu Roy, "Reservation-The Safety Valve", *Frontier,* Vol. 25, N. 21, January 1993, p. 12.
2. *Ibid.*
3. Marc Galanter, *Competing Equalities,* Delhi: Oxford India Paper Back, 1984, p. 7
4. Government of India, *Report of the Second Backward Classes Commission* 1980, Vol. II, p. 2.

5. D.N. Shandanshiv, *Reservation for Social Justice,* Bombay, Current Law Publisher, 1989, p. 24.
6. *Constituent Assembly Debates,* Vol. I, pp. 58–60.
7. D.N. Shandanshiv, *op.cit.,* p. 50.
8. Marc Galanter, *op.cit.,* p. 132.
9. R.C. Verma, *Indian Tribes through the Ages,* New Delhi, The Director Publication Division, Ministry of Information and Broadcasting, Government of India, 1990, pp. 41–49.
10. Government of India, *Special Report of Commissioner for Schedule Castes and Schedule Tribes,* January 1998, New Delhi; Government of India Press, 1998.
11. S.R. Maheshwari, *The Mandai Commission and Mandalisation: A Critique,* New Delhi, Concept Publishing Co. 1991, pp. 10–15.
12. Marc Galanter, *op.cit.,* pp. 5–6.
13. B.K. Roy Burman, *Beyond Mandai and After,* New Delhi, Mittal Publication, 1992, p. 3.
14. Government of India, *Backward Classes Commission,* 1980, Vol. 1, Part 1, p. 52.
15. Ramaiah, "Mandai Commission Recommendations", *Mainstream,* Vol. XXVIII, No. 43, 18th August 1990, pp. 55–56.
16. Government accepts Mandai Panel Report: 27 per cent Quotad for Backward Classes, *Indian Express,* Delhi Edition, 8th August 1990.
17. B.K. Roy Burman, *Beyond Mandai and After,* New Delhi, Mittal Publication, 1998, P: 43.
18. "Decision to Implement; Political Parties in a fix", *Indian Express,* Delhi Edition, 22nd August 1990.
19. B.K. Roy Burman, "The Missing Data", *Indian Express,* 23rd August 1990.
20. Upendra Baxi, 'Reflection on Reservation Crises in Gujarat', *Mainstream,* 8th June 1985, p. 22.
21. Sarala Gopalan, *Towards Equality: The Unfinished Agenda Statues of Women in India, 2001,* National Commission for Women, 2002.
22. Robert A. Dahl, *Democracy in the United States,* Boston: Houghton Miffin, 1981, p. 107.
23. Sushila Kaushik, 'Women and Political Participation', *Women in Politics: Forms and Processes,* New Delhi: Friedrich Ebert Stifting, 1992, p. 36.
24. Jayati Ghosh, 'Women in Indian Politics', *Frontline,* 8th October 1999, p. 103. For 1999 data the source is www.parliament of India.
25. *Manushi,* No. 96 Sept.-Oct. 1996, p. 26.
26. Abhilasha Kumari and Sabina Kidwai, *Crossing the Sacred Line: Women's Search for Political Power,* New Delhi, Friedrich Ebert Stifting, 1996, p. 2.
27. Letter to the Premier from Sarojini Naidu and Begun Sh. Nawaz, in *Indian Journal of Gender Studies,* New Delhi, Publications, No. 6:1, 1999, pp. 126–128.
28. Margaret Alva, 'Whither Indian Women', *Seminar* 45, 7th September 1997, p. 36.
29. Kamlesh Sharma, 'Women in Panchayat's, in Madhya Pradesh', *Kurukshetra,* Vol. 47, No. 6, March 1999, p. 33.
30. Government of India: *The constitution Eighty First Amendment Bill,* p. 2.
31. Reservation in Parliament, *The Pioneer,* 2nd October 1996.
32. Opposition Allies want quota within quota, *The Pioneer,* 10th July 1998.
33. Women's Bill jumps the first hurdle but has miles to go, *The Economic Times,* 1st December 1998.
34. Madhu Krishwar, 'Out of the Zenana Dabba, *Manushi,* Nov. 96. No. 62, p. 24.
35. Government of India, *Report of the Backward Classes Commission,* Ist Part, Vol. 1 and 2, 1980, p. 42.
36. Gurpreet Mahajan, *Democracy, Difference and Social Justice,* Oxford University Press, Mumbai, 1998, p. 494.

35

Education in India

Sonali Chitalkar

British rule in India has been interpreted in various ways in the overall framework, within which colonialism and imperialism have been understood. This framework ranges from the 'political economy' approach of Adam Smith and Ricardo and includes the Marxist-Leninist interpretations of imperialism and colonialism. Significant advances in understanding colonialism were made by Hobson, Hilferding and Luxemberg. After World War II and the national liberation movements which followed, most former colonies won national independence. This led to the dissolution of empires and to the end of colonialism. Most post-war Marxist approaches to imperialism consider that ex-colonies and developing countries are still subordinated to imperialist countries through dependency relations. Thus, a special type of development of the countries dependent on imperialism is the characteristic of the international capitalist division of labour within the framework of the world capitalist system. The dependence created by colonialism is still manifested in all the key spheres of the developing countries' economic life. Dependency theories, the world-systems theories of hegemony, in the world economy have all illuminated current concerns with imperialism and colonialism.

Though different in nature and content, almost all these understandings centre on the link between colonialism and the development of capitalism. Interpretations of colonial education policies, had for a long time, curiously glossed over this link. For instance, in India, colonial education policies were rather simplistically linked to the British need for a 'brown sahib' to aid in the administration of colonial India. This essay sketches how notions like that of a 'brown sahib' was one of the many desired outcomes of colonial education policy in India. British education policy was a part of the overall colonial enterprise which was essentially rooted in the then current liberal-capitalist political philosophies. The achievement of freedom from British rule did not end this association. It is argued that post-colonial education policies are also an extension of colonial education policies in a neo-liberal manifestation.

I

❑ Education Policy Under Colonial Rule

The Beginnings

Till the English victories in the Battles of Plassey (1757) and Buxar (1764), the English East India Company was a trading body. It was not interested in social reform and education in India, which were largely missionary concerns. The Charter Act of 1813 was significant not only for restricting the Company's monopoly over Indian trade but also because it provided a sum of one lakh rupees annually to be 'set apart for the introduction and promotion of a knowledge of indigenous sciences among the inhabitants of British territories in India'. The focus in this period was on the Indian knowledge and science and not on European education. The Charter of 1813 is considered significant as an enunciation of the principle of State responsibility for education in India.

Between 1823 and 1835

This clause of the Charter Act of 1813, however, remained inoperative till 1823 when the famous Anglicist-Orientalist erupted over the content and medium of education in India. The former pushed for the promotion of English and modern education, while the latter for Oriental subjects and vernacular languages. Macaulay's minutes of 1835 settled the controversy in the favour of the Anglicists.

The teaching of English started in several Government schools and colleges after the establishment of the General Committee of Public Instructions (GCOPI) in 1823. This Committee drew up a plan for establishing a preparatory English school in every district and a College in every division. Whereas the schools were supposed to teach English, the colleges were expected to impart education in European knowledge and science.

A radical change was introduced in the education policy of the then Government of India, when Macauly assumed the Chairmanship of the GCOPI following the 1833 Charter of the Company. As has been mentioned already, Macauly advocated a more aggressive policy for teaching English and European knowledge and science, gradually replacing the teaching of Sanskrit, Arabic and other local languages by English and prohibiting the publication of books relating to oriental learning. After his proposals were approved by Lord William Bentick in 1935, schools and colleges teaching English and European knowledge and science became entitled to receive Government aid. This inevitably had an adverse effect on the traditional educational system in India.

Wood's Dispatch and After

A significant development, in the effort to spread English education and teaching European knowledge and science, was the Charles Wood's dispatch of 1854, the highlights of which were:

- The purpose of education in India would be the spread of European knowledge and science.
- Oriental learning was not necessary for progress; vernacular education would continue to get Government aid.
- English would be the medium of instruction in higher classes.
- Each Presidency would have a Department of Education under a Director of Public Instructions. Under him would be various Inspectors of Schools.
- A University would be established in each of the Presidency towns of Calcutta, Bombay and Madras.
- Government grant would be available to only those schools which provide secular education and which are under Government inspection.
- Educational qualification would be an important condition for appointment to Government jobs.

It would be significant to pause and unravel colonial education policies in the light of these seven significant policy declarations on education that have been mentioned above.

The year 1830 in England saw the ascendency of the Whigs (referred to as the Liberal party after 1834) came to power. This political change had significant impact on India. Though the construction of the 'colonial citizen' was already under way, through the development of railways and telegraph, education policy in India served to nourish its liberal roots in England. Thus much of the content and form of colonial education policies can be understood if we appreciate that 'the state's role according to liberalism was to assist civil society to fulfill its goal of ensuring individual rights, particularly the right to hold and increase property'. Thus the cultivation of a colonial citizen, through the formation of a civil society in India, of the type that existed in England, became the core enterprise of colonial education policy. What was this colonial citizen and how was he similar to his English counterpart?

In England, the idea of a civil society and the ideal of rational behaviour was a valued ideal. Its most central tenet was that 'rational behaviour meant translating the concern for the safety of property into the desire to strengthen the State's efforts to establish order'. Education policy in India was structured to facilitate this process in the colony. However, 'in India ... the dream of the English bourgeoisie merely provided the vocabulary with which a miniscule civil society could legitimize its rise in the midst of exploitation of the working population'.

Thus the language of 'mass education', 'civil society' and 'citizen' used in policy in colonial India 'gave a very long life to eighteenth century English diction, in which 'people' and 'citizen' meant only men of status or property.

Hereafter two core themes emerge in education policy in India and they carry forward to present day education policies. The first was the division that colonialism engineered in India, between the small educated elite which was the beneficiary, 'the citizen' in colonial India and the masses.

The other was the gender dimension of education policy in colonial and independent India.

The main education policies after the Woods dispatch were as follows:

- The Education Commission of 1882 also called the Hunter Commission
- The Universities Commission of 1902
- Government Resolution on Educational policy in 1913
- The Calcutta University Commission of 1917
- The Hartog Committee of 1929
- The Sapru committee in 1934
- The Aboot-Wood report 1936-37
- The Zakir Hussain Committee report 1937
- The Sargent Report of 1944

The main policy framework that is indicated in these reports leads to the emergence of the following themes in policy.

Firstly, a gradual withdrawal of the State from the direct support and management of institutions of higher education can be evidenced. Secondly, there is evidence of tracking into vocational and technical education as a separate stream for those who were unfit for general education. Thirdly, with the exception of the Zakir Hussain Committee's Report and the Sargent Report, policies focused on the development of secondary and higher education thus privileging the already privileged classes who had benefited from colonial education policies. This was not a policy without deeply iniquitous outcomes. It led to 'the unplanned, haphazard and indiscriminate expansion of secondary and higher education'.

Overall, India has been more successful in meeting secondary and higher education targets rather than primary education goals. Literature touts this as an achievement.

This 'achievement' is again a reflection, of the social, political and economic forces at work. Thus 'the class-base of political power naturally led to a greater emphasis on secondary and higher education which benefit the 'haves' rather than the 'have nots' so that the expansion programmes at these stages received early attention, greater priority and more adequate allocations than those of mass education.'

The Zakir Hussain Committee deserves special mention in policy as it stands out as the only colonial education policy recommendation that attempted to reorient colonial education policy towards the benefit of the masses rather than the colonial elite. It focused on free and compulsory education for seven years and on a nation-wide scale envisioned that the medium of instruction be the mother- tongue. The scheme of education suggested by it is popularly known as the "Wardha Scheme", the main features of which are as follows-

- A Basic Craft was to serve as the centre of instruction. The idea is not to teach some Handicraft side by side with liberal education, but a craft or vocation was to become the basis of education;

- The core of the Wardha scheme was that it was supposed to be self-supporting to the extent of covering teachers' salaries and making pupils self-supporting after the completion of their course;
- Manual labour was insisted on so that every individual may learn to earn his living through it in later life;
- Pedagogy was closely coordinated with the child's life, i.e., his home and village crafts and occupations.

The Gandhian vision of education proposed by the Wardha scheme was promptly disowned both by the colonialist and nationalist discourse. Since 'nationalist discourse drew heavily from the Brahmanical tradition it could not provide room for non-esoteric forms of knowledge' as proposed by Gandhi. Further, 'practioners of the nationalist discourse, as it matured towards Indian Independence could afford to be paternalistic in the style of English administrators'. This paternalism is observed in post colonial education policies in India.

Educational Policy in Independent India

After independence, the University Education Commission of 1948 was appointed by the Government of India under the Chairmanship of Dr. S. Radhakrishnan. The Commission made important suggestions for improving the standard of university education in the country such as the introduction of a three-year degree course for the first university degree, greater use of tutorial system of instruction, formulation of new aims, emphasis on developing critical thinking. The Radhakrishnan Commission had surveyed the field of secondary education in a passing manner and had admitted that 'our secondary education remains the weakest link in our educational machinery and needs urgent reform'. This fact was the reason d'être of an All India Commission for Secondary Education appointed in 1952 under the chairmanship of Dr. A. Lakshmanswamy Mudaliar.

However, between these two commissions came the forty-fifth amendment to the Indian constitution, 1949, which states 'The State shall endeavor to provide, within a period of ten years from the commencement of this constitution, for free and compulsory education for all children until they complete the age of fourteen years'. All subsequent policy formulations in education need to be seen against this amendment.

The Mudalair Commission of 1952 offered a number of suggestions to adjust secondary education with the new goals and needs for free India. The aim was now to train youth for intermediate leadership and for democratic citizenship. Secondary education was to be a terminal stage for a large majority of the nation's youth, who would take up their places in society after their school education and provide leadership to the general masses. The Commission was equally concerned with qualitative improvement of the schools. To develop individual talent, curricular offerings were extended and diversified. To achieve the new aims of education, changes in methods of teaching were suggested. New trends in examination, guidance and extracurricular work were brought into the school programmes. Multipurpose secondary school was a new concept recommended by the Commission. Inclusion of craft, social studies and general science in the curriculum was aimed at orienting students towards an industrial and science-centred democratic life.

The Government of India in October 1964, set up the Kothari Education Commission, to deliberate on the national pattern of education and on the general policies for the Development of education at all stages ranging from the primary to post-graduate stage and in all its aspects, besides examining a host of educational problems in their social and economic context.

Based on the recommendations of the commission, the National Policy on Education, 1968 was passed by the Government of India. The National Policy of 1968 marked a significant step in the history of education in post-Independence India. It aimed to promote national progress, a sense of common citizenship and culture, and to strengthen national integration. It laid stress on the need for a radical reconstruction of the education system, to improve its quality at all stages and gave much greater attention to science and technology, the cultivation of moral values and a closer relation between education and the life of the people.

However the most significant aspect of the 1968 policy was the promise of schooling of equitable quality for all. The Common School System was accepted in the first National Policy on Education-1968 (i.e., NPE-1968) in order to 'equalize educational opportunity for all children and to promote social cohesion and national integration'. Subsequently the National Policy on Education 1986 made the following commitment:

> *The concept of a National System of Education implies that, up to a given level, all students, irrespective of caste, creed, location or sex, have access to education of a comparable quality. To achieve this, the Government will initiate appropriately funded programmes. Effective measures will be taken in the direction of the Common School System recommended in the 1968 policy.* (National Policy on Education-1986, Section 3.2 also retained in the policy revised in 1992).

It is in the background of the National Policy on Education 1986 that a dichotomy between policy and practice in education is revealed.

Gradually through practice there was the abdication of constitutional obligation and steady dilution of policy relating to free education of equitable quality. The policy framework of NPE-1986 and the programme design of POA-1986 and Programme of Action 1992 contained the promise of school education of equitable quality for all, was 'designed to basically promote exclusion of crores of children from elementary education and introduce inequality by institutionalizing low-quality multiple tracks or parallel streams of education. It was this character of NPE-1986 that provided both the foundation and the necessary socio-political space to international funding agencies, including the World Bank, to exacerbate abdication, accelerate the pace of exclusion and further marginalize people's aspirations for a Common School System and genuine Neighbourhood Schools'.

Thus the NPE, 1986, institutionalized non-formal education for out of school children and girls who could not come to formal schools, permanently relegating them to the margins of the educational and social system.

The next big policy formulation in education has been the Right to Free and Compulsory Education Act, 2009 (RTE, 2009). In conceiving the RTE Act, has perpetuated the differential tiers of schooling institutionalized by the NPE 1986. As a result, children of different sections of society have access to varying quality of schooling in accordance with their socio-economic status or ability to purchase schooling in the market. This is evident from the very definition of "school" in clause (n) of Section 2, which provides for four categories of schools of varying quality and provisions.

The Act insists on compartmentalizing the fundamental right to education of every child from 6 to 14 years in these categories. For instance, Section 5 provides for the right of the child to seek transfer to another school under certain circumstances. However, at the same time, it restricts the right of the child to seek transfer to schools of "specified category" (that is, Kendriya Vidyalayas, Navodaya Vidyalayas and other similar elite schools) and private, unaided schools.

This implies that the majority of the children in the 6-14 age groups shall be denied education in schools which the State itself considers, rightly or wrongly, as providers of higher quality education. This goes against the very basis of education as a Fundamental Right.

In the Act there is the provision of 25 per cent seats being reserved in schools of "specified category" and inprivate schools, aided or unaided (Section 12), for "children belonging to weaker section and disadvantaged group in the neighborhood". This amounts to the declaration that at present private schools are not only of higher quality compared with Government schools but shall remain so even after the Act is implemented.

II

Elementary Education Policy in India

The neo-liberal agenda on education can be most clearly seen in elementary education in India. Firstly, the Government of India announced a proposal (September 2009) to set up model schools under the Public-Private Partnership (PPP) Model. Secondly, Public expenditures on education in general and particularly on elementary education in India are steadily showing a declining trend.

The privatization agenda is being pursued in elementary education on the basis of empirical research is that in no way justify policies for privatization. Such empirical researches selectively highlight deficiencies in public school education. It is important to understand how a 'coalition of interests' are engaging in the alteration of common sense in elementary education in India and effectively pushing privatization and school choice policies.

The arguments for privatization of elementary education are organized around four key issues. The key claim is that a large and underestimated private sector already exists in elementary education in India. The importance of this sector is underlined by showing that this sector is popular amongst the poor. A group of studies demonstrate that private schools are more effective and efficient and finally that the efficiency of this sector rests on lower relative costs.

It is estimated that a very large number of private un-recognized schools exist that are not counted.

The importance of this sector is demonstrated by studies which say that in urban India, Government and aided schools together absorbed only 39 per cent of the new primary enrolment over the period. The remaining 61 per cent is being absorbed in low fee paying private schools. With regards to the popularity of these schools amongst the poor, findings from the MIMAP survey, 1996 in India show that, of all school-enrolled, children aged between 5-10 years old living below the poverty line, 14.8 per cent attended private schools (8 per cent in rural and 36 per cent in urban India). These findings have been supported by Pradhan and Subramaniam (2000), PROBE Team (1999) and by Tooley and Dixon (2003) for Andhra Pradesh. These studies demonstrate that the use of private schools is greatest at the primary level.

One of the focal points in the literature favouring privatization is that private schools are more effective in terms of achievement. This conclusion is reached on the basis of survey results based on standardized testing. Private schools are considered more efficient in terms of controlling teacher absenteeism etc. Teacher absenteeism is identified as one of the major problems in Government schools.

Lastly, a major point of debate is the lower cost advantage of private schools. This is mainly due to market-clearing teacher salaries and lower cost per unit attainment. Attainments in these studies are measured on the basis of standardized testing on small sample surveys.

Most of the studies described above are looking at cost advantage from the supply side. The main cost component used is teachers salary and Pupil Teacher Ratios. It is more accurate to look at demand side costs for private schools. Not doing so may conceal higher complementary costs (e.g., textbooks, private tuitions, capitation, extra-curricular, rents illegally siphoned off by private managements etc). Most important, average cost incurred by the households on tuitions fees is likely to be high as compared to cost calculations based on teachers' salaries. Similar conclusions have been reached by an important group of studies that have undertaken demand side computation of cost. Household survey in Rural Areas reveals that private education is more costly, in rural areas. It is worth noting that in urban areas this figure might be higher.

An Eight-State survey of schools and households is revealing in terms of quality of schooling. In the eight states surveyed, almost 90 per cent students go to government schools except in UP (73 per cent) and TN (74 per cent). Pupil Teacher Ratios's are high in government schools.

Government schools also have a higher percentage of trained teachers. A comparison can be made by looking at the percentage of untrained teachers in government schools with private schools. In Andhra Pradesh there are only 8.6 per cent untrained teachers in Government schools whereas there are 62 per cent untrained teachers in private schools. In Assam the same ratio is 32.5 per cent as compared to 75 per cent. Similarly in Bihar it is 1 per cent as against 68 per cent. In Madhya Pradesh the same ratio is 18 per cent and 74 per cent. Rajasthan, Tamil Nadu, Uttar Pradesh and West Bengal reveal similar trends.

The same study also reveals that private schooling is a burden for households.

Thus per pupil cost advantage of private schools, claimed by many studies may be washed away, if we look at demand side measures and use differential measures for computing cost of private and public schooling.

As mentioned above a number of studies demonstrate that almost 15 per cent of all school-enrolled children aged between 5-10 years old living below the poverty line are opting to study in low-cost private schools. Further it is asserted that 61 per cent of all the increase in total primary school enrolment in the period 1986-1993 was 'absorbed' by private schools. Both these assertions are significant if taken at face value. Especially if almost one-seventh of the BPL population in India finds private sector education a better option than public schools then it an obvious matter of concern.

The veracity of BPL estimates is a disputed fact for India. In India, the official poverty estimates dropped from 37.6 per cent in 1993-94 (NSS–50th Round) to 27.7 per cent (NSS-55th Round). However, experts estimate higher levels of poverty for the NSS-55th Round. Based on expert estimates, India's corrected headcount ratios for the 55th NSS Round ranges between 30.6 per cent and 37.1 per cent. There is indeed a large gap in the estimates provided officially and those by the experts. Popli use parametric, semi-parametric and non-parametric approaches to obtain the headcount measure of poverty for the year 1999-2000 based on Household Expenditure Survey data of 1993-94 and show that there is a decline in India's poverty by about 5 per cent, which is less than that estimated officially (9.9 per cent).

Thus not only are BPL estimates skewed, studies show that these are biased as well. The major issue is the implementation of the census in which there is high level of exclusion of the genuine poor households from the BPL list, thereby leading to under-representation and mis-representation in identification of poor households and distortion of ground realities. Ground level studies in west Bengal have shown how the implementation of the BPL Census has been blatantly managed in favour of non-poor households by the Panchayats.

Thus, the sweeping conclusion is that low-cost private schools are preferred by the poor especially that BPL is a sweeping conclusion to say the least. Are those opting for low cost schools really BPL?

Further data on absorption of new enrollees utilized by Kingdon was examined where simulations have been used to project the astounding figure of sixty-one per cent for urban India. Firstly this needs to be weighed against the availability of public schooling in the area. Secondly, simulations in themselves are a crude tool of estimating increase in enrolment. The response of enrolment to population growth both in the private and public sector are not as causally defined or as simplistic as demonstrated by Kingdon.

One of the major points for critique of public schools is that they are more effective per unit cost of attainment.

A variety of methods have been used for demonstrating this result. One common feature of these studies is that they are one time small sample surveys mostly based on tools developed by Pratham. The tools used for these surveys are simple and have been standardized on a large sample. Based on these surveys, it has been demonstrated that students in Government schools do not have basic skills in numeracy and language. Studies like Kingdon and Jimneez and Lockheed have tried to control for background factors and have then concluded that private schools have a greater per unit cost attainment.

The methodology of the studies described above flies in the face of educational learning theories that are the basis of the educational system in India since the NCF 2005. Standardized, one shot surveys are not the most efficient way of measuring attainment which is individualized and constructively attained to say the least. Further the most important criteria, for measuring the quality of schools, is the quality of constructive teaching-learning process which has not been assessed by any of the studies mentioned above.

The second point of critique is that the studies described above take no note of the fact that education has inter-generational benefits and it is not correct to compare subjects on the basis of one shot surveys. Controlling for background factors might take care of statistical validity of results but fails to capture the inter-generational effects of schooling. Starting with the Coleman Report there is a long history of school quality research in different contexts, particularly in the United States, which suggests that much of the apparent differences in schools are due to parental choices that propel children from certain backgrounds into certain types of schools. Thus school effects are yet not conclusively proven. Standardized testing may not be the best way of measuring and comparing achievements. Household factors and selectivity bias need to be accounted for while drawing conclusions on effectivity.

The other major point of debate in the push for privatization is that private schools are more efficient. Public schooling is seen as being inefficient in terms of how it uses resources and particularly in ensuring teacher presence.

Almost all the literature on efficiency of private school quotes the World Bank Harvard study of teacher absence. The main finding of this study which is picked and repeatedly quoted is that almost 11 to 25 per cent of public school teachers are absent from work on any particular day. It further found that private school teachers are 2-4 percentages more likely to be present in school than Government school teachers. The World Bank study mentions many more results which are ignored while selectively quoting it on teacher's absence.

Some of the results of the study mentioned above are stated below.

- Teacher compensation has little effect on absence; infrastructure provides a stronger incentive to attend school and improving monitoring increases the marginal cost of teacher absence.
- There is little evidence to suggest that greater local ties are associated with lower teacher absence.
- Teachers in private schools and contract teachers, who face very different incentives, have similar or slightly lower absence rates while being paid a fraction of Government teachers' salaries. None of these conclusions signal privatization *per se*.

These results show that teacher absence is not just found in Government schools and is obviously a more complex phenomena requiring deeper study and thicker descriptions and not necessarily market based solutions.

Studies like those of Kingdon, 1996, have pegged their criticism of public schools solely on the criteria of teacher absenteeism and teacher unionism. There is a concern here as has been demonstrated by Panchmukhi and Mehrotra that the oversupply of potential teachers (trained or untrained) may push the market clearing wages for teachers too low. The response to this concern has been that market-clearing wages are desirable for teachers and have even demonstrated that market clearing wages are sufficient for generating a decent standard of living in Uttar Pradesh.

The further argument is that teacher salaries constitute an economic rent because of their absence from school. While the argument for enforcing teacher presence in schools is a valid one, the argument on economic rents needs to be scrutinzsed. The privatization process has to ensure that these rents are eliminated. Privatisation will simply imply that economic rents are being shifted from the teacher to the private sector. It will not ensure that rents are eliminated. Teacher's presence and effective teaching are variables that beg a deeper analysis.

From the above critique it becomes very clear that there is no clear logic for privatization in elementary education in India. Indian education policy is situated within an overbearing economic and political context of international competitiveness as is evident from the clear push towards privatization in all sectors after the Structural Adjustment Policies of 1991. However, policy in any sector is not a positive prescription and has certain very well defined normative aspects to it.

Some of the questions which are relevant in the context of policy are as follows: What are the social relations, subject positions and opportunities generated within education policy?

Answers to this from the Indian context are as follows: One of the primary subjects in elementary education in India, whether in the private or public sector, is the teacher. The other prime subject is the student-parent. In the public sector the teacher is considerably unionized and empowered. Thus social relations are not exploitative in the public sector and could be highly exploitative in the private sector as shown in previous sections.

It is, when one looks at opportunities generated by the policy of privatization, that the direction of policy making in India becomes clearer. Privatization already exists in elementary education in India through the medium of private unaided schools. The massive expansion of private unaided schools and private unrecognized schools, as some of the studies documented above reveal, has been phenomenal in the last few years. It would be worth asking if private school managements have heavy direct and indirect political involvement and whether further opportunities are being generated for this section.

The rush for privatization is being pursued as a policy imperative and can be explained by Olson, who theorizes that "only a separate and 'selective' incentive will stimulate a rational individual in a latent group to act in a group-oriented way"; that is, only a benefit reserved strictly for group members will motivate one to join and contribute to the group. This means that individuals will act collectively to provide private goods, but not to provide public goods. The selected 'elite' group of policy makers, that is, acting collectively to privatize education; it is also the group that is benefitting from commercialization of education.

Olson also predicted that small distributional coalitions tend to form over time in countries. Groups like cotton-farmers, steel-producers, and labour unions will have the incentives to form lobby groups and influence policies in their favor. Since the benefits of these policies are selective incentives concentrated amongst the few coalition's members, the costs are diffused throughout the whole population, the "Logic" dictates that there will be little public resistance to them. Hence as time goes on, these distributional coalitions accumulate in greater and greater numbers.

Both the theoretical insights provided above find their way in explaining the push for privatization in elementary education in India. Privatization will ultimately lead to the transformation of education into a private good and cooperation will ensue amongst coalitions to ensure that this actually happens despite little logic for the policy thrust. Since the benefits are restricted and costs are diffused, little resistance is seen to the policy of privatization in India and the policy rolls on.

Supported by an international pressure and strong internal coalitions there emerges a strong privatization narrative.

There are a few important dynamics of this narrative. There is 'scaffolding of these privatization narratives into institutions and operative networks'. This is followed by constant talk of privatisation. Fairclough (2000) theorizes that much of the action of Governments is the language. In India this 'talk' can be noticed in the Government's policy position on elementary education which is 'dichotomous and even contradictory'. On one hand there is a commitment to EFA and on the other a rollback of resources. Thus statements and fragments of government policies do not make a coherent whole. This is followed by a discourse of derision to pathologize the public sector. The slew of researches on the 'sick and dispensable' character of publicly provided elementary education in India needs to be evaluated in this context.

The working of the PPP model in education can also be illuminated through theory of the 'Corporate Welfare complex'. The Whitfield complex can be identified in India. Wipro (Azim Premji Foundation), Pratham, ICICI Lombard, Teach India (Bennet-Coleman), Educomp to name a few have taken up education related activities in a major way and are leading examples of Corporate Welfare.

Whitfield further identifies three features of this complex: There emerges a relationship between public (client) agencies and private contractors to whom a number of State functions are outsourced. Slowly these contracts get so over extended that private interests start to take control over public facilities thereby altering the very nature of the cotract. Regulatory and financial concessions to private interests, tax breaks and subsidies follow the development of this public private partnership. The call for PPP in elementary education in India can be explained against this theoretical background. Entities like Pratham which are not for profit are slowly tying up with State Governments for improving the delivery of education under tie-up schemes. The cutting edge of such collaborations and their effectiveness are a matter of research.

Thus clearly, privatization in elementary education is not justified simply on arguments of efficiency and better quality of private provision. It is established above that it is based on research that is contestable in its outcomes. It is still being pursued by a coalition of interested classes for private benefit.

An important outcome of this relentless attack on public education has been the 'alteration of common sense'. Private schools are universally considered 'more efficient' and as undisputed deliverers of quality education. There is a sense of empowerment being offered to parents as consumers while policies like the creation of a publicly funded Common school system through neighbourhood schools could have delivered the constitutional promise of 'education of equitable quality to all'.

III

Gender in Education Policy

The principle of gender equality is enshrined in the Indian constitution in its Preamble, Fundamental Rights, Fundamental Duties and Directive Principles. The constitution not only grants equality to women, but also empowers the State to adopt measures of positive discrimination in favour of women.

Within the framework of a democratic policy; our laws, development policies, Plans and programmes have aimed at women's advancement in different spheres. From the Fifth Five Year Plan (1974-78) onwards there has been a marked shift in the approach to women's issues from welfare to development. In recent years, the empowerment of women has been recognized as the central issue in determining the status of women. The National Commission for Women was set up by an Act of Parliament in 1990 to safeguard the rights and legal entitlements of women. The 73rd and 74th Amendments (1993) to the constitution of India have provided for reservation of seats in the local bodies of Panchayats and Municipalities for women, thus laying a strong foundation for their participation in decision making at the local levels.

India has also ratified various international conventions and human rights instruments committing to secure equal rights of women; mainly among them is the ratification of the Convention on Elimination of All Forms of Discrimination Against Women (CEDAW) in 1993.

The Mexico Plan of Action (1975), the Nairobi Forward Looking Strategies (1985), the Beijing Declaration as well as the Platform for Action (1995) and the Outcome Document adopted by the UNGA Session on Gender Equality and Development & Peace for the 21st century, titled "Further actions and initiatives to implement the Beijing Declaration and the Platform for Action" have been endorsed by India for appropriate policy follow up.

However, there still exists a wide gap between the goals enunciated in the constitution, legislation, policies, plans, programmes and related mechanisms on the one hand and the situational reality of the status of women in India, on the other. Gender disparity manifests itself in various forms, the most obvious being the trend of continuously declining female ratio in the population in the last few decades. Social stereotyping and violence at the domestic and societal levels are some of the other manifestations. Discrimination against girl children, adolescent girls and women persists in parts of the country.

The underlying causes of gender inequality are related to social and economic structure, which is based on informal and formal norms, and practices. Consequently, the access of women, particularly those belonging to weaker sections including Scheduled Castes/Scheduled Tribes/Other backward Classes and minorities, majority of whom are in the rural areas and in the informal, unorganized sector to education, health and productive resources, among others, is inadequate. Therefore, they remain largely marginalized, poor and socially excluded.

Gender represents a unique concern in India. Gender is 'the key narrative of the nation and has been central as an issue, as a crisis or a problem from the times of the colonial encounter.' In colonial times not only did the 'native' require to be emancipated but 'the woman' shackled by patriarchy was also a target of rescue. Thus 'awakening, progress and change are the key terms used in the context of women's education from the nineteenth century onwards.' It seems that both the colonial state as well as the nationalist discourse was steeped in reformist zeal towards improving the overall condition of women.

Thus for colonial rulers, 'the atrocities practiced against women in India became at once a confirmation of their own modernity and a moral ground on which the civilizing mission could be launched'. However an immediate ambivalence is noticed when policies for education for women are the question. Two core contradictions can be identified as the roots of this ambivalence. The first contradiction is the pure-impure dichotomy closely followed by the public-private duality in relation to women in India. Women were and are regarded as pure due their fertility and role as mothers. Thus they also become repositories of family honor, the protection of which is possible only in the private space of the household. Thus there is a distinct discomfort with pulling the woman out of the private space of the family and household into the public spaces of education.

The public-private dichotomy has dominated the discourse of girl's education through colonial times to present times. Restricting women to the private domain ensured control over their sexuality, whereas 'formal education involves moving into public spaces or interaction with males and socialization as boys moving away from the eventual goal of wifehood and marriage.' Despite this complex interplay of push and pull factors in women's education it had 'definitely come to be a public issue by the 1920s. However there was no radical break with the contradictions identified earlier. Apart from Gandhi, who bought women into public spaces in a significant way, there was little done to alter the centuries' old discourse on women and their education in India.

In the absence of such a radical break there is virtual silence on Gender issues in education policy in India. The post-colonial state has preferred to develop policies to advance girls education. Thus special programmes like Mahila Samakhya have been launched. However even policies like the Right to Free and Elementary Education Act 2009, do not document and emanate a gender concern.

That social structures restrict the ontological view of a female is evident if education policy is reviewed in India.

Women have been conceived as mothers and nurturers ot only in India but in most of Asia. This view was current till the 1960's and was reflected in the differentiated curricula for boys and girls in schools. The Hansa Mehta committee on differentiation of curricula for boys and girls (1964) came down strongly on this view. The committee viewed differentiation as a perpetuation of existing traditions of unequal division of labour, and rejected differentiation on grounds of gender difference as 'unscientific'.

The Kothari commission Report (1964-66) shifted the policy discourse on women's education by coming down on gender differences as socially constructed and unscientific. It looked upon women's education as a contribution to national development and as instrumental to reproducing future citizens.

The National Curriculum Framework of 1975 taking a cue from the Kothari Commission report advocated the 10 + 2 + 3 system. The first 10 years would comprise a common curriculum for all students. Thus the issue of differentiation of curricula on a gender basis was laid to rest at least at the policy level. The Kothari Commission had recommended that adopting science and technology education was essential for social and economic transformation.

The year 1975 was significant for the declaration of the International Women's Year by the United Nations and the setting up of the Committee on the Status of Women in India (CSWI) by the Ministry of Education. The report of the CSWI was a landmark document that substantively shifted the discourse on women's rights. While bringing to focus the entrenched inequities on which women were located, it moved away from generalizations and stressed the different experiences of women from different economic sections of society. It concluded that women's productive roles had hitherto remained unacknowledged in policies and consequently their needs had remained unaddressed.

The committee pointed out that in the realm of social values and attitudes, formal education had failed to initiate change and that if anything, education had served to deepen class differences between women since independence. The committee problematized the notion of relevance of knowledge for women. It sought to extend the definition of knowledge to the hitherto and unexplored domain of local and specific needs of women. The committee pointed out that the premise that education should equip women for roles within the domestic sphere negated their substantive contributions within the productive sphere.

The *Shrama Shakti* report, or the report of the National Commission on Self-employed Women and Women of the Informal Sector, was the first committee which made visible the role and contribution of women in the unorganized sector of the economy.

Education for this large section of women workers needed to address their 'contextualized' and 'diverse' needs. The Commission noted that to promote equality it will not only be necessary to provide for equal opportunities for all, but also its conditions of success.

It recommended that syllabi need to be made more relevant for children of rural areas, by offering practical subjects like animal husbandry and cattle care as options along with subjects like history and science. It also recommended that textbooks be revised to bring women into greater focus.

The National Policy on Education, NPE (1986), has been hailed as a path-breaking document as it emphasized the re-orientation of the national education system to play a 'positive interventionist role in the empowerment of women... the development of new values through redesigned curricula, textbooks, training and orientation of teachers, decision-makers and administrators....'

Coming as it did in the wake of the women's movement, the vision of the NPE echoed the demand that education be 'used as an agent of basic change in the status of women'. Textbooks were revised at various levels following the NPE's recommendations. The NCERT also brought a series of teachers' handbooks to address gender equality in classrooms through curricular transactions.

Analysis of post-NPE textbooks shows, however, that revisions were few, piece-meal and utterly cosmetic.

The NPE Review Committee pointed out that although the NPE (1986) gave prominent space to education for gender equality, there was no reference to gender in the entire chapter on the 'content and process of school education', except for a mention that 'equality of the sexes' is to be one of the ten core curriculum areas. Indeed, the NPERC recommended that a gender perspective be explicitly built into the entire curriculum, including the hidden curriculum.

While the National Curriculum Framework, 2000 was largely seen as regressive for gender equality, the National Curriculum Framework, 2005 focuses on Gender and education of marginalized groups.

Thus a review of policy shows that "education", "equality" and "empowerment" of girls have been used as words in policy and educational documents for long without there being a Gender perspective being built into policy.

For "Equality" as a goal, strategies adopted have focused on increasing representation of these notions of gender in educational material sensitive portrayals of discrimination that girls and women face, portraying positive role models and enacting role reversals of stereotypes neutralizing texts of any gendered references, the formal or sameness approach that focuses on equal treatment rather than equality of outcome.

Parity has been the major objective, not just in terms of enrolment or retention of girls, but also in terms of the curriculum and content. Equality, in this formal approach, is seen as mere parity or identical treatment across gender. Parity is a concept that deals with boys and girls being offered equal access to school, equal facilities and even equal representation in the curriculum and textbooks, but all in numerical and formal terms. Such identical treatment dictates that all practices be gender neutral. This does not necessarily recognize the specific concerns of women in education.

Thus, while ideas of empowerment led to the formation of specific programmes like the Mahila Samakhya Programme for adolescent girls and women, the question however remains if targeted programmes in the' girls education' framework can be an alternative to paradigmatic changes in the system of education for Gender equality of women.

IV

Vocational Education and Skills Development

The emphasis on vocational and technical education is evident from the era of Dalhousie in colonial India. In 1847, a Civil engineering college had been established in Roorkee. Dalhousie sought to replicate this in all the three presidencies with the aim of supporting the colonial Government's expansion in railways and telegraph in India. The Dispatch of 1854; for the first time, recognized the need of giving the people an education of "such a character as may be practically useful to the people of India in their different spheres of life." In 1904, the Governor General, Council of Indian Education, made resolution regarding technical education and its promotion. The Hartog Committee (1929) proposed the diversion of more students towards industrial or commerce career at the end of middle stage. Similar emphasis was found in the Sargent Plan (1944).

In recent years skill development has emerged as a key outcome of concern for secondary education in India. Secondary education itself now is seen as a key stage in the skills development framework. Unlike before where it was seen merely as a conduit to higher education now secondary education has to be effective enough to act as a terminal stage in education. Thus it is charged with creating a threshold level of skills in a graduate. Inevitably skill development is being linked with vocationalisation of education. In policy, skills development is also being underpinned by an ideological thrust on the knowledge economy.

The second half of the nineties decade saw an immense thrust on the idea of a knowledge society with the OECD and the world bank defining "*knowledge-based economies*"–as 'economies which are directly based on the production, distribution and use of knowledge and information' (OECD 1996). Clear identifying features of the knowledge society are codification of knowledge and its transmission through information technology, employment demand for a highly skilled workforce and emphasis on collaborative networks for diffusion of knowledge. The hinge on which the knowledge society operates is science and technology. The key transformational tool is Government policy, specifically State education policy.

Thus societies must transform in at least four areas for becoming knowledge economies. Overall education systems have to be capable of 'skilling human capital'. Collaborative networks are also an essential feature of knowledge economies and have to be created. Thus 'Know-who' involves information about who knows what and who knows how to do what. It involves the formation of special social relationships which make it possible to get access to experts and use their knowledge efficiently.' Curriculum must change accordingly to focus on science and technology. Finally policy has to orient itself to skill development and vocationalization.

Skill development policy has been pursued by the Ministry of Labour and Employment (MoLE) and Ministry of Human Resource Development (MHRD) in India. They formulate policies for the Vocational Education and Training (VET). The MHRD is assisted by the All India Council for Technical Education (AICTE) and National Council for Education Research and Training (NCERT).The AICTE prepares curriculum and imparts vocational higher education through polytechnics while the NCERT prepares curriculum and imparts vocational education at school level and through open schools.

The MoLE is assisted by Directorate General of Employment and Training (DGE & T) which imparts vocational training through Craftsmen Training Scheme (CTS) and Skills Development Initiative Scheme (SDIS). The CTS provides training to 1.2 million people through Industrial Training Institutes (it is). SDIS provides training to 1 million people through Vocational Training Providers (VTPs).

Both the ministries are developing separate frameworks called National Vocational Qualification Framework (NVQF) and National Vocational Educational Qualification Framework (NVEQF) for curriculum design, standardization and certification.

All these initiatives are underpinned by National Policy on Skills Development (NPSD) which is the main driver policy. It has set a target of providing skills training to 500 million people by 2022. Under NPSD, National Skill Development Corporation (NSDC), a Public Private Partnership (PPP) has been set up to provide funding, facilitation and advocacy by means of 21 Sector Skill Councils (SSCs). All policies are framed at the Centre and implemented at State level by the States.

The National Policy on Skills Development, 2009, clearly reflects the focus on skills development and on the role of schools in advancing skills development in India. It enumerates a range of employability skills, including vocational skills as essential to skills development. It also mandates that curricula be repositories of these skills. Thus if Skill Development is treated as the core process, in India as in the rest of the world, policy envisages vocationalization as a route to skill development.

Vocationalisation of education has historically been seen as a route to skill development in school. It aims at laying foundations for the world of work. UNESCO associates Vocational Education (VE) with the upper secondary stage of education and defines it as education designed to prepare skilled personnel at lower level of qualifications for one or group of occupations, traders or jobs. Recognizing this, The National Policy on Education of India in 1986 made in education system, apart from organizing the education structure into 10 + 2 + 3 pattern, it majorly promoted vocational education at +2 stage as a separate stream.

Accordingly the NCERT proposed a scheme for introduction of vocational education. A Centrally Sponsored Scheme (CSS 1988) was introduced in 1988. This policy was further revised by NCERT in 1992, for the purpose of creating skilled manpower. The focus of this revision was to orient vocational education for the creation of highly skilled workers and to make education job-oriented and relevant for which curriculum restructuring was undertaken. Significantly there was the urgency to integrate academic and vocational skills and bring vocational education under a national qualification framework, to increase vertical mobility.

The scheme is again under review to attune policy to the needs of a globalized knowledge economy. The focus of this revision is on furthering the agenda underscored above. Additionally there is a focus on inculcation of lifelong learning, public-private partnership, tracking at lower secondary level of education etc.

Despite the policy focus on vocational education, it was realized that the vocational education stream is quite small enrolling less than three per cent of students at the upper secondary level. Additionally there were problems even in skills outcomes of vocational education courses. The main issues in vocational education were low enrollment, weak labor market outcomes and lack of employability skills in students graduating from vocational courses.

The World bank further advises that 'to make the existing vocational education system relevant to market needs, a major restructuring of the system and how it is managed will be needed'. Further the policy direction suggested by the World Bank includes *ensuring private sector participation in management of institutions and curriculum design,* moving from a system which is exclusively financed by the Government to a system which is increasingly financed by the private sector and by students paying user fees, *ensuring that vocational education is not a dead end* is not seen as an option of last resort by prospective students etc.

Separate tracking failed to deliver outcomes in India as in the rest of the world. This led to a multi-pronged policy attempt to restructure secondary school education for skill development. At least two policy agendas have been analyzed above. The National Curriculum Framework for school Education, 2005, governs the academic content of school education. The National Vocational Education Qualifications Framework governs vocational education in Indian schools up-to higher levels of education.

Accordingly, currently policy is seeking to operationalize the National Vocational Education Qualifications Framework (NVEQF) to facilitate lateral and vertical mobility for students. Four main issues give rise to a rationale for a National Qualifications framework.

The National Vocational Educational Qualification Framework (NVEQF) is expected to bring school level vocational education and polytechnics under its purview. One of its objectives is to facilitate international recognition of national standards and that of Indian qualifications from secondary to doctorate levels of education. The framework will have a competency based modular approach with provision of credit accumulation and transfer. There will be collaboration with industry for development of quality standards, model curriculum, assessment and testing procedures. It aims to facilitate vertical and horizontal mobility of students and provide them options of multiple entry and exit through schools, colleges and institutes of vocational education.

The NVEQF serves as an instrument for classifying qualifications according to a set of criteria for levels of learning outcomes. It has specified levels of learning achievements, arranged in ascending order from 1 to 10 levels which depend on the complexity of learning; 1 is the least complex and 10 the most complex.

Levels 1-2 are of the standard of secondary education and basic vocational trades training. Levels 3-4 are similar to advanced trade certificate or vocational certificate. Levels 5-6 are approximate to diploma, and graduate certificates/advanced diploma qualifications. Levels 7-10 approximate to qualifications of graduate and postgraduate standard.

Each level on the NVEQF is described by a statement of learning known as a level descriptor. The level descriptor provides a broad indication of learning outcomes that are appropriate to a qualification at that level. They are designed to support the reviewing of specified learning outcomes and assessment criteria in order to develop particular modules and units and to assign credits at the appropriate level.

The NVEQF has been piloted in Haryana and it involves the extension of vocational education to secondary level (classes 9-10), in addition to higher secondary level in Government schools (classes 11-12). This in itself is a controversial policy decision.

In India, the National Curriculum Framework for School Education, 2005, (henceforth NCF, 2005) provides a reference point for understanding the policy context of curricular and structural changes for skills development. The focus of the NCF (2005) is on restoring 'dignity of labor' and repositioning the fundamental elements of Nai-Talim or Gandhian Basic Education. In this model, 'work' at school had myriad applicability. It could be used pedagogically to link the context of the learner to the subject matter at hand. In the process it would become a medium of skill-formation. This beautiful integration was ruptured by policy in two ways. Firstly the Kothari Commission (1964-66) introduced the concept of work experience that later got extended to the idea of Socially Useful Productive Work (SUPW). Operationalized in this manner, 'work' got relegated to a few allocated time slots in the school day. Later the National Policy on Education (1986) created two distinct streams at the secondary level-the vocational and the academic.

In order to remedy this rupture, the NCF, 2005, positions the idea of 'work centered education'. This formulation gives place to generic competencies, also identified by the World Bank as markers of employability in the globalized 'knowledge economy'. The position paper of the National Focus Group on Work and Education clearly identifies some generic competencies that a child would acquire throughout the primary and middle stages of Education. It is here that Indian curricular policy reforms paradigm clashes with the skills-development approach of the OECD-World Bank. Despite the core agreement on generic skills, the NVEQF looks at competency based outcomes, whereas The National Curriculum Framework clearly pushes curriculum policy towards a Gandhian work based skills development approach.

Theoretically both these policy frameworks are in opposite directions. Competency based curriculum theories see curriculum as a body of knowledge to be transmitted; and attempts to achieve certain ends in students-the product. The view of curriculum, as a product, implies that objectives are set as a plan drawn up, and then applied, and the the outcomes (products) measured. It is a way of thinking about education that is concerned with competencies. Franklin Bobbitt (1918) and Ralph W. Tyler (1949) are two theorists that dominate theory and practice within this tradition.

This approach to curriculum theory involves detailed attention to what people need to know in order to work, live their lives and so on. A restricted, example of this approach can be found in many training programmes, where particular tasks or jobs have been analyzed-broken down into their component elements-and lists of competencies drawn up.

Bobbitt's work and theory met with mixed responses with one sayin criticism that was made, and can continue to be made, of such approaches is that there is no social vision or programme to guide the process of curriculum construction. It is a technical exercise.

The attraction of this way of approaching curriculum theory and practice is that it is systematic and has considerable organizing power. Central to the approach is the formulation of behavioral objectives, providing a clear notion of outcome so that content and method may be organized and the results evaluated. The NVEQF clearly pulls in this direction.

Another way of looking at curriculum theory and practice is via process. In this sense curriculum is not a physical thing, but rather the interaction of teachers, students and knowledge. In other words, curriculum is what actually happens in the classroom.

Lawrence Stenhouse (1975) theorized the process model of curriculum theory and practice. He defined curriculum tentatively: 'A curriculum is an attempt to communicate the essential principles and features of an educational proposal in such a form that it is open to critical scrutiny and capable of effective translation into practice' which we will now implement.

As Cornbleth (1990) has argued, curriculum cannot be taken out of context, and the context in which it was formed was the school. Curriculum theory and practice only makes sense when considered alongside notions like class, teacher, course, lesson and so on. It is not a concept that stands on its own. Apart from its Vygovtskian roots the National curriculum framework is based on the above theoretical structure.

Thus in India policy basically pulls in two different directions as far as curriculum policy for skill development is concerned. This has implications for teacher's quality and capacity and teacher's education, both of which are central to skill development. The curriculum and qualifications framework envisaged by the NVEQF demands that along with vocational trainers there is a need for teachers who can understand and implement the integration of general and academic streams of education. Teachers need to be trained to recognize competencies and assess them, all of which are essential to skill development outcomes.

Like in other areas, policy in skill development and vocationalization are underpinned by an urgency reflected in arguments of dismal quality and scores. In a departure from past policy, two Indian states-Himachal Pradesh and Tamil Nadu participated in the PISA 2009+. The results of the assessment have since then been referred to for pushing a skills development agenda in India.

PISA tests students in reading and numeracy, key skills required for a knowledge economy. The average reading literacy score for Himachal Pradesh, one of the educationally better states in India, was the lowest average reading score observed in PISA 2009 and PISA 2009+. In Himachal Pradesh, 11 per cent of students are estimated to have a proficiency in reading literacy that is at or above the baseline. It can be tentatively said that 89 per cent of students in Himachal Pradesh are estimated to be below this baseline level as compared to 81 per cent of student performing at or above the baseline level in reading in the OECD countries. In Tamil Nadu, 17 per cent of students are estimated to have a proficiency in reading literacy that is at or above the baseline. This can be roughly interpreted to mean that 83 per cent of students in Tamil Nadu are estimated to be below this baseline level.

Students in the Tamil Nadu attained a mean score on the PISA mathematical literacy scale as the same observed in Himachal Pradesh. In Tamil Nadu-India, 15 per cent of students are proficient in mathematics at least to the baseline level. This compares to 75 per cent in the OECD countries, on average.

Scores on scientific literacy scale in the same assessment were as follows. In Himachal Pradesh 11 per cent of students are proficient in science at least to the baseline level. Students in Tamil Nadu in India were estimated to have a mean score on the scientific literacy scale, which is below the means of all OECD countries, but significantly above the mean observed in the other Indian state, Himachal Pradesh. In Tamil Nadu-India, 16 per cent of students are proficient in science at least to the baseline level as compared to 82 per cent in the OECD countries, on average.

Proficiency in English language is also considered an important skill in the globalized knowledge economy. Advantage in English language communication is one of the key factors parents consider while opting for private school education in India. Do Indian graduates really acquire this skill in schools? The Wall Street Journal describes the difficulty that many organizations are having in recruiting able graduates in India. It states that the number of high school and college graduates who come through the door and who can communicate effectively in English is staggeringly low and that many lack a grasp of educational basics such as reading comprehension. It cites a Customer Contact company that can hire just three out of 100 applicants.

It is accepted that English is important in Indian schools. However, some of the literature surveyed surprisingly claims that most of the population does not gain this skill through the secondary school system. Many secondary schools still rely on an outdated grammar-based approach to teaching English that does not prepare students to communicate effectively in the language.

Thus, with contestable evidence of falling scores in science and mathematics and lack of proficiency in English, amongst Indian secondary school and university, graduates a sense of pessimism created around education, creating a discourse for policy shifts of the kind outlined above.

V

Higher Education Policy in India

Higher education has been 'the one area where we have always exceeded our targets'. However, this 'achievement' is again a reflection of, not so much a result of coherent and well planned policies. Since colonial times 'the class-base of political power naturally led to a greater emphasis on secondary and higher education which benefit the 'haves' rather than the 'have nots' so that the expansion of programmes at these stages received early attention, greater priority and more adequate allocations than those of mass education'.

Expansion of education in the colonial times and early years of independence can also be explained on the basis of the expansion of industry, both in public and private sectors, and the large expansion of the services sector (including governmental services at all levels). This created an immense demand for the products of secondary schools and universities.

Higher education policies take a sudden critical turn in the 1990's which was a decade of turmoil in higher education; and the government approaches meant almost 'killing of higher education'. The defining characteristics in higher education after the 1990's are a clear absence of policy in higher education accompanied by public sector disinvestment in this sector.

Like in elementary education the roots of the turn policy in higher education can be traced to the National Policy on Education (1986).

According to the NPE-86 "Higher education provides people with an opportunity to reflect on the critical social, economic, cultural, moral and spiritual issues facing humanity. It contributes to national development through dissemination of specialized knowledge and skills. It is therefore crucial factor for survival. Being at the apex of the educational pyramid, it has also a key role in producing teachers for the education system." Therefore, it proposed, "in the near future, the main emphasis will be on consolidation of, and expansion of facilities in the existing institutions. Urgent steps will be taken to protect the system from degradation."

The NPE however proposed raising of resources by "mobilizing donations", "raising fees", "effecting some savings by efficient use of facilities", "levying a cess or charge on the user agencies". The policy document clearly stated that all these measures will "reduce the burden on State resources" and create "a greater sense of responsibility within the educational system."

In the NPE, higher education would work only through the "creation of a system of performance appraisals of institutions according to standards and norms set at the National or State levels" The policy also upheld the creation of "the spirit of autonomy for educational institutions".

The paradigm reflected by the National Policy on Education, 1986, follows exactly the policies prescribed by the World Bank's for restructuring of higher education in developing countries. (World Bank 1986). From the eighties the World Bank positioned a picture in higher education through all their documents and publications. The general picture painted positioned a shortage of funds. The only way out was for students to bear a large part of the burden of education costs. It was argued that only the relatively better off students were able to enter higher education; subsidizing those makes for inequality and not egalitarianism; if the same subsidy were shifted instead to primary education, the effect would be towards equality. The World Bank had suggested cost recovery from students (parents), educational loans to students desirous of higher education, and pure private educational institutions, which would charge fees sufficient to meet costs and make a profit.

A least the following key points emerge from the World Bank initiated prescriptions for higher education.

- Higher education should not have the highest priority claim on incremental public resources available for education in many developing countries, especially those that have not yet achieved adequate access, equity and quality at the primary and secondary levels.
- The social rates of return on investments in primary and secondary education usually exceed the returns on higher education.
- Cost recovery may be increased for public institutions by means of elimination of subsidies.

- Strong participation of the private sector because for such sector the creation of such institutions might be more attractive due to a low cost per student.
- Even though governments must establish a general framework for the functioning of private institutions, the World Bank advised "the avoidance of regulation on the cost of enrollment and tuition", and "the establishment of accreditation and evaluation mechanisms for such institutions."
- The World Bank recommended that the representatives of the private business sector should be included in the "Government agencies that work with public and private universities."

The government took several measures and constituted several committees for the implementation of the National Policy on Education and for gradual withdrawal of subsidy to higher education as dictated by the World Bank. Among the significant steps that it immediately took are:

- Freezing budgets for higher education.
- Financial reforms to raise resources through the creation of self-financing courses, the creation of student loans lie any other consumer goods loans without any social vision.
- The reclassification of higher education as a Merit good and subsequently as a Merit 2 good.

An indication of the influence of cororates in higher education was the Ambani-Birla report "A Policy Framework for Reforms in Education" which was invited by the government and was tabled in April 2000. Considering education as a very profitable market, these two industrialists made a case for full cost recovery from students and immediate privatization of entire higher education except those areas of education involving "liberal arts and performing arts."

Clearly there is a privatization agenda being pursued by the Indian state for higher education. There is clear and persistent statement of this agenda in Plan documents. The approach paper to the twelfth five year plan states that 'private initiatives in higher education including PPP models will be actively promoted'. Both the eleventh and the twelfth plans are pegged to the concept of inclusive growth. However despite there being no clear and established link between inclusive growth and privatization, PPP is the policy that is proposed by both plans. This is a clear case of contradiction. Six directional statements are made in the twelfth plan that indicates a move towards privatization. These are:

- Removal of entry barriers for private participation.
- Encouragement of PPP.
- Reexamination of the not-for-profit tag in higher education.
- Access of public funds to private players.

- Creation of large education hubs in the country under public sector enterprises but supported by private sector.

Thus 'many of the recent policy initiatives mark a transition in the history of higher education in India ... from a system imbedded in welfare statism to a system based on neo-liberal market philosophy.' In a final word, the transition seems to be complete and dangerously irreversible.'

Five higher education bills proposed after 2000 clearly indicate the Indian states policy shift towards privatization in higher education.

- The Foreign Educational Institutions (Regulation of Entry and Operations) Bill, 2010 was introduced in the Lok Sabha in May 2010.
- The Educational Tribunals Bill 2010.
- The Higher Education and Research (THER) Bill 2011 and was introduced in the Rajya Sabha in December 2011. An all powerful commission is sought to be created for the centralization of all aspects related to higher education including starting of a university.
- Another draft bill for starting innovation universities was also circulated. It also re-modified as Universities for Research and Innovation Bill, 2012 and was introduced in the Lok Sabha in May 2012.
- The Prohibition of Unfair Practices in Technical, Medical Educational Institutions and Universities Bill does not fulfill the objective of social control over self-financing or private unaided institutions. The fees and salaries to teachers will not be regulated as the minister assured private school principals.

VI

Conclusion

Thus, there is a clear continuity from the colonial era in Indian education to the present policy regime constructed by the Indian state. The educational ideal of the colonial times was not a brown sahib but a colonial citizen who was subservient to the needs of the colonial state. This citizen was dressed in concepts of rational behavior and practiced in the norms of civil society. Education provided the site for this dressing and practice. However, whereas the liberal ideal of civil society was based on 'equality, autonomy, freedom of entry and exit, contract, deliberative procedures of decision making...'. In the colonial state 'the domain of civil social institutions is restricted to a fairly small section of citizens.' Colonial education policy is also underpinned with a problematic notion of gender which has carried down to present times. Gender as a category of educational policy analysis has been replaced by girl's education as the central concern of policy.

Education has also become a site where technological change of the recent decades is entrenched and proliferating. A key element of this technological change is the centrality that Information and Communication technology has come to acquire in India. This change in technology is coupled with the increasing emphasis on professionalization of education. The themes of 'skill', 'quality', 'efficiency' and 'privatization' are the doors through which this technological change has entered education policy discourse in India. While technological change itself is natural to human progress, the issue of equity takes precedence over technology. Thus we see a digital divide which is economic, social or cultural deprivation generated by missing ICT access and skills. In the modern knowledge and information based world, economic opportunities, such as employability, depend on ICT access and skills, further privileging the elite over the deprived sections of Indian society.

In India, the State has thrown its weight behind the educational and technological needs of the elite. Apple (1979) reveals how the State's powerful investment in education can disrupt the dissemination of knowledge in society, not only by projecting a particular ideological position, but also by excluding particular demands, interests and knowledge-forms, preventing them from crystallizing as sources of contradiction and dissent. The knowledge of the ruling class, sets stringent limits on other knowledge production, in order to restrain forms of cultural and political response that could undermine their powerful position in society.

The neo-liberal project in fact involves 'an immense task to create a truly organic ideology, one that seeks to spread throughout society and to create a new form of national popular will'. Thus 'what has been accomplished has been a successful translation of an economic-doctrine into the language of experience, moral imperative and common sense'.

Apple thus draws attention towards the process by which 'elements of ideologies of groups in dominance become truly popular'. The popularity of these ideas is achieved by pushing them in a 'rupture' in the beliefs of 'historically' less powerful groups. This rupture is used to build a 'shift in common sense'. This rupture originates from real and contradictory experiences of a large portion of the population. They connect with real needs, fears and hopes of a group of people.

In education policy in India, policy makers have been able to latch on to the concern that parents have about the economic future of their children. This has been combined with a sustained effort to shift 'common sense' associated with schooling. Through sustained 'construction of commonsense', private schools have been equated with 'efficiency and quality' whereas public school have been equated with inefficiency and low quality. Government schooling does suffer from problems of state failure and thus pose a real problem, but these necessitate a different set of policy responses rather than a simplistic move towards the market. Education policy has found and utilized a rupture in the lives of ordinary people and has 'cemented conservative educational positions into our daily life.'

This cementing is being done on the basis of research that contains preconceived notions of the efficacy of markets.

No matter how radical some of these proposed reforms may be but they have redefined the terrain of debate for all things educational. Understanding this redefined terrain is essential for analysis of the discourse of educational policy reform in India.

Thus education aids in the formation of a 'subservient citizen'. Under the colonial State the ideal citizen was the subservient citizen. Colonial education policy also aimed at implanting 'civil society' in India. While colonialism had its run in India till 1947 in post-independence, the ideal of a subservient citizen continued to dominate education policy. In the era of structural readjustment policies, the idea of subservient citizen has undergone change. Now the citizen is the consumer whose commonsense has been so altered that 'now equality means guaranteeing individual choice in a free market'. The role of the State now is not merely administrative and coercive and an arm of capitalism but rather as 'educative and formative.' It 'exercises moral and educative leadership of a new hegemonic bloc by gaining active consent over those it rules'. As a result, education policy is shifting to display at least the following key features:

- A shift towards Public-Private Participation in elementary as well as higher education.
- Imposition of standards in education thus centralizing government control over curriculum, teaching and research.
- The growing pressure to make the needs of business and industry into the primary goals of the education system.

Notes and References

Popov, Y. (1984), *Essays in Political Economy, Imperialism and the Developing Countries.* Moscow: Progress Publishers, p. 119.

Grover and Grover (1998), '*A new look at Modern Indian History*', S. Chand & Co. Ltd.

Ghosh S C (2009), '*The History of Education in Modern India 1757-2007*', Orient BlackSwan.

Kumar Krishna, 2005, '*Political Agenda of Education: A Study of Colonialist and Nationalist Ideas*', Sage.

Naik, 1974, '*Policy and Performance in Indian Education*', K G Sayyidin Memorial lecture.

Sadgopal, 2010, '*Right to education Vs Right to Education Act*', Social Scientist.

Reddy, A. (2008). '*Public financing of elementary education in India*' Indian Journal of Social Development, Vol 8, No. 1, pp. 19–36 and De A & Endow T, (2008), '*Public Expenditure on Education in India: Recent Trends and Outcomes*', RECOUP Working Paper No. 18, p. 8.

Public Report on Basic Education in India, 1999, Oxford University Press. See also Pratham's Annual Survey of Education reports published since 2005.

Apple M, 2006, '*Educating the "Right" Way*', Routledge, for a complete analysis of how a coalition of neo-conservative forces are leading to the alteration of commonsense.

Kingdon, Geeta G. (2005). '*Private and public schooling: The Indian experience*'. Conference paper Co-sponsored by the World Bank Kennedy School of Government, Harvard University, October 5-6, 05, pp. 1–22 and Tooley J & Dixon P '*Private education for low-income families: results from a global research project*' in Srivastava P, Walford G's ed. (2007), 'Private chooling in Less Economically developed countries, Symposium, pp. 15–41.

Jimenez and Lockheed, 1995, '*Public and Private Secondary Education in Developing countries: A comparative study*', World Bank Discussion Paper no. 309, World Bank.

Kingdon, Geeta G. (1996). '*Private Schooling in India: Size, Nature and Equity Effects*'. Economic and Political Weekly, Vol 31, No. 51 pp. 3306–14.

Pradhan, B K and A Subramanian (2000): '*Education, Openness and the Poor*', Discussion Paper 14, NCAER, New Delhi and others.

Tilak JBG, (2000).' *Determinants of household expenditure on education in rural India*' NIEPA, NCAER Survey on human development in India, p. 68.

Mehrotra S & Panchamukhi PR '*Universalising Elementary Education in India: Is private sector the answer*' in Srivastava P, Walford G's ed.(2007), 'Private Schooling in Less Economically developed countries, Symposium, pp. 112–129.

Popli G, Parikh A, Richard Palmer–Jones, A. (2005). '*Are the 2000 poverty estimates for India a myth, artefact or real?*', Economic and Political Weekly, 22nd October, pp. 4619–4623.

Chaudhury N, Hammer J, Kremer M, Muralidharan K, Rogers F. H. (2004). '*Teacher absence in India: a snapshot*' Journal of the European Economic Association Vol 9, No 5, 04, pp. 2–10.

Olson, M. (1998) '*The Logic of Collective Action: Public goods and the Theory of Groups*', Harvard University Press, p. 9, 22, 23 for more on how individuals come together to derive common benefits.

Ball, S. (2007). '*Education plc: understanding private sector participation in public sector education*', Taylor & Francis.

Fairclough, N (2000*). 'New labour, new language?*. Taylor & Francis, p. 157.

Whitfield, D (2001). '*Public services or corporate welfare: rethinking the nation state in the global economy*' Pluto Press, pp. 130–33.

Sen S, ' *Towards a Feminist Politics: The Indian Women's Movement in Historical Perspective*' in Kapadia K, ed 'The Violence of Development, the politics of Identity, Gender and Social Inequalities in India, Kali for Women.

Chanana K, in '*Hinduism and Female Sexuality: Social Control and Education of Girls in India*', Sociological Bulletin, Vol 50, no. 1, March 2001.

OECD, 1996, '*The knowledge-based economy*', OECD.

World Bank 2006, '*Skill development in India: The Vocational Education and training system*' Human Development Unit, South Asia.

NCERT, 2007 '*Position paper on Work and Education*', NCERT.

Bobbit J F, 1918, '*The Curriculum*', Hougton Mufflin

Tyler R W, '*Basic Principles of Curriculum and Instruction*', U. Chicago Press.

Stenhouse L, 1975, '*An introduction to curriculum research and Development*', Hienemann.

Cornbleth C, 1990, '*Curriculum in Context*', Falmer Press

Chitalkar S, 2010, '*The Politics of Education Policy Reform: A Stakeholder Analysis*', Unpublished Thesis, NUEPA.

Tilak JBG, 2004 '*Education in the UPA government Common Minimum Programme*', EPW, October 2004.

World Bank, 1986, '*Financing of Higher Education in Developing Countries*', The World Bank, Washington D.C.

World Bank, 1994, '*Higher Education: The Lessons of Experience*', The World Bank, Washington D.C.

Government of India, April 2000, '*A Policy Framework for Reforms in Education*', a report submitted by special subject group on 'Policy Framework for Private Investment in Education, Health and Rural Development' constituted by the Prime Minister's Council on Trade and Industry with Mukesh Ambani (Convenor) and Kumarmangalam Birla (Member), New Delhi.

Tilak JBG 'Higher education policy in India in Transition EPW, Vol XLVII No. 13, 31st March 2012.

Chatterjee P, 2001, 'On civil and Political society in post-colonial societies' in Kaviraj and Khilnani ed, Civil Society, History and Possibilities, Cambridge University Press.

Apple M, (1979) *Ideology and Curriculum*, London: Routledge & Keegan Paul.

Apple M, (1999) *Official Knowledge: Democratic Education in a Conservative Age*, London: Routledge.

Bukharin, N. (1917) *Imperialism and World Economy.* London: The Merlin Press, 1972.

Hilferding, R. (1910) *Finance Capital,* London: Routledge and Kegan Paul, 1981.

Jha P, Das S, Mohanty S, Jha N, .(2008), '*Public provisioning for elementary education in India*', Sage.

Kingdon, Geeta G. (1996). 'Private Schooling in India: Size, Nature and Equity Effects'. Economic and Political Weekly, Vol 31, No. 51 pp. 3306–14.

Kingdon, Geeta G. and Mohd. Muzammil (2003) *The Political Economy of Education in India: Teacher Politics in Uttar Pradesh*, Delhi: Oxford University Press.

Kingdon, Geeta G. (2005). '*Private and public schooling: The Indian experience*'. Conference paper Co-sponsored by the World Bank Kennedy School of Government, Harvard University, October 5-6, 05, pp. 1–22.

Lenin, V.I. (1917) *Imperialism: The Highest Stage of Cappitalism: A Popular Outline.* Beijing: Foreign Languages Press, 1973.

Marx, K. (1867) *Capital,* Volume One. Harmondsworth: Penguin, 1976.

Marx, K. (1894) *Capital,* Volume Three. Harmondsworth: Penguin, 1981.

Milios, J. (1994) "Marx's Theory and the Historic Marxist Controversy on Economic Crisis (1900–1937)", *Science and Society,* Vol 58, No 2.

Mukherjee, N. (2005). '*Political Corruption in India's Below the Poverty Line* (BPL): *Grassroots' perspectives on BPL in perpetuating poverty and social exclusion & good Practice in people's participation and BPL exercise from Bhalki Village*'. Development Tracks in Research, Training & Consultancy, p. 3.

Ricardo, D. (1821) *The Principles of Political Economy and Taxation*. Cambridge: Cambridge University Press, 1951.

Smith, A. (1776) *An Inquiry into the Nature and Causes of the Wealth of Nations*. London: Ward, Lock & Co, no date (reprint of the 1812 edition). Tilak, J BG.(1985).' *Analysis of costs of education in India'* NIEPA Occasional Paper No. 10.

Tilak, J BG.(2000).' *Determinants of household expenditure on education in rural India'* NIEPA, NCAER Survey on human development in India, p. 68.

36

Policy and Planning for Health Services

Indira Chakravarthi

Most of the countries across the world have developed a healthcare and medical care system in a planned and organized way. In addition to this, some countries have also attempted to use the system to advance other social goals, such as to reduce inequities and corruption. The provision of medical care has been viewed and undertaken as a part of the larger policy and planning processes, and has largely been provided through non-profit mechanisms, as a basic right of citizens, and is the most important social security element in the welfare state.

It is useful to make a distinction between 'health' and 'health services system', even though much of the discourse on health is largely about health services for the provision of medical care. It is an accepted fact that health is more than the absence of illness and it is a dynamic concept involving the biological and social dimensions of the well-being of all individuals and populations. Healthcare refers to prevention of illness, protection from illness and promotion of health in populations. It is about paying attention to the availability of sufficient food, clean water, shelter, hygienic living and working conditions, and a clean environment, in short, all the aspects conducive to prevent illnesses and diseases in a population and to keep people healthy. Hence, healthcare is much more than merely organizing health services for medical care. However, provision of medical care to sick individuals is essential and critical as a preventive measure for spread of infectious diseases, as well as for provision of cure and relief from pain, and support to disabled and chronically ill individuals. The health services system is a complex of education, research and delivery systems for providing curative, preventive, promotive and rehabilitative services to the population[1].

There is a substantial amount of literature and discourse on the health status of the Indian population, on the health policy and planning process in India, on the status of health services infrastructure, on medical education, and so on. A comprehensive account of the developments in the health sector requires several volumes; it is impossible to do justice to this vital, critical area of social policy and inter-disciplinary study within the confines of a single chapter. Here, an attempt is made to present a bird's eye view of the salient features of the health sector, and the various forces that have shaped the developments thereof.

This chapter deals with the organization and provision of health services in India in the post-1947 period. It does not touch upon several important components of the health services system, namely medical education, production and supply of medicines, vaccines, medical devices and equipment-based medical technologies. Incidentally, production of drugs and pharmaceuticals in the country is administered by the Ministry of Chemicals and Fertilizers, Department of Pharmaceuticals.

❑ Health Policy and Planning in India

A broad range of economic and social rights, and 'development' have been endorsed and officially acknowledged, at national and international levels, to be central to health. Article 21 of the constitution of India, 'Right to Life', has also been interpreted widely to include in its ambit rights to health, shelter, food, education, etc.

The constitution outlines the division of responsibilities in the health sector among the state, central and local governments, with the state essentially responsible for the delivery of health care. The sixth item in the State List in the constitution of India vests responsibility for 'Public health and sanitation, hospitals and dispensaries' on the state governments. However, a number of items related to health are listed in the Concurrent List; Items 20 and 20A in the List, on Economic and Social Planning and Population Control permit both the State and the Union to function in these areas. In practice, much of the directions, plans and priorities, as well as resources go from the Centre and its role is therefore important. Over time states have became increasingly dependent on the centre for financial assistance to implement disease control programmes and community-based health services. In turn, the centre has increasingly gained financial and programmatic control of these areas, adversely affecting the development of technical and organizational capacity in the states.

> *It is only when the description of the present structure of the health sector is preceded by a historical analysis of its varying components and the forces that determine it can one understand the current values and meaning of present experiences.*[2]

I

❑ Public Health and Health Services in Colonial India

The foundations for the present-day health policies, plans and programs originated in the late 19th and early 20th century during the colonial rule and in the course of the nationalist movement against it.

"The initial phase of this effort, from 1700 to 1835, was guided by an open policy of learning from the Indian medical systems and their practitioners, but after 1835, the British policy became more dominating. Not only were the schools teaching both ayurveda and allopathy asked to abolish the former, but English was also made compulsory in medical schools. British standards were rigorously imposed and all support to traditional systems was withdrawn. This period, is one of major changes when the pre-existing medical systems were completely over-shadowed by allopathy in India. However, there have been certain areas of continuity as well, which are more crucial...".[3] Namely, hospitals in the pre-colonial period were run more as charity institutions for the poor, while the rich availed the services of private practitioners at home; the major patrons of Ayurveda were the courts and the urban elite; famous practitioners like *Dhanvantari, Charaka, Susruta, Atraya,* were all court physicians and lavishly rewarded for their services. These features remained in the colonial period and continue till today i.e., of elitism in medical services and availability of private practice for those who could afford it.

Right through the first half of the 19th century, the focus of the colonial government in provision of healthcare services was on armies and European civilian populations. The Indian Medical Service (IMS) was primarily a military medical service, constituted for maintaining the health of the army. The professional medical men, both in the IMS and the civil medical services, did not show much interest in the sanitary matters unless there were epidemics. Before the 1860s sanitary arrangements for the civilian population was not given much attention. Any efforts for local improvements, such as removal of filth, or repair of wells and drains, depended on the individual official in-charge.

Sanitation and hygiene as one of the preventive health measures can be considered to date from the 1859 Royal Commission appointed to inquire into the sanitary state of the army in India. The Commission recommended measures not only for the army but also for the civilian population. It reported that the health of the army could not be separated from the sanitary conditions of the neighbouring population, and that proper measures for water-supply, drainage, paving, cleansing and general constitution in these towns would be most beneficial to the health of the troops living near them. In accordance with the suggestions of the Commission, Commissioners of

Public Health were established in 1864 in Madras, Bombay and Bengal. In Madras and Bombay, public health services were initiated through the municipal and district boards. The Commissioners put forward far-reaching recommendations, which included employment of trained public health staff in towns and districts. But these recommendations were not carried out and no comprehensive policy was laid down with regard to development of preventive health services. Not much progress was actually made and in 1869 the sanitary commissions were practically abolished. The reasons given for this lack of performance ranged from lack of funds, to unsatisfactory legislation, to apathy of the people. According to Jeffrey, little was achieved partly because sanitary concerns were restricted to official circles, and technical disputes about the relationship between sanitary measures and medical science hindered the implementation of policy, especially with respect to the role of clean water in preventing cholera.[4] The doctors of the Indian Medical Service argued that the sanitary commissioners would unnecessarily limit the functions of army medical officers, and through the Indian Medical Gazette waged a war against the appointment of a layman to head the Bengal Sanitary Department. Sanitary Commissioners were expressly excluded from any concern with the cantonments and the European civil lines which remained the responsibility of the army. The measures proposed to deal with cholera were implemented for the army and cholera mortality dropped in the 1870s (to 3 per 1000). However, when medical men came to deal with civilian cholera they invoked excuses such as the superstition of the natives. Increasingly, the towns had local municipal committees, which focused on activities like conservancy, by employing sweepers to collect sewage and bury it, and on transportation. However, because of financial constraints these committees could not impact much on sanitation. In 1888, in view of the then recently created local bodies – in municipal and in rural areas – the Government of India issued a resolution drawing their attention to their duties in matters of sanitation, and the task of sanitation was entrusted to these local bodies in many parts of the country. The training in hygiene and sanitation was expanded, and graduates were brought into sanitary work. Most of the activities were severely restricted however, by a shortage of funds, and by blaming the poor natives for their ignorance, superstitions, etc., to be the reason for their sickness and ill-health. There was opposition from local politicians for taxation for sanitary purposes.[5]

The report of the Plague Commission in 1904 recommended the strengthening of public health services and the establishment of laboratories for research and for preparation of vaccines and sera. The action taken on these suggestions included: (1) creation of a Medical Research Department under the Central Government; (2) establishment of the India Research Fund Association for promoting research into medical problems; and (3) annual grants from the central funds to the provinces to assist execution of public health works, such as drainage and water supply, and strengthening of public health personnel, such as appointing Deputy Sanitary commissioners and health officers in local bodies (Health Survey and Development Committee 1946). The success of such 'preventive' sanitation efforts were negligible, except in the larger cities. Sanitary policy was restricted to towns and military areas, as the Royal Commission was to consider improvements for the towns in proximity to military stations.

In the early 20th century, capitalist development and rapid unplanned increase of the urban population led to slums, overcrowding and urban squalor in India just as it had in Europe over the previous century. There was a large-scale urbanization in India after the First World War, with Calcutta, Bombay, Madras, Kanpur, Ahmedabad, Madurai and Coimbatore becoming major industrial centers. There were an estimated 7-8 million industrial workers. There was an overcrowding on an unprecedented scale, largely associated with influx of rural population, which constituted the urban industrial working class. The urban industrial worker lived in abysmal conditions in the *bastis* (slums), which lacked all civic amenities. The Second World War aggravated the existing conditions in all industrial areas. It was expected that this would aggravate further in the post-War period with further development of industry, unless adequate measures were taken, such as laying down minimum standards of housing for workers. Even in the towns most directly amenable to the British influence and action, the conditions were appalling, with very high morbidity and mortality.

After the 1900s, the state became increasingly active in the provision of public health for the general population, by funding measures such as small pox vaccination and loans and grants-in-aid for sanitation. The two Acts of 1919 and 1935 transferred medical administration (namely that of hospitals-dispensaries), medical education, and public health activities to the provinces. Decision-making in matters of sanitary and medical policy were devolved to Indians who were also employed as municipal health officers and surgeons in the civilian wing of the Indian Medical Service, which underwent a drive towards 'Indianization' after 1919.[6] While such measures led to greater public health activity in the provinces than before, however, they continued to be plagued by a lack of adequate resources and personnel.

While public health measures were not a priority, this was not the case as far as medical services were concerned. Medical colleges had been established as early as in 1835 in the three Presidencies namely Bombay, Calcutta and Madras, and they followed the guidelines laid down by the General Medical Council of England. The rudimentary medical services provided by the medical officers of the East India Company to its army as well as to British civilians got consolidated as the Indian Medical Service soon after 1857. In addition, several eminent Indian medical professionals also set up a variety of medical colleges and hospitals in different parts of the country. As a result, many Indians were exposed to and received 'western' medical education since the beginning of the 20th century.

According to the Annual Report of the Sanitary Commissioner (1910), there were in-patient, out-patient and surgical treatments being offered in all of the 2670 hospitals and dispensaries (both funded by state as well as by private sources). The number of such institutions increased to 2707 in 1911, and in addition there were 829 special hospitals of the state, for example the Railway Hospitals. We learn from this Annual Report that at that time private dispensaries were also far more common in India than anywhere else, approximately 706 in that period. By the 1900s it was common in most cities and towns to find men making their living from practicing Western medicine.[7] There were also 4 medical colleges offering University degrees and 14 schools offering diploma courses. While these numbers may not have been sufficient for the large population, they indicate that the institutions being set up provided allopathic services and served to propagate it further.

Western medicine has had a long and complex history in this country; it was not simply an 'imposition' of the British colonizers. Before the 1800s western medicine had made few inroads into India and was largely confined to European enclaves and the major port cities. A dramatic transformation took place over the next hundred years, whereby it became the dominant system within the realm of state medicine and public health. In the late 19th century the exposure to English education led to the growth of an English-educated, elite class of Indians in the country. By the 1900s western medicine had started gaining in prestige and popularity among the western educated middle class. The medical profession proved attractive to many Indians, who sought a career in the subordinate branch of the IMS. Indians started joining the Indian Medical Service after 1855. The western medicine came to enjoy formidable degree of authority and ultimately became the universal system. While the policies and actions of the colonial government contributed in a large measure to the process by which it acquired its privileged position, yet 'the adoption of western medicine was punctuated by resistance, negotiation and participation'.[8] After the passing of the Montagu-Chelmsford reforms of 1919, the British expected the Indian ministers of health and education to try to support indigenous medicine, since the Indian National Congress had begun to pass resolutions in its support. While some ministers did support the Indian system of medicine on both patriotic and economic grounds, some (in Bombay and Punjab for instance) resisted nationalist pressures and used their limited funds to support modern scientific medicine and surgery and make it accessible to all. While the Congress and non-Congress parties never committed themselves exclusively to one or the other side, leaders like Nehru supported the spread of western scientific medicine. By 1920 many middle-class practitioners of western and indigenous systems of medicine were also involved in Congress.

'Western medicine' became the established mode of providing medical care, and was also followed by the dominant Indian classes. Accordingly, the medical education also gave priority to the teaching of western medicine, and was supported by not only the colonial state, but also by the indigenous private philanthropic organizations, as well as the Rockefeller Foundation. The other medically related ideas that evolved in the west and the various measures that were adopted in England got 'imported' to India. Sanitation, hygiene and vaccination became the 'public health' measures, and the Factories Act was introduced to regulate industrial working conditions, and thereby ensuring the health of the workers.

Some of the erstwhile eminent medical professionals, such as Dr B C Roy, Dr A R Ansari, Dr Khan Saheb, Dr Jivraj Mehta, Hakim Ajmal Khan, and Dr N M Jaisoorya, occupied leadership positions in the national struggle. Inspired by the welfare state movement in England and the socialized health services in the Soviet Union, they articulated a demand for a more egalitarian health service system, and made this an important demand in the anti-colonial struggle.

Dr B C Roy's presidential address at the All India Medical Conference in Lahore in 1929 gave an idea of the issues that merited attention, according to sections of medical professionals back then, such as that of inclusion of practitioners of indigenous systems of medicine (*vaids* and *hakims*) in the Indian Medical Association. He said, "Should we restrict the membership to such persons only as follow the western system of Medicine? ...If we take medicine merely as science it may be argued that only those who are trained in scientific methods prevalent in the west should be eligible to be members. But to my mind it is taking a very narrow view of the whole matter. On the other hand, if we define science as a systematized branch of human knowledge we cannot ignore other systems…it is not for us to be cut off from the past systems but it is necessary for us to resuscitate them and to develop them…. We cannot ignore them…". There was also a call for efforts to promote self-reliance and self-confidence and to make medical education relevant to Indian conditions, "We do not desire to depend on others. We therefore desire to utilize such powers as the Universities and the Councils of Medical Registration in different provinces have given us for the purpose of developing medical education in our own way". Dr Roy concluded his speech with the assertion that the Association had an important role in the ongoing political struggle of that time: " ...It has been asked often whether a member of the profession should interest himself in any matter outside the four corners of his professional life, whether this Association should take up matters which, in common parlance, are dubbed political….In India we have never regarded the various affairs of life as being in watertight compartments: politics, technically so called, is intermixed with economic, social and medical problems. If politics means the science of organization for the purpose of securing the greatest good for the largest number, I declare, we members of the profession dare not keep away from politics".[9]

The Rockefeller Foundation (RF) was also interested in promoting 'western medicine' and associated medical practices such as nursing in India.

It focused on plantations in different parts of Asia and Latin America to increase the productivity with scientific inputs, including control of diseases, which affected labour productivity. In India the RF began its activities in 1915, with control of hookworm disease in the tea gardens of Assam, initiated by Heiser. One of the interests of the RF in India was medical education. According to the RF, officials who visited India in that period would be more desirable to co-operate with the Indians than with the British, as education was under the control of Indians. The RF supported the establishment in Calcutta of the All India Institute of Hygiene and Public Health, which was formally opened in 1932. The RF also provided fellowships that enabled Indians to receive training in laboratories in the United States of America.

Interestingly, vaccine research, development and the production of vaccines in India was an area where institutions which were established here in the same period, started gaining importance and various institutions were being established in the other parts of the world for the same. As recommended by the Plague Committee research, institutes were set up in the early decades of the 20th century. The organization of medical research in India started with vaccine research in British India, with the objective of primarily protecting the imperial army from infectious diseases. The first bacteriological institute in India was founded in 1892 at Agra, followed by the establishment of the King Institute of Preventive Medicine, Madras, and the Haffkine Institute, Bombay, both in 1898; the Central Research Institute, Kasauli, in 1905, and the Pasteur Institute, Coonoor in 1907. There were also a few private companies that produced vaccines and sera, such as Bengal Chemicals and Pharmaceuticals, Bengal Immunity, and Smith Strain Street and Co. all in Calcutta. Indigenous vaccines and sera were produced against rabies, tetanus, diphtheria, pertussis, cholera, smallpox, typhoid and anti-snake venom. India was considered to be at par with the rest of the world in vaccine technology till the 1930s.

In the process of putting in place the public health structure described above, while the Sanitary Commissioners had inadequate support, the main emphasis continued to be on the development of medical relief, based on the system of western medicine. It received much more attention than the development of those preventive health measures which were collectively termed as 'public health activities', which too was derived from modern medicine.

Interestingly, the Director-General of the Indian Medical Service in the early 1930s argued that excessive reliance on medical intervention was 'one-sided' and 'dangerous'. That 'even if public health services were to achieve success in stamping out malaria, cholera, tuberculosis and other diseases, there would still be deaths from starvation if nothing was done to increase the production of food or restrict the growth of the population'.[10]

This points to the important issue of the occurrence of famines in the colonial period and their impact on the nutrition, and the health of the Indian population. In fact, the close link between famine and/or economic (agricultural) crisis and soaring malaria mortality was a frequent reference in the historical records of the pre-1910 colonial period. Most provincial sanitary commissioners throughout the 19th and early 20th century began their annual reports by quoting the price of staple food grains, followed by the wage rates, and then the state of the harvests. The then prevailing economic conditions were thus seen as central to interpreting the data on vital statistics that were given in their report. Most famine inquiries of the late 19th century refer specifically to the selectively greater malaria mortality among the starving.

As in England, in the Indian sub-continent too, linkages between ill-health and factors such as food availability, poverty, and urban living conditions, were raised by certain sections of the colonial administration. However, the public health here too was restricted to environmental hygiene, to sanitary and other technical/legal measures. So the model adopted here was that of 'assimilation and application of knowledge of medical science' to public health, as had happened in Great Britain and other industrialized Western countries.

II

❑ 1950s to 1980s: Planning for Healthcare Services Through Five-Year Plans and Committee Recommendations

Various political groups participating in the nationalist movement drew up plans in the 1940s for development of health services, as part of their overall planning for the economic development of the country. In 1938 the National Planning Committee of the Indian National Congress set up a sub-committee on Health, known as Sokhey Committee. There were three other plans namely, the Gandhian Plan of Economic Development, the Bombay Plan of Economic Development, and the People's Plan of Economic Development of the Indian Federation of Labour. Except for the Bombay Plan, the other two focused on agriculture and health of the rural people. The Bombay Plan focused on urban services for industrial growth and proposed to deal with rural problems through proper instructions and education, and a well-organized propaganda. Interestingly, the system of medical and health care envisaged by all these plans was also based upon modern medicine, and along similar lines namely that of a network of dispensaries for rural areas, maternal and child health centres, and hospitals for urban areas, to be staffed by trained doctors and nurses. It was not very different from that of the Bhore Committee set up by the colonial government.

The Sokhey Committee report, submitted in 1948, stressed that the maintenance of the health of the people was the responsibility of the state, and called for integration of curative and preventive functions in a single state agency. It recommended a scheme of having large number of community health workers with training in practical community and personal hygiene, first aid and simple medical treatment, with stress on social aspects; for drawing in Ayurveda and Unani practitioners, and self-reliance. This committee endorsed the findings and recommendations of the Bhore Committee that had submitted its report in 1946.

Post-1947 - Bhore Committee: Idea of a National Health Service System

The British government too set up the Health Survey and Development Committee in 1944 to make (1) a broad survey of the existing position in regard to health conditions and health organization in British India; and (2) recommendations for future development. The need for such a survey had arisen from the need to make plans for postwar development in the health field. The report of this Committee, popularly known as the Bhore Committee in four volumes, gives a picture of the state of public health and of the existing health organization in the country in the years preceding the Second World War, and made detailed recommendations and measures for setting up a national health system in the country.

The Bhore Committee was influenced by the development of national health systems in countries such as the erstwhile Soviet Union and England, wherein the trend was that of provision by the State to provide a complete health service which was treated as a matter of right. According to the Report in drawing up a health plan, in the first place certain primary conditions which are essential for healthful living must be ensured. These were:

- Provision of adequate health protection to all covering both curative and preventive aspects, irrespective of their ability to pay for it.
- Improvement of nutritional standards qualitatively and quantitatively.
- Suitable housing, sanitary surroundings, and safe drinking water.
- Elimination of unemployment.
- Provision of a living wage for all workers.
- Improvement in agricultural and industrial production and means of communications, particularly in rural areas.

In addition, the measures for a healthy community life and for physical and mental recreation must also receive serious consideration. There must be practical co-operation of the people themselves in the improvement of public health. It concluded that:

> "Under the conditions existing in the country, the medical services should be free to all without distinction and that the contribution from those who can afford to pay should be through the channel of general and local taxation. It will be for the governments of the

future to ultimately decide whether medical service should remain free to all classes of people or whether an insurance scheme would be more in accordance with the economic, social and political requirements of the country at the time".[11]

The Bhore Committee envisioned a National Health Service system for a provision of comprehensive primary health care. Some of the salient features of this system were to be:

- It would provide universal coverage, free of charges, through a comprehensive,[12] state-run, salaried health service.
- No individual should fail to secure adequate medical care, curative and preventive, because of inability to pay.
- It was planned for rural population.
- Services to be as close as possible to people in order to ensure their maximum use by the community.
- The district as the unit, and the district health scheme to be organized in a three-tier unit.
- Special provisions will be required for certain sections of the population, such as mothers, children, mentally disabled.
- Health organization to be such so as to provide for co-operation between health personnel and people.
- There should be no attempt to isolate and implement specific parts of the plan, on grounds of lack of funds, as component parts were inter-related.

Given the need for a vast health service for the largely rural population and the difficulty experienced in the past in attracting medical practitioners to the countryside, it concluded that the most satisfactory way of meeting the situation was to provide a whole-time salaried service, which would enable government to ensure that doctors are made available where their services are most needed. It also concluded that these whole-time salaried doctors employed by the State should be prohibited from private practice. If private practice by these State employed doctors was not prohibited, their preventive duties in the peripheral institutions would not receive adequate attention. It suggested scales of pay to provide adequate remuneration for their services. The Doctor, the leader of the health team should be a 'social physician', who should combine remedial and preventive measures, and the future doctors should be trained to equip them for all such duties.

The health plan was drawn up in two parts – one a comprehensive long-term programme for the somewhat distant future (also known as the three million plan), and the other a short-term programme covering two five-year periods.

The recommendations were rather comprehensive: they addressed subjects such as health services (which included services for specific diseases, for mother and children, dental services, etc), occupational health, environmental hygiene (issues such as town and village planning, housing, water supply, general sanitation, and vector control), nutrition, medical education and research, requirements of drugs and medical equipment, establishment of standards for medical institutions and equipment, measures to address the "population problem", regulation of the medical and related professions, and budget for such a health service system.

The Committee stressed the organic unity of the component parts of the programme it had put forward. According to the Committee, "Large scale provision for the training of health personnel forms an essential part of the scheme ... Side by side with such training of personnel, we have provided for the establishment of a health organization which will bring remedial and preventive services within the reach of the people, particularly of that vast section of the community lies scattered over the rural areas and which has, in the past, been largely neglected from the point of view of health protection on modern lines. We have drawn attention to these aspects of the health programme because we feel that it is highly desirable that the plan should be accepted and executed in its entirety. We would strongly deprecate any attempt, on the plea of lack of funds, to isolate specific parts of the scheme and to give effect to them without taking into consideration the inter-relationships of the component parts of the programme. Our conception of the process of development of the national health services is that is will be a co-operative effort in which the Centre, acting with imagination and sympathy, will assist and guide a co-ordinated advance in the Provinces. We therefore look forward to a pooling of resources and of personnel, as far as circumstances permit, in the joint task that lies before the Governments".

While the Bhore Committee made such detailed suggestions for the organization of the government health services, however, it did not say anything about private practitioners and private hospitals/institutions, their place in the health system they envisaged, and their regulation.

It is important to take note of the position of the Bhore Committee regarding the indigenous systems of medicine.[13] It acknowledges that these systems have played a part in the long distant past in influencing the developing of medicine and surgery in other countries of the world. However, it goes on to say, "We do, however, say quite definitely that there are certain aspects of health protection which, in our opinion can be secured wholly or at any rate, largely, only through the scientific system of medicine. Thus, public health or preventive medicine, which must play an essential part in the future of medical organization, is not within the purview of the indigenous systems of medical treatment as they obtain at present. This in no way reflects upon these systems. It has, however, to be recognized that great improvements have taken place in the field of public health as the result of many discoveries of science, which are and can be implemented only through the scientific system of medicine, and through personnel trained in such a system.... It is necessary to prominently keep before our eyes the intimate relation between science and the advancement of medicine... no system of medical treatment which is static in conception and practice, and does not keep pace with the discoveries and researches of scientific workers the world over, can hope to give the best available ministration to those who seek its aid... [Modern medicine] must be regarded as neither Eastern nor Western but as a corpus of scientific knowledge and practice belonging to the whole world and to which every country has made its contribution".

Thus, the Bhore Committee clearly favoured the Western medicine for medical relief, as also for public health activities. It also envisaged public health as part of medical organization. It was this Report, and not any of the others that had been made by the Indian nationalist groups, which became the basis for the health system in India after 1947.

The Chopra Committee on the Indigenous Systems of Medicine (1946) was set up to rectify the marginalization of those in the Bhore Committee, which recommended a mutual learning between allopathy and the indigenous systems; and that some practitioners of each should impart education in the other systems, and an attempt be made to evolve an integrated knowledge system.

In the post-World War II period, the newly independent states of Africa and Asia undertook a programme of planned economic transition to development, within a liberal-welfarist approach. In 1950, the new government embarked upon a planned effort for economic progress and development of the country. Economic progress was to mean much more than building up an efficient apparatus for production of material goods; it also encompassed provision of social services, widening of opportunities for the common people, social equality and justice. Development Planning was adopted to achieve the social objectives enshrined in the Constitution, to bring about economic growth and development, to promote a rapid rise in the standard of living of all the people, by efficient exploitation of the resources of the country, by increasing production, and offering opportunities to all for employment in the service of the community. The overall objective was rapid economic development oriented towards establishing social justice, by refashioning existing economic and social institutions.

Health planning was made an integral part of the overall planning for socio-economic development. In the initial years the planners recognized the need for addressing the problems of unemployment, malnutrition, social justice, housing and environmental sanitation, along with the need for developing integrated health services for the entire population. Within the health sector of the developing countries such as India the vision and goal was that of universal provision of curative, preventive and promotive health services by the state, by creating and extending primary healthcare infrastructure, especially in the rural areas where much of the population lived.

1950s-1970s: Vertical Programs versus Comprehensive Primary Health Care: Increasing Rural-Urban Gap In Infrastructure

The Five Year Plan (FYP) recommendations of various Committees, and proceedings of the Central Council of Health and Family Welfare, have largely provided the framework for development of health services infrastructure, medical education and research.[14] The Five Year Plans have, by and large, looked upon the health sector as constituted by various schemes that had targets to be fulfilled. Each Plan gives a picture of the state of affairs and progress, the focus areas/plans for the period under consideration, of the various components placed under the health sector, and the financial outlays. It was not until 1983 that India adopted a formal or an official National Health Policy, which was revised in 2002.

The First FYP (1951-56) proposed the following health services:

- Network of peripheral primary health units to provide both preventive and curative services.
- Secondary units and district units to provide better and more complete facilities.
- Mobile dispensaries to be associated with these rural health units in order to provide medical care and specialists services to the rural population.
- Population control to be a part of the public health programme.

With respect to finances, the plan proposed that the Central government would be responsible for the overall development of primary health services in the country as a whole, for higher education and research, for specific programmes; while local authorities would execute medical and public health programmes.

The priorities for the first plan period were:

- Provision of water-supply and sanitation.
- Control of malaria.
- Preventive health care of the rural population through health units and mobile units.
- Health services for mothers and children.
- Education, training, and health education.
- Self-sufficiency in drugs and equipment.
- Family planning and population control.

In the 1950s the Primary Health Centres (PHCs) were established as part of the broader strategy of rural development through the Community Development Programme (CDP). The CDP was to address agriculture, rural industry, education, communication, transport, nutrition, sanitation, and water supply. The PHC was to provide a curative, preventive, promotive services, and hence its functions covered: provision of medical care, control of communicable diseases, promotion of maternal and child health; collection of vital statistics; protection of water supply and promotion of environmental sanitation; conducting school health programmes; and providing family planning services.

Attempts were also made to bring about a social orientation of education and training of health workers, and to make them more relevant to the conditions prevalent in the country. An upgraded department of preventive and social medicine was established in medical colleges, and was expected to provide a wider academic base than the conventional hygiene, public health, and a social-cultural-economic context to clinical medicine.

While the Bhore Committee and the initial plans proposed development of the district level integrated health unit, the practice was at variance with these proposals. In the 1950s and the 1960s the entire focus of the health sector in India was on management of epidemics. As communicable diseases formed the bulk of the health problems back then, in view of the limited resources, it was considered best to tackle them initially through separate mass campaigns, each campaign directed against a single disease. The national programs were launched for eradication of several communicable diseases. The international agencies supported this approach and separate countrywide campaigns with a techno-centric approach were launched against malaria, smallpox, tuberculosis, leprosy, filaria, trachoma and cholera. Separate cadres of workers were trained in each of these vertical programmes. They were termed 'vertical programs' as each of them was run through a single-purpose, country-wide organization, each with an independent line of command from national to village level. The National Malaria Eradication Programme (NMEP) alone required the training of 150,000 workers spread over 400 units for the prevention and curative aspects of malaria control. These campaigns tended to be highly techno-centric, owing to availability of 'miracle' tools like DDT (Dichloro Diphenyl Trichloroethane), BCG (Bacille Calmette Guerin), and small pox vaccines, mass X-ray units and chemotherapeutic drugs like streptomycin, and penicillin.

The policy of launching mass campaigns was in continuation with the policy of colonialists who subscribed to the ideas then of modern medicine that health could be looked after if the germs which were causing it were removed. In the first two Plans, the bulk of the resources which were allocated for the health outlay was for these programs. These programs depended on international agencies like UNICEF, WHO and the Rockefeller Foundation for supplies of necessary chemicals and vaccines. Along with financial aid came political and ideological influence. Experts of various international agencies decided the entire policy framework, programme design, and financial commitments etc.

In that period malaria was considered an international threat. The NMEP was started in 1953 with an aid from the Technical Cooperation Mission of the USA and technical advice of the WHO. The DDT spraying operations were one of the most important activities of this programme.

The tuberculosis programme involved vaccination with BCG, TB clinics, and domiciliary services and after care. The emphasis however was on prevention through BCG.

The Mudaliar Committee, set up in 1959 to evaluate the progress made in the first two plans and to make recommendations for further development of health services, recorded that the disease control programmes had some substantial achievements in controlling certain virulent epidemic diseases. Malaria was considered to be under control. The deaths due to malaria, cholera, smallpox etc., were halved or sharply reduced and the overall morbidity and mortality rates had declined. The death rate had fallen to 21.6% for the period 1956-61, and life expectancy had risen to 42 years. The Mudaliar Committee also recorded that the PHC programme was not given the importance it should have been given right from the start. Most of the PHCs were understaffed, large numbers of them were being run by ANM's or public health nurses in charge. The fact was that the doctors were going into private practice after training at the public's expense. The condition of the secondary and district hospitals was the same as that of the PHCs. The report showed that the majority of the beds and various facilities were located in the urban areas. The Committee recommended that in the immediate future instead of expansion of PHCs, consolidation should take place and then a phased upgrading and equipping of the district hospitals with mobile clinics for the treatment of non- PHC population. But the urban health infrastructure continued to increase to meet the growing demands for medical care and this was where the state government's funds were getting committed. An important observation of this Committee was that dealing individually with diseases such as tuberculosis, small pox, cholera, leprosy and filariasis would not be conducive to the organization of unified efforts that would be needed for promotion of total health care. According to this Committee the health personnel engaged in such mass campaigns must be trained to tackle all health problems in any area; it was neither possible nor desirable to have separate agencies to deal with separate diseases.

It also suggested measures to improve the service condition of doctors and other personnel in order to attract them to rural areas, and recommended promoting education in the Indian systems of medicine; and giving attention to tribal and backward areas, such as suitable tribal student to be selected even while at school for training as doctors, duty in tribal areas for limited areas should be made compulsory for members of the Central and State Health services.

The Third Five Year Plan (1961-66) also highlighted inadequacy of health care institutions, doctors and other personnel in rural areas as being the major shortcomings at the end of the second Five Year Plan. While the third plan did give serious consideration to the need for more auxiliary personnel, no mention was made of any specific steps to reach this goal. In the actual training and establishment of institutions for these people, inadequate funding became the constant obstacle. On the other hand, the proposed outlays for new medical colleges, establishment of preventive and social medicine and psychiatric departments, completion of the All India Institute of Medical Sciences (AIIMS), and schemes for upgrading departments in medical colleges for post graduate training and research continued to be at a high. The plan also suggested "that a new short term course for the training of medical assistants should be instituted and after these assistants had worked for five years at a PHC they could complete their education to become full-fledged doctors and continue in public service". The Medical Council and the doctors lobbied to oppose this and hence it was not taken up seriously.

Ignoring the Mudaliar Committee's recommendation of consolidation of PHCs this plan period witnessed a rapid increase in PHCs numbers but there was not much improvement in their condition. However, there was an army of special uni-purpose health workers under the vertical programmes. In the same geographical area there was an overlap and duplication of work.

The major diseases affecting the Indian population, such as diarrhoea, amoebic dysentery, cholera, typhoid, and jaundice were water borne, and they also spread due to lack of basic sanitation. To address this problem in 1960 the National Water Supply and Sanitation Committee (Simon Committee) was formed to review the progress made under the national programmes in the first two plans.

India was the first country in the world to adopt a policy of reducing population growth through a government sponsored Family Planning (FP) program in 1951. In the first two plans, the FP program was mainly run through voluntary organizations, under the umbrella of Family Planning Association of India. The program was guided by the Central and State Family Planning Boards. Faced with a rising birth rate and a falling death rate, the Third Plan stated that "the objective of stabilizing the growth of population over a reasonable period must therefore be at the very center of planned development". Hence it was stated that greatest stress has to be placed in the Third and subsequent Plans on the program of family planning, through intensive education, provision of facilities and advice on the largest scale possible and widespread popular effort in every rural urban community. Family planning was to be undertaken, not merely as a major development programme, but as a nation-wide movement. In this, the central feature was to be the integration of family planning with the normal medical and health services, especially those rendered through the primary health centres. To an extent, such services could also be made available through voluntary agencies, mobile units, industrial and other establishments. The distribution of simple contraceptives and general advice could be entrusted in a much larger measure to voluntary organizations, to paramedical personnel and to people specially trained in family planning work. In the urban areas it was proposed that greater use should be made of private medical practitioners in providing advice, distributing supplies and, to the extent possible, in undertaking sterilization. It was during this period that the camp approach was tried out and government agencies began to actively participate in pushing population control. Family Planning became an independent department in the Ministry of Health. The heavy emphasis on population control was due to the influence of various developed countries, but especially the United States of America. In 1966 a UN advisory mission visiting India strongly recommended that the directorate (health and family planning) should be relieved from other responsibilities such as maternal and child health, and nutrition.

This was a fundamental change in India's health policy. This policy change, though it had its own inner compulsions, was more so due to the influence of foreign agencies. To endorse this strategy The Special Committee to Review the Staffing Pattern and Financial Provision under Family Planning was appointed also known as the Mukherjee Committee. This Committee indicated that the camp approach had failed to give the family planning program a mass character and hence the availability of the Intra-Uterine Contraceptive Device (IUCD) was a great opportunity. This committee recommended introduction of target fixation, payments for motivation and incentives to acceptors. It suggested reorganization of the FP program into a vertical program like Malaria.

The Chadha Committee in 1963 and the Committee on Integration of Health Services in 1967 recommended the integration of health and family planning services. The idea of integration of preventive and curative services was first mooted in 1937 in India. According to the latter Committee, an integrated health service would have a unified approach for all problems instead of a segmented approach for different problems, and medical care of the sick and conventional public health programs should function under a single administrator and operated in a unified manner at all levels of hierarchy with due priority for each program obtained at a point of time. According to the Committee parallel services, whatever may be the historical reasons, they are wasteful and are primarily the result of lack of planning or bad planning. Among the advantages of integrated services was that they laid the basis for comprehensive health service and the health of the total community was looked after more effectively and more economically. The Committee foresaw that attempts at unification would be resisted; and many virtues of separate cadres would be invoked.

The Fourth Plan (1970-1975) continued on the same line as the third plan. The importance of PHCs was felt to consolidate the maintenance phase of the communicable diseases programme. This was due to the fact that the entire epidemiological trend was reversed in 1966 with the spurt in incidence of malaria which rose from 100,000 cases annually between 1963-65 to 149,102 cases. The FP continued to get more emphasis with 42% of health sector plan allocation going to it. During this period the water supply and sanitation were separated and allocations were made separately under the sector of Housing and Regional development.

Committee on Multipurpose Workers (Kartar Singh Committee) 1972

We see that through the 1960s and 1970s the vertical programs in health, family planning and nutrition were being run almost independently of each other by staff recruited under each; there was little or no co-ordination between the field workers of these programs and even at the supervisory level. In 1972 the government constituted a Committee to study the question of feasibility of having multi-purpose workers in the field. The Committee found that clearly people were not happy with so many workers visiting their houses and making enquiries for individual programs. The community leaders were of the opinion that a single worker delivering both health and family planning services would be more welcome. It was also mentioned that the existing health & family planning workers were not able to provide remedies even for simple ailments like headaches, cuts and burns, and the village people had to resort to either the village quack or trudge long distances to get relief at the PHC. The ANMs and malaria and small-pox workers, all endorsed this view, and further added that their acceptability to the community would be increased if they were in a position to provide a rudimentary treatment for minor ailments.

According to this Committee having multi-purpose workers for delivery of health, family planning and nutrition service to the rural communities was both feasible and possible. After an integrated training, each health worker should be given a first-aid kit and also some medicines for minor ailments. These medicines should be replenished at regular intervals. The workers must be taught when to refer cases beyond their competence to the PHC doctor. It recommended that each PHC (covering a population of 50,000) should have at least two doctors, wherein one of them should be a female. This Multi-Purpose Workers' Scheme was launched in 1974, with the objective of re-orienting uni-purpose workers serving in vertical public health programmes like malaria control, etc., into multipurpose health workers.

As mentioned in the previous section, during the colonial period the early leaders in modern medicine, also prominent in nationalist politics, had called for an inclusive medical registration system and the admission of indigenous practitioners in the medical association. However, in the course of the dispute over the formation of an all-India medical council, it became clear that international recognition of medical degrees by the General Medical Council in London depended on a very clear distinction between doctors trained in western medicine and the rest. By the mid-1930s many of these medical practitioner-leaders withdrew their support for indigenous medicine and took up positions in the new Indian Medical Council, which excluded indigenous practitioners. Thus, 'the future of western medicine came to lie, not with the English colonizers, but with India's emerging elites, who took it up after 1914, as part of their own hegemonic project'.[15] The adoption of 'western' medicine by the Indian middle-classes and the training received by those who went to the West had created an elite class of medical practitioners. They reproduced those patterns of education and thinking, continued to maintain their professional links, and all this was only reinforced and strengthened in the post-1947 period. Given that some of these medical practitioners had also been active in the nationalist politics, it was this system that got state patronage, as clearly enunciated by the Bhore Committee. State promotion and patronage for 'western' medicine continued after the colonial period, and also received support from various western institutions and foundations. Thus, the hegemony of western medicine was retained and extended by influential sections of the nationalist leadership and the medical profession after 1947. Since then the state and these elites took over the task of modernizing the country, through modern medicine and through modern science and technology. India received aid and grants in the early years of Independence for the health sector from several institutions such as WHO and private foundations from the west such as Rockefeller and Ford Foundations, largely towards research and training. In the post-Independence period too, India received grants from Rockefeller Foundation (RF) to varying institutions to aid research. The combined outcome of all these actions was such that by the early 1970s the government was trying to address the issue of the essentially urban orientation of medical education in India, which heavily relied on curative methods and sophisticated diagnostic aids.

Group on Medical Education and Support Manpower (Srivastava Committee) 1974

Although the number of doctors had steadily increased over the successive plan periods, the alienation of these doctors from the rural environment had deprived the rural communities of total medical care. The Fifth Plan had stated that teaching in medical colleges required a radical change. The undergraduate medical education would have to be re-oriented towards the needs of the country and emphasis would have to be placed on community care rather than hospital care. A change in the structure of medical education was therefore called for to meet the changing requirements and to provide adequately for future needs, particularly of the rural community. At the same time, improvement in the delivery of health services by integration of health, family welfare and nutrition services though multi-purpose workers was also being attempted. Keeping these in mind the government set up a Group on Medical Education and Support Manpower to devise a suitable curriculum for training a cadre of Health Assistants, and to suggest suitable ways and means for implementation of recommendations of earlier Committees on Medical Education.

This Committee felt that in spite of the substantial investments made and the impressive results particularly in the field of medical manpower, the health status of the Indian people was still far from satisfactory. It put forth a framework for development of a universal and an egalitarian health service for India. It admitted that so long as stark poverty persisted, the benefits of even the meager investments made in the health services would not reach the people. Hence there was no alternative to making a direct, sustained and vigorous attack on the problem of mass poverty and for creation of a more egalitarian society. A nation-wide program of health services should be developed side by side as it would support this major national endeavour and be supported by it in turn.

The committee also pointed out that 'the over-emphasis on provision of health services through professional staff under state control has been counter-productive. On the one hand, it is devaluing and destroying the old traditions of part-time semi-professional workers, which the community used to train and throw up and proposed that with certain modifications it can continue to provide the foundation for the development of a national program of health services in our country. On the other hand, the new professional services provided under state control are inadequate in quantity and unsatisfactory in quality. With regard to medical education the committee cried for a halt to opening of new medical colleges and emphasized that there was no point in thinking that doctors would go to rural areas because there were a number of socio-economic dimensions to this issue. Thus, the option for rural areas was the Community Health Worker (CHW) scheme.

The Committee suggested having para-professional or semi-professional health workers from the community itself to provide simple preventive, promotive and curative health services which are needed by the community. It also recommended having a referral services complex, in which the PHCs as well as taluk/tehsil, district, regional and medical college hospitals should each develop living and direct links with the community around them well as with one another within a total referral services complex. Finally, it recommended the establishment of a Medical and Health Education Commission.

In the Fifth Plan period (1975-80) there was a re-thinking on the social, and technological basis of the development of health services. The government acknowledged that despite advances in terms of infant mortality rate going down, life expectancy going up, the number of medical institutions, functionaries, beds, health facilities etc., were still inadequate in the rural areas. There was serious dissatisfaction with existing model of hospitals, specialties and super specialties and highly trained doctors which were limited to urban areas mainly for well-to-do lifestyle. An attempt to search for alternative models was made with the Srivastava Committee recommendations to train health workers from the community, to link this basic services within the community with the infrastructure of dispensaries and hospitals through a well-organized referral system.

In accordance with the recommendations of the Study Group on Medical Education and Support Manpower (1975) two centrally sponsored schemes *viz.*, (1) Community Health Workers and (2) Re-orientation of Medical Education were initiated in 1977. These schemes were to be continued in the Plan.

In October 1977 the Community Health Worker (CHW) scheme was introduced with the objective of providing a trained community health volunteer selected by the community itself for every village or a population of 1000 people. These were part time workers selected by the village, who were then trained for three months in simple promotive and curative skills, both in allopathy and indigenous systems of medicine. They were to be supervised by MPWs, and the programme was started in 777 selected PHCs where MPWs were already in place.[16]

Reorientation of Medical Education

The scheme for Re-Orientation of Medical Education (ROME) was introduced with the objectives of:

1. Introducing community bias in the training of undergraduate medical students with emphasis on preventive and promotive services.
2. Re-orientation of the role of medical colleges so that they became an integral part of the health-care system and did not continue to function in isolation.
3. Re-orientation of all faculty members so that hospital-based and disease-oriented training was progressively complemented by community-based and health-oriented training for providing comprehensive primary health care.
4. The development of effective referral linkages between PHCs, District Hospitals and Medical Colleges.

The scheme was implemented in its first phase, in about 106 medical colleges. In spite of a one-time grant-in-aid of about ₹16 lakh to each of the participating institutions, the objectives of the scheme could not be achieved to the desired extent. This was largely due to (1) a lack of commitment to the programme at all levels, (2) slow progress in the utilization of Central funds, and (3) absence of efforts in the restructuring of teaching and training programmes at the college levels.

The Minimum Needs Programme (MNP) was introduced in the first year of the Fifth Five Year Plan, to provide basic minimum needs and improve living standards. The basic needs identified for this programme were Elementary Education, Adult Education, Rural Health, Rural Roads, Rural Electrification, Rural Housing, Environmental Improvement of Urban Slums, and Nutrition. The health infrastructure was to be strengthened and expanded through this MNP.

Shortage of Doctors for Rural Areas and the Steps to Address This in the Sixth Plan Period

Despite the high yearly turnout of medical graduates and growing unemployment among them, in several States, doctors were not available to serve in the rural primary health centres/hospitals. The Centrally Sponsored Scheme of Re-orientation of Medical Education was to be continued and the present deficiencies noted in the implementation of the schemes set right. The Medical Council of India has also prescribed service in rural medical institutions for six months as part of the compulsory internship. In addition, reforms in other directions like modification of the curriculum, training of medical under-graduates in certain fields relevant to the problems of rural health care, community orientation etc, were to be given an adequate attention in the Sixth Plan. The other measures proposed to address the shortage of doctors for rural areas were mainly incentives to work in rural areas, and steps to encourage private practitioners to work in rural areas.

In the middle of the Fifth Plan a State of National Emergency was proclaimed and during this period (1975-77) population control activities were stepped up, with compulsion, force and violence characterizing the FP program. In the midst of all this the National Population Policy was announced whose core aim was a "direct assault on the problem of population rise as a national commitment." This was a stark contrast to the statement made at the Bucharest Population summit in 1974 by the erstwhile health minister that "development was the best contraceptive."

Overall, it is seen that between 1950 to 1965 there was a period of growth at several levels of health services. Medical colleges with tertiary-level hospitals, advanced research institutions and Primary Health Centres (PHCs) were set up, while sub-centres at the village level lagged behind. Vertical disease control programmes grew while general health services received inadequate attention. Similarly, courses in college for medical education grew while training of nursing and other health personnel lagged behind. A significant number of institutions of indigenous medicine and homoeopathy were set up, but with nominal resources as compared to the allopathic institutions. From 1966-1980, there was a growth of village level services with the institution of several village health worker schemes and some feeble attempts to Re-Orient Medical Education (ROME scheme) to rural conditions. A massive program of expansion of primary health care facilities was undertaken in the sixth and seventh Five Year Plans. Yet, all plans and recommendations for an integrated, comprehensive health service have largely remained on paper, and the focus has remained on single-issue programmes. Among vertical programmes too, the Family Planning programme has occupied centre-stage, and larger proportion of the resources.

Vertical Programmes: Significance and Impact – Alma Ata Declaration on Comprehensive Primary Health Care

Few issues relating to the organization of health systems and service delivery have been discussed so much as the pros and cons of vertical versus integrated health programmes. Vertical programmes involve an exclusive/

selective targeting of specific interventions against a specific disease or problem through a single-purpose machinery, and they are not fully integrated in the health systems. In vertical approaches (also referred to as stand-alone, disease management or disease control programmes), interventions are provided through delivery systems that typically have separate administration and budgets. In the integrated model (also known as horizontal approaches or programmes), services do not have separate administration or budgets and are typically delivered through health facilities that provide routine or general health services.

The debate on the comparative effectiveness of vertical versus more systemic approaches can be traced back to the 1960s, and it has persisted and emerged time and again, such as following the 1978 Declaration of Alma-Ata on primary health care; in the 1980s with the success of the smallpox eradication programme; and with the proposal of the 1993 *World Development Report: Investing in Health for "Essential Packages of Care"*. More recently, the debate has been rekindled due to the growth in funding which were targeted at specific diseases and services, from sources such as the Global Fund to Fight AIDS, Tuberculosis and Malaria (GFATM) and WHO's emphasis on strengthening health systems and primary care.

The arguments for vertical programmes are, in the main, driven by the assumption that concentrating on a few well-focused interventions is an effective way to maximize the effect and time response of the available resources rather than waiting for changes in the health system so that the delivery of better services would be viable. The arguments against vertical programmes tend to assert that they are value driven, often have limited chance of sustainability and have negative spillover effects on health systems and non-targeted populations. Despite the wide-ranging discussion over the past 50 years, evidence on the relative benefits of vertical versus integrated service delivery is limited.

The Vertical programs have had a major influence on the development of health services in India. In the 1940s–50s it was thought that a unipurpose mass campaign approach, involving a single line of command was the most effective mechanism for tackling several communicable diseases that accounted for substantial mortality and morbidity then, such as small pox, malaria, tuberculosis, filariasis, etc. The programs for control or eradication of communicable diseases were taken up on lines of a military operation, involving preparation for the operation (Preparatory Phase), launching a strong attack on the disease (the enemy) (Attack Phase), consolidating the gains made through the attack (Consolidation Phase), and surveillance to ensure that the disease does not come back (Maintenance Phase). Vertical approaches to public health problems were favoured by WHO, international aid agencies, and the technical co-operation missions of the industrialized countries of the West. They presented opportunities to provide 'services of experts', supply equipment, drugs, insecticides, and vehicles. While India was dependent on these foreign sources for vital supplies for the programs, it had to bear bulk of the costs for such programs. Vertical programs were also favored by the local political leadership as they gave results within a short time for widely prevalent problems, and offered a simpler alternative to establishing a permanent network of comprehensive health services across the country. Except for the National Smallpox Eradication Program, other mass campaigns have not yielded the expected results. While there are several reasons for the failure of these vertical programs, a major casualty has been the stunted development of a comprehensive health infrastructure across the country. The preoccupation with running of vertical programs has lead to neglecting the development of permanent network of health institutions in the rural areas and diversion of the inadequate human resources to these programs. In turn, the weaknesses in the general health infrastructure have made it difficult to maintain a disease at a low level of incidence after the attack and consolidation phases of a program.

After many such expensive failures and loss of time, it was finally accepted by the administration and political establishment that a permanent rural health infrastructure employing multi-purpose workers was a better alternative to mobile units with uni-purpose workers. However, before the health system could recover from the pernicious impact of the vertical programs, an even more extensive program was launched in the form of the Family Planning Program.

The Declaration of Alma Ata on Primary Health Care was an outcome at the international level of the adverse impacts of vertical programs of the 1960s in many parts of the world, and the general disillusionment with modern medicine in the 1970s and its 'inability to address the needs of the developing countries'. The Alma Ata Declaration together with the slogan of "Health for All by 2000 AD" (HFA) proposed at the 1976 World Health Assembly, is considered to be the major public health initiative of the 20th century. It was made at the International Conference on Primary Health Care, jointly sponsored by two UN organizations – WHO and UNICEF, and held at Alma Ata (now known as Almaty), Kazakhstan, in erstwhile USSR.

The priority of WHO in the 1950s and 1960s was the eradication of malaria which was largely promoted by the U.S government, and also control of certain other communicable diseases. Criticism of the malaria eradication program began in the 1960s from those who felt that the development of health services was suffering due to the attention being given to malaria. The Soviets took the lead in calling for a review of the campaign, which took place in 1969 and essentially led to the abandonment of the eradication program. The Alma Ata Declaration arose from the observation of failings of the Vertical Programs, as well as the positive results from community health programmes in countries such as Nicaragua, Costa Rica, Guatemala, Honduras, Mexico, India, Cuba, Bangladesh, the Philippines and China (barefoot doctors). In other developing countries, as in India, during 1950s-1970s, it was the period of population control programs and of technological transfer to the less developed countries by the developed countries (S&T assistance as instruments to resolve world poverty). There was questioning of the hospital-centered bio-medical model of healthcare services from many quarters. In that same period Christian medical missionaries had trained villagers as health workers, and the Chinese Cultural Revolution had thrown up the concept of 'barefoot doctors', and there had been large-scale expansion of rural medical services in China. In India too, villagers were being trained as community health volunteers and trained birth attendants, and indigenously formulated programs were being implemented, by non-governmental groups and doctors working in rural areas. In general, the 1960s and 1970s were a period of social ferment, and there were calls and movements for alternative technologies, for 'appropriate' technology, 'intermediate' technology, as also opposition to ideologies of a 'technological imperative'.

The Alma Ata Declaration placed health within a global and political context by calling for peace, reduced military expenditure and a 'New International Economic Order' to reduce the health status gap between developing and developed countries. The main features of the Primary Health Care (PHC) approach that was articulated were: healthcare is a fundamental human right and a responsibility of the government; and has to be equitably distributed; essential health care should be based on practical, scientifically sound and socially acceptable methods and technology, made universally available to the community though their full participation at a cost that the community and country can afford to maintain at every stage in the spirit of self-reliance and self-determination. Furthermore, the PHC approach extended far beyond narrow medical activities to living conditions in general, such as ensuring sufficient food, water, sanitation, etc. In the years immediately after Alma Ata, the District Health System (DHS) model was formulated as an organizational framework for a health care system to deliver the PHC Approach.[17] This PHC approach was to be the means to achieve 'Health For All by 2000 AD'.

As a signatory to this Declaration and as the guidelines enunciated, it provided another opportunity to the Indian government to put in place a system of basic health services (that had been envisaged in the earlier planning periods), based on local needs and capacities (self-reliance), and to shift from use of highly sophisticated medical technology to less sophisticated or locally appropriate ones. However, this did not happen. That the comprehensive proposals of the Alma Ata were never seriously implemented is a well documented fact. On the contrary, the selective PHC approach promoted by international institutions was adopted, which brought in more technological interventions into the rural primary health care system in developing countries, specifically in areas of maternal and child health, and some infectious diseases. These were to be delivered through community health workers.

As pointed out by Banerji, in the *History of Public Health in Western Countries* virtually no such Vertical Programs were employed to tackle communicable diseases. The changes in the ecological conditions brought about by socio-economic development have been the principal factors which led to control or eradication of communicable diseases prevalent there.[18]

(This) focus on the health sector without analysis of the socioeconomic system that determines it assumes an autonomy and near independence of the health sector that is both unempirical and unhistorical. Moreover, it leads to conclusions that are also empirically invalid and ineffective policy-wise. This is most clear in international health studies, where pieces of and individual experiences in the health sector are usually perceived as meriting "export" to other countries. A recent example of this is the present attention given to the Chinese barefoot doctors' experience. Much has been written concerning that use of personnel in the People's Republic of China. Consequent to that interest many national and international agencies, including the World Health Organization, are encouraging the export of that specific Chinese experience to other countries. Oblivious of China's socioeconomic determinants that may explain the success of the barefoot doctors, those exporters have tried to transform what is basically a political phenomenon into a mere managed one. Not surprisingly, the export of the Chinese barefoot doctors' experience has failed to grow in those countries where the socioeconomic determinants were different ones. Indeed, that experience assumes and presumes a series of economic and political parameters that determine its success. The purpose in citing this example and many others is not to question the value of international studies, but rather to stress the great importance of analyzing the nature of the health sector within a country's broader economic and political parameters which determine it.[19]

ICSSR-ICMR Study Group on an Alternative Strategy for Health Services in India in 1981

In the late 1970s the two major funding agencies in medical sciences and social sciences, Indian Council of Medical Research (ICMR) and the Indian Council of Social Science Research (ICSSR), respectively came together to prepare an alternative strategy for health services in India. This report stated that for achievement of health for all by the year 2000, a radical change was called for, and it was necessary to develop a comprehensive national policy on health. A major program for the development of health care services, through an alternative model and not by expansion or tinkering with the existing system, was necessary but not sufficient. Simultaneously, there was need for integrated overall development, including family planning; and for improvement in nutrition, environment and health education. The objectives of overall development, through rapid economic growth, were to eliminate poverty and inequality, to spread education, and to enable the poor and underprivileged to assert themselves. The alternative model of health care services was to be strongly rooted in the community and one that replaced the existing "top-down, elite, curative and urban-oriented, centralized and bureaucratized system".

1980s – Rhetoric of comprehensive PHC – Reality of 'Selective' PHC – re-incarnation of Vertical Programmes

The principles of PHC were taken largely from experiences in developing countries of community based health programmes, such as the barefoot doctor experience in China arising from a political and cultural revolution, and in other countries it were part of larger struggles for political reform, for rights and well-being of all, and awareness of social and economic dimensions of poor health. So the implementation of PHC had socio-political implications to an extent that governments had to address the underlying social, economic and political causes of poor health. Despite being a signatory to such principles, it was not implemented seriously by the Indian government.

In 1979, a conference was sponsored by the Rockefeller Foundation with assistance from the World Bank at Bellagio, Italy, with the President of the World Bank, Vice President of Ford Foundation, USAID, and UNICEF officials. This conference advocated an alternative concept to that of the Alma Ata Conference – that of Selective Primary Health Care; meaning limited focus on certain health care interventions, as distinct from comprehensive or holistic health care. The arguments of this group for selective PHC were: that the comprehensive PHC of Alma Ata was too unrealistic and costly, and that it should be postponed. If health statistics were to be improved, high risk groups must be targeted with carefully selected cost-effective interventions for a limited number of diseases. Until health care systems are adequately resourced and organized, it is better to deliver a few proven interventions of high efficacy at high levels of coverage, aimed at diseases responsible for the greatest mortality. Selective PHC was simply a re-incarnation of the earlier 'vertical programmes', and a packaging of the scientific and biomedical orientation that emphasizes the delivery of 'medical technologies' amenable to vertical programmes as the only remedies for disease and illness.

By the early 1980s, WHO, UNICEF and major bilateral donors, notably USAID, also endorsed this selective approach, epitomized by the 'Child Survival Revolution' launched in 1982. This prioritized seven child health interventions: growth monitoring, Oral Rehydration Therapy (ORT), breast-feeding, immunization, family planning, food supplements and female education, which collectively became known as the acronym GOBI-FFF. This emphasis on a limited set of technological interventions detracted attention from a more comprehensive approach to child health that would prevent the occurrence of diseases in the first place. For example, treating children with acute diarrhea disease would not be accompanied by interventions to improve childcare, nutrition of mother and child, or access to clean drinking water. The biomedical orientation resulted in the promotion of manufactured oral rehydration salts rather than more appropriate and accessible rehydration fluids that could be prepared locally. In many countries, the selective health care approach has manifested itself as a set of multiple, parallel programmes, not very different from the vertical programmes of the previous decades.

Although selective health care was advocated on the grounds that basic health care infrastructure is inadequate, it is rarely implemented in conjunction with a plan to strengthen such infrastructure at the same time. As a result, many selective and vertical programmes have short-lived results because they are not accompanied/followed by the establishment of permanent health services to sustain the on-going control and prevention of diseases. In practice, they actually undermine the development of health care systems. Mass immunization campaigns such as the Pulse Polio programme, have been prioritized to such an extent that other services have been disrupted and the long-term development of sustainable routine immunization services have been hindered.[20, 21]

Currently, selective approaches are a prominent feature of the international health policy landscape. Many of the selective health care initiatives now operate as global Public Private Initiatives (PPIs), introducing a much higher level of involvement from the commercial/private sector. This brings in private financing and technical solutions, but at the same time provides the commercial sector with further public subsidies, and the opportunity to capture a share of the resulting market for their products. Some of these global PPIs are Global Polio Eradication Initiative (GPEI), Stop TB, Global Alliance for TB Drug Development, Roll Back Malaria, Global Fund to fight AIDS, Tuberculosis, Malaria (GFATM), and so on.

The **Sixth Plan (1980-85)** conceded that "there is a serious dissatisfaction with the existing model of medical and health services with its emphasis on hospitals, specialization and super specialization and highly trained doctors which is availed of mostly by the well to do classes. It is also realized that it is this model which is depriving the rural areas and the poor people of the benefits of good health and medical services". The plan emphasized the development of a community based health system. The strategies advocated were: (1) provision of health services to the rural areas on a priority basis. (2) the training of a large cadre of first level health workers selected from the community and supervised by MPWs and medical officers of the PHCs. (3) No further linear expansion of curative facilities in urban areas; this would be permitted only in exceptional cases dictated by real need or priority. The objective of strengthening the Health and Family Planning infrastructure was also towards realization of the objectives of family planning and population control.

National Health Policy 1983

The National Health Policy brought together and re-iterated much of the elements of the previous recommendations and the Alma Ata Declaration, and called for an integrated comprehensive approach towards the future development of health services infrastructure, medical education and research.

It observed that between the 1950s and 1970s "a network of dispensaries, hospitals and institutions providing specialized curative care had been established; a large stock of medical and health personnel of various levels were available; and there was significant indigenous capacity for production of drugs, vaccines and hospital equipment". Yet poor health status of the people remained a cause of concern. Along with factors such as poverty, ignorance, and lack of safe drinking water, the high population growth rate was identified as one of the contributory factors for the high mortality and morbidity, and high levels of malnutrition. The adoption of the western model of hospital-based curative care was considered to be inappropriate and irrelevant to the prevailing socio-economic conditions of the country as there was neglect of preventive and promotive aspects of public health and no involvement of the community in the planning, identification, and implementation aspects of the health services. According to this Policy, "To ensure that the approach to healthcare does not merely constitute a collection of disparate health interventions but consists of an integrated package of services seeking to tackle the entire range of poor health conditions on a broad front", there was need to restructure the health services infrastructure based on epidemiological needs, re-orientation of existing health personnel, decentralization, development of the indigenous systems of medicine and their involvement in the overall health system, and a meaningful integration of the indigenous and modern systems of medicine. In addition, there was also a need to phase out private practice by government doctors and a need to utilize the private practitioners and private voluntary organizations particularly in rural areas and urban slums. The NHP 1983 also pointed out that there was a need to pay attention to food distribution systems, to generate productive employment, to improve purchasing power, along with having special schemes to address chronic nutritional disorders.

Over the years, through the five-year plans, the central government has been setting the priorities and targets, financing, and implementing the family planning, immunization, and 19 national disease control programs, and the expansion of primary care services to rural areas under the minimum needs program across the country. Despite the rhetoric to integrate programs and strengthen local decision-making, the funding system has reinforced a series of parallel disease control programs and separation of health and family welfare programs. It has also institutionalized a centrally-based rigid approach for planning of personnel and health facilities based on population norms. Whereas, the state governments have been responsible for the implementation of the national programs and providing curative care through their respective departments of health. So, in practice both the centre and the state are involved in the provision of medical and public health services.

Currently, the role of the central government is as follows:

- Sets policy and legal framework, national goals, develops national health laws.

- Regulates medical and dental education, manages national institutions for medical, nursing, and public health education, training and research, and manages national public health institutions.
- Financing–provides funds to states through taxation revenues, and through funds from external development assistance.
- Provides curative services through national hospitals, clinics and regional cancer hospitals etc., and through services in specialized projects, such as the reproductive and child health projects, tuberculosis, kala azar, etc., which are provided through the three-tier network of rural health centres.
- Provides public health services through 19 National Health Programs implemented through the rural health facilities, and IEC (Information, Education and Communication in Health).

❑ Structure of the Health Services System

The health services system in rural areas is a three-tier system comprising of Sub-Centres (SCs), Primary Health Centres (PHCs), Community Health Centres (CHCs), which are set up on a population basis. The Sub-Centre is the most peripheral facility located in rural area, and first contact point between the primary health care system and the rural community. Each Sub-Centre is required to be staffed by at least one Auxiliary Nurse Midwife (ANM) / Female Health Worker and one Male Health Worker. These workers in the Sub-Centres are assigned tasks relating to communication in order to bring about behavioral change and provide services in relation to maternal and child health, family planning, nutrition, immunization, diarrhea control and control of communicable diseases programmes. Since 2005 there has been a provision for a voluntary, community level health worker (Accredited Social Health Activist - ASHA), who is expected to assist the ANM in her tasks in the village. Unlike all the other health workers, the ASHA does not receive any salary but is paid based on performance/case-basis. The Union Ministry of Health and Family Welfare provides Central assistance to all the Sub-Centres in the country in the form of salary of some staff, rent, drugs for minor ailments, contraceptives, and vaccines. The salary of the Male Worker is borne by the State Government. The PHCs and CHCs are the referral facilities, staffed by doctors and other support staff, and are to be equipped to provide a range of curative services. Together with the District Hospital, these facilities form a referral network, to be equipped to cater to the curative and preventive needs of the population of the district.

The health needs of large urban slum populations in India have been left to the local municipalities. While a metropolitan city such as Delhi will have health departments for provision of health services through big and small municipal hospitals and local clinics, etc., to provide a wide range of services, most municipalities have budget deficits and have difficulty even paying for staff salaries, leaving most curative health care in urban areas to the private sector.

Although a significant expansion of rural healthcare infrastructure did take place during the 1980s, this remained grossly under-utilized because of poor facilities, lack of doctors and support staff, low attendance by medical staff, inadequate supplies, insufficient hours, lack of community involvement and lack of proper monitoring mechanisms. The Primary Healthcare Approach was never implemented in its full form, and selective vertical programmes have been pushed as a substitute for comprehensive health system development. We see that there has been a colossal divergence between the policy rhetoric and actual implementation. At the same time there has been a massive expansion of an unregulated and unaccountable private sector.

III

❑ Private Medical Care Sector

Throughout these years the private sector has grown unchecked to fill in the gap in availability of public health services, with little attempts by the governments to regulate its activities. Government policies in the health sector have always been favourable for the growth of the private sector. There has been direct support in form of customs duty exemption and reduced duties on imported equipment, concessional loans, land at subsidized rates for construction of hospitals, etc. There has been indirect support, by accommodating private interests in the government healthcare sector for purchase of drugs, supplies and equipment, and allowing private practice by government hospital doctors. Since 1990s, the growth of the private sector has taken place through various PPP arrangements, medical tourism, and offering tax holiday for setting up hospitals in tier II cities/towns.

Apart from such direct favourable policies, other reasons indirectly contributing to the huge growth of private medical sector have been:

- Neglect of public services in general, including public health services, leading to stagnation, and quantitatively and qualitatively inadequate services.
- Growth of middle-classes in urban areas, as also in rural areas due to green revolution; subsequent emergence of a 'globalized' middle class, with aspirations different from the large sections of the poor. These classes found the public sector inadequate and moved to the private sector. This class not only comprises a large market for corporate hospitals and the insurance sector but has also justified and pushed neo-liberal moves towards privatization[22].

The private medical care sector in the country is extremely diverse and fragmented. Over the years the private sector has grown phenomenally, as well as diversified its operations. The private sector in India has a dominant presence in all the sub-sectors – namely, medical education and training, medical technology and diagnostics, pharmaceutical manufacture and sale, hospital construction and ancillary services and, finally, in the provisioning of medical care.

The private sector can be characterized in the following ways.

- Based upon training/qualification as Formal Providers or Informal Providers.
- Based upon orientation of the provider(s) as For-Profit and Not-for Profit.

The **Formal for-Profit** can be further classified based upon ownership as:

- Formally qualified as individual practitioners of all systems of medicine, such as allopathy, ayurveda, unani, homeopaths, etc.
- A range of small and big healthcare facilities, namely nursing homes, hospitals, specialty centres, diagnostic laboratories and pharmacies, owned by individual practitioners, or small groups of practitioners, or franchised by larger 'brand' healthcare companies.
- Large corporate hospitals, specialty hospitals, diagnostic and imaging centers, set up by industrial houses or listed on the stock market.

The **Informal for-Profit** sector comprises:

Individual practitioners with no formal training in any particular system, who have picked up skills through apprenticeship with a formally trained practitioner; compounders, practitioners of folk traditions, birth attendants, traditional healers, small chemist shops, quacks; largely located in slums and working class colonies in cities and in villages lacking in any health facility.

The **Not-for-Profit** sector comprises:

Religious organizations, charities, social organizations and other non-governmental institutions that offer a range of health services. These institutions are not motivated by profit, but may impose charges to recover cost of services. Some are dependent upon funding from government or from non-governmental local or overseas sources.

It is only in 2011-12 that the government made steps towards regulation, by enacting the Clinical Establishments Act for registration of private healthcare institutions. However, there are still no effective measures for regulation or monitoring of the private sector, and its quality has never been adequately established in comparison to the public health services. In the absence of regulations for the private sector regarding elements such as location, standards, pricing, nature of care to be provided, private facilities are set up, operate in marketplaces, residences/residential colonies, pharmacy shops, with freedom to provide any kind of service, of whatever quality and at exorbitant cost, which varies from facility to facility. The medical councils of the various systems of medicine perform only the jobs of registering qualified doctors and issuing them the license to practice. There is no monitoring, continuing education, price regulation, etc., either by the councils, or by the government.

The steady corporatization of medical care is another development, not totally unrelated to the liberalization-privatization regime of the early 1990s. Since the early 1990s, when healthcare was seen as a 'sunrise industry', several big corporate houses, Fortis Healthcare (promoted by Ranbaxy Labs), Wockhardt Hospitals (promoted by the pharma company Wockhardt) and Max Healthcare announced plans to set up hospital chains across the country. In addition to these big hospital chains including the oldest one, Apollo Healthcare Enterprises Limited (AHEL), a large number of other private hospitals and specialty facilities, such as for cardiac care, renal care, eye care, laparoscopy, pathological laboratories, imaging facilities, etc., have also come up. The International Finance Corporation (IFC), a member of the World Bank Group, is providing loans for expansion of private hospitals and for setting up hospitals in smaller cities and towns in the country (such as to Apollo, Max and Rockland groups), as part of its strategy to invest in health care, and to promote private sector involvement in healthcare in India.[23]

Increasingly over the past decade, healthcare has come to be viewed as a 'big business opportunity' and an 'engine of growth' and there is much discussion about the rising 'healthcare industry'[24] in India. There is strong advocacy and promotion by the industry of the idea that, "health care infrastructure should not just be viewed as a social good but also as a viable economic venture with productivity". The PPPs are being viewed as having potential to create 'an enormous market with a reliable, multi-year revenue stream for private investors'[25]. In fact the industry views the scenario thus: "*The first wave of healthcare provision in India was the government run healthcare network. The influx of the private players defined the second wave. Now a discerning and interconnected nation demands a new incarnation: Healthcare 3.0, which will transform the ground rules of healthcare...... Healthcare 3.0 will ordain that revenues are linked to patient satisfaction............Seamless public-private partnerships will be the backbone of the new dispensation, emerging as fundamental to growth.*"[26]

IV

❑ Low Public Financing of Health

The primary source of public financing is the general tax and non-tax revenues, including grants and loans received from both internal and external sources. In addition to tax revenues, a meagre amount is also raised through user charges, fees and fines from the sector. This pool of resources is used to finance the programmes of the Centre and the States. In the case of local governments, the respective state governments largely finance their health programs. Local governments do raise resources through user charges and certain fees, though the quantum varies widely from state to state.[27]

One of the reasons underlying the poor state of health care facilities in India happens to be the very low levels of public expenditure in health sector, which happens to be among the lowest in the world. In terms of resource allocations, almost throughout the post-independence period, the governments at the centre treated the social sectors- like health, education, housing, water and sanitation as being inferior to the Economic Sectors. The scenario has worsened since the beginning of 1990s, with the fundamental shift in the Central Government's policies. As of 2004-05 expenditure on health accounted for less than 2% of the total central government expenditures. Among states public expenditure on health formed 3-4 % of total expenditure, except in Maharashtra where it was 2.88%. Public spending on health in India gradually accelerated from 0.22% in 1950-51 to 1.05% during the mid-1980s, and stagnated at around 0.9% of the GDP during the later years.

Out of the total expenditure in India on health, almost 80% is private spending, with only 20% coming from government sources. In the public spending component the central government spending accounts for only 6.7%, while spending by the state government's accounts for 12%. The local bodies are accounted for less than 1% of the total government spending on health. In 10 states, private spending on healthcare is between 81 to 90%. Kerala had the highest private spending at 90%, followed by UP and West Bengal at 86%, and Maharashtra at 83%.

The State government's list consists of health and is financed primarily by the State Government, and is financed through general tax and non-tax revenue resources, as the cost recovery from the services delivered has been negligible, at less than 2%. As a result, resource allocation to this sector is influenced by the general fiscal situation of the State Government. Public spending on the health sector in the states increased to about 0.9% of the GDP in 2003-04, from 0.8% in 1975-76. It was during 1975-85 that public spending on health registered a substantial increase and reached a high of 1.05%. But shortly after, it deteriorated steadily due to general fiscal stress during the late 1980s followed by the reform measures initiated in the 1990s.The severity of the fiscal strain during the late 1980s forced the State Governments to introduce austerity measures and the soft sectors such as health were targeted for expenditure compressions. When reform measures were initiated at the Centre during the early 1990s, fiscal transfers to states were compressed leading to reductions in health sector allocation.[28]

External aid comes from bilateral and multilateral agencies as grants/donations and/or as loans from World Bank. Such aid comes largely for different programmes or schemes, such as for reproductive and child health, immunization, family welfare, AIDS control. Out of the total external aid in

2004-05, 68.49% came to central government, 10.73 % came to state governments, and 20.78 % was as grants to NGOs.

The deficiencies of the existing public healthcare system could have been rectified and it could have been transformed into an universal, efficient, effective and accountable healthcare system by providing adequate financial, human, and material resources, and guided by principles of comprehensive Primary Health Care that evolved in the 1970s. Instead, they have been used to justify imposition of a series of Health Sector Reforms (HSRs) aimed at accommodating the vast private interests and creating healthcare markets, in the name of health system strengthening for equity and universal health coverage.[29]

V

❑ New Public Health from 1990s Onwards: Entry of the World Bank in 'International Health'—Structural Adjustment Programs and Health Sector Reforms (HSRs)—Transition from Health Service as a Basic Right to Healthcare Markets

By the late 1980s, the worldwide economies were beginning to be restructured and an ideological shift had taken place vis-à-vis provision of welfare services by the state. The economic reforms initiated overturned the planned expansion of welfare and led to introduction of policies of liberalization, globalization, and privatization. Such resolution of the economic problems had significant implications for healthcare and for the social sector in general. It gave rise to a restructuring of health services in the name of social efficiency. Health sector reforms were initiated in many advanced capitalist countries, as well as developing countries, that had a public healthcare system, irrespective of whether it was funded by taxation or by insurance, and there has been dismantling and privatization of national health care systems in several countries in the name of these reforms or pressure to do so.

The State is identified as the cause of the crisis, due to its inefficiency in managing the productive enterprises and services, and its growing social expenditures. Hence there is need for reforms and restructuring. There is a 'social construction' of a new 'common sense' at the ideological and economic level. In the new context the 'new common sense' that is being constructed is that of health as a private good to be acquired, and is not a public good or universal right, nor is it a state responsibility.

Changes over the past have targeted this service sector for privatization and rapid global integration. These processes have been facilitated by the developments in communications and information technologies in the past two decades. Over the past decade the processes of globalization, mainly through privatization and expansion of corporate entities and market-led activities, have increased. The integration of commerce, investments and finance into the global economy has become the major force in the setting of public policies, including those in the health sector[30].

The economic recession of the late 1970s and the crisis in developing countries namely the inability to pay earlier loans and an increase in debt were used by Indian state also to restructure the economy. The inefficiencies of public sector were used to justify introduction of neo-liberal economic policies and market-based solutions. The already highly unsatisfactory situation in the health sector in the country only worsened with the onset of such neo-liberal policies. A significant shift was affected from provision by the state of comprehensive health services through a publicly funded, universal, national health system, to free provision of just a minimum, essential package of services only to those identified as poor by the state. Overall, there has been a considerable impact of globalization on healthcare services.

The 'Washington Consensus' of WB-IMF-US treasury came up with the Structural Adjustment Programs (SAPs) in 1980s for recovery from the crisis. The provision of new loans to repay earlier loans, became the main subject to implementing the SAPs. The World Bank also started playing an increasingly dominant role in the health sector in developing countries, through SAPs and conditionalities attached to grants, loans and debt relief.

VI

❑ Significant Presence of World Bank and Other Donor Agencies in Health Sector

The World Bank's *World Development Report 1993: Investing in Health,* spelt out the guidelines for the Health Sector Reforms (HSRs), for restructuring health services in developing countries. According to this report good health increases the economic productivity of individuals and the economic growth rate of countries; hence investing in health is one means of accelerating development. Moreover, good health is a goal in itself. Based on such ideas and on estimations of the global burden of disease and cost-effectiveness of interventions, the report also devised measures for priorities in health spending. The report advocated a threefold approach to health policy for governments in developing countries and in the formerly socialist countries:

1. 'To foster an economic environment that will enable households to improve their own health. Policies for economic growth that ensure income gains for the poor are essential'.
2. Limit public health expenditure.
3. Governments in poorer countries should focus their scarce public resources on providing a free 'basic' or 'minimum' package of preventive and curative services for the poor, while withdrawing from the direct provision of other services. In other words, 'redirect government spending away from specialized care and toward such low-cost and highly effective activities such as immunization, programs to combat micronutrient deficiencies, and control and treatment of infectious diseases. By adopting such packages of public health measures and essential clinical care, developing countries could reduce their burden of disease by 25 percent'.
4. Cost-recovery mechanisms in public sector, by enforcing charges for health services.
5. 'Encourage greater diversity and competition in the provision of health services by decentralizing government services, promoting competitive procurement practices, fostering greater involvement by non-governmental and other private organizations, and regulating insurance markets'.

Such reforms, according to the WB could translate into longer, healthier, and more productive lives for people around the world, and especially for the poor people who account for more than 1 billion of the population.

These were structural and functional reforms in financing, governance related; through mechanisms for decentralization and involvement of the private sector through Public Private Partnerships (PPPs) in various forms in providing medical care. The reforms also stressed a change in management approach, aimed at redressing the issue of poor rural health infrastructure and increasing efficiency and effectiveness in implementation of the centrally administered programmes. These measures were piloted in the donor-funded projects, such as the Reproductive and Child Health Project and some of the disease control programs, or through the European Commission which funded the Sector Investment Program.

Some of the specific institutional mechanisms that were initiated to improve functioning of rural health facilities were:

- Deploying community health workers who would be paid based on performance and achievement of set targets (Mitanins in Chhattisgarh).
- To address the shortage of doctors by initiating steps such as re-orientation, skill upgradation, redeployment of existing doctors, hiring part time or contractual staff.

- The involvement of local practitioners in provision of RCH services through franchising of NGOs/private providers, contracting out diagnostic and other services.
- Rogi Kalyan Samitis (RKS)/Patient Welfare Societies for autonomous hospital management; decentralization measures, and district health plans.
- Other decentralized management structures such as State Health Society, State Programme Management Units (SPMUs) and District Programme Management Units (DMUs) were being set up with various key personnel to manage finances and programs professionally.
- Performance-based funding by the Centre to the states had been taken up as part of the EC-SIP programme.
- Capacity building, for preparation of district health plans.

While most of the official development assistance comes largely through the national government, since the 1990s the central government enabled development assistance agencies such as the Department for International Development (DFID), European Commission (EC) and United States Agency for International Development (USAID) to work at the state level in the health sector. There is significant presence of multiple bi-lateral and multilateral donors, UN agencies and World Bank, all referred to as *development partners*, in the health sector, both at the state levels and in the union ministry of health. Several states had agreements with donor agencies, which defined Health Sector Reform (HSRs). The largest such state level projects have been the State Health Systems Development Projects (HSDPs) implemented in several states with loans from the World Bank – Andhra Pradesh, Punjab, Karnataka, West Bengal, Orissa, Tamil Nadu, Maharashtra, Uttar Pradesh, Uttaranchal and Rajasthan. Specific objectives of the HSDPs were: constructing/improving infrastructure at secondary levels; policy reforms; development of management skills; and improving the performance of the healthcare system. DFID had such programmes for West Bengal, Orissa, Madhya Pradesh and Andhra Pradesh. USAID was running projects in Uttar Pradesh, Uttaranchal and Jharkhand. European Commission was present in Rajasthan, Chhattisgarh, and MP.

While donor assistance forms a small proportion of the health budget, yet there is presence/participation of donors in financial, personnel and policy areas and deployment of donor consultants in supportive roles within the ministry. Bilateral and multilateral funding agencies have come to dominate an area of health sector financing which is now defined as financing of technical assistance.

DFID started working in the health sector in Madhya Pradesh in 2004, and it started funding the development of a comprehensive Health Sector Reform Programme (HSRP) in 2007. The objectives of the reform programme were: improving quality and accountability of health services, developing human resource management, increasing financial allocations and effective use of same, regulation of private providers and improving services to reduce malnutrition and to improve child health. DFID contracted with development sector consultancy firms to form a Technical Assistance Support Team (TAST) to work with government departments to implement this programme. As per the 2007 Memorandum of Understanding for MP-HSRP (between Government of MP, India, and DFID), DFID was to provide a total of up to £60 million to Government of MP, over a seven year period beginning 2007.

Evaluation of some of these reform programmes have indicated that at the end of the project period, the States had not developed comprehensive State policies and strategies, and the project components to develop capacity in policy, planning, and management had also not taken place adequately.[31]

Another development was the involvement of the numerous divisions of the World Bank in driving privatization in healthcare, through projects, investments and institutional support for multinational and local companies. Specific loans from the World Bank or IDA often involve, and are conditional upon, privatization of the relevant services. The International Finance Corporation (IFC) is a division of the World Bank that invests solely in the private sector – it has a declared policy of extending the role of the private sector in public services including healthcare. As of May 2009 it had invested about $200 million in the private healthcare sector in India. Since 2002 IFC has extended loans to Apollo Health Enterprises Limited, as well as to other hospitals such as Max, Rockland, Artemis, and Duncan-Gleneagles.[32]

Since the 1990s Global Public-Private Partnerships (GPPPs) have become common in the international health arena. Earlier international public health was dominated by the public sector through the World Health Organization (WHO) and other UN agencies and bilateral organizations, with NGO participation. Today there is much more involvement of the private corporate sector and private philanthropic foundations in health programmes, with the involvement of the Bill & Melinda Gates Foundation being the most visible: by 2012 Gates Foundation had invested more than $1billion in programs 'to fight disease and poverty in India'. The Foundation gives funds to the central and state governments, non-governmental organizations and the private sector in the country. It began with funding the AIDS control program and has since expanded to areas such as maternal and child health, nutrition, vaccines and routine immunization, family planning, control of infectious diseases, and agricultural development. The Foundation is spending several millions of dollars to promote the use of vaccines for diseases such as diarrhea, influenza among children, diseases which can be more easily prevented by providing clean drinking water, improving sanitation, nutrition. The Foundation has significant presence in states like Bihar and UP, where it has an investment of ₹250 crore in medical, health and family welfare sectors, to provide technical and management support to the state health ministry.

VI

❑ Policy Measures Since Liberalization

National Health Policy 2002

According to the National Health Policy 2002, the previous policy of 1983, "in a spirit of optimistic empathy for the health needs of the people, particularly the poor and underprivileged, had hoped to provide *Health for All by the year 2000 AD*, through the universal provision of comprehensive primary health care services. In retrospect, it is observed that the financial resources and public health administrative capacity which it was possible to marshal, was far short of that necessary to achieve such an ambitious and holistic goal… it would be appropriate to pitch NHP-2002 at a level consistent with our realistic expectations about financial resources, and about the likely increase in Public Health administrative capacity…". The NHP-2002 made a break with the policies and vision of the past, to set out a new policy framework "within the socioeconomic circumstances currently prevailing in the country". Among the recommendations made were:

- The increase in the aggregate public health investment through a substantially increased contribution by the Central Government; given the extremely difficult fiscal position of the State Governments, the Central Government will have to play a key role in augmenting public health investments.
- By levying reasonable user charges for certain secondary and tertiary public health care services, for those who can afford to pay.
- Despite all that may be guaranteed by the Central Government for assisting public health programmes, public health services would actually need to be delivered by the State administration, NGOs and other institutions of civil society.
- In principle, the state would encourage the handing over of public health service outlets at any level for management by NGOs and other institutions of civil society.
- The policy welcomed the participation of the private sector in all areas of health activities – primary, secondary or tertiary. Its contribution would be substantial in the urban primary sector and the tertiary sector, and moderate in the secondary sector.
- In the context of the very large number of poor in the country, it would be difficult to conceive an exclusive Government mechanism to provide health services to this category. A social health insurance scheme, funded by the Government, and with service delivery through the private sector, would be the appropriate solution.
- The setting up of an organized urban primary health care structure, the funding for which would be jointly borne by the local self-government institutions and State and Central Governments.

- The national health programmes be implemented through autonomous bodies at State and district levels. The relative distancing of the programme implementation from the State Health Departments would give the project team greater operational flexibility.
- The alternative systems of medicine — Ayurveda, *Unani*, *Siddha* and Homoeopathy — have a substantial role. Because of inherent advantages, such as diversity, modest cost, low level of technological input and the growing popularity of natural plant-based products, these systems are attractive, particularly in the underserved, remote and tribal areas.

National Commission on Macro-economics and Health 2005

Following the publication by the World Health Organization (WHO) in 2001 of its Report on Macroeconomics and Health, in 2003 the Government of India established a temporary National Commission on Macro-economics and Health to assess the place of health in national economic development. This Commission was co-chaired by the two ministers for health and finance. Among the objectives of this Commission were a critical appraisal of the existing health system—both private and public— and suggested ways for strengthening it to improve access to a minimum set of essential health interventions for all. It also looked into the issue of improving the efficiency of the delivery system and encouraging public-private partnerships in providing a comprehensive health care. According to this report, "Selective, fragmented strategies and lack of resources have made the health system unaccountable, disconnected to public health goals, inadequately equipped to address people's growing expectations and inability to provide financial risk protection to the poor.... The reasons for this failure can be attributed to three broad factors: poor governance and the dysfunctional role of the state; lack of a strategic vision; and weak management, unrealistic and non-evidence-based goal-setting, lack of strategic planning and inadequate funding". The Commission recommended a reform process to overhaul the existing system that was dominated by low-quality health care, was costly and unaffordable for the majority of the people, and where the public sector was under-funded, poorly equipped and constrained by bureaucratic procedures. It recommended that public spending be increased from the current level of 1.3% to 3% of GDP in the next few years; gradually shift the role of the State from being a provider to a purchaser of care; try out innovative financing models to provide a basic minimum package of interventions – such as targeting only the poor for publicly funded care, cost sharing through capitation, vouchers, and insurance.

National Rural Health Mission (NRHM) 2005

The National Rural Health Mission (NRHM) was announced in April 2005 as 'an articulation of the commitment of the Government to raise public spending on Health from 0.9% of GDP to 2–3% of GDP.' The Mission aimed 'to undertake architectural correction of the health system to enable it to effectively handle increased allocations as promised under the National Common Minimum Programme and promote policies that strengthen public health management and service delivery in the country'. Among the core strategies of the mission were training and enhancing capacity of Panchayati Raj Institutions (PRIs) to own, control and manage public health services; and provision of a female health activist in each village, named ASHA (Accredited Social Health Activist). The ASHA is an honorary volunteer, receiving only performance-based compensation for promoting universal immunization, referral and escort services for Reproductive and Child Health (RCH) services, construction of household toilets, and other healthcare delivery programmes. She is also given a Drug Kit containing generic AYUSH[33] and allopathic formulations for common ailments. ASHAs are trained periodically to act as a bridge between the ANM and the village population, and are accountable to the Panchayat. The Centre provides funding for key components in the 18 high focus States. The states were expected to increase contribution to Public Health Budget (preferably by 10% each year), and increase devolution to Panchayati Raj Institutions as per 73rd Constitution (Amendment) Act.[34]

The NRHM aimed at strengthening Health Infrastructure and human resources with a special focus on Reproductive and Child Health (RCH) services, but also including other Disease Control Programmes. Though largely restricted to rural areas, many programs such as the RCH program, Janani Suraksha Yojana (JSY) and Malaria Control were extended to urban areas. The strategy consisted of strengthening Sub-Centres, Primary Health Centres (PHCs) and Community Health Centres (CHCs) for improved curative care which conform to Indian Public Health Standards (IPHS). Strengthening the institutions involved both the creation and improvement of physical infrastructure as well as recruitment of health personnel.

The NRHM essentially functions as an omnibus broadband programme, comprising of four distinct budgetary components: the Reproductive and Child Health Programme, the various disease control programmes, the immunization programme, and the NRHM additionalities, which is the only new feature of NRHM. These additionalities consist of the ASHA programme, untied funds and maintenance grants for the district planning and maintenance of rural health facilities. Except for the NRHM additionalities which was purely tax-based, all the other three were supported by a large consortium of development partners comprising the World Bank, USAID, DFID, EC, UNFPA, UNICEF, and JICA. The immunization programme also had the WHO and GAVI (Global Alliance for Vaccination and Immunization). In the implementation of these programmes all the reform measures mentioned earlier were being adopted in all states.

NRHM focused on 18 states, with poor infrastructure and low public health indicators, namely the 8 Empowered Action Group (EAG) states

-(Bihar, Jharkhand, Madhya Pradesh, Chhattisgarh, Uttar Pradesh, Uttaranchal, Odisha and Rajasthan), 8 North Eastern States, and Himachal Pradesh and Jammu and Kashmir. As part of the Mission's mandate of review and concurrent evaluation of the program, a Common Review Mission (CRM) has been set up. This CRM consists of Public Health Experts, Representatives of Development Partners, Civil Society Members, and officials, and is conducted annually. There was also an international advisory panel for NRHM, convened by the Earth Institute of Columbia University, USA, to review NRHM operations, assess progress, conduct evaluations and make policy recommendations.[35]

In view of the crisis in the health system in India and the appalling condition of the rural health services, some of the measures such as the promise of increased budgetary allocations, providing some untied funds and grants to the rural facilities, some increase in staff, increase in budgets for drugs, inclusion of some monitoring and accountability mechanisms were seen as positive steps towards systems strengthening, although inadequate. However, the ideas of providing only some basic services through these government facilities, targeting of the services, and privatization as the option for delivering curative services continue to remain. NRHM has approached the reform/re-organization of the health services system as solely a technical and financial issue, for which certain organizational and management changes aimed at internal reform of the system are being adopted.

The High Level Expert Group (HLEG) on Universal Health Coverage and 12th Five Year Plan

Since 2005 the WHO has invoked the idea of Universal Health Coverage (UHC) in the international health discourse, urging all countries to achieve UHC as soon as possible.

We need to remember that the idea of UHC is not a new one. The provision of a comprehensive, universal health service, namely the same quality of curative and preventive services available to all irrespective of their ability to pay, as a right, through a publicly funded national health service system had been a central feature of welfare states, as also of the planning process in India since the 1940s.

In October 2010 the Planning Commission constituted a "High Level Expert Group on Universal Health Coverage for India" (HLEG) with the mandate of developing a framework for providing easily accessible and affordable healthcare to all Indians. This HLEG defines universal health care as "ensuring equitable access to all Indians, to affordable, accountable, appropriate healthcare services, with the government being the guarantor and enabler, although not necessarily the only provider of healthcare and related services". The HLEG recommended that general taxation should be the principal source of healthcare financing and that there should be no fees of any kind for health services; and that Government (Central government and states combined) should increase public expenditures on health from the current level of 1.2% of GDP to at least 2.5% by the end of the 12th plan, and to at least 3% of GDP by 2022. It also said that, "Purchase of all health-care services under the UHC system should be undertaken either directly by the central and state governments through their Departments of Health, or by quasi-governmental autonomous agencies established especially for the purpose". Thus, the HLEG recommended a market approach entailing separation of financing and provisioning, and "purchase" of services from a fragmented system consisting of competing providers, instead of the system envisaged since the 1950s (but never effectively implemented), of a fully publicly financed, integrated health system, planning for and providing universal, comprehensive health services. However it also recommended that insurance companies or other independent agents should not be used to purchase health care services on behalf of the government[36].

The Twelfth plan for health proposes a 'new strategy' as part of a longer term reform of the system over the next decade. It records that shortages remain in infrastructure and human resources for the health facilities; and proposes that there must be substantial expansion and strengthening of the public sector healthcare system, and that expenditure by the Center and the States, both plan and non-plan, will have to be substantially increased. According to this Plan, the health system will continue to have a mix of public and private service providers and the two need to coordinate for delivery of a continuum of care. That given the reality of public-private providers, there can be a network of public and private providers to attain universal coverage. It is suggested that various options of financing and organization should be explored by states and they be encouraged and financed to run one to three pilots to test out the models. Such as, "The pilots could explore different models for providing universal access to an essential health package (EHP) including ... a combination of public and private facility networks. In areas where both public and private contracted in providers co-exist, patients shall have a choice in selecting their provider. Networks of such integrated facilities at different levels will be encouraged to provide a continuum of care ...". There is also the proposal of granting financial and administrative autonomy to public facilities, encouraging them to raise their own resources, and more direct privatization measures to set up facilities to provide medical care.

This Plan suggests that various options of financing and organization be explored by states and they be encouraged and financed to run one to three pilots to test out the models. There is also the proposal of granting financial and administrative autonomy to public facilities, encouraging them to raise their own resources; and more direct privatization measures to set up facilities to provide medical care, to set up private sector medical colleges, to meet the requirements of skilled personnel. A strong regulatory system would supervise the quality of services delivered by such networks.[37]

Thus, we see that instead of asking why the government health system is so weak and ineffective, and why there is such a vast private sector, the Planning Commission serves it as a *fait accompli* and proposes to "strengthen" the public health system (for universal health coverage) by accommodation of the private sector within the health system, rather than explore other options. While the induction of the private sector into the healthcare system has thus been legitimized, yet these documents remain silent on the diverse nature of the private providers, the growing presence and influence of corporate providers, on the difficulties and negative experiences faced by other countries with corporate hospitals, and on how exactly they are going to be regulated. It is also noteworthy that the corporate sector and the policy makers are speaking in the same language.

The discourse on health systems is currently dominated by discussion on health financing mechanisms and on what is the best way for the government to organize purchase of health services. There are several demand side financing measures in the area of maternal health services meant to promote delivery in health facilities. These measures are intended to supplement traditional 'supply-side' financing by channeling resources directly to service users – a transfer of 'purchasing power'. There are unconditional cash transfers, conditional cash transfers, short term payments to offset the costs of accessing services, and vouchers for maternity services; the Janani Suraksha Yojana is an instance of a conditional cash transfer scheme, where payments are made to woman on undergoing delivery in an accredited health institution. The Chiranjeevi Scheme of Gujarat and Sambhav Scheme of UP are voucher schemes in which private providers have been contracted to provide cashless maternity services to designated groups of women.

❑ Summing Up

Universal health services coverage of the population through some health plan is well established today, whether this be through social health insurance or tax-funded national health services, or a combination of these. Most developed countries, capitalist or socialist, and some developing countries, have insured through either of the above means, a minimum standard of health care for their population. The experience of the pre-reform National Health Service (NHS) of UK shows that, although the system was far from perfect, yet, it was possible to have a taxation-based national health system, and undertake planning for large populations, avoid wasteful duplication and achieve efficiency, and secure comprehensiveness, universality and equity of health services, provided free to all as a right.[38] However, such assured universal coverage of health care has not emerged in any satisfactory manner in the developing countries such as India.

For various reasons – largely political and administrative that have been analyzed in great detail by many public health researchers, scholars and activists, the goal envisaged in the post-Independence period for the health services in India has not been fully realized. As pointed out by Banerji, 'considerable thought has been given to re-orienting this health service system and over the years several commissions, committees and study groups have pondered over it. Almost all of them have emphasized the need for radical change'.[39]

However, there has been a large gap between policy-planning and actual implementation. The public health services in India did not grow as envisioned due to factors such as lack of political will; inadequate budgets; pressure from international agencies such as WHO to implement vertical programmes for population control and against specific diseases such as malaria; corruption; and reluctance of doctors and specialists (trained in urban medical colleges oriented to western standards) to work in the rural health facilities lacking in basic infrastructure and amenities. The planning process itself has been top-down and highly centralized with little accountability, and dominated by the 'techno-managerial model of healthcare'. While there is substantial infrastructure, personnel, technology, well-equipped institutions for education and research, and production capacities in the public and private healthcare sector ('world-class'), they are riddled by several problems. The public health infrastructure, with a potential to provide primary health care, has been largely usurped by the family planning programme and some vertical disease programmes, which have strong political and administrative backing, and receive aid and assistance from the international development institutions, and most bilateral as well as UN agencies. An overview of the health system, whether public or private, reveals that despite repeated declarations to serve all especially the rural poor, the system is riddled with unevenness and inequalities of resource distribution, access, participation, and of health status. In addition it lacks an epidemiological approach (namely one catering to the disease and illness patterns), based on use of inappropriate technology, has a top-heavy organization, and the hierarchical structure matches the hierarchies in the larger society. No matter what the slogans and promises, the effective result has been and continues to be that the benefits of the health services, as well as the profits from the supporting drug and equipment industries reach only a small section of the population. Further, this pattern is not unique to the health services system, but permeates every facet of development in the country.[40]

As has been pointed out in the context of Latin American countries, in India too, "The underdevelopment of health and health services (in these countries) is brought about by the same determinants that cause underdevelopment in general, the pattern of control over resources of these countries in which the majority of population has no control over their resources".[41] This scenario is a reflection of the values of the decision-makers, planners and those engaged in implementation, who largely belong to the elite upper classes and hold all the political and economic power. Hence, the path to another approach to health service development can be one towards bringing about radical changes in all other social and economic spheres, as has happened in countries like Cuba.

Notes and References

1. Health services system can be looked upon as the combination of resources, organization, management and financing, for providing organized medical care and health-related services to populations at large.
2. Navarro V. (1977) *Social Security and Medicine in the USSR: a Marxist Critique*. Toronto, Lexington Books, p. xviii.
3. Qadeer, I. (2011) Health Services System in India: An expression of socio-economic inequalitites. In: I. Qadeer *Public Health in India: Critical Reflections*. Daanish Books, Delhi, pp. 81–82.
4. Jeffrey, R. (1988) *The Politics of Health in India*. University of California Press, Berkeley, pp. 94–95.
5. Pati, B., and Harrison, M (2001) (eds) *Health, Medicine and Empire – Perspectives on colonial India*. Chapter 1: Introduction. Orient Longman, Hyderabad.
6. *Op. cit.*, 5
7. *Op. cit.*, 5
8. Arnold, D. (1993) *Colonizing the Body: State Medicine and Epidemic Disease in 19th century India*. Oxford University Press, Delhi, p. 12.
9. Cited and discussed in Banerji, D (1985) Chapter 2: Colonialism, the National Movement and Health Services. In: D. Banerji: *Health and Family Planning Services in India: An Epidemiological, Socio-Cultural and Political Analysis and a Perspective*. Lokpaksh, Delhi, pp. 14–15.
10. Cited in Kumar, D (2005) Perceptions of Public Health: A study in British India. In: AK Bagchi and K. Soman (eds.) *Maladies, Preventives and Curatives: Debates in Public Health in India*. Tulika Books, N Delhi.
11. In: Health Survey and Development Committee (1946) Vol. I, Chapter II: History of Health Administration of India. Manager of Publications, Delhi.
12. Services covering and meeting all kinds of healthcare needs, from infancy to old age; and not just for specific illnesses or physical illness only, but also preventive and curative.
13. In: Health Survey and Development Committee (1946) Vol. II Chapter XXIII: Indigenous Systems of Medicine. Manager of Publications, Delhi.
14. The WHO Country Office for India and the Ministry of Health and Family Welfare, Government of India have brought out two compilations of a large number of health related documents. The documents were identified and sourced from various individuals, libraries and documentation centres, across the country over a span of three years. These were thereafter, digitized or reproduced, as required. The first compilation, 'Health Committee and Commission Reports, 1946-2005' is available at: http://nrhm-mis.nic.in/ Publications. aspx. It provides full access to reports of the various committees and commissions which include Sokhey; Mudaliar; Chadha; Bajaj, amongst others. The second compilation of Health Legislation in India is available at http://202.54.104.236/intranet /eip/legislation /index.php. This brings together over 200 health and health-related acts and rules, applicable at the central level, across broad categories. Key health related international covenants and guidelines have also been included.
15. *Op. cit.*, 8, p. 294.
16. See Phadke, A. (1992) Is CHV (community health volunteer) relevant today? Medico Friend Circle Bulletin July-August No. 184-185. Available on www.mfcindia.org.

17. The principles of the PHC Approach are as relevant today as they were nearly 30 years ago and provide a guide not just for the organization of health care systems, but also for how health care systems could act as an engine for promoting health and development more generally, and as an instrument for promoting equity and empowering the poor.
18. Discussed in Banerji (1985), *op. cit.*, 9, p. 136.
19. *Op. cit.*, 2, p. xviii.
20. Werner, D. (1994) The Life and Death of Primary Health Care. Medico Friend Circle Bulletin May-June No. 206-207. Available on www.mfcindia.org.
21. Chakravarthi, I. (2012) Immunization: Need for Caution. SEMINAR no. 631 March, pp. 63–67
22. Baru, R. (1998) *Private Health Care in India: Social Characteristics and Trends.* Sage Publications, New Delhi.
23. Discussed in Chakravarthi, I (2010) Corporate presence in the healthcare sector in India. Social Medicine, Vol. 5 no.4, pp. 192–204. (available on www.socialmedicine.info).
24. The term "healthcare industry" is used as an umbrella term while referring to hospitals, diagnostic centers, drugs and pharmaceutical industry, medical equipment and devices industry, and the health insurance industry. The hospitals sector is reported to form the major segment of this industry; and hence the term healthcare industry is often used while talking about corporate and other big private hospitals.
25. Discussed in Chakravarthi, I (2013) The emerging "healthcare industry in India": A public health perspective. Social Change Vol. 43 no.2, p. 165.
26. In: Bakshi, A., Prathipati, S., Sriram, S., and Vaidya, M. (2010) Gearing up for Healthcare 3.0. Background Paper for CII Seventh India Health Summit, 2-3 December 2010, New Delhi. McKinsey and Company. Downloaded from: http://www.mycii.in/image/eventimages/eventmainimages/E000012424_Gearing%20up%20for%20Healthcare%203.0%20-%20SECURED.pdf.
27. Elaborated in Government of India (2009) *National Health Accounts India 2004-05.* Ministry of Health and Family Welfare, National Health Accounts Cell, Delhi. Available on www.mohfw.nic.in
28. See for example: Singh, N.D. (2010) Rural Healthcare and Indebtedness in Punjab. Economic and political Weekly Vol. 45 No. 11, pp. 22–25.
29. Balasubramanian, P. (2004) Who should India emulate in Health Care — United States or Cuba? Medico Friend Circle Bulletin August-September, No 306, pp. 10–14. Available on www.mfcindia.org.
30. In: Sen, K. (2003) Introduction: Restructuring Health Services – Public Subsidy of Private Provision. In: K. Sen (ed.) *Restructuring Health Services: Changing Contexts & Comparative Perspectives*, London, Zed Books and European Commission, pp. 2–3.
31. Ravindran, T.K.S. (2007) World Bank and India's Health Sector. Medico Friend Circle Bulletin July-September, No.323–324, pp. 1–7. Available on www.mfcindia.org.
32. Chakravarthi I., Roy B., Mukhopadhyaya I., and Barria S (2017) Investing in Health: Healthcare Industry in India. Economic and Political Weekly, Vol. 52(45) pp. 50–56
33. AYUSH stands for Ayurveda, Yoga and Naturopathy, Unani, Siddha, and Homeopathy. The Department of Indian Systems of Medicine and Homoeopathy (ISM&H) was created in 1995, and renamed as Department of AYUSH in 2003, with a view to focusing attention to development of Education and Research in these systems (www.indianmedicine.nic.in).
34. For details on NRHM see http://www.mohfw.nic.in/NRHM/Documents/Mission_Document.pdf.
35. www.mohfw.nic.in/NRHM.htm

36. See: Government of India (2011) High Level Expert Group on Universal Health Coverage for India. Planning Commission.
37. Government of India (2012) Twelfth Five year Plan, Chapter 20 HEALTH. Planning Commission. See sections 20.19, 20.42, 20.43, 20.44, 20.46, 20.48, 20.57, 20.58 in this.
38. See Pollock, A. (2005) NHS plc. London, Verso
39. See: Chapter 29: Summary. In D Banerji (1985) *op. cit.*, p. 9.
40. *Op. cit.*, p. 3.
41. Navarro, V. (1981) Introduction. In V. Navarro (ed.) Imperialism, Health and Medicine. Baywood, New York.

CONCLUSION

37

India Since 1947

Bipan Chandra

The leaders of India's struggle for freedom and the founders of the Indian Republic were moved by the vision of an independent national economy based on modern technology and social justice and equity. Indian economy was, moreover, to be built within a world-wide perspective. It was not to be autarchic. It was to be an integral part of world economy. But the question was what type of integration?

From Naoroji and Ranade to Jawarharlal Nehru, national leaders realized that Indian underdevelopment was the result of a particular type, *i.e.*, the colonial type, of integration with the world capitalist economy. India was incorporated into the world economy as a supplier of low-technology, low-wage produced raw materials and as a market for high-technology, high-wage produced manufactures. Independence from colonial rule was desired, above all, with a view to reverse this colonial economic relationship with the metropolis and put an end to the colonial structure of Indian economy.

What we in India have attempted after independence was guided by our perception of India's weaknesses during the colonial period. India was a typical dependent economy. For nearly two centuries it had been subservient to the needs of the British economy. Its surplus had been drained or expatriated in various forms ranging from direct appropriation through taxation and plunder to an unequal exchange of commodities and investment of foreign capital, all of which was, in reality, a small part of the capital which was being drained out of India.

Indian agriculture had been stagnating for decades both in production and productivity. While overall agricultural production per head fell by 14 per cent between 1901 and 1941, the fall in per capita production of food grains was over 24 per cent. While yield per acre of all crops remained stagnant, the yield of foodgrains declined by 0.18 per cent per year between 1891-1941. Nor was this accidental. In 1949, only 19.1 per cent of area sown was irrigated, and less than 8 per cent was under improved seeds.

The industrial base of Indian economy was very weak. In 1950, industry and other constituents of secondary sector contributed only 16.1 per cent of the national income. Within the industry, the emphasis was on labour-intensive, low-technology, low-skill, low-wage products. There was near complete absence of capital goods and machine industries and total dependence on imports of machine tools and machinery. Of the total industrial output, the engineering, electrical, metallurgical, and chemical industries contributed only 13.5 per cent. Thus, the entire industrial structure was based on a light industry which was in turn based on imported machinery. Moreover, foreign capital had a stranglehold over Indian economy. As late as 1951, it controlled nearly 50 per cent of the modern industrial and banking structure. Thus, it controlled more than 50 per cent of the capital invested in petroleum, jute, tea, coal and other mines and rubber factories and more than 30 per cent of capital invested in banking, electrical industries, engineering industries, food industry and coffee plantations. It had more than 20 per cent share even in cotton-textiles and sugar industries. Indian capital had, of course, been struggling against this stranglehold and, taking advantage of the weakening of links with the metropolis during the two world wars and the Great Depression during the 1930s, had grown to sizeable proportions. Unlike the situation in other colonies and semi-colonies, Indian capital had not only grown but grown as independent capital and not as comprador capital.

The net result of colonial rule was the prevalence of abysmal poverty and degraded quality of life, for the vast majority of the Indian people. Famines and epidemics carried away millions.

Independent India set out to overcome its colonial under-development on the basis of modern industry and technology and scientific agriculture. India was still to develop as an integral part of the world economy but the basis of this integration was to be different—it was to be based on the needs of India's autonomous development, free of subordination to the metropolitan interests or of domination by foreign capital. This could not be accomplished through the unhampered working of the market forces and private enterprise. It required planning and massive reliance upon the public sector. Simultaneously, poverty was to be banished and equity and social justice promoted.

Let us be very clear on what India tried to achieve, especially after 1955. India set out to achieve an integrated national economy based on a national industry catering primarily to its domestic market. Socialism was also an objective. It inspired the people and the leadership. But the heart of India's effort was not socialism but the structural transformation of Indian economy leading to an independent national economy. And this effort at self-reliance had to be on a significantly large scale. Any small-scale effort would be aborted by population growth and the pressures of the metropolitan economy for perpetuating India's colonial integration with the world economy.

The technological and productivity levels of Indian agriculture and industry had to be constantly and rapidly raised to the levels of the most advanced sectors of world capitalist economy. Merely to increase production on the basis of existing, low-level technologies might represent economic growth, as had occurred in India in many earlier periods including the Mughal period, but it would not represent economic development or self-sustained economic growth.

What was the result of our 55-year long effort and where did we go from there?

The post-1947 agrarian legislation marked a basic transformation of agrarian relations, though from above, and with the active involvement of the peasantry. In this respect the path followed has been similar to that followed in Britain, Germany, Italy, and Meiji Japan. In fact, India has been in the mainstream of the capitalist mode of transforming agriculture, only France providing a partial exception. The erstwhile *zamindars* were permitted to resume large chunks of land for self-cultivation. This led to large-scale eviction of small tenants. In parts of the country, landlordism, semi-feudal tenancy and share-cropping continued for a long time and were only gradually eroded.

However, while the post-independence agrarian legislation hardly benefited the mass of poor peasants and agricultural labourers, it did not amount to preserving semi-feudalism; it marked, over time, a structural change in agriculture. *Zamindari* abolition put large chunks of land in the hands of the old occupancy tenants, many of whom became substantial owners of land who gradually took to capitalist agriculture as rich peasants or large-scale capitalist farmers. Their ranks were also strengthened when many of the erstwhile *zamindars* and landlords took to capitalist agriculture on the lands they had resumed for self-cultivation. Tenancy and *anti-zamindari* legislation also augmented the ranks of small and middle-landowner cultivators who already constituted over one-third of the Indian peasantry during the colonial period. India always had a large class of non-landowning agricultural workers. Their number increased sharply due to the colonialization of the Indian economy. Large-scale evictions as a result of *anti-zamindari* and tenancy legislation and the rapid rise in population have now made it the largest social class in the country.

Thus, while semi-feudal landlordism has survived, though on diminishing scale, in some parts of the country-agrarian structure today basically consists of a class of capitalist farmers and rich peasants at the top, a large number of middle peasants in the middle and the mass of small peasants and agricultural labourers at the bottom.

Unlike the colonial state, the post-independence state has put massive resources into the development of agriculture in the form of irrigation, rural roads, electrification, scientific research, price-support, and fertilizer production. The result has been a more or less satisfactory agricultural growth-2.54 per cent from 1950-51 to 1984-85 and nearly 3.5 per cent form

1985-86 to 1989-90. This has made India self-sufficient in food grains and agricultural raw materials, though oil seeds and pulses have remained work points. All the same cereal availability per head per day has gone up from 334.2 gm in 1951 to 456.2 gm in 1989 and food availability, including pulses, from 394.9 gm in 1951 to 496.6 gm in 1989.

Indian industry has grown physically as well as undergone basic structural transformation. Industrial production is today ten times of that in 1951. The rate of industrial growth during the Seventh Plan (1985-86 to 1989-90) and subsequently has been more than 8.5 per cent per year. A major reversal has occurred in terms of the growth of basic and capital goods and increased their share in total industrial production. While the annual rate of growth of consumer goods from 1950-51 to 1981-82 has been 6.6 per cent for basic goods and 8.45 per cent for capital goods. This structural change is also reflected in changes in the shares of major industry groups in the industrial sector. Between 1956-57 and 1980-81, the share of consumer goods has come down from 48.37 per cent to 23.65 per cent, but that of basic goods and capital goods has gone up from 22.13 per cent and 4.71 per cent to 39.42 per cent and 16.43 per cent respectively.

A major weakness of Indian industrial effort is the technological dependence on the metropolis, especially where advanced technology is concerned. Among the Indian economists, A.K. Bagchi has been stressing this aspect for several years now. The struggle of independent technology today is the most important part of the struggle for independent development. But even in this respect, some progress has been attempted. An effort to develop independent technology has been made over the years. National expenditure on research and development has been rising year after year. It has been, moreover, several times more than the expenditure on the purchase of imported technology through royalty and technical fees, the relevant figures of 1979-80 being ₹324.5 crore and 39.6 crore respectively. A major achievement in this respect has been the rearing of a large cadre of scientific and technical manpower. For example, in 1986-87, the number of students enrolled in engineering and technology colleges was 184,421 and in engineering and technology schools 506,821.

Of course, today there can be no economic autarchy or self-sufficiency, and least of all in the field of technology. A large part of advanced technology has to be borrowed. The nature of technological dependence depends on what is borrowed on what terms and to what use it is put. This is a rather large question, and not an easy one to deal with. But it can be pointed out that in India most of the imported technology is bought outright without equity participation. And, as pointed out earlier, the net outflow on the purchase of imported technology has so for been kept at rather low levels, being 9.9 crore rupees in 1965-66 and 39.6 crore rupees in 1979-80.

The growth in agriculture, industry, and services gets summed up in Net National Product or National Income. At fixed prices, it has grown more than four times since 1950-51. Per capita national income has grown by about 90 per cent. This growth has been unsatisfactory from the point of view of the needs of the Indian people. But this does show that India has broken through colonial economic stagnation. Moreover, it compares favourable with the growth of Western Europe and the United States, both during the comparative period of their development and their overall period of development. For example, in Britain, the rate of growth of national income from 1855-64 to 1963-67 was 22.8 per cent per decade, per capita income growth rate is 13.4 per cent per decade. For France, the two figures for 1861-71 to 1963-66 were 20.5 and 17.0; for Germany from 1950-59 to 1963-67, they were 31.0 and 19.3; for the USA from 1934-43 to 1963-67, they were 42.4 and 17.5.

By any reckoning, India had to weaken the stranglehold of foreign capital on the Indian economy, if it was to develop an independent national economy. There could be no economic independence and little political independence if giant foreign companies, industrial and finance, were to control they key economic positions in the country.

What has been independent India's record in this respect? But before we try to answer this question, let us focus on two features in the Indian situation which are not to be found in other non-socialist, post-colonial societies and states. For one, already in the colonial period, a considerable indigenous capitalist class had been formed which was basically independent and not comprador, *i.e.*, it was not an intermediary between British capital and the Indian market or a junior partner of the British capital. In the main, it did not develop an organic link with British capitalism; it was not, as a class, integrated with foreign capital in a subordinate position even when the Indian economy as a whole was. Its dominant sections had no noticeable alliances or partnerships with British or international finance capital or the emerging giant international corporations.

Second, from 1880 onwards, the Indian national movement opposed the entry of foreign capital into trade, industry and finance. Foreign capital, the nationalists argued, did not develop but exploit and dominate the country. One way of keeping out foreign capital, it was believed, was to develop a strong state or public sector as a protective wall against the much stronger international capital. The government should pioneer those industries which indigenous capital could not. And if foreign capital was needed, the state should borrow capital abroad on the security of its revenues and either employ it to undertake industrial development on its own or lend it to local capitalists. Thus, the conception of the public sector as an instrument for avoiding domination by foreign capital was strongly entrenched by 1947.

The result is that Indian economy has so far developed as an independent economy. Foreign capital no longer has a stranglehold on it. Neither foreign industrial capital nor finance capital plays dominating or an increasing role in it. Import-substitution industrialization strategy has not led, as has been the case in Latin America, to a more incisive penetration by multinational corporations. Instead, it has promoted Indian capital-owned and controlled industries. This is borne out by the following statistics: Foreign-controlled firms contributed only 10.8 per cent of the total value added in the factory sector of mining and manufacturing in 1983-84. If non-factory manufacturing is also taken into consideration, this figure would be 7.7 per cent. In terms of total volume, the total accumulated foreign private investment in India until 1974 was ₹1,943 crore. This was less than 20 per cent of the net domestic capital formation of only 1974. The Foreign private capital inflow was expected to constitute only about four per cent of the total corporate investment in the Seventh Plan. In 1985, total foreign investment approved was only about ₹122 crore. Around 1981, of the top 25 industrial units of India in terms of sales, including public sector units, only four were foreign, and they occupied 13th, 14th, 21st, and 24th positions. In 1981, of the top 20 industrial (private) houses (conglomerates), only two were foreign, occupying 4th and 14th positions. In 1985, of the first ten industrial houses, not even one was foreign; and not one of the foreign-controlled units would figure in the first 25 in terms of total capital employed. In 1983-84, total assets of the branches and subsidiaries of foreign companies were ₹5136.7 crore, while in 1985 the assets of Birla's and Tata's alone came to ₹4,112 crore and 3,699 crore respectively.

What is equally important, not a single major or economically strategic sector of the Indian economy is under the control or domination of foreign capital. This applies to iron and steel, other metals, coal, cement, engineering, heavy machinery and electricals, chemicals, defence industries, petroleum production and refining, textiles, jute, tea, coffee, cycles, fans, sewing machines, radios, scooters, automobiles, tractors, and refrigerators. Foreign capital has a large presence in drugs and pharmaceuticals, tobacco, rubber goods, typewriters, batteries, bulb, and explosives. Its domination over soap and detergents has been eroded in the last few years. This process is also taking place in the other industries, except drugs, mentioned above.

Foreign capital plays hardly a role in banking and insurance. As early as 1970, public sector banks controlled 84.7 per cent of total deposits while foreign banks controlled only 8.9 per cent. No foreign insurance companies have operated in India since 1973 when the general insurance business was nationalized. The branches of Indian banks have gone up from 4,239 in 1950 to 54,600 in 1987; the branches of foreign banks have increased from 66 in 1950 to 136 in 1987.

The size of foreign aid, including grants and concessional loans, has also been declining since the mid-sixties and was in 1988-89 about 1.5 per cent of India's national income and 9.5 per cent of its plan outlay.

It is at the level of social justice, equality and equity that India's record has been very poor. Even though the extreme poverty and starvation of the colonial period no longer prevail, there has been the failure to effect in a meaningful manner the life and standard of living of the bottom 40 per cent to 50 per cent of the people. Their social needs have not been met even at a minimum desired level. There has been some progress in some of the indices of quality of life. For example, expectation of life at birth has gone up from 32 years in 1941 to over 58 years in 1986-91; literacy from 13.9 per cent in 1941 to 36.2 per cent in 1981; and infant mortality has come down from 227 per thousand births in 1941 to 95 in 1985 and death rate from 31 per thousand in 1941 to 10.9 per thousand in 1987-88; the number of registered medical practitioners has increased from 1.7 per 10,000 of population in 1950-51 to 4.3 in 1986-87. But, as is evident, all this is utterly inadequate. Illiteracy in India is one of the highest in the World. National Sample Survey, 42nd round, covering the period July 1986-June 1987, reveals some interesting statistics. In rural areas, the public distribution system gives full coverage to only 14 per cent of the population in rice, 26.5 per cent in wheat, 4.5 per cent in oil, 36 per cent in sugar and 44 per cent in kerosene. Only 25 per cent of the rural population got treated through the public health system. For urban areas, this figure was nearly 27 per cent. Only 20.6 per cent of rural children took polio vaccine and 15.5 per cent the Triple-antigen vaccine. Even for urban children, these figures were only 46.3 and 37.1 in rural India 80.5 per cent of births took place within the houses, that is, not in a hospital. Of these, less than 10 per cent were attended to by a doctor or government midwife. About 33.4 per cent had no attendance and 29.16 per cent were attended to only by family members, neighbours, etc.

In this respect, it is important to remember that effective poverty removal programmes were initiated only in 1975 and have been vigorously, though inadequately, pursued only since 1984-85. Even so, nearly 30 per cent of Indian people are still living below the poverty line.

What of the future? Certainly, India is faced with certain major problems of the short-run variety, *e.g.*, the situation of the external and internal debt trap, the fiscal crisis of the state and balance of payment crunch. But we are also faced with certain long-teams issues; our approach towards them will have far greater consequences for our social, economic and political development.

The makers of modern India, especially Jawaharlal Nehru, rightly made an attempt to catch up in the economic realm with what we had missed out during the long two-centuries of colonial rule. Based on economic thinking of the 1930s and 1940s, this meant transforming Indian economy on the basis of capital goods industry, planning and public sector. Nehru was right in his basic thrust, and whatever we have achieved so far is the result of the foresight of the Nehru generation. But just as it will be a folly to abandon the Nehru spirit and approach, it will also be a folly to try to stick to the specific prescriptions of the Nehru era. For as the world changes, so must our efforts to adapt to those changes even when keeping the earlier vision and broad objectives intact. The thinking of the 1930s, 1940s, and 1950s would prevent any real consideration of the emerging political and economic reality. And the lack of innovative thinking would prove very costly at this juncture because of the sudden weakness of political and class structures and institutions that have supported and been responsible for India's independent national development. The inspiration and ideological-political structuring provided by the national liberation struggle are increasingly receding; the Congress party is directionless and in shambles; the secular opposition parties and groups are unable to cohere; the left is dissipated and bereft of any fresh idea; communal parties and groups are growing and becoming respectable; the bureaucracy is demoralized and politicized, *i.e.*, it caters to whosoever is in power; the intelligentsia has defaulted and abdicated its social role, nor is it anymore trusted by the people—it is increasingly becoming irrelevant; the bourgeoisie has grown rapidly but has lost cohesion—this is signified by the absence of a dominant leadership of the class; the working class is fragmented by a multiplicity of trade union centres as also by the pattern of industrial development so that there is a small well-paid section in technologically advanced industries, a medium-paid section in traditional industries such as cotton-textiles, jute, sugar, and tea and of free plantations; and a vast mass of tender-paid, unorganized workers in the informal, small-scale sector, the rich peasant is fighting for hegemony over non-social development; the vast mass of agricultural labourers and poor peasants are completely disorganized and atomized; and the middle classes, gripped by consumerism, are losing their ideological edge and have abandoned all pretence of being guardians of social values and societal welfare, being increasingly engulfed by individual greed and social pessimism.

India, in this situation, needs fresh and rigorous thinking in all fields, but above all in the economic field. We are at the beginning of a new momentous phase in world history. The First Industrial Revolution was based on technical innovations, particularly in textile-production and Watt's steam-engine. Second Industrial Revolution, from 1815 to 1850s, was based on machine-making or capital-goods industry when machines to manufacture machinery and locomotives were invented. During the third stage of the Industrial Revolution in the last quarter of the 19th century, science was joined with technology and electricity, petroleum, the internal combustion engine and steel became the engines of economic growth. The post-First World War period witnessed the development of petrochemicals, electronics and nuclear energy. In recent years, the thrust areas are those of the microchip, biotechnology and new sources of energy. Throughout these four phases India and other parts of the colonial world went on under-development which meant above all that the technological gap between them and the advanced capitalist, metropolitan countries went on increasing.

India under Jawaharlal Nehru tried to bridge the gap by combining the second and third stages of the Industrial Revolution by manufacturing machines to produce machines and by developing steel, cement, and electricity production. This was a necessary task, for we had to compress in a decade or two what Europe had achieved in 150 years. But this was not enough of a task. For while we run to catch up with the past, the present in the advanced world is moving into the future.

The current phase of development has been described by Andre Gunder Frank as that of "the production of technology by technology of the production of productive techniques". Giovanni Arrighi has put it equally well. The advanced sector of the world economy now deals with and has a monopoly over "strategic (economic) decision-making control and administration, research and development, and other 'brain' activities." Execution, including the production of consumer and producers' goods, can be shared with the Second and Third World. In other words, the brain activities are to be concentrated in the core or advanced European countries, U.S.A. and Japan and the Second and the Third Worlds are to concentrate on "muscle and nerves activities." However much the multinational corporations take their productive activities to other countries, they concentrate the 'brain activities' or production of 'productive' techniques in the core countries.

It is this new situation we have to face and conform to. This means that the vision and the objective of the Nehru era—that of 'catching up with the West' and on that basis to build a more egalitarian and just society—must continue on inspiring us, but the means and the goals of technological transformation must undergo a change. The real option before all of us are as Immanuel Wallerstein put it as early as 1980, "For the 1990s the basic policy issue is who will gain the competitive edge in the new technologies of microelectronics, biotechnology, and energy resources. Success will be determined by an interlocking triplet of research and development innovations; reduction of real costs of production; and increased access to markets for the older sectors of production—formerly high-profit sectors, now medium-profit sectors such as electronics, automobiles, and even computers."

Once the objective and the path to reaching it are clear, the quick mastery of the new leading sectors of economic activity—several contemporary economic issues beginning to become clear. First, planning and active state role in economic development, including role of public sector in production, still retain their primacy, for without them no Third World country can hope to compete in the new technology sectors. Second, if the new phase of Industrial Revolution is based on brain-activity, then education, especially higher education, acquires a critical significance. Moreover, not only quantity but the quality of education must also be treated as urgent tasks. Any populist effort, in its many guises, to neglect the quality of education must be opposed, for the cost of neglect here is as great as the neglect of machine-making and other capitalist goods industries in he earlier periods.

Third, the drain of capital and resources, which is a case of India is, in any case not significant, is bad but worse is the brain-drain to which the country has been subjected in recent years. The ways and means must be found to prevent and reverse the brain-drain to the USA and Europe.

More than NRI capital we need the physical presence of the present NRIs in India and the checking of others becoming NRIs in a continuous flow. India also suffers from internal brain-drain. One, there is the continuous non-utilization of the brains of crores of rural and urban poor children and youth who are given such poor education in the schools that their further mental and intellectual development is scotched in the very beginning. Two, there is the growing reservation in schools, colleges and technological institutions and in jobs which will keep out a major segment of our brain-power and force it to migrate. Three, even those who stay to work in our universities, research organizations, and factories are rapidly frustrated in their efforts to grow or contribute to technological and industrial production because of the hierarchical and bureaucratic organization of these institutions.

Fourth, it becomes clear that those who oppose, with whatever argument, the development of modern science and technology are contributing to India's underdevelopment and recolonization in real terms no less than those who helped the company of merchants conquer India in the 18th century, leading to India missing out the first four phases of the Industrial Revolution.

Our analysis also shows the US demand on Super 301 in its true light. For, with the emphasis on control and administration, R&D, financial and investment decision-making, *i.e.*, on brain activities in general, in the latest phase of Industrial Revolution the role of the service sector, research and innovation and patents acquires not only increasesing importance but systemic significance from the point of view of independent capitalist development.

Fifth, the role of foreign capital and multi-national corporations has to be seen in the broad context discussed above. On the one hand, India has to, and has no choice but to, participate actively in the world capitalist economy. On the other hand, its own economic development has not reached a stage where its incorporation in or integration with world capitalist economy no longer faces the danger of subordination and subservience to metropolitan capital. So long as what Marxists describe as the stage of primitive capital accumulation and Rostow as the pre-take-off stage is not fully transcended and the process of autonomous capital accumulation fully established, the danger of renewed subordination will continue. Today there is no doubt that this danger still takes the form of domination through the investment of foreign capital.

But it is also obvious that not all foreign capital investment poses this danger. Indian economy, Indian capitalist class, and the Indian state have reached a stage where they can certainly absorb a certain degree of foreign capital especially to serve the dual purposes of absorption of technology and organizational structures and skills and provide a degree of competition to indigenous entrepreneurs, private or state. What we have to avoid is the pattern of Latin American style dependent development where the multinational corporation control key economic positions and determine the predominant patterns of international exchange. There is the great danger that, though foreign capital investment would result in industrial development, it should simultaneously perpetuate technological backwardness relative to the advanced capitalist countries. While some industries of the second, third, and fourth phases of Industrial Revolution would be transferred to India, the advanced brain-activities would continue to be kept out of it and would remain the monopoly of the First World. In other words, while our former hostility to foreign capital should be moderate, our policy of controlling its direction and role has to be continued.

What about equity and social justice? Jawaharlal Nehru was absolutely correct in linking development and rapid industrialization with equity and social justice. Removal of poverty and reduction of social inequality depend upon increasing supply of mass consumption goods and creation of employment through industrialization. But the opposite is also true. Creation of a mass market for products of modern industry, including recent-most durables which ease the burdens of household running or bring entertainment to the door, depends upon reduction of social inequality via better distributions of income.

This means, above all that a high rate of economic growth and removal of poverty should not be counterpoised, the two are interlinked and interdependent. It is not accidental that the socialist and humanist Nehru was not able to take any concrete steps towards poverty-removal or devoted any substantial resources to the task; while the much more financial resources could be devoted by Manmohan government to such poverty-removal programmes as the Integrated Rural Development Programme (IRDP). The difference lies in the availability of greater social surplus in Rajiv Gandhi's India made possible by Nehru-led planning and development.

In the absence of any short-term prospects of a socialist system coming into being, what is today needed is to rapidly increase the rate of economic growth on the basis of latest technology, but not depend on the already exploded trickle-down theory that the poor will be also somehow benefitted. Active steps should be taken to devote a part of the increasing social surplus to programmes such as the Employment Guarantee Scheme. But this also will not happen on its own. It will require immense pressure by the organized and mobilized poor. Hence the significance of the maintenance and deepening of democracy and civil liberties. The other side of the medal is the need to avoid populism by unscrupulous or heedless political forces which would emphasize the immediate needs and demands of the masses at the cost of long-range economic development. For the basic needs of the masses may not be fulfilled by economic development, but they cannot be fulfilled without economic development either. The social need is to combine maximization of the rate of capital accumulation, both social and individual, and therefore of economic growth with increasing welfare of the masses which means, in our conditions, the lower 50 per cent of the population. This perspective should also determine the mix of modern industry-based on the latest technology and small-scale and rural industry, and of brain-activities and mass welfare. And in no case can we accept the World Bank recipe that we should confine our economic policies to the satisfaction of basic needs while leaving the latest technology and its development to the First World, for that is a sure recipe for keeping India a permanent part of the Third World, of the periphery, of the neo-colonial world, whatever nomenclature one may use.

38

Micro-movements and Future of Politics

D.L. Sheth

The scene in which grassroots movements in India occur is varied and complex. The natural temptation is to begin with a discussion of definitional and morphological issues involved in identifying the phenomenon called "grassroots movements". We shall avoid this temptation as far as we can, for such an exercise may end up in drawing abstract conceptual boundaries around a phenomenon that is fluid and growing. Instead, we will directly describe the phenomena that we view as grassroots movements, although a better term could be found for it, no doubt. To be sure, anything that happens at the base of politics and acquires some political salience can be described as a political happening at the grassroots, and if it acquires some durable organizational form, one may even be tempted to describe it as a social movement.

For the present, however, my interest is limited to describing a particular genre of the grassroots movements which became politically visible in the mid-1970s and to examine its potential for transforming Indian politics, an avowed goal of these movements. Whatever may be their own self-perceptions, these movements, in the view of some observers of the grassroots scene in India have over the last decade or so been growing into the 'Fifth Estate' of Indian politics. For others, they represent bubbles on the political surface of India, which appear, burst and reappear from time to time without leaving much impact on the ongoing political life of the country. For still others, they represent seeds of change, with a potential to transform the nature of Indian politics.

Before forming a judgment, one way or the other, let me describe the phenomenon. We shall do this first by locating these movements in the political space from which they operate and which they have created for themselves. We shall then describe the issues they have raised in Indian politics, and the organizational forms they have evolved to tackle these issues. Having done this, we hopefully shall be in a better position to judge their potential for transformation of the Indian polity.

❑ THE DECLINE OF INSTITUTIONAL POLITICS

A large number of these movements occupy social spaces created by the decline of the conventional mainstream politics of legislatures, elections, political parties, and trade unions. This decline, although it began earlier, became visible during the Emergency (1975-77) and has continued since.[1] The result is the retreat of democratic institutions from open, competitive politics where they continually sought to establish their claims for legitimization, into the pure politics of power and manoeuvre.[2] In the process, the political parties lost their national character, both in political and geographical terms. Their role in inducting new groups onto politics through waging struggles for their legal and political rights was considerably reduced. Their ability to process issues arising in the economy, society and culture declined greatly.

The parties failed to convert the economic demands of the poor and the deprived into effective political demands. Instead, some parties took the easy course of ethnicizing and communalizing the economic issues for electoral gains. The result was that the political process, which in the 1950s and 1960s worked for inclusion of the middle castes into the mainstream of Indian politics, got halted in the mid-1970s, keeping out large sections of ex-untouchables, the tribal people, the occupationally marginalized and economically extremely poor groups from among the ritually low-ranking Hindu castes, and the other poor and landless among the minorities. Of course, they were approached for their votes but only with all kinds of electoral gimmicks—the 1971 elections being the biggest of them all. Being leaderless, their struggles were sporadic and local in character and for that reason, their survival and dignity ceased to be issued in mainstream politics. The populations involved in these struggles were dispersed and fragmented on many dimensions besides that of class. For that reason, they were written off by the parties, especially those of the left, as unorganizable. In sum, the parties prematurely gave up their "movement" aspect, becoming increasingly just electoral machines operating with make-shift arrangements at the grassroots at election time. Having lost the capacity to retain the durable social and economic support they had once built, they have sought to forge such support anew at every election since 1971. The elections became more like referenda, and electoral mandates lost their appeal, at least, they ceased to inform the process of government formation and policy for any party elected to power.

The trade unions, which to begin with were like labour wings of the political parties, with the little autonomy of their own; became virtually bargaining counters between the people of the same class, supposedly representing different interests. The unions showed a complete incapacity to expand their activities in the growing informal and unorganized sector of the economy. Workers in this unorganized sector had little to offer, either electorally or in membership fees. Whatever ideological incentive was still there for expanding the activities of the trade unions to incorporate the workers outside the big factories and white collar establishments, got eroded as trade unions' incomes grew ever larger from the frequently raised membership fees and not infrequently from the wheeling and dealing of the leadership. Tired after long years of struggle, the union leadership got used to a cushy lifestyle and to a mentally non-taxing bureaucratic mode of functioning. In all this, their activities assured a sound financial base to the parties to which they belonged. So party leaders had no reason to complain.[3]

The legislatures reflected this change in the wider politics. Gone were the days when a Ram Manohar Lohia could raise and sustain a protracted debate on poverty in the Indian Parliament. The parliament increasingly becomes a handmaid of the executive branch, with the ruling party using the brute force of its majority to silence any debate on issues it considered inconvenient and uncomfortable for the government or its leaders. The net result was, the executive became the most powerful branch of governance and the judiciary a final arbiter of all political disputes. The political discourse began to be increasingly inform by narrow constitutionalist positions held by the executive and often endorsed by the law-courts rather than by issues emerging from democratic politics.[4] The Indian constitution which was held not only as an instrument of government but also as an agenda for social transformation became a document sanitized from the flesh and blood of social and political movements which enriched democratic politics.

The Context

It is in this context of the decline of institutional politics that the grassroots movements emerged on the Indian political scene. They moved into niches yielded by the retreat of institutional politics. They took up issues and constituencies abandoned by the political parties and the trade unions, and those ill-served by the bureaucracy. In the process, they reformulated the issues and expanded their constituencies in a framework of politics that was non-electoral; the organizational form that evolved was not of a political party or a pressure group. It was a participative and mobilizational form of politics which sustained struggles on issues articulated by the people themselves and worked for their empowerment. Through these struggles, they expanded the meaning of constitutional politics insofar as they sought to justify their struggles in terms of the Directive Principles of State policy—a chapter in the constitutional provision of which are not justifiable in courts of law.

Although they share common political arenas and a broadly similar perspective on social transformation, the grassroots movements vary a great deal amongst themselves. The differences are with respect to their political lineage, size, geographical level of operation which may vary from a highly local to the provincial and national levels, the importance they attach to some issues over others, the populations they work for, and the organizational form they adopt. There are sporadic, short-term movements addressing a particular issue, like the liberation of bonded labour. There are also the long-term movements, with a developed organizational form, working for a specific constituency, like the farmers' movements. Then there are a series of single-issue movements active at the national, state, and local levels. These include the human rights organizations, working both in urban and rural areas. The most widespread ones are those that can be described as the "movement groups of social activists". These are groups of committed social activists forming themselves as a nucleus and working self-consciously as 'agency' for social and political transformation. Through involving and mobilizing people, to begin with on issues concerning them directly, they seek to harness the social energy so released, to a long-term movement for transforming power relations in the society.

In the decade after 1975, these groups of social activists multiplied into thousands and spread into different parts of the country.[5] They are now led by young men and women, usually from the middle or lower-middle classes, who have left their professional careers and founded or joined these movement groups in the rural areas and the tribal belts of the country. They take up various causes on behalf of the marginalized populations of the dalits, the tribal people, the landless, and women. They work on a long-term basis in small geographical areas for the goal they describe as "empowerment of the people". Some socially committed professionals and social activists have organized themselves for national-level campaigns for the right to shelter and to work.

Then there are legal aid groups, the groups for better health care for the people, popular culture and people's creativity groups, and popular science movements. There also are the new trade union movements launched by small groups of social activists organizing workers in the informal sector. These include organizations for self-employed women, the *beedi* workers (involved in hand-rolling of Indian cigarettes), workers in construction and public works, and those working in the small industrial and semi-industrial units like the powerloom and handloom factories. Included in this list, which is incomplete, are only those grassroots movements that self-consciously see themselves in the role of creating social transformation by using new means of political action. The traditional philanthropic and welfare organizations, the non-political developmental organizations, various front organizations of political parties and the sect-like organizations of the religious movements have been excluded, although the line dividing some of these organizations and those described above as grassroots movements is often thin.

The central thrust of these grassroots groups and movements is the politics of issues. They have not only raised new issues but have kept alive the old unresolved ones, issues long since given up by the political parties. These include such broad issues as human rights, women's rights, child labour, ecology, and communalism (chauvinism based on caste/religious identities or sentiments). More specific issues are also raised by different movements. These include bonded labour, atrocities perpetrated by the dominant castes on the dalits and tribal people, and the rights of the populations displaced by the big development projects of the state, private companies, and multinational corporations.

Long-term issues are also addressed by the movement groups at the micro-level but these have yet not acquired political salience at the national level. These issues pertain to the legal rights of the landless to minimum wages and working conditions, the access of the tribal people to the forest and forest products, and the poor people's rights to the village commons, such as to village grazing land, use of the so-called "wastelands", tilling dried-up lakes, ponds, and water reservoirs, fishing rights in common waters, and so on. Social issues are also taken up involving political mobilization around such controversies as dowry deaths (murdering of the wife by the husband and/or his kins for the inadequate sum of dowry received or for re-marrying another woman for dowry), burning of widows, rapes, and child labour. The list goes on and on.

The important fact is that almost all issues raised by the grassroots movements are ones on which the state is committed to act positively as ordained in the Directive Principles of the State Policy in the constitution but, being non-justiciable, they are not resolvable through recourse to the law-courts. Direct action by the people on these issues becomes, therefore, a preferred means of political action for the movement groups. Today, there is some group or the other working on these issues even in the most remote rural and tribal areas of the country. And yet the reach of the grassroots movements remains limited, both politically and geographically.

The enormity of the problems the grassroots movements have taken upon themselves is so great, that one wonders how long they can withstand the pressures and trials of their efforts, to continue to serve as a buffer between the state's growing coercion and the chaos in Indian society. It is the inability of the state, its bureaucracy, and its institutionalized politics to process these problems into their own arena that has created this overwhelming situation that the grassroots movements feel they are required to tackle. The activities of these movements are constantly on the move, spending most of their time and energy on firefighting; this leaves them little time for reflection or for interaction with those in movements other than their own.[6]

Micro-Movements and Local Politics

While they operate at the base of the Indian polity, the movements are not a part of what is conventionally understood as local politics. Until recently, that is while the one-party dominance of the Congress party reigned, local politics was vertically, even if loosely, coordinated by the macro-institutional structure of politics. The *panchayats* (village councils whose members are periodically elected through universal adult franchize), the cooperatives, the block development committees were also operated and politically coordinated through holding diverse caste-based factions into the politically accommodative structure of the Congress party. The factional alignments characterized the party system at the local level. But local politics has substantially changed, especially since the 1971 elections. This change, often attributed to the breakdown of one-party dominance is, rather the result of changes that have been taking place at the base of the society. And these changes have created new political space at the local level, which has now been occupied by the movement groups.

Let us quickly index only a few of such changes. The relations between castes, which often are hereditary occupational groups, hitherto based on the principle of a barter-like reciprocal system of goods and services (the *jajmani* system), have been fully monetized. A much greater proportion of the rural population over two-thirds now lives in bigger villages, with populations of over one thousand. At the same time, the bulk of the population in an average village now consists of owner-cultivators and the landless labourers. The other categories such as the priestly, trading and artisan castes, are either moving out of the villages into the nearby towns or are getting absorbed into the ranks of owner-cultivators or the landless labourers. The Indian village, which was primarily a social system within which economic activities subsisted, is now acquiring the character primarily of an economic organization in which social relationships are getting defined in terms of relations between employers and employees, between wage-labour and capital. The so-called "caste conflict" is now mainly between the dominant castes of the owner-cultivators and the castes of the landless labourers, with the former having lost their traditional claim on the labour of the latter.

The changes in the village social structure have changed the nature of conventional local politics, the political parties, operating on the old assumptions, have not been able to address themselves to the new issues that have sprung up in rural India. Instead, as we saw earlier, the issues are being taken up by the movement groups operating from outside such institutions of local politics such as the panchayats, the cooperatives, and the local units of the parties.

Micro-Movements and Mainstream Politics

From this description of the micro-movements, the political spaces they occupy, the issues they articulate, and the organizations they have spawned, it should be clear that they represent a fairly heterogeneous but vigorous element of political action at the grassroots of Indian politics. But they function as disparate micro-movements, each zealous in guarding its identity, autonomy, and territory. They resent any effort by a macro-organization, even by a non-party political formation, at the national or regional level to coordinate their activities or federate them into a larger political entity. They align with some others on issues, join up for common causes, even create joint fronts. But they do all this only around specific issues and for the duration for which the struggle lasts. They refuse to become organizational parts of, or to create for themselves, any larger long-term movement. This, despite the fact that many among them share a common perspective on problems, especially in terms of their critique of the existing political and social order and the model of development. Not only this, in their programmes and activities they manifest a common approach and methodology of struggle. They work on similar issues and for the same types of constituencies, albeit in different geographical areas. There may be cultural explanations for such a strange situation of separation, but they will not be resorted to for the present.

The important fact is that there seems no possibility, in the foreseeable future, of these micro-movements emerging as a larger nationwide political movement by forging coalitions, alliances, and mergers among themselves. It is for this reason that the activists and intellectuals of the political parties and some observers of the grassroots scene in India do into attaching much political significance to the micro movements. In this view, any movement that does not make a visible impact, either on government policies or electoral politics, has no political future. The activists of the movement, however, do not share the view of conventional revolutionary politics, in which movements, are conceived and carried out with the ultimate objective of capturing state power.[7]

For them, the capture of state-power is not a precondition for social transformation. There indeed are some differences within the micro-movements on whether they should completely rule out, even from a larger-term theoretical perspective, the goal of acquiring or capturing state-power, however remote that possibility might appear today. As we shall see later, this particular issue has become quite important, linked as it is with the issue of the use of violence, and the controversy has resulted in the splitting of some groups and movement. But a large number of the movement groups, including those inheriting the Marxist-Leninist tradition of struggle, prefer to leave this issue dormant, if not to ignore it totally. They believe that a premature and excessive concern about capturing state-power suppresses the real issues of politics and social transformation, distorts the priorities in the struggle, and gives rise to authoritarian tendencies within the organizations of the movements.

The groups belonging to the Gandhian *sarvodaya* (a neo-Gandhian movement which emphasized cooperation as against conflict between classes as a means of social transformation), socialist, and even liberal traditions, however, clearly reject capture of state-power, even as an ideal.

They find the concept overly political and distracting from the long-term struggles for the decentralization of economic and political power. According to them. This can only be achieved through changing the forms of organization and building peoples' own capabilities, rather than through changes, if achieved in the broader society and culture, may ultimately result is the transformation of the state itself.

Whatever the nuances of their positions on the issue of state-power, in practice the micro-movements of all types, function away from mainstream politics. Theirs is the politics of issues, of winning rights, and of changing the consciousness of the people. This often brings them into a confrontation with the state, the bureaucracy, the law and order machinery, the local power structures, and sometimes even with the political parties and established trade unions. They view such confrontations as an aspect of the large, long-term struggle for political and social transformation, and not as a means of directly competing with the political parties for the legitimacy-claims in the prevalent system. Instead, they emphasize withdrawal of legitimization, by separating themselves from the institutions of mainstream politics and devoting their energies to building the people's own organizations. In the process, they view situations of conflicts as the means of raising people's consciousness and building the awareness of the people, rather as the means of capturing state-power.

This, however, does not mean that they are opposed to the institutional framework of Indian democracy. In fact, they consider institutional democracy as a necessary condition for their functioning, but not a sufficient condition for their long-term goal of political and social transformations.[8] For this goal to be achieved, they believe that the political battleground needs to be shifted away from the mainstream politics into the society and culture. In this sense, while they do not view the functioning of institutional democracy as representing forces hostile to their agenda of social transformation, working within and for it is not something high on their agenda. Their political agenda, instead, is further democratization, not only of the political institutions but of the family, the community, the workplace, and the society at large.

Micro-Movements and the Politics of Transformation

The self-perception of these grassroots movements is, thus, not merely of being pressure groups working for the rights and benefits of specific constituencies. They view themselves as movements for political and social transformation, and their methodology consists in involving the people in redefining the basic issues concerning the relationship between society and politics. Let us illustrate this point briefly with a reference to the three major grassroots movements: the human rights, the ecology, and the feminist movements.[9]

The issue of human rights as viewed by the activists of several human rights groups is not limited to the conventional legal notion of civil liberties;

it also extends to situations in which individuals and groups are denied the satisfaction of their basic needs. The poorest among the poor have in their view lost out in both respects. Thanks to the model of development adopted by the state, the poor are neither entitled to become full wage-earners in the economy nor full-fledged citizens in the polity. The politics of micro-movements, therefore, lies not merely in fighting particular infringements of legal rights of citizens, but in creating and expanding new political and civic spaces for them by converting the survival and development needs of the poor and the deprived into struggles of their economic, political, and cultural rights and these not only of individuals *qua* individuals but of groups and communities surviving on the margins of the civil society. In the process, the activists link rights of access to and benefits from the development process with the issues of ethnic identity and human dignity, and view the satisfaction of material needs as a pursuit not detached from the spiritual and cultural aspects of human existence. Several movement groups that are not single-issue organizations for human rights relate to human rights movements through such a perception of rights.

Similarly, the ecology movements do not view ecology as merely a cost factor in development, as many ecology academics do. Nor are they interested in specifying tolerable levels of ecological destruction necessary for achieving higher levels of economic development as modernizing regimes tend to do.[10] Instead, they view ecology as a basic principle of human existence, which, if reactivated, can yield higher level principles for reorganizing the economy in human terms and refocus development in terms of well-being, in which, to use Gandhiji's well-known phrase, "everybody shall have enough for his or her need, but not for his or her greed".

The activists of the women's movements have lately been defining their problem not merely in terms of achieving equal benefits and access for women is the present system. They self-consciously take up such issues mainly for finding entry points to the submerged world of Indian womanhood: but their long-term goal, as they put it, is to change the working of the gender principle itself in the economy and society, such that both society and economy become more just and humane. They find the ecological worldview of the movement more aligned with the feminine principle. The fusion of the ecological and gender principles, they argue, is conducive for a more humane economic and political organization of the society than that of development which, in their view is founded on the principle of male-domination over all aspects of human life and nature. Their project, working together with the human rights and ecology movements, is thus to change the forms of organization and consciousness in society.[11]

Guided by this broad perspective, these movements are often able to forge links with each other in fighting for issues at the grassroots. It is not accidental that ecology movements like the Chipkoo movement have the participation of women, and that the Bodhgaya movement for the rights of the landless in Bihar is viewed by its participants as a movement for total revolution in which women play significant leadership roles. Women are in the movements fighting for the rights of the population displaced by development projects, especially in Madhya Pradesh and Maharashtra. Similarly, human rights organizations often team up with women's organizations on issues of dowry, *sati* (self-immolation of a widow by burning herself on her husband's funeral pyre), rape, and equal wages. Similarly, activists in women's groups took on an active role in mobilizing and assisting the victims of the Bhopal chemical disaster. At no time in independent India, in the movements led by the parties and trade unions, was there ever such a high degree and such a sustained level of participation by women as one witnesses today in the non-party political movements at the grassroots.

Even as these movements seek to acquire greater perspective and coherence, they confront situations of division and splits within their own organizations. Currently there is active debate among these groups on five issues which has resulted in splitting some groups and joining together of some others. The issues are over the appropriate attitude the grassroots movements should adopt towards (1) the use of violence, the specific issue being violence as a justifiable means of self-defence for the people versus complete reliance on non-violent methods of *satyagraha* as a mode of conducting struggles; (2) acquiring/capturing state-parties in the electoral politics versus engaging themselves solely in the non-electoral and non-party politics; (3) the kind of relationship the groups/movements should maintain with the political parties in the conduct of their own struggles; (4) cooperating with the state in implementing certain development schemes that may provide immediate short-term benefits and relief for the poor; and (5) accepting foreign funds.

These controversies have resulted in some activists leaving the movement and joining political parties; some have formed themselves into apolitical-type NGOs. The issue of violence has, for example, split an old movement in the Bodhgaya but it has also given rise to the larger formation of two types of movement groups in Bihar—those who believe in the inter-racial use of violence and those who assert their faith in the *satyagraha* type of non-violent struggle.

This review of the large, almost 'overwhelming', canvass of the grassroots movements suggests that the grassroots movements in India can best be viewed as stirrings within the civil society which, by acquiring self-conscious organizational forms, expand the frontiers of the civil society to include the vast population on its periphery. Their long-term objective, it seems to me, is to bring the modern state in India, which has hitherto remained away and above the society, under the command of the civil society.

Such stirrings indeed are noticeable in many countries of the world today.[12] The moot question is whether the world constitutional order will emerge and expand through the process of the formation of a civil society at the global level, with concommitant growth of global citizenship, or will it be imposed top-down *a la* the GATT, the International Monetary Fund, the World Bank and now the new Eco-regime which may be fabricated in the post-Rio Earth Summit politics of big powers. The grassroots movements in India, as do the 'new movements' in other parts of the world, represent a powerful counterveiling force to the top-down process which has acquired a new clout in the post-cold war world. If there is still any hope for achieving a just and peaceful order for the world as a whole, the thinking on the constitutional order has to align with the new politics of movements.

Notes and References

1. On 25th June 1975, Internal Emergency was imposed in India by the then Prime Minister Mrs. Indira Gandhi as a stratagem to continue in power after she was disqualified from her membership of the Indian Parliament on being found guilty of electoral malpractice by a High Court judgement delivered on June 12. During the Emergency, which lasted for two years, the constitutional rights of citizens including some Fundamental Rights were suspended. The Emergency regime was stifly resisted by several political parties and social activists. For an account of how the constitutional rights were undermined by the emergency regime, written during the Emergency, see Rajni Kothari, "End of an Era", *Politics and the People: In Search of a Humane India,* Delhi, Ajanta Publications, 1989, pp. 235–250.
2. For an illuminating analysis of the decline of the institutions of democratic governance in India, see Rajni Kothari, "Decline of the Moderate State", *State Against Democracy: In Search of Humane Governance,* Delhi, Ajanta Publications, 1988, pp. 15–36. An incisive account of the decline of political parties can be found in Kothari's "Decline of Parties and Rise of Grassroots Movements", *State Against Democracy, op. cit.,* pp. 33–51.
3. The decline of the Trade Union Movement is graphically illustrated by Sandip Pandey. See his "The Datta Samant Phenomenon", *Economic and Political Weekly,* Vol. 16, Nos. 16-17, April 1981, pp. 1–8.
4. For an account of the erosion of the legislative and judicial institutions in the decade of the 1970s, see Rajni Kothari, "Taking Stock of the Seventies", *Politics and the People: In Search of Humane India, op. cit.* pp. 343–353.
5. The political and historical context from which these groups emerged and their typology is provided in my "Grassroots Stirrings and the Future of Politics", *Alternatives,* Vol. 9 No. 1, March 1983.
6. The problems faced by the activists of grassroots movements are discussed in my "Grassroots Initiatives in India," *Economic and Political Weekly,* Vol. 19, No. 6, February 1984.
7. For a critical assessment of the role of grassroots movements in the politics of social transformation, see Harish Sethi, "Groups in New Politics of Transformation", *Economic and Political Weekly,* Vol. 14, No. 7. 18th February 1984, pp. 305–316.
8. For a more comprehensive discussion on this point see my "Alternative Development as Political Practice," *Alternative,* Vol. 12, No. 2, April 1987.
9. The political thinking and positioning of the movements described in this section is based on my participation in about a hundred dialogues with social activists in different parts of India in the early 1980s, sponsored and organized by *Lokayan.*

10. For a critical assessment of attitudes and thinking of various ecological movements in India, see Harish Sethi, "Some Consideration on Ecological struggles in India", *Asian Exchange,* Vol. 4, No. 1, pp. 49–74.
11. The leading exponent of this position is Vandana Shiva. See her *Staying Alive: Women Ecology and Survival in India,* New Delhi, Kali for Women, 1988.
12. For a comprehensive statement on the global potentials of social movements, see Richard Falk, "The Global Promise of Social Movements" Explorations at the Edge of lime," *Alternatives,* Vol. 12, No. 2, April 1987.

Index

B

C

G

Q

R

T